SYNTHESIS IN SL TEACHING

SYNTHESIS

IN

SECOND LANGUAGE TEACHING

AN INTRODUCTION TO LANGUISTICS

HECTOR HAMMERLY

Simon Fraser University

Volume 1 of the Series in Languistics

Second Language Publications

P O Box 1700 Blaine, Wash. USA 98230

P O Box 82370 N. Burnaby, B.C. Canada V5C 5P8

To my wife Ethel,
without whose support and
encouragement this book
would not have become
a reality.

ISBN: 0-919950-01-9

Printed in the United States of America

ACKNOWLEDGMENTS

This book would not have been possible without the support and generous help of several colleagues and friends in the Department of Languages, Literatures and Linguistics of Simon Fraser University.

I am particularly grateful to Barrie E. Bartlett and Isabel Sawyer, who read the whole manuscript with great care. Substantial improvements resulted from their suggestions. Pierre Trescases, Edward R. Colhoun, and Tai Whan Kim also read portions of the manuscript. The comments of all these colleagues and friends were most helpful; I must, however, assume responsibility for any shortcomings in the final product.

Student feedback played an important role in the production of this book. My gratitude goes to all the students who over the years reacted to the various ideas discussed herein. A special word of thanks is due Maria Ruscher and Beatrice Stadler, two graduate students who read the manuscript and also wrote some of the drills that appear in Appendix B.

My wife Ethel provided essential help with bibliographic research and typing.

A final point: being a synthesis, this book has benefited from the ideas published by numerous scholars in the past. In fact, it is impossible to write a synthesis of our field without referring to, and occasionally quoting, the work of others. My only regret is that I cannot acknowledge all the sources of the thoughts expressed in this book.

ABOUT THE AUTHOR

Hector Hammerly started his teaching career as an Instructor in Spanish at the Foreign Service Institute, U.S. Department of State, in Arlington, Virginia. In 1961 he completed an undergraduate major in French, spoken natively by his father. From 1961 to 1964 he was an NDEA Graduate Fellow in Linguistics. He has been teaching applied linguistics and second language methodology since 1963, first at NDEA summer institutes for teachers of French and Spanish, then at Simon Fraser University, where he is an associate professor in the Department of Languages, Literatures, and Linguistics.

Professor Hammerly received his Ph.D. in applied linguistics ("foreign language education") from The University of Texas at Austin in 1970, with a dissertation on the teaching of second language pronunciation. He has since published numerous articles in a variety of professional journals, including *The Modern Language Journal, The Canadian Modern Language Review/La Revue canadienne des langues vivantes, Hispania, Foreign Language Annals,* and the *International Review of Applied Linguistics*. He also edited and co-edited, respectively, the 1974 and 1975 pedagogical proceedings of the Pacific Northwest Council on Foreign Languages.

This is Professor Hammerly's second book. His first was *The Articulatory Pictorial Transcriptions: New Aids to Second Language Pronunciation* (Blaine, Wash.: Second Language Publications, 1974).

Hector Hammerly and his wife Ethel (*née* Pidoux) make their home in Coquitlam, British Columbia. They have a (trilingual) son in medical school in Mexico.

CONTENTS

INTRODUCTION

This book has been written for all those who are interested in the theory and practice of second language teaching and learning.

This field has seen in recent years frequent and at times drastic changes. The voices of numerous leaders from within and without our discipline have resounded with claims and counterclaims calling second language teachers to follow them. It has even been argued, on the basis of demonstrably poor results at many institutions, that second languages can be learned but cannot be taught --as if poor teaching were proof that good teaching is impossible!

As a consequence of all this, there is much understandable confusion. Many members of our profession seem to have lost their "bearings" and to be running here and there, from fad to fad to fad, not hitching their wagons to a star but rather to any passing meteorite.

It is the purpose of this book to help re-establish a sense of direction by redefining our discipline and giving it a principled orientation. What is needed at this time is not further panegyrics to the latest methods nor additional clarion calls to return to the old. What is needed is a reasoned synthesis based on the available facts and combining into a harmonious whole the best of well-established and new approaches to second language teaching.

For despite confusion and negativism, there is reason to be optimistic --excellent results in second language teaching/learning *can* be attained, and not just by the best teachers and students, by means already available to almost everyone in our profession.[△] It is just a

----

[△] For example, standardized test data obtained over several years from my second- and third-semester university students of Spanish (whom I seldom taught myself) shows that their *average* scores corresponded to the

question of consistently following certain principles and procedures, with adaptations, of course, to the characteristics of the learners and the situation.

It is the main goal of the author of this book to share with the reader the principles and procedures that can ensure success in second language teaching, to help elaborate a sound theory of second language teaching/learning to which such successful practice can be related, and to take the first steps toward making ours an autonomous discipline. If even minor progress takes place in these areas, the effort will not have been in vain.

HECTOR HAMMERLY

---

following percentiles (percentage of examinees outscored):

Semesters	Listening	Speaking	Reading	Writing
Second	94	95	92	86
Third	92	88	91	92

Their communicative competence also developed nicely, as shown by their performance in Foreign Service Institute-type interviews. (The standardized tests used were the Modern Language Association Cooperative Spanish Tests LA and LB, MA and MB; note that the third-semester students were compared with fourth-semester norms.)

Almost all the teaching was done by assistants, under fairly typical conditions. The point of this is that anyone who meets our basic professional requirements could establish a similar program and obtain similar results, provided he followed sound principles and procedures.

1

SYNTHESIS IN THE FIELD WITHOUT A NAME

Many influences, many distortions

For much too long, the field of second language teaching and learning has been subordinated to, or closely associated with, one or more other disciplines, with a few beneficial but many negative effects. The second language field has been, among other things:

--an appendage to the classical languages, with Latin rules foisted on modern language students;

--an accessory to literature, with the written language emphasized to the exclusion of communication;

--an annex of phonetics, with second language students learning precise pronunciation but unable to speak;

--an application of linguistics (round one: "structural"), with easy distortion into an excessively mechanistic pedagogy, insufficient attention to the written language, and so forth;

--an assumption of psychology (round one: "behaviorist"), with preoccupation with the avoidance of errors and determination to teach via analogy, never analysis;

--an adjunct to education, with our field losing its uniqueness in general trends and being drowned in mindless jargon;

--an afterthought of linguistics (round two: "transformational"), with rejection of drill and gradation, proclivity for overly complex and abstract explanations, disinterest in performance, anti-empiricism, and much more;

--an article of faith of psychology (round two: "cognitive"), with disapproval of correction, encouragement of linguistically unsupported creativity, and, more generally, the equation of formal learning with natural acquisition; and

--an assertion of psychiatry, with students mixing the two languages freely and being asked to sit on comfortable armchairs and listen to the second language to the rhythm of Baroque music.

No wonder the second language field is in such a

state of confusion! If instead of being a field of study it were a person, the result would have been the same --the stress of frequent major changes and of many conflicting relations and the pressure of much contradictory advice would make anyone confused and distraught.

But it does not have to be that way. The second language field/"patient" can break off hurtful entanglements and find its identity (it does not even have a fitting name of its own!), overcome its inferiority complex, and assert itself by pursuing its own goals in its own way.

But it will not be easy. As Mackey [1973:13] put it, language teaching will continue to be subservient to linguistics and psychology until, like any science, it weaves its own net, so that it can say, "What my net can't catch isn't fish."

There is much in a name

A field is unlikely to become autonomous as long as its name or names are unclear or subordinate it to other disciplines. The oldest name for our field, "foreign language teaching" is inappropriate in that it does not mention learning and, more seriously, in that it calls "foreign" the languages spoken by numerous native citizens,[△] making them feel like aliens in their own land. Calling a language "foreign" is misleadingly applying a political label to what is basically a social phenomenon. Reference to a "target" language, while very graphic, has undesirable military connotations. The symbol "L2" sounds too much like a chemical compound if read as "ell-two"; and if it is to be read as "second language" why not spell it out that way and abbreviate it "SL"? It seems therefore that what we teach our students should be referred to as "second languages." A "second language" can be defined psycholinguistically as "any language other than the learner's native language," that is, any language learned after language acquisition in early childhood. (This use of the word "second" in this book must be kept distinct from its chronological use.)

[△] In the United States, for example, a 1976 Bureau of the Census report estimates that at least 8,000,000 inhabitants speak a language other than English as their native language and that, in addition, at least 17,000,000 speak such a language as a second language. Canada, though officially bilingual, is also a multilingual nation.

That still leaves the problem of what to call the field that can be defined as "the theory and practice of second language teaching and learning." The name "second language teaching" is too long and conveys only some of the ideas involved, among other things leaving out theory. "Applied linguistics" is a very undesirable term because it subordinates our field to linguistics even though linguistics has very different aims and methods from our own and can hardly be "applied" at all. The label "foreign language education" or even "second language education" is unfortunate in that it makes our field a part of education, when as we shall see our subject is pedagogically unique and is often taught outside the purview of educators.

Fortunately, years ago Nelson Brooks [1964:231] coined a single-word name for our field which our profession would do well to adopt --for it is a convenient and distinctive label-- and which will be used in this book: "languistics." *Languistics* is hereby defined as "the science of second language teaching and learning." A language teacher is not necessarily a "languist," for a *languist* is "someone who has completed graduate studies in languistics" (for an outline of such studies see Appendix D).

On keeping the feeder disciplines at arm's length

Having gained a sense of identity from a name and a self-definition, the next step in securing autonomy for languistics is to establish a new relationship with those disciplines that can contribute insights to it, that is, its feeder (*not* "parent") disciplines. This relationship, as several authors have noted, should be similar to that which medicine --also an applied science-- has with its feeder disciplines. Medicine is not a part of biology, chemistry, physiology, etc. but uses whatever it finds applicable in them and simply ignores the rest. Similarly, languists should decide what is applicable to their discipline from feeder disciplines such as linguistics, psychology, education, etc. and ignore the rest.

The feeder disciplines of languistics, from which languists draw upon as needed, can be seen in Figure 1.1. They are the disciplines that concern themselves with language (linguistics), learning and the psyche (psychology), teaching (education), and culture. The culture-related disciplines break down further into those having

LANGUISTICS AND ITS FEEDER DISCIPLINES

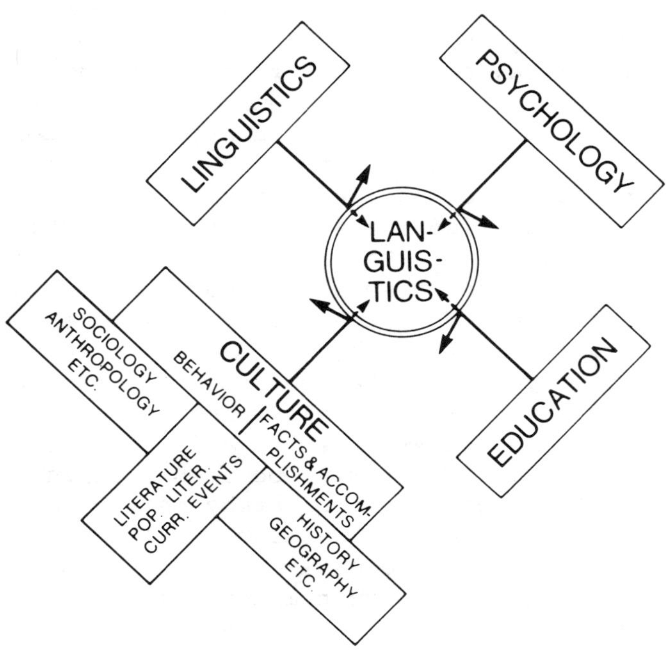

Figure 1.1

to do with culture as behavior (sociology, anthropology, religious studies, etc.); those having to do with culture as facts about, and accomplishments of, a society (history, geography, archeology, political science, economics and commerce, philosophy, fine arts, etc.); and those fields from which insights are available for both types of culture (literature --both belletristic and popular-- and current events).

Languistics needs to avoid too close an association with any of these feeder disciplines, for it has its own subject matter, its own goals, and its own procedures. Too close an association with any other discipline leads to: (1) overemphasis on the concerns, however irrelevant, of that discipline; (2) subjection to the winds of change in theory in the other discipline and to the expectation that all its theories should somehow be applied, even if inapplicable; (3) a tendency to disregard the contribution of other disciplines and to see everything in terms of one "parent" discipline --a kind of tunnel vision--, with the consequence that the training of specialists in the subordinate field lacks balance; and (4) bias in the delimitation of research issues and the selection of research techniques. These are major reasons why languistics must be autonomous rather than --as we shall see below-- a part of, or very strongly influenced by, linguistics, psychology, education, literature, or any other discipline.

The case of linguistics

Because linguistics is the science of language, and languistics is concerned with the teaching and learning of language, it has been assumed that linguistics can make a greater contribution to second language teaching than any other discipline; but the points of view and concerns of linguists and languists are so different that in fact linguistics may have less to offer second language teaching than psychology or education. The activities of second language programs include description, selection, gradation, presentation, explanation, practice, and evaluation. Of these, linguistics can help only with language description, and even that *indirectly*, for before it can be used in languistics, a linguistic grammar, being very abstract, must be radically changed into a (pedagogical) languistic grammar, which should be far more concrete and less ambitious. A contrastive linguistic grammar should equally undergo major changes before it can be used in second language teaching. So linguists have a very limited role to play in the field of languistics; as linguists, even if they call themselves applied linguists, they are not qualified to say anything about how second languages (or first languages for that matter) should be taught. Indirect --and anecdotal-- proof of this is that there have been excellent second language teachers who knew no linguistics and there are excellent linguists who do not know the first thing about second language teaching.

To the limited extent that linguistics may be indirectly applicable to second language teaching, the linguist is further at a loss in deciding which grammar of a language to adopt as the basis for his work. In addition to Chomsky's Revised Standard Theory, there is Tagmemics, Stratificational Grammar, Relational Grammar, Role and Reference Grammar, Case Grammar, Equational, Functional, Montague, Realistic, Arc-Pair, Corepresentational, Cognitive, and Dependency Grammars, Epiphenomenal Syntax, and many more theories of grammar. There are similarly many schools of phonology and semantics.

Furthermore, each theory may differ from another in numerous ways, and certain theories of language are contradictory. And each theory can yield several descriptions of the same language.

Sorting out what will be used from what description of a language according to what theory is therefore a very difficult, nearly hopeless task. Matters need to be simplified, and one way of doing that is to concentrate primarily on the main theories of language --traditional, structural, and generative-transformational--, even if this means reducing drastically one's initial choice; then one's base can be broadened by adding what may be useful from other theories.

It would be a serious mistake, however, to decide blindly that the most modern or the most dominant theory of language must be the most useful one. In fact, the dominant school of linguistics, generative-transformational grammar, seems to be the least applicable to practical concerns [Lamendella 1969, Krohn 1970, Spolsky 1970, Roulet 1978]. This is because, as shown in Figure 1.2, the interests and attitudes of the generative-transformational (G-T) linguist are quite different from, and often opposite to, those of the languist.

	CONCERNS OF G-T LINGUIST	CONCERNS OF LANGUIST
1	A theory of language	The theory and practice of second language teaching
2	A description of languages (explanatory adequacy)	The teaching of languages (pedagogical adequacy)
3	Universal characteristics of language	Characteristics of particular languages
4	Ideal native speaker competence only	Real non-native speaker transitional competence *and* performance
5	Abstract rules involving abstract forms	Concrete behavior involving actual utterances

Figure 1.2

It should be obvious from this partial list of differences between the concerns of the linguist and the languist that "it is impossible to base [second language] teaching materials or a teaching methodology upon linguistics" [Selinker 1972-a:8], for in languistics "we are concerned with language as the rightful property of language users, not as the special preserve of the linguist" [Widdowson 1980:169], who may describe it in terms of rules and elements that exist only in his mind.

In view of the present orientation of linguistics, there is no question of equating second language teaching with "applied linguistics" and much less of making it part of "educational linguistics" [Spolsky 1978-b], i.e., part of a subfield of linguistics. Terms such as "applied linguistics" have simply outlived their usefulness, especially now in the age of post-structural linguistics.

Still, what the languist says about the language must be linguistically valid, so he cannot disregard linguistics entirely. Post-structural linguistics has had the effect of turning most second language specialists away from linguistics [Bolinger 1972]; but if an eclectic approach to linguistic theory is adopted, by drawing whatever is applicable from whatever source, it becomes clear that linguistics remains a useful source discipline.

Linguistics can be quite useful to the languist if he will only choose carefully from among what the various schools of linguistics, past and present, have to offer. Beyond language descriptions, linguistics can offer certain valuable insights, such as the distinction between form and meaning, the differentiation of speech from writing, the central importance of structure, and so on.

It would be very unfortunate if the second language profession's disenchantment not only with post-structural linguistics but with any linguistics were to intensify to the point where linguistics is totally abandoned as a source discipline. Already some negative effects can be seen, such as the current stress on communication at the expense of accuracy, and the resurgence of many discredited traditional teaching procedures.

To a great extent, of course, it is the linguists who have painted themselves into a corner of irrelevance. It is to be hoped that this situation will change. As Lakoff [1976:222] has put it, "it will be increasingly recognized [in linguistics] that theory severed from applications is suspect...." When this recognition becomes a reality and linguists once again try to develop a science rather than inhabit a philosophical realm, on that day, and not before, linguistics will again become really relevant to the discipline of languistics. (More on linguistics in Chapters 2 and 4.)

Other feeder disciplines

As with linguistics, much the same with psychology. There are probably as many theories of learning and of the nature of the psyche as there are theories of language. But at least psychologists have not tried to make second language teaching a part of their discipline (witness the absence of an "applied psychology" in our field), at least not yet anyway. However, with the disestablishment of linguistics has come, at about the same time, the emergence of several second language methods directly derived from psychological views.

As with linguistics, too close an association with different schools of psychology has resulted in one-sided practices in second language teaching. Adherence, for two decades, to the simplistic, mindless conditioning of supposedly passive learners was the result of slavishly following the behaviorist psychology of the day. More recently, application of cognitive psychology has led to the other extreme, that is, to the view that learners are infinitely varied and creative and that they cannot be conditioned at all but must be taught everything in a second language as an intellectual exercise first.

As with linguistics, extreme positions in psychology lead to extreme, unwise procedures in languistics. This is unfortunate, because a careful selection of psychological concepts from various theories would illuminate such essential languistic matters as learning processes, intelligence, motivation, attitudes, personality, and so forth. (More on psychology in Chapters 3 and 4.)

Education provided a home for languistics during the mid-sixties, as the Chomskian revolution in linguistics was being won, and as a result second language teaching has come to be known in many quarters as "foreign (or 'modern' or 'second') language education." Having been left homeless by the linguistic revolution, the confused wayfarer --Second Language Teaching-- should be grateful that it was provided with lodgings by Education. But the guest should not become a manservant. He should leave his temporary quarters and settle in a house of his own. For languistics is no more, and maybe less, a part of education than it is a part of linguistics, psychology, literature, or any other discipline.

The reader might be wondering, "If our field is 'second language teaching and learning' isn't that part of education the way 'mathematics education' or 'English education' are part of it? Shouldn't it therefore be called 'second language education'?" No, because there are several important differences. First, what the students have to learn in our field is considerably different from any other subject. The study of the native language calls for the expansion and creative use of a known code; the study of mathematics involves learning a new code via a nonconflicting known code; it is only in second language study that a new code must be learned despite the conflicting demands of a known code. As a consequence of this difference, second language teaching and testing procedures are unique. Secondly, this is the only field of study for which adequate professional preparation means (a) taking several courses in each of a considerable number of disciplines outside education and (b) developing proficiency in a subject well beyond the level that universities can offer, possibly having to go to another country in order to attain it. Third, and most important, no other subject is offered in so many settings clearly beyond the jurisdiction of educators --colleges, universities, government institutes, commercial schools, self-instruction, and living abroad. (Too, note that even the second language teaching that does fall within the purview of educators has been rather unsuccessful.)

It makes no sense to subordinate languistics to education, for it would mean keeping a unique field of study as part of another one with much broader concerns and with jurisdiction over only one instructional setting and a minority of the successful learners. Languistics should encompass *all* the settings in which second language teaching and learning takes place and should not be defined and named just in terms of the education-controlled and largely ineffective elementary and secondary school settings.

There are several additional disadvantages in the education "connection." Undergraduate and graduate education programs reflect the fact that most professors of education have *general* interests of little relevance to languistics (perhaps to any particular teaching field). One result of this is that within faculties of education both languists and second language teachers have to take many education courses that represent an unprofitable use of time in terms of their particular concerns. To the extent that education is emphasized, other disciplines may be neglected; thus, it is frequently the case that in faculties of education second language teachers and languists receive minimum or no training in linguistics, psychology, or the culture fields essential to a well-balanced professional second language background. Moreover, with many laudable exceptions, professors of education tend not to be empirically oriented, so if a field is part of education it will naturally suffer from the general disinterest in objective, careful, data-oriented research.

With regard to the field of literature, which can be defined as "the study of esthetically-superior creative writings," it should be clear just from its definition that its goals, concerns, and research methods are very different from those of languistics. The literature specialist is primarily interested in the esthetics of language use, the languist in functional communication, and this initially at a very simple level. The literature specialist concerns himself mostly with written language, the languist with all modalities but especially with the spoken language. The literature specialist leans towards a very subjective approach to his field, the languist tries to be very objective towards his. The literature specialist's research is based on texts, the languist's primarily on the observation of audiolingual data and experimentation. It is hard to imagine two fields of specialization more different than these two.

It should be obvious, therefore, that even if literary studies can give insights about other cultures, a specialization in literature is not, of itself, at all adequate as a qualification for the second language field. (Of course, many literature specialists do learn something about second language teaching from experience, quite apart from their literary studies.)

It follows, from the marked differences between the two fields, that languistics should never be subordinated to literature or it will suffer numerous negative effects. The view held by many literature specialists is that the only worthwhile reason for learning a second language is to study its literature. This view, when taken to its logical conclusion, makes language secondary --and something anybody can teach--, for all pedagogical and communication considerations are cast aside in order to introduce second language students to literature as soon as possible. The results probably sound familiar to many readers: the students learn neither to communicate in the second language nor to enjoy its literature.

There are really only two useful points of linkage between second language learning and literature. First, when pedagogically suitable to languistic goals, certain literary texts may be selected (and possibly adapted) by languists for use as reading material. Second, once the students have attained the necessary advanced level of proficiency, as determined by languists, one of the most culturally and esthetically self-enriching uses they can put the second language to is the study of literature, and some might even decide to become literature specialists --but this connection with literature comes after the second language program itself is completed.

As we have seen, even the traditional source disciplines of second language teaching are of questionable relevance and often harmful to languistics. And yet, some hold an invalid position of "pedagogical ecumenism," according to which "*any* discipline can be made to seem relevant to foreign language teaching" [Quinn 1974:331]. The disciplines we have discussed have some relevance, but there are many disciplines that can make no such claim. An example is philology. As interesting as it may be to occasionally give a historical insight about a sound, word, or rule to our students, such facts are digressions that have nothing to do with the task of learning a second language. Another example is psychiatry. Our students are, by and large, and despite occasional impressions to the contrary, emotionally normal, so a field that studies abnormal behavior can hardly have relevance for us. Psychology of the normal person gives us all the insights we need into the cognitive and emotional makeup of our students. To claim the backing of psychiatry for methodological practices in languistics --something currently being done for at least two methods-- is to appeal to the authority of a field that is quite unrelated to our concerns. It is as unjustified as an appeal to the authority of religion would be.

Note that neither linguistics, nor psychology, nor education, nor any particular combination of theories from them has brought the second language profession much closer to a solution of our practical problems. In each historical period in our field --Wardhaugh [1974:129-35] classifies them into "prelinguistic," "linguistic" and "contemporary"-- prevailing views on language, learning, and educational goals have been united to produce a particular pattern of language teaching, but no such combination has produced very good results. The reason should by now be clear: to be successful, second language teaching must weave and cut its own cloth, not wear a borrowed multicolored collection of patches barely held together by the pins of fashion.

More on languistics

Languistics can be said to have had its start as a comprehensive and systematic field of study in 1899 with the publication of Henry Sweet's *The Practical Study of Languages* [1899, 1964]. As early as 1917 Harold Palmer [1917, 1968] was calling for the establishment of a "science of language-study." The subtitle of Robert Lado's well-known 1964 book on language teaching is "A Scientific Approach." And yet, our field is far from being a science, for bias and subjectivity pervade it and pervert it.

To be a science, languistics will have to break with much of the past, to develop its own theory and to apply it according to its own principles and procedures. To be a science, languistics will have to dedicate itself to (1) data collection, description, and analysis, (2) the making of explanations that account for the data, (3) the making of predictive hypotheses, (4) experimentation to test the hypotheses, (5) integration of confirmed hypotheses into a theory, and (6) application of the theory in the form of controlled methods, procedures, and techniques. But far from being such a science, our field suffers from limited and subjective observation, contradictory generalizations, little valid prediction, haphazard and limited experimentation, leaving no basis for the confirmation or rejection of hypothesis, their integration into a theory, and the controlled application of the theory.

Without a scientific approach there can be no generally accepted principles, for such principles can be derived only through the objective steps just outlined. And without scientifically derived principles consistent success is impossible. Even those facts already known are not being integrated and applied systematically to second language teaching and learning.

The science of languistics involves interaction between languists, authors of second language materials (who should preferably be languists too), second language teachers (whose preparation should include a good number of languistics courses), students of languistics, and second language students; in addition, there is indirect interaction with feeder disciplines as discussed earlier. The goal of languistics, in addition to optimizing these interactions, consists of (1) optimizing results in second language teaching and learning through (2) the development of a sound languistic theory and (3) its application in the form of valid principles, procedures, and techniques. The goal of second language teaching is to impart (1) linguistic, (2) communicative, and (3) cultural competence to second language learners.

Neither a revolution nor a new orthodoxy

What the second language profession needs is neither another revolution nor a new orthodoxy but an enlightened synthesis that can serve as the basis for a new beginning.

Revolutions have a way of coming and going without leaving many lasting effects. The audiolingual revolution, for example, saw a sharp increase in modern language enrollments but followed the pattern of most revolutions --initial "sale" by its pioneers/leaders, widespread adoption even by many who don't understand the new ideas, resultant misapplication and distortion, disappointment, and abandonment almost *in toto*, throwing "the baby out with the bath water." As Warriner [1980:86] put it, "we never gave the audiolingual revolution a fair chance of succeeding"; among others, a highly mechanistic distortion took the place of the originally successful methodology. It seems to be the same with all new methods, techniques, aids, and devices --once they leave the hands of their originators they are misused, too much is expected of them, and then disappointment sets in, followed by abandonment.

Theoretically based orthodoxies have an equally negative effect. The advocates of new orthodoxies --for example, Jakobovits, Lakoff, Diller, and others for the transformational cognitive approach-- tend to see all in black and white and to condemn all ideas based on previous paradigms --in our example, condemning any manifestation of empiricism, structuralism, and behaviorism. No compromise is allowed. The past is dead. Long live the new orthodoxy. Nothing is really known about second language teaching and learning and nothing will be known until the new prophets reveal it.

New orthodoxies establish tyrannies of what their leaders think should work, on theoretical grounds, regardless of what really works or doesn't. It is only reluctantly that people like Jakobovits [1970-b:34] admit that there seems to be a "curious paradox" in that what seems to work in practice should not, and the better and more powerful theories do not yield practical applications. (One can't help but wonder if perhaps there may be something wrong with some of the new theories.)

Towards enlightened eclecticism

What languistics needs is enlightened eclecticism, leaving behind extreme and unproductive positions and slogans and carrying over from the various positions into the more productive middle ground only those aspects that are logically defensible and demonstrably useful. Such a process of synthesis is very much needed in a field which, like ours, has been disrupted by major revolutions every two decades and lesser changes every three to five years. No doubt change is essential to progress; however, the kind of frequent and radical change there has been in second language teaching, not unlike a pendulum gone berserk, while creating the impression of purposeful movement has been mostly misspent energy leading to confusion.

The need for synthesis, however, should not lead languistics into any haphazard combination of theories and practices. For hasty synthesis can lead to misguided eclecticism, and that would be worse than no synthesis at all. Certain pitfalls must be avoided and certain principles followed.

Misguided eclecticism characteristically shows disregard for some of the evidence, whether factual or logical. It may uncritically accept any procedure that is propounded with sufficient salesmanship, "trying everything in the hope that something will work" [Joiner 1974-c:168]. It may be an excuse for remaining in comfortable ruts. It may combine, from various sources, elements that do not support or even contradict each other. It may consist of blind compromise, automatically choosing the midpoint between any two views --or adopting both-- regardless of merit. Lacking principles, it is philosophically close to the ever-present faddism. Clearly, such eclecticism is undesirable and lacks intellectual respectability.

"Enlightened eclecticism," a phrase coined earlier in another context [Ornstein *et al.* 1971:64], is a better alternative. Something "enlightened," to paraphrase Webster's Third, has been freed from ignorance and misinformation and is based on full comprehension of the problems involved --certainly worthwhile goals. But for enlightened eclecticism to be possible in languistics, three essential conditions would have to be met.

The first condition --already discussed-- is that languistics be viewed as a separate discipline. Only thus will it be able to reject decisively all unacceptable "implications" and inexpedient "applications" of theories in other disciplines. The second condition is an agreement on the goals of second language study. It may be the least difficult condition to meet, for while there can be many second language programs with many different goals, it seems to be recognized that the overall goal of second language study is "communication plus," that is, linguistic, communicative, and cultural competence.

The third condition for the introduction of enlightened eclecticism in languistics is that empirical research on second language teaching and learning be conducted scientifically rather than attempting to fit a particular paradigm. There is no reason for our field to be a form of philosophy in which data are made to fit speculation. It is by interposing bias-free empirical research between theory and practice that informed views based on observable evidence will again weigh more than subjective theorizing. We must be reasonably sure of our facts before we can use them wisely, as wisdom is the right use of knowledge, not the haphazard application of speculation.

After meeting these three conditions, enlightened eclecticism can become a reality by the implementation of the characteristics of its definition: enlightened eclecticism is *the gathering, from all reliable sources, past and present, of the best fact-supported elements that can be combined into a harmonious whole, adapting it to all appropriate variables and aiming it at the efficient and effective attainment of the stated goal*.

It may have been this kind of eclecticism that numerous other second language specialists [Anisfeld 1966, Hanzeli 1968, Ney 1968, Boswell 1972, Hok 1972, Quinn 1974, and many others] had in mind when they proposed an eclectic solution to our problems. It is this kind of enlightened eclecticism which, if adopted, would terminate a long period of confusion, disharmony, and near-anarchy in the second language field. It would open the way, in the discipline of languistics, for the only tyranny that any science can accept --the tyranny of what is true and truly works.

2

LANGUAGE

A definition of language

The wartime Prime Minister was ending a speech before the House of Commons:

> We shall defend our island whatever the cost may be. We shall fight on the beaches, we shall fight on the landing grounds, we shall fight in the hills, we shall never surrender....

This part of the speech given by Winston Churchill on June 4, 1940 set the House of Commons in an uproar, and it is claimed that no one who heard this passage can forget it.

Language.

A charming little fellow points an uncertain, stubby finger toward a four-legged creature in perpetual motion and exclaims, full of glee, "Dawggee!"

Language.

Two extreme examples of it, perhaps; and yet both are readily recognized as occurrences of language. For language ranges from the first one-syllable words of the infant to the eloquent speeches of famous orators, and from the hesitant scribblings of a first-grader to the brilliant writings of widely-read authors.

But just what is language?

Everyone seems to have a more or less vague idea of what it is. Through the centuries, many definitions of language have been proffered by philosophers and literary authors, and more recently by psychologists and linguists. As we turn to linguistics --the science of language-- we find however that there are almost as many definitions of language as there are linguists.

It is nevertheless possible to cull from those numerous linguistic definitions a composite one with which a substantial number of linguists would agree. Such a definition is as follows:

> *A language is a complete, complex, changing, arbitrary system of primarily oral symbols learned and used for communication within the cultural framework of a linguistic community.*

The rest of this chapter is a discussion of the eleven

elements of this definition and of their most important implications for languistics.

A language is complete

The statement that a language is "complete" does not mean that it is a closed system but rather that it is completely adequate for the changing needs of its linguistic community. Until the early twentieth century there were missionaries and travelers who reported coming across exotic languages that were so underdeveloped and limited that their speakers were forced to communicate mostly by gestures. What such reports proved was that the persons making them were linguistically unsophisticated observers, for in each case the language in question was later found to be quite developed and perfectly adequate for the communication needs of its speakers.

Languages are complete for the needs of their communities. In the case of the lexicon, for example, when the members of a linguistic community see the need for a new word or phrase, they readily add it to their language. This may be done by borrowing it from another language, as in the case of *patio, savoir faire* and *blitz* in English. Or a word may be brought into the everyday language out of the comparative obscurity of scientific terminology, as in *antenna*, from entomology, and *satellite*, from astronomy (which after a while replaced the borrowing *sputnik*, at least as far as non-Russian satellites are concerned). Or a word may be created, usually through the combination of existing meaningful parts, as in *television*, but sometimes by other means, as in *radar* (from "*ra*dio *d*etecting *a*nd *r*anging").

The relationship between lexical variety and the needs of society is seen even more clearly when the vocabularies of two or more languages are compared.[△] Thus, in Quechua (spoken by Indians of the former Inca empire in parts of Peru, Bolivia, and Ecuador) there are many words for

---

[△] The hypothesis that lexical variety depends on the needs of society is related to the "Whorfian hypothesis" [Whorf 1956], which holds that each language system correlates to a system of thought that determines the speaker's view of the world. A weaker version of the hypothesis limiting the lack of correspondence between the expressions of two languages to certain lexical fields of social importance seems more valid.

"corn," while English speakers manage with only two. This difference apparently depends on the fact that being able to distinguish clearly between many varieties of corn and stages in its development and use is much more important to the survival of Quechua-speaking Indians than to that of English-speaking peoples, for whom corn is only one among numerous staples.

Language completeness is also relative to the needs of the individual. While a language continues to be learned throughout life, no person knows the whole language and some know far more than others. A manual laborer, for example, seldom needs the degree of language control that a journalist or a politician needs, and as a result he may never develop it.

A language may be temporarily quite incomplete, both for a society and for the individual. Thus, a technologically underdeveloped society will lag behind developed ones in its use of appropriate technological terms. As for the individual, one example of linguistic incompleteness is the situation in which the young child often finds himself --it will probably never be known how many tantrums and other forms of negative child behavior result simply from the frustration of the child at not having the verbal tools to express clearly his thoughts and feelings. Another example is the adult whose thoughts occasionally run ahead of the language at his command or whose communicative performance suffers as a result of faulty linguistic recall.

Among the implications of the completeness/incompleteness of a language for languistics are the following:

(a) No language is better than any other on the whole, since each expresses quite adequately the needs of its society.

(b) Given that far less than the whole language can be taught in the second language program, it becomes necessary to select very carefully what will be taught, so as to make the second language as complete as possible for the communication needs of the learners.

(c) In order to avoid wasting the students' time and forcing them into frustrating situations, they should not be asked to participate actively in communicative activities for which the basic linguistic tools have not been provided.

(d) In cases of faulty recall, language students should learn the technique of circumlocution and, when that is not possible, elicit from the teacher the word or expression they have failed to recall.

A language is complex

Language is the most complex natural system of communication. It is composed of a relatively small number of meaning-free but functionally important sound units, but these occur in many combinations forming many thousands of meaningful word parts and words, and these in turn can be combined into an infinite number of sentences.

By way of contrast, the so-called animal "languages" found in nature consist of a small number of unitary messages --that is, each message seems to be an indivisible unit rather than a combination of meaningful parts that could enter into other combinations and thereby convey different messages. Gorillas have about twenty vocal messages. Dolphins, baboons, and bees --the latter by dancing in the hive-- seem to have even fewer than that. It is evident from this that human language is immeasurably more rich and complex than such animal systems. Codes more complex than human language, such as intelligence codes, do exist, but they are based on language (or on mathematics, which is language-related).

The complexity of languages as systems has at least two implications for languistics:

(a) Second language learning is a complex and long-term task. This realization makes one see how ridiculous are the claims of those who advertise that they can teach a language in a small number of hours ("Learn to Converse in French in Two Weeks!") or with a few recordings ("Learn German the XXX Way: Three Records, $9.95").

(b) Second language teaching must proceed by steps, that is, by emphasizing the various aspects of the complex system in turn as well as integrating the parts learned during communicative activities. A complex system with numerous rules and elements cannot efficiently be learned as a whole, especially after the favorable conditions of early childhood no longer exist.

A language changes

Being a social phenomenon, a language is in a constant state of change, although certain parts of language change faster than others.

Vocabulary is the most changeable part of language. Not only do words and idioms come and go, but words can radically change their meanings over the years.

Examples of lexical disappearance in English are: *twenty-three skiddoo*, which twenty-three skiddooed (skiddid?) away long ago; *running board*; and a word as recent as *lem* (for "lunar module" --remember?). And that recent phrase, *punk rock* --how long will it last? Slang is, naturally, the fastest-changing type of vocabulary; no doubt the reader will be able to think of several examples of slang expressions that came into the language, had their day, and then disappeared.

Many words have changed meanings in English. For example, *awful* used to mean "amazing," and *artificial* used to mean "perfect, skilful." Over three hundred words in the King James Version of the Bible (published in 1611) have changed meaning, with the result that it has become as difficult to read as an income tax form and numerous modern versions have appeared.

In a way, however, changes in the lexicon are not changes in the system of a language but only in some of the units used within that system.

Grammatical changes, though far less frequent than lexical ones, do occur and have a more fundamental effect on the system. An example from English is *thou* and its related forms, which disappeared several centuries ago except from period literature, Christian worship, and the speech of a few isolated communities. Another example is the growing acceptance of *It's me* --though not, of course, by teachers of English!

Phonological changes also occur occasionally. In the eighteenth century, for instance, the pronunciation /š/[△] was substituted for /ty/ in words such as *nation* and for /sy/ in words such as *issue*. Another example is the loss of the distinction between /t/ and /d/ in the North American pronunciation of words such as *latter* and *ladder*.

The changeability of language leads to four main implications for languistics:

(a) For students whose primary or only goal is learning to communicate in a second language, the current, modern form of the language should be presented. Current French is not learned by reading *chansons de geste*. For the student who wants to learn current Spanish, Cervantes' *Don Quijote de la Mancha* would hardly be indicated. Students of English as a second language would find Shakespeare nearly incomprehensible and largely irrelevant to their linguistic needs. (The study of literary masterpieces

----

[△] Slant lines enclose phonemic symbols. Phonemes --functional units of sound proposed by structural linguists-- are discussed in Chapters 4 and 15.

written in an older form of the language has its own intrinsic value --cultural, historical, and literary-- but it should not be confused nor allowed to interfere with the learning of the current form of the language, which should be assured first.)

(b) Data from historical (or "diachronic") linguistics may be quite interesting but it is largely irrelevant to languistics. Any information about a previous state of the language is unessential to the second language program.

(c) Because languages change, language teaching materials must also change. This does not mean that they should attempt to include the latest slang --a hopeless task, since by the time the manuscripts are published, much of the "latest" slang would be obsolete. But language materials should be kept up to date with regard to the more established colloquial forms of the language, and this makes new editions necessary at least every ten years.

(d) Second language teachers should keep up, if not with the latest slang, at least with the most current colloquialisms in everyday use.

Language systems are arbitrary

There are, to be sure, certain features which various languages share --otherwise no comparisons would be possible-- and also a few features that seem to be characteristic of all languages and may therefore be called "language universals." But language universals are hardly a concern for the second language learner, whose goal is to master the *particular* characteristics of the language he is studying.

As a social phenomenon, each language has its own set of phonological, lexical, and grammatical conventions which, at least at the surface level of actual utterances, differ from those of any other language.

The following are some examples of arbitrariness in grammar:

--The third person singular possessive pronominal adjectives agree (a) with the gender of the possessor in English, as in *his house* and *her house*; (b) with the gender of the possessed in French, as in *sa maison* and *son bureau*; and (c) with neither in Spanish, as in *su casa* and *su libro*.

--Demonstratives are divided into three distances/relationships in Spanish, as in *este libro, ese libro,* and *aquel libro,* two in English, as in *this book* and *that book,* and have only one in French, *ce livre,* which only optionally may be expanded into *ce livre-ci* and *ce livre-là*.

--In subordinate clauses, the verb remains in its main clause position in English, Spanish, and French, but it shifts to final position in German:

E: I know he'*s going* to Toronto.
S: Sé que *va* a Toronto.
F: Je sais qu'il *va* à Toronto.
G: Ich weiss, dass er nach Toronto *geht*.

--Hungarians do not use prepositions but postpositions; the Hungarian equivalent of *in the garden* is *a kocsiban*, that is, *"the garden-in."[△]

--In Japanese, nouns are seldom marked for plurality and never after a number; thus, the way of saying *three cars* in Japanese is the equivalent of *"three car." (When one thinks about it, one cannot help but conclude that the noun plural marker used in English after a cardinal number is quite redundant; but it is in the nature of social conventions that they are seldom logical.)

In terms of vocabulary, different languages divide the same reality differently. Some examples follow:

--English *to know* has *two* equivalent words (that is, its meaning is divided between two words) in Spanish (*saber* and *conocer*), French (*savoir* and *connaître*), and German (*wissen* and *kennen*).

--*Sensible* means very different things in English and Spanish or English and French.

--There is no one-word way of saying *shallow* in French or *afford* in Spanish.

The following are instances of arbitrariness in phonology:

--English and German /p/, /t/, and /k/ are aspirated (that is, followed by a sudden release of air) at the beginning of stressed syllables, but French and Spanish /p/, /t/, and /k/ are not.

--The sounds [s] and [z][☆] can make a difference between one word and another in English, French, and German, but not in Spanish.

--English and French use the word-initial consonant sequences /sp-/ and /st-/, but standard German normally

----

[△] An asterisk precedes an utterance that does not normally occur in the language being used.

[☆] Square brackets enclose phonetic symbols; a complete list of those used in this book appears in Appendix A.

does not and Spanish never does.

One linguistic implication of the arbitrariness shown by these and numerous other differences between languages is that little or no appeal can be made to logic. The reason why a Frenchman, for example, speaks the way he does is simply that his parents, his grandparents, and so on spoke in almost exactly the same way --assuming, of course, no shift in geographic or social dialect. So, most student questions of the type "Why do they say it this way?" have to be answered with "Because." If an historical explanation were attempted, how far back would it have to go --Proto-Indoeuropean? Note that even that would not really answer the question "Why?"

The main linguistic implication of the arbitrariness of languages is that learning a second language consists primarily in learning to use phonological, grammatical, and lexical conventions different from one's own. Of course, the learner must also practice what he has learned of the second language, together with what is common to both languages, as an integrated whole, for otherwise communication would be impossible.

A language is a system

As a system, a language is made up of interrelated parts or subsystems. These subsystems have to do with either *form* or *meaning*, although form and meaning almost always go together.

With regard to *form*, a language has the interrelated subsystems of word order (*syntax*), word formation (*morphology*),[Δ] and sounds (*phonology*), which most linguists organize variously into *components* and some linguists call *levels of analysis*.

An example of a pattern of *meaning* is the subsystem of antonyms, such as *tall/short*, *fat/skinny*, and *wide/narrow*.

(Linguists have described language systems in many ways, the major two approaches in North America being the structuralist and the generative-transformationalist. The pros and cons of these two approaches and their implications for second language teaching will be discussed in Chapter 4.)

In language learning, form and meaning do not always go together. Thus it is possible to have:

[Δ] These two subsystems are so closely interrelated that they are often merged into *morphosyntax* or simply *grammar*.

--knowledge of form without knowledge of meaning, as when a person hears a new word and can repeat it but does not know what it means; and

--knowledge of meaning without knowledge of form, as when a listener knows from the context, intonation, or gestures what is meant but cannot repeat accurately one or more words.

The fact that form and meaning do not always go together in language learning provides further justification --in addition to the fact that "it works"-- for the second language teaching practice of temporarily separating form and meaning when such a temporary separation facilitates the learning process. This refers to echoic activities where attention to meaning would detract from full attention to form.

The fact that language systems have a limited number of formal rules but an extremely large number of lexical elements suggests that the formal rules should be the basic framework around which the lexical elements fit. This in turn implies that most second language teaching, at least in the early stages, should be directed towards the learning of that basic framework of linguistic structure, both through drills and communicative activities. It would be a mistake to place early emphasis on the learning of much vocabulary, for at least two reasons:

--Although vocabulary is important for communication, it is the easiest component of language for a learner to acquire mostly on his own, and thus such acquisition can take place mainly outside the instructional program.

--With a good control of structure and a limited but carefully selected vocabulary, much can be said, with considerable accuracy; in the opposite situation --a large vocabulary but little structural control-- much that is said is unintelligible and much of the rest is socially unacceptable.

A language is primarily oral

There are several reasons why many people think that the written form of a language is primary and the spoken form a somewhat corrupted derivation of it. Among them are the following:

--The greatest concern of educators has been the imparting of literacy and the greatest educational goal of peoples and individuals has been its acquisition.

--Until recently, the written form of the language was the only one having any permanence.

--Many important concerns of people are associated with written documents, not only personal legal documents but also those having to do with religion (the Bible, the Koran, etc.), politics (constitutions and manifestoes), and so forth.

--An aura of superiority for the written form of the language comes from the fact that it is the vehicle for cultural, intellectual, and artistic pursuits, such as literature, philosophy, and so on.

But careful observations about the nature and use of language lead to the conclusion that, while in literate societies the spoken and written forms interact, speech is the primary form of language and writing is based on it. Some of the considerations leading to such a conclusion follow below.

First, a worldwide look at languages reveals that, of about 3,000 languages, only a few hundred are normally written. The unwritten languages are nevertheless languages in the full sense of the term, generally as complex, expressive, and sophisticated as the ones that have a written form.

Second, the written forms of languages appear to have developed historically much later than their spoken forms, which again would make speech more basic.

Third, speech is much more dynamic. In many languages the written form lags decades or even, in some respects, centuries behind well-established features of the spoken language. For instance, such English spellings as *name* and *spoon* were a good representation of the spoken forms [na:me] and [spo:n], pronunciations that were standard until the "great English vowel shift" of the fifteenth century changed them into /neym/ and /spuwn/ without, unfortunately, a corresponding change in spelling.

Fourth, the distinction between speech and writing and evidence that speech is basic can be seen in the fact that when languages have undergone a change in their writing systems, no change whatever has occurred in the way people have expressed themselves orally. An example of this is the change in the Turkish alphabet, from Arabic to Roman, that took place in 1929.

Fifth, note that a language may be written in several ways. In Japanese, for example, it is possible to write the content words with ideographs (*kanji*), or with two different syllabaries (*katakana* and *hiragana*), so the spoken language cannot be a derivation of the written.

A sixth point is that the opposite situation is also

found, that is, two or more languages may be written in the same way, further demonstrating the relative independence of speech and writing. Chinese ideographs, for instance, can be read as very different words in Chinese and Japanese. To give an example, 人 ("man") is [ǰɛn] in Mandarin Chinese and [hi'to] in Japanese.

Seventh, learning to speak his native language is a natural part of the cognitive and social development of the young child --he is not *taught* the spoken language but by the age of four or five he has mastered it. The written form of the language, however, is not learned naturally, as a result of social interaction, but must be taught.

Eighth, in teaching a child to read and write his native language, writing is presented as a representation of *spoken* language that the child has *already* learned, with only occasional exceptions. That is to say, writing represents spoken language, not the other way around.

Ninth, far from speech being a corrupted form derived from the written language, it is writing that is generally a poor representation of speech. Even in the case of "phonetic"[△] languages like Spanish, there are considerable inconsistencies, and ease of interpretation may be (a) unidirectional --letters to sounds but not sounds to letters-- and (b) available to native speakers only, at least initially. For instance, Spanish *bota* and *vota* are both pronounced ['bota]. In less "phonetic" languages, i.e., languages with a poorer fit between sounds and spelling, there may be many such examples. In French *sent, cent, sans,* and *sang* are all pronounced [sɑ̃]. In English, the phoneme /f/ may be represented by *f*, *ff*, *ph*, or *gh* (*enough*). Conversely, several sound units may be represented by the same letter or combination of letters; for example, English *ea* may stand for /iy/ (*sea*), /e/ (*leather*), /ey/ (*steak*), and /ɑ/ (*heart*).

A tenth point is that not only is the written language a poor representation of what it does represent of the spoken language, but it may not even represent at all certain very important features of speech such as intonation contours, stress patterns, rhythm, syllabification, etc. In some languages, this lack of representation may even apply

---

[△] This is a popular use of the word "phonetic," to mean "having a good fit between sounds and letters"; of course *all* living languages are "phonetic" in the sense that they have "phones" (sounds) and phonetic features.

to consonant and vowel sounds. In English, for instance, the by far most frequent spoken vowel unit, the mid-central /ə/ as in the first syllable of *about*, has no written representation of its own and is represented variously with all five written vowels plus the letter *y*.

Finally, even in highly literate nations such as the United States and Canada the percentage of spoken communication far exceeds that of written communication. Back in the 1920s, long before the development of all-pervasive media like television, it was estimated that oral communication was more than 75 percent of all communication.

It seems clear from the above points that, while the two forms of language are relatively independent, the written language is based primarily on the spoken, rather than the other way around, and that speech is therefore the basic form of language. This leads us to the conclusion that speech should be emphasized in second language teaching and that the distinction between speech and writing should be carefully maintained. In addition to the general reasons given above, three practical arguments can be offered for this position, as follows:

First, several studies have shown that speech and the written language pull the attention of the second language learner in different directions [Richards and Appel 1956, Foster and Williams 1960, Muller 1965, Roland 1966, Hammerly 1970-a, many others]. While exposure to reading from the start may help speech recall in a general way and may support, also broadly, listening comprehension, these studies clearly show that early and sudden exposure to the standard written language interferes with sound discrimination and speech accuracy in a number of important particular ways. (A few studies [Estarellas and Regan 1966, Lipton 1969, Hawkins 1971] claim different results, but they have had confounding variables or an inadequate evaluation of the students' pronunciation.)

Second, simultaneous or temporally contiguous information from several senses is popularly believed to facilitate learning, and it seems indeed to facilitate certain learning tasks. But when information from one sense *contradicts* information from another sense, the result is not facilitation but either confusion or rejection of one sense in favor of the other, regardless of the consequences. In second language learning, the sense of sight often contradicts the sense of hearing rather than the two being mutually reinforcing. The result, given the greater eye-dependency of most literate persons, is that when the two senses contradict each other they disbelieve their ears and follow the written code, but according to the interpretation given in their *native* language to the letters of the written code.

Third, several studies have indicated that beginning second language students are more interested in developing audiolingual[△] skills than in reading literature or in writing [Agard and Dunkel 1948:292, Politzer 1953, Scherer and Wertheimer 1964:24, Hammerly 1971-b]. The percentage of beginners with audiolingual goals has been between 80 and 90 percent in those studies in which preference was quantified. Interestingly, students who prefer audiolingual goals may do so even though they are fully aware that they face a harder learning task than would be the case if they limited themselves to reading and writing [Hammerly 1971-b].

Of course, the learning strategies of literate students are bound to differ from those of preliterate young children, so it would seem unwise to treat the older learners, who may be largely visually dependent, as if they were young children. They need to be given some kind of visual reminder of what they have heard and said, or they will have difficulty practicing and remembering it. But this visual support should be fully supportive, unlike the misleading standard spelling (what this visual support should be is explained in Chapter 15).

From the discussion in this section, the following implications for languistics emerge:

(a) The main stream of the second language program should offer all four intralingual language skills --listening, speaking, reading, and writing-- but with emphasis on the spoken language throughout, for the large majority of students who prefer such an emphasis. Those who only want to learn to read should have such an option; but it should be made clear to them that such a choice may mean they will never be able to speak the language fluently and accurately.

(The remaining implications apply to the main, oral stream.)

(b) In describing the second language to the students, a clear distinction should be maintained between statements

----

[△] Throughout this book the term "audiolingual" is used in the sense of "listening and speaking" [Brooks 1975]; only when followed by the words "method" or "approach" does it refer to teaching procedures.

that apply to the spoken language and those that apply to the written language only. For example, the statement that "an *e* is added to the masculine of French adjectives to form the feminine" applies to the written language only. Similarly, spoken English noun plurals are *not* formed by "adding -*s* and -*es*."

(c) Since the standard written language tends to interfere with phonological accuracy in the spoken language (while the opposite is seldom the case), the two forms of language, audiolingual and graphic, should be kept temporally separate and learning to read should be a gradual activity preceded by the establishment of a spoken foundation. This implies two practices: (1) training second language learners so that they can again rely primarily on hearing rather than sight, and (2) providing, as a temporary "crutch," a visual reminder of pronunciation, intonation, etc. that does not result in phonological interference of its own and that leads gradually to spelling.

(d) An audiolingual emphasis must be maintained throughout the program, for most language communication, by far, is spoken rather than graphic. Programs that start with an audiolingual emphasis but gradually shift to an emphasis on reading and writing will naturally tend to produce parallel results in student proficiency, from an adequate early speaking proficiency through its gradual loss and replacement by passive reading skill.

(e) Skill in reading and writing, despite such claims in the early sixties, does not automatically result from audiolingual proficiency. While audiolingual proficiency seems to greatly facilitate the learning of the graphic skills (assuming an alphabet), apparently far more so than the other way around, reading and writing must be taught.

(f) Since only a small minority in any culture is interested in literature and since most second language students are mainly interested in *communication*, literary studies should not be the only kind of advanced language study available. The advanced language student should have a number of options open to him.

(g) The greater motivation of students to learn to speak rather than just read, and their willingness to work harder toward a spoken communication goal should be taken full advantage of by providing satisfying activities in the process of reaching such a goal. Spoken communication of a limited nature can and should start quite early, and it can gradually become more and more sophisticated. Any considerable length of time without spoken communication can result in a major loss of motivation.

A language is composed of symbols

All symbols are, by definition, "arbitrary meaningful conventions."

The symbols of language are not letters (though in another context letters can be referred to as "graphic symbols"), for a letter is not meaningful in itself. Neither are they sounds, for sounds *per se* have no meaning. (The /ə/ of *a book* has meaning not as a sound but as a morpheme; proof of this is that it means nothing in *allow*.) The symbols of language are its "minimal meaningful units" or *morphemes*, of which in English there is only one in, for instance, *Mississippi* or *Saskatchewan*, and three in *pompously* --the noun stem *pomp*, the adjectival suffix *-ous*, and the adverbial suffix *-ly*.

The form of language symbols, which with very few exceptions are social conventions inherited from previous generations, is arbitrary in the sense that there is no direct relationship between their sounds and what they refer to. With a different set of historical circumstances, *table* might mean "chair" and *chair* might mean "table"; furthermore, there is nothing in the sounds of these two words to suggest the objects to which they refer. The very few exceptions to this arbitrariness are onomatopoeic words such as *boom, meow, ping-pong,* etc., which imitate noises. But even with these words there is some arbitrariness --to a Spanish speaker, for example, a dog does not bark *bow-wow* but *guau guau*, and never *arf*; to a Japanese speaker, a dog goes *wan-wan*, with a quite arbitrary nasal.

There are cases where two or more languages have certain language symbols with very similar form and very similar or identical meaning, that is, *cognate* words. *False cognates (faux amis* is the picturesque French name for them) are very similar in form but have different meanings --as in Spanish *lectura* or French *lecture* vs. English *lecture*-- and their teaching presents problems that will be discussed in Chapter 18.

Among implications for languistics, the fact that the meanings of language symbols are social conventions of each linguistic community should lead one to be wary of assuming vocabulary equivalences across languages. However, the lack of equivalences has been grossly exaggerated. (This matter will be discussed further in Chapter 14.)

Languages are learned

There is lively debate on such questions as how the native language is acquired, whether some aspects of language are innate, how much second language learning resembles native language acquisition, and so forth. These and other related questions will be considered in Chapters 5 and 11, and a theory of second language teaching/learning will emerge as this book progresses. At this point, however, some general observations and their implications can be stated.

There is no reason to believe that specific features of a language are inborn. It seems that only the *ability* to learn language(s) is innate, given the requisite minimum intelligence, and that this ability has a particular specialized locus in the brain from well before birth.

The ability to learn very limited language-like communication systems is also present in higher animals like chimpanzees and gorillas, as a number of experiments have shown. They can be taught systems containing up to about 300 "words" --not verbal but in the form of signs or button pressing-- and can even produce certain "grammatical transformations" and "novel sentences." Four important differences remain: (a) this is not a natural social development, (b) the systems are quite limited, (c) animals seem unable to refer to something removed from their environment, and (d) they are unable to pass this learned knowledge to their offspring.

Learning a language is a relatively difficult, time-consuming task. It means developing such a degree of control over its phonological and grammatical patterns or rules that most can be used automatically. It means learning a vocabulary large enough to permit effortless communication on a broad range of topics. It means that, each minute, at the normal rate of speech of about 150 words, the speaker must be able to make several hundred lexical, grammatical, and phonological choices or distinctions, most of which must necessarily be unconscious and automatic, for otherwise communication would be impossible, since his attention needs to be almost exclusively on *what* he wants to say and is saying rather than on *how* he will say it. The fact that almost all children accomplish this by the age of four or five says much about the enormous capacity of the human brain.

A languistic implication of the fact that even children with a fairly low IQ acquire their native language is the following: While learning a second language may be difficult and time-consuming, given sufficient motivation and the right conditions all normal people can do it. This does not detract from the evidence that some second language learners are better at it than others [Naiman *et al.* 1975].

Furthermore, second languages are learned mostly as the result of teaching. Thus the languist and the second language teacher do not have to pay much attention to rather demoralizing turns of phrase such as "...that people can teach, is an interesting hypothesis, but unsubstantiated" [Jakobovits 1971:91]. There is evidence that some second language teachers are more effective than others, and some of the characteristics of the better teachers have been isolated [Politzer and Weiss, n.d.]. Moreover, there is also considerable evidence that major differences in methodology produce marked differences in outcome as long as the methods are kept clearly distinct.[△]

It would seem therefore that unlike native language acquisition, which occurs to a fairly advanced level without instruction, second language learning is greatly facilitated by instruction, which can speed up the learning process by selecting, organizing, grading, and (when desirable) explaining the linguistic data to be learned. Such facilitation and speeding up of the language learning process are available neither to the native language acquirer nor to the second language acquirer who is simply surrounded with the ungraded language in a "sink or swim" approach.

[△] This has been the case in a good number of studies, of which the following are examples: (1) Delattre 1947; (2) Scherer and Wertheimer 1964, i.e., the results for the first year, as during the second year there was no methodological distinction; and (3) Hammerly 1965. That the Pennsylvania Project [P. D. Smith 1970] showed no marked differences is due to a considerable number of deficiencies, of which the following are examples: (a) inadequate teacher retraining, pp. 27-31; (b) assignment of many teachers to the method not wanted by them, the "functional skills" method, p. 20; (c) insufficient distinction between methods to begin with, p. 62, etc; and (d) inadequate adherence to methods, p. 188, coupled with a poor system of observation. (Experimental studies in second language methodology are discussed in Chapter 24.)

A language is primarily used for communication

While perhaps less than half of all communication is verbal --it has been suggested that as much as 70 percent may be visual, in the form of pictures, body language, etc.--, the most frequent use of language, by far, is for interpersonal communication. The progress in telecommunications and the increase in international travel have only made it more so. When one considers that a performer can be said to be communicating to his audience and an author to his readers, few uses of language not involving communication are left. (Among the latter are the echoic uses of language --singing in the shower, for instance-- and its use in very deliberate thought.)

Communication with other people is not only linguistic but also social. Among other things, a speaker can avoid negative social reactions by speaking accurately, realizing that getting his thoughts across in any old way just won't do. Strictly linguistic communication, without regard to negative reactions, is possible even with numerous errors thanks to the redundancy of language. It should be kept in mind, however, that (a) the greater the number of errors the lesser the redundancy and therefore the intelligibility, and (b) even a single error can occasionally result in linguistic misunderstanding.

Languistic implications of the preceding discussion include the following:

(a) Second language programs should take advantage of the students' motivation to communicate and offer opportunities for communication from the start, even if very limited and simple at first.

(b) Through careful selection, organization, and presentation of the linguistic data, and through the correction of student errors, second language learners should be encouraged to be as accurate as possible in their use of the language, keeping in mind that accuracy enhances both the intelligibility and the acceptability of communication.

A language is used within a culture

Culture and language are inseparably intertwined. Even though for analytic purposes it is possible to distinguish between verbal and other forms of behavior, such a separation is largely artificial.

Knowledge of a language must entail, to be functionally adequate, knowledge of the cultural connotations of words, the gestures, and the appropriate verbal and nonverbal behavior for the various situations in which the language is used in the second culture.

The languistic implication of the above is that it is not enough for the second language program to impart linguistic competence and communicative competence; it must also impart cultural competence. (Cultural competence is discussed in Chapter 20.)

A language is used in a linguistic community

It is hoped that the reader will forgive the unavoidable circularity of this subtitle. Linguistic communities must be discussed in terms of the languages used in them and the languages themselves in terms of the communities in which they are used.

The boundary between two languages is based on the criterion of lack of mutual intelligibility between speakers. Sometimes in geographically contiguous languages --as in areas between France and Italy or between Germany and the Netherlands-- the linguistic boundaries are not clear-cut but there is a gradual shifting from one language to the other; but usually the boundaries are clear.

Linguistic communities can be of several types: (1) regions within a country or countries where another, official language is spoken, as with Catalan, Basque, and Quechua; (2) regions within a country where two or more official languages are spoken, as with French in Canada and Belgium; (3) regions corresponding to political boundaries, as with Icelandic and Swedish; and (4) regions embracing several countries or parts of countries, which may even be widely separated, as with English, French, and Spanish, or adjoining, as with German.

Within a linguistic community there are usually several mutually intelligible varieties of the language or *dialects*, a term without pejorative connotations. Dialects can be defined geographically ("dialects" in the narrow sense), occupationally ("registers"), or socially ("styles"), in most cases approximately. The Spanish dialects spoken by a *madrileño*, a *porteño* from Buenos Aires, and a *mexicano* are geographically distinct dialects. The French dialects spoken by a Parisian member of the *Académie Française* and by an uneducated Parisian butcher are examples of socially distinct dialects (registers-styles).

While the speaker of a language can usually manage quite well by being able to speak a single (educated) dialect, he needs to understand the various dialects he will come in contact with if he is to be a successful communicator.

Dialects differ in at least three other dimensions, as follows:

--The number of their speakers.

--Their internal simplicity, in terms of structure. A dialect may have, for example, one or several fewer sound units than another dialect.

--The prestige they enjoy among the members of the linguistic community.

Languistically, a frequent question is: Which dialect(s) of language X should be taught? The answer is not simple, but the following suggestions are relevant:

First, only one dialect --with several registers and styles-- needs to be taught for active use. However, second language students should be exposed to a variety of dialects for comprehension purposes, preferably at the late intermediate or advanced levels so as to avoid confusion.

Second, the three factors of number of speakers, structural simplicity, and cultural prestige should be weighed, perhaps in that order, keeping in mind that the needs of the students are more important than tradition. "Latin American" Spanish, for instance, has many more speakers and a simpler structure (both phonologically and morphologically) than Castilian Spanish; these two factors should have greater weight than the traditionally greater prestige of the Madrid dialect --except, of course, when a group of students is learning Spanish in preparation for a sojourn in Spain. Similarly, standard Southern French offers certain pedagogical advantages --a simpler sound system, etc.-- over Parisian French, though not its prestige.

A final point is that sometimes the best solution to the dialect question is to teach a *hybrid* "dialect" that combines features common to most dialects and eliminates regionalisms. "Latin American" Spanish is just such a hybrid dialect, for there is not one but many dialects of Spanish in Latin America. Listeners may wonder where the speaker of a hybrid dialect comes from, but the advantage of learning such a dialect is that the speaker would be understood everywhere.

3

LEARNING

The multiple facets of learning

(1) A dog learns to salivate when a bell rings. A child learns to withdraw his hand when his mother cries "Hot!" This is classical conditioning [Pavlov 1927] or *signal learning*.[△]

(2) A monkey learns to press a lever to get a peanut. A child learns that saying "Ma" or "Pa" will get him a hug. Here we are dealing with *stimulus-response learning* [Watson 1914, 1919; Skinner 1938, etc.].

(3) A chicken learns to play a tune on the piano by pecking at the keyboard. A child learns to tie his shoelaces. Both are instances of motor *chaining* (Skinner 1938, etc.].

(4) An American school child learns to recite the Pledge of Allegiance. A student of French learns to reproduce a previously unknown dialogue sentence. These cases of verbal memorization are examples of *verbal association* or verbal chaining.

(5) A young child learns to differentiate between dogs, cats, horses, and cows. This is a case of *multiple discrimination*. The same would be true of the student of French who learns to discriminate between [ü] and both [u] and [i].

(6) A young child learns to respond to all dogs as "dogs" regardless of size, age, breed, color, etc. This is an instance of *concept learning*. Involved is a generalization based on concrete stimuli.

(7) A child grasps the concept of "justice." A student of Spanish learns one of the rules affecting the choice of *ser* versus *estar*. Abstract concept formation and rule learning, both of which are based on combinations of previously learned concepts, are examples of *principle learning*.

△ This term, together with the other italicized terms about types of learning given in this section, is taken from Gagné 1977.

(8) A child figures his way through numerical data, applying previously learned rules, and comes up with the solution to a problem in arithmetic. A translator takes into account numerous rules, many of them consciously, and produces an English version of a paragraph in German. In both cases, what is involved is *problem solving*, the result of thinking in which previously learned concepts and principles are combined consciously to focus on unresolved or ambiguous events.

Toward a definition of human learning

The eight types of learning --from the most mechanical to the most cognitive-- briefly discussed above are an indication of the fact that learning is a very complex activity and one that does not lend itself to easy definition. This should not lead us to the discouraging position taken by some, namely, that little is known or will ever be known about learning; for as Carroll [1974-b:113] noted, while there is much we do not know about learning, there is also much we *do* know, not only about learning in general, but also about second language learning in particular. Lately, especially, much is being done to study learning, as opposed to just teaching, which was the emphasis of the educational literature since the Renaissance.

It is clear, from the fact that animals are incapable of performing the more cognitive types of learning activities humans can perform, that a definition of learning based on animal behavior would be too restrictive to include all forms of human learning and a definition based on human cognitive activities would include much that animals cannot do. Furthermore, a definition of human learning should be broad enough to encompass a range of laws of learning, for trying to establish *the* laws of learning would be analogous to a medical researcher attempting to develop a single vaccine for all diseases [Asher 1972:162].

Human learning can be defined as "a relatively permanent change in knowledge or behavior that results from experience." Note that learning in humans is usually but not always observable. Furthermore, the learning experience may be formal, as in the case of instruction, which results in "learning" in its narrow sense, or informal, as in the case of the non-instructional environment, which can be said to result in "acquisition" in its narrow sense. We should further distinguish [Corder 1968] between "learning to know" or "cognitive knowledge," which involves a change in mental organization that may not be observable, and "learning to do" or "performative knowledge," which involves an observable change in behavior, mediated by practice and possibly taking cognitive knowledge as its point of departure. (Note that practice can also result in a change in mental organization, which must always be present at some point.)

Toward a definition of second language learning

Second language learning, unlike native language acquisition or second language acquisition, can be defined as "a relatively permanent improvement in second language knowledge or behavior resulting from instruction." Second language learning is controlled by the teacher or the teaching materials. Native language acquisition and second language acquisition are not controlled directly by anyone and only very indirectly by the sociolinguistic environment.

We can say that second language learning involves the following factors:

Who learns: The learner and his characteristics (see Chapter 6).

Why he learns: The learner's motivation (also Chapter 6).

How he learns: The learner's cognitive processes (in this chapter).

What he learns: The language (Chapters 2, 4, and others).

From whom he learns: The teacher (Chapter 8).

By what means he learns: By being taught (Chapter 7) through a variety of methods (Chapter 12), and so forth.

Behaviorism or cognitivism?

It is clear from our discussion so far that neither behaviorism nor cognitivism accounts fully for the processes of human learning or, more specifically, second language learning. The more extreme behaviorists reduce human beings to bundles of responses and adopt, in order to be "scientific," the unreasonable convention that the mind does not exist. This naturally leads, in second language teaching, to an emphasis on mindless conditioning. Perfectly intelligent human beings are treated as if they were pigeons or rats, with stress on repetition, the avoidance of explanations, and the attempt to eliminate all possibility of error. We can say, with the wag quoted by Mowrer [1960-a:*x*], that a behaviorist psychologist is "an individual who thinks that the human race is directly descended from the white rat" --many second language teachers seem to have had the same belief.

But if it is unscientific to adopt the convention that the mind does not exist, when the results of mental processes are constantly evident, it is equally unscientific to go to the other extreme and state that imitation, practice, reinforcement, and generalization are no longer valid concepts in our field [Jakobovits 1970-b:24], i.e., that language acquirers/learners are not conditioned at all. *Once* a language is known, it seems clear that it is *used* in a largely "stimulus free and innovative" manner [Chomsky 1966:46], but it seems equally clear that *while* it is being learned stimuli, practice, reinforcement, and generalization play a very important part in the learning process.

The important thing to remember is that conditioning --not mindless but intelligent conditioning-- "works" in the second language teaching/learning process, as second language learning means, among other things, the automatization of numerous rules. If it "works," it is obviously theoretically sound and productive regardless of its critics. Of course, the key is the word *"intelligent"* conditioning. The mind of the human learner is quite active during all but the simplest learning processes.

In answer to the question that heads this section, therefore, we must conclude that practice without understanding (the extreme behaviorist approach) is not conducive to creative linguistic competence, and understanding without practice (the extreme cognitive approach) is conducive to neither fluent nor accurate linguistic performance. What is needed is intelligent practice or practice with understanding; what is needed is both cognition and behavior; what is needed is a synthesis in the form of what, for lack of a better term, we can call *cognitively-based behaviorism.*

Such a theory would recognize a variety of types of learning, with the complex types based on but qualitatively different from, the basic types. If analyzed into its ultimate and simplest elements, even the most complex and cognitive type of learning would be based on conditioning of one form or another. As it refers to formal second language learning, conditioning accounts directly for an important part of the process, but far from all of it; another important part consists of various types of conceptual learning (*ultimately* based on conditioning).

Conditioning

In its simple form, conditioning consists of the repetition of a stimulus, a response, and a reinforcement (serving to strengthen the association between the stimulus and the response) to the point where that particular response to that particular stimulus comes to be reasonably expected. More complex conditioning involves learning to produce discriminative responses to discriminative stimuli. That this is effective in second language teaching/learning can easily be demonstrated by teaching a morphological agreement rule such as the one illustrated by the following Spanish sentence:

Hay un chico alto aquí.
/a /a /a
/os /os /os
/as /as /as

With proper teaching, such a pattern can be internalized in a few minutes. Such teaching would emphasize correlation drills (see Chapter 17 and Appendix B); of course, the conditioning would be "intelligent" or cognitively-based, as the students would know that they are making gender and number agreements.

A *stimulus* ("S") is usually external, i.e., something to respond to or act upon. Internal stimulation is also possible, as the responses themselves may stimulate further responses of that nature. A stimulus is said to be a *discriminative stimulus* ("S^D") when it indicates what response will be reinforced, that is, when it signals reinforcement for a particular response. Note that, while stimulus-response ("S-R") association is ultimately the basis for all learning, it is not very evident in humans because, except for young babies, they have learned much already and therefore more complex forms of learning are in evidence. In second language teaching/learning, we seldom deal with the learning of one particular response to one particular stimulus via one particular reinforcement; instead, it is normally a matter of discriminating between groups of stimuli with several responses that are rewarded in a variety of ways. For that reason, the simplest S-R findings from psychological experiments are not directly applicable to second language teaching/learning.

A *response* ("R") can be overt or covert. In the second language classroom, as in most other situations, only overt responses can be evaluated and overtly rewarded, thus resulting in the most effective type of conditioning. It should be noted, however, that observers who are responding covertly may also be reinforced by what has been called "vicarious reinforcement" [Bandura 1970]; that is, upon observing the reinforcement for someone else's response, they learn how to respond themselves.

Reinforçement ("Reinf.") is not just any kind of reward but an act that by choice increases or decreases the occurrence of the behavior it follows. Positive reinforcement increases the likelihood of the behavior it follows; its removal ("non-reinforcement") decreases the likelihood of the behavior it follows. A negative reinforcer can be applied ("punishment" or "correction"), in which it decreases the likelihood of the behavior it follows; an aversive condition can also be removed (this is, technically, "negative reinforcement"), in which case the likelihood of the associated behavior increases.

Note that for conditioning to be effective, reinforcement must occur after the correct response and not after other responses; in other words, reinforcement must be *contingent* upon the desired response. For human learners are cognitively active and perceive whatever follows their responses to stimuli as the reinforcement for those responses --second language students, for example, are always looking for knowledge of the results of their responses.

Thus essential linguistic reinforcement --knowledge of the rightness or wrongness of the response-- should be prompt in coming or other intervening acts will be interpreted as reinforcing. To put it differently, reinforcement must be immediate to be effective, especially at the beginning of any conditioning sequence. Reinforcement can be effective even after a delay of 30 or so seconds, but only where there is no confounding intervening activity, something that is only possible in an artificial laboratory environment.

As the conditioning sequence progresses, reinforcement of correct responses should become intermittent, as it has been shown that this makes the learned behavior more resistant to extinction --the "Humphreys effect" [Humphreys 1939]. So reinforcement should be gradually phased out, since we want the conditioned behavior to continue to occur even in many situations where it will not be specifically reinforced. What happens in effect is that the learner becomes more resistant to the frustration of not being reinforced [Mowrer 1960-b:18-20]. So reinforcement should be discriminate in frequency: at any point in the second language program we would positively reinforce all correct uses of the new rule being learned, many uses of the rule learned before that, some uses of earlier rules, and none of the correct uses (while still correcting errors) of previous rules that by then should be thoroughly learned. Of course, reinforcement should be geared to the individual student --if a student never quite mastered an early rule, his correct uses of it should be positively reinforced.

Many in the second language profession believe that in order to make an incorrect response disappear, all that is needed is not to reinforce it positively, that is, to ignore it. It may disappear that way, and again it may not, for positive communicative reinforcement --being understood-- can form a powerful combination with linguistic noncorrection, giving the learner the impression that nothing is wrong. It has been thoroughly demonstrated experimentally that "punishment" (correction) makes an unwanted response disappear much more effectively than the withholding of positive reinforcement. (Granted, there are effective and ineffective ways of correcting in second language teaching/learning, something that will be discussed later.)

Note that some learning *can* take place without reinforcement, through the contiguity of two or more stimuli or of a stimulus and a response. Probably much native language vocabulary is acquired that way.

A further distinction is made between *primary reinforcers*, which fulfill physiological needs (food, water, etc.) and are much used in laboratory experiments with animals, and *secondary reinforcers* such as praise, grades, money, which are related to the relief/nonrelief of fear and the fulfillment/disappointment of hope and are frequently used with human learners. Money, or tokens, for example, have been very effectively used in behavior modification [Craighead *et al.* 1976:114] and even in second language teaching.

Practice --repetition of the S-R-Reinf. situation-- results first in a trace being formed; further practice leads to the establishment of an association between stimulus and response; more practice turns the association into conditioning; still further practice makes the conditioning into a habit; practice in the combined use of related habits results in a skill. In the opposite direction, what is not used or is corrected is reduced in strength from habit to conditioning to association to trace to unlearned (at least consciously).

Note that the most effective way to decondition a

learner (that is, to overcome in him the interference of previous learning) is to teach him a new response in the presence of an old stimulus-response association. This would seem to indicate that in order to overcome native language interference, second language learners should learn second language responses in the presence of the native language rather than trying to ignore it. (Of course, our aim would not be for our students to unlearn their native language.)

More on intelligent conditioning

As stated earlier, there are few learning acts in which human beings are cognitively passive or inactive. Cognitively mature learners (younger learners only gradually learn this skill) participate intelligently in the learning process, that is, through cognitively controlled discriminative responses to discriminative stimuli. In fact, the mature learner is mentally active throughout the process --paying attention before the stimulus, perceiving or understanding the stimulus, considering the possible responses, choosing one from among the likely responses, monitoring the chosen response as he produces it, paying attention to the reinforcement, and evaluating the correctness of his response on the basis of the reinforcement given by the teacher/interlocutor/environment. It would thus be possible to represent the learner's cognitive mediation ("CM") as pervading the learning act; with this understanding, it is only for the sake of convenience that we will represent it as occurring between the stimulus and the response, as follows:

S - CM - R - Reinf.

The formula would not be complete, however, if we failed to represent the conditions that make cognitive mediation possible. For cognitive mediation to be effective or even possible, physical conditions ("P") must be favorable, with no permanent or temporary impediment to the response (more generally, with no major discomfort); there must be no interfering emotional state ("E"); and the learner must be volitionally ("V") inclined to respond. This can be added to the formula, which becomes then:

S - (P-E-V Cond.) CM - R - Reinf.

Evidence of the negative effect of physical discomfort on learning is the fact that learning is much less effective when one is very hungry or near suffocation from lack of fresh air. (Emotional and volitional factors will be discussed in Chapter 6.)

Note that, in native language acquisition, conditioning --association, reinforcement, generalization, etc.-- is not readily observable because the environment acts for the most part indirectly upon the acquirer. In second language teaching/learning, however, conditioning can be used quite directly and overtly, with the result that what Wilga Rivers has called "skill-getting" can be made very effective. Having made all the mechanical aspects of the second language automatic, they need not be attended to during "skill-using," but the attention can be instead where it should be, on the meaning, not the form, of the message.

More on reinforcement (feedback)

"Feedback" is not a technical psychological term, but it is a useful word whereby we can refer broadly to the way the environment/interlocutor/teacher responds to the behavior of the learner.

Feedback is essential to learning. Without feedback, practice does not allow any new learning, only a rather ineffective and diminishing maintenance of what has already been learned. When correct and incorrect responses are indistinctly rewarded, the learner cannot differentiate between them. Learning increases with the precision of feedback. This was shown long ago in experiments in which subjects learned to draw three-inch lines progressively better in conditions of no feedback, nonsense syllable feedback, "right"/"wrong" feedback, and exact feedback (amount and direction of error) [Thorndike 1927, Cason 1932]. This seems to indicate that second language learners would benefit more from knowing the nature of their errors than from just knowing that they were wrong.

In the second language program, feedback occurs at three levels:

1) *Affective feedback:* "I like you" or "I don't like you," e.g., "when you are a discipline problem";

2) *Communicative feedback:* "I understand what you said" or "I don't understand what you said"; and

3) *Linguistic feedback:* "What you said is linguistically correct" or "What you said is linguistically incorrect."

The learners should be assured of constant positive affective feedback, that is, of a supportive emotional atmosphere that will remain so as long as they adhere to normal classroom discipline. Within that supportive feedback, they should be aware, however, of the difference between communicative and linguistic feedback. Negative linguistic feedback --the correction of linguistic errors--need not discourage second language students from speaking if offered in a kind, matter-of-fact manner and if they understand clearly that the other two types of feedback remain normally positive. If these conditions are met, the learner will see linguistic corrections as help, not as punishment --as applying specifically to his utterance, not to himself as a person. On the other hand, if a linguistically incorrect utterance is rewarded globally because of its communicative value, the incorrect elements or misapplied rules in it are being learned, as what is incorrect is being positively reinforced along with the larger message. This is not to say that every small linguistic error should be corrected at all times, for this would be discouraging to the students. What it means is that we should create an atmosphere in which the students will want to talk but not one in which they will want to talk while disregarding accuracy.

Incidentally, the fact that native language acquirers do eventually eliminate errors from their speech without frequent correction in no way applies to the situation of the second language learner. The native language acquirer has far more exposure to many more accurate linguistic models and far greater motivation to conform to sociolinguistic pressures --under these conditions, errors have no chance of surviving. The second language learner, if anything, has pressure to conform to the error-laden interlanguage of his classmates; so if his errors are not corrected they will naturally become habitual. (More on second language errors and their correction in Chapters 7, 9, and others.)

Chaining and shaping

In chaining, a particular sequence of responses is learned, in which each response becomes a stimulus for the next, the individual responses being already known. An example is the memorization first, of the words in a line and then of the lines of a poem.

In shaping, a new response is learned (or relearned) through the reinforcement of successive approximations. As each approximation is performed consistently, only a closer approximation begins to be rewarded. An example of this is the behavior modification process whereby a mental patient who is oblivious to everyone and everything can be taught to leave a corner of his room, go to the hospital cafeteria, and serve himself a meal. Another example is the speaker of French or German who can be trained, by means of successive approximations, to change his pronunciation of English /r/ from a uvular fricative [ʀ] to a retroflex palatal [ɹ].

Both chaining and shaping are based on the concept of *contingent reinforcement* developed by Skinner in particular. Some language laboratory materials and most programmed learning are based on the same principle.

Motor skills

Certain aspects of second language learning --if not, mistakenly, the whole process-- have been compared to the development of motor skills like typing or swimming. Actually, only the pronunciation of a second language and the mechanics of writing constitute motor skills, and even these can be helped by adopting a reasonably cognitive rather than a purely mechanical approach to teaching them.

A motor skill involves movements or combinations of movements. These do not have to be learned holistically --the parts can be learned separately and then combined (e.g., in second language pronunciation, attention can be paid to individual phonetic features one at a time). The learning of a motor skill in an instructional setting involves three phases:

(1) understanding of the task;

(2) association and integration of part skills; and

(3) autonomous phase, where the motor skill is used automatically while attention is on something else [Fitts and Posner 1967].

During phases (1) and (2), motor skill development is helped by verbal instructions, pictures, and demonstrations; during phase (2) there needs to be considerable practice with feedback, leading gradually to phase (3). Motor skill development does not benefit from very concentrated practice; practice should instead alternate with periods of rest.

Habit formation

As already indicated, sufficient practice beyond intelligent conditioning will ensure that control over most elements and rules of a second language becomes automatic --that is, habitual-- and no longer requires conscious attention. In other words, it is not enough to grasp linguistic rules and elements cognitively; they must be internalized through practice into habits. Note that linguistic habits are not restricted to particular utterances but facilitate the generation of an infinite number of different sentences --one can speak thus of "*generative* linguistic habits."

Once a linguistic rule has been internalized --that is, once it has become habitual-- the speaker/hearer is generally unaware of it but can apply it correctly when higher-level decisions call for its use. It is only when habits are looked upon as mindless conditioning to particular stimuli [Chomsky 1966:44] that the notion of language as a habit structure must be rejected. When habits are considered from the frame of reference of the synthesis we have called "cognitively-based behaviorism," it is clear that the internalization of a linguistic rule would probably start as cognitive activity but would eventually result in automatic linguistic behavior --a habit. Without linguistic habits we could not possibly communicate, as we would have to pay conscious attention to a myriad rules, elements, features, etc. --hundreds per minute.

When certain linguists and second language specialists have referred to the necessity of forming linguistic habits then, what they have meant is the establishment of a permanent and strong tendency to act linguistically in a particular way, not the memorization and use of particular sentences via particular stimuli. (Note in this regard that both Skinner's views as presented in *Verbal Behavior* [1957] and Chomsky's attack of those views in his 1959 review of Skinner's book represent extreme positions, neither of which is tenable --more on this in Chapter 4.) Whether a rule is internalized deductively by starting from a *verbal* rule, or inductively by manipulating sample sentences embodying the rule, the important thing is to succeed in establishing in the learner a *behavioral* rule or linguistic habit through intelligent practice.

Practice for the formation of habits needs to take primarily the form of numerous associations. The greater the number of associations, the faster habits are formed and the longer they are retained. This applies both to vocabulary (word associations) and grammar (association between rules and numerous sentences illustrating their use). Note also that conscious attention to the crucial element of the habit to be learned seems to be particularly helpful as an early step to habit formation.

Conceptual learning

In Gagné's progression from simpler to more complex

forms of learning, several types of conceptual learning are listed at the cognitive end of the hierarchy, and they are supposed to be based on simpler forms of learning.

Conceptual learning includes discrimination, generalization, principle or rule learning, and problem solving.

Actually generalization occurs in all types of learning, even in learning a particular response to a particular stimulus, in which case the generalization is: "Because X was followed by Y n times, Y always follows X" [Mowrer 1960-a:438]. More commonly, generalization means responding in the same way to other stimuli similar to the original one, which can be called "one-many generalization" [Mowrer 1960-a:439]. There can also be response generalization, where one learns to respond with many similar responses to the same stimulus.

Discrimination is the opposite side of the coin from generalization. One learns to discriminate by learning different specific responses to different stimuli or stimulus clusters which until that point were not distinguished. Like generalization, discrimination is involved in many types of learning.

Discrimination provides a corrective to overgeneralization. Thus, it is mostly through discrimination that the limitations of a rule can be learned. The skillful performer differs from the poor one in that the former makes finer discriminations between what he is doing and what he should be doing.

Problem solving is largely dependent on previous knowledge and it involves understanding essential features and formulating and testing hypotheses. It is related to intelligence and develops gradually through exposure to a variety of learning experiences. There is evidence that bright children and college students have a greater tendency to test hypotheses than average children and, of course, higher animals --more intelligent humans are mostly *sudden* learners and problem solvers, while average children and higher animals do both gradually.

It seems that a solution to a problem arrived at without much help is remembered better than if it is given for memorization from the start. This would mean that it may be better to handle second language teaching/learning as a series of guided problem-solving situations. No doubt such an approach would also be more motivating for most students.

What facilitates learning

1) High motivation and positive attitudes

(To be discussed in Chapter 6.)

2) Gradation

A few second language learners can learn by leaps and bounds, more or less haphazardly, with emphasis on communication throughout; the great majority however benefit from a gradual, step-by-step process of learning, one structure and one task at a time. Of course, only some elements or rules of a language need to be learned in a particular order; teaching the rest in a fixed order would make their retrieval from memory more difficult.

3) Organization

The human mind naturally organizes data. For example, if asked to list thirty countries, it is highly likely that the resulting list will have some sort of organization. Organization facilitates learning by grouping what is to be learned into related and manageable "chunks."

4) Highlighting the crucial

This is related to organization. If the learner is aware of which are the crucial elements of the learning task, this greatly facilitates the learning process, as it allows the learner to attend to the most important aspects of the task and to subordinate the less important elements to them.

5) Practice

We learn by doing, but by doing intelligently. Without practice there can normally be no learning, only a slight and passive awareness that cannot be translated into the corresponding behavior. As Bloomfield [1942:16] put it in reference to second language learning: *"Practice everything until it becomes second nature."* And Nida [1957:20] said that we cannot "learn to swim merely by reading books about swimming.... We learn by doing."

One of the problems with second language teaching is that the more creative students are reluctant to practice enough to form linguistic habits --they want, instead, to use the language creatively from the start. They may need to be convinced, via a demonstration, of the necessity of systematic practice.

6) Meaningfulness

The more meaningful the material, the easier it is to learn it. For example, high-meaningful words in a passage of prose can be recalled three to eighteen times better than low-meaningful words [R.E. Johnson 1973]. From hardest to easiest, words are learned in isolation, in pairs, in phrases, in sentences, in sentences with linguistic context, and in sentences with both linguistic and nonlinguistic contexts. Also, the more ways new material relates to previously learned material, the easier it is to learn it. All of this means, for instance, that during the internalization phase of second language dialogue learning, students should be fully aware of the meaning of each sentence.

For meaningful material massed practice seems to be more effective, and for nonmeaningful material distributed practice, with frequent periods of rest or alternate activities, seems to be better. Since second language learning is mostly meaningful learning, this would seem to support the idea of intensive language training.

7) Pleasantness and ease of the task

Some learning tasks are inherently easier and more pleasant than others. Television, among other things, has gotten North American youth used to the idea that most problems can be pleasantly and quickly solved. As teachers cannot compete with the media, perhaps they should not even try to be as entertaining and quick to solve problems in their teaching as television stars are in their shows.

There is no way second language learning can be made into a quick and easy learning task, so students should be made to see it for what it is --long-term and difficult-- or they will soon get discouraged as they do not see immediate fluency develop (many students quite unrealistically expect to be fluent after two years of high school or two semesters of college language study). Perhaps we should give up even trying to teach second languages to students who are not motivated to put in the major, long-term effort required to develop second language competence.

Note also that if a learning task is too easy, too undemanding, many students get bored and lose respect for the teacher and the program. They may complain at difficult work, but they would rather be challenged by it than bored by work that is too easy. Furthermore, with easy learning tasks --such as some of the easiest drills-- the students may not be learning anything. Such learning tasks are similar to tests in which the correct answers to multiple-choice questions are predictable from the pattern of their distribution.

8) Transfer of training

Previously acquired knowledge or habits facilitates new learning --transfers positively to the new task-- if it is identical or very similar in nature. To the extent that it differs within a background of similarity it will cause negative transfer or interference. If totally different or quite different, transfer will be zero or near zero. (A discussion of this is found in Chapter 9.) Learning strategies can also be transferred, not always appropriately.

Deduction and induction

Much has been said about the relative merits of deduction (learning from the general to the particular) and induction (learning from the particular to the general) but neither has been demonstrated to be inherently superior. Which is better would seem to depend on the nature of the particular learning task and on the cognitive preference of the learners.

Deduction would seem preferable where there is conceptually complex material, so it has a limited role to play in second language learning. But by and large, time spent on elaborate analysis, on the formulation of verbal rules for their own sake, is mostly wasted, although some analysis seems to facilitate learning. Where a second language rule is very different from anything in the native language, analysis and deduction might be indicated. There is nothing wrong in knowledge *about* the language as long as it is transformed into performance *in* the language --in fact, adequate knowledge can speed up and give the right direction to the development of the corresponding performance. But just knowledge of a rule as a theoretical item can inhibit its use in performance [Lawler and Selinker 1971].

Induction means discovery of a rule without guidance. It would seem appropriate when the rule is simple enough or evident enough that it can be readily discovered. But for most second language rules, reliance on unguided discovery --induction-- is quite inefficient, as they are not readily discoverable by any student and never quite discovered by some students.

We conclude then that for a few rules induction is possible and for a few deduction is necessary. What should be done with the majority of second language rules? The answer seems to be *guided discovery*, an intermediate process whereby the students are neither handed a rule formulation to apply nor asked to inefficiently test false hypotheses. Instead, through the careful selection and presentation of examples and well-chosen questions about them, the students are led to the right hypothesis within a very short time. This combines giving the learner guidance with giving him the satisfaction of discovery, of controlled problem-solving.

Memory

Memory is the retention of information or a response, i.e., of knowledge or behavior. Some psychologists recognize three types of memory, short-term, which lasts up to about 20 seconds; intermediate, lasting a few minutes; and long-term, which can last for a lifetime. An input remains initially available in short-term memory, but other than in echoic learning it must be manipulated and reorganized if it is to be retained. (Incidentally, the fact that it remains available for 20 seconds means that there can be a fairly lengthy pause between a model and a repetition without harm to the latter.)

Nonechoic material is reorganized into "chunks." These, depending on the level of proficiency of the learner, may be very simple bits of information such as phonemes or more complex ones such as syllables, words or phrases. Short-term memory can hold 7 ± 2 such "chunks" at any one time [G. Miller 1956]. For something to go into intermediate or long-term memory it has to be further reorganized, practiced with effort (not merely repeated mechanically), associated with other items, and if possible used with understanding.

Studies are needed on the number and frequency of reintroductions of a second language item necessary for it to become established in long-term memory and readily retrievable. Memory increases with age, up to a point --it has been found, for example, that a three-year old can remember three digits, a seven-year old five, and a 16-20-year old eight [G. Miller 1951:210]. It has also been determined that what is stored in memory together tends to be remembered together; this underscores the importance of "cross-filing" second language material in memory, through communicative activities, so that recall will not be dependent on a single context.

Strictly speaking, nothing is forgotten completely --a "trace" remains, as proven by the fact that what has been apparently forgotten is more rapidly re-learned with each try. While people vary greatly in their ability to learn, it seems that they all tend to forget what they have not fully mastered at about the same rate. Forgetting seems to be related to (a) the degree of learning, which is based on the amount of (meaningful) practice,

(b) the distribution of the practice, and (c) the interference of intervening cognitive activities, with more similar material inducing more forgetting. That is, we forget mostly because of the interference of earlier or later learnings, if the "interference theory" of forgetting is right [Postman and Underwood 1973]. Also the absence of appropriate recall cues accounts for much forgetting [Tulving 1974].

Thought

Some have expressed the view that "without language there seems to be nothing like explicit thought whatever" [Langer 1951:38]. Whorf, as we have already noted, saw language as the shaper of ideas. At the other extreme, some believe that the mind functions independently of language.

There can be no question that thought encompasses more than language. It includes several language-unrelated activities such as music and painting and certain activities which are only indirectly related to language, such as gestures and abstract thought. The fact that the same thought can be expressed in different words and in different languages is in itself proof that thought and language are distinct. Further evidence of the relative independence of thought from language comes from research with the deaf and studies of text recall. Lado, who conducted some of the latter, concluded that it is thought and not language that provides "the continuity and congruence of any connected series of sentences" [Lado *et al.* 1971]; he saw thought as central and language as "a symbolic system that refers to [thought] in various ways" [Lado 1970].

Research

In conclusion, let us note that second language learning is a nearly ideal field for psychological research. The reason psychologists have preferred to study learning in animals is that animals can be bred in such a way that they can reach the researcher having learned very little before the experiment, and by their behavior they can reveal basic, biologically given laws of learning [Mowrer 1960-a:9]. Two types of human subjects --infants and second language learners-- can be said to meet that condition, although of course the second language learner is only starting the second language, not learning in general, "from scratch."

Thus second language teaching/learning would be a very

suitable field for psychological research (if only psychologists could be "weaned" from their excessive interest in paired associates), providing a testing ground for both linguistic and psychological theories and possibly leading to their reformulation.

4

STRUCTURALISM-BEHAVIORISM OR GENERATIVISM-COGNITIVISM IN LANGUISTICS?

A short short story

Two linguists, one a structuralist, the other a generativist, were dropped by parachute into the unknown land of Upper Slobbovia so that they might describe the language spoken there. Their task necessarily involved a process of observation, notation, segmentation, and analysis.

The structural linguist, trained in phonetics and field methods of observing and describing unknown languages, felt comfortable about this work. The generative linguist, however, felt very frustrated about this work, for his training directed him, as soon as possible, to make abstract deep structure generalizations about Slobbovian syntax and produce a logical explanatory grammar of the language --something he could not do without acquiring a thorough knowledge of Slobbovian first.

Having inventoried the sounds of the language, the structural linguist proceeded to observe, and to elicit by pointing, etc., recurring sequences of sounds, and then to compare and contrast these sequences in order to determine which sounds or groups of sounds were capable of making a difference in meaning. After analyzing the sound system, the structural linguist proceeded to a grammatical analysis of the language, by segmenting phrases and sentences into grammatically and lexically meaningful sequences, and describing in increasing detail the functions of those segments and how they were joined together into phrases and sentences; he also ascertained and listed the meaning of all segments, phrases, and sentences. As the next step, he made a list of the various types of sentences he found, giving examples of each in horizontal formulas and charts with possible substitutions at each point. Finally he prepared a list of the rules according to which the various types of sentences could be combined into more complex sentences, paragraphs, and discourse.

At the end of a few months, the structural linguist had learned enough about the Slobbovian language to produce a working grammar of it. He did so by proceeding from the particular to the general, from the readily observable to the abstract, without preconceptions, increasing the sophistication and abstractness of his analysis as his own knowledge of the language developed --in other words, he *discovered* the language, *just as a second language learner needs to discover the second language.*

The structuralist's grammar of Slobbovian was far from perfect. It had certain shortcomings that a generative grammar would eventually overcome and go beyond --it left certain unusual sentences unaccounted for, except in footnotes; it could not generate all the sentences of the language; being as concrete as possible, it was intentionally repetitive at places; it did not fully develop all the possible relationships between sentences; and so forth. But it was a very useful working description, particularly useful for anyone who wanted to learn the salient facts about Slobbovian or who wanted to learn the language itself.

In the meantime, and for several years to come, the generative linguist was quite unable to produce anything other than a few broad generalizations, since he had to learn the language quite well, to near-native ability, *before* he could start to analyze it in terms of abstract generative rules. For unlike his structuralist colleague, the generativist had to rely on introspection rather than the eliciting of data, and had to go from the general to the particular and from the abstract to the observable (at least in his output). When he, years later, produced a grammar of Slobbovian, it went beyond and was more complete and precise than the structuralist's working grammar; but it was also too abstract and too involved to be of much use to anyone but other generative linguists specializing in Slobbovian.

Two main schools of linguistics, again

No doubt certain principles and findings of linguistics are useful to languists. They may also find application for many concepts in psychology. But which linguistics? And which psychology?

Regarding linguistics, there is considerable wisdom in Halliday's [1964] observation that the value of a linguistic description depends on "whether it has proved useful for the purpose for which it is intended." From the point of view of our concerns as languists, the question is then: Which linguistic description has proved most useful for the purpose of second language teaching/learning? Although there are many linguistic theories and corresponding descriptions, the main ones have been in existence --and have been "applied"-- long enough that our question becomes answerable. At the same time, note too that this question may also have to be answered eclectically.

We can speak of two main schools of linguistics, already identified as structural and generative. The generative school --of which Chomsky and Katz are leading figures-- is rationalist, deductive, and its followers believe that language is creative, stimulus-free, rule-governed behavior (although in a sense most linguists have believed that). An offshoot of this school is Case Grammar [Fillmore 1968], an attempt to establish a deep base composed of universal semantic relationship in the form of cases --Agentive, Objective, Instrumental, etc. This was potentially applicable to second language teaching [Nilsen 1971], but unfortunately more and more cases have been postulated, with the result that Case Grammar has become too unwieldy for our purposes. (Note that Case Grammar, being semantically based, has some claim to psychological reality.)

The structural school --of which Bloomfield was the leading exponent-- is empiricist, inductive (data-based), and its followers believe that language is a largely conditioned set of habits (which, when properly understood, most linguists believe, even many who are reluctant to admit it).

Alliances between linguistics and psychology

Linguistics and psychology have tended to form alliances --holy and unholy-- because they are closely related disciplines, both having an interest in human behavior, of which language is an important part.

Structural linguistics has been closely associated with behaviorist psychology. This was more a case of historical accident than anything else, for if the circumstances had been different, structuralism could have formed a combination with other learning theories [Wardhaugh 1974:123]. Be that as it may, the alliance was established with behaviorism, and in this chapter we shall refer to the resultant school as "structuralism-behaviorism."

The generative school of linguistics has been closely allied to cognitive psychology. One of Chomsky's [1959] earliest writings was an attack on the views of neobehaviorist Skinner, in the form of a review which according to some "demolished" the latter. Readily ignored is the fact that, as MacCorquodale [1969,1970] showed, Chomsky's rather caustic attack grossly distorted what Skinner had said. (This is not a defense of Skinner's more extreme views.) Through the years generativists have shown a close association with cognitivists, to the point that Chomsky [1968] wrote that linguistics is "a branch of cognitive psychology." In this chapter this alliance between linguistics and psychology will be referred to as "generativism-cognitivism."

Differences between structuralism-behaviorism and generativism-cognitivism and their languistic implications

First it should be noted, as Stevick [1971:11] did, that these two schools have a number of things in common. Both recognize similarities and differences between languages (although structuralists emphasize the differences and generativists the similarities); both adopt a nonprescriptive attitude toward language rules (although this nonprescriptiveness is more evident among structuralists); both agree that the behavior of the language user should be the source of the data (although the structuralists rely on informants while the generativists rely on introspection); both believe that the second language learner should be able to produce accurately and unhesitatingly an infinite number of sentences (although structuralists emphasize accuracy and generativists creativity); and so forth.

But the significant contribution of these schools lies in that in which they disagree, for it is here that we find a choice of implications and possible applications to our field. These psycholinguistic or linguistic differences will therefore be surveyed at this time.

1) Is language stimulus-free or conditioned?

Radical behaviorists, Skinner among them, have taken the position that because cognitive processes cannot be observed they must be ignored; the result is that they see not only language acquisition but language use as mindlessly conditioned, a position adopted to a considerable extent by structuralists. The generative-cognitive school goes to the other extreme and sees no need for the concept of conditioning either in language use or in language acquisition --or, by extension, in second language teaching/ learning, where conditioning procedures *are* eminently useful.

On this issue, we can say that there is a range between the extreme represented by Skinner and the extreme represented by Chomsky and that fortunately most linguists and psychologists place themselves somewhere away from the extremes. Skinner discovered a very effective way of controlling certain aspects of animal and human behavior; his error was to extend his valid findings about the artificial process of induced learning to the rather unrelated natural processes of language acquisition and use. Chomsky based, on his partially valid observations about natural processes of language acquisition and use, an unjustified rejection of conditioning under *any* circumstances.

For we must make a clear distinction between *getting* control of the language "instrument," as Rivers called it, and using it creatively. Furthermore, getting control of the instrument can be divided into *natural acquisition*, in which the environment acts on the acquirer rather indirectly, and *induced learning*, in which the teacher and the media act on the learner directly, with the result that in the latter conditioning can be quite effective. Language *use* is largely free of conditioning (whatever conditioning of rules is necessary has taken place beforehand) and unpredictable, for the stimuli are largely within the speaker's mind and not amenable to observation. In language use, people generate at least partially novel sentences while their attention is on meaning and maybe broad higher-level syntactic choices, lower-level rules falling into place automatically. In language learning, students need to devote concentrated effort to the task of making precisely those lower-level rules automatic; this is best done through intelligent conditioning.

This brings us again to the question of linguistic habits. It seems clear that when structuralists-behaviorists defined a language as a system of habits they were emphasizing only one aspect of language to the exclusion of others, that is, they were right insofar as this described the automatic use of lower-level rules, both in coding and decoding, but wrong in ignoring the higher, cognitive, creative aspects of language use. Generativists-cognitivists are equally wrong in rejecting the notion of habit because they happen to emphasize other things. Surely generativists-cognitivists can find nothing wrong in the idea that once a rule has been used it is easier to use it again, and once it has been used X times it becomes internalized, i.e., can be used automatically when called for. That is all a linguistic habit is --a rule that has been internalized through (intelligent) practice to the point of automatism. A linguistic habit is the behavioral link between unconscious knowledge of a rule (which is part of competence) and the accurate and fluent realization of that rule in sentences that incorporate it (which is part of performance).

The languistic implications and applications of extreme structuralism-behaviorism or extreme generativism-cognitivism have been negative, shifting from excessive reliance on mindless drill in the case of the former to rejection of all mechanical drill,with nothing to take its place, in the case of the latter. Less extreme advocates of structuralism-behaviorism have contributed quite a variety of types of conditioning drills and exercises. A good contribution of generativists-cognitivists has been the idea that exercises should be done with full learner awareness of what is involved.

Again it seems that synthesis is desirable, for learning a second language is both a question of habits and cognition, of skills and intellect, of mechanics and communication.

2) Discovery or generation?

As illustrated in our short short story, structuralists and generativists proceed quite differently in their analysis of a language. Structuralists start with phonetics and go from there to phonemics, morphology, syntax, meaning, and discourse levels; generativists may start with discourse considerations and move from there to semantic, phrase structure, lexical, transformational, and morphophonemic components, the last of these yielding the phonetic output.

Note that these two opposite orders of analysis correspond respectively to the order of discovery and the order of generation --that is, in learning a language one discovers it, beginning with concrete sounds and ending with syntactic and semantic abstractions and discourse considerations; but in generating sentences (once the corresponding features of language have been learned), one goes in the opposite direction, from discourse and general semantic considerations to the phonetic output.

Discovery versus generation is an important difference to languists, for the appropriate model needs to be used in second language teaching. It seems clear that the second language *learner* finds himself, *vis-à-vis* the language to be learned, in the position of language *discovery* resembling the order of structural analysis of an unknown language rather than the order the generativist uses in analyzing a language thoroughly familiar to him. On the other hand, the second language *user* --which the second language learner becomes more and more as he learns the language-- finds himself generating sentences with discourse and semantic rather than phonetic decisions involved in the conscious control of his speech acts.

We conclude therefore that both approaches to language are useful, the structural (with emphasis on discovery) for language *learning* and the generative (with emphasis on generation) for language *use* once the language or parts thereof have been learned.

3) Emphasis on competence or emphasis on performance?

The generativists' distinction between competence and performance is a useful one. Linguistic competence is the mostly unconscious knowledge of a language that an ideal native speaker/hearer has; it allows him to understand novel sentences, reject ungrammatical ones, disambiguate ambiguous ones, ignore performance errors, etc. Performance is what speakers of a language actually say, systematic errors and unsystematic mistakes included. But note that these concepts refer mostly to the language *user*, not the language *learner*.

Given the preference of generativists for the cognitive realm and their much lesser interest in actual behavior, it seems natural that they have developed grammars of competence, not of performance. A theory of competence results in grammars that are abstract and complex and that make explicit rules such that a native speaker could not understand, much less express. Such grammars are hypotheses based on introspection, unlike grammars of performance, which could be based on observation --for example, a grammar of competence posits rules with infinite recurrence, a grammar of performance would not. It may be that grammars of performance would be based on rules quite different than those used in grammars of competence.

It is possible to have mechanical performance (mechanical linguistic behavior) without competence (linguistic knowledge). An example of this would be someone singing Italian opera without any knowledge of Italian; another example would be a second language student imitating a dialogue sentence without knowledge of its meaning or of the rules involved in its production. It is not possible to have competence without performance, either one's own or that of others, which would lead to the formation of one's competence. (So, it is a mistake to expect much competence-based performance early in a second language program.)

The performance of others and his own performance --mechanical and competence-based-- lead the second language learner to the internalization of rules that constitute his transitional competence. The importance of this is that second language performance is essential to the development of second language competence. In the second language classroom, one of the earliest and the longest step in the mastery of each rule should be mechanical performance, in the form of manipulation of sentences, and this is the usual doorway to the internalization of the rule (or formation of the habit) into the transitional competence of the learner.

From the point of view of languistics, therefore, the generativist tendency to regard competence as all-important and performance as rather unimportant --"trivial" is the usual word-- is most unfortunate. In the second language program it is linguistic behavior or performance that must be emphasized, and intuitive linguistic knowledge or competence, however crucial in underlying novel linguistic behavior, should develop from performance. Otherwise the result is second language students who know all the rules of the language but cannot perform.

It makes little sense to talk about teaching a second language "for competence," since competence is the *unconscious knowledge* of the *ideal native* speaker, and second language learners proceed *consciously, lack knowledge,* are *far from ideal* and are *not native*; that is, these two "people" in no way resemble each other, so one cannot serve as a model for the other. (Neither can native language acquisition --as we shall see in Chapter 5-- be a model for second language learning.)

4) Linguistic creativity and sentence generation

According to the generativists-cognitivists, language behavior is characterized by creativity. This should not be taken to mean creativity in its usual sense, as in the arts or literature, where the major component of creativity is originality. There is seldom originality in speech. There is nothing original in recombining previously memorized words and phrases according to thoroughly learned rules and sentence patterns. Perhaps the word "creativity" is inappropriate for linguistic activity and instead of "linguistic creativity" we should speak of "linguistic *recombinatory power*."

Not everything we say is recombined afresh, "from scratch"; much is based on learned sequences of words and their modification --these sequences are referred to as "routines" and are found in the early speech of native language acquirers and young second language acquirers [e.g., Hakuta 1974, 1976]. So language exhibits a continuum from automatic, "formula" utterances which are not recombined afresh to novel recombinations. It seems, however, that the latter evolves from the former, that is, novel communication is not independent from formulaic speech in the form of routines and patterns but evolves from it. Novel sentences are based on known sentence patterns, which are used over and over again.

Generating a sentence involves high-level decisions about discourse, style, meaning, and perhaps overall syntactic pattern, and for someone who knows the language well these decisions are followed by lower-level automatic consequences that take care of all the remaining syntactic details and of all the morphological and phonological details. The lowest-level consequences, phonetic ones, are the most automatic. But as has already been stated, "creative" recombination "from scratch" is not the way in which sentences are generated, especially not in a language one does not know very well.

There are at least two important implications in this for languistics. The first one is in the form of a danger. It can be quite harmful to second language learners to emphasize unbridled linguistic "creativity" from the start of the program. This will usually lead the students to try to generate numerous sentences "from scratch" even though, unlike natives, they do *not* have automatic control of lower-level structure or of basic sentence types --the result is the making of very many errors, which in a short time become ingrained or "fossilized."

The second implication is that, since native language acquirers and users make use of a considerable number of memorized phrases and of a number of sentence patterns, this lends further theoretical support to the second language practice of teaching sentences and sentence patterns and doing the drills necessary for the internalization of the high-level rules that underlie them. (Not that this further support is essential --these practices are also fully supported by learning theory and by the fact that they "work.")

5) Deep and surface structure, ambiguity, and sentence derivation

Generativists distinguish between "deep structure," the rules of arrangement of functional elements, and "surface structure," the arrangement of elements in actual sentences. Thus, *The boy sees the girl* and *The girl is seen by the boy* differ at the surface level but have the same deep structure, while *John is eager to please* has the same surface structure but different deep structure from *John is easy to please.*

As further proof of the difference between deep and surface structure, many ambiguous sentences are quoted in the literature. It is curious that the generativists' insistence on dealing with isolated sentences --much like the structuralists do-- has led them to posit numerous ambiguities where there aren't any. For except for intentional ambiguities such as those created in a humorous vein, ambiguities very seldom occur. All the "classic" linguistic examples of ambiguity, such as *They are flying airplanes, The students are revolting, The shooting of the hunters,* etc. lose their ambiguity when placed within the context of discourse and nonlinguistic referents. In those circumstances, people will not even think of the "other" meaning.

Another aspect of the relationship between deep and surface structure is the derivation of sentences from the former to the latter. Certain generativists would say, for example, that the sentence *John shaves himself* derives from the deep structure sentence *John shaves John* (both occurrences of *John* referring to the same person), which then becomes *John shaves him* (same reference) and finally *John shaves himself*. It seems clear, however, that we do not think that way to produce such a sentence, that is, that this process lacks psychological reality. Another example, from French, is deriving *Je les ai achetés* from *J'ai acheté les livres* through the intermediate step **J'ai acheté les*, again an intermediate nonexistent sentence having no psychological reality (it is true that logically both deletion and transposition are involved, but the human mind is quite capable of doing both at the same time). We see that according to the generative-transformational paradigm, then, sentences are understood and produced in terms of other, even nonexistent, sentences --this is quite circular, unnecessary, and psychologically unreal.

What are the implications of this for languistics? First of all, our students are quite aware of meaning and seldom need to refer to deep structure rules; they will *not* say **Pleasing John is very eager* or **John is easy to participate* if they are at all paying attention to what they are saying; nor will they need "command of an abstract grammatical rule" [Saporta 1966] to accept *I eat fresh fish* and reject **I eat fresh well* --their knowledge of reality will lead them to reject the latter. Second, almost all surface ambiguities disappear when attention is paid to discourse constraints and meaning, so there is no need for the "disambiguation exercises" that some generativist applied linguists have proposed. Third --although this could be shown within structural grammars--generativists have contributed the idea that sentences having the same surface structure but different deep structure should not be part of the same drills but should be drilled separately. For example, *John is eager to please* could have such substitutions as *anxious, to help out,* and *to participate,* while separately *John is easy to please* could have such substitutions as *hard, impossible,* and *to fool,* etc. This is a useful application of generative-transformational theory. (In fairness to structural textbooks, they seldom mixed deep structures.) Fourth, rather than try to teach the production of sentences through the intermediate step of other sentences or even of nonexistent sentences, we should lead our students to the correct abstractions about the language through manipulation of surface structures. (Derivation "trees" in particular are very difficult to manipulate.) An abstract grammar cannot somehow be injected into our students so they will start generating sentences from deep structure; practice must necessarily start with concrete surface structures. The relationships between sentences should be practiced by means of transformation exercises that allow students to change one surface structure into another directly, without intermediate deep structure steps.

6) The ideal native speaker versus native informants

Unlike structuralists, who determine what people actually say by observing the spontaneous or elicited speech of native informants, generativists produce grammars of the competence of the "ideal native speaker" mostly by introspection and intuition. Insofar as he is his own informant, the generativist probably makes use of his intuition the way less highly trained people do --by a process of analogy, not analysis, that is, by very quickly going over his memory storage of similar sentences in order to answer the question "Is this said?" The problem with the linguist relying on self-generated data is that it is easy for him to lose scientific objectivity and produce a distorted analysis; it is nearly as bad as a surgeon operating on himself.

The generativist's idealization of the native speaker, which deprives him of sex, age, and socioeconomic status, added to his tendency to ignore meaning and discourse constraints, makes of the ideal native speaker no more than "a grammar machine" [Di Pietro 1978-b:150].

As far as languistics is concerned, two implications arise. One is that second language grammars should refer to the speech of real native speakers, warts and all. They should not be based on some ideal nonperson but on typical speakers; they should be based on the observation of systematic performance (surface performance minus unsystematic mistakes), not on introspection. The second point is that our students do not have and cannot have for a long time a native speaker's intuition about the language --they lack both the linguistic memory storage and the linguistic competence. That being the case, we should not expect them to learn the second language intuitively or to use it intuitively, at least not until they reach a very advanced level of proficiency.

7) Abstractness or concreteness

Being closely tied to the observation of actual utterances, structural statements are as concrete as possible. A generative grammar, on the other hand, being an attempt to generate all possible well-formed sentences with an integrated set of nonredundant rules, is necessarily abstract and complex.

To take syntax as an example, structuralists produce easy-to-understand horizontal "slot and filler" phrase and sentence formulas. Generativists instead produce "trees" --a kind of reverse parsing-- that are very hard to follow and many transformations which, as we have seen, may lack any psychological reality.

As to phonology, structuralists organize the system into a relatively small number of phonemes, allophones, and distribution rules. Generativists, instead, propose numerous complex rules --English, in one analysis [Chomsky and Halle 1968], has more abstract rules than the number of phonemes-- and even derive certain common sounds through rules (in the same analysis, [ə], the most common English vowel, is not part of the basic sound system but is derived through rules); moreover, the phonetic output of a generative grammar is not simply phones but columns of pluses and minuses corresponding to a list of features.

It should be clear from this --and the reader is invited to look for himself-- that a generative grammar is generally too abstract to be applicable to second language teaching. On the other hand, a good structural grammar may not be fully *comprehensive* but is easily *comprehensible* to the average second language student.[△]

8) The order of rules

In a structural grammar the rules are separated into levels but within each level they have few restrictions as to their order. But the need for integration and non-redundancy in a generative grammar means that its rules must be applied in strict order. This means that a sentence must be a statement before it can be a question, or it must be active before it can be passive, etc.

This strict order is not related, except by occasional coincidence, to the order in which, for example, transformations are learned by native language acquirers or second language learners. A child learns to use noun phrases with adjectives ("Good boy!") long before he can say "The boy is good," a sentence which is supposed to come first and underlie the other. A second language learner is exposed to questions from the start, long before he can produce the statements that supposedly underlie the questions. Subject pronouns are acquired or learned before the noun phrases that "underlie" them. And so on.

There is, therefore, no reason why transformations, or anything else, in a second language should be taught in the order in which rules appear in a generative grammar.

9) Emphasis on syntax versus emphasis on phonology and morphology

Generativists emphasize syntax, to the point that morphology and phonology seem to have been unimportant afterthoughts. Structuralists emphasize particularly phonology but also morphology, to the detriment of syntax (until recently neither paid much attention to meaning or discourse).

A school of linguistics that has emphasized phonology and morphology can contribute much to the beginning level in second language learning, when much time is devoted to sounds and forms. A school that has emphasized syntax no doubt has many insights to offer for the intermediate level of second language learning, when most of the syntactic rules are learned. A school that emphasized vocabulary,

---

[△] This is not to say that some structuralists have not indulged in needless abstractions. See, for example, A. Hill's [1958:145-52] treatment of English pronouns.

meaning, and discourse would have much to offer for the advanced level of second language teaching/learning.

The main contribution of generativists to languistics is then in the field of syntax, within which they can show most of the relationships between sentences in terms of transformations. Surface-to-surface transformations can be the basis for many useful exercises.

10) A global view versus separation into levels

While structuralists separate language rules and elements strictly into several levels, generativists deal with the whole language in a global, integrated manner.

The global view can have a very negative effect on second language teaching if it is interpreted to mean that a second language should be learned globally, without dealing with selected parts one at a time. The basic pedagogical principles of selection and gradation cannot be abandoned with impunity. The result of abandoning them is that nothing is learned thoroughly.

At times it is useful, in the second language class, to deal with one aspect or level of language to the temporary exclusion of other levels. Thus, at certain points during the learning of the sound system, progress is facilitated by disregarding meaning. Separation of meaning from structure can be carried to extremes, however, as in the case of Morton's [1961] Spanish course, in which meaning does not intervene until after about 100 hours of instruction --only a captive and well-paid audience of experimental subjects could work without meaning for so long.

Generally, then, occasional separation by levels is useful; at the very advanced level, the global view of language becomes applicable.

11) Spoken and written language

Following their global view of language, generativists would not separate speech from writing. According to them, language is not primarily speech but the internal symbolization of thought, which may express itself in speech or writing, with complex interrelationships between them.

As part of a global view of language, there is nothing wrong with this. As something to apply to second language teaching, there is much that is wrong with it. For example, it led, in the late sixties, to a resurgence of the idea that writing should be taught from the start and not kept separate from speech.

Second language students need to develop some degree of mastery over the spoken language before they are exposed to the interfering effect of the inconsistencies of spelling. Written English, for example, may be a "near-optimal" system for generative linguists [Chomsky and Halle 1968], but as any beginning ESL teacher can testify, it creates grave problems for the beginning second language learner. The same thing is true of other alphabetic languages. Writing is imperfect, distracting, and confusing to the learner, as seen in Chapter 2.

The clear distinction between spoken and written language associated with the structuralists is one that every teacher of an alphabetic second language would do well to maintain, especially at the beginning level. At the advanced level the students could benefit from generative rules that relate spellings to sounds and stress patterns, as those showing the relationship between *condemn* and *condemnation* or between *telephone* and *telephonic* (most of the words to which such rules apply are infrequent or learnèd, that is, advanced, anyway); such rules may be useful generalizations for the learner even though they may lack psychological reality for the native speaker.

12) Universals versus particulars of language

Generativists are especially interested in the universal characteristics of language; structuralists have tried to analyze each language without preconceptions, as if it were unique, while of course recognizing at the same time that all languages have phonemes, ways to refer to actions and objects, and so forth.

Generativists see the peculiarities of each language as particular manifestations of universal principles. One problem with this is that anything can be modified into anything by transformation rules, thereby making this position cheaply unassailable. Another problem is that, just like in earlier times "universal principles," categories, etc. were based on Latin, modern "universal principles," far from being universal, are based mostly on English.

It would seem logical that whatever language universals there may be, they would simply reflect universal human experience and communication needs. All humans have certain characteristics, knowledge, and needs in common. All must name objects, describe actions, ask questions, express disagreement, and so on.

Language universals, being so broad in nature, are of no interest to the languist, whose concern is limited to the features of two languages, the language of the learner and the language to be taught/learned. Universals are not even needed for contrastive analysis, which can be done strictly with reference to the two languages involved. The second language learner, rather than wonder about universals, should be urged to drop all preconceptions before starting the study of the language. As for second language learning proceeding from the universal to the particular, it cannot --at all times, particular utterances must be referred to, for a second language is not learned in the abstract. Even when fairly abstract rules are being taught, the use of concrete examples is essential to success.

13) The use of contrasts and distributions

A most useful concept from structuralism is that of contrasts and distributions, one that is not given overt importance by the generativists. Contrasts and distribution rules are a basic kind of information that any learner --even subhuman ones-- requires. It is quite basic to know whether X is equal to Y or contrasts with Y and where X and Y are found.

Second language students need to know what contrasts with what and what does not. For learning a second language is, among other things, learning a system of contrasts and distributions different from that in one's native language. This applies to phonology and also to morphology, syntax, semantics, and discourse.

14) Practical applications

To conclude this list of comparisons between structuralism-behaviorism and generativism-cognitivism, we shall consider specifically the application of both schools of linguistics-psychology to the development of drills and exercises for the second language classroom.

It has been said that structuralism can help second language teaching only in the area of pronunciation and of "slot and filler" (substitution) drills. It is true that structural applied linguists developed a good number of types of pronunciation drills. It is also true that for the teaching of grammar some structuralists made extensive use of simple substitution drills, as inadequate as such drills are for the practice of most rules. But it is also true that many structuralists have made use of quite a variety of grammatical exercises, including several new types of transformation exercises based on surface structure transformation rules. (The use of transformation exercises in second language teaching preceded both generativism and structuralism.)

By way of contrast, generativism has not contributed to second language teaching a single useful type of drill or exercise. The claim that it would result in better transformation exercises has not materialized. The only possible candidate for an innovation, the "disambiguation exercise," is as we have seen quite useless. This inapplicability of generativism to second language teaching is a natural result of the former's concern with the unconscious mental activity of the ideal native speaker and of its disregard for performance as superficial and trivial. Such a concern may provide a useful logical way of checking the validity of generative rules, but it is quite unrelated to the concerns of languists.

More on the abstractness of linguistics

Linguists of *any* school need to deal with language with a degree of abstractness that is excessive for the second language student who, after all, has not been trained in linguistics. For the student, it is as if linguists wanted to make the simple unnecessarily difficult, although we can be sure that is not the case. But the high degree of abstractness of linguistic grammars --much higher in the case of generative grammars than in most structural grammars-- explains why generally speaking linguistic findings cannot be applied directly to second language teaching.

More on the psychological reality of linguistic rules

In the case of generative grammar, abstractness has led to the point where contact with the language "as she is spoke" has almost been lost. Despite the fact that it has been claimed that "the rules of [rationalist] grammar are psychologically real" [Diller 1971:21], there is no evidence that they are. Opposite evidence is both logical and based on common sense. One can compare a generative grammar to the circuit of a calculator, which no one would claim is organized according to the way people add, subtract, multiply, and divide [Lamendella 1969].

As Politzer [1972:46] noted, one cannot imagine that a speaker would first generate strings of abstractions at the syntactical level, then select lexical items, then apply transformational rules, and finally convert this into sounds. In this respect, Chomsky [1965:9] has been wiser than some of his followers, for he wrote: "When we say that a sentence has a certain derivation with respect to a particular generative grammar, we say nothing about how the speaker or hearer might proceed, in some practical or efficient way, to construct such a derivation."

It would thus be unreal to say that someone must think

of a statement before he asks a question. It is unreal to say that a speaker derives the stress and vowels of *photographer* from *photograph* --the psychological unreality of such stress rules as proposed by Chomsky and Halle [1968] is evident in the fact that native speakers of English very often misplace stress in polysyllabic words when they first acquire them.

On the other hand, such structural concepts as the phoneme and the allophone seem to have psychological reality, as seen by the fact that untrained native speakers produce a list of sounds similar to a phonemic inventory and are as well largely unaware of allophones (their difficulty, if literate, lies with the graphemes).

Synthesis: Linguistic (generative) versus languistic grammars△

We have seen that generative grammars do not have much direct application to language teaching/learning, both because of their great abstractness and because they are grammars of idealized competence, not of real performance. Of course, they were never designed to facilitate the teaching/learning process, so their inapplicability to it is perfectly understandable. Facilitating second language learning is the function of languistic grammars.

A languistic grammar adapts knowledge from linguistic and traditional grammars to the task of second language teaching. It readily sacrifices certain desirable features of linguistic grammars for the sake of facilitating the language teaching/learning process.

(It should be remembered, of course, that while languistic grammars select, simplify, and modify what is provided by linguistic grammars, the former should not include major distortions of the latter --"a grammar of housewiring that distorted the principles of electricity to the extent that the would-be housewirer ran the risk of electrocution would lack both pedagogic value and theoretical validity" [Bartlett 1979:186].)

The contrastive characteristics of generative and languistic grammars are listed in Figure 4.1.

△ The usual dichotomy between "scientific" (for "linguistic") and "pedagogical" grammars is terminologically unacceptable. A grammar for teaching purposes is also *scientific*, though not linguistic --it follows scientific languistic principles.

COMPARISON OF LINGUISTIC (GENERATIVE) AND LANGUISTIC GRAMMARS		
1	Describe the competence of ideal native speakers	Describe the systematic performance of everyday speakers
2	Concern themselves with the code itself	Concern themselves with the teaching and use of the code
3	Comprehensive	Selective
4	Refer to one language	Refer to two languages --native and second
5	Ordered generatively	Order according to the steps of discovery of the second language
6	Abstract	Concrete
7	Complex	Simple
8	Follow theoretical considerations	Adapt themselves to pragmatic factors
9	Concerned with universals	Concerned with particulars
10	Emphasize economy and avoid redundancy	Emphasize clarity, with redundancy if necessary for clarity
11	Based on one theory	Eclectic
12	Very accurate	Allow "rules of thumb"
13	Have no particular skill emphasis	Emphasize the spoken language
14	Make no particular use of contrasts	Emphasize contrasts, both within and across languages
15	Rules symbolized in algebraic formulas and tree diagrams	Rules verbalized, with minimal symbolization
16	Sentence generation "stimulus-free"	Sentence generation largely conditioned

Figure 4.1

One cannot help but conclude, from the previous discussion and from a look at Figure 4.1, that a generative grammar and a languistic grammar are very different things indeed.

This brings us to the question: What particular combination of theories should be reflected in the eclectic content of languistic grammars? In other words, what particular combination of structural, generative, traditional, or other grammars seems to perform well as a languistic grammar?

For phonology, I would recommend articulatory phonetics (acoustic phonetic information is not readily observable or depictable and cannot easily be translated into sound production), the structural concepts of the phoneme and allophone, and, at the advanced level, some generative phonological rules.

The treatment of morphology would be based on the treatment of phonology. All three types of grammar being discussed (structural, generative, and traditional) have useful insights.

The syntactic characteristics of simple sentences can best be dealt with by means of tagmemic ("slot and filler") formulas [Allen and Widdowson 1975:57-8].[△] The relationships between sentences and the way simple sentences can be combined into more complex ones can be expressed by means of transformations. Here generative grammar can contribute useful insights, although it must be remembered that pedagogical transformations are from surface structure to surface structure, not from deep structure to surface structure. Traditional grammar can also contribute insights to the pedagogy of syntax.

Lexicon and semantics cannot be effectively dealt with by generative semantics in a languistic grammar. Generative semantics is again too abstract and tends to "atomize"

[△] A "tagmeme" is a form-class correlation, i.e., a correlation between a grammatical function or "slot" and the class of items or "fillers" that can perform that function at that level. Note that tagmemics has several advantages: (1) the formulas are simple and require little explanation, (2) learners readily accept the concept of a number of simple sentence patterns from which more complex sentences can be derived, (3) it is reasonably easy to represent the formulas diagramatically, and (4) it is easy to convert tagmemic formulas into language drills.

meaning into minute components that are too small in scope for second language teaching. The entries in good monolingual and bilingual dictionaries plus contextual translation equivalences are perfectly adequate for our purposes. Equivalences within situational contexts can be the basis for developing in our students an understanding of discourse constraints.

This combination of insights from structural, generative, and traditional grammars seems to result in an effective languistic grammar. I have used such an eclectic grammar with considerable success. Others also claim that such eclectic grammars are successful [e.g., Dalbor 1972]. It is natural that this should be so --grammars based on pragmatic considerations are far more likely to contribute to a practical task than grammars that rigidly and pristinely follow a single theory of language.

5

SIX TYPES OF LANGUAGE ACQUISITION/LEARNING

Is learning to be based on acquisition?

Should the second language teaching/learning of linguistic adults proceed by imitating the way children acquire their native language? Should it attempt to imitate the way infant bilinguals acquire two languages?

Regarding the first of the two questions above, Di Pietro [1975:195] wrote:

> In the twentieth running of the Grand Prix you can tell who [the runners] are because each....has a distinctive lettering on his jersey. [Some runners]...are wearing two jerseys at the same time and are claiming that our venerable Grand Prix is really two races in one and should be retitled "the 20th Grand Prix on Both First and Second Language Acquisition."

This claim that native language acquisition and second language learning involve the same psycholinguistic processes has been increasingly made in recent years [e.g., by Newmark and Reibel 1968, V. Cook 1969, Tucker and d'Anglejan 1972, Ervin-Tripp 1974, Macnamara 1975]. Yet it has been made one-sidedly, by emphasizing the similarities between the two processes and ignoring a large body of data that shows important differences. It has even happened, occasionally, that an author presents data supporting the conclusion of important differences but claims the data support the opposite view.

Others see that there are marked differences between the two processes. Strevens [1978:180], for example, wrote that native language acquisition and second language teaching/learning "belong in different universes of discourse which overlap in only limited ways." It seems necessary, then, to consider in some detail the similarities and differences between these two processes.

Types of language acquisition/learning

The issue is only made more confused by dividing language acquisition/learning into the traditional two types --native language acquisition and second language learning--

when in fact there are six common language acquisition/learning types, as follows: (1) native language acquisition from infancy; (2) infant bilingualism, or the acquisition of two or more languages from infancy; (3) adult second language learning, that is, the formal learning of a second language by a linguistic adult (about twelve years of age or older) in the second language classroom; (4) adult second language acquisition, that is, the acquisition of a second language by an adult in the environment, "sink or swim" fashion, without the benefit of effective instruction; (5) childhood second language acquisition; and (6) childhood second language learning.

There are, of course, a number of similarities between these six types of language acquisition/learning. In all of them the learner must process, one way or another, an enormous amount of language data of various kinds. In all of them, in order to be successful the acquirer/learner must have motivation to acquire/learn the language and communicate in it --without sufficient motivation, the young child's linguistic development will be poor, the language student will fail the course and drop from the program, and the immigrant, unable to communicate in the dominant language of the community, will keep himself within native language enclaves.

But beyond these and possibly other broad similarities, there are a number of important differences between these types of acquisition/learning whose importance as factors simply should not be minimized.

The language acquisition device and hypothesis testing

In 1965 Chomsky proposed (in *Aspects of the Theory of Syntax*) that the process of native language acquisition is guided by an innate "language acquisition device" ("LAD") containing knowledge of language universals. Many mentalist psycholinguists have supported this idea. Among them, McNeill [1966] specified four functions or faculties of the LAD: (1) distinguishing speech sounds from other sounds, (2) organizing linguistic events into classes, (3) containing knowledge that only a certain kind of linguistic system is possible, and (4) having the ability to constantly evaluate and simplify the linguistic system being constructed. Note that of these four functions, (3) is unnecessary to learn a language, and (1), (2), and (4) can result from the application of general principles of learning and cognitive development.

Many have disagreed with the idea of innate knowledge.

Among them, Piaget [1967] and Slobin [1973] wrote of language acquisition as resulting from special capacities arising out of general cognitive development rather than being innate. Hebb *et al.* [1971] saw the child born with a predisposition to talk and the capacity to learn how to do it but attributed any universal characteristics of child language not to a LAD but to universal experience.

In fact, there is not an iota of evidence that native language acquisition is guided by a LAD, that young children test hypotheses rather than discriminate and generalize, that the process goes from base to surface, or that imitation and the linguistic environment play unimportant roles. Why should knowledge about language categories be innate? Does it not make sense to expect it to develop from experience? Why should infants be born with analytical skills that linguists must acquire through long years of painstaking academic effort? It makes no sense. But then, it does not have to make sense. As Ambrose Bierce [n.d.:104] put it: "The doctrine of innate ideas is one of the most admirable faiths of philosophy, being itself an innate idea and therefore inaccessible to disproof."

It is the rejection of the principles of learning that has led to the creation of this preposterous LAD. And in creating it, Chomsky and others are admitting that they do not know how a language is learned; they cannot explain it, so they appeal to this magical LAD. In any case, the languist is too busy with the observable to waste his time with fables.

Regarding the testing of hypotheses, Chomsky [1968:76] would have us believe that, on the basis of "meagre and degenerate data" a two-year-old compares hypotheses about a particular language with innate knowledge and accepts or rejects the hypotheses depending on whether they are congruent with the principles of universal grammar found in the abstract deep structure. This claim borders on the ridiculous. To test hypotheses, the child would have to be able to engage in abstract reasoning --this a two-year-old cannot do. To test hypotheses, the child would have to intentionally try several ways of saying something to find out which is accepted --it doesn't seem the child goes about intentionally doing this. Furthermore, young children do not respond to correction, so it should be obvious that they are not actively testing hypotheses and correcting them accordingly. To assign knowledge of a linguistic theory and the ability to test hypotheses based on it to a two-year-old is the height of unreasonableness. It is also a "cheap" theory, as it is not subject to direct empirical confirmation or rejection.

Many scholars have rejected the idea of a hypothesis-testing infant. Among them are Braine [1971], T. Quinn [1974], and R. Clark [1975]. Quinn said that the child is not cognitively capable of proceeding like a speculating linguist, i.e., positing hypotheses, making predictions, comparing data with predictions, then confirming or rejecting the hypotheses. He added [1974:340] that that is "language learning as perceived by someone interested in speculative theory construction" rather than in "the observable reality of the nursery and the classroom." Clark [1975:322] claimed that language acquisition seems to be based on "a range of very simple strategies" rather than "a complex device for forming and evaluating hypotheses."

The young child clearly makes structural generalizations which allow him to produce novel sentences. But both these generalizations and his occasional overgeneralizations leading to errors can be explained in terms of the laws of learning; there is no need to posit a complex hypothesis-testing LAD.

As to adult second language acquirers/learners, although they have the cognitive apparatus to engage in the testing of hypotheses, most seldom do so. Immigrants do not set out to test hypotheses, that is, they do not produce incorrect utterances in order to find out if the feedback is negative; instead, they produce the best utterances they can and distinguish then between positive and negative feedback.

Second language learners in the classroom should not simply be surrounded with the language and expected to figure it out by testing hypotheses. They should be guided all the way. If a second language learner were simply exposed to varied linguistic data and expected to form correct hypotheses about them without any guidance, he would (1) base his hypotheses on his native language and (2) be unable to correct them due to (a) insufficient exposure to the language and (b) insufficient interaction with native speakers/models.

Input, interaction, and feedback

The language addressed to young children, far from being "meagre and degenerate," is abundant and mostly well formed [Bellugi and Brown 1964, Drach 1969]. It is, to be sure, repetitive and simplified [Snow and Ferguson 1977];

it is also easy to understand, marked by intentional clarity [Slobin 1975]. In other words, "motherese" or "caretaker language" is graded to the growing linguistic ability of the child and goes maybe only slightly beyond it [J. Phillips 1973]. Similarly, the language of the second language classroom should be carefully graded to the knowledge of the students.

Young children are strongly affected by the linguistic environment and clearly respond to it. Thus, it has been shown that the items children would use could be predicted to a very high degree by the frequency of occurrence of those items in their mothers' speech [R. Brown and Hanlon 1970]. Of course, the action is mutual --the environment acts on the acquirer and the acquirer acts on the environment. Communicative interaction seems essential to the internalization of the language. This is a powerful reason for making sure that second language students frequently engage in communicative activities.

Part of this interaction is feedback. The young child does not get much direct linguistic feedback nor can he respond well to it --it is very hard to get a child to imitate a linguistic correction. He acquires his language, instead, on the basis of communicative feedback or what we could call the system of "Uh?s" and "Ah!s" The second language learner can learn not only from direct feedback but also by observing what other students say and how the teacher reacts to that [Allwright 1975]. For the second language learner, the rewards of correct linguistic behavior are far more concentrated and can be far more explicit than for the native language acquirer. Furthermore, native language acquirers neither understand nor want linguistic correction, but well-motivated second language learners both want it and understand it.

Imitation, analogy, and practice

While a few words are acquired by the infant by trial and error --what Thorndike called "babble-luck"-- and a few are created ("baby words"), almost all the words are learned by imitation. Echoing is quite noticeable in early language acquisition, and so is analogizing. It has been found that while some young children imitate about ten percent of what they hear, others imitate up to 40 percent or more [Bloom *et al.* 1974]. At more advanced stages of native language acquisition imitation and analogy lose their importance as the attention is almost exclusively on meaning, to the point that children become poor imitators of surface structure. Parallel to native language acquisition, second language learning also requires considerable imitation and analogy in its early stages.

Young children practice structures, as shown by Weir's [1962] study of "language in the crib." They enjoy practicing the language, even practicing skills that have been almost perfected. Herein lies a lesson for the older second language learner, who prefers to keep practice to a minimum.

Steps in language acquisition/learning

The very young child, before one year of age, develops first some knowledge of communicative function --such as expressing requests, approval, disapproval, etc.-- before he develops language [Halliday 1975]. When language acquisition begins, the development of meaning precedes that of form, so that semantically-based marked forms are acquired earlier than arbitrarily based ones [Adiv 1980-b]. Even the child's imitation and practice, which are crucial to further linguistic development [R. Clark 1975:322-3], are contextualized. For the second language learner, there are at times overriding criteria that determine that they should go from form to meaning, not from meaning to form. The need for communication, so overpowering in the case of the native language acquirer, can be temporarily subordinated to other pedagogical needs in the case of the second language learner.

It has been found that young children acquire the rules of two languages in about the same order [Kessler 1971]; this would seem to be a function of the universality of communication needs. Unmarked forms emerge first, both in native language acquisition [Slobin 1973] and second language acquisition [Swain 1976, Tarone *et al.* 1976, Adiv 1980-b]; in both cases words (free forms) are acquired before sub-word elements (bound forms). Studies of the acquisition of morphemes by many native language acquirers show approximately the same order of acquisition, apparently determined by both grammatical and semantic complexity [R. Brown 1973, DeVilliers and DeVilliers 1973]. Dulay and Burt's [1974-b] claim of a universal order of morpheme acquisition by *second* language acquirers, however, has been disproved by longitudinal studies such as Hakuta's [1976] and Rosansky's [1976]. In second language teaching/learning the order of rules should follow pedagogical principles; there is no reason for it to follow any detailed "natural" order, except in the broad sense that it should meet the needs of communication.

In native language acquisition, phonology is not acquired by mastering individual sounds and then combining them. Early utterances (single words) are quite variable in their pronunciation and only gradually come to match adult pronunciation. Unlike this, adult second language learners can be taught to master sounds one at a time --in contrast with other sounds-- and to match second language standards as each sound is learned.

The child apparently makes considerable use, in early acquisition, of holophrases consisting of more than one word, which are "acquired as invariable routines and retained intact for some time before the internal structure is modified in any way" [R. Clark 1975:320]. These segments are memorized at the surface level without awareness of their internal structure. These unanalyzed sequences are also referred to as "prefabricated patterns" [Hakuta 1974, 1976] or "formulaic expressions." L. Fillmore [1976] found that five children learning a second language used formulaic expressions for 52 to 100 percent of the utterances in the early stages and still for 37 percent of the utterances by the lowest user at the end of the first year. She also found that formulaic speech gradually became creative language, under pressure of communication needs. It seems that what the child does is combine set phrases or make them part of simple sentences, generating novel sentences by the extensive manipulation of a very limited vocabulary --a simple operation for the child and yet these sentences would have complex linguistic analyses if they were treated as generated by the child "from scratch." How simple sentences can be combined is learned by the child through analogy based on adult models.

This process of sentence generation has long been used with considerable success in second language teaching. The learner is asked to learn thoroughly a small number of sentences, as in a dialogue, then these "prefabricated patterns" are manipulated and varied to produce many other simple sentences, and finally they are combined with other sentences to generate more complex sentences. Rules are derived from formulaic speech by analysis based on analogy.

The child may attend to different aspects of the language at different points in his development. He may concentrate at times on pronunciation and not attend to meaning or structure, or he may attend to global meaning without paying much attention to structure, or he may pay attention to structure and disregard everything else [R. Clark 1975:323]. Similarly, the second language learner needs at times to concentrate his attention on one component of the language only, to the temporary exclusion of the others.

A difference between language acquisition and language learning is that acquisition is mostly unconscious and learning mostly conscious. But they both move in the opposite direction --in school, the native language acquirer becomes conscious of some of the characteristics of his language; in the second language program, good teaching will lead conscious knowledge to become unconscious through directed communicative practice. Note that unconscious acquisition is a very inefficient process that takes a great amount of time, far more than the second language learner can devote to the task. The unconscious language acquisition process involves acquiring through use; the conscious language learning process involves first learning, then using.

In terms of order of native language acquisition, we can divide it approximately into three periods:

(1) From about age two to age six, the child acquires the sound system, most of the syntax, and mostly concrete vocabulary.

(2) Between about ages seven and ten, he acquires the more complex phonological rules, especially those relating sounds to the written language, complex syntax, and further vocabulary.

(3) From about age eleven on, there is mostly vocabulary acquisition, especially the words for abstract semantic concepts.

As it can be seen, this order of acquisition only very roughly parallels the usual order in second language teaching, in terms of broad mastery of components. One difference, among several, is in vocabulary --beginning adult second language learners are quite capable of dealing with abstract vocabulary from the start.

Motivation

We come now to the first variable for which a clear distinction can be made between the various types of language acquisition/learning. The native language acquirer has an extremely strong motivation to acquire the language, for, if not his physical needs, certainly the satisfaction of his emotional needs and of his need to act on the environment depend on communication with those who surround him. He is also highly motivated to become integrated into the speech community, as seen by how quickly the older child adopts the accent of those in it. In the case of the infant developing bilingually, motivation may vary from very good to outstanding, probably depending on his emotional communication needs in each language.

For the adult, motivation to learn a second language can vary from no motivation at all, as in the case of some high school or university students and some of the government employees who are *required* to study a language, to fairly good motivation; but this motivation seldom, if ever, has a strength even approaching the infant's. This is natural --the second language learner has satisfied all basic ego needs (he has a social and linguistic identity already) and can satisfy almost all of his communication needs in his native language.

For the older child, whether acquiring a second language or learning it in school, motivation is much weaker than for the native language acquirer. It can be enhanced by emphasizing the use of the second language as the means of communication.

In second language learning, spoken face-to-face communication seems to be the greatest motivator for about 80 percent of the students [Politzer 1953, Hammerly 1971-b, D. Quinn 1971], so it should occur frequently.

What the acquirer/learner starts with

Infants start the language acquisition process with a *tabula rasa*, that is, "the mind before impressions are recorded upon it by experience" [*Webster's New World Dictionary*] --we have rejected innate knowledge, although not the idea that humans are born with special capabilities for processing language. In older children and adults, on the other hand, there is a previously acquired set of linguistic habits or "system of internalized unconscious rules." This is important because it is easier to learn something new than something at odds with previously acquired knowledge.

So in this factor, too, infants have an advantage over older learners. It is not, however, a totally one-sided advantage, for the awareness that older learners may have of the general characteristics of language and of the characteristics of their specific native language may be used --should be used-- to facilitate second language learning.

Exposure

A conservative estimate is that the preschool child has over 18,000 hours (10 hours a day x 365 days x 5 years) of contact with his native language between the ages of one and six. Furthermore, he has many models and rarely any colearners at the same level. During that time, if he speaks for only one hour a day, he will speak for a total of over 1,800 hours.

In an instructional program, the second language learner would have about 200 hours of contact per school year, for a total of 600 in three years --*one thirtieth* of the total for the child. Moreover, the learner has only one live model and 20 or 30 colearners at the same level all competing for the attention of the one model. And if he speaks for five minutes each hour, which is unlikely, he will speak for a total of 50 hours --*one thirty-sixth* of the total for the child.

Put in another way, in terms of time one year of second language instruction (200 hours) is equivalent to about three weeks of the child's native language acquisition (10 hours a day x 7 days x 3 = 210 hours). Thus, the five years of exposure to the language preschool children get are equivalent to about 90 years of language instruction!

It should be obvious that, despite the greater efficiency of the adult as a learner (to be discussed below), he cannot hope to accomplish in 600 hours what the young child attains in 18,000 hours (if he uses the same learning process as the child). It should also be obvious that with such a major difference in exposure to the language (1) trying to imitate the slow native language acquisition process in second language teaching would be a very inefficient use of the limited time available, and (2) what is needed in the second language program is the use of all sensible shortcuts. Random exposure to the second language is very inefficient. Careful grading, organization, and presentation of the teaching materials, the judicious use of all the capabilities of the learner (including his knowledge of his native language), and exercises of various kinds are some of the shortcuts available in second language teaching.

The limited exposure of the second language learner to the language can be supplemented by a program of extracurricular activities. Much additional exposure can be obtained through language clubs, pen-pals, subscribing to second language publications, seeing films, visiting restaurants, conversing with visiting speakers, and so on.

Linguistic interference during the learning process

Interference does not exist in native language acquisition, occurs from occasionally to fairly often in infant bilingualism, can be seen to increase with age in the case of older children, and can be quite marked in the second language speech of adults.

Interference at various stages of second language learning is most readily observable in the phonetic output, seldom seen in the morphology but frequently observed in the syntax, and perhaps less observable, though still frequent, in the area of vocabulary. This interaction between languages should be taken into account, as second language teaching seems to be more efficient when it is based on a careful comparison of the two languages [Fries 1945:9] as well as on an effort to counteract native language interference by means of appropriate exercises. This is not to say, of course, that work at the points of interference is enough; integration of the language as a whole is also needed.

It should also be noted, in relation to interference, that it is impossible to keep the native language out of the second language learning situation --even when the native language is carefully avoided in the instructional process, it is at work in the learner's mind. This was suggested long ago [Sweet 1899, 1964:198, Palmer 1917, 1968:63], and some empirical evidence of it is available [Butzkamm 1973, Hammerly 1974-c]. Accepting the inevitable, we can conclude that there is nothing wrong in making such limited, overt use of the native language, in second language teaching, as may improve the efficiency of the teaching/learning process.

Language ego, anxiety, and inhibitions

Young children have a flexible "language ego," i.e., identity *vis-à-vis* the language they speak [Guiora *et al.* 1972-b]. As a result of this flexibility, they have no anxiety about language acquisition and no inhibitions about language use. This means they can be quite relaxed, even in the presence of contradictions and ambiguities.

Adults, with an established identity and language ego, can find second language learning to be a traumatic experience. Adults acquiring a second language in the environment may overcome their inhibitions because of their great need to communicate; but this is seldom the case with second language learners.

Inhibitions, and the anxiety related to them, seem to start at age nine or ten. The pressure to produce appropriate responses, the fear of ridicule, etc. cause many older learners to have such a degree of anxiety that it interferes with learning. Psychological studies have shown clearly that, while some anxiety facilitates verbal learning and other complex tasks, much anxiety blocks such learning [Korchin and Levine 1957, Gorsuch and Spielberger 1966].

Ways must be found, in second language programs, to reduce excessive anxiety. An encouraging and helpful attitude on the part of the teacher, the elimination of guessing and ambiguities from the teaching process, and the assurance that there will be no surprises in the testing program can all go a long way toward solving the problem of excessive anxiety. At the same time, care must be taken that some anxiety does exist, for it seems that in the totally relaxed classroom very little is learned.

Flexibility of the brain

Until brain lateralization --the functional specialization of each side of the brain-- is nearly completed by about age five [Krashen 1973], the brain of the child retains a degree of flexibility that is much greater than that of the adult. This flexibility or plasticity of the brain can be seen in the fact that aphasic lesions occurring before the age of nine leave no permanent language deficit; that is, the speech function is transferred to the other side of the brain, in almost all cases from the left side to the right. After that, some impairment of speech function remains, quite severe in the case of adults.

The flexibility of the brain may account in part for the greater facility of children in acquiring pronunciation and intonation, a superiority that begins to fade away at age nine or ten, with extremely few acquirers older than thirteen or so being able to acquire a native-like accent, that is, without thorough guidance. On the other hand, this advantage of the younger learner seems to apply to the phonology only, as Carroll [1960] pointed out. Much can be done in this respect for the older learner by means of carefully guided and structured phonological instruction, rather than by resorting to the almost useless old standby, "Imitate me carefully."

Memory

It is well known that great musicians, athletes, and others requiring much muscular dexterity start their specialized activities in childhood. Perhaps the reason why children are better than adults in the area of motor skills is that children have better motor memory, that is, once they have produced a particular combination of muscular movements they remember it better than adults do. My experience with adult second language learners is that, given adequate guidance, they can produce any second language sound; but then they seem to have difficulty in remembering the new combinations of muscular movements and so revert to familiar articulations.

Motor memory seems to be the only aspect of memory at which adults are at a disadvantage. In other aspects of memory they seem to outperform children. Adults may have a difficult time learning, but they remember what they learn better than children, in part because they try to make sense out of everything, which helps recall. Young children seem to learn easily, but they also forget with great ease.

Spelling-boundness

The young child is not spelling-bound in his approach to language acquisition. Children in the third grade are still quite happy to learn a second language orally, but by the sixth grade they have become spelling-dependent to the point that they insist on being shown the written forms [Kirch 1956]. The spelling-boundness of linguistically adult second language learners can negatively affect the development of intonation, fluency, etc., but its negative effects are particularly evident in the area of pronunciation, as it has been repeatedly shown experimentally [Richards and Appel 1956; Foster and Williams 1960; Muller 1965; Roland 1966; E.F. Garcia 1966; Hammerly 1970-a, 1975-b; and others].

Experienced teachers of English as a second language, for example, are forced to reject statements such as the one by Chomsky and Halle [1968:49] that "conventional orthography is....a near optimal system for the lexical representation of English words," as good as such a statement may be from the point of view of linguistic theory. Even in native language acquisition/learning, the fact that some high school graduates of normal intelligence can hardly read would seem to indicate that such a statement is very, very far removed from the realities of language acquisition, literacy, and language use. For other languages, including a "phonetic" language like Spanish, a familiarity with the numerous problems that standard spelling poses to the second language student also leads necessarily to the rejection of similar statements.

Spelling-boundness is, therefore, a factor in which the young child has an advantage over the literate adult. The preliterate child has the advantage of not having to overload his perceptual mechanism --I am tempted to say "short-circuit" it-- with two complexly interrelated systems, the phonological system and the graphemic one, that often pull the attention of the learner in opposite directions.

If the adult second language student is so spelling-bound that he *must* see something --and this seems to be the case for most students-- then he should be given a visual "crutch" that does not lead to phonological errors and that can be gradually phased out in favor of standard spelling. Purely pedagogical transcriptions, based mostly on new principles, have already been proposed in another book [Hammerly 1974-a] and are presented in summary form in Chapter 15.

Structuring of input

A further difference refers to the structuring of the language data --items and rules-- to which the acquirer/learner is exposed. Although, as we have seen, the young child is not exposed to data haphazardly, he can hardly be said to have carefully graded and systematically planned input. The same can be said for adult second language acquisition, in which, as in early childhood, exposure to data is determined by communication needs and not by structural criteria.

Within a second language teaching program, however, it is possible to use careful grading and planning in the presentation of language data to the students. As Lane [1962:2] put it, "...second language learning is what we make it," a statement that is still true insofar as it refers to those factors in the second language teaching situation that are controllable. Since a structured learning task is easier to accomplish than an unstructured one, careful structuring of second language input can give the second language learner a marked advantage over acquisition situations.

A system of concepts

The young child develops concepts at about the same time and rate as he acquires the words for them; this is a slow process requiring many associations. The linguistic adult already has a system of concepts, so he does not have to learn to think all over again. With not too many modifications, the older learner's system of concepts can be used to speed up the learning of second language vocabulary and grammar. This means that his native language should be used, at least in the early stages of second language teaching, in order to facilitate learning.

This is not to say, by any means, that second language teaching should go back to the old practice of having students with little performative knowledge of structure or of how to use a dictionary translate texts word by word, *à coups de dictionnaire*. The poor results of that are well known and most second language teachers have their favorite examples.[△]

Linguistic awareness

The young child develops structural control unconsciously, without linguistic awareness --proof of this is that no amount of explanation will make him use a syntactic rule which lies beyond the scope of his productive system. The linguistic adult, on the other hand, can grasp structural relationships consciously. He has the advantage of being able to talk *about* language, and if he cannot he can be led to acquire and refine the ability to do so; in other words, he can use a metalanguage. He can therefore be aided consciously by the process of guided discovery or, when necessary, by deductive explanations.

Linguistic accuracy

The young child develops precision in the use of his native language very gradually and slowly, through interaction in communication. Linguistic accuracy does not

---

[△] One of my favorite ones is the following set of instructions for the post office printed on a catalogue envelope originating in Luxembourg:

> "SENDING NON CLOSED, MAY BE OPENED FOR CONTROL BY THE POSTAGE SERVICES. FOR OPEN DECOLLATE THE SLAP. FOR CLOSE PUT DOWN THE SLAP AGAIN."

"Decollate," incidentally, means "decapitate."

seem to matter to him --all he wants to do is communicate. For instance, it takes him several years to master the sound system. He shows a similarly slow development of accuracy, as seen from the adult point of view, in grammar. It also takes him fairly long to narrow down the meanings of words from their initial very broad semantic fields. For example, for some time /dada/ may mean not only "father" but also "any man," "I'm happy," "I want to play peekaboo," and so forth. Furthermore, as already mentioned, direct correction of the young child's speech is ineffective.

The linguistic adult, in contrast, has the advantage that at least at the start of the study of a second language he has a desire for accuracy and is capable of being accurate if properly helped. But the second language student should be made to maintain a high standard of linguistic accuracy from the beginning rather than be allowed or encouraged to develop accuracy slowly and gradually. The classroom environment is not such as to lead to a gradual improvement in accuracy. If high standards of linguistic accuracy are not maintained, what the student really does, out of his desire to communicate, is to settle for an error-laden interlanguage that allows him to communicate ideas with his equally inaccurate classmates and with an indulgent teacher or with patient bilingual speakers, but which sounds like ridiculous gibberish to most native speakers of the language. In the second language class, therefore, correction must be offered, consistently and persistently.

Overall learner characteristics

Psychologists have known for a long time that adults are more efficient learners than young children [Thorndike *et al.* 1928]. Adults have learned how to learn, that is, they have developed learning strategies which are generally more sophisticated and more efficient than those of young children. They have greater concentration. They have far more understanding of learning tasks and can aim their efforts at specific short-term and long-term goals. Their analogical processes are not "hit or miss" affairs but can be guided through reasoning. They are superior at learning morphology and syntax --as opposed to young children who are superior at acquiring pronunciation [Fathman 1975]. They have a better capacity for restructuring information for storage in long-term memory, something that substantially helps recall. Their short-term memory is capable of accommodating longer "chunks." Their attention span is longer and they are less subject to frequent distrations. They are far more capable than younger learners of steady work of a routine nature, something that may be an unavoidable type of activity in an efficient second language program.

All of these characteristics of the older learner help account for the fact that more of the second language can be learned in one semester of college than in over one year of high school or in several years of elementary school. Even children of different ages show this difference --Ervin-Tripp [1974] found that children seven to nine years of age learned French faster than four to six year olds.

It seems, therefore, that there is no global "critical period" during which a second language must be learned. Instead, different aspects of second language learning are easy or difficult at different ages [Ervin-Tripp 1974] --one can speak of a "sensitive period" [Lamendella 1977]. The ideal age to start the study of a second language, other than in immersion programs, would seem to be about twelve years of age, when the learner still possesses some of the advantages of young children but has already acquired most of the advantageous learner characteristics of the adult.

Conclusion No. 1

The differences between young children and adults that have been discussed in this chapter --and which are summarized in Figure 5.1-- make it clear that the response to the first basic question posed at the beginning of this chapter must be negative. The second language teaching of linguistic adults *should not* imitate the way children acquire their native language, for, despite the general similarities between the two processes, there are many fundamental differences, and such imitation would result in a tremendous loss of efficiency.

Bilingualism

As for the second basic question, that of making infant bilingualism a model for second language teaching, much about the differences has already been indicated in the preceding discussion.

A discussion of bilingualism in any detail would be beyond the scope of this book, but a few ideas can be commented upon.

ADVANTAGES AND DISADVANTAGES IN SIX TYPES OF LANGUAGE ACQUISITION/LEARNING						
	(1) NLA	(2) Inf. Bil.	(3) Adult SLL	(4) Adult SLA	(5) Child SLA	(6) Child SLL
Motivation	A	A/a	D/d	a/d	a	d
What the learner starts with	A	A	d	d	d	d
Exposure	A	a	D	a	a	D
Linguistic interference during the learning process	A	a/d	D	D	d	d
Language ego, anxiety, and inhibitions	A	A	D/d	D/d	a	a
Flexibility of the brain	A	A	D	D	a	a
Motor memory	A	A	D	D	a	a
General memory	d	d	A	A	a	a
Spelling-boundness	A	A	D	D	a	d
Structuring of input	D	D	A	D	D	A
Possession of a system of concepts	D	D	A	a	a	a
Linguistic awareness	D	D	A	a	d	a
Linguistic accuracy	D	D	A	a	d	a
Overall learner characteristics	D	D	A	A	d	d

(5) and (6) refer to children about 7-11 years old.

"A" = major advantage
"a" = advantage
"d" = disadvantage
"D" = major disadvantage

Figure 5.1

The by-now-classic distinction between "compound" or "interdependent" bilinguals and "coordinate" or "independent" bilinguals is misleading as far as second language teaching/learning is concerned and has been misapplied within our field.

It is misleading because the so-called "compound" bilingual, who thinks in one language and speaks in another, is not really bilingual --he does not meet strict criteria for bilingualism either linguistically (lack of interference) or psychologically (direct thought-to-expression processes).

The concept has been misapplied to the field of second language teaching/learning by confusing the *goal* of second language teaching --the development of coordinate bilinguals-- with the *process* for attaining that goal. Thus, those who want to imitate bilingual acquisition in second language teaching urge the building of a wall of separation between the two languages which is never to be crossed, not even in the early stages of second language instruction. As we have seen, this is an impossibility, because that artificial wall will be frequently crossed by the students in their minds anyway. Not only that, but a careful study of bilingual development from infancy on [Hammerly 1964] shows that, even when specific persons and environments are consistently associated with each language in the mind of the child, there is considerable linguistic interaction. In this case, phonological interference was evident until the age of four, grammatical interference until the age of ten, and the two lexicons continued to interact into adulthood. In other words, it seems that a coordinate bilingual emerges slowly from an at least partially compound system.

Conclusion No. 2

In answer to the second basic question at the beginning of this chapter, the second language teaching of linguistic adults *should not* be based on the characteristics of the bilingual development of young children, as this would be very inefficient.

Instead of trying to imitate the way in which young children acquire one or more languages, which is an impossibility, second language teaching should try to compensate for the disadvantages and fully exploit the assets that the linguistically adult learner brings to the second language program.

6

THE LEARNER

Adapting instruction to the learner

It has been noted that the concept of adapting instruction to the characteristics of the learner is not new, going back at least to Montaigne in the 16th century [Hosenfeld 1975]. It is only in recent times, though, that the characteristics of the learner have been studied in some depth.

Students are different in a hundred ways. Good teachers have always adapted to individual student characteristics; it is part of being a flexible and creative teacher.

Programs, however, cannot offer more than a limited number of options, although computer-assisted instruction could greatly increase the number of possible tracks to reach the same goals. Within one classroom, the needs of the group dictate that there can be only one instructional track (unless it is a fully individualized classroom), but within that one track there should be full attention to individual differences. Few teachers can operate simultaneously a multiplicity of programs, but most teachers ought to be able to run successfully a highly adaptable single program.

Learners differ in (1) what they bring to the learning task, and (2) how they proceed to learn. It is mostly the latter that can be manipulated in teaching. However, the rest of this chapter will discuss both types of characteristics, on the assumption that both can give insights into the second language learning process.

Biological characteristics

1) Age

Age has already come under discussion in Chapter 5, so here only a few additional comments are presented. Each age seems to have peculiar advantages and disadvantages --second language acquisition/learning is possible at any age, though not in the same way or at the same speed. The only aspect in which younger learners are consistently superior is in the *acquisition* of second language pronunciation --older children are superior to younger children in its *learning*.

A number of studies have shown that older learners are at an advantage in formal second language learning in the classroom [Ervin-Tripp 1974, Fathman 1975, Genesee 1978, Snow and Hoefnagel-Höhle 1978, Cummins 1979]. Dodson [1967], for example, found that adults required half as many imitations than primary school children to master a sentence, that is, to be able to reproduce it. Catford's [1969] conclusion was that adults are about five times as efficient as children in learning second languages.

2) Sex

When large groups of students are considered, the average scores of females are consistently higher than those of males in second language aptitude and achievement. The difference is most marked at the senior high school and college levels [Cloos 1971]. It is, however, a small difference.

Cognitive characteristics

1) IQ

Pimsleur [1980:3] estimated that intelligence accounts for only 16 percent of success in second language learning. IQ seems to be primarily related to academic second language skills like reading, grammar, and vocabulary rather than to oral production [Genesee 1976].

It has been known for some time that intelligence is not a major factor in success. It has been determined, for instance, that the distribution of IQ scores of high school dropouts is the same as that of high school graduates and that career success among geniuses is the same as among the general population [Terman *et al*. 1947].

2) Second language aptitude

Scores in Carroll and Sapon's [1959] Modern Language Aptitude Test have been shown to relate to success in second language learning in the classroom, even to the point where subtest scores relate to specific second language skills [Gardner and Lambert 1965]. Pimsleur [1966-b] found that his Language Aptitude Battery [1966-a] scores plus grade point averages correlated at r .72 with success in second language courses.

These aptitude tests are composed of several factors, perhaps the most significant of these being auditory ability [Pimsleur *et al*. 1964]. Other important factors are grammatical sensitivity or language analysis ability, memory, and verbal intelligence.

Aptitude can have a marked effect on progress in a

second language program. Thus, at the U.S. Army Language School high aptitude students are able to reach the advanced level of proficiency in half the time needed by average students. The spread of aptitude is considerably greater than that, as these students are from the chosen top third rather than average students.

Aptitude, however, seems to be more relevant in a formal second language learning situation than in an acquisition situation. In the latter, attitude seems to be more important than aptitude.

Interestingly, it is possible to train students so that they will get higher scores in the auditory ability sections of both the Modern Language Aptitude Test [Yeni-Komshian 1965] and the Pimsleur Language Aptitude Battery [Hatfield 1966]. This would seem to indicate that at least this component does not measure a stable characteristic of the learner.

3) Learning strategies

There is considerable evidence that there are individual cognitive strategies in face of a learning task, with each learner having a whole repertoire of strategies that he uses for different tasks. Some favor induction and analogy, others deduction; some can work orally, others must have something written; some learn vocabulary by hearing, others visualize spelled words, others visualize the meanings, still others respond kinesthetically; some rely on immediate feedback from the teacher, others internalize that feedback and learn to judge their own performance. Low-aptitude students learn better with a more behavioristic approach, but better students learn better with and prefer a more cognitive approach [T. Mueller n.d.]

Faced with all these differences in learning styles, what is the teacher to do? Perhaps the answer is to make instruction varied enough so that all students have an opportunity to make full use of their repertoire of learning strategies.

It should be kept in mind, however, that some common learning strategies are quite inappropriate for second language learning. One does not learn to pronounce and speak a second language fluently by relying on spelling, so students who have this strategy should be retrained to rely on their ears. Other strategies from which second language students should be "weaned" are translating word by word, wanting to have every little thing explained, wanting to be creative with the second language from the earliest lessons, and so forth. In other words, the student cannot be told to just be himself --he will have to adapt to the program as much as, or more than, the teacher has to adapt to the student's characteristics.

4) Previous knowledge: his native language

As discussed in previous chapters, the student's native language is a very important factor in second language learning. Furthermore, it has been found that proficiency in the native language correlates positively with success in second language courses.

5) Previous knowledge: his educational background

Other things being equal, the more successful a learner has been in his previous schooling, the more likely he is to succeed in a second language course. If his educational background is nil, that is, if he is illiterate, the learner might have fewer interference problems in learning the spoken language but would have a major learning task when it comes to reading and writing.

6) Previous knowledge: knowledge of other second languages

Knowledge of more than one language seems to facilitate the learning of additional languages. This is especially true if a language previously learned is closely related to the new one.

7) Reasoning: field independence/field dependence

Field independence is the ability to concentrate on relevant details of a learning task and ignore the rest. There is some evidence that this is related to success in any kind of learning and in second language courses in particular, especially in learning elements and rules of structure. Field dependence, the ability to ignore details and pay attention to the whole, may be useful during communicative activities.

8) Reasoning: broad/narrow categorization

The narrow categorizer may make some categories too narrow, thereby forcing himself to avoid what is excluded from them. The broad categorizer tends to overgeneralize, to include too much in each category. Thus the broad categorizer will make many errors.

Affective characteristics

1) Attitudes

Attitudes --beliefs, feelings, and intentions affecting behavior towards a social object-- can have a marked effect on second language learning. The learner's attitudes toward second language study, the teacher, the method of instruction, and second language speakers and their culture can all affect the outcome of second language teaching.

In North America, there is a considerable amount of ethnocentrism, with second language minorities and foreigners viewed with some suspicion and even, in some cases, contempt. Foreignness is rejected, and for many knowledge of a second language is to be kept hidden, as it might indicate membership in a minority group. This affects especially the study of languages whose speakers have a low socioeconomic status.

Fortunately, just as attitudes are learned, especially from parents, they can also be unlearned and replaced by more positive ones. Second language study itself seems to improve the attitudes of learners toward the speakers of the language [Riestra and Johnson 1964, Jonas 1969]. Success in second language study, if allowed to follow its normal course, will lead the learner through Valette and Disick's [1972:17] five stages of attitudes --receptivity, responsiveness, appreciation, internalization, and characterization.

In his studies of attitude, Lambert concluded that the factor of attitude and motivation is as important as intellectual capacity in determining success in second language learning. However, his conclusion is based on studies conducted in quasi-bilingual communities in Quebec, where a large component of *acquisition* was involved. Savignon [1972], in a study in a monolingual environment, found no correlation between communicative competence and attitude toward France and French-speaking peoples. She concluded that attitudes are important in an environmental situation because they determine the degree of contact with speakers of the second language; but attitudes are not relevant in a remote situation. Another study found a similar lack of correlation between communicative competence and attitudes for German [Bartz 1974].

Student attitudes should not be the only basis for methodological decisions. The fact that some students do not like a method should be a reason to adapt it, not to change it drastically if it is based on sound principles.

"Attitudes" can refer to more than social situations. A second language learner can have an "attitude of perseverance," an "attitude of accuracy," an "attitude of independence," and so forth.

2) Motivation

We can think of motivation as an internal force that

propels a person toward a goal. It is largely based on attitudes. It is crucial to learning --without motivation there will be no responses or unwilling responses, the former a situation in which there can be no feedback, the latter one in which feedback has little or no effect. Motivation cannot be dictated; it belongs personally to the learner.

Perhaps we should give up trying to teach second languages to students who do not want to learn them. It seems pointless. Without interest there can be little or no effort and without considerable effort there can be no success in second language learning. Perhaps the only required course in the second language field should be an introductory course to the study of language, the main purpose of which would not be to teach a language but to create the necessary motivation to embark on the learning of one.

Carroll, however, wrote [1974-b:121] that "even unmotivated students can learn, as long as they attend actively to the learning task." Elsewhere [1963:729], he listed among the aspects of perseverance the desire to please others, to get good grades, and to feed one's self-esteem. This would be to rely basically on extrinsic motivation, at least at the beginning of the program. (*Extrinsic* motivation is outside the nature of what is taught and includes relations with other people, plans for the future, grades, etc. *Intrinsic* motivation is more closely related to the nature of what is being learned and includes the need to achieve, the desire to communicate, and feelings like the need to improve one's self-image and to reduce anxiety.)

Students have a natural desire to excell, to achieve highly in all their endeavors. Most also have considerable intellectual curiosity that can be the basis for encouraging them to learn a second language.

As a second language program progresses, the teacher has many opportunities to enhance the initial motivation of his students. Motivation leads to learning and is enhanced by learning; it is a reciprocal process. Success in reaching partial goals, the opportunity to communicate in the second language, the use of humor by the teacher [Fleming 1964-a, 1964-b] --all of these are highly motivating. The student who is satisfied with the second language program and his progress in it will be sufficiently motivated to persevere in his efforts. If he has not done well in other subjects, starting the study of a second language can be highly motivating to the student, for it is like a new start, on a par with more academically successful students.

Yet, in our desire to motivate students we should not go to extremes. Trying to motivate them through affective means should stop short of adopting therapy techniques that belong in the psychiatrist's office and not in the second language classroom.

Several studies have shown that second language students are motivated first of all by spoken communication. This was found by Agard and Dunkel [1948], although they also found that students were quite bored by the relentless use of memorization and simple mechanical drills that characterized postwar aural-oral courses. A study at the University of Texas at Austin [Solé 1973] showed that two-thirds of the lower-division Spanish students wanted to *use* the language audiolingually, reading skill coming in a poor third. A survey from grade three to college found communication and travel to be the most frequent reasons for second language study given by California students [McEwan and Minkle 1979]. It is therefore essential to provide frequent opportunities for communication, for otherwise the students will lose motivation as they will think that their second language study is useless.

Another important distinction in the study of motivation is that between *instrumental* and *integrative* motivation, introduced by Gardner and Lambert [1959]. Instrumental motivation is the desire to learn a second language for some useful purpose, such as a job, travel, and so forth. Integrative motivation is the desire to learn a second language in order to communicate with its speakers.

Lambert [1963] asserted that an integrative orientation leads to better results in second language learning than an instrumental one. Such better results for an integrative motivation have been found in environmental second language learning situations where contact with speakers and therefore acquisition was an important factor. Examples of that are the learning of French in Montreal or the learning of English by foreign students at American universities [Spolsky 1969-a]. This is because an integrative motivation will lead to making more personal contacts with native speakers and therefore to greater second language acquisition.

But instrumental motivation can be quite strong and,

indeed, decisive. Through primarily instrumental motivation, U.S. Foreign Service officer candidates work very hard in order to reach the level of proficiency that will guarantee them a commission. Successful students of Hebrew who are preparing for the rabbinate can also be said to depend on a mostly instrumental motivation. In many Third World countries English may be learned best by those with the highest instrumental motivation, since the language is learned in order to have access to scientific and technological information. These may be extreme examples, but the point is that much second language learning can succeed on the basis of instrumental motivation.

There is considerable evidence that whether integrative motivation will be very important or not in the classroom situation may depend on sociocultural factors [Gardner *et al.* 1979]. In the remote second language learning situation, basically a monolingual situation with no access to a second language community, classroom factors have been found to outweigh by far environmental factors [Myers 1979].

In conclusion, we can say that second language motivation is psychologically complex: partly extrinsic and intrinsic, partly instrumental and integrative. It may be that doing well in second language learning is the primary reason why extrinsic gives way to intrinsic motivation and instrumental tends to become integrative motivation.

3) Other emotions

The experience of second language learning gives rise to many emotions. It is emotionally trying to go back to dependency, to be unable to express oneself, to be exposed to much that is strange and different and ambiguous, to not know what to expect, to have to concern oneself over making errors, and so on. Second language learning puts us in the role of being ignorant and having to express ourselves childishly. Severe social adjustment is required, as second language learning is not just an intellectual experience but an intense personal encounter.

When strong negative emotions are allowed to develop, they interfere with learning. But much can be done to reduce negative emotions to manageable proportions. Student frustration at the inability to express themselves in the language can be reduced by allowing them, once in a while, to express themselves in the native language about the classroom activities and the program in general. Student insecurity can be reduced by making students conscious of the fact that the teacher is in control and knows what to do. Causes of anxiety --undue severity on the part of the teacher, unpredictability of the content of exams, especially oral exams, ignorance of how to respond to different values-- can be largely eliminated. There is no reason why second language learning cannot be a largely positive experience, despite the emotions it arouses.

To sum up, learning benefits from emotional commitment, as affective factors may have as much or more effect on learning as cognitive ability. In second language teaching we need therefore to "involve the whole learner" [Disick and Barbanel 1974]. This does not mean, however, that we have a right to make emotional demands on our students or to expect them to share with us their most intimate feelings.

Personality characteristics

1) Introversion/extroversion

Extroverts seem to learn second languages faster than introverts, but this may be because they get more practice through getting more turns in class. Careful studies are needed, however, to determine the relationship between this personality trait and second language accuracy, for while extroverts may be more fluent and talkative, they may be so interested in communication that they disregard accuracy. A recent study showed that talkativeness and sociability among elementary school students of French was *negatively* correlated with ability to understand the language [Swain and Burnaby 1976].

The second language teacher should not be so pleased that a few (extroverted) students are saying something in the language that he neglects to correct their errors. Extroverts, unlike some introverts, tend to respond well to criticism. If anything, an effort should be made to encourage introverts to speak more and to restrain extroverts from saying much outside of what they have learned.

2) Impulsiveness/reflectiveness

Impulsive learners learn mostly intuitively, while reflective learners are given to learning systematically. Reflective learners tend to be more accurate. A study of the speech of adults learning to read English as a second language showed that reflective students were slower but more accurate than impulsive students [Doron 1973]. Again, for the second language teacher it is a question of discouraging the extremes.

3) Perfectionism

Perfectionist tendencies have been found to correlate

with good performance in a second language even among young children, in this case learning French in an immersion program [Swain and Burnaby 1976]. Another study found concern to do well and fear of making mistakes among grade one children [Genesee and Hamayan 1979]. As with the two other traits discussed, extremes are bad. An excess in perfectionism has negative effects --reluctance to speak, out of fear of making errors, etc.-- and the other extreme, not caring about making errors, results in the fossilization of a fault-ridden pidgin.

4) Empathy

Being able to put oneself in the place of the foreigner and play the role to the hilt, gestures and all, seems to help second language learning, as one is identifying with the goal of study. An empathy test based on identifying changes in expression in a face on film was found to successfully predict accuracy in second language pronunciation, thus showing the importance of empathy [Guiora *et al*. 1972-b]. The development of empathy towards speakers of the second language can be subtly helped by the use of drill, dialogue, and situational sentences that help the students to visualize themselves as proficient speakers of the language.

5) Self-concept

Students with a poor self-concept are poor learners, and a high level of self-esteem facilitates learning. The second language teacher should therefore do everything possible to enhance his students' sense of self-worth.

For teenagers with a hazy self-concept, the experience of learning a second language can be an opportunity to experiment with a new identity [Disick and Barbanel 1974]. (Of course, if they see the second language program as an imposition from the parental/educational establishment they will resent it rather than want to experiment with it.)

6) Tolerance for ambiguity/need for structure

Younger learners are more tolerant of ambiguity --they don't mind if everything is not perfectly clear. As they mature, they either remain relatively tolerant or more rigidly want to have everything clearly structured. Since clarity and structure cannot be considered faults in a second language program anyway, they should be provided throughout. There is no reason why second language learners should be submitted to a great deal of ambiguity, which few can tolerate, even if some are emotionally equipped to withstand it.

Social characteristics

1) Sensitivity to the influence of others

Different learners are influenced more or less by parents, peers, the community, and school figures. All of these exert pressure to conform. In young children's native language acquisition, pressure to conform results in the adoption of linguistic norms. In older children's second language learning, however, peer pressure to conform may mean that they will not try to excell, to be different from the average, in order to avoid rejection. It seems that an attitude of conformity correlates with high achievement in a formal second language teaching situation and with low achievement in more informal, acquisition-type immersion second language programs [Hamayan *et al.* 1977].

2) Socioeconomic background

Different socioeconomic backgrounds are accompanied by sets of attitudes some of which may adversely affect second language learning.

3) Need for an authority figure

This need is most evident among young learners; but even older children and adults tend not to learn very well in an overpermissive atmosphere.

4) Capacity to study alone

Some students cannot learn very well alone; they need to study in a group or at least with a "buddy." The second language program should be flexible enough to allow practicing the language in a variety of social situations, giving the learners some choice.

Goal characteristics

Student goals vary in many respects. For example, in terms of quality, some want to speak the second language accurately while others are quite happy with an inaccurate interlanguage. In terms of quantity, some want to develop a comprehensive knowledge, others aim at a rudimentary one. As to modality, some want to learn all four language skills, others want to be able to speak a little, still others just want a reading knowledge. One of the functions of the second language teacher is to convince his students that they should aim at the higher goals.

Unfortunately, while many students have some goal or goals --personal usefulness, career, school requirements-- and while the goal of most students is communication [Papalia 1973], there are students who lack any goals. For these, who have no long-term goals, the mechanical activities of a second language program would be unbearable if they were not provided with attractive short-term goals. All students in fact need short-term goals, for it is virtually impossible to persevere towards a distant goal without frequently feeling a sense of accomplishment on the way. One of the functions of the second language teacher is therefore to present his students with a whole series of short-term goals that are reasonably attractive and that can be reached with relative ease. At the same time, they must require some effort to reach, for any attempt to make second language learning effortless is doomed to failure.

The needs of the learner

In Maslow's [1970:35-58] holistic-dynamic theory of human motivation, there is a hierarchy of basic needs that humans must meet. In order --and generally they must be satisfied in that order if the person is to be able to proceed to higher ones-- they are the following:

1) Physiological needs

Students who haven't had breakfast or who have had a sleepless night cannot learn very well. When there are unsatisfied physiological needs, everything else takes second place.

2) Safety needs

Children prefer routine and a predictable and orderly world out of their need for safety. Less obviously, the adult also "prefers a safe, orderly, predictable, lawful, organized world..." [p. 41] and shows preference for familiar rather than unfamiliar things.

The second language classroom should be such an organized, predictable microcosm; but not all the time, for people also like, for "spice," an occasional exposure to the unknown and unorganized. There is such a thing as feeling too safe in the second language class, when there is no challenge, no correction, no need to pay much attention for there is nothing unpredictable.

3) Belongingness and love needs

These needs involve both giving and receiving love. In the second language classroom what needs to be emphasized is a sense of belonging to the (usually small) group of students that want to learn the second language well, not to the group of those (usually in the majority) who do not care for second languages and do not want to sound like second language speakers.

4) Esteem needs

This refers to both self-esteem and the esteem of

others. A danger in the second language classroom is that by approving and rewarding poor performance we may foster a false sense of self-esteem.

5) The need for self-actualization

Self-actualization refers to doing what one is individually best-suited for, to becoming everything that one is capable of becoming. Involved here is the achievement of goals and obtaining satisfaction in life. Success in second language learning can partially fulfill self-actualization needs.

As the lower basic needs are satisfied, higher basic needs emerge. Most behavior, however, is multimotivated [p. 55], as several or all of the basic needs apply simultaneously. (And much behavior is not motivated, as it responds to external stimuli.)

Other needs --not basic-- are (1) the desire to know and understand, which plays an important role in learning, and (2) esthetic needs [pp. 48-51].

The good second language learner

Several studies have tried to describe the characteristics of the successful second language learner, on the assumption that fostering the development of such characteristics will increase the effectiveness of our endeavors.

General factors such as second language aptitude --as measured by standardized aptitude tests-- and attitudes and motivation seem to account each for about one third of the variance in terminal second language scores. Additionally, general intelligence seems to account for about one sixth, leaving only one sixth for other factors. Such findings would seem to indicate that methodology is unimportant; this, however, would be an erroneous conclusion.

How the language is taught affects all of the factors involved in success in second language learning. Standardized second language aptitude test data apply primarily to oral methods, so a traditional method would not be making much use of the student's second language aptitude as measured by such tests. While initial attitudes and motivation are not amenable to control, second language teaching of the right kind can markedly improve the student's attitudes and motivation. Even the factor of general intelligence is filtered through the language teaching method, as some methods make much more use than others of the learner's intelligence. So methodology is an important factor affecting all other factors.

More specifically, Bartz [1974] found correlations between communicative competence in German and Pimsleur's Language Aptitude Battery verbal and interest scores, years of second language study, and the age of the student (though these last two did not correlate with linguistic competence). Also correlated with good communicative competence were, for oral communication, introversion, soberness, and self-sufficiency; for written communication, imagination, placidness, and low anxiety; and for overall competence, attitudes toward the study of German, though *not* attitudes toward Germany and German-speaking people.

Rubin [1975] came to the conclusion that good second language learners (1) are willing to guess and guess accurately, (2) want very much to communicate, (3) are uninhibited and risk making mistakes, (4) pay attention to form, (5) practice, (6) monitor their production and compare it to native standards, and (7) pay attention to meaning in its social context.

Field independence and tolerance of ambiguity have also been found to correlate successfully with second language learning [Naiman *et al.* 1975]. In an acquisition situation, good learners perceive their social distance from the second and the native culture as not too close nor too great [Acton 1979]. It has also been shown that high self-esteem correlates with better performance in oral second language production [Heyde 1979].

Pimsleur [1980] concluded that the more successful second language learners refuse to depend on their eyes, avoid constant one-to-one word translation, listen to the language extensively, and do not plunge into constructing sentences without knowledge.

The good second language learner needs to be the subject of further studies. Two considerations that need to be taken into account in such future studies are the differences between the learning and the acquisition situation and the considerable importance of *controllable* factors. What cannot be controlled can be of only little interest to us; it is in the manipulation of controllable factors that our profession can find room for improvement and the opportunity to help every second language learner become a good second language learner.

7

TEACHING

Towards a definition of teaching

A broad definition of teaching is "helping someone to learn." In this broad sense, not only teachers but also parents, ministers, journalists, even policemen, teach. In a narrow sense, as it will be used in this chapter, teaching is the interaction between a teacher and his students whereby planned learning takes place by the latter. Teaching can be to groups or individuals, but only individuals can be said to learn. Teaching, the attempt to induce learning, as we all know, does not always succeed --the suggestions in this chapter are intended to help make it successful.

In order to teach successfully, one has to be able to answer with considerable precision a number of questions. Among them are the following:

1) What is to be learned? In our case the answer is, the second language, and one must understand its nature very well in order to be able to teach it effectively. An answer to this question would produce as its final output a list of rules and elements that the students are to learn, i.e., a linguistic grammar.

2) When is it to be learned? It is not enough to select what will be taught. One must also organize it in a well-ordered progression.

3) What are the characteristics of the learner? In addition to such characteristics as age, learning strategies, motivation, etc. that were discussed in Chapter 6, one should in particular find out the learner's "entering behavior," that is, what he already knows.

4) How is the material to be taught? Here one has to consider the teacher and the methods, materials, and techniques he may use.

5) Was it learned? This involves both informal assessment and testing.

6) If not, what can we do about it? If a particular point or lesson or unit was not learned, it should be taught again, preferably in a new way. If the whole program is failing to produce learning, it should be revised accordingly.

There are other important factors that do not fit in this list of questions. Among them are the setting (classroom, etc.), the social milieu, the time available for instruction, and, of special importance in second language teaching, the opportunity for the students to communicate and the availability of technological aids.

Some remarks on second language teaching

The rest of this chapter deals more specifically with second language teaching.

Some mentalist psycholinguists would argue that in the strict sense of the term --helping learning-- second language teaching is impossible. Jakobovits, among them, claims [1970-b:144-5] that the impossibility of teaching a language is due to our inability to state specifically how a language is learned and what it is to know a language. But we do know enough to proceed to teach and to do so quite effectively. As Strevens [1978:180] put it, "teaching *can* affect learning." To be successful, of course, teaching must apply what is already known about learning and second language learning in particular --we should be challenged but not intimidated by what we do not know or by what some people claim we do not know.

Rather than trying to justify what we do on theoretical grounds, we should determine whether it works or not. On that practical basis, the assertion that second languages are not being taught effectively has some validity. A number of studies indicated that in many programs the number of hours or years of instruction is not a strong predictor of oral fluency [Upshur 1968, Mason 1971, Saegert *et al.* 1974]. Second language teaching in North American public schools has been largely a failure, to the point that Shuman [1971] suggested the discontinuation of language teaching in the schools in favor of specialized regional language centers.

Yet the existence of many second language programs yielding poor results in no way denies the equally real existence of excellent second language programs in which the students do learn to communicate in the second language. The value of formal second language instruction is also seen in the fact that it is mostly those immigrants who receive formal instruction who go beyond a low level of proficiency.

Second language teaching/learning differs in nature and objectives from other school subjects. This should be made clear to the students from the start. The main difference is that in second language learning one learns a new code that conflicts with a known code, not something new via a known code. As a result of this, very little new information is exchanged and feedback is mostly about formal accuracy rather than about the truth value of messages.

Second language teaching/learning is unavoidably artificial, so no activity conducive to learning should be rejected on the sole grounds that it is not "natural." Motivation and exposure to language data are not sufficient conditions for learning a second language. Among other things, the exposure must be of a certain kind and the learner must be induced to interact with other speakers of the language; furthermore, selected data must be presented and manipulated, and the process of rule formation must be guided through explanations as needed and through differential reinforcement. Learning implies systematic study, for if it is not systematic it is acquisition, with all its disadvantages. Left to themselves to acquire the language, that is, to proceed according to their own "syllabuses," many acquirers do not know how to proceed, enter numerous dead ends, and form poor linguistic habits. Such results are found even in immersion acquisition, where the acquirer does not get constant feedback from a host of good models around him.

The four major steps in the teaching of second language items are (1) presentation, (2) understanding, (3) manipulation (practice), and (4) use in communication. These steps should be followed for each new rule and element that is taught. For some rules, several classes will be needed to go through the four steps. As we shall see in Chapter 12, different methods organize and emphasize these four steps differently.

The second language lesson

The second language lesson should follow a series of steps which usually include the four just mentioned. These steps are listed below:

(1) "Warm-up," that is, review of previous material and some conversation based on it.

(2) Sometimes, quiz over laboratory work or homework.

(3) Presentation of new material. The hardest new material should be presented early in the lesson, when the students are most alert.

(4) Understanding of new material --make sure the

students understand the words, sentences, and rules.

(5) Manipulation of new material, both in the form of mechanical drills and meaningful exercises.

(6) Use in communication of all that had been learned up to that point, in communicative activities.

(7) Sometimes, repetition of steps (3) to (6) for other new material.

(8) Description and preparation for laboratory work or homework assignment.

Sometimes, not in all classes, games, songs, and other "fun" activities would be included in the lesson. Sometimes tests would also be done, preferably early in the class period.

Of course, this is not meant to be a rigid schedule. Flexibility should be maintained, as all classes are not the same, varying in ability, background, motivation, and so on and therefore calling for the adaptation of procedures.

The class should not duplicate homework. It should have clearly stated objectives. Students should be kept on their toes with a variety of activities presented at a fairly fast pace.

Some pointers on class management

Such matters as how to relate to students and how to maintain discipline are outside the scope of this book, as they are covered in general education courses. However, a few pointers on class management that have particular relevance to the second language class are offered below.

For the sake of a greater sense of security, students need considerable control on the part of the teacher. But as Stevick [1980:17-8] has noted, there is no reason why nearly 100 percent control on the part of the teacher cannot be combined with the learners exercising nearly 100 percent initiative. It is a question of freedom within structure. As Stevick [1980:33] put it: "Absence of structure, or of focus on the teacher, may be all right in certain kinds of psychological training, but not in our classrooms."

To maintain attentiveness on the part of the students, the teacher should not give away who will be the next student called to respond. This means that students should not be called on in a predictable pattern (around the table, by rows, etc.). It also means that, when asking questions, who is to answer them is not to be indicated in advance --ask the question, let all have a moment to think of the answer, and then call on a student to respond.

Do not allow distractions. There should not be private discussions, in class, between the teacher and a student. As for student questions, resist the temptation to answer them all. Students ask questions for many reasons, among them to show off or to get a break in the learning activities or to test the teacher's knowledge. The teacher should not allow the students to get him into such useless lengthy digressions. More relevant questions may refer to grammatical points that will be studied in future lessons; in such cases, the best policy is simply to tell the students that that point will be explained in lesson such-and-such, not to try to explain it prematurely.

As for the classroom atmosphere, it should be positive, with considerable use of praise. A moderate amount of anxiety should be created, with students competing for personal satisfaction in excellence rather than for grades. Excessive linguistic experimentation going beyond the bounds of the known should be discouraged, but experimentation that fully exploits what is known should be encouraged.

Some principles of second language teaching

The following list of principles of second language teaching is not intended to be exhaustive, nor are the principles all necessarily ordered according to their importance.

1) Long-term and short-term goals should be established

Teaching can only be haphazard if one does not first determine what the learner should do in order to go from what he knows to what he should know. This has to be the first step, for everything else depends on it.

The main long-range goal of second language programs is to develop a knowledge of the second language in our students. But what is a knowledge of a second language? We can say that someone knows a second language when he can decode and encode messages in it at conversational speed and without systematic errors. More broadly speaking, the goal of second language instruction can be defined as "communication plus" --the ability to communicate fluently and accurately in the language plus an understanding of the second language, of one's own language and of language in general, plus an understanding of the second culture, one's own culture, and culture in general.

While the student may have initial choice of overall goals, once he has chosen one of the alternatives offered by the program it should be up to the expertise of the teacher, not the ignorance and bias of the student, to determine the subgoals and detailed "route" needed to reach the long-term goal of the student. The teacher is much better qualified than the student to determine what ought to be learned, when, and how. For example, left to themselves, the students may give greater importance to immediacy of application ("Can I use this immediately?") than to the gradual building up of competence.

Short-term goals are psychologically essential. Very few students can work persistently towards a long-term goal without the satisfaction of reaching partial ones. Since second language learning is a very long-term task, frequent short-range satisfaction is essential to student morale. Work should therefore be divided into units of no more than a few hours each.

To maintain motivation, all goals should be clear and the students should be provided with ample feedback. Learning is more efficient when the learner knows precisely what the objectives are every step of the way. This specification of objectives for the learner has been the subject of several books in our field, on "performance objectives" [Valette and Disick 1972, Steiner 1975]. (More comments on performance objectives will appear in Chapter 23.)

2) Selection should be used

This principle is closely related to the first. Teaching activities must be selected to fit the goals of instruction.

Vocabulary has been the object of considerable selection research, but some research of this nature has also been done with grammar. In both cases, the need is to concentrate on what has the greatest potential application. In the case of grammar, not all rules need to be taught or can be taught --some are still being discovered-- but all of the frequent and some of the less frequent rules should be taught.

In a full-fledged second language program, we should teach approximately 99 percent of the phonological rules and elements, 80 percent of the grammatical rules and patterns, and about three to five percent of the total vocabulary of the second language. Obviously, careful selection is called for.

3) Gradation should be used

This is a fundamental principle of all teaching. It consists, as Palmer [1917, 1968:81] put it, in passing *"from the known to the unknown by easy stages, each of which will serve as a preparation for the one immediately following."* Or, as Jespersen [1904:129] expressed it: "One thing at a time, and that done well."

Gradation has long been seen as fundamental to all teaching. Comenius enounced the principle of gradation in 1648 [*Orbis pictus*:123, quoted by Kelly 1969:224], as follows:

> Let us teach and learn: the few before the many; the short before the long; the simple before the complex; the general before the particular; the nearer before the more remote; the regular before the irregular.

To these we can add: the concrete before the abstract; the analogous before the anomalous; the easy before the difficult; the imitative before the creative; and the mechanical before the communicative.

Structural and communicative gradation are in general mutually compatible. There are, however, certain problems. For instance, it is sometimes necessary to teach something difficult early because it is very common --the English verb *to be* is a case in point. But despite such difficulties, the principle of gradation should never be abandoned. After all, the learner is in this respect not unlike a piano, which has to be tuned one note at a time.

Very few rules and elements need to be learned in a particular order, and even those that do, need to be practiced in the rather random order of communication. The tendency of the learner, if he has learned something in a particular order, is to have difficulty recalling it unless what preceded it in the original presentation occurs first. But if every structure is used in communication, it becomes readily accessible to the learner.

Selection and gradation should be based on pedagogical grounds (teachability), on linguistic grounds (complexity), and on the communication needs of the learner (utility). Of these, the linguist only has something to say about the second [Corder 1968].

4) Flexibility within structure should be used

While flexibly adapting to the characteristics and needs of the learners, the second language teacher should provide them with a high degree of structure. Structure gives the learners a sense of security and comfort.

Early second language instruction in particular should be fairly directive, with the students being told what to do. Later they can become more independent.

5) Process and outcome should be distinguished

What may have ultimate priority, that is, the desired terminal behavior, should not necessarily be emphasized first. Examples of mistakenly emphasizing the eventual outcome from the start are: the teaching of the four language skills together from the beginning because they "reinforce each other," the emphasis on vocabulary as opposed to structure from the start, and the early emphasis on free communication before linguistic habits have been formed.

The best way to get our students to learn something well may not be the most direct way; sometimes certain indirectly related learnings should be prerequisites to the goal activity. An example of this is the need to develop a fairly good control over the sound system of the language before engaging in free speaking. The terminal behavior should not always determine directly the teaching procedures.

6) Guidelines about how to learn should be provided

Most second language students have no idea of how to learn a second language or, worse yet, come to the learning process with the wrong ideas. At the very start of the program, therefore, the teacher should point out what the common misconceptions are and what learning strategies would be more productive.

7) A brisk pace should be kept

There is a tendency to teach far more than can be assimilated, a tendency that is reinforced by the fact that most teaching materials have too much content per unit and are meant to cover too much of the language per level. To be successful, the pace must not be too fast or too slow. The reaction of the students is the best indication of whether we are proceeding at the right speed. If they make many errors, we have been going too fast; if they look bored, we have been going too slow. Generally a brisk pace is much better than a slow one.

8) A variety of activities should be offered

A variety of activities is essential to prevent boredom, even if some of the activities do only that. There should rarely be more than about ten minutes spent on any given activity. If an activity requires more than ten minutes, it should be broken up into segments, with brief interludes for other activities.

9) The minds of the learners should be used

We should make full use of what the learners already know and of their capacity to understand and reason. They know their native language and culture, although it may be necessary to help them make their knowledge more overt and precise. For example, it may be necessary to make sure beginners understand basic grammatical concepts before they undertake the study of related rules.

Understanding the nature of a learning task and conscious attention to its crucial aspects will facilitate learning. This is one reason for keeping memorization limited. It is also a reason for making sure that the students understand the point of every drill.

The problem-solving abilities of the students should be fully exploited. Much in a second language can be presented as problem-solving situations for which the data are provided and the students are encouraged to figure out the rule --that is, discover how the language works in a given area and state it in their own words. After all, they should gradually learn to be what they will eventually have to be --unaided listeners and self-monitored speakers of the language. ("Grammar" and "rules" are discussed further in Chapter 17.)

10) Examples for future reference should be memorized

In the presentation of each rule, one or two good examples should be learned thoroughly for future reference. It helps greatly the correction process to be able to say "This is as in sentence such-and-such, remember?"

11) The rules should be kept simple

Rule statements should be kept as simple as the need for accuracy and future reference will allow. When necessary, explicit use should be made of rules of thumb. If a rule statement accounts for about 80 percent of the data, it is quite useful, provided that the learners are aware of its limitations and of the fact that the remaining 20 percent will be dealt with later.

12) The complex should be broken down

Complex rules should be broken down into their parts and these should be taught one at a time. But note that no rule or subrule is useful if it applies to only three or four words. (Linguists have a tendency to enunciate such limited rules, but it would be a mistake to teach them to second language students.)

13) Contrasts should be used

Any sounds, grammatical rules, or vocabulary items that experience has shown tend to be confused should be contrasted and the right choice practiced. Nothing is gained by ignoring such difficulties. On the other hand, contrasting items that are not normally confused can lead the students to see difficulties where there aren't any.

14) Sentences should be generated through analogy and analysis

Second language students should be taught to generate novel sentences by taking as a model samples of the language (analogy) whose structure is understood (through analysis). Samples are needed because random exposure to the second language would be inefficient and because most students need to base the production of sentences on something concrete.

15) The teacher should be demanding

Pimsleur [1963] found that second language students prefer teachers who are fair, patient, and reasonably demanding. Being reasonably demanding is a question of balance --one should be neither so strict as to cause students to fail nor so soft-hearted as to hand out the students unmerited "successes," which for them are as demeaning as failures. While success breeds success, it must be real, not ersatz success.

Being demanding involves the use of mastery learning --not leaving a rule entirely, for example, until 80 or 90 percent of the students can use it correctly 80 or 90 percent of the time. While it is true that "to require perfection at once is the great imperfection of most teaching" [Gattegno 1972:31], there is nothing wrong in requiring a high degree of accuracy within the small but gradually growing area of what has been studied. (More on mastery learning will be presented in Chapter 23.)

16) Allowance should be made for the occurrence of errors

"Error-free" second language learning would have to be so repetitive, so mechanical that it would not lead to the free use of the language. While it is better to keep errors to a minimum, if the students are going to be able to communicate freely they will need to make increasingly freer choices and increasingly freer use of the language, and this means that errors will occur.

Rather than be very concerned about the occurrence of errors, the teacher should make sure that he provides feedback to the student. The teacher should also take care not to shift suddenly from mechanical to free use of the language; such a sudden shift will cause more errors than can effectively be corrected.

17) Continuous feedback should be provided

The need to provide feedback has already been discussed.

18) New material should be introduced in class

It is during the introduction of new material that the student needs the teacher most. This is where questions may occur and where understanding of the material must be ensured. It seems senseless to give new material as homework without any preparation. (Of course, self-instructional programs cannot follow this principle.)

19) Homework should be made relevant

For students to want to do homework, its successful completion should be essential to success in class the following day.

20) Material should be reintroduced cyclically and in many contexts

All elements, rules, and expressions should reappear at increasingly longer cycles if there is going to be reinforcement and active mastery. These reappearances of the material should be in a variety of situations, for otherwise the learners will be unable to use these elements, rules, and expressions freely.

21) An atmosphere favorable to classroom interaction should be created

It helps if the teacher shows a difference between learning activities and communication by visibly relaxing for the latter. Classroom interaction can be facilitated by dividing the class, during part of the hour, into small conversation groups, although this should not be done with complete beginners. Depending on the communicative activity, the teacher should talk most, some, or none of the time. The tendency of most teachers is to talk too much, thus pre-empting student interaction.

22) The attainment of all goals should be evaluated

This can be in the form of informal assessment, based on students' responses to questions, etc. or more formal tests. In either case the students need to know whether they have in fact attained a given goal. In either case, if the goal has not been attained there should be further instruction for its attainment. (Chapter 21 deals with testing.)

23) Student opinion should be sought

Students' evaluations of teachers, methods, textbooks, and programs should not be considered demeaning --they can be most illuminating, and should be obtained on a regular basis. This can be done formally, by means of a questionnaire, and informally, by simply giving the students a chance to talk in class about the learning activities, etc. The best arrangement is to do both, informal expressions of opinion at reasonably frequent intervals and formal questionnaires once or twice a year.

During informal opinion sessions, the students should feel at ease, so they should be allowed to speak in their native language; furthermore, the teacher should listen attentively but not contradict, as this would create further alienation rather than *rapprochement*.

The greatest value of seeking student opinion is that it makes the students aware that their views are valued and helps them feel that the teacher is seriously interested in their learning. (On student evaluations, see Walker 1976:133-40.)

24) Constant evaluation of the teacher's and program's effectiveness should be undertaken

Teachers need, on a continuous basis, to evaluate their lessons to determine whether they are successful or not and why, as well as what can be done to improve them in the future. It is not enough that a teaching approach or procedure should work --we must be constantly on the lookout for procedures that work *better*. It has been said that "good is the enemy of best."

The outstanding teacher who gets good results "with any method" does so by adapting poor methods in many significant ways. In evaluating the results of his teaching, the teacher should therefore be as objective as possible, not only in testing his students but also in observing himself. He should ask himself, "What is it that I actually do (regardless of the 'method' or textbook I'm using)?"

The teacher's techniques and the program's methods and procedures should be modified according to the results of this ongoing process of evaluation.

The teaching materials

The textbook is traditionally the most important tool in teaching. For second languages, this is unfortunate, for it shifts the emphasis from speech, where it should be, to the printed word, where it should seldom be. It is paradoxical that the second language profession, of all people, has not welcomed the communication revolution and insists on relying on the mute textbook. The availability and low cost of cassette tape recorders, to give only one example, should long have made the second language textbook obsolete, replacing it with inexpensive, disposable workbooks as adjuncts to recorded programs.

For the time being, however, reliance on the textbook may continue to be the norm, so we should at least consider some implications of the textbook as a pedagogical tool.

The first point is that the teacher should not be impressed by the physical characteristics of the textbook. If I have learned one thing about second language textbooks it is that a beautiful, sturdy binding, the best paper, full-color illustrations, carefully selected type fonts, and so forth, are all pedagogically meaningless. Some wonders of the art and technology of publishing lead to very poor results in the classroom.

Any textbook should be compared, before adoption, with one of the several checklists that have been proposed [e.g., Rivers 1968:368-71, Bruder 1978, C.A. Tucker 1978]. The use of such checklists makes textbook evaluation far more objective than a perusal of the book, however careful.

But even the "ideal textbook" needs to be adapted [Madsen and Bowen 1978], for teaching conditions and the needs of the students are constantly changing. As Madsen and Bowen [1978:viii] pointed out, it is not enough for a text to be well written --it must also be compatible with the teaching goals and style of the teacher and with the student level in the course or program. Adapting a second language textbook includes removing flaws, improving its realism, and making it fit the characteristics of the learners and the goals of instruction.

The textbook is only one of the many types of materials that can be used in the second language classroom. Many teachers rely on their own materials rather than published ones. But there are just so many materials teachers have time and energy to create. Ultimately most teachers must rely primarily on the textbook, as things now are.

The creation of supplementary materials can be made into an opportunity for student participation. All students can participate in creating visuals, and advanced students can create, with teacher supervision, language texts for cassettes, video tapes, skits, and other activities. Being able to contribute in this way to the second language program gives students a sense of attachment to the program which may not be attained in any other way.

To conclude this section, it is to be hoped that second language programs of the future will not rely on textbooks, with their deadening effect on communication, but on audio materials with visual support. There is no reason why the absence of a textbook should plunge teachers and students into a state of confusion. It should, instead, free them to enjoy unhindered communication in the spoken language.

8

THE TEACHER

The importance and functions of the second language teacher

The teacher is the most important factor in the success or failure of the second language program. Well-motivated learners can be "turned off" by the rigidity and lack of enthusiasm of a poor teacher; on the other hand, most unmotivated learners seem to be able to gain an adequate degree of motivation if they come under the influence of a teacher who knows what he is doing and does it with enthusiasm and imagination. We can therefore place both successes and shortcomings in second language programs at the feet of the teacher.

While the teacher and the student are equal in many respects, they are *not* equal in knowledge of what constitutes reasonable second language goals, in knowledge of how to learn a second language, in knowledge of the second language itself, usually in general knowledge, and often in emotional maturity allowing the right decision-making processes. Also the fact that there is one teacher and many students creates a certain degree of dependence of the students on the teacher.

The teacher's functions include the following:

--guiding activities and procedures;

--motivating the students;

--being a model;

--facilitating communication in the second language;

--establishing an atmosphere conducive to learning;

--determining goals and seeing to it that most students can reach them;

--participating in activities;

--using technology;

--conveying an understanding of the second culture;

--providing the recall schedule needed by students to establish words and rules in memory;

--monitoring the students and providing them with feedback;

--organizing resources and being a resource person;

--researching the second language learning process and learning more about it; and

--participating in professional organizations.

Despite all these important functions he must perform, the teacher needs to resist the impulse to monopolize class time. While at the very beginning of the second language program he may need considerable time speaking himself, the proportion of this time should gradually diminish, so that by the advanced level no more than about ten to twenty percent of the time should be taken up by teacher talk.

Maintaining flexibility is essential. Carroll [1966-a: 96] found, for example, that many teachers are so rigid that they find it difficult to change any of their behavior, to the point that some do not even learn to change from systematic to random calling on their students, even after being instructed to do so. Flexibility applies in particular to methods. Many teachers tend to settle down to teaching the way they were taught, whether or not effective and appropriate in their present situation. The flexible teacher does not follow a method slavishly but adapts it and deviates from it as the need arises. He keeps trying new things, after learning about them in the professional literature or through colleagues, and retains what works. He refuses to develop strong emotional attachment to methods, regardless of claims and bandwagons, and tries instead to practice a form of enlightened eclecticism.

The qualifications of the second language teacher

1) Proficiency in the second language

Proficiency in the second language is a *sine qua non* of second language teaching. The practice of allowing teacher certification to someone who has only taken a few second language courses has done incalculable harm. The attitude of some administrators who will put anyone, regardless of his lack of practical qualifications, to teach a second language is unforgivable.

Proficiency in the second language refers to both performative knowledge *of* the language and cognitive knowledge *about* the language; the former is important for modelling, the latter to present and explain language structures in the classroom.

The teacher's knowledge of the language he teaches should be advanced, at least four on the Foreign Service Institute scale (see Appendix C). His control of the sound system should be native-like; if it is not, he should not serve as a model but make use of recordings or paraprofessionals. An excellent performative control of the grammar is also essential; but the vocabulary does not have to be as extensive as the usual level-four speaker's, provided that there is native-like accuracy and fluency. (It should be obvious that in order to reach this level of proficiency, at least six months of residence in the foreign country are normally necessary.)

The importance of the teacher's knowledge of the language can be seen in the fact that Politzer and Weiss [n.d.] found a positive correlation between teacher listening comprehension and three out of seven measures of student achievement. They also found that the teachers with the best command of French had students with better attitudes toward the study of French, probably the result of the teacher feeling more secure.

The best teachers/models, unlike the usual practice, should be assigned to the first course in the sequence. This is where the foundation is established, and it must be solid.

The teacher should speak a standard dialect of the language. If he is a native speaker who speaks a nonstandard dialect, he should make a little effort and use a standard dialect in class. It is not very difficult for a native speaker of Buenos Aires Spanish, for example, to stop using the [ž] and the *voseo* typical of that nonstandard dialect.

The limitations of the teacher's knowledge of the second language impose limitations on what he can do in the classroom. For instance, if he does not speak the language well, how can he be successful with an oral method? Such limitations should be overcome by diligent study of the second language and by spending as much time as possible somewhere where the language is spoken. Even after attaining an adequate level of proficiency, there should continue to be occasional visits to second language areas, as his constantly hearing inaccurate language from his students can lead the teacher's language to deteriorate to the point where he is using an impoverished interlanguage.

Above all, the teacher should be conscientious enough to realize that he has no right to impose his language limitations on his students and that he has to do everything possible to overcome them.

2) Proficiency in the native language of his students

Where a single native language is common to all students, a teacher who knows that language will be able to understand their problems much better and therefore teach far more effectively. He will also be able to communicate with them far more efficiently.

3) Knowledge of the structures of the two languages

It is not enough to know the structure of the second language. Since a great many of the difficulties of the second language learner are due to the influence of his native language, the well-qualified second language teacher will take care to learn about the phonology, grammar, lexicon, and semantics of the native language and in particular about the ways in which the two languages differ. Where the class is linguistically heterogeneous, the conscientious teacher will make an effort to learn the key facts about the phonology and grammar of the native languages of his students.

4) Knowledge of the psychology of learning

This was discussed in Chapters 3 and 4.

5) Knowledge of methodology, testing, and technological aids

Such knowledge has its theoretical aspects, but what matters primarily is to have a practical knowledge in terms of procedures and techniques.

6) Knowledge of the second culture and the native culture

Again a comparative knowledge is most useful.

7) Some facility in consecutive interpretation and written translation

Proficiency in the two languages does not guarantee the ability to translate, something that most second language teachers are often called upon to do in their teaching. Some formal training in this skill would be desirable.

8) An understanding of communicative needs and functions

Even if a second language program is structurally graded rather than organized around communication acts, an understanding of communicative needs and functions can help in the choice and conduct of progressive communicative activities.

The personality and attitudes of the second language teacher

It has been pointed out that second language teachers need to have strong personalities, for they are different from other teachers --they have chosen unpopular majors as undergraduates and because of their specialization have to teach largely in isolation [Goddu 1976:327]. Unfortunately the tendency for persons with strong personalities is to be inflexible. For example, many second language teachers refuse to adopt better methods or techniques, regardless of how successful they may be, because they do not suit their personalities.

Successful second language teaching requires flexibility, sensitivity to the point of compassion, and a well-developed sense of humor. The teacher must like people and be interested in relating to them, without which no amount of professional preparation is sufficient.

The teacher should not make an effort to be popular with his students. If he is an effective teacher and helps them on an individual basis he will in time earn their respect and possibly their liking. He cannot help but arouse emotions in his students, and these emotions cannot all be positive --the important thing is to arouse a constructive combination of emotions.

The teacher is in a position to either humiliate or encourage the student, but he should never humiliate him. In terms of Transactional Analysis [Berne 1964], the relationship between the teacher and the student should be, depending on the latter's age, that of Natural, Nurturing Parent and Natural Child or that of Adult-Adult, rather than that of Controlling, Bossy Parent and Adapted or Rebellious Child. (Of course, the need for discipline in some classrooms upsets the ideal relationships.)

It goes without saying that the teacher's attitude towards second language study should be one of enthusiasm. The good second language teacher will not consider his subject to be primarily a mental discipline to be available to an intellectual elite of students --he will gladly help any student who shows a desire to learn. He will be, as already discussed, reasonably demanding. He will consider second language teaching not just a job but a challenging, interesting, and fulfilling career.

A second language teacher should be judged by his output, that is, by the fluency and accuracy of his students, not in one class, but over the years. Conscientious teachers will not be afraid to be judged on that basis, for they will be confident that their students will succeed if they really try, and they readily accept that they have much to do with whether most of their students really try or not.

The good teacher will value efficiency. Many teachers look down upon efficiency as something associated with impersonal, dehumanized factory assembly lines; but much can be done to increase efficiency in second language teaching while maintaining a personal, empathetic approach.

Toward his students, the teacher should have sensitivity to individual differences, should evaluate them fairly, should not play favorites, should guide them according to their needs and no further, and should involve them all actively in the learning and communication process.

In order to satisfy the need for security of his students, the teacher should be strong and stable, a reliable source of information and reassurance. He will impress on his students what is important for them to learn rather than let them wander unguided through the second language curriculum. He will make sure that the students develop the right attitudes toward second language study, toward accuracy and communication, and he will counteract student tendencies toward negative transfer, eye dependence, and constant translation. He will not hesitate to correct his students, doing so not as an adversary but as a helpful guide. At the same time, he will convey the message "You can do it," for unstated lack of confidence in the students can have such negative effects --what has been called the "Pygmalion effect" [Rosenthal and Jacobson 1968]-- that "the teacher who does not expect much of his students disqualifies himself as their teacher" [C. Brown 1974:16].

The paraprofessional and other assistant teachers

It has often been said that a native-speaking assistant with the right background can perform quite well many of the functions of a teacher, especially one whose proficiency in the language is weak. This is possible, but the native-speaking assistant must have the right personality, some training, and he must be provided with specific teaching objectives which he is to attain by closely adhering to appropriate materials. This is the basis on which native paraprofessionals teach in such places as the Foreign Service Institute and the Defense Language Institute. Furthermore, the native paraprofessional should have had recent contact with the second culture, be able to identify with students, be objective about his own culture, and be familiar with school procedures [Hammelmann and Nielsen 1974].

Native paraprofessionals should be used for what they can do best --engage in controlled and free communication with the students. It is a misuse of native-speaking talent to put them to do drills, which a laboratory machine can do.

Other "assistant teachers" can be preservice personnel (student teachers, teaching interns), laboratory monitors (usually native paraprofessionals), and advanced students.

Apprentice teachers can be used rather easily and well in a second language program. The cost is low and they are very enthusiastic, as performing that function carries some prestige among their fellow students.

The use of advanced students should concentrate on helping the weaker lower-level students who are having difficulties with individual study. Advanced students are generally quite willing and even proud to help lower-level students, but to be fair they should be granted some form of credit for their contribution. Even high school students enjoy assisting the teacher --for instance, a program in which high school Spanish students spent two days a week for one month helping to teach elementary school students proved quite motivating [Beach 1973].

The training of the second language teacher

It has been said that "teachers are born, not made," but most good teachers develop their good qualities (other than personality) through training and experience, given a basic interest in teaching and a reasonably high intelligence.

But it is not enough for the prospective teacher to take a number of courses, complete a program, and obtain a certificate, especially when it is the practice to give certificates to all those who are admitted to the program. Emphasis in teacher training, as in second language teaching, should be on enabling a certain level of performance, not on courses completed. Performance should be measured at key points in the program, and those whose knowledge, attitudes, or behavior are inadequate should be led through remedial subprograms and, if still inadequate, dismissed from the program. Mastery rather than hours sitting in class chairs should be the decisive criterion for certification.

The academic component of the teacher's program should consist of a combination of courses about language (linguistics), learning (psychology), general teaching (education), second language teaching/learning (languistics), and culture (sociology-anthropology, area studies, and some literature).

The linguistics component is more important for the teacher than for the student. A second language student does not need to know phonetics or grammar except as the teacher may present it on an *ad-hoc* basis; but the teacher has to know both on a systematic basis if he is to be able to guide his students through the language. Of course, even teachers who have never formally studied linguistics make use of linguistic notions such as *verb, noun, sound, agreement, subject,* etc.; but these and other linguistic concepts can be understood better and applied more effectively in the classroom if they are explored as part of a series of courses in linguistics. Such a series does not need to be too long: after an introduction to linguistics, all the prospective teacher really needs is a course in phonetics, a course on the structure of the native language and one or two courses on the structure of the second language, and, if available, a course on contrastive analysis and error analysis. There is no need at all for much linguistic theory for the teacher *qua* teacher, although of course some theory would be useful if he wants to do research, etc.

In terms of psychology, future second language teachers should take, after an introduction, a course in learning theory and courses on cognition, memory, and personality, and, if available, psycholinguistics.

From education specialists, the prospective second language teacher would do well to take courses in teaching theory, educational psychology, and classroom management.

The languistic component of teacher training programs would consist of several courses. First there should be a general methods course, then courses on the psychology of second language learning, on second language technology, and on second language testing. Finally there should be a methods course relating to the specific language to be taught and introducing the practical aspects of the program.

Practice teaching would start with observation in connection with the specific-language methods course. As suggested by Mackey [n.d.], *observation* could consist of watching an experienced teacher on video tape, with subtitles labelling what is going on; then watching identical video tapes without subtitles, with the trainee identifying the behavior; this would be followed by group discussion of why the teacher proceeded that way. After the observation phase, the trainee would *plan and practice* the same type of lesson. The third phase would be *performing,* that is teaching a lesson under controlled conditions. In regard to the planning and practice and the performance phases, teaching by the trainee could proceed from teaching peers (for example, via microteaching) to teaching real classes. The technique of microteaching, pioneered by Politzer at Stanford University [n.d.] and used extensively at several other institutions [Jorstad 1973], can be a very useful part of the practice component. Microteaching involves teaching material limited to a single concept, for five to ten minutes, to a small group of students, while the microlesson is observed and usually video taped. After the microlesson, the student teacher first, and then the methods class as a whole, watch the video tape and discuss it. Of course, upon completing his academic preparation, the prospective teacher should spend a few months as an intern following classes and doing part of the teaching daily under the supervision of a successful classroom teacher.

Before starting to do practice teaching, before doing the bulk of his specialized course work, however, the prospective second language teacher should be required to demonstrate, via appropriate standardized tests and Foreign Service Institute-type interviews, that he has an advanced proficiency in the second language he plans to teach. In fact, future second language teachers should not be allowed to reach advanced courses in languistics before they have demonstrated objectively their proficiency in the language. To facilitate meeting this language requirement, there should be a required period of residence in the second language environment for all future second language teachers, unless they have managed to attain advanced proficiency (F.S.I. level four) by other means.

Highly desirable as additional preparation for future teachers would be taking one or two semesters of an unknown language and taking a course on translation. The classes in an unknown language could be very illuminating for the prospective teacher if efforts are made to let him see not only good teaching but also the effects of bad teaching from the point of view of the learner. For example, a piece of difficult material could be first taught too fast, allowing too little practice --this "shock treatment" can be more effective than any amount of lecturing in making future teachers aware of the need to go slow, to observe reactions, not to expect too much from the students [Moskowitz 1975]. The course on translation, necessarily specific to the two languages involved, will enable future teachers to provide their students with better, more precise interlingual equivalences.

Teacher training should be a continuous, career-long process in which certification is followed over the years by graduate courses, workshops, institutes, and so forth. Unfortunately many university departments consider teacher training not "academic" enough for their faculty, and the few faculty members who are interested in teacher training are looked down upon by their literature- or linguistics-oriented colleagues. But despite its low priority and bad reputation, teacher training is interesting enough and rewarding enough to attract enthusiastic practitioners.

(A possible program in languistics at the graduate level is discussed in Appendix D.)

The second language teacher and the profession

Powers [1971] has questioned the existence of a second language teaching profession, as there seems to be no agreement on goals, no systematic treatment of its body of knowledge, no agreement on how to teach languages, no standards for membership in the profession nor elimination of incompetents, no system for rewarding high attainment, and no unified organization. According to Jarvis [1976:2], many second language teachers "see themselves at the center of a whirlwind of dizzying confusion. Little in which they once believed is secure, stable, or sacred." There is "at close range a blur --a whirl of controversial (even irreconcilable) strategies, ideas, theories, societal pressures, curricula, methods, goals and philosophies" [*ibid.*]. For many this results in "a sense of threat and a loss of equilibrium" [*ibid.*].

To the extent that a profession exists in North America, it consists of "a very heterogeneous collection of approximately 80,000 people" [Jarvis 1974-a:1] in the United States and about 10,000 in Canada. Many of these 90,000 teachers unfortunately do not seem to take our profession very seriously. They either teach the way they were taught or mindlessly follow fads, in either case without giving much consideration to the results of their teaching. It would be helpful for them to concentrate their attention on the issues involved --thus seen, in terms of its problems and their ramifications, second language teaching can be a challenging continuum of problem-solving situations.

The lack of unity in the profession is seen in the fact that only a small minority of those 90,000 teachers are members of professional organizations. If all were members, and spoke with a more united and louder voice, perhaps such debacles as the great loss in enrollments beginning in the late '60s --and due to the call for immediate "relevance"-- could have been prevented.

The second language teaching profession has a tendency to ignore its history; it keeps "rediscovering" what had been discovered earlier. It is far too affected by the overabundance of Pied Pipers who try to lead it their way. In following trends and fads, it ignores the wise advice of cooler heads and ignores or even attacks those who do not slavishly follow the latest trends.

The secret of stability and progress in our profession is principled methodology. Until basic principles are accepted, second language teaching will keep on jumping from one method to the next, rejecting them in turn to revert to neotraditionalism. And that for those who care; those who do not care continue undisturbed and unperturbed their ineffective traditional teaching.

No wonder that every fifteen or twenty years North American governments have to take action regarding the shocking state of second language teaching. Unfortunately, such interventions have never had very long-lasting results; perhaps the majority in our profession are too recalcitrant to change. For example, in the United States in the '60s there were 587 N.D.E.A. institutes attended by 30,000 elementary and secondary school language teachers [Cloos 1971:249]; yet very few effects remain, and the undergraduate curriculum for language teachers changed in very few colleges and universities, even of those where institutes were held [Axelrod 1966].

In their next intervention in the field of second language teaching, perhaps the U.S. and the Canadian governments could aim at the establishment of model regional centers where a variety of teaching procedures and techniques could be demonstrated on a continuing basis, for teacher training and retraining. I doubt very much that our profession will ever be sufficiently united in purpose to establish such regional centers without government initiative. These regional centers could also engage in the controlled comparison of methods and other research, something that again our profession has been rather reluctant or unable to do.

9

CONTRASTIVE ANALYSIS, ERROR ANALYSIS, AND INTERLANGUAGE

Examples of interference

I recall, with amusement and some embarrassment, the time I told my first class in applied linguistics that I had come from South America to North America on a *sheep*. Phonological interference is evident even in people who have mastered a second language to a high degree, as seen in certain public figures.

Grammatical interference is also quite evident in second language learner speech, as seen in Spanish-to-English **Did you liked it?* and English-to-French *...*son grand-mère*. Lexical interference can be seen in such utterances as French-to-English **Don't cry, Louise; you're too sensible*.

Toward a definition of contrastive analysis

Interference can be predicted and/or explained by comparing the two languages in question and determining how the second language differs from the native language of the learner. This type of study, which in modern times was preceded by the work of Weinreich [1953] and Haugen [1953], can be said to have started with the publication of Lado's *Linguistics Across Cultures* [1957]. It is part of applied linguistics, not pure linguistics, for although it borrows most heavily from linguistics it also draws much from psychology, sociology, and so forth [James 1980: 7].

Contrastive analysis makes explicit the differences between two languages [Di Pietro 1978-a:2]; ideally, it should also list those items which are the same in the two languages, since facilitating positive transfer is as important as counteracting negative transfer. (Such an analysis should perhaps be called "comparative" rather than "contrastive.")

It is possible to carry out not only pedagogical contrastive analyses but also theoretical ones, which are simply comparisons of two or more languages without pedagogical implications or applications. Such theoretical studies do not concern us here.

Contrastive analysis is of great value in languistics. It reveals the points where we can expect difficulty, it suggests the likely degree of those difficulties, it can give insights about how to overcome them, and it explains most of the errors that occur. Although the predictive power of contrastive analysis is somewhat limited, it has fairly precise explanatory power.

The second language teacher who knows the cause of an error is much better equipped to deal with it, both in terms of prevention and correction, than the one who does not. Unawareness of interference means not being able to know what is wrong. But through contrastive analysis the teacher can have a fairly precise idea of what is wrong; as Lado [1957:4] pointed out, the professionally trained teacher will notice clear-cut, specific distortions, not just a "foreign" accent or an "incorrect" form.

Contrastive analysis has become very controversial, for reasons which have little to do with its validity and practicality. Some have severely criticized contrastive analysis, claiming that interference plays a very small role in second language learning [Whitman and Jackson 1972, many others]. Many have objected to contrastive analysis on the grounds that it cannot predict all errors [Newmark and Reibel 1968, many others], although such an absolute predictive power was never proposed. The state of contrastive analysis is illustrated by the fact that in a recent issue of the *International Review of Applied Linguistics* [Vol. 18, No. 2, 1980] there were three articles devoted to contrastive analysis and error analysis --the first [Ghadessy 1980] questioned the value of interference studies, the second [Sheen 1980] showed the importance of interference, and the third [Abbott 1980] called for greater rigor in such studies!

The bases for contrastive analysis

Contrastive analysis has been called "sound practice in search of a sound theory" [James 1980:166]. It is doubtful, however, that a single theory of contrastive analysis will emerge, as contrastive analysis is based on propositions from various sources --the ideas that (1) while languages have much in common, they also differ in many ways, (2) these similarities and differences can be described, and (3) they are the sources of positive and negative transfer for the second language learner.

What two languages have in common ranges from broad

linguistic universals to specific phones. There is enough in common between any two languages to permit comparison. But in contrastive analysis there is less interest in linguistic universals than in specific differences --after all, it is the differences that cause difficulty for the second language learner, provided that they are accompanied by sufficient similarity to cause transfer. Between any two languages there are many content or meaning similarities and few expression or form similarities.

The notion of contrast is basic to contrastive analysis and to any learning. Contrast consists of "difference seen against a background of sameness" [James 1980:35]. In the second language learner, awareness of contrasts leads to understanding, which in turn leads to the avoidance of errors. That contrasts are fundamental to learning has been stated by Carroll [1966-a:104], who claimed that it is a psychologically established fact that "the frequency with which an item is practiced per se is not so crucial as the frequency with which it is contrasted with other items with which it may be confused." Contrasts can be interlingual, intralingual, or both; making use of both seems to give the best results.

Contrastive analysis is based on transfer theory, which describes "the impact of prior experience upon current learning" [Ausubel 1963:28], that is, the fact that the learning of task A will affect the subsequent learning of task B, for new knowledge is acquired on the basis of old knowledge. In second language learning in particular, the knowledge we are interested in is primarily performative knowledge or behavior, as opposed to just cognitive knowledge. This is related to the role of habits in learning, which we can say, with Hok [1972:266], is a very important one, as "all learning...is at some point habit learning in the sense that once performed it can more easily be performed again."

The relationship between contrastive analysis and transfer theory was expressed by Lado [1957:2] in terms of a tendency of individuals to transfer forms, meanings, and their distribution from their native language to the second language. Note that Lado described this as a tendency, not as a process involving perfect predictability.

We can speak of three types of transfer: positive, negative, and zero. Positive transfer or facilitation occurs to the extent that two learning tasks are the same, especially in terms of responses. Note that the second language learner needs to be informed when two structures are identical, for if this is not confirmed for him he may tend to avoid identical structures in his effort to differentiate between the two languages. Negative transfer or interference occurs to the extent that two learning tasks are different but related. Zero transfer occurs when the two learning tasks are unrelated.

In terms of transfer theory, it can be said that learning a second language consists of (1) facilitating positive transfer to the second language of all items that are identical to native language items, (2) overcoming interference for those items that differ in the two languages, and (3) integrating all second language items into a working whole.

This process of facilitating positive transfer and counteracting negative transfer is not a passive one from the point of view of the learner. Throughout the new learning task his mind is constantly generating associations and organizing the relationships from the known to the unknown. However, the process will not work too well unless the right learning strategies for going from the known to the unknown are encouraged by the teacher. It would be very inefficient to overtly ignore previous knowledge. (In many places second language teaching is the only field of teaching where, to its detriment, previous learning is ignored.)

Interference can be seen as interlingual and intralingual. Interlingual interference is based on differences in categories, constructions, elements, rules, and meanings across languages. Intralingual interference usually takes the form of overgeneralizations from what is already known of the second language, overgeneralizations which are based on second language irregularities, complexities, and asymmetry.

Interference on an interlingual basis can be *preclusive* or *intrusive*. *Preclusive interference* occurs when the lack of something in the native language interferes with or precludes the learning of something in the second language. For example, the lack of articles in Chinese interferes with the learning of the system of articles in English by Chinese speakers. That this is true interference, due to the relationship of new learning to old knowledge, is evident from the fact that speakers of French, German or Spanish have no problem (or only minor problems) with English articles. *Intrusive interference* refers to the situation where something in the native language intrudes or appears in the second language, for example, the use of the English Adjective + Noun word order in French as a second language. Many people consider only the intrusive type to be interference, but it should be clear from the example given earlier --and many other examples are possible-- that preclusive interference is just as much interference as intrusive interference.

The relationship between interference and difference/similarity is somewhat paradoxical. At one end, it would seem that the more different two structures are the more learning difficulties they would cause, and yet this is not so --if the two structures are different to the point of being unrelated, there is zero transfer. At the other end, if two structures are identical there is maximum positive transfer but if they are slightly different there is maximum interference. Thus, interference is maximal when the two learning tasks are slightly different, diminishes as their difference increases, and disappears when the difference is total. Limited evidence of this was obtained in a study which showed that speakers of languages having non-Roman alphabets had less difficulty with English spelling than speakers of other languages with Roman alphabets [Oller and Ziahosseiny 1970]. That the markedly different nature of a new task makes it easier to learn has been known for a long time; it was found that making something stand out makes it easier to learn, a principle that is known as the "von Restorff effect" [von Restorff 1933].

A realistic version of the contrastive analysis hypothesis

In recent years, following Wardhaugh [1970-b], it has become fashionable to talk of several versions of the contrastive analysis hypothesis, varying in strength from strong to weak.

The strong version of the contrastive analysis hypothesis is said to state that contrastive analysis can predict all problems and that interference from the native language is the sole cause of difficulties for the second language learner. Such a hypothesis is obviously unreasonable and contrary to the facts. It is a strawman designed to condemn contrastive analysis as invalid. Furthermore, the insinuation by association that early proponents of contrastive analysis like Lado and Fries favored such an unreasonable hypothesis is quite unfair. It is true that occasionally statements that are too strong were made. But such statements were rare and did not come from the leaders of the contrastive analysis movement.

Those who reject the trumped-up strong version go to the other extreme and propose a weak version that they find more acceptable. The weak version states that contrastive analysis can only help to explain certain errors after they have occurred and that it has little or no predictive power. It is clear that such a hypothesis is useless, for it takes away from contrastive analysis the ability to contribute to the preparation of language materials, the overcoming of interference, the preparation of tests, and so on. Moreover, as we shall see, contrastive analysis has been proven to have considerable predictive power in the sense of "*pre-identifying*" [James 1980:145] what will cause difficulty.

The only realistic version of the contrastive analysis hypothesis, that is, what should be *the* contrastive analysis hypothesis, is a moderate one that states that most difficulties in second language learning can be pre-identified and explained in terms of the relationships between the two languages. This is, incidentally, very close to the original hypothesis. Lado did not say that individuals *always* transfer forms and meanings but that "individuals *tend* [my italics] to transfer the forms and meanings..." [1957:2] from the native language to the second language. And while it is true that contrastive analysis has been found occasionally to predict difficulties that do not materialize and to fail to predict some that do, Lado did not claim perfect predictive power. On the contrary, he intimated the need for error analysis by saying [1957:27] that certain problems could not be fully accounted for without actual observation of the speech of second language learners.

Contrastive analysis has sufficient predictive power to serve as the basis for the preparation of first-generation second language materials. At that point, there is hardly any other basis on which to proceed. But contrastive analysis is not enough. It should be supplemented by error analysis, on the basis of which teaching materials can be revised and improved.

Confirmation of the contrastive analysis hypothesis

From the preceding discussion, it is evident that we can disregard the strawman "strong" version and the useless "weak" version and refer to the moderate version, from now on, simply as the contrastive analysis hypothesis.

Very many studies have confirmed the validity of the

contrastive analysis hypothesis. Preliminary evidence of its validity comes from studies of languages in contact showing that the linguistic distortions of bilinguals correspond to differences between the two languages involved [Weinreich 1953, Haugen 1953]. Many studies have shown that foreign accents differ according to the native languages of the speakers. The obvious difficulty that English speakers have with the French subjunctive is not shared, except in minor details, by Spanish speakers, whose language has a subjunctive mood (in English there is only vestigial subjunctive syntax and no subjunctive morphology). A study showed that learners of English as a second language who had articles in their native languages performed significantly better than those whose native languages did not have articles in their use of that English category [Oller and Redding 1971]. French-dominant bilinguals have been found to lag behind English-dominant bilinguals and English monolinguals in the acquisition of certain English prepositions [Canale *et al*. 1978]. More generally, since no language is inherently difficult --all children master them at about the same age-- the differences in time needed by English speakers to master various languages can be attributed to the relationship of each language to English.

Interference works even in reverse. After long exposure to a second language, the native language begins to show characteristics of the second language as well as instances of avoidance. I have found myself saying **intrínsico* rather than *intrínseco* in Spanish, under the obvious influence of *intrinsic*. Having first learned English *obsolete*, I have avoided Spanish *obsoleto*, assuming it to be an anglicism, which it is not.

The evidence in favor of the contrastive analysis hypothesis and the importance of interference is overwhelming. Contrastive analysis will therefore outlive its critics and probably much of modern linguistics. It is definitely not a fad of the past.

The predictive power of contrastive analysis

Contrastive analysis cannot predict all difficulties --after all, some are intralingual, occurring within the second language. Contrastive analysis predicts in the sense of pre-identifying *what* will cause difficulty, to a lesser extent it predicts the *form* the errors will take, and it never predicts with 100 percent certainty *when* they will occur in the speech of a language learner. In other words, what contrastive analysis predicts is variable transfer rules, which when applied result in error but which are not consistently applied. Contrastive analysis compares competences, and that is why great precision in the prediction of performance errors is not possible, as many factors intervene in second language performance other than the two competences.

At times contrastive analysis can only predict that there will be difficulty without being able to predict exactly what the error will be. As an example [Wilkins 1972], it can be predicted that French speakers will have difficulty with English /θ/ and /ð/, but not whether they will pronounce /θ/ as /s/ or /t/ and /ð/ as /z/ or /d/ (for reasons unknown, it seems that French Canadians substitute the dental stops and European French speakers the alveolar fricatives).

Phonology is most amenable to prediction, perhaps because it is a psychomotor skill [H.D. Brown 1980:157-8]. In grammar and vocabulary, the variability of cognitive activity makes prediction less certain. But even in phonology, no one that I know of has ever claimed that all errors could be predicted, again a strawman attacked by certain generative phonologists [e.g., Tarone 1978].

Considerable evidence of the predictive validity of contrastive analysis is available. Some examples follow. Significantly high correlations were found between contrastively predicted and observed errors in the verb systems of English and Hiligaynon [Ruiz 1963]. It was found that contrastive analysis allowed prediction, to a large extent, of the English composition errors made by Tagalog speakers [Aguas 1964]. A prediction of English errors by Japanese speakers was confirmed [Ota 1971]. Schachter, after studying the difficulties of different groups of foreign students with English relative clauses, concluded [1974:212] that the evidence strongly supported the predictive validity of contrastive analysis, as the learners seem to base their second language hypotheses on their knowledge of the native language. Two of my own studies [Hammerly 1970-a, 1975-b] have confirmed the contrastive analysis hypothesis, at least for phonology.

The percentage of interlingual errors

Further confirmation of the contrastive analysis hypothesis and of its predictive power comes from error studies showing the percentage of interlingual errors versus intralingual errors.

Interference is the chief source of difficulty, but obviously not the only one. This difficulty manifests itself most clearly in the initial errors of beginners --that is, the great majority of their pronunciation errors and over half of their grammatical errors-- and in the persistent errors of near-bilinguals, almost all of which are of the interlingual type.

Politzer [1965:131] reported on a study of errors by hundreds of students of French at the University of Michigan. The vast majority of errors on the examinations were found to be based on false extensions of English-French correspondences. Another study [Dušková 1969] determined that native language interference caused most of the errors in written English by Czech students (especially difficult were categories lacking in Czech, like the articles). In another study [Buteau 1970], a large number of errors by English speakers in a French grammar test were found to show the influence of English. In still another study [Tran-Thi-Cahu 1972, 1975], interference accounted for 51 percent of the errors made by second-year high school English speakers learning Spanish; interference from French, previously learned by some of the students, was also found to cause errors; and there was a high correlation (r .69, $p < .005$) between student ratings of grammatical difficulty and the occurrence of errors. Another study [Powell 1975] showed that at the end of the second year of high school French, 223 volunteers showed much more interference from English, the native language, than from French. Even when a "noncontrastive" approach to error analysis is used, the majority of errors turn out to be interlingual --Richards [1974] found 53 percent interlingual and 31 percent intralingual.

Among *advanced* students in a second language program, interlingual errors play a smaller role. They have been found to constitute 36 percent of the errors in one study [Grauberg 1971] and estimated at one third by another author [George 1972]. But when it comes to errors that persist into the near-bilingual level, they have been found to be overwhelmingly interlingual. According to B.D.W. Hocking [1973], it is not uncommon to find speakers of English as a second language whose only surviving errors are all interlingual. Recently a study [Sheen 1980] of French-English near-bilinguals confirmed this, showing that interference from the native language was by far their most important source of errors, many of which were fossilized.

Several studies have shown that from the beginning to the advanced level in a second language program interlingual errors gradually decrease and intralingual errors gradually increase [B.P. Taylor 1975, Dommergues and Lane 1976, Seah 1980]. This is in perfect harmony with transfer theory. Second language learners, like all learners, rely primarily on what they have learned previously. At the beginning of the program the second language learner, lacking competence in the second language, is forced to rely primarily on his native language --quite naturally, since it is all he knows. As he learns the second language, he comes to rely more and more on it, and as a result interlingual errors decrease and intralingual errors increase. Due to faulty or insufficient feedback, however, some interlingual errors become fossilized, with the result that they constitute the majority of errors among near-bilinguals who have long overcome most early interlingual and almost all intralingual difficulties.

Note, however, that at any point in this process an error cannot be called intralingual if its "source" is a second language rule that the learner does not know. Just keeping this in mind would lead to reclassifying many errors in error studies from intralingual to interlingual. Some such studies, such as Dulay and Burt's [1974-d], have approached errors with an anti-interference bias and have been shown to have attributed to the influence of the second language errors that were clearly interlingual [Abbott 1980].

Difficult and less difficult languages

The fact that interference affects similar tasks but does not affect what is very different is seen in the different problems faced by learners of related and unrelated languages. There is little grammatical interference for an English speaker learning Chinese [Lee 1968] because structurally the two languages are very dissimilar. On the other hand, there is considerable interference for a Spanish speaker learning Portuguese or for a German speaker learning English, and this is due to the fact that these pairs of languages are closely related.

Yet, structural interference is not the key factor in determining how long it takes to learn a language, since Foreign Service Institute experience [Wilds 1962] shows that for an anglophone beginner to reach the 2+/3 level of proficiency in intensive courses, four to six months of intensive study (about 600 hours) are needed in languages like French, Spanish, and German, longer for less related languages like Greek and Hindi, still longer for less related languages like the Slavic languages, and longest (about a year of intensive study) for Arabic, Chinese, and Japanese, which are very different from English. It seems that the magnitude of the lexical learning task, far greater with unrelated languages, is what determines the length of study needed to reach a given level of proficiency.

When two structures are very different then, as in negation in Japanese (unlike English, a bound morpheme attached to the verb stem), there is no interference. This is the reason why there is little interference when the two languages are unrelated and more when they are related [Kellerman 1979, Adiv 1980-b]. With unrelated languages, learning is slower but greater accuracy is more attainable. With related languages, learning is faster but considerable inaccuracy is likely.

Of course, whether similarities between related languages will cause much or little interference will depend primarily on whether the differences between the similar structures are pointed out and drilled in the second language program. With understanding and practice, interference can be overcome and accuracy maintained.

Interference with a further second language

Whether the native language or a previously learned second language will interfere more or less with the learning of a further second language (chronologically the third, fourth, etc. language) will depend on the relationship between the languages. If the native language is English, the chronologically second language Spanish, and the chronologically third language Italian, Spanish is much more likely to interfere with Italian (and facilitate the learning of its vocabulary) than English. In this case, the degree of mastery of Spanish would be relevant, for if it is only slight, English might interfere more. Note, however, that there is an "I'm-speaking-a-second-language" syndrome, according to which the language learner is likely to draw primarily upon any previously learned second language, even if weak and unrelated to the new one, because he feels he must sound foreign and avoid his native language. It may also be that the interference of previously learned second languages is primarily in the forms of lexical items while that of the native language is primarily structural. This whole question needs to be researched much further before firm conclusions can be reached.

Some objections to contrastive analysis and their rebuttal

Some scholars who object to the contrastive analysis hypothesis have proposed other explanations for the errors of second language learners. Newmark and Reibel [1968] claimed that ignorance rather than interference was the cause of most errors. But ignorance does not explain the fact that learners' errors persist after they have learned the corresponding second language rules, and even into the near-native level. The ignorance hypothesis also fails to account for the fact that learners learn to control some second language items much more easily than others, although equally ignorant of them all at the start and equally instructed in all of them later [James 1980:22-5]. Also, there can be not only interference without ignorance but also ignorance without interference, as in positive transfer to unknown rules and in the frequent strategy of avoiding difficult (not thoroughly known) rules [Schachter 1974]. No, ignorance is not an adequate explanation for most second language errors. As James [1980:22] put it: "Ignorance is not an alternative to interference, but at best a precondition for it."

Another alternative hypothesis posits that difficulties are due to cross-associations based on redundancy within the second language [George 1972]. According to this view, for example, the reason why distinguishing between French *savoir* and *connaître* is difficult is that the distinction is semantically redundant. But the proof that this is not a valid explanation lies in the fact that speakers of German (*wissen/kennen/können*) or Spanish (*saber/conocer*) have no problem with this French distinction, while speakers of English (only *know*) do.

Another objection is the claim that there are low correlations between students' perception of difficulty (determined via questionnaire), contrastive analysis predictions, and the incidence of errors. First, recall that a correlation of r .69 was found between perception of difficulty and incidence of errors [Tran-Thi-Chau 1972, 1975], which is fairly high considering the unreliability of subjective estimates. But even if there were very low correlations, it should be kept in mind that students may find difficult certain structures with which they make no errors and find "easy" some with which they make numerous errors; furthermore, they may simply avoid difficult structures --a form of error--, with the result being recorded as "no error." The degree of difficulty of structures should be determined not by asking the students but by submitting them to a production test that does not allow room for avoidance.

Another objection to contrastive analysis comes from the evidence that students of English as a second language from many language backgrounds seem to make very similar errors. But aside from the fact that communication needs are universal and largely determine the order in which structures will be acquired within a second language acquisition situation, we should keep in mind that it is very likely that students from many linguistic backgrounds make similar errors because all their languages differ from English in respect to those structures. Moreover, proficiency tests tend to obscure the variation among learners of different language backgrounds because such tests may have only one or two questions for each second language rule, not enough to show any differences, with respect to those rules, between students of different language backgrounds [Hatch 1978-a:60].

Hierarchies of difficulty based on interference

Contrastive analysts not only want to pre-identify difficulties, they also want to classify them according to degree of difficulty, that is, into principled hierarchies.

The best-known of these hierarchies of difficulty is the one proposed by Stockwell and Bowen [1965:16], based on whether an item or structure is obligatory, optional, or absent in each of the two languages. Unfortunately, it is rather inadequate. For example, many of the items classified as "optional" are hardly optional --there is nothing optional about using the /r̃/ of Spanish *perro* when referring to a dog, nothing optional in the choice of *tú* versus *usted*, and most of the so-called "optional" transformation rules in the grammar are not at all optional in the context of communication. Another difficulty is that, while the addition of semantics to the grammatical hierarchy [Stockwell *et al.* 1965:284] makes the scale very complex, it does not prevent it from having easy and difficult items within the same order of difficulty. Thus, within the first order of difficulty (L1=Ø, L2=Obligatory) appear things of greatly different difficulty, such as the choice between Spanish preterite and imperfect past tenses (difficult) and verb form concord (easy).

One thing that is clear is that different hierarchies are needed for phonology, grammar, and vocabulary. While grammatical and lexical items are within the awareness of the learner or can be easily brought to his awareness, much in the phonology is below the level of awareness and tends to remain there. This has important consequences for the hierarchy of difficulty of each of these different language components.

The next three sections present my own hierarchies of difficulty --one experimentally confirmed, the other two tentative-- for second language phonology, grammar, and vocabulary.

A hierarchy of phonological difficulty

The basis for contrastive phonological analysis should be both functional (phonemes and allophones, etc.) and phonetic, that is, related to articulatory similarity. A purely functional comparison can hide many difficulties. A purely phonetic comparison would fail to account for how speakers use the sounds. Furthermore, contrastive phonological analysis should take the syllable, not the word level as its basis --the mistake of taking the word as the unit of analysis led to Lado's [1957:17] wrong prediction that word-initial French /ž/ would be difficult for English speakers, when in fact it is not difficult because it occurs in syllable-initial position in English. A hierarchy of phonological difficulty should also take into account suprasegmental and spelling factors in increasing interference.

Of course, it should be kept in mind that while interference causes most pronunciation problems, there are other problems not caused by interference but by such things as a tendency to tongue centralization [F. Johansson 1973], a tendency to a consonant-vowel syllable pattern, and emotional states like anxiety and so forth [Tarone 1978:25].

Care should be taken when classifying errors into phonological and grammatical. What may seem like a grammatical error, as in a Spanish speaker saying *like* for *liked*, may be phonological, in this example due to the fact that the sequence /kt/ does not occur in final position in Spanish. Also note that while one interference error may not cause misunderstanding, the cumulative effect of two or more interference errors can seriously affect comprehension. Thus, if a Spanish speaker mispronounces the /ɪ/ as /i/ *or* the /d/ as /ð/ in *hidden* he is unlikely to be misunderstood, but when both errors are made he will very probably be understood as having said *heathen*.

My hierarchy of phonological difficulty based on interference is presented in Figure 9.1.

There are six types of phonological relationships and three aggravating factors that may make a particular

<table>
<tr><th colspan="6">HIERARCHY OF PHONOLOGICAL DIFFICULTY</th></tr>
<tr><th></th><th>Native language</th><th>Second language</th><th colspan="3"></th></tr>
<tr><td>1</td><td>Allophone</td><td>Ø</td><td rowspan="6">Phonetic differences</td><td rowspan="6">Spelling interference</td><td rowspan="6">Suprasegmental interference</td></tr>
<tr><td>2</td><td colspan="2">Different distribution or function of native language allophones</td></tr>
<tr><td>3</td><td>Ø</td><td>Allophone</td></tr>
<tr><td>4</td><td>Ø</td><td>Phoneme</td></tr>
<tr><td>5</td><td colspan="2">Different distribution or function of native language phonemes</td></tr>
<tr><td>6</td><td>Phoneme</td><td>Ø</td></tr>
</table>

Figure 9.1

problem worse. The six types of relationships are listed as 1 (most difficult) to 6 (easiest) and the three aggravating factors are listed vertically. Note that by "most difficult" problems I mean most *persistent*, not necessarily most important for communication.

To begin the discussion of this hierarchy, observe that allophonic problems are higher in difficulty than phonemic ones. This is because generally speaking the learner is more aware of phonemes than allophones, especially in the native language where allophones are largely automatic variants. Within the three problems having to do with allophones, the most difficult one therefore is stopping the use of a native language allophone, of which there may be no awareness, and the least difficult one is learning a second language allophone, something that can more easily be brought to awareness by means of explanations and drills. It is easier to learn a new psychomotor habit than to unlearn an old one. Within the phonemic problems, the order is inverted, for learning a second language phoneme that does not exist in the native language represents more of a learning task than simply stopping the use of a native language phoneme. It is more difficult to establish a new perceptual category than to stop using a known one.

Problems of type 1 in the hierarchy are not very serious from the point of view of communication but constitute the most persistent problems, the ones that even after many years of second language learning and acquisition can still be observed, the ones that cause a retention of a foreign accent in the second language. These are situations in which the native language has an allophone that the second language lacks and where the native language allophone is substituted for the correct second language allophone. Examples of this situation are the use of English aspirated [pʻ], [tʻ], and [kʻ] or of "dark l" ([ɫ]) in French and Spanish.

Problems of type 2 --native language allophones having counterparts with different distributions or functions-- would include Spanish [s] and [z], which are allophones of one phoneme in Spanish but different phonemes in English, and English [ç], which has a limited distribution as an allophone of /h/ in *human, hue*, etc. and a more extensive and quite different distribution in German, where it can be considered an allophone of /χ/ after front vowels, etc., as in *Ich* and *schlecht*.

The third type of problem, in order of difficulty, is the situation where a native language phoneme lacks a certain allophone that the corresponding second language phoneme has. An example of this is English and Spanish /b/, which has basically one allophone ([b]) in English but two allophones, [b] and [ƀ], in Spanish. The English speaker will therefore tend to use his only allophone in all cases, regardless of the distribution rule in Spanish.

Note that failure to produce accurate second language allophones can result in phonemic misunderstandings, not just in an accent. The English speaker who says Spanish *cada* with his flapped allophone of /d/ will be heard as having said *cara*. The Spanish speaker who uses his unaspirated allophone of /p/ in English *pat* may be heard as having said *bat*.

The fourth type of problem in order of difficulty, but one that is most important from the point of view of communication, is the situation where the native language does not have a certain phoneme that the second language has. Examples of this are, for English speakers, the front rounded vowel phonemes of French and German (/ü/, /ø/, etc.) and the /r̃/ in Spanish. For French and Spanish speakers learning English, examples of this type of problem are the /ɪ/ in *bit* and *ship* and the /æ/ in *cat* and *sat*. For French and German speakers learning English, /θ/ as in *thin* and /ð/ as in *that* present a similar problem. It is this type of problem that causes the most difficulties in communication and often results in amusing or embarrassing errors.

Problem number 5 --a different distribution of phonemes in the two languages-- is what causes Spanish speakers' difficulties with the English initial consonant clusters /sp-/, /st-/, and /sk-/, resulting in words such as **eschool* --these consonant sequences exist in Spanish, but not in initial position. This type of situation is the reason why an English speaker finds it difficult to produce French, Spanish or German /e/ and /o/ in final position without gliding them, as well as the reason why he finds it difficult to produce such German consonant clusters as /pf-/ and /-tst/.

The sixth type of problem, where the native language has a phoneme that the second language lacks, may lead to occasional intrusions of native language sounds in the second language. Examples are the need for the English speaker not to use /ǰ/ in French, /æ/ in French or Spanish, /ə/ or /v/ in Spanish, /w/ in German, and so forth.

Three aggravating factors that can turn a relatively easy situation into a more difficult one are phonetic differences, spelling interference, and suprasegmental interference. Thus, it is because of phonetic differences and spelling interference that the English speaker finds it much harder to master, for example, French /ʀ/ and Spanish /r̃/ than French or Spanish /ñ/, which is very close phonetically to a quick rendition of the English sequence /-ny-/ as in *canyon* and *onion*. There are also phonetic intrusions, such as the glottal stop [ʔ] by speakers of English and German learning French or Spanish.

Spelling interference can combine with any of the six phonological problems and make it more serious. Thus, the mispronunciation, by English speakers, of French and German /ʀ/ and of Spanish /ř/ and /r̃/ as palatal fricatives and their use of [v] in Spanish are to a great extent the result of the misinterpretation of spellings according to native language sound-spelling correlations. It is also spelling interference that turns an easy sequence like German /šp-/ into a persistent difficulty for English-speaking students. But spelling interference is not limited to consonants and vowels. It is spelling that causes many of the problems in syllabification in French and Spanish by speakers of English. Thus, the conventional separation between written words contributes to the pronunciation of

**E | se | hom | bre | es | es | pa | ñol,*

in eight syllables, with syllabic rhythm pauses between the words as opposed to the normal syllabification

E | se‿hom | bre‿e | s‿es | pa | ñol,

in six syllables. The same can be said for the rendition of French *Robert est ici* as

**Ro | bert | est | i | ci*

rather than the correct

Ro | be | rt‿es | t‿i | ci.

In intonation, the written question mark causes the voice of the learners (and of native informants!) of various languages to go up at the end of questions in which the voice is supposed to go down, as in information questions (as opposed to "yes/no" questions) such as Spanish *¿Dónde está el libro*? and French *Qui est là?*

Suprasegmental interference, other than suprasegmental problems of a phonemic or allophonic nature, can be seen in certain tendencies related to stress, intonation, etc. An example is the strong English tendency to have a mid-central (/ə/) or high-central (/ɨ/) vowel in unstressed syllables, a tendency that, when carried into Spanish or French, results in numerous errors affecting comprehension, for it eliminates the contrasts between, for instance, Spanish *señores* and *señoras* or French *le livre* and *les livres*.

Finally, it should be noted that this hierarchy of phonological difficulty has generally been confirmed, at least as far as English and Spanish are concerned, by an experimental study that analyzed pronunciation errors after nine weeks of university beginning Spanish instruction [Hammerly 1975-b].

A hierarchy of grammatical difficulty

My tentative hierarchy of grammatical difficulty based on interference is presented in Figure 9.2.

This hierarchy applies primarily to the commonly taught Western languages. Even so, it should be obvious that it is much too simple and that further research would result in its elaboration. Note that syntactical problems are far more serious than morphological ones, the latter causing rather little interference [Dušková 1969, LoCoco 1975]. Since the learner is generally *aware* of grammatical items, tasks that represent learning something new (types 1 and 5) are listed as more difficult than tasks

HIERARCHY OF GRAMMATICAL DIFFICULTY		
	Native language	Second language
1	∅	Syntactical pattern or category
2	Differences in word order	
3	Syntactical pattern or category	∅
4	Agreement, concord, etc.	
5	Divergent morphological pattern	
6	Convergent morphological pattern	

Figure 9.2

in which the use of something known should be stopped (types 3 and 6).

The first type of problem is the situation where the second language has a syntactical rule lacking or largely lacking in the native language. Examples of this are, for English-speaking learners, the French and Spanish subjunctive mood and multiple past tenses, the system of Japanese honorifics, and the case systems of German and Russian. For Chinese speakers and others whose languages do not have articles, the article system of English represents also a problem of type 1. So does, for Spanish speakers, the English use of subject pronouns, used only emphatically in Spanish, and the syntactic rules governing the use of certain English prepositions. For learners of English, the use of the tense-carrying *do* also falls under this category. Such problems are most persistent, and some learners show difficulties with them even after many years of language study.

Problems of type 2 involve differences in word order. Examples of this are, for English speakers, the different order of object pronouns in Spanish, French, and German, the non-use of prepositions at the end of sentences in French and Spanish, the use of the German verb at the end of subordinate clauses, and the order of nouns and adjectives in French and Spanish.

The third type of problem is the reverse of type 1, that is, the situation where the native language has a syntactical rule that is lacking or largely lacking in the second language. A good example of this is the non-use of progressive constructions in French, with the result that often English-speaking learners of French use the construction *être en train de...* much more often than speakers of French do --a covert error in usage. The use of English-to-Spanish **Estoy yendo a México mañana* for Spanish *Voy a México mañana* is another instance of this type of problem. So would be the use of Spanish subject pronouns in non-emphatic sentences by English speakers.

The next type of problem --number 4-- involves agreement between nouns and articles and adjectives, concord between subjects and verb forms, etc. The concept of such agreements is learned rather easily, but because they are largely redundant, errors continue to be made for a long time. There is some interference, as in the case of the English speaker who makes a possessive with French *femme* agree with the possessor, as in English, and says **Son femme*.... In the case of noun gender and its agreement with articles and adjectives, the problem is basically lexical --the student did not quite learn its gender along with the noun when he first learned the noun. Here again there is some interference, as for the Spanish speaker learning French who must remember (and usually cannot) that in French the words for *nose* and *milk* are masculine, the opposite of Spanish. (And what sense is there in calling Charlie Chaplin *une vedette* and a soldier *une recrue*?)

The fifth type of grammatical problem involves the learning situation where the second language has more morphological contrasts than the native language. Examples of this are the numerous verb endings (not the agreement) in French, Spanish, and German, and the case forms (not when and how to use them, which is a type 1 problem) in German, Latin, Russian, etc. In other words, these are difficulties involving the learning of grammatical forms and transfer may take the form of non-use or avoidance. Morphemes which are most redundant, such as the third-person *-s* in English (whose function is already expressed by the subject), seem hardest to learn. (The noun-plural *-s* is not redundant but the fact that it has the same form as the third-person *-s* only adds to the confusion of learners of English.)

Grammatical problems of type 6 involve situations where the native language has more forms than the second language, so that at times the former may be transferred to the latter. Actually transfer in this situation seems to be rare. An example would be the inappropriate use of the English adjective prefixes *in-*, *im-*, and *dis-* in German, which has the single adjective prefix *un-* (and the suffix *-los*).

In English, morphological errors are much less serious than syntactical ones; but languages differ markedly in the amount of information they convey through the morphology or the syntax. Chinese, for example, expresses almost all grammatical meaning through its syntax, while Latin expresses most grammatical meaning through its morphology and allows considerable syntactic freedom.

A hierarchy of lexical difficulty

Hierarchies of lexical difficulty have been proposed by several scholars, among them Higa [1965] and Rodgers [1969]. My tentative hierarchy appears in Figure 9.3.

The most difficult type of problem (type 1) is the situation in which forms are similar and their meanings, while within the same broad semantic field, are different. In this situation, the learner falsely assumes similarity

HIERARCHY OF LEXICAL DIFFICULTY		
	Native language	Second language
1	Similarity in form Difference in meaning within the same semantic field	
2	Similarity in form Similarity but divergence in meaning	
3	Similarity in form Similarity but convergence in meaning	
4	Difference in form Similarity but divergence in meaning	
5	Difference in form Similarity but convergence in meaning	
6	Similarity in form Identity in meaning	
7	Difference in form Identity in meaning	
8	Identity in form Identity in meaning	

Figure 9.3

in meaning to match the similarity in form. Examples abound; they include English *lecture* vs. French *lecture* and Spanish *lectura* and English *library* vs. French *librairie* and Spanish *librería*, that is, the so-called false cognates or, as colorfully called in French, *faux amis* ("false friends"). Note that when words of similar or identical form have widely different meanings there is little or no interference, as with German *List* ("cunning") or *link* ("left") and the corresponding English false cognates.

The second type of problem, one that applies to few words, represents similarity in form where there are more words in the second language than in the native language. For example, Spanish *radio* divides into English *radio*, *radius*, and *radium*. Problems of type 3 are the converse of type 2, that is, they refer to situations where the native language has more than one word similar in form to a second language word. The example of *radio* in the opposite direction applies. Another example would be the distinction in English between *piece* and *apiece* vs. French *pièce (Une pièce de 10 francs, Ça coûte 5 francs pièce)*; note that *room* vs. *pièce* is basically a type 7 problem.

The fourth type of problem, which with type 5 applies to a good number of words even in cognate languages, is the situation where form is different but meaning, while similar, is covered by more words in the second language than in the native language. Examples of this are English *know* vs. French *savoir* and *connaître*, Spanish *saber* and *conocer*, and German *wissen* and *kennen*; English *leg* vs. French *patte* and *jambe* and Spanish *pata* and *pierna*; French *dire* vs. English *say* and *tell*, etc. The fifth type of problem is the opposite of type 4, that is, there are more words in the native language than in the second language. As convergence is easier to deal with than divergence, type 5 problems are less of a learning task than type 4 problems.

The sixth type of relationship is that of true cognates showing minor differences in form. Many scientific terms fall under this category, as, for example, *mathematics*, *physics* and other international words taken from Greek or Latin. Any interference here is due to whatever differences in form there may be. Thus, an English speaker may say **físicas* instead of Spanish *física*, and a Spanish speaker may say **matematics* for English *mathematics* (note that in this last example the difficulty could be phonological).

The seventh type of situation applies to most of the vocabulary to be learned, except perhaps in very close cognate languages such as Spanish and Portuguese. This is where the form is different and the meaning is the same, at least insofar as the basic denotations are concerned. Examples of this are English *horse* vs. French *cheval*, Spanish *caballo*, and German *Pferd*, and English *head* vs. French *tête*, Spanish *cabeza*, and German *Kopf*. If there is interference, it is to the extent that words differ in their various contextual uses, not in their basic denotations; thus, these languages may use entirely different words for *the head on a beer*, *the head of the bed*, and *the head of an organization* [Mackey 1965:95], even though *head* = *tête* = *cabeza* = *Kopf* as the top of the body.

Finally, there is the very rare situation where two words are the same in form and meaning (basic denotation), and where no learning is therefore involved and no interference can occur. An example of this is French *hôtel* and Spanish *hotel* in their basic denotation of "inn," although even here there is a difference in spelling, so the form identity exists in the spoken language only.

Of course, Figure 9.3 applies primarily to languages that are to some extent related. In the case of completely unrelated languages, probably only relationships 4, 5, and 7 would apply, with possibly a few coincidental false cognates and very few true cognates related to onomatopoeias.

Interference also operates at the level of discourse rules. Schmidt and Richards [1980:146-8] pointed out, for example, that Japanese callers talk first on the phone, that French *bon appetit* sounds unusual to English speakers, and that in Thai *How are you?*, unlike English, requires an answer while *Where are you going?* is a greeting that does not. Formulas can differ in meaning not only across languages but also across dialects of the same language; for example, *Gracias* is used in some dialects of Spanish to accept something and in others to decline it. Discourse differences may also make the learner insensitive to nuances in usage; for instance, the Spanish speaker who is told that in English there is no distinction in formality like his *tú* and *usted* tends to disregard the many subtle ways in which such distinctions are expressed in English.

The point of reference for grammatical contrastive analysis

While the point of reference for comparing two

phonologies is ultimately articulatory phonetics, a universal common ground, and while lexical comparisons can be made on the basis of semantic features, another universal common ground, there is no agreed point of reference for the comparison of two grammatical systems. Candidates are surface structure, deep structure, and translation equivalence.

Early contrastive analyses dealt with surface structure comparisons. This is the reason why generative linguists have tended to shun contrastive analysis --a paradox, since transformational grammar with its emphasis on universals would seem to offer a better basis for it [Politzer 1972:88-9]. Since contrastive analysis emphasizes the differences between two languages, and since these differences are greatest at the surface level, being at least in theory nonexistent at the universal deep level, it follows that contrastive analysis should focus primarily on surface structure, where the language-specific categories exist. At the same time, a strict surface structure comparison can be quite misleading --it can lead, for example, to equating English *He read a book* with French *Il lut un livre* rather than with the equivalent *Il a lu un livre*.

Some consider transformational grammar as a *sine qua non* of contrastive analysis. Its contribution, however, does not consist in insights about deep structure, for "the notion of deep structure itself is extremely uncertain" [Wardhaugh 1970-b:128], as "there is little agreement among leading transformationalists on just what deep structure is" [Oller 1973-c:39]. According to James [1969:86], the study of deep structure is irrelevant to a pedagogical contrastive analysis because it does not contribute to second language learning, although of course not-too-deep rules would be involved in transfer problems. A pedagogical contrastive analysis does not benefit from ordered rules or "branching" rules, both features that make a transformational grammar hard to follow. A grammar that is hard to follow is not suitable for teacher training or for second language teaching. The usefulness of transformational grammar in pedagogical contrastive analysis consists in making the comparison of transformation rules possible; but such comparisons should be expressed in terms of how each transformation rule affects surface structures. Transformation rules are transferred across languages just like everything else. But note that merely comparing transformation rules can lead to the generally false equation of English *He has read a book* with French *Il a lu un livre* --so transformational grammar by itself is not an adequate grammatical point of reference either.

Contrastive grammatical analysis on the basis of translation equivalence has been carried out for a long time. Most bilinguals agree on translation equivalents of contextualized simple sentences, so that can be a valid point of reference, more so than surface structure or deep structure analysis, both of which pay little attention to meaning. Since second language learners also identify common items and sentences across languages, contrastive analysis, being concerned with what learners do, should take such translation equivalents into account. In fact, in his book *Contrastive Analysis* James concluded [1980:178] that of all three bases for grammatical comparison, translation equivalents, if rigorously defined in terms of both semantic and pragmatic equivalence, are the best point of reference.

Translation equivalents have the further advantage that they would allow the conduct of limited and simple contrastive analyses by the second language teacher without much specialized training in linguistics. This differs radically from theoretical contrastive analyses of an extensive and detailed nature, which require the cooperation of teams of highly qualified linguists.

Applications of contrastive analysis

Contrastive analysis has a considerable number of applications. Among them are the following:

1) The preparation of teaching materials

Contrastive analysis provides a principled basis for the preparation of first-generation second language teaching materials. According to Fries [1945:9], the most effective language teaching materials are based on a careful comparison of parallel scientific descriptions of the two languages. Elsewhere [1949] he noted that each linguistic background requires special materials, as second language teaching involves teaching a specific second language to students with a specific native language background. Despite its abandonment in today's heterogeneous ESL classes, nothing has changed the basic validity of this principle.

Contrastive analysis provides the basis for the *selection* of most of the rules to be taught. Thus, second language teaching should concentrate on the problems, on the "points of interference." There is no need for an English speaker to have drills on French *Il est bon,* which is the same as English; but *Il a froid,* which contrasts with English, should be drilled [Politzer 1965:28-9]. Of course mastery of the problems is only rarely attained through strictly mechanical practice --most often cognitively-based practice is necessary.

When the students have different language backgrounds many of their problems will differ and some exercises will be irrelevant to them a good part of the time. To avoid this situation, special exercises by language background should be prepared and the class should be divided part of the time into subgroups for work by language background.

Contrastive analysis provides part of the basis for *gradation.* The question is: Which should come first in the second language program --rules that differ or rules that are the same across languages? If the early lessons emphasize what is the same, the danger is that the learners will assume that the two languages are much closer than they really are, that is, such an order of presentation would confirm the erroneous "equivalence hypothesis." Politzer conducted an experiment which supports the view that parallel constructions should not be taught first [1968-a]. The point is that, in order to know what is not parallel and should be presented early, contrastive analysis is necessary.

Once a set of teaching materials has been used for some time in the classroom, it can be modified and adapted on the basis of error analysis, but contrastive analysis provides the only sound basis for the original development of the materials.

2) The presentation of second language materials

On the basis of contrastive analysis, the teacher can know what in the materials to emphasize, what types of supplementary drills to write and use in order to counteract interference, and how to correct errors. With respect to the latter, note that a contrastive approach to error correction often makes it necessary for the teacher to imitate a student error in order to make the contrast clear --this does not disturb the learning process provided it is clearly signalled as a discriminative rather than an imitative activity.

3) Understanding the learner

A knowledge of contrastive analysis can greatly help the teacher to understand the problems of the learner. The beginning learner thinks in the native language and tries to express in the second language which he is learning the meanings he has in his native language. To overcome interference, the learner must be brought to awareness of the differences between the two languages. Interference is not eliminated by ignoring it; it must be actively counteracted so as to prevent most errors and correct the rest. In an acquisition situation it may be necessary to butcher the second language first; but this is not at all necessary in a second language learning situation.

As to the learner's age, adults show more interference than children, especially in the sound system. But even young children show some interference. Perhaps one reason there is less interference in childhood is that children are less capable of transfer than adults, that is, not only of negative transfer but also of positive transfer.

4) Second language testing

By pre-identifying the problems of the learner, contrastive analysis provides a basis for the selection of test items and multiple-choice distractors, and for the degree of emphasis each language item should be given. This, as in the case of teaching materials, applies to the first generation of a test; revised versions would be produced on the basis of error analysis. Note that there is no excuse, with modern technology, for having standardized second language tests that are not geared to specific native language backgrounds; as James [1980:151] pointed out, it is quite feasible, in this age of computers, to establish a universal bank of test items each designed for a specific native language background and to give language-specific tests.

5) Research in languistics

By making problems quite specific and observable, contrastive analysis facilitates linguistic research. One of its advantages is that it is methodologically neutral, although of course methods of second language teaching that ignore the students' native language cannot make use of contrastive analysis.

(For further reading on contrastive analysis see especially Lado [1957], Di Pietro [1971, 1978-a], James [1980], and Fisiak [1981].)

Definition and significance of error analysis

As defined by J. Richards [1971:12], error analysis deals with the differences between the speech of second language learners and that of adult native speakers of the language. The purpose of error analysis is to understand what errors occur, why, and how, in order to use that knowledge to better understand and improve the second language teaching/learning process.

Changing attitudes toward second language errors

From the early '40s to the mid-60s an error was considered something to be avoided. There was an unrealistic view that if teaching and learning were adequate there would be no errors. More recently, errors have come to be considered unavoidable. When rules have not been perfectly learned or are temporarily forgotten --which is bound to happen-- the learners will make errors, despite our best efforts.

Since the mid-60s, under the influence of cognitive psychology, second language errors have increasingly been seen as manifestations of the learner's grammar and as not only useful but necessary for learning the language by means of testing hypotheses. As we shall see, this is also an unrealistic view, for while it seems to accommodate some of the facts about second language acquisition, it does not suit the facts of second language learning.

Second language errors, acquisition, and learning

The linguistically-adult second language acquirer may need to engage in the free testing of hypotheses in order to construct his own grammar, so he may need to make errors in order that, through feedback, he may learn the limitations of rules and thereby modify his hypotheses accordingly. The second language learner does not need to test hypotheses, as the rules are provided to him and whatever hypothesis testing he may do is limited and controlled; so instead of making errors in order to learn a rule, he makes errors if he has not learned it.

The second language acquirer's errors are evidence of his transitional second language system --they, along with correct utterances, show what he knows. In the second language learning situation, we know what the transitional system should be at all times, that is, the sum and integration of all the rules taught to any point in the program. In the learning situation, errors show therefore either that the learner has not thoroughly learned something he should have learned or that he has ventured into unfamiliar linguistic territory, where he would naturally rely on what he knows --native language rules or overgeneralizations of the second language rules with which he is familiar. The learner's transitional system equals what has been taught of the program system, minus faulty learning, plus interlingual and intralingual transfer from the known to the unknown.

Most concepts in the error analysis movement apply to second language acquisition, not second language learning. But error analysis itself is applicable to second language learning, for it can show what, of that which should have been mastered, has been learned, and to what extent.

The description of errors

Error analysis involves comparing utterances with their interpretations and reconstructions --"authoritative" when there is input from the learner or "plausible" when he cannot be consulted [Corder 1974:127-8]. As a minimum, grammatical and lexical error data should include the native language equivalent, the interlanguage utterance, and the second language reconstruction, as in the example below:

NL		IL error		SL
for the man	/	*por el hombre	/	para el hombre

Phonological error data need only identify the two languages and list both the target and the interlanguage utterances.

Further thoughts on error analysis

One problem with error analysis is that most analysts seem to set out to confirm their views. Since many follow the principle that "whenever possible errors should be assigned to causes other than interference," it is no wonder that many error studies tend to discount the importance of interference.

The native language of the learners must be taken into account in error analysis. Learner groups analyzed should have the same native language background and be fairly homogeneous in educational, social, aptitude, and attitude characteristics. Studies of errors made by linguistically heterogeneous groups are worse than useless --they are misleading.

Every attempt should be made to discover what errors are systematic. This includes calculating the percentage of the time that a structure is used wrongly (*vis-à-vis* the total number of attempts to use it) as well as estimating the times it is avoided. It may be that the only way to obtain fairly precise estimates of the latter would be by administering production tests, not by analyzing spontaneous speech or writing, in which much avoidance is possible.

Abbott [1980] has suggested error analysis procedures that will make analysis more consistent and will make its data and results accessible to others.

Types of errors

There are as many types of errors as there are causes of errors. Second language learners' errors may be due to native language interference, second language overgeneralization, strategies of learning, strategies of communication, teaching techniques or teaching material presentations, ignorance, carelessness, and emotional states such as anxiety, stress, anger, fatigue, etc.

One basic distinction between error types is that made by Corder [1967] between *errors* and *mistakes*. *Errors,* he said, are systematic, while *mistakes* are not; the latter are due to chance circumstances --slips of the tongue or pen-- and they are errors of performance rather than competence.

A distinction we have already made is between *interlingual* and *intralingual* errors. A difficulty with this is that the division between interlingual and intralingual errors is not clear-cut --many errors may have multiple causes. In that case, rather than follow bias the logical thing to do is to assign the error to that which the learner knows best at that point, since the learner will rely on what he knows. Thus, what is wrong in analyzing many errors as overgeneralizations is the assumption that the learner relies more on the very little he knows of the second language than on his thorough knowledge of the native language.

With respect to their effect on comprehensibility, errors have been classified into *global* and *local* [Burt and Kiparsky 1974]. *Global* errors are those that cause a native speaker to misunderstand or not to understand the message in the context given; thus, they interfere with communication. *Local* errors are not communicatively serious for, given the context, they do not interfere with comprehension of the message. (Note that the degree of offensiveness of errors, to be discussed in Chapter 13, does not correspond to their effect on communication.)

From the point of view of the learner in a second language program, I think it is very important to distinguish between those errors involving rules that have been taught and should have been learned, for which I propose the name *distortions,* and those errors involving what has not yet been taught, which can be called *faults*.

Errors can be *structural* or *of appropriateness* [Corder 1974:123-4]. Errors of appropriateness can be *referential* (e.g., calling a *hat* a *cap*), errors *of register* (e.g., calling a Navy *ship* a *boat*), and *social* errors (e.g., greeting your professor with *How are you, old man?*) [*ibid.*].

In terms of their mechanics, the mathematical possibilities of errors are limited to *addition, omission, substitution,* and *transposition.* Note that for each of these there is a corresponding type of grammatical drill --addition, deletion, substitution, and transposition-- used in second language teaching.

Selinker [1972-b] and J. Richards [1973] discussed four types of intralingual errors. The most common of these is *overgeneralization,* which is also frequently found in native language acquisition. Examples are **goed, *catched, *childs* and **I said him so* for *I told him so.* Overgeneralization errors show that the learner has mastered a second language rule but not its limitations. Another type of intralingual error is that due to *transfer of training.* This includes *induced errors* [Stenson 1974] such as where a learner of English may talk about **worshipping to God* after the teacher has told him that "*Worship* means *pray*"; another example is the error often made in early directed dialogues:

Teacher: *Tell Jimmy that he should stop talking.*

Student (to Jimmy): **That you should stop talking.*

Strategies of learning can also be the source of errors. One common strategy is to overdifferentiate the two languages in order to avoid interference. This is what leads some French speakers to stress English *attack* on the first syllable even though its stress matches French, or to say **composed with* even though if they followed the French pattern they would get it right. Errors result also from *strategies of communication.* J. Richards [1971] reported, for example, that in learning French in Quebec he was forced to refer to the future before having learned the appropriate tense, so he used much more than natives, and at times inappropriately, the construction *Je vais + infinitive.*

To conclude this discussion of types of errors, we should consider *avoidance errors* [Schachter 1974]. These "silent" errors [Rojas 1971] are covert in nature and manifest themselves by the learner using a structure much less than is normal usage among native speakers. Avoidance may involve sounds, rules, words, or even whole topics. This means that even when there are no overt errors the speech of the learner deviates from that of the native speaker. As a corrective measure, when avoidance is suspected, the teacher should ask: What is another (a more direct and more common) way of saying that?

Contrastive analysis and error analysis

It should be clear by now that contrastive analysis and error analysis complement each other. The predictions of contrastive analysis, useful as they are, cannot be confirmed or rejected without error analysis. On the other hand, the suggestion that we should directly do error analysis, without contrastive analysis, has to be rejected --without contrastive analysis, error analysis would not be able to explain any of the overt interference errors, and would not even be able to identify any of the covert interference errors --errors such as *Will* for *Shall* in *Will we go for a walk?* under the influence of German *wollen* or French-to-English *I visited her grandmother* when *I visited his grandmother* is intended [James 1980: 186-7]. Contrastive analysis and error analysis are both important, and ideally contrastive analysis should come first. (For further reading, J. Richards [1974] is a good book on error analysis.)

Interlanguage

Selinker [1972-b:222] defined *interlanguage* as a "separate linguistic system" based on the output of a second language learner. Corder [1971] emphasized the fact that such systems have some rules particular to individuals by calling them *idiosyncratic dialects*. Nemser [1971] stressed their deviancy from native norms by calling them *approximative systems*.

We should keep in mind that such systems are *not* separate but consist of combinations of second language rules, native language rules, and ad-hoc rules adapted from either one or both languages. Furthermore, a language is rather static as a system, so perhaps the term inter*language* is inappropriate as a reference to changeable, transitional systems and should be reserved for the final plateau, that is, for that point in which the system becomes fixed short of native control of the second language system.

Maybe it would be more useful, in the context of the second language learner in the classroom, to speak of a series of *transitional second language systems* of additive and integrated rules, starting with the learning and integration of the first two rules in the sequence and ending with the last system in the program, still short of native speaker competence. The rules in these systems are variable; that is, some are learned better than others and at various times more or fewer errors may be made with each. Good second language teaching would consist of teaching the second language rules and preventing the formation of approximative rules. Throughout, no system except perhaps the last one can be considered well-established and distinct enough that we can speak of a separate linguistic system. Even the last one is not really separate, for it comes close to matching native speaker competence.

Fossilization and backsliding

Fossilization refers to approximative rules that do not go away but become part of a stable interlanguage. This happens when feedback is positive despite errors and there is therefore no monitoring [H.D. Brown 1980:183]. It can be seen clearly in the speech of many immigrants who, as soon as they learn to communicate, settle down for an error-laden interlanguage, that is, a stable system with fossilized approximative rules.

Pseudofossilization can be said to occur when a temporary plateau with approximative rules is reached but this approximative system is later replaced by a better one as a result of further learning.

Backsliding refers to the fact that under conditions of stress or extreme relaxation approximative rules and items that had been overcome may reappear. This is readily observable in phonology. I recall, for example, an instance in which under the urgency of the moment I mispronounced the English word *bus* as [bus], influenced by Spanish, even though for many years I had pronounced it correctly.

Selinker and Lamendella [1978:245] gave a challenging list of research questions about fossilization. An important point is the need, in such research, to differentiate between the acquisition and the learning situation.

10

COMPETENCES, PERFORMANCES, SKILLS, COMPONENTS, AND LEVELS

More on second language learning

For the layman, learning a second language means learning words and how to use them in communication --the important role of phonological and grammatical structure is ignored. For many linguists, learning a second language is learning its structure --the important role of vocabulary and of the communicative functions of language is neglected.

What is needed is an attitude towards second language learning that takes into account both form and meaning, structure and communication. There must be an understanding that language learning is not an either/or proposition but a complex activity having many facets and involving the learner at many levels of his conscious and unconscious mind. Language learning ranges from the development of simple mechanical skills to abstract cognitive activities, all co-occurring in the same messages [Lado 1964:7]. And this process, which must be developed to the point where hundreds of phonological, grammatical, and lexical choices are made per minute [*ibid.*], has as its aim nothing less than "the bilingualization of monolinguals" [James 1980:8].

In this chapter we will discuss a number of aspects of this complex process of second language teaching/learning.

Competence and performance

Competence is internalized knowledge, performance is the use to which that knowledge is put. For example, in the case of linguistic competence, performance is what is actually said and is based on internalized knowledge of the linguistic code. Performance is thus the application of competence; it is competence in action.

This is true of the person who knows the language. For the second language learner, the process is reversed: he develops competence through performance, first performing mechanically without competence, then performing with some competence, and finally basing his performance on competence.

Three types of competence

Linguistic competence is not enough to participate in discourse --one must also have communicative competence and cultural competence. Without communicative competence, the second language learner will not know what to say, to whom, when, and where. Without cultural competence, his linguistic and non-linguistic behavior will be inappropriate, he won't understand the behavior of others, and he will show ignorance of culture-wide knowledge.

It follows from this that second language teaching should attend to all three types of competence --linguistic, communicative, and cultural.

Linguistic competence

Linguistic competence involves the accurate and fluent use of four of the components of language --phonology/orthography, grammar, lexicon, and semantics-- and its four intralingual skills --listening, speaking, reading, and writing. (The fifth component of language, discourse, is basically the substance of communicative competence.)

In terms of sentence generation and second language learning, the order of the five components of language is from discourse to phonetics and from phonetics to discourse, respectively. This is shown in Figure 10.1.

Sentence Generation and Learning

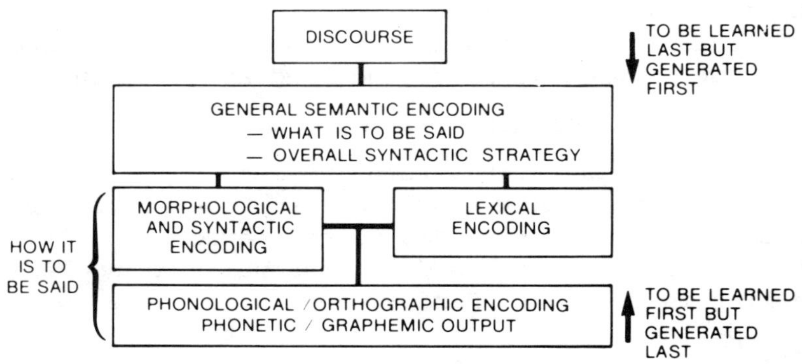

Figure 10.1

In terms of the four skills, it seems that a distinction can be made between comprehension competence and production competence. Neufeld [1980] found evidence for such a dual model of linguistic competence in the fact that advanced learners of French could perceive native pronunciation performance but could not match it. A unitary model of linguistic competence seems therefore inadequate. Perhaps we should posit different models of linguistic competence for each of the four intralingual skills.

Three types of linguistic performance

We can distinguish among three types of linguistic performance: surface, systematic, and mechanical. *Surface performance* is performance that contains mistakes (unsystematic errors) such as false starts, slips of the tongue, hesitation sounds, etc. It should be obvious that the linguist does not base his analysis nor the young child his acquisition nor the second language learner his learning on surface performance but they abstract from it what is systematic. Surface performance minus mistakes constitutes *systematic performance,* the basis for all language analysis, acquisition/learning, and use.

A third type of linguistic performance is *mechanical performance*. This can be *echoic* in nature, as when a nonspeaker of Italian sings opera or a second language learner imitates an utterance, or *manipulatory,* as when a second language learner performs drills. Since the speaker cannot generate such utterances by himself in communication situations, we can say that mechanical performance is not based on competence. At the same time, we should keep in mind that mechanical performance with increasing structural and semantic understanding usually leads to sentence-generating competence.

Communicative competence

Communicative competence has to do with the ability of a speaker to generate appropriate and effective messages, that is, situationally relevant and appropriate for a variety of communication acts. In other words, communicative competence is concerned with the discourse component of language.

The term "communicative competence" was coined by Dell Hymes in reference to sociolinguistic theory; communicative competence, unlike Chomsky's "linguistic competence," does not operate in a social vacuum and is concerned with appropriateness.

Speech acts can be classified according to many criteria, among them functions, situations, roles, topics, modalities, formality levels, domains, and levels of communication. According to functions, communication acts may persuade, amuse, show respect, inform, etc. Roles are, generally, those of speaker, hearer, and participant in inner speech, and more specifically, a child, a mother, a professor, a salesclerk, a taxi driver, etc. Modalities correspond to the four interlingual skills of listening, speaking, reading, and writing. Formality levels range from intimate (e.g., "on the ball") to "frozen" (e.g., "astute"). Domains include the home, the school, the bus, etc. As to levels of communication, Powell [1969] distinguished five: (1) clichés, the most superficial, (2) facts, (3) ideas and judgments, (4) feelings, and (5) peak communication, the deepest and most open.

In a sense, of course, communication is much broader than the use of language implies. We can communicate in quite a variety of nonlinguistic ways. We can say that "a person cannot *not* communicate. One's presence communicates" [C. Brown 1974:14].

In terms of second language teaching, communicative competence is one of three primary goals (the others being, as already stated, linguistic competence and cultural competence). Thus, it should not be neglected; but neither should it be overemphasized at the expense of linguistic competence and cultural competence.

Cultural competence

Cultural competence is the knowledge about his culture and civilization that the average educated native speaker has plus the ability to behave as he behaves. So both cognitive knowledge and performative knowledge of linguistic and non-linguistic behavior are involved (presumably the behavior itself should be called *cultural performance*).

Cultural competence is quite important, for even a proficient speaker, or perhaps *especially* a proficient speaker, will not easily be forgiven for cultural errors or *faux pas* --the more proficient he is, the more is expected of him in terms of cultural competence.

There should be therefore cultural instruction along with linguistic and communicative instruction, right from the start of the second language program, and especially intense instruction prior to any visit to second culture countries.

There is, of course, some overlap between linguistic and communicative competence and between communicative and cultural competence. The division into three competences is however justified in terms of their three different emphases --the language code, its use to convey messages, and the behavior and knowledge of its native speakers. (Cultural competence is discussed further in Chapter 20.)

The eight language skills

For a long time there has been recognition of four language skills --listening comprehension, speaking ability, reading comprehension, and writing ability. These are the main language skills. They are intralingual in nature, that is, described from the point of view of one language only.

Four other language skills, which are also important, are interlingual in nature --oral translation from the second language to the native language, oral translation from the native language to the second language, written translation from the second language to the native language, and written translation from the native language to the second language.

The three language modalities

Language skills can be organized into three modalities, audiolingual (listening and speaking, oral translation), graphic (reading and writing, written translation), and nonverbal.

It has been claimed that nonverbal messages transmit 65 percent of meaning, in the form of kinesic behavior (gestures), paralanguage (voice qualities, laughing, yawning, etc.), and proxemics (spatial factors) [Applbaum *et al.* 1974). All these nonverbal elements are an important part of the communication act. An awareness of kinesics, paralanguage, and proxemics can be taught through practice in observing speakers, on video tape for example, in those three respects.

It should be noted that the audiolingual modality is basic and the graphic modality derivative. The nonverbal modality accompanies the audiolingual modality but is only partly derived from it.

The four intralingual skills and second language teaching

The four intralingual skills can be represented graphically as seen in Figure 10.2.

Note that the former division into "passive" and "active" skills is misleading. The listener is far from passive. While he listens, he is actively echoing the utterance in his mind, processing the linguistic data, trying to predict what will follow, and, if interested in

THE FOUR INTRALINGUAL SKILLS		
	Receptive or decoding ("Passive")	Productive or encoding ("Active")
Audiolingual Modality	Listening	Speaking
Graphic Modality	Reading	Writing

Figure 10.2

retaining part of the message in long-term memory, he is restructuring it for such storage. Even when listening for the sole purpose of something as "simple" as imitation, the listener is active, echoing, segmenting, and perceiving the elements of the utterance. Reading is similarly an active process in which the reader brings into service interpretive skills that include the recall of rules, meanings, and spelling-sound correlations. So, instead of referring to listening and reading as "passive" skills, we shall refer to them as "receptive" or "decoding" skills, and instead of describing speaking and writing as "active" skills, we shall label them "productive" or "encoding" skills.

Note that of these four skills, speaking is central and underlies the others. It seems that we cannot understand what we cannot somehow say to ourselves, since subvocal speech production is involved in the listening process. Similarly, until we become highly proficient readers we say to ourselves, subvocally, what we read. As for writing, we can only write what we can say to ourselves first. So speaking is *the* crucial skill, either at the center of or underlying all language activity. This means that speaking in its various forms should take up much of the class time in a second language program, for with rare exceptions students who can speak well can also perform well in the other skills, but the converse is seldom true.

There have been various approaches to the development of the four intralingual skills in second language programs. One that has been used for a long time is a sequence in which reading and writing are emphasized first, followed later (sometimes much later, if at all) by the addition of listening and speaking. This can be represented graphically as follows:

$$R + W \longrightarrow (L + S)$$

Such a sequence has long been associated with the traditional or grammar-translation method. As practiced in a more or less extreme form, the result of such a sequence is that the students learn to read fairly, write rather poorly (as they lack the oral basis for writing), and their listening comprehension and speaking ability are minimal. (Naturally, students learn mostly what their program emphasizes.)

A serious problem with this sequence is that the echoic behavior of the students is not available for correction. Numerous experiments have shown that there is subvocal activity or *silent speech* during reading as well as apparently during writing and listening [e.g., Edfeldt 1960, Locke and Fehr 1970]. As a result of this unchecked silent speech, second language students can develop a set of very inaccurate pronunciation, stress, intonation, etc. habits even without actually uttering a single word. At the time when they finally start hearing and speaking the language, therefore, the phonological aspect may be ruined for them and they have to be taught new habits in a remedial fashion, which is far more difficult than getting them to develop correct habits from the start.

The sequence of intralingual skills in which the students first listen to the language for some time, then also speak it, then learn to read it, and finally add the writing skill may be represented as follows:

$$L \longrightarrow S \longrightarrow R \longrightarrow W$$

This sequence, advocated by a number of scholars [e.g., H.R. Cook 1967, Burling 1968, Postovsky 1971], represents an improvement over the traditional sequence discussed previously, but it is not without problems. For one thing, it has been shown that when listening to unusual combinations of sounds there is subvocal speech --the reader probably recalls having had this experience upon first hearing an unusual name. In listening to a second language, *everything* sounds unusual at first and is therefore accompanied by subvocal speech. But if the students do not produce vocal speech, their defective echoic subvocal speech is not available for the necessary corrective feedback by the teacher. Wrong habits are therefore very likely to be formed, and they become evident only after they have become well established, that is, when the students begin to speak the language.

Listening and speaking are two sides of the same audio-lingual coin and are intimately related, in fact inseparable. One cannot have one without the other, whether overt or covert. Speaking practice, even if only imitative in nature, gives familiarity with processes of segmentation and short-term retention that are essential for listening. Only the repetition of sentences will demonstrate that they have been retained in short-term memory. Listening involves the reconstruction of messages; but how can messages be reconstructed accurately if one does not have practice in constructing them? One can understand what one can say much better than if one cannot say it; for example, the reason many second language students cannot understand informal speech with its elisions, assimilations, etc. is very likely that they have not been taught how to produce it. A final argument is that our students want to express themselves orally as soon as possible, even if in terms of very simple phrases.

(Of course, carefully prepared listening exercises *can* lead to the formation of correct discrimination habits and comprehension, provided they indirectly control sub-vocal speech. But it is much easier to control vocal speech directly.)

A sequence of intralingual skills that has also been recommended is one in which some time would be spent working only on the receptive skills, only later adding the productive skills. This can be represented as follows:

$$L + R \longrightarrow S + W$$

The difficulties with such a sequence are the same as the ones with the preceding one, plus the interference of sub-vocal pronunciation based on spelling misinterpretations. Such can hardly be considered a desirable set of circumstances.

The two types of presentation most widely used today can be represented as follows:

(1) $L + S \longrightarrow R + W$ and (2) $L + S + R + W$

Both of these approaches are based on the false assumption that the audiolingual and the graphic skills "reinforce each other," and the second one may be influenced by generative-transformational linguistics, in which no separation is made between speech and writing.

In the first of these approaches there is a very short delay between the audiolingual presentation of new material and exposure of the students to its graphic form in standard spelling. The delay may consist of only part of the class hour, with the audiolingual presentation at the beginning of the hour and the graphic work at the end of the same hour. Or there may be an overnight delay, with the students reading and writing the materials presented audiolingually as homework or with a graphic presentation the following day. In either case, what happens when the graphic exposure follows so quickly the audiolingual exposure is that, for example, after the teacher of English worked hard and succeeded in getting his Spanish speaking students to say correctly

(1) ['gʊd "mɔɹnɪŋ 'mɪstəɹ "smɪθ]

after the students have read

(2) Good morning, Mr. Smith.

their production becomes something like

(3) ['gu:ð "mɔřnin 'mistɛř es"mi:ð]

To give examples from English speakers learning Spanish, French, or German, the following sentences will suffice to point out what may happen when (1) correct oral production is influenced by (2) standard spelling to become (3) a very inaccurate utterance the following day or at the end of the class:

English to Spanish:

(1) ['kyeřo přesɛn"tařle̯a la se'ñořa ðe "galƀɛs]
(2) Quiero presentarle a la señora de Gálvez.
(3) ['kʿiy ey'ɹow 'pʿɹ̥ɪzn̩"tʿɑɹley ɑ: lɑ: 'sɪ"nowɹə 'dey 'gæɫ"vɛz]

English to French:

(1) [žvu'dʀɛ vu pʀezɑ̃'te mə'syø 'pɔl lə"lɔ̃]
(2) Je voudrais vous présenter Monsieur Paul Lelong.
(3) ['ǰey və'dɹey vuw 'pʿɹ̥iyzn̩'tʿey 'mɑ̃nzyəɹ 'pʿɔɫ "ley'lɔ̃ŋ]

English to German:

(1) [ɪç 'mʊs 'ɑynn̩ aʀ"tʿi:kl ɪn dəʌ "tsaytʊŋ "zu:χn]
(2) Ich muss einen Artikel in der Zeitung suchen.
(3) [ɪk 'mʌs 'aynn̩ "ɑɹ'ţɪkɫ ɪn dɛɹ "zɑyţŋ "sʌčn]

Obviously, no one sentence is likely to have all these errors, but the errors themselves can all occur.

Examples such as these, and many others, are attested to in the professional literature. The results of many studies lead one inevitably to the conclusion that the audiolingual skills, far from being "reinforced" by the graphic skills, suffer considerable interference from them.

The erroneous belief that the graphic and the

audiolingual skills reinforce each other is based on the fact that *generally* people learn better the more of their senses are involved in the process. But of course they learn much worse when data from two senses contradict each other, in which case the two senses should not be used together. The graphic modality is psychologically and physiologically very different from the audiolingual modality; it is for that reason that the graphic skills interfere with the formation of good audiolingual skills.

When conflicting data from two senses reaches the mind, the learner is forced to go with one sense and reject the other. In the presence of the written second language, the student, accustomed to relying primarily on visual data, disbelieves his ears and follows the visual stimuli instead, however wrong [Hammerly 1970-a]. As Politzer [1965:93-4] put it: "In the initial stages of learning [the graphic and the audiolingual skills] interfere with each other and pull the learner's attention in opposite directions." Pimsleur [1980:35] also referred to this problem, saying that second language learners must learn to trust the spoken word and must set as their goal to learn the sounds rather than their written representation, believing in the way words sound rather than the way they look when there is a conflict.

The negative effects of reading on pronunciation have been noted in many experiments. To refer to only one, Muller and Muller [1968] showed a marked advantage in pronunciation for a group of students who studied Portuguese audiolingually for four weeks over a group that saw the written symbols from the start.

The degree of influence of spelling on pronunciation can be seen in the fact that even sounds that exist in the native language --that is, that are the same in the two languages-- will be replaced under the influence of spelling. In a study that I have previously alluded to [Hammerly 1970-a], it was found that English speakers would correctly pronounce the /s/ in Spanish *zapato,* the /m/ in *quedan pocos,* the /b/ in *verdad,* and the [∅] ("silent *h*") in *habido* while they did not see them in writing but mispronounced them, substituting another English phoneme, as soon as they could read the words.

In view of this, the claim that adults cannot learn to pronounce a second language well hardly seems justified. If adults are submitted to contradictory stimuli, if nothing is done to counteract native language interference, and if there is hardly any phonological instruction, what else can we expect but poor pronunciation? How can we glibly claim that adults cannot pronounce a language like natives if we don't properly teach them how?

Different languages present different degrees of difficulty in this respect. English may be the worst culprit, for as Viëtor put it, its orthography is "an international misfortune." The generative phonologists' claim that it is close to optimal shows a total break with reality. Thus, while it is true that if one knows word stress one can predict a high percentage of English phonemes from graphemes, such a finding is quite useless in view of the fact that English orthography does not indicate stress. Almost all generative phonological rules are equally useless for the nonlinguist trying to learn the surface relationships between English spelling and pronunciation. To give an idea of the complexity of the task, consider that the 24 consonant phonemes of English are realized by at least 176 different graphemes or grapheme combinations, and that the 14 vowels and diphthongs are realized by at least 265 different graphemes or grapheme combinations [Mazurkiewicz 1976]. No wonder that even native speakers of English have problems, at first sight, deciding how to pronounce words such as *caste, frigate,* and *archives*. The problems of the learner of English as a second language are of course much worse, for they are both intralingual and interlingual.

The standard spelling of a second language may be most misleading when it is "deceptively familiar," as is the case of Spanish spelling for speakers of English [Bowen and Stockwell 1957]. Some words in Spanish, when pronounced under the influence of English spelling-sound interpretations, do not have a single sound in common, as is the case with

(1) [bɛř'ðað]   (2) verdad   (3) [vɹ'dæd]

In languages like English and French, speech based on spelling is incomprehensible (and spelling based on speech hardly readable). For example, the French word that sounds like *feess*, when seen to be written as *fils*, results in mispronunciation that makes the word unintelligible.

To have a chance to develop an acceptable pronunciation, the speaker of English learning another language should not even look once at its standard spelling or serious problems will arise. As Pimsleur [1980:39] put it in regard to one problem sound: "Never look at the letter *r*." This is excellent advice to the language learner which can be extended to include most of the alphabet.

We conclude then that early access to a second language through its written form --if it has an alphabet-- guarantees the formation of bad pronunciation habits. Access to the written language does speed up learning and retention but this is at the cost of a major sacrifice in accuracy, for students who learn the written form from the start tend to see the spoken form as a distortion and tend to distort it themselves.

So it isn't enough to tell the students which sounds are represented by which letters and drill them on that. The strength of the habitual native language sound-spelling correlations is such that the only hope of students developing an accurate pronunciation lies in training them audiolingually in the absence of the standard written language. The solution to the problem is therefore to learn first the rules governing the sounds of the language, and *then* the rules that govern its spelling, that is, the sound-spelling correlations. But both sets of rules must be presented and practiced systematically --there is much transfer from sounds to spelling but it is not automatic.

This brings us to the following skill sequence:

$$L + S \longrightarrow R \longrightarrow W$$

This sequence, teaching audiolingual skills only first, has been advocated in modern times since the 1960s by the strictest audiolingualists. However, study beginning with the audiolingual skills existed "at least as early as the beginning of the Middle Ages" [L. Kelly 1969:214].

Emphasis should be on the audiolingual skills for several reasons. Students are mostly motivated to learn to speak. Speaking is basic to all the other skills. Speaking allows greater productive practice per period of time than writing. At least 75 percent of linguistic communication is audiolingual, an estimate made during the pre-television era [Rivers 1975:58]. Speaking is more difficult than reading or writing, so more time should be spent on learning the most difficult skill if the skills are going to be balanced at the end of the program.

The motivation factor is particularly important, as the learners will work harder, and therefore are more likely to succeed, when the second language program matches their goals. N. Brooks [1964:264] stated the problem by saying that second language learners desire and need training in speaking the language, a form of training they are generally denied in our schools and colleges. A survey in Iowa showed that 60 percent of first-year university students had speaking fluency as their objective, with only 13 percent having primarily a reading goal [Thogmartin 1971]. Further surveys by Rivers [1973, 1976:184-223] and Reinert [1974-b] confirm the motivational primacy of speech for both high school and college students.

Another advantage of early exclusively audiolingual teaching is that, although the order of skills makes no difference to the high aptitude students, low aptitude students seem to find an audiolingual-graphic sequence easier than a graphic-audiolingual one. Low aptitude students prefer listening to reading and retain more from listening [S. Taylor 1964] and they benefit more from an audiolingual than from a cognitive approach [Chastain and Woerdehoff 1968].

Another reason for early audiolingual teaching is that there is much greater transfer from speech to the graphic skills than the other way around. Knowing how to speak enormously facilitates learning how to read and write (given an alphabetic system). A recent study, for example, showed high transfer just from listening to reading [Reeds *et al.* 1977]; transfer from speaking is considerable higher. As evidence of the lack of transfer in the opposite direction, consider the hundreds of thousands of second language students who have found, after years of exposure to reading and writing, that this did not transfer to functional audiolingual ability when they visited a country where the second language is spoken. My own experience was that after seven year-long courses in English as a second language via a traditional method, when I arrived in the United States I could neither understand nor say anything.

Second language students should be eased into some form of speaking the language from the first day; there is no need to wait until there is a sophisticated receptive knowledge of the language. All that is needed is to keep early speaking very simple and it can start from the first day of class, going from mechanical to creative and gradually becoming functional. If speaking is postponed, the students lose much of their motivation, form wrong notions about the spoken language, and develop inhibitions against its use.

For many students --even for native-speaking teachers who have forgotten their long years of preschool language acquisition-- language *is* reading and writing, that is, what is found in books. They need to be convinced that the pronunciation, stress, intonation, word formation, and word order of the *spoken* language are the basic components of language.

Other students may be convinced of the need to concentrate on the spoken language but may be very eye-dependent. Second language teaching should not be a question of catering differentially to those students who have auditory preference or visual preference in learning. It should not be up to the student to decide if he is going to learn through the ear or through the eye --if he enrolls to learn a living *language,* as opposed to just learning to read a language, he *must* learn primarily through the ear. If he is too visually dependent, he needs to be auditorily retrained, not patronized. Students *can* learn or rather relearn (for they did it in childhood) to rely on auditory stimuli and to manipulate language orally without the dubious and misleading "support" of the standard written language. Otherwise they can become so visually oriented that in order to say anything they have to "write" it in their minds and read it word by word, with disastrous effects on their speech. (A special visual support to pronunciation and recall usable during early second language teaching will be discussed in Chapter 15.)

One mistake in many second language programs is that after an introduction emphasizing audiolingual skills the emphasis of the program is allowed to shift to the graphic skills. In some "audiolingual" programs there is far too much emphasis on reading and writing at the intermediate and advanced levels, with the result that whatever facility in speaking was developed at the beginning is gradually lost. Emphasis in speaking should be retained throughout the program, not for the beginning levels only. After all, with the right kind and amount of auditory and graphic materials available to him, the second language student can develop the listening, reading, and writing skills mostly on his own; for the speaking skill, however, he depends on classroom activities.

The prereading period

Implied in the L + S ⟶ R ⟶ W sequence of skills we are discussing is a period of time during which the students have no access to the written form of the language. This has been called the *prereading period.*

The prereading period was first advocated by Pestalozzi (1746-1827), a Swiss educational reformer. After World War II, the first scholar to experiment formally with a prereading period was Delattre [1947], during the 1944-45 school year at the University of Oklahoma. He found that the experimental group that worked only with records for twelve weeks was markedly superior in French pronunciation and speaking, at the end of one and two semesters, to a group that worked with textbooks from the start. Other studies involving a prereading period produced similar results --for instance, Scherer and Wertheimer's [1964] study with German at the University of Colorado and my own study with Spanish at Ohio State University [Hammerly 1965].

Of course, a prereading period does not help if it is not accompanied by intensive phonological instruction and followed by a gradual introduction of sound-spelling correlations. Furthermore, no matter how long the prereading period is, it seems that serious interference problems occur the moment the written language is introduced, if this introduction is sudden [Marty 1962].

My study, during the 1964-65 school year, involved an experimental group that was not officially exposed to written Spanish until after twelve weeks of audiolingual work. The study showed certain weaknesses inherent to the prereading period. After about three weeks, the students in the experimental group began to forget early material, because they had no easy way to review it. Furthermore, spelling pronunciation errors began to appear by the third week, as some students began to borrow the printed materials from friends or relatives and others started to write in their own, very inaccurate "transcriptions" as soon as the class was over. This led me to the conclusion that some kind of strictly pedagogical (as opposed to linguistic) transcription should be used as an aid to recall.

So a strict prereading period cannot be continued for more than a few weeks (without a pedagogical transcription), after which certain serious problems would emerge, such as the already-mentioned student "transcriptions," difficulty in learning (especially memorizing) material, difficulty in remembering previous material because there is no easy way to review, and considerable anxiety among the more visually-dependent students.

Delattre himself must have realized the difficulties involved in a long and strict prereading period, for by 1962 he was advocating a prereading period of only three weeks rather than twelve. In recent years, the practice has been to make the prereading period very short or to eliminate it altogether. This is regrettable, for if only the prereading period were supplemented by the right kind of pedagogical transcription, it could live up to all its original expectations and be as long as necessary to ensure audiolingual ability without graphic interference, while also providing the visually-dependent students with the support they need.

The ideal sequence of skills

This brings us to the order of intralingual skills that seems ideal, taking into account all the facts discussed so far. It is as follows:

L + S + Pedagogical Transcription ⟶ R ⟶ W

The students would first work audiolingually, including being trained in listening comprehension, but would have access to a pedagogical transcription as an aid to phonological recall and to visual aids as an aid to the recall of meanings (the native language can also be used for the latter purpose). Then they would be gradually introduced to the written symbols and reading and finally the writing skill would also be gradually added. This sequence of skill development can be represented graphically as shown in Figure 10.3, with "PT" standing for "pedagogical transcription" (the definition of the three levels of second language learning appears later in this chapter).

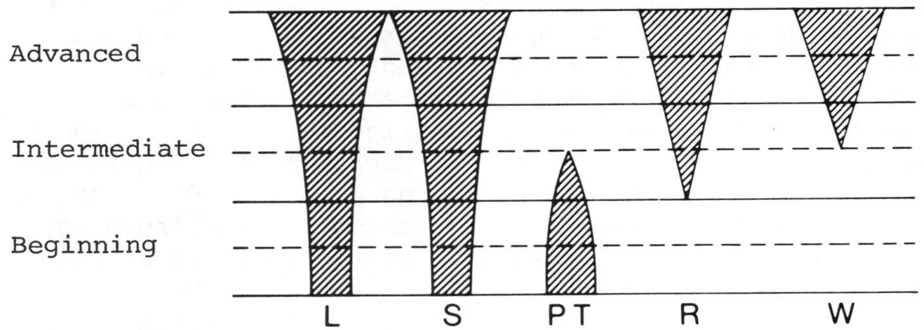

Figure 10.3

Incidentally, the idea that there should be an audiolingual introduction is not based on the poor argument that this is the way the child learns his native language. We have rejected native language acquisition as a model for second language teaching/learning. If we adopted it, we would have to go along also with errors not being corrected, gradual semantic differentiation, no use of the native language, no explanations, no order or gradation of linguistic data, and all the other serious disadvantages of the native language acquisition situation.

Much better arguments for an audiolingual introduction are the fact that language is primarily oral, that reading and writing are based on the audiolingual modality rather than the other way around, and so forth; but the strongest reason for proceeding in this manner is that the graphic form of the language interferes with the accurate learning of the audiolingual skills, as has been demonstrated.

Students of course must be taught the relationships between sounds and spellings, as there is no automatic transfer. It has been demonstrated that systematic instruction in this respect is much better than simply exposing the students to the written language after a prereading period [Estarellas and Regan 1966]. The transition is naturally more successful when done gradually, as is possible by the use of a pedagogical transcription that moves step by step from pronunciation to spelling.

Once all four intralingual skills have been introduced, it is a good idea to have activities that call all of them into use. For example, it is possible to read a story, tell it, have other students listen to it, write about it, and so on. Such work should be reserved for the late intermediate and advanced levels. At such levels, lessons can be staggered so that while audiolingual work is done, say, on lesson 19, reading work is being done on lesson 18, and writing work on lesson 17.

The three levels of second language teaching/learning

It is traditional to refer, within second language programs, to a beginning level, an intermediate level, and an advanced level. The problem is to define them in a way that will be generally accepted by the profession.

Ideally, the only logical basis for defining levels would be by the criterion of linguistic attainment. Usually, however, the criterion of time spent studying the language is used. There are at least three reasons why the time-spent criterion is inadequate: (1) there are different approaches to teaching, such as the cyclical vs. the mastery approach, (2) there are individual differences in attainment, and (3) there are major differences in the time commitment required by different languages.

The two major approaches to language teaching in terms of coverage of material are (1) cyclical, covering the basic rules of the language quickly, once over, at the beginning level, and doing them again, in the form of a review, at the intermediate and advanced levels, and (2) mastery-based, covering everything more slowly and thoroughly once and taking care that the materials are cumulative so that everything that has been learned up to any point in the program reappears with a certain frequency in new combinations. I prefer the second of these two approaches, for it seems to me that it is better to learn each item thoroughly the first time around than to have the students go through repeated cycles of insufficient learning, half-learning all items only to make numerous errors and need several reviews (which are avoidable). Still, even if the second approach were generally accepted, that would not solve the question of defining levels of second language learning, for different materials present the rules of any given language in different orders.

Individual differences in attainment within lockstep second language programs make the meaning of levels very imprecise, for within the same time commitment one student may attain much higher proficiency than another. It is only in self-paced, individualized programs that mastery can be made the condition for further progress and therefore a meaningful level criterion.

The differences in time commitment required by different languages are quite marked. While in 600 hours (400 hours of class + 200 hours of study) the average college student can develop a functional knowledge of spoken Spanish (about 2/2+ on the F.S.I. scale), attainment of the same level in Russian or Chinese requires a much greater time commitment. Wilds [1962] estimated that in order to reach F.S.I. level 3 in both speaking and reading about 1,100 hours are needed for the Romance and Germanic languages, 2,600 hours for the Slavic languages, and 4,400 hours for Arabic, Chinese, and Japanese.

So the semester or the school year is not an acceptable measure of learning. Definitive second language levels, when they emerge after the necessary research is done, will have to specify mastery of particular aspects of each language and would be able to indicate time commitment only very roughly.

And yet, after all this has been said, we are unfortunately still left with the need to define levels in some practical way. In the absence of the necessary research and teaching conditions, I am forced to define levels on the basis of curricular realities --semesters and years of study. The reader should keep in mind, however, that for the average student three years of Spanish or French or German represent twice the linguistic coverage of three years of, e.g., Russian and four times the linguistic coverage of three years of, e.g., Chinese.

So we shall define the levels on the basis of the commonly-taught Western languages. In those terms, the *beginning level* is approximately the first year or 250 hours of class/study in college, the first two or three years in high school, and the first four or five years of elementary school study of a language as a school subject. The *intermediate level* is approximately the second year or the next 200 hours of class/study in college, the next two or three years in secondary school, and it can be reached but seldom completed in non-immersion elementary school study. The *advanced level* represents the third year of language study or 150 hours of class/study in college, is a level that is seldom reached in high school, even at the end of the twelfth grade, and is never reached in elementary school (except in immersion programs). We could also speak of a *very advanced level*, but this would be in all respects a continuation of the work of the advanced level, with emphasis on acquisition.

In regard to curricular content, the first 15 or 20 hours of the beginning level should consist of an introductory minicourse the main purpose of which is to teach control of the sound system. (Since most language teachers lack the necessary expertise in teaching pronunciation, the phonological component of the introductory minicourse should be semiprogrammed, that is, partly self-instructional.) Other functions of this introductory minicourse would be to get acquainted and eliminate excessive anxiety; to determine the learning strategies of the students, explain to them how a language is best learned, and therefore encourage certain learning strategies and reject others (for example, to discourage the strategy of memorizing individual words and encourage learning by phrases); to develop or redevelop the ability to imitate sentences accurately; and to engage in some memorization activities and the learning of a few grammatical rules and a very small but very useful core vocabulary. Beyond this introductory minicourse, the beginning level should concentrate primarily on phonology and essential grammar --not all but about half the grammatical patterns to be taught in the program. Vocabulary should be kept small and functional. Everyday language is to be learned, as more sophisticated and intellectual forms of language are based on it. Literature, philosophy, and other such creative or intellectual pursuits have no place at the beginning level. A start should be made, however, toward understanding behavior in the second culture.

If a good foundation is not established at the beginning

level, especially in the early beginning level (first semester of college, first year and a half of high school), bad habits are formed and the damage is done, for corrective measures are largely ineffective. This is why in the professional literature much more space is devoted to the beginning level than to what follows it. Like the foundation of a building, the success of the whole second language program depends on establishing a good foundation at the beginning. The beginning level is of supreme importance.

During the early intermediate level (third semester of college or equivalent), residual attention to phonology via the use of a pedagogical transcription can be phased out and reading can be phased in. During this sublevel the study of grammar would be essentially completed, leaving for more advanced levels certain infrequent rules and stylistic considerations. It is primarily at the intermediate level and beyond that intensive courses are most suitable, as at the beginning level most students are reluctant to make such a major commitment; also, beginning-level classes include many low-aptitude students who would not do well in intensive courses (of course the beginning level can successfully be offered intensively to well motivated students of average or high aptitude). By the late intermediate level (fourth semester of college or equivalent) there could be a taste of quite a variety of options for the student in terms of modality, content, and so forth; these options can be offered in the form of semiprogrammed minicourses --by then, the students have learned how to learn, know what they want to learn, and are well motivated, so it is possible to rely far more on individual responsibility.

At the advanced level the students, familiar with the options available, should be encouraged to pursue their choices fairly freely. (One advantage of the use of minicourses is that it allows small schools to offer advanced courses as frequently as there is demand regardless of scheduling and staffing problems.) Also at the advanced level, reading, which was started at the early intermediate level, and writing, which was started at the late intermediate level, should be intensified, although not at the expense of audiolingual activities, which should remain dominant, but mostly as activities performed outside of class. The advanced level should also allot time to a systematic study of the second culture. Other possible activities at the advanced level and beyond it are language analysis, both intralingual and interlingual, interdisciplinary studies and the study of current events, and the study of both popular literature and literary works --all in the second language, of course.

Levels and components

Figure 10.4 presents the relationship between the three levels of language learning and the five components of language.

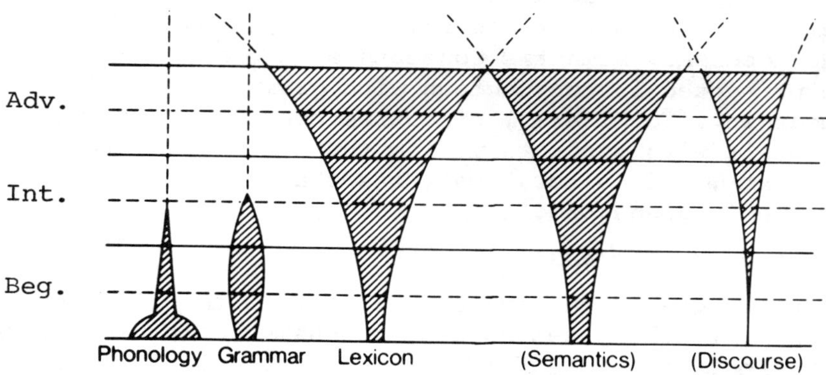

Figure 10.4

As already explained, control over the sound system must be established as early as possible, for whatever the student says later reinforces his early pronunciation, good or bad. Phonological instruction should therefore take place from the first day of class, be particularly emphasized during the first 15 to 20 hours, and continue to receive some attention throughout the beginning level and into the early intermediate level. But even during the introductory phonological minicourse of 15-20 hours there should be other activities, for only a captive, well paid group of subjects would be willing to work hour after hour on phonology only --other, more meaningful activities should break the monotony of phonological instruction.

There should be attention to grammar --morphology and syntax-- throughout the program, with special emphasis on it especially during the first three sublevels, the late beginning level and the early intermediate level in particular. Then emphasis would shift to extensive vocabulary learning (with attention to minor grammatical rules) from the late intermediate level on.

It used to be said that vocabulary should be kept to the minimum required to do phonological and grammatical work [e.g., Lado 1964:52]. However, very few students are sufficiently motivated to keep on studying a language while their vocabulary is so minimal that they cannot engage in any communication with other members of the class. So, while vocabulary does not need to be emphasized at the beginning level --emphasizing it would lead to an undesirable neglect of structure--, enough should be taught so as to enable the students to have some limited conversation from early in the program.

There is no need to teach semantics systematically. All the necessary semantic concepts of the second language can be presented in conjunction with grammatical and lexical learning. Similarly, discourse considerations need not be dealt with separately from the linguistic situations, texts, and cultural patterns that form the core of the second language program.

The first hour of class

Second language teachers usually devote the first hour of class to teaching second language names, linguistically complex greetings, or a full-fledged dialogue. All of these have phonological complexities which, if introduced prematurely, only help launch the students on the path to defective phonological habits. The students should be *eased* into the language, not thrown in the middle of it pell-mell.

The first hour of class should be devoted to learning only two or three new sounds and a very few short phrases based on the new sounds plus any sounds the two languages have in common. In addition to that, part of the first hour of class should be devoted to getting acquainted and having the students fill out information cards (both in the *native* language) and providing a brief orientation on rules for the classroom (especially for younger learners), on how to study for the course and how to use the teaching materials, on the objectives of the course and the nature of the testing and grading, and if possible, the teacher should squeeze in something interesting about the second culture (ideally something very brief about the second culture should be presented in each hour of class). Of course, most of the orientational activities require parts of several class hours, spread through the introductory minicourse.

The four steps of the teaching cycle

Beyond the first hour of class and beyond the introductory minicourse on phonology of the first 15-20 hours, each hour of class should normally be composed of (1) a warm-up and review, (2) one or more teaching cycles, and (3) assigning and preview of homework. A teaching cycle has four steps, which are: (1) *presentation* of a dialogue, text, or examples of a grammatical rule; (2) *understanding*, that is, making sure that the material or the rule have been understood, although of course the conveyance of meaning is part of the presentation; (3) *manipulation,* that is to say, practice under controlled conditions, from mechanical to fairly free, a practice that includes integration of the latest point learned with everything learned previously; and (4) *communication,* whereby the students apply creatively what they have learned to the free production of their own messages, within the limits of what they know.

These four steps take the learners from what they are asked to say to what they want to say. A teaching cycle may take more than one class; conversely, one class may include several teaching cycles. Note also that some rules require a series of progressive teaching cycles over a period of many hours before they are fully mastered.

As will be seen in Chapter 12, different methods organize and emphasize the four steps of the teaching cycle differently.

Speed of coverage

At the beginning, progress should be slow, so that a good foundation can be established. The tendency in most programs is to cover material much too fast, thus not allowing its thorough internalization. An unreasonable pace may get a class to cover a textbook, but that will be superficial, not thorough learning. It is better to have limited ambitions and fulfill them fully than to be overambitious, overload the students' processing ability, and have them fail to fully master anything.

As the program progresses, if it is based on a solid foundation it will be possible to gradually speed up the learning process. Thus, to take vocabulary as an example, the first semester should not attempt to teach more than about 450 words, but then from the second to the sixth semesters the pace can be increased to, respectively, about 550, 650, 800, 950, and 1,100 words, for a total of about 4,500 words in six semesters.

More on options

In addition to the demanding long-term programs with general objectives there should be, for those who want them, short-term courses with limited objectives --some of the recently developed special purpose courses fall under this category. Naturally, anyone who will make use of a language in free communication situations should be directed to enter a general program rather than a very limited special purpose course.

Another matter in which there should be more options is in the languages available for study. All important languages of the world should be available to our students; those for which regular classes are not possible should be available in the form of semi-independent study --there are adequate materials for such study for most important languages. Given the social, economic, and political realities of the world, it is scandalous that only a tiny number of students in North America are studying languages other than French, Spanish, German, Italian or Latin. Computer-assisted language instruction offers a practical alternative to full staffing and would, in conjunction with recordings, allow anyone to study any language, especially if conversation sessions with a native speaker can be arranged.

Beyond the advanced level

Beyond the advanced level, second language learning per se gives way to second language acquisition via the use of the language for a great variety of purposes. In other words, beyond the advanced level there is skill-getting through skill-use rather than separate skill-getting as such.

It is unfortunate that at this point in the learner's progress most college language departments limit his options to one, the study of literature. There should be, instead, very many options, all the options that the second language and culture have to offer. There is no reason, for example, why a language major could not specialize in language and culture rather than language and literature.

It is at this point, or at the earliest after completion of the intermediate level, that the opportunity for the language student to visit a country where the language is spoken should be facilitated by any means possible.

Going prematurely to a country where the language is spoken is harmful because, lacking a foundation and a systematic knowledge of the language, the learner is forced to improvise incorrect utterances and is seldom corrected for them --in other words, it has all the initial disadvantages of acquisition as opposed to learning. Much more can be learned in another country, in the same period of time, after four to six semesters of good instruction at home than without such a background. Note that not only an intermediate linguistic competence but also a basic cultural competence are needed [Morain 1971, Gordon 1974]. (Study abroad has been discussed in detail in several sources [e.g., Bourque 1974, Reynolds 1975, Allouche and Ervin 1976, Conner 1977].)

More on textbooks

One of the most harmful factors in a second language program is excessive reliance on textbooks. Textbooks, unfortunately, tend to dominate second language teaching. They are always there, setting an unreasonably fast pace, always open, interfering with the development of the audiolingual skills and reinforcing the wrong notion that *the* language is what is found in books. The belief that a second language can be learned from textbooks is most damaging to second language learning and needs to be eliminated. Much would be gained by banning textbooks from the second language classroom, reducing them to homework and laboratory workbooks subordinated to cassette tape recordings.

Articulation

Attrition in second language programs is very high, with only about ten percent of those enrolling in the early beginning level going on to enroll in the late intermediate level. Most students do not study long enough to develop even minimal proficiency.

While there are many reasons for this situation, one of the most unnecessary and annoying is the inability of the second language profession to articulate the progress of language students across and within schools. Articulation is a scandal. Large gaps are allowed to occur in a student's progress and nothing is done to fill those gaps. High schools make elementary students start again at the beginning and colleges do not recognize what has been learned in high school. It is a wonder that not all language students are completely discouraged. Within schools, articulation is not much better. Different teachers follow different methods, and materials that in no way provide continuity are used from one course to the next.

The solution would be to have progress and placement, from kindergarten to graduate school, on the basis of demonstrated proficiency --demonstrated via standardized proficiency tests which, unlike the ones now available, would measure performative knowledge of specific aspects of the language. As for gaps in the sequence, the solution would be to fill them with independent or semi-independent skill maintenance minicourses, which would be modules preferably geared to individual interests.

A preprogram alternative: the exploratory course

It is the obligation of the educated person to go beyond the boundaries of his own language and culture and to explore the variety available throughout the world. The second language program is for most students the only opportunity in their lives to become acquainted with the languages and cultures of the world.

It seems, therefore, a disservice to the student to channel him immediately into only one second language and culture and not give him a full opportunity to explore many of them. For that reason, some feel that, regardless of the age of the learner, he should first be exposed to an exploratory course, which we can call "Languages and Cultures," before he undertakes the systematic and long-term study of any particular language.

The exploratory course Languages and Cultures could last one semester or one year and its activities could include the following (based partly on Pei [1973] and Bourque and Chehy [1976]):

--a look at the language situation around the world, chief languages spoken, their characteristics, their location and number of speakers, etc.

--a look at foreign elements in the native language: foreign words and place names, and foreign cultural elements;

--teaching a limited amount in each of the languages offered by the school: numbers from one to ten, greetings, a brief dialogue, some very limited communication;

--teaching about language learning and dispelling such myths as the primacy of writing, the word as the unit of learning, one-to-one interlingual matching in meaning, etc.

--offering some insights into the nature of language, with examples of sounds, sound-spelling correlations, morphemes, syntactical rules, etc. from several languages, including in particular the native language;

--providing insights into human behavior around the world, with emphasis on the identification of differences between the North American culture and other cultures; and

--as a project, each student could research a cultural area of interest to him.

Such a course would best be taught by a team of faculty from the language department, if possible with some cooperation from other departments. Note also that it is more likely to be successful if considerable use of media is involved.

(For more on exploratory courses, see Adcock [1976:314-7] and Brannon and Cox [1976:164-70].)

11

MODELS OF SECOND LANGUAGE ACQUISITION, LEARNING, AND USE

Many models, many purposes

Many models of second language acquisition, learning, and use have been proposed in recent years. From the fact that most deal with only one or two aspects of the language acquisition/learning or use processes one can reach the conclusion that a single model will not account for all aspects and that several models are necessary --one to represent the mental processes of the learner, one to represent the way the native and the second language relate, one to represent sentence generation, and so forth.

Models of second language acquisition/learning

The models of second language acquisition/learning that have appeared so far are only partially applicable to learning (as opposed to acquisition), if they do not fail to distinguish at all between these two processes.

Selinker's [1972-b] Interlanguage Model, already discussed in Chapter 9, presents learner language as a system or series of systems between the native language and the second language and sharing characteristics of both. This model can be represented graphically as in Figure 11.1.

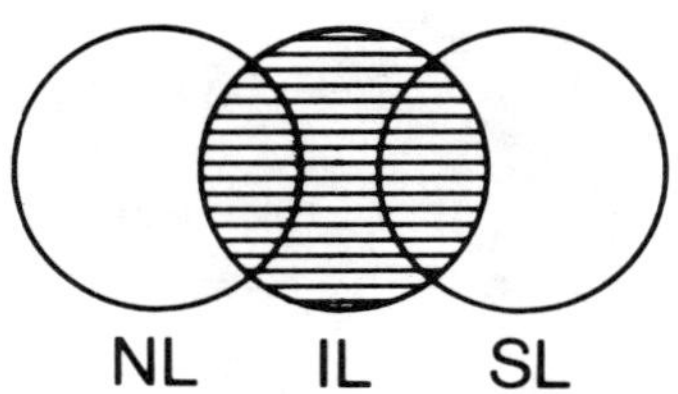

Figure 11.1

Unfortunately this model is too simple to distinguish between acquisition and learning or to give any details about the relationship between the two languages and the second language learning process. Furthermore, it is wrong in representing the two languages as being apart.

Dulay and Burt have contrasted a simplistic Restructuring Hypothesis, according to which the second language is constructed on the basis of the native language, with their Creative Construction Hypothesis [1974-a, 1974-c], which posits the "creation" of the second language independently of the native language. The problem with this hypothesis is that it is based on a questionable concept of a natural sequence of acquisition [Dulay and Burt 1974-b, Bailey *et al.* 1974]. Another problem, more fundamental, is that overwhelming evidence proves that the native language does indeed influence second language acquisition/learning, although not of course to the point of being the sole basis for second language development.

Schumann [1976] observed that there are certain similarities between second language learners' interlanguages and pidgins. He proposed therefore a Pidginization Hypothesis of second language acquisition/learning. But while a process of simplification and reduction similar to pidginization may occur in a second language acquisition situation, there is no reason for it to occur in a second language learning situation, unless we allow unrestricted and uncorrected communication from the start.

From Schumann too [1978] we have the Acculturation Model, according to which second language acquisition is just one aspect of the social and psychological integration of the acquirer into the second language society. Such a model, as Schumann himself allows [1978:50], would be particularly applicable to acquirers under conditions of immigration to or extended sojourn in the second language area. It would simply not be true that second language *learners* need acculturation in order to learn the language.

More relevant to the second language program, Valdman [1978] proposed a cyclical syllabus model in which subparts of a grammatical point are presented at different times, and Brumfit [1980] conceived of the second language program as a ladder-like grammatical core surrounded by a spiral of notional-functional-situational activities.

A Two-Cone Model of second language teaching/learning

The focus of this chapter is on a model that aims to describe the most important aspects of the process of second language *learning* resulting from formal teaching and leading to the development of a fairly high degree of linguistic, communicative, and cultural competence. Certain features of other models will be related to it.

The name of the model is the Two-Cone Model because each of the two languages, native and second, is represented by a cone. Within each cone (see Figure 11.2), phonology ("P") is shown primarily at the apex, grammar ("G," for morphology and syntax) appears in most of the central area, and vocabulary and semantics ("V") are shown all along the periphery but mostly at the base of the cone.

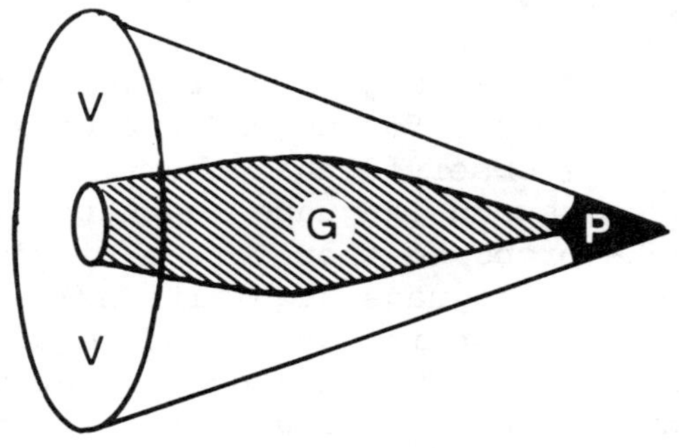

Figure 11.2

This order of second language subsystems corresponds to their logical order of emphasis in teaching/learning --first we teach control over the sound system, the language subsystem which has the smallest number of rules and elements and which is present in all utterances; then we tackle the morphology and syntax, the next subsystem in increasing number of rules, along with some vocabulary learning; and then, once the structure of the language is well under control, we emphasize the learning of vocabulary, the language subsystem with the largest number of elements, a learning task that continues indefinitely beyond the second language program.

Note that this order of emphasis for the language subsystems corresponds to the order of discovery, which is the opposite of the order of generation. (Much misleading discussion has arisen in our field because of a failure to differentiate between the order of discovery or learning and the order of sentence generation.)

Initial contact between two languages is therefore at their most superficial levels, that is, phonetic. Figure 11.3 represents such contact by the touching of the apices of the two cones. As the learning of the second language progresses, the second language cone can be represented as entering the native language cone and

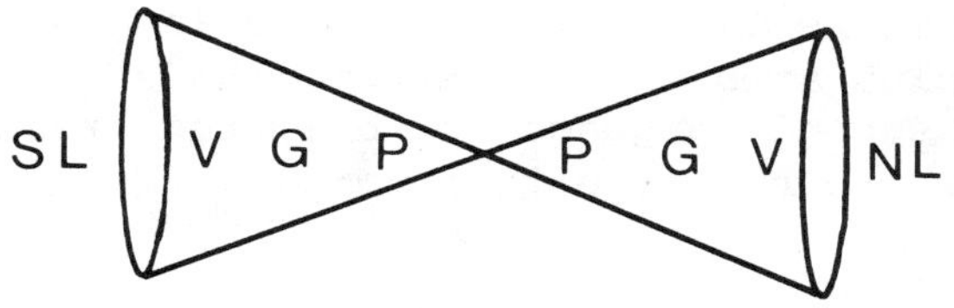

Figure 11.3

emerging gradually from it (Figure 11.4, -a, -b, and -c). The intent is to represent simultaneously both the learning of the second language and the overcoming of the interference from the native language.

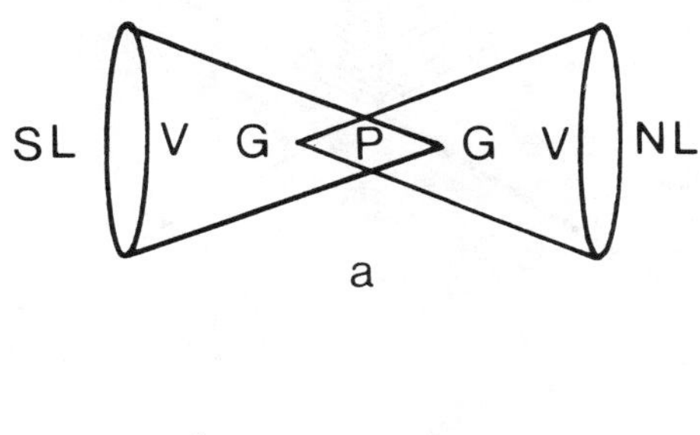

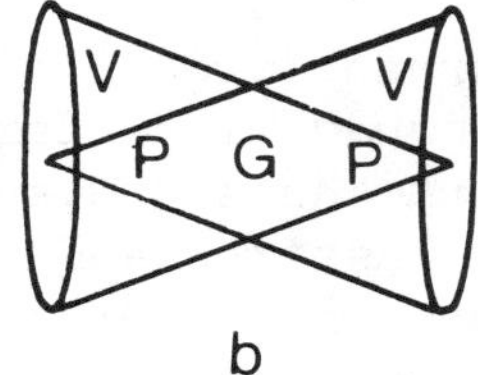

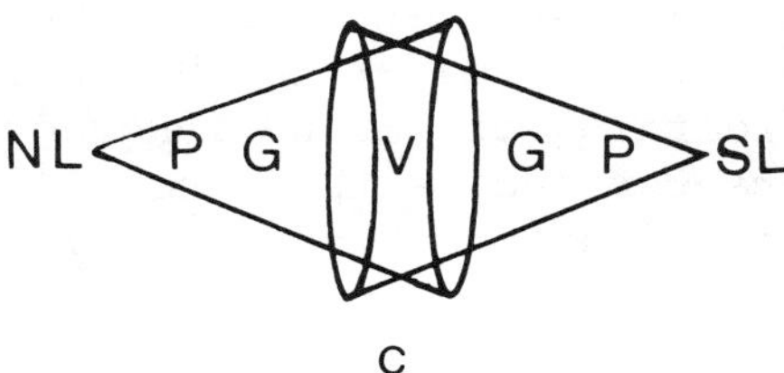

Figure 11.4

As the sound system of the second language is learned (Figure 11.4-a), something that, for better or for worse, occurs quite early,[△] certain elements and rules (shaded area A-1 in Figure 11.5) of the native language sound system (area A plus area A-1) interact (shaded Area B-1) with the emerging second language sound system, resulting in both positive and negative transfer.

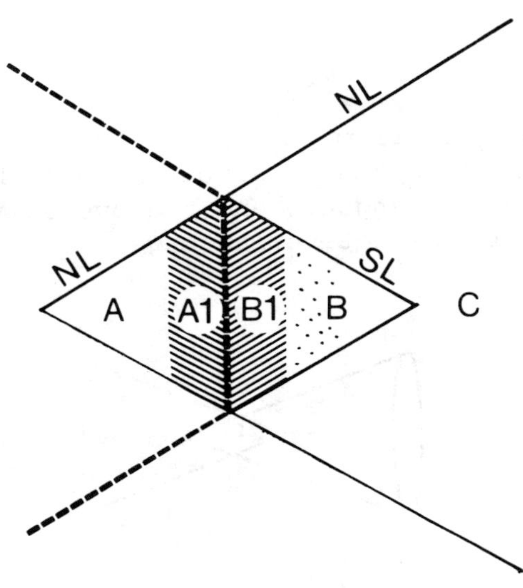

Figure 11.5

If what emerges as learned (area B) is fully mastered, it is free from native language interference. Frequently, however, especially with the sound system, the rules and elements are not fully mastered and are not completely free from native language interference, with the result that the learner's system contains fossilizations [Selinker and Lamendella 1978]; in addition, errors that had apparently been overcome can recur as backslidings under conditions of stress, anxiety, etc. Both such errors are represented as dots (in area B) in this model.

The teaching/learning of second language grammar can be similarly characterized as the second language emerging from contact with the native language (Figure 11.4-b).

△ Of course, it should be kept in mind that not all aspects of the sound system are learned early, only the most overt ones --certain generative phonological rules cannot be taught and learned (or acquired) until there is a considerable control over the language as a whole.

But at this point, in addition to interlingual errors there is a growing number of intralingual errors as the learner increases his knowledge of the second language and relies more and more on it. Interlingual and intralingual errors are made in regard to both new rules being learned and to incursions into linguistically unknown territory.[△]

If we apply Figure 11.5 to the learning of second language grammar, area A represents that part of the native language whose interference has been overcome and for which second language rule counterparts have been learned (area B). Shaded area A-1 represents those rules of the native language grammar that are currently interacting with equivalent second language rules being learned. Shaded area B-1 represents the latest rules being learned; during this learning there are interlingual errors due to the influence of the native language (which could be represented as an arrow pointing right from area A-1 to area B-1) and intralingual errors based on what is already known of the second language (these could be represented as an arrow pointing left from area B to area B-1). Areas A-1, B-1, and B correspond approximately to the linguistic area covered by interlanguages.

As the second language program progresses, what is known of the second language (area B) increases in size and influence, causing a corresponding increase in intralingual errors. Interlingual errors, on the other hand, tend to decrease. They are maximal for new elements and rules as these are being learned, gradually decrease, and disappear --other than in backslidings-- if the second language item is fully mastered and integrated (of course, it may not be fully mastered, in which case errors fossilize). Any incursion outside of what is known will result in both interlingual errors, under the influence of

----

[△] Incursions into linguistically unknown territory should be discouraged because they cause very many errors, more than can be effectively corrected. Such incursions in no way facilitate learning, which is not based on free hypothesis testing, even though such incursions are essential to the acquisition process. In the learning process, we do not enlarge our knowledge by blindly operating beyond our capacities but by operating fully within our capacities and gradually and systematically developing new capacities.

the rest of the native language cone (area C), and intralingual errors, the incorrect application of known second language rules. The trend, as already noted in Chapter 9, is for more interlingual errors to occur at the beginning level and more intralingual errors to occur at the advanced level, as reliance on previous linguistic experience shifts from the native language to the second language.

Since the whole system of a language cannot be taught or manipulated at once, it is necessary to teach and manipulate parts of it, one at a time, cumulatively. This learning one by one of the second language rules results in the emergence of a series of additive and integrated second language transitional systems (TSs), which are shown in Figure 11.6. These transitional systems go from TS-1, after the first two second language rules have been learned and integrated, along with bilingual rules,[△] to TS-n, corresponding to the maximum second language competence offered by the program according to its specific objectives. TS-n is short of full second language native competence, which can only result from advanced second language acquisition.

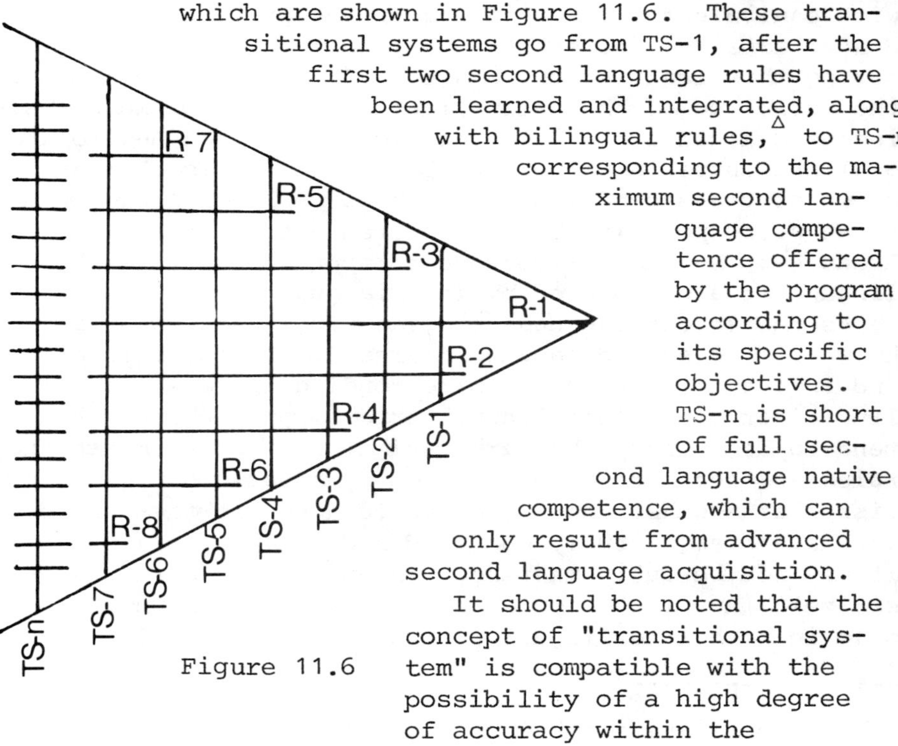

Figure 11.6

It should be noted that the concept of "transitional system" is compatible with the possibility of a high degree of accuracy within the

----

[△] Throughout this discussion when referring to rules and elements to be learned the intent has been to refer to those that differ from the native language so as to cause interference; those rules and elements that are the same in the two languages ("bilingual" rules and elements) need not be studied or learned, although they do need to be acknowledged and integrated into the TSs.

limitations of the system, unlike "interlanguage" with its implication of unavoidable interlingual errors and "approximative system" [Nemser 1971] with its implication of general inaccuracy. That learners tend not to learn many rules thoroughly and to venture often outside the limits of what they know, thereby making many errors, in no way negates the theoretical possibility of totally overcoming interference and being quite accurate within the expanding limits of transitional systems. (Of course such control is much more likely with mechanical activities than with freer uses of the language.) Note also that TSs are not only additive but also integrative --without the latter they could not be considered to be systems [Sampson 1978].

The sequence of second language rules to be learned --and therefore the sequence of TSs-- is based on pedagogical considerations and principles. A natural sequence of acquisition, if any, would be dictated by communication needs, and communication needs are only one of the many factors weighed in determining the pedagogical sequence of a second language program.

As Figure 11.7 shows, each second language rule should go through the four teaching steps identified in Chapter 7 --(1) presentation ("Pres.") in some language sample; (2) understanding ("Und."), that is, making sure that it has been grasped cognitively; (3) manipulation ("Man."), composed of mechanical drills ("MD") and meaningful exercises ("ME"); and (4) communication ("Com.") in terms of communicative activities ("CA") and free or real communication ("FC") [cf. Paulston and Bruder 1974].

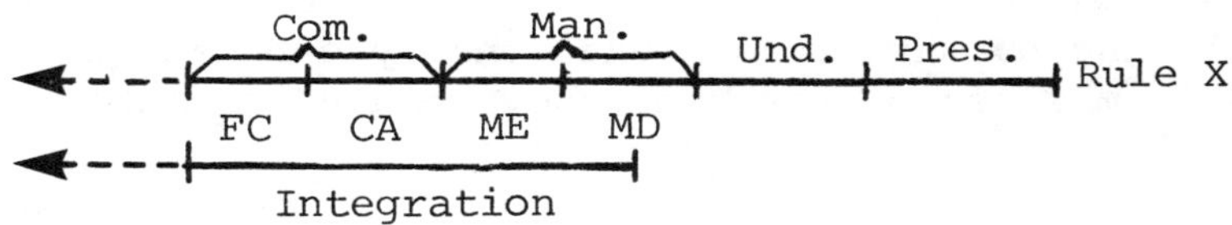

Figure 11.7

The process of integration with previously learned rules and bilingual rules begins in the latter part of the mechanical drills and is especially evident in the communication phase.

For each rule the Monitor function△ passes from the

△ The Monitor Model is discussed later in this chapter.

teacher to the learner during the mechanical drills and can become internalized to the point of becoming unconscious with the right amount and kind of meaningful practice, beginning with meaningful exercises and progressing with communicative activities and free communication in that teaching cycle and further practice throughout the program.

The learning of second language vocabulary is part of the process of second language learning almost from the start;[△] but, for the reason already explained (vocabulary being the largest and most unwieldy subsystem), plus the fact that early emphasis on vocabulary detracts from adequate attention to structure, vocabulary learning should be mostly an advanced task.

At the end of the second language learning process, the structures of the two languages are largely apart (to the extent that native language interference has been overcome) but the two languages remain indefinitely in contact lexically and semantically (Figure 11.4-c). Proofs of this are (a) the evidence of lexical-semantic interference in near-bilinguals [Sheen 1980] and (b) the ease with which bilinguals "plug in" words from language Y within language X syntactic structures while speaking in language X with other X/Y bilinguals.

It should be noted, by the way, that although the Two-Cone Model is meant to apply to second language learning, in general terms it also applies to the process of bilingual differentiation in childhood [Hammerly 1964]. Figure 11.4 can be interpreted as showing that a bilingual child separates the two sound systems first, by about age four (Figure 11.4-a); then by about age ten he finally succeeds in separating completely the two syntactic systems (Figure 11.4-b); and no matter how functionally separate the two languages may become for him, they remain in contact lexically and semantically (Figure 11.4-c).

The Two-Cone Model is not a "sunburn" model [Lane 1966] such that emphasis is on unsystematic exposure to the second language through mimicry and memorization. It is instead a "behavioral" and a "structural" model in which learners are led to competence in the second language by a series of carefully coordinated steps chosen according to a fairly specific description of terminal behavior (TS-n).

[△] A good case can be made for meaning-free phonological instruction, i.e., the early phase of it.

The Two-Cone Model is also a "cognitive" model, for rules should be learned with understanding, as grammatical awareness facilitates performance [Hammerly 1977]. It is also a "generative" model, because each TS is a system capable of generating an indefinite number of novel sentences (provided, of course, that its rules are properly related). Finally, the Two-Cone Model is also a "communicative" model, as communication is the last phase of each teaching cycle and each rule and element, together with all previously learned rules and elements and bilingual rules and elements, is used frequently in communication.

The Two-Cone Model seems to be valid whether the second language is spoken in the environment (*environmental* second language learning, often called "*second* language learning") or is not spoken in the environment (*remote* second language learning, often rather inappropriately called "*foreign* language learning"). A representation of the language spoken in the environment can be added to the Two-Cone Model in the form of a rectangle, as seen in Figure 11.8

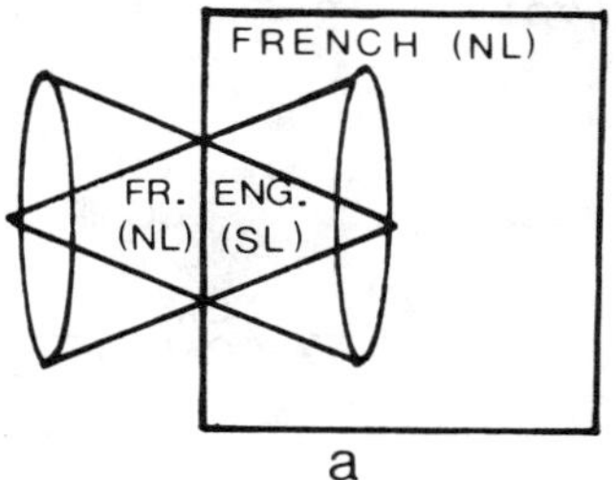

a

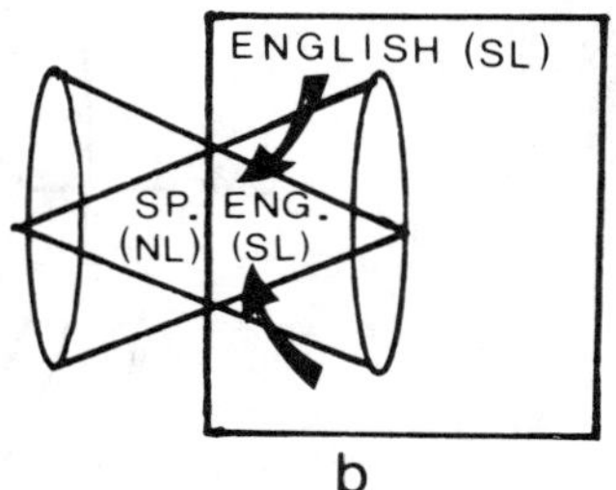

b

Figure 11.8

In the remote second language learning situation, as in the case of a French speaker learning English in a French-speaking environment in which English is not spoken (Figure 11.8-a), there is a pure process of second language learning, with no acquisition involved. In the environmental second language learning situation, as in the case of a Spanish speaker learning English in the classroom within an English-speaking environment (Figure 11.8-b), varying degrees of second language acquisition are bound to accompany second language learning (in fact, they may have preceded it, in which case a substantial part of second language teaching may have to be remedial).

In the environmental situation, exposure to the second language outside the second language program contributes to the development of second language competence (and incompetence), but it does so through the filter of the learner's native language (see the arrows in Figure 11.8-b).

In other words, the learner/acquirer automatically and mostly unconsciously compares with his native language any rule or element that he acquires from the second language environment, although this tendency to compare gradually diminishes as the learner/acquirer's competence and confidence in the second language develop.

In regard to the three types of competence --linguistic, communicative, and cultural-- that should be the goals of second language programs, the Two-Cone Model as described to this point represents primarily linguistic competence. It is possible, however, to add to it outer layers for communicative competence and cultural competence respectively (Figure 11.9).

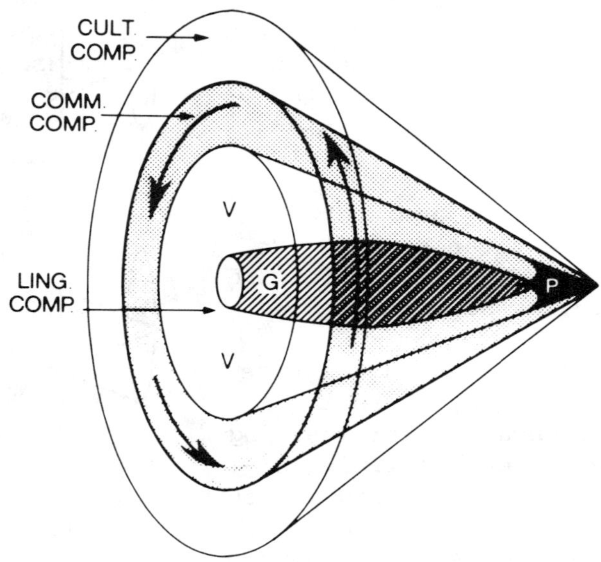

Figure 11.9

With these additions, the second language cone represents the learning of the structure and vocabulary of the second language (linguistic competence), the communication based on it (communicative competence), and the cultural context in which that communication takes place (cultural competence). That is, communication occurs within a cultural context and consists of the cyclical reintroduction of communicative acts and situations around a structural core.

(While the Two-Cone Model represents linguistic competence as the core in each cone, communicative and cultural competence are not separate components but are integral parts of each of the two cones. They are outer layers of each cone, inseparable from the core and with complex interrelations with the core and between themselves. In other words, a second language should not be taught apart from communicative and cultural considerations; communication makes use of a language within a cultural context; and cultural instruction should preferably be done in reference to the second language and its communicative uses.)

The Two-Cone Model of second language learning should prove more useful than previous models of second language acquisition/learning, as it seems to depict clearly various aspects of the second language learning process such as the relationship between the second language and the native language, the sequence of learning second language subsystems, rules, and elements, the development of second language transitional systems, the place and origin of errors, the influence of the linguistic environment, and the relationship between the three types of competence that constitute second language competence.

Models of sentence generation and use

Krashen [1978] proposed a Monitor Model of second language sentence generation. According to this model, second language acquisition and second language learning are separate processes, acquisition being naturalistic, unconscious, the basis of a "feeling" for the language, and the source of sentences, while learning is artificial, conscious, the basis of "rules," and does not originate sentences. What is learned is available only as a Monitor of the output of acquisition, given knowledge of the rules, adequate time --for example, the Monitor operates during writing activities but not during rapid speech-- and a focus on grammatical form.

There are several problems with the Monitor Model. First, it minimizes the role of learning, assigning to it only trivial functions. Learning can and does originate sentences, the majority of sentences, at least in a remote second language learning situation. Furthermore, if the monitoring function is internalized through practice, so that it shifts from conscious to unconscious, the Monitor can operate during rapid speech. As to grammatical focus, it has been shown that the Monitor operates even when there is weak focus on form [Shuldberg 1981].

It seems that in second language learning sentence

generation does not result from acquisition (which may be nonexistent, as in the remote second language learning situation) nor can it be said to follow the steps of a generative-transformational grammar. Instead, sentence generation in a second language program seems to proceed from the learning of fixed routines --simple phrases and sentences-- to the learning of semifixed patterns and, through the modification of the latter via analogy and reference to meaning, to creative speech. This kind of generative grammar, unlike a transformational grammar in which all sentences are formed from elements, produces most sentences by "chunking together" and modifying ready-made phrases --it is therefore a "phrase grammar" [Nattinger 1980]. An infinite number and variety of sentences can be produced this way, by combining a limited number of well-learned simple phrases and patterns. This is what allows us to say that the generation of sentences can be based mostly on learning rather than exclusively on acquisition.

Stevick [1980:277] proposed an improved Monitor Model, which he called the "Levertov Machine." It is an improvement in that it establishes some connections between learning and acquisition; but it still fails to establish any connection between learning and the sentence "generator." Furthermore, it stores items with different strengths in separate learning and acquisition storages instead of storing them in a single storage with a continuum from conscious to unconscious. I am quite sure there is no such separation in the mind of the learner/acquirer.

It is to be hoped that through the development, improvement, and integration of models, a clearer idea of the principles underlying second language learning will emerge.

12

METHODS AND APPROACHES[△]

Corn growing and second language methodology

Suppose many North American corn growers refused to accept any modernization and continued to grow corn with nineteenth century methods; suppose, further, that many other corn growers abandoned proven methods every few years to follow unsubstantiated claims about new methods and techniques from Podunk, Bolivia, and Timbuktu; suppose, moreover, that an anti-equipment movement took hold of the rest, so that they left their plows and corn pickers to rust in the fields --you would not think much of such farming, would you?

And yet, this is precisely what the second language teaching profession has done. A substantial number of language teachers are so traditionally oriented that they still teach with methods that have not changed much since the nineteenth century. Others are ready to abandon reasonably successful methods to follow unproven methods and techniques from strange sources and distant places. Most seem to have joined an anti-machine movement, with the result that language laboratories have been abandoned *en masse*, there is very little use of portable cassette machines, and computers are avoided like the plague.

This methodological traditionalism from some, bandwagonism from others, and nihilism from still others, has done incalculable harm to second language teaching in the United States and Canada. It is no wonder our enterprise is a disaster. And it will continue to be a disaster until we adopt the real attitude of farming, industry, and business --continue to gradually improve upon demonstrably successful eclectic methods, making use in the process of the best technology has to offer.

△ Portions of this chapter are from my article "Recent Methods and Trends in Second Language Teaching," *The Modern Language Journal*, Vol. LV, No. 8 (© 1971 by the Regents of the University of Wisconsin), pp. 499-505; used by permission.

The importance of methods and approaches

Some would say that methods and approaches are unimportant, since statistically they seem to account for only 15-20 percent of variance in success in second language learning. What we should keep in mind is that most of the other factors in success, such as verbal intelligence, modern language aptitude, and grades in other subjects, are beyond our control. Of the factors that we can control, methodology is the most important. Other things being equal or beyond our influence, methodology is what we can most readily change to effect success in second language learning.

There are also those who downgrade the importance of methods and approaches because certain methodological studies have shown little or no difference in the results obtained with different methods [e.g., P.D. Smith 1970, known as "the Pennsylvania Project"]. To this we can say that most methodological experiments have suffered from serious defects, not the least reason for poor research being the fact that many teachers do not adhere to the procedures and techniques they are supposed to use in the experiment. Furthermore, some methodological studies *have* shown marked differences in the results obtained with different methods [e.g., Scherer and Wertheimer 1964, Hammerly 1965], so the conclusion that methodology is an important factor is fully justified.

Some definitions

We can define a *second language method* as a set of procedures and techniques that agree with basic assumptions about the nature of language and the purpose and process of second language learning, that deal with such matters as selection and gradation of second language rules and elements, the presentation of teaching materials and the nature of practice, and that aim at the development of linguistic, communicative, and cultural competence.

While a method is practical and specific, an *approach* is philosophical and general. An approach can be defined as a way of directing activities that agrees with one or more general assumptions or principles. Thus, within one approach, oral for example, there may be several methods --in this case Direct, Structural, Audiolingual, Audiovisual, etc.

Procedures are general, method-wide ways of doing things. For example, the teaching of dialogues is a procedure in the Audiolingual Method. *Techniques* are specific ways of implementing procedures. For each procedure there may be several techniques of implementation, and different teachers use different techniques. Of course, research may enable us to determine not only the relative superiority of methods and approaches but also which procedures and even techniques are most successful.

A *syllabus,* as in "notional-functional syllabus," is a British term that refers to a specification of the content and content sequence of courses. The closest North American terms are *course outline* for one course and *curriculum* for a program of courses.

Incidentally, since we are discussing terminology, I might point out that it is curious that the advocates of certain sets of procedures that fit clearly under any definition of "method" insist on calling their methods by strange new names, or calling them "approaches," "ways," etc. One wonders if they are afraid to have their methods referred to as "just another method." Anyway, in this book we shall consider them for what they are --methods.

Other variables in methodology --apart from those in our definition of *method*-- are based on assumptions about the process of second language teaching, about the role of the teacher, and about the role of the learner. The relative weight given to structure and communication is a further variable. Methods and approaches also differ as to whether they are global rather than graded step by step --the Natural Method, the early Direct Method, the Functional Approach, and Community Language Learning are global, ungraded; the Traditional or Grammar-Translation Method, the Audiolingual Methods, the Cognitive Approach, the Silent Way, and Suggestopedia are graded.

A little background to modern times

There is evidence [L. Kelly 1969:59] that in classical times and up to and during the Renaissance, Latin and other languages were taught by many inductively and with emphasis on communication. At the same time, attention to grammar --in the form of declensions, conjugations, etc.-- and the use of translation also existed, as language teaching procedures, from ancient times. As Latin became a dead language, modern languages also came to be taught as if they were dead, although through this period some pioneers such as Montaigne in the sixteenth century and Comenius and John Locke in the seventeenth century advocated modern ideas.

Despite the efforts of a few enlightened scholars, the

trend to teach modern languages as dead languages continued to intensify and resulted in the coalescence of grammar and translation procedures, bringing together longstanding traditions and resulting in the establishment of the Traditional or Grammar-Translation Method.

The Traditional or Grammar-Translation Method

The Traditional or Grammar-Translation Method reached its zenith in the nineteenth century in Germany with the work of Seidenstücker (1785-1817) and Plötz (1819-1881), closely followed by others such as Ahn and Ollendorf; however, much traditional teaching in Germany and elsewhere had preceded them, in the eighteenth century and earlier. This method came to dominate second language teaching in the whole Western World. It is still used, with some modifications, in many educational institutions.

This method is based on the assumptions (1) that language is primarily graphic, as already seen a view resulting from the teaching of classical languages as dead languages; (2) that the main purpose of second language study is either as a tool for literary research or for the development of the learner's logical powers (the latter leading to such oddities as schools requiring "either mathematics or a foreign language"); and (3) that the process of second language learning must be deductive and must be carried out with constant reference to the native language of the learners.

The procedures of this method, at least in its most extreme form, are as follows:

--The language skills given emphasis are reading and writing, with listening and speaking taught, if at all, at an advanced level. A common result of this emphasis is, for example, the Spanish major who can read the *Cantar de Mio Cid,* Cervantes, and García Lorca but cannot communicate in spoken Spanish.

--Pronunciation is usually ignored. If attended at all, it is referred to on the basis of spelling and native language sounds (e.g., "French *é* is pronounced like the *a* in English '*fate*'") --this leads to very poor pronunciation. To remedy this situation, advanced pronunciation courses may be offered, something that is seldom useful for the students, since by that time their pronunciation habits, whether good or bad (usually bad), have long become firmly established.

--Grammar is taught through the memorization of rules --the memorization of conjugations is an example-- which are then applied deductively and practiced in translation exercises. Such procedures cannot result in fluent oral production. They mean, instead, that when the learner is asked, for example, *Quand partez vous?*, he must think "*Quand...? quand...?* --oh, yes, *when--*, *partez?* --hmm, that must be from *partir;* now, let's see: *je pars, tu pars, il part, nous partons, vous partez...;* that's right, I'm supposed to answer *nous partons;* OK, the French word for *tomorrow* is...," etc., by which time the person who asked the question is on a journey of his own, either real or of the mind. In terms of actual learning, this process of deductively applying rules is very inefficient. As a case in point, Pimsleur [1980:49-51] showed that students who had spent *60 minutes* practicing French sentences with object pronouns in the language laboratory did slightly better in a production test than students who had spent about *six hours* in deductive instruction with written exercises.

--Vocabulary is emphasized in the Traditional Method from the beginning and is taught by means of bilingual word lists and practiced in exercises with isolated sentences. Having learned such word pairs and armed themselves with a bilingual dictionary, but being only vaguely aware of multiple meanings, idioms, and acceptable grammatical patterns, the students are only too ready to produce incorrect and frequently unintelligible one-to-one word equations between the two languages. As Jespersen [1904:11] put it: "Disconnected words are but stones for bread; one cannot say anything sensible with mere lists of words." Disconnected sentences are not much better. Such words and sentences lack both linguistic and communicative context. And yet, quite recently, some [Heilenmann 1977, Westphal 1977] have been calling for a return to vocabulary list learning.

--The native language is used most of the time in the Traditional Method. It is constantly used in class and is the door to the second language. Emphasis is placed on similarities rather than differences between the two languages. (As we shall see, this excessive use of the native language led to an extreme reaction against any use of it at all. This is unfortunate, because the limited and wise use of the native language can perform a number of very useful functions in second language teaching. A similar extreme reaction took place, by the way, against the teaching of grammar.)

The approach of the Grammar-Translation Method to sentence generation is quite poor. Moulton [1966:18-9] referred to it as the "cookbook method," in which grammatical rules are the recipe, new vocabulary the ingredients, and written sentence translations the cake, which is usually atrocious. We can say that the evil of the Traditional Method is not translation (although its tendency is to overuse it and misuse it) but the constant attempts to construct sentences word by word according to memorized grammatical rules. As Dodson [1967:39-40], who favors translation, pointed out, the reason the deductive Grammar-Translation Method does not work is that it is not possible to communicate when sentences are generated that way; for example, he notes that the German sentence *Der Jäger kann das Tier sehen* ("The hunter can see the animal") requires 17 grammatical decisions for its production! It is obvious one cannot proceed to communicate deductively but must internalize the rules, that is, make them into linguistic habits.

The standard order of presentation in Traditional Method textbooks is (1) rule, (2) word list, and (3) translation exercises. With respect to the four steps of the teaching cycle, the order is (1) understanding, as the method is deductive, (2) presentation of illustrative language material and of vocabulary, (3) limited graphic practice, and (4) no communication.

The typical Grammar-Translation program is unbalanced in that it pays no attention to pronunciation, overemphasizes spelling and vocabulary, provides a theoretical rather than a practical knowledge of grammar, and ignores the communicative function of language. As a result, graduates of Grammar-Translation programs have a cognitive knowledge *about* the language, but not a performative knowledge of *how* to use it. Exposure to (for many years), and observation of, the Grammar-Translation Method leads me to the conclusion that it can result in an ability to read fairly, but it usually produces very little habit formation and no ability to communicate.

All of the above leads to the inevitable conclusion that the Traditional or Grammar-Translation Method is quite unacceptable as a method of second language teaching. But perhaps the reason why it continues to be used is that it has certain practical advantages --it can be used by language "teachers" with little knowledge of the language or of teaching techniques; it is inexpensive, as it allows classes of any size and class periods can be few; it is easy to administer, control, and apply; teaching is neither physically nor emotionally tiring; testing is easy; and so forth. Of course, we know that given its poor results, all of these "advantages" and more are mostly illusory and in no way justify the use of this method.

The Natural Method

The poor results of the Grammar-Translation Method led to a series of reactions to it, the first major reaction being the Natural Method. Although its forerunner was Pestalozzi, the Natural Method did not gain much momentum until the 1850s and '60s, with the work of Marcel, and especially Heness and Sauveur. It was a movement carried out in special language schools in particular; it failed to make inroads into the educational establishment.

The Natural Method tried to imitate the process whereby the young child acquires his mother tongue. Its procedures included monolingual teaching with active demonstrations of meaning, emphasis on the spoken language, and inductive learning --that is, translation, rules, and explanations were entirely avoided.

Natural methodists, unlike the Direct methodists who followed them after three or four decades, did not attempt to elaborate psychological or linguistic rationales for their practices. We know, from our discussion in Chapter 5, that such a method could not be an efficient method, for there is no possibility of, nor advantage in, reproducing the process of native language acquisition in the second language classroom.

The Series Method

Another reaction to the Traditional Method took place beginning in the 1880s under the leadership of Gouin. In his main book [1880], Gouin proposed a method based on the observation of how his small son talked to himself and acted out each sentence after a visit to a flour mill. (This is therefore a type of Natural Method, as it tries to imitate child language acquisition.) The method is called the Series Method because it divides a variety of activities into series of short sentences that are repeated and acted out.

An example would be the Gouin series on "I open the door" [from Diller 1971:51-66], which would include a total of fifteen sentences, with emphasis on the verbs, as follows:

(1) I walk towards the door,	I walk
(2) I draw near to the door.	I draw near
(3) I draw nearer to the door.	I draw nearer

(4)	I get to the door.	I get to
(5)	I stop at the door.	I stop
(6)	I stretch out my arm.	I stretch out
(7)	I take hold of the handle.	I take hold
(8)	I turn the handle.	I turn
(9)	I open the door.	I open
(10)	I pull the door.	I pull
(11)	The door moves,	moves
(12)	the door turns on its hinges,	turns
(13)	the door turns and turns,	turns
(14)	I open the door wide,	I open
(15)	I let go the handle	I let go

There is no question that older children and adults would find such an atomization of an action into its minute components boring, silly, and quite useless. Furthermore, the Series Method was based exclusively on the description of activities and questions and answers derived from the sentence series; there was no careful gradation in vocabulary and grammar, and the grammar --other than the learning of verbs-- was relegated to a secondary role.

Still, this verb-centered method can be the basis for active verb practice. Such practice should not be in the form of series of sentences, however, but in the form of narrations, with mime rather than full actions used to act out the verbs.

Other reformers and pioneers

In 1882 Wilhelm Viëtor published a booklet in German, under a Latin pen name meaning "How much longer?," which was to be instrumental in fostering the reform movement that finally succeeded in the 1890s. For that reason, Viëtor has been erroneously called the "father of the Direct Method" --in fact he was not opposed to the reasonable use of translation and his call for reform did not advocate any of the extreme practices that Direct methodists later urged and implemented.

Other pioneers of the late nineteenth century and early twentieth century, who again were not Direct methodists but reasonable reformers (and who, curiously enough, have been called Direct methodists by several language teaching historians), were Henry Sweet (1845-1912), Otto Jespersen (1860-1943) and Harold Palmer (1877-1949). Men of considerable vision, their works [Sweet 1899 (1964); Jespersen 1904; Palmer 1917 (1968), 1921, 1922 (1964); Palmer and Redman 1932 (1969)] can still be read with much profit.

The Direct Method

Unfortunately, after centuries of domination by the Grammar-Translation Method, the leading second language teachers of the late nineteenth century were not ready to follow calls to reasonable reform. Instead, as it often happens with reactions, they went from one extreme to the other. They condemned all the "tools" of the Grammar-Translation Method without considering that what was wrong was the way these tools were used.

Whereas the Traditional Method made excessive use of the native language, the Direct Method prohibited it altogether. Whereas in traditional teaching much time was spent on the deductive teaching of rules, in Direct methodology no rules were taught. Whereas traditionalists explained everything, Direct methodists explained nothing. Whereas the Grammar-Translation Method was carefully graded, the Direct Method abandoned gradation in favor of vague intuition as a guide in going from simple to complex.

The Direct Method is based on two correct assumptions and a wrong one. But the wrong one invalidates the whole method. The two correct assumptions are (1) that language is primarily oral and (2) that the main purpose of second language study is communication. The wrong assumption is that the process of second language learning must be like the process of native language acquisition, that is, inductive, monolingual, and so forth. As Paul Passy, a leading French Direct methodist, put it [1899:8, my translation]:

> That is, in effect our obvious model: the simple fact that the baby learns his language and can learn several shows us that he has a good method and that we would do well to take it as our guide.

But as we have already stated, it is neither possible nor efficient to imitate the native language acquisition process in our classrooms.

The Direct Method, at least in its early form, includes the following procedures:

--Listening and speaking are the skills emphasized, but reading and writing are usually presented with them.

--Pronunciation is supposed to be acquired by imitation, without formal teaching in the form of rules, explanations, or drills and usually without a transcription (some Direct methodists did use phonetic transcriptions).

--Grammar is supposed to be acquired inductively, without formal teaching in the form of rules, explanations, or drills and at least originally without a particular order of presentation. By rejecting the use of explanations, the Direct Method puts adults at a great disadvantage, since adults, as a result of their education and their cognitive maturity, have learned to base much of their learning on analysis and synthesis. The later Direct Method development of allowing explanations *but* in the second language is hardly an improvement --the purpose of explanations is to make something clearly understood, not hazily guessed at in an unfamiliar language.

--Vocabulary is emphasized from the beginning and is object-centered, starting with objects in the classroom. But much of that early vocabulary --pens, pencils, blackboards, desks, pieces of chalk-- is not useful for communication. Talking about objects in the classroom has no function whatever outside of class and therefore should have none in the second language class. In what circumstances are you going to talk, for example, about chalk, the ceiling, and the blackboard?

--Meaning is conveyed in the Direct Method inductively, without reference to the native language. Use is made, instead, of objects, pictures, and actions. Of course, this does not succeed in keeping the students from making second language-native language associations in their minds. Furthermore, this procedure turns the comprehension of meaning into an ongoing guessing game, at which some students are not very successful.

--The use of the native language by either the teacher or the students is expressly forbidden. This is in fact what gives the Direct Method its name; it is its defining characteristic. Franke [1884] and other Direct methodists theorized, as shown in Figure 12.1, that the use of the native language as a way of conveying meaning is a more "indirect" device than associating second language words "directly" to the objects, actions, etc. to which they refer --that is, the route Concept-Foreign Language Word

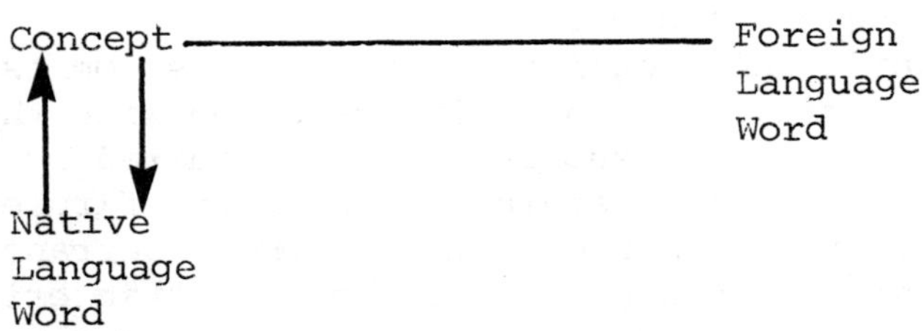

Figure 12.1

was claimed to be shorter than the route Native Language Word-Concept-Foreign Language Word (and the direct route Foreign Language Word-Native Language Word was rejected). The fact that certain Direct methodists [e.g., Passy 1899: 16] admitted the possibility of some use of the native language in extreme circumstances does not invalidate the statement that the primary feature of the Direct Method is its prohibition of the use of the native language.

Of course, a strict application of the injunction against the native language can result in much frustration. Students may go for months without knowing the meaning of many words, so all they can do is guess. And what does a student feel when he does not understand something, asks for an explanation, and the teacher replies --alas!-- in the second language? What he feels is frustration and what he does is get an inaccurate "explanation" from his classmates, after class, in the native language. Psychologist Roger Brown [1973:5] reported on this kind of frustration, the result of his experience in a Berlitz course in which hours were spent to put the meaning of a few words of Japanese across when it would have been so much easier and better to provide their native language equivalents. But frustration is not the only disadvantage. Such a procedure fails to make use of the student's knowledge; it neglects to take advantage of contrastive analysis to counteract interference overtly; and it precludes the use of understandable, complete, and accurate rule formulations.

One reason given for prohibiting the use of the native language is that its use would make it impossible to think in the second language. Thinking in the second language was a goal of Direct methodists, as seen in the following statement from Passy [1899:11, my translation]:

> ...it is necessary, from the beginning, to set ourselves as a goal to be attained as rapidly as possible that of leading our students *to think in the foreign language*.

The problem with this is that expressing one's thoughts directly in the second language cannot be achieved in a short time, even in conditions of total immersion. So procedures and efforts aimed at the early direct expression of thoughts in the second language are misdirected.

One of the disadvantages of the Direct Method is that it requires mature learners to return to childish ways of learning and behaving; many cannot successfully do that. This infantilization of the learner, which is quite unjustifiable, is a characteristic that the Direct Method shares with the Natural Method.

With respect to the four steps of the teaching cycle, the Direct Method follows the order (1) presentation and (2) communication, such as it is. There is little concern for ensuring understanding of rules and elements as such; the emphasis is on the understanding of communication. As to manipulation, it has been only recently that some Direct methodists added drills to their programs.

Success with the Direct Method is possible, but it depends on having a very skillful teacher and plenty of time, neither of which conditions is normally present. In regard to the time factor, Direct methodists seem to be totally unconcerned about efficiency --Passy [1899:18], for example, would have been satisfied if beginners learned two or three words per lesson.

Where classes are heterogeneous in language background *and* there aren't appropriate materials available for each language, some sort of monolingual method becomes necessary. But we should not confuse such necessity with virtue --there is no reason why a Direct Method should be used with linguistically homogeneous classes, like almost all school and college classes.

The Direct Method represents an extreme reaction to an extreme situation. However, 90 years is enough time to overreact to the excesses of the Grammar-Translation Method; judicious use of the native language and explanations and (where needed) deductive instruction can facilitate and speed up the second language learning process. Basically, one should be wary of any absolute prohibitions, such as the multiple prohibitions of the Direct Method --there will always be particular circumstances in which even the most defensible prohibition needs to be set aside in second language teaching.

The Reading Method

The Direct Method became official in France and Germany in 1902. In North America, where education is decentralized, there was no such official method adoption, but many teachers tried to implement the Direct Method.

The problem was that in the United States and Canada the second language sequence, unlike Europe, was short, usually only two years in duration. In two years a slow and inefficient method like the Direct Method could not produce tangible results.

It was this consideration that led the authors of

the Coleman Report [Coleman 1929, 1931] to propose an adaptation of the Direct Method for the more attainable single goal of reading proficiency. This adaptation came to be known as the Reading Method, which was widely used until the 1940s and to a lesser extent the 1950s, when second language study sequences became longer and more ambitious goals became possible.

As a type of Direct Method, the Reading Method did not allow the use of the native language. One of its characteristics was the careful grading of vocabulary, with new lexical items being presented in the context of numerous known words. This method seems to have been moderately successful in attaining its single goal of reading proficiency.

The Structural Method

During World War II the urgent need arose to impart second language communication skills to a large number of government personnel. The Traditional Method very seldom resulted in fluency. The Direct Method could impart communication skills, but much too slowly. The task of developing a new approach was given to a group of structural linguists working under the aegis of the American Council of Learned Societies.

These structural linguists followed the assumptions (1) that language is primarily and basically oral, an emphasis-on-speech American tradition going back to George Ticknor (1791-1871) and Henry Longfellow (1807-1882); (2) that the main purpose of second language study is communication; and (3) that the second language learning process is more efficient if it combines induction with explanations, if it makes use of the native language, if the teaching materials are based on a careful analysis of the contrasts between the two languages, and if there is intensive practice.

Although these structural linguists were reluctant to say they had developed a new "method" and would refer, at most, to a "linguistic approach," it seems obvious that when similar materials were produced[△] and similar teaching procedures were used for dozens of languages a method *was*

[△] The "Spoken Language" series published by Henry Holt and Company beginning after the War included 22 languages. The similarity in the set of procedures used in each language fully justifies calling this a "method."

developed. For lack of a better term, we shall call it the "Structural Method."

The forerunners of the Structural Method were Sweet, Jespersen, and Palmer. Palmer proposed many of the types of drills that later became part of this method. As to its philosophy, it has been expressed in part by two statements. The first, by Delattre [1947:243], identified the main problem with language teaching as one of *order*, of putting the cart before the horse by providing graphic before audiolingual training, rules before examples, and quantity before quality, ignoring in the process the fact that "[a] language is first of all 'speech.'" The second statement, by Moulton [1961:86-90], listed the linguistic principles of the then new second language teaching as "'Language is speech, not writing'....'A language is a set of habits'....'Teach the language, not about the language'....'A language is what its native speakers say, not what someone thinks they ought to say'....and 'Languages are different.'" Such statements of broad principles do differentiate the Structural Method from certain aspects of the Grammar-Translation Method, but they are too general to differentiate it from other methods --for example, Direct methodists would not disagree with any part of these statements, even though the Structural Method differs markedly from the Direct Method.

The Structural Method can be said to have the following procedures, which have evolved considerably since World War II:

--The oral skills are emphasized throughout, with the development of the graphic skills being delayed until an oral foundation has been established.

--Pronunciation is taught by means of mimicry (and since the midfifties via orally-based pronunciation drills), with explanations, the correction of errors, and a transcription as an aid.

--There is team teaching in small classes. One member of the team is a "native informant," an educated native speaker of the second language who serves as linguistic model, drill master, and conversation leader. The other member of the team is an academically-trained linguist who follows the progress of several groups of students and visits their classes in order to give explanations and answer questions. The size of the classes is about six to eight students.

--Grammar is taught by induction but with explanations of grammatical patterns available to the students, both in printed form and through the help of the linguist.

The early tendency was to rely excessively on induction, perhaps under the influence of such leaders as Bloomfield, who stated [1942:12] that "the command of a language is not a matter of knowledge" but "a matter of practice." Originally explanations were given, if at all, as "summaries of behavior," that is, at the end of drill sessions. This seems to have been partially motivated by a desire to discourage grammatical discussions between the students and their linguistically-untrained native informants. Gradually, however, the printed explanations moved up closer to the beginning of the units or lessons, so that by the early sixties they appeared, in U.S. government language school textbooks [e.g., Desberg *et al.* 1960], just after the examples.

Grammatical practice consisted in doing structural drills. At first these were limited in variety and number, but as the years went by new types of drills were added, so that by the late fifties there was quite a variety, and the typical unit included many pages of drills. Another late development was making sure that drill sentences were all understood, by providing native language equivalents where necessary.

Note also that the structure of the second language, in contrast with that of the native language, is the basis for progression in course content. Nevertheless, linguistic competence is not the only goal pursued --frequent communicative activities foster the development of communicative competence.

--Vocabulary is not emphasized early in the program and is taught in context --that is, within sentences within dialogues within situations-- with native language sentence equivalents.

--The teaching of dialogues, which the students have to imitate and memorize, is, although not new, characteristic of this method (although some structuralists use teaching materials without dialogues). Dialogues are the means of introducing the students to new vocabulary and examples of phonological and grammatical patterns. These examples are then the basis for drills. In the early materials (i.e., during World War II), the dialogues were very long. As time went by, the dialogues became shorter, so that by the late fifties we find some government textbooks with dialogues of about 18-20 sentences.

--The native language is used as little as possible but as much as necessary to facilitate and increase the efficiency of the second language learning process. It is used, for example, in dialogue sentence equivalents, in certain pronunciation and grammatical drills, and in explanations. This is, therefore, a bilingual method. The native language is not, however, the door to the second language in the sense that it is used as the basis for sentence generation (as in the Traditional Method). Emphasis is placed on differences rather than similarities between the two languages.

The term "mim-mem" was used, mostly in a derogatory manner, and especially during the War and post-War years, to refer to this method. While there was some justification for the term (there were then very long dialogues for *mim*icry and *mem*orization), the term is imprecise in that it emphasizes only two of the numerous activities that took place in the classroom under the early Structural Method.

In a number of ways, the Structural Method is balanced; it is, for example, at neither extreme of the deduction/induction spectrum and more or less at the center on the question of the use of the native language. The Structural Method can also be said to have some scientific basis, as the science of linguistics and, in particular, contrastive analysis, is the basis for the preparation and presentation of teaching materials.

The results obtained with the Structural Method in its early form varied considerably, for as part of the Army Specialized Training Program classes supposedly using this method were offered at many universities, in most of which there were no linguists trained in the use of the method. Where the Structural Method is used under the supervision of properly trained applied linguists, as at the Foreign Service Institute of the U.S. Department of State, the results are excellent, with habit formation (or "rule internalization"), overt structural understanding, and a fairly high degree of communicative competence. Fluency in the use of the language depends on how well the instructor builds the bridge between mechanical language work, such as the memorization of dialogues and the performance of drills, and the free use of the language. Unfortunately, in the later adaptations of the Structural Method for use in schools and colleges few teaching materials provided this essential bridge-building practice, most leaving it up to the imagination of the teacher, which generally was not adequate to the task.

One last point. The Structural Method does not owe its success to intensive programs and small classes. My teaching experience has proved to my satisfaction that the Structural Method can be just as successful at the rate of only five, not 30, hours of class per week. Moreover, it can be adapted to large classes, by performing some activities with the whole class (although with many individual responses) and dividing the class into smaller groups for communicative activities.

The Audiolingual Methods

During the late 1950s a group of leading American language teachers, some structurally-oriented but most of them Direct methodists, adopted and adapted for the schools, to various extents, some of the procedures used in the Structural Method. These various combinations of Direct and Structural methodology came to be known as the Audiolingual Method, even though when Brooks coined the word "audio-lingual" he simply had in mind a term that would indicate emphasis on the listening and speaking skills, not a particular method.

In fact, we have to talk of Audiolingual Method*s*, because from the start of this process of adaptation and adoption there were at least three varieties of the Audiolingual Method: (1) a structurally- and situationally-oriented bilingual variety, with a balance of dialogues, drills, and communicative activities and close to the Structural Method;[△] (2) a situationally-oriented variety with numerous dialogues, minimal use of the native language, and virtually no drills;[☆] and (3) a variety close to the Direct Method, in which no use was made of the native language but dialogues and drills were used extensively.[◇]

Given these varieties, it is hard to pinpoint the assumptions and practices of the Audiolingual Methods, so most will have to be listed as ranging over a certain spectrum. The three main assumptions are as follows: (1) some Audiolingual methodists consider language primarily and basically oral, and favor a prereading period, while

---

[△] E.g., the first edition of the *A-LM* series published by Harcourt Brace, from 1960 on.

[☆] E.g., the *Entender y hablar, Ecouter et parler,* etc. series published by Holt, Rinehart, Winston in the early sixties.

[◇] E.g., the materials developed by Scherer for the University of Colorado experiment [Scherer and Wertheimer 1964].

others think of language as both and about equally oral and graphic; (2) the main purpose of language study is assumed to be the development of communicative ability, an assumption on which there seems to be unanimous agreement among Audiolingual methodists (although in practice communication is de-emphasized by the intermediate level); and (3) most Audiolingual methodists seem to consider that second language learning is primarily inductive, as seen in the continuation of the early Structural Method practice of giving explanations as summaries of behavior, if offered at all.

The procedures of the Audiolingual Methods are as follows:

--Some Audiolingual methodists think that the development of oral skills should precede that of graphic skills; but a considerable number think that reading and writing should be taught together with or in immediate alternation with listening and speaking.

--Pronunciation is supposed to be acquired primarily or exclusively by imitation, an obvious Direct Method practice; a notable exception is Bolinger *et al.*'s *Modern Spanish* [1960, 1973] and Desberg and Kenan's *Modern French* [1964], which include some of the types of pronunciation drills used in the Structural Method. For other materials, especially those for secondary schools, pronunciation drills appeared later (if at all) in the teacher's manuals, with the result that they were seldom done in class.

--Since the team teaching of the Structural Method is not possible in most school and college classrooms, audiolingual materials attempt to give the teacher the functions of both linguist and native informant. As very few teachers have studied linguistics, and not many speak the second language like natives, their performance of both these functions is difficult and often impossible. As to the size of classes, the much larger size of school system classes led to the practice of relying heavily on group responses, an unfortunate and unnecessary development --unnecessary because even in school-size classes it is possible to rely primarily on individual responses (followed occasionally by group imitations); unfortunate because it led to the overuse of repetition and very simple, mindless drills.

--Grammar is taught primarily by oral "pattern drills" and induction. Although the individual teacher can change the order of presentation and give explanations earlier, first-generation audiolingual textbooks discouraged the giving of explanations by not offering them or by restricting them to very brief charts or discussions at the end of each drill section or even at the end of the whole unit. This reluctance to give explanations shows the influence of the Direct Method and of strict behaviorism. Unlike the Direct Method, which simply exposes the student to the language, the Structural Method is supposed to organize and explain the data, from which the learner systematically internalizes the rules. In the Audiolingual Methods, the use of drills to practice grammatical rules varies greatly, from the structurally-oriented Audiolingual Method using a large number and variety of drills, to the situationally-oriented Audiolingual Method using very few drills and those of basically one simple type. The latter method relies mostly on repetition and substitution, with no cognitively-oriented drills.

--Vocabulary is not emphasized early and is taught in context, with native language sentence equivalents appearing somewhere in most textbooks and provided to the students in class, by some, but usually avoided by many Direct methodist teachers, this avoidance resulting in considerable problems in comprehension. Note that meaning has an important role in the Audiolingual Methods. True, it isn't sufficiently emphasized in drills; but dialogues, readings, and conversational exchanges are supposed to be understood. There is no minimization of understanding, only of vocabulary.

--Dialogues are used, usually at the beginning of each textbook unit; this is a procedure on which all three Audiolingual Methods agree. A good development was that, in adapting the use of dialogues (in the Structural Method) for the schools, dialogues were usually shortened considerably from their length of about 20 sentences to about 12-14 sentences. (In later audiolingual textbooks, the trend toward shorter dialogues is still more evident, as dialogues have come to be six to ten sentences in length.[△]) The dialogue sentences are the basis for grammatical drills, lexical variation drills, conversation, etc., although they have not been fully exploited.

--The use of the native language varies with the three Audiolingual Methods. The structurally-oriented one is basically a bilingual method, like the Structural Method,

---

△ E.g., the second and third editions of Harcourt Brace Jovanovich's *A-LM* Series.

that is, it makes moderately frequent use of the native language. The other two methods use the native language very little or not at all.

Given the variety of Audiolingual Methods and the fact that most teachers are poorly qualified to use them (through lack of training), it is not surprising that results have varied tremendously, from excellent to poor. Further distortions of the Structural Method soon arose. In some colleges, in an apparent attempt to justify a role for professors, lectures were added --this even though there is no function for lectures at all in the Structural Method. In many places, audiolingual teaching meant mostly audio for the students and lingual for the teacher, another distortion [Nachtmann 1973]. But the worst distortion is the common practice of reducing audiolingual teaching to a very mechanical sequence of dialogues and drills followed by more dialogues and drills, that is, without developing communicative competence. This defeats completely the purpose of audiolingual teaching, as it substitutes mindless repetition for manipulation and communication with understanding.

This communication-less audiolingual teaching is a contradiction in terms. As Brooks [1964:235] stated: "The new orientation is toward language *as* communication and *for* communication." In accordance with this orientation, most early audiolingual textbooks did offer many opportunities for communication --personalized questions, free replacement, rejoinders, conversation stimuli, topics for reports, etc. [Stanislawczyk and Yavener 1976:2]. But few teachers felt secure enough in their knowledge of the second language to embark on such procedures, and as a result they stayed within the safer (and stultifying) ground of rote memorization and mechanical drills. Structuralist-behaviorists, generally speaking, have written in favor of communicative activities and "liberated expression" rather than of a mechanical approach to language teaching. It was the numerous teachers who were linguistically unqualified and therefore preferred to "stick to the book" who reduced their students to the status of "Skinnerian rats."

When students in poor audiolingual programs (the majority of audiolingual programs) realized how mechanical and devoid of communication these program were, many lost their initial preference for audiolingual goals and decided they would rather have an emphasis on grammar and reading and writing. When those who had graduated from such audiolingual programs found, upon visiting a foreign country, that their neat little dialogue sentences for all occasions just didn't serve for free communication situations, discouragement was strengthened. Finally, when methodological comparisons did not show any advantage for audiolingual teaching --no wonder, because its goals and procedures were never defined, teacher training and certification were haphazard, articulation was a shambles, the use of technology was poor and minimal, and the experiments themselves were defective-- the second language teaching profession became disenchanted almost in its entirety.

Not disenchanted were those whose audiolingual teaching was based on sound principles and who were getting excellent results from carefully implemented programs --but these constituted a small minority. In other words, among the great majority who were practicing mindless audiolingual teaching there was a small minority who were practicing enlightened audiolingual teaching, with very good results. This minority still exists and teaches very successfully, despite the general rejection of audiolingual methodology. The Audiolingual Method, in its cognitive, bilingual, structural-communicative variety has not failed --it just has not been widely tried.

Of the methods discussed so far, the Traditional Method and the Direct Method represent respectively the two extremes of the methodological spectrum, the Structural Method its approximate center, and the Audiolingual Methods a range going from the center to near the Direct Method extreme. In practice there have been, of course, many combinations of the basic assumptions and procedures of these methods, so that second language teaching can be said to have taken place at any point in this spectrum.

The Cognitive Approach

As a result of the disappointment with the (distorted) Audiolingual Methods, especially with their mechanical, communication-less variety, there was a reaction during the midsixties which acquired considerable momentum by the late sixties and into the early seventies. This reaction took two forms --a return to a more Direct methodist orientation, basically in the form of the Audio-Visual Method, and a return to a deductive neotraditionalism, in the form of the Cognitive Approach.

The Cognitive Approach should be considered an approach and not a method because there never has quite been an agreement on a set of procedures but a loosely defined language teaching philosophy. Carroll's [1966-a:101-2] specification that the "cognitive code-learning theory" stresses conscious control of patterns through study and analysis, and that this constitutes a "modified, up-to-date grammar-translation theory" is perhaps the closest we can come to defining this approach; but note that such conscious control of patterns in no way conflicts with what Carroll [*ibid.*] called the characteristics of the "audiolingual habit theory" --audiolingual emphasis before graphic instruction, habit formation, and the automatization of habits through practice. It is clear that cognition can be combined with habit formation. It is possible therefore to speak of "cognitive habit formation" [Carroll 1971] and of a "cognitive audiolingual approach" (see Chapter 24).

The Cognitive Approach can be said to be located, in the methodological spectrum, between the center and the Traditional Method extreme. To judge from certain second language textbooks that claim to have a cognitive orientation, the Cognitive Approach is characterized by roughly the following procedures:

--All four skills are given about the same emphasis, although communication is a major goal.

--The teaching of accurate pronunciation is de-emphasized.

--Grammar is taught deductively, by first giving rules and then practicing them in meaningful situations. Habit formation drills are rejected, for language is not seen as a set of habits but as conscious, creative activity. The emphasis is on deduction and on contextualizing language as soon as the students' comprehension can be verified. There is much use of questions and answers.

--Vocabulary is emphasized from the beginning, as it is thought by some proponents of this approach that much vocabulary is needed in order to allow meaningful communication.

--Mechanical activities, such as mimicry, the memorization of dialogues, or the performance of drills, are avoided.

--The native language is used more than in the Structural or the Audiolingual Methods.

The Cognitive Approach is mostly a call to return to deductive teaching based on the view that language is "rule-governed behavior." But the rule-governed behavior of which generative-transformational linguists speak is unconsciously acquired and largely unconsciously engaged in, so it has nothing to do with second language behavior derived from the memorization of rules as in the Grammar-Translation Method.

The Cognitive Approach is the second language teaching approach most directly influenced by generative-transformational grammar. As a result, its procedures emphasize certain things at the wrong time and fail to emphasize certain things that should be emphasized, as can be seen in the preceding discussion of procedures.

Cognitive teaching continues to be done at some schools. However, it should be kept in mind that cognitive learning and habit formation are not mutually exclusive and that an ideal eclectic method would make use of both.

The Audio-Visual Method

Another direction that the anti-audiolingual reaction of the late sixties took was toward the Direct Method. By then the Direct Method had been supplemented by better visual aids, thanks primarily to such efforts as those in France by the Centre de Recherches pour la Diffusion du Français (CREDIF), which developed a variety of the Direct Method called the Audio-Visual Method.

Two varieties of the Audio-Visual Method need to be recognized. First, as developed by CREDIF and evident in the first edition of their *Voix et images* materials, there is the Audio-Visual Method used with classes in a French-speaking environment and with students of heterogeneous language backgrounds. Such materials do not make use of contrastive analysis and have few or no drills. Unfortunately, materials for students with a homogeneous language background, such as English, were prepared with an equal disregard for the native language.

A second variety of the Audio-Visual Method is that in which the materials, though making no overt contrasts between the two languages, are based on contrastive analysis and include both pronunciation and grammatical drills of various types resulting from that analysis. Such materials [e.g., Capelle and Capelle 1969] can also be said to be, in terms of the use of the native language (nil), Direct Method materials; but in terms of other considerations they can be placed between the Structural Method and the Direct Method, since they borrow from the Structural Method the contrastive basis and the drills.

The effectiveness of the Audio-Visual Method varies considerably with the ability of students to guess the meanings portrayed by the visual aids. Some students are good at this and seem to experience only minor comprehension problems; others are poor at guessing and seem to spend most of the classtime in great frustration, having to ask their classmates, after class and in the native language, what was going on. The Audio-Visual Method, even when the visuals are understood, can easily degenerate into speaking about what someone does on a filmstrip without involving oneself in the communication process. Even at its best, this method is clearly slower than the bilingual Structural Method or its descendant, the bilingual structurally-oriented Audiolingual Method, in producing communication skills.

The Bilingual Method

As a reaction to the slowness and relative ineffectiveness of the Direct Method and the Audio-Visual Method, Dodson [1967] proposed a Bilingual Method that makes considerable use of oral sentence translation (interpretation).

The Bilingual Method is based on the fact that all sentences are translatable, and that by translating them orally it is possible to greatly speed up the process of second language learning, both in conveying meaning and in ascertaining comprehension. The translatability of sentences should be self-evident. It is unfortunate, but not a valid counterargument, that the Grammar-Translation Method gives the wrong impression that sentences are translatable word by word, which they seldom are.

The claim of the Bilingual methodists is that there is a proper and specifiable role for translation in second language teaching. This is a limited but very important role. And there is no reason why the proper use of translation should lead to its misuse and overuse as in the Traditional Method.

Dodson conducted several experiments and concluded, from his studies and those of others, that the Bilingual Method leads to better and faster results than the Direct Method or the Audio-Visual Method.

The Total Physical Response

This is a Direct Method with a twist or two. Psychologist Asher [1977], after observing that young children acquiring their native language learn to respond first to commands, physically, and after further observing that the child's listening comprehension is always ahead of his speaking ability, decided to adapt these facts to the second language teaching/learning situation. This resulted in a method whose three basic principles are as follows: (1) listening comprehension should be developed before speaking; (2) listening comprehension can best be developed through responses to physical commands; and (3) learners will spontaneously start speaking when ready.

The use of commands to teach listening comprehension was pioneered by Palmer and Palmer [1925]. The way the procedure is carried out in the Total Physical Response is as follows: (1) the teacher gives a command and then carries out his own command; (2) then the class responds to the command, first as a group, then individually; and (3) at first the commands are very simple, but gradually they become very complex.

Asher has accumulated evidence from numerous experiments --in several languages and from kindergarten to college-- over a period of 20 years, proving the validity of this method for the development of listening comprehension. He has shown that listening comprehension as developed by this method is very significantly superior to that attained by other methods in a similar length of exposure to the language and equal or slightly superior to the listening comprehension of students under other methods after much longer exposure to the second language. There are films available showing this method in action.△

Probably the reason why the Total Physical Response succeeds so well in teaching listening comprehension is that it requires active responses. Involvement, some kind of active response, is essential to memory. Asher's studies have demonstrated "the powerful effect that the kinesthetic sensory channel has in making a second language learnable for most children and adults" [Asher 1977, Foreword].

Unfortunately, students exposed to the Total Physical Response make, when they eventually start speaking, numerous errors which have become fairly well engrained.☆ This should not surprise us, knowing what we do about subvocal speech and about the fact that such errors become engrained if they are not corrected from the start. But Asher has some strange notions about the speaking

---

△ Four films are available from Sky Oak Productions, 19544 Sky Oaks Way, Los Gatos, California 95030.

☆ I analyzed the sound track of the German demonstration film and found the speech of the students to be plagued with errors even after 30 hours of instruction.

skill. According to him, the ability to speak a second language cannot be taught directly [1977:26]. When students start speaking, after about 20 hours of exposure to commands, they are not to be corrected ("penalized"!) for their errors. Asher thinks [*ibid.*] that the distortions will gradually disappear --but why allow them to develop in the first place? As to pronunciation, Asher takes the defeatist attitude that "...the probability is extremely slight that one will achieve a near-native pronunciation if the language training starts after puberty" [*ibid.*] --a statement that is generally true of untutored second language acquisition but need not be true at all of second language learning that results from instruction.

Another basic weakness of this method is its exclusive reliance on commands, at least during the first 20-40 hours. Many basic language patterns, so common in any language that they should be taught quite early, are not commands --in fact commands constitute a very small minority of all utterances. The use of commands extends even to practice with abstract words. Rather than talk about justice and honor, Asher's students have the words "Justice" and "Honor" written on cards and ask each other: "Hand me *Honor*!" or "Pass me *Justice*!," something that might be fun as an occasional game but is totally unrelated to the communicative function of the words.

Another problem is that, unlike experimental subjects who get paid to do whatever the experimenter asks them to do, most school students are quite self-conscious about not looking ridiculous and would therefore dislike the idea of responding physically to commands, at least to certain commands that may appear silly to them; perhaps children in the early grades would be more willing to engage in such activities. Furthermore, physical response activity should be only one of several activities, and included among the others should be speaking; otherwise, there is no control over the silent speech of the students and they may be forming bad covert pronunciation and grammatical habits, through silent speech, that cannot be corrected by the teacher.

Despite its shortcomings, the Total Physical Response can make a great contribution to other, more eclectic and well-rounded methods. This contribution would be in the form of incorporating into other methods, especially during the beginning level and with some regularity, what has been called "audio-motor units" [Kalivoda *et al.* 1971] --that is, total physical response activities of five to ten minutes' duration. This would help enhance the listening comprehension of students taught by any method. Of course, many teachers have long used imperative drills as part of their pedagogical arsenal. (By the way, it seems that, for the purpose of kinesthetic activity aiding listening comprehension, audio-motor units do not require the students to act out the commands --apparently just miming them produces the desired effect.)

The Comprehension Approach

Asher has not been the only one to favor a method that would develop listening comprehension only for quite a while, before speaking. Gauthier [1963] had the students respond to questions in the native language first, until they felt confident enough to use the second language. Others favoring the teaching of only comprehension first are Winitz and Reeds [1973, 1975], and Gary and Gary [1978, 1980].

The problems we have already discussed --uncorrectable subvocal speech leading to the formation of bad habits, and the frustration of the students' desire to speak from the start, which is their greatest motivation-- apply to all comprehension methods. (A book of readings favorable to the Comprehension Approach is Winitz 1981.)

The Situational Method

A method in which emphasis is on situations and there are no grammatical explanations and very few drills has been advocated by some. As it is, the situationally-oriented Audiolingual Method did just that. Such a method may be suitable for young children in that they may not be capable of sustained structural practice or of understanding structural explanations. But older learners can do both.

Situations should not be emphasized at the expense of structure and structural learning should not exclude situational practice. The ideal method pays proper attention to both structure and communication (and culture). In fact, the Structural Method and all three Audiolingual Methods have made considerable use of situational material.

The Modular Approach

According to this approach, which can be used with any method, the program is divided into modules, which the student can take up in various combinations. This makes possible much second language teaching *à la carte,* according to the communication needs of each learner. For those who are not interested in options but in a general, standard program, most of the modules can be arranged in linear order for that purpose.

Given the fact that many students have specific reasons for studying a second language, the use of a Modular Approach makes sense. It could be used, for example, in English as a Second Language, to attend to specific purposes such as biology, police work, medicine, nursing, waiting on tables, etc. within the framework of a more general program.

The main problem with the Modular Approach is that it is not suitable for beginners. Basic skills must be mastered before the use of modules becomes appropriate. This means that the Modular Approach is only partially implementable by the intermediate level and not fully implementable until the advanced level.

Culture-based Methods

Some would place primary emphasis on culture and define second language courses "in terms of cultural themes or topics rather than the grammatical concepts 'covered'" [Strasheim 1981:68]. Supposedly this would be more highly motivating. But there is here the same distortion as in other methods --emphasizing one thing at the expense of another important thing or things. Second language teaching should not be a question of this rather than that, but a matter of teaching all three of linguistic, communicative, and cultural competence. Besides, although culture should be included in the second language program, culture does not offer, like linguistic structure, a logical basis for the selection and gradation of materials. Second language programs can offer interesting, challenging, and motivating cultural topics while at the same time centering their progression on a grammatical core.

Some would say that culture should be taught when we have the students, that is, in the first two years of secondary school or first year of college. But if it is taught to beginners, culture has to be taught in the native language --if this is in the form of occasional comments there is nothing wrong with it, but if it is a matter of general emphasis it is quite counterproductive, as there would be little *language* learning. Most students do not seem to be highly motivated by culture in any case, as what they want first and most is to develop the ability to communicate fluently and accurately in the second language, with cultural insights welcome only if they contribute to that goal.

Relevant cultural insights should be given from the start, and eventually cultural topics can be studied systematically; but *emphasizing* culture at the beginning level to the detriment of structure --when structure is far more important for communication-- is just as bad as rushing the students quite early into the second language literature, encouraging them to communicate with disregard for accuracy, or teaching them the language as a series of mechanical drills. All distortions are to be equally avoided.

The Neo-Natural Method

Terrell [1977] has proposed a "Natural Method" which has some interesting features. To differentiate it from the Natural Method of the nineteenth century, from which it diverges in several important respects, we shall call Terrell's method the "Neo-Natural Method."

The Neo-Natural Method is based to a considerable extent on a model of second language acquisition by adults in the language environment. Its procedures are as follows:

--Classes are used for communicative activities only, with emphasis entirely on content and not on form. This resembles the second language acquisition environment.

--To facilitate communication, the acquisition of a large vocabulary and the development of listening comprehension are emphasized from the start. (But a large vocabulary with very limited structural control is an open invitation to inaccurate communication.)

--Any practice of structure is done outside of class, in the form of carefully structured taped and written drills and exercises which provide the correct answers. (This is a good idea, but it is not possible in the public schools, where very little or no homework is assigned.)

--No errors are ever corrected in class. The idea is that the correction of errors interferes with the desire to communicate. (This of course reduces the motivation for not making errors and for practicing the homework exercises to the point of mastery. As to the effect of correction on the desire to communicate, there are ways and ways of correcting....)

--The students should feel free to respond in the native language, in the second language, or in any mixture of the two. (The possibility of responding at any time in the native language, however, would seem to reduce the motivation to learn how things are said in the second language.)

As shown by my parenthetical remarks, I cannot agree with most of these procedures. Yet I see much value in the idea that classtime should be devoted to communicative activities --not exclusively, but primarily. After all, it is only in the classroom that students in remote second language learning situations can engage in conversation in the second language. Explanations and structural drills and exercises can be made available on cassette tapes and workbooks for work outside class, so there is no reason for teachers to turn themselves into living tape recorders and spend most of the classtime presenting drills. At the same time, it seems that students benefit from having structural patterns introduced first in the classroom, where, if there is any confusion, it can be cleared up on the spot; then they can do the bulk of practice on their own.

The value of self-instruction combined with communicative activities has been confirmed, at least for outstanding adult second language learners, who indicated their preference for such an approach during a series of intensive interviews [Naiman *et al*. 1975]. Such an approach would seem to be of value for many second language students.

The newer psychologically-based methods

While all methods have had certain psychologically-based procedures, and while the Total Physical Response is largely based on psychological considerations, there are three methods --which have certain things in common-- which were designed by psychologists and psychotherapists and which reflect the ideas in those fields rather closely. They are the Silent Way, Community Language Learning, and Suggestopedia; they are the brain-children of, respectively, Gattegno [1972], Curran [1976], and Lozanov [1978]. The fact that there are so many psychologically-based methods now shows that, as linguists have become more theoretically inclined and have tended to move out of the field of second language teaching, psychologists and psychotherapists have moved in, exerting, for better or for worse, a growing influence, and proposing methods based on their theories.

The work of Gattegno, Curran, and Lozanov has in common the fact that they all attempt to reduce the psychological defenses of the second language learner as a condition to successful learning. All three also try to create in language classes a "community feeling" in which all students pull together and help each other. All three methods are "student-centered," emphasizing the attitudes of the students toward the teacher and the learning task and stressing self-reliance.

One problem with student-centered methods in which students have greater freedom but also greater responsibility is that only a small minority of students --mostly adults-- would really welcome the greater responsibility that such freedom entails. Most students prefer thorough guidance under a teacher who assumes full control. The maturity, self-reliance, autonomy, and responsibility that these methods require are shown mostly by adults --though by no means by all-- but by very few children. Language teachers who attend demonstrations of such methods should keep in mind that these tend to succeed because they (the teachers) are used to directing their own learning and are very interested in learning despite major demands and drawbacks that these methods may impose. In the normal school situation, pressures to pass, inexperience in self-directed learning, lack of high motivation, the need for order, the desire for efficiency, constant anxiety, all militate against these methods.

Any uncritical praise for these methods should therefore be taken with a large grain of salt.

The Silent Way

This method, developed by Caleb Gattegno, gets its name from the fact that, throughout, the teacher is almost totally silent, and oral production by the students is based on their discovery of what they should say, aided by charts and colored rods. Thus it represents a reaction to much teaching in which the teacher monopolizes class time, certainly a bad practice. But, like most reactions, it is extreme --it goes from excessive modelling to insufficient modelling, from a teacher who monopolizes speech production to a virtually silent one.

The Silent Way is a Direct method with special procedures. Typically a Silent Way course includes the following steps:

--The sound-spelling correlations of the language are learned by reading spelled out words aloud from a color-coded letter-sound chart (a "fidel"), sometimes starting with a native language fidel and then transferring that letter-sound knowledge to the second language. During this early phase, the teacher models each word at most once or twice. There is no direct imitation of the teacher, but the students observe each other's production and the differential feedback it gets --a nod or smile, or calling on another student--, so that in effect the students attempt to imitate the best production by another student. There is no direct correction.

--Words are read aloud from a chart. Again, as in the previous step, the teacher merely points at the words with a pointer but says little or nothing. The words read from the word charts may include numbers up to a billion or higher.

--Shortly after the reading aloud of words begins, the use of colored rods is introduced. These are rods of different colors and sizes that the teacher uses to get the students to produce various sentences involving, for example, spatial relationships, size comparisons, temporal relationships, and so forth. For a fairly long time, the word for "rod" may be the only noun used in the course.

--More advanced activities and materials are fairly standard and include in particular a series of carefully selected readings.

Throughout a Silent Way course, there is no repetition, no memorization, and no translation. Furthermore, such courses claim to subordinate teaching to learning, although at all times the teacher is very much in charge.

Regarding the rods, it is said that, unlike various objects, they give free rein to the imagination, as they can become anything that the speaker wants, that is, they have great representational flexibility. Still, I cannot see the point of spending many hours talking about colored rods. Sentences about rods, such as "Take a blue rod and a green rod and give her the blue one and give him the green one" [Gattegno 1972:42], or even far more complex ones, are the epitome of uselessness, regardless of the merits of their legth, diction, etc. For students to reach that level of syntactic proficiency by talking only about rods, they must have an unusual resistance to boredom. Equally useless are very long numbers [*ibid.*, p. 46]. The idea of occasionally using something neutral such as rods (or some other neutral object) for the imaginative generation of sentences is sound and should be part of a good eclectic method. But the idea that second language instruction should center for many hours around a single type of object is quite unsound, for such teaching makes even the simplest meaningful communication in the classroom impossible.

With regard to the four skills, Silent Way methodists emphasize speaking, of sorts (is reading aloud following a pointer and producing inane sentences about colored rods speaking?); they have virtually no listening, except to other students (remember that the teacher is silent over 90 percent of the time); and they introduce reading from the start and begin writing quite early. This is hardly an ideal emphasis or order of skills, because of the lack of listening to natives, the mechanical nature of speaking, and the early introduction of reading and writing with their deleterious effects (it is not enough to introduce sound-spelling correlations and practice them all for an hour or so).

The teaching of pronunciation is particularly questionable. Gattegno considers imitation a minor factor. But second language learners cannot invent the language --they must either imitate somebody or read it aloud, the latter having serious negative effects (even if errors are indirectly corrected, why put the students in a position where they will make many errors in the first place?). As it is, Silent Way methodology offers the worst of both --the students read aloud and imitate each other. The reading aloud, by the way, is not only misleading but lacking in natural rhythm, intonation, pauses, etc. If anything about second language pronunciation is true, it is the fact that we should never "encourage production of the student's own brand of the sounds," and yet this is what Gattegno [*ibid.*, p. 37] recommends. Students learn second language pronunciation best by imitating a good guiding and kindly correcting model, not by reading aloud and imitating each other, even if offered some guidance.

The fact that silence can be used effectively and that a learner can derive benefit from a brief utterance followed by silence should not be lost on us. A good eclectic method would benefit from the use of silence, from not submerging the learner in a barrage of second language utterances that make it impossible for him even to think clearly. In addition to leading us to reduce the percentage of teacher talk, the Silent Way can contribute, to an eclectic method, the idea of a "silent unit," a period of five to ten minutes, to be used two or three times a week, during which the teacher remains silent and elicits sentences from the students by means of various visual aids, objects, etc. Silent units could start at the late beginning level.

Note that while Silent Way methodists oppose direct correction, they do practice differential reinforcement. When a student says something correctly he gets a nod or a smile; when he says something incorrectly he receives a "reject call" and another student is asked to say it. (Of course, eliciting a corrected utterance from the erring student immediately, while he still remembers the criteria underlying his answer, would be better.)

Despite this feedback, there is generally too little guidance in this method. Most students need more direct expressions of approval or disapproval. Many students cannot handle all that silence without answers from the teacher. Few students can assume so much responsibility for their own learning --general skills may be there, but they need to be guided in acquiring the specific tools for second language learning. The Silent Way throws the students back on their own devices --but what devices? Second language teachers may have good devices, but the devices most learners bring to the second language learning task are largely inappropriate and should be replaced by better ones. The students should be shown what devices to use and how. The result of the insufficient guidance provided by the Silent Way is much frustration, which disappears only if the student decides to go along with this unusual method, despite its shortcomings.

The Silent Way asks students to rely on themselves in matters for which they need expert advice (pronunciation, etc.) and does not let them rely on themselves in matters for which they should (early sentence generation, which should be the result of modifying and combining model sentences in the mind, not of having words pointed out).

This method does not require active participation from any student. Students are allowed to be passive until ready to participate. This is another reason why the Silent Way would not work in high school or college --without being urged to participate, some students would not participate at all.

Gattegno has shown considerable lack of linguistic sophistication (and this is reflected in his method). For example, he talks repeatedly about the "feel" and "spirit" of the language, which are linguistically unacceptable vague terms. He refers to 21 English vowel sounds (!). His method lacks any scientifically-based control or gradation.

While Stevick [1976-a:135-47] has reported good results with the Silent Way, no carefully controlled experiments have been carried out. I seriously doubt that this method, with its various shortcomings, can develop in students linguistic and communicative competence efficiently and effectively, especially so in the case of school classes.

At the same time, we should not forget that the Silent Way can contribute two very useful concepts to second language teaching with an eclectic method --cutting down on teacher talk in general, and the "silent unit."

Community Language Learning

This method, developed by Charles A. Curran, is the application to second language teaching of Couseling-Learning, which is an overall approach to education developed by the same psychologist and based on the principles of nondirective counseling.

The basic procedure of Community Language Learning is a small group (six or so learners) recording session in which the students (called "clients") talk with each other in the second language and then listen to the tape recording they made, write the sentences, and analyze them with the help of the teacher (called "knower" or "counselor"). For these recording sessions, the students sit around a table and the teacher stands behind each speaker to help him as needed, moving to stand behind the next speaker, and so on. After the conversation has been recorded, the students first of all talk about the experience (in the native language), sharing whatever feelings they have about it. Then they all listen to the recorded conversation, first without interruption (a five-minute conversation may mean only 30 or so seconds' recording), and then sentence by sentence. During the latter stage, the sentences are written on the board and the students make their own copies. Then the teacher helps the students analyze the word parts, words, and structure of the sentences, after which the group is ready to start recording another conversation.

In the first or "embryonic" stage, the student says what he wants to say in the native language and the teacher standing behind him provides him with the second language equivalent, which he repeats and records. In the second or "self-assertion" stage the student tries to say things in the second language without waiting for the teacher's help, then he gives the class the native language equivalent. In the third or "birth" stage the student speaks independently in the second language and only gives the native language equivalent if another group member asks for it. In the fourth or "adolescent" stage, after much instruction, the learner is finally considered "sufficiently secure to take correction" [Curran 1976:30] --by then, of course, it is too late for most errors, which have become engrained. In the fifth and final stage, called the "independent" stage, the teacher provides, in addition to correction, better idiomatic expressions as well as stylistic insights.

The fact that students say what they want to say apparently makes their practice more meaningful and prevents fatigue. Herein lies a lesson for any method --at least part of the time second language students should be encouraged to say what they want, with help as needed.

Another important feature of Community Language Learning that can be part of any good method is the idea of letting the students, at frequent intervals, express their feelings and views about the second language learning process and the problems they are finding with it. Such opportunities to comment about classroom activities and their participation in them serve to clear the learners' minds of worries and conflicts and thereby facilitate learning. Of course, to be effective this has to be done in the native language.

Both the feature of allowing students to ask for second language equivalents (in the native language) to incorporate in their conversation and the feature of recording short conversations for analysis can also be quite useful within an eclectic method if used with moderation.

It should be noted, as H.D. Brown [1977] has pointed out, that the role of the teacher-counselor in Community Language Learning is too narrow in being so strongly nondirective --counseling psychologists do not agree that the role of a counselor should be nondirective. It is at the early stages, when he is most helpless, that the learner most needs direction. A teacher does not have to assume a nondirective role to be a good counselor. As Brown [*ibid.*, p. 368] put it: "...a teacher can assert himself, be a 'leader,' and even control the material and pace, and still be an excellent, empathetic, and understanding counselor." Lack of direction, the emphasis on self-directed inductivity, means that for weeks the students may be frustrated by confusion, until they begin to "see the light." This is perfectly avoidable. A structured course, unlike Community Language Learning, gives learners a sense of security, especially at the beginning when they most need it. At a more advanced level students can be more self-directed.

It should also be clear that by always letting students

say what they want, from the beginning, this method abandons the fundamental principles of selection and gradation. It also leaves the students without essential corrective feedback until an advanced state in their learning, when correction becomes remedial and ineffective.

As far as the use of this method in the schools is concerned, there are two practical shortcomings that make it impossible. First, small classes are required, of six or at most eight students each; very few schools can arrange that. Second, each small class must be directed by a teacher who must have several uncommon qualifications: he must be thoroughly bilingual, he must be excellent at consecutive interpretation and translation, he must be able to explain any aspect of the language at any time (as anything at all may come up at any time during the recording sessions), and he must be trained in counseling; such persons would be very hard to find. So Community Language Learning cannot be normally used in school teaching and must be reserved as one possible though defective way of teaching small groups of adults under expert supervision.

As to the results of Community Language Learning, I am not aware of any careful comparative research.

Suggestopedia

This method, developed by Bulgarian psychotherapist-educator Georgi Lozanov, is in current use in certain second language centers in Eastern Europe and the U.S.S.R.; it has also been tried in Canada and the United States. It is part of Lozanov's philosophy of learning, called "Suggestology."

Suggestopedia attempts to break barriers to suggestion, and therefore to inductive learning, by means of (1) the prestige and authority of the teacher, who is fully in control, (2) music, (3) dramatic readings, (4) a relaxed, living-room-type atmosphere, with soft lighting and comfortable armchairs, (5) the presentation of second language learning as a pleasant, easy, and natural activity, (6) techniques of relaxation, and (7) emphasis on communication, not accuracy.

The basic suggestopedic course has ten units, each with a long dialogue (75 sentences or longer); each unit is studied for six hours, for a course total of 60 hours. A total vocabulary of 2,000 items is taught in the course.

Students meet for four hours per day, four 45-minute classes plus breaks. For each unit, new material is introduced during a presession, during which the dialogue is studied along with its native language equivalent, a session (or "séance" or "concert") during which the dialogue is read by the teacher with two kinds of background music, and a postsession, during which the dialogue is exploited via questions and answers, role playing, and other elaboration techniques. There is no mechanical practice. The emphasis is on the memorization of vocabulary.

Neither the presession nor the postsession have anything different from widely used methods. It is the session or concert that is different. The concert consists of two parts, during both of which the students relax. In the first part, while the teacher reads the dialogue "solemnly, slowly, with clear diction" [Lozanov 1978:270], the students listen to it and to classical music of an emotional nature. "Between the first and second part of the concert, there are several minutes of solemn silence" [*ibid.*, p. 272]. In the second part of the concert, with books closed, the students listen again to the dialogue, this time read as normal speech, while classical music of a more philosophical nature is played. "At the end, the students silently leave the room" [*ibid.*].

The class is usually made up of six men and six women. They meet in a living-room-type area with pastel walls, soft lighting, curtains, etc. and sit in comfortable armchairs --the idea is to facilitate a relaxed atmosphere that fosters learning. This idea of a relaxing atmosphere could be used in any method (provided the relaxation is not so great that nothing is learned).

It seems that if anything makes any difference in the Lozanov method, it is the music. As he himself put it: "The active session [listening to the teacher read the dialogue without music] was dropped because it did not produce the same satisfactory results as the concert session" [*ibid.*, p. 269]. The music seems to be selected with some care [*ibid.*, p. 333], although there is in Lozanov's book no mention of any careful experiments to determine the effect on learning of various types of music. (His use of music with psychiatric patients led him to the conclusion that Baroque music has a very relaxing effect.) So Lozanov's major contribution to second language learning might be the finding (so far not experimentally corroborated) that relaxing music helps learning. But this is not a particularly novel finding, in view of the long-known favorable effects of certain types of music on industrial production (and plant growth, egg laying by chickens, and milk production by cows). Still, it would seem highly advisable for the second language profession to conduct controlled experiments on the effect of various types of music on different second language learning activities under a variety of conditions.

The dialogues, which are very long, are not to be memorized but just studied in class and read for 20 minutes at bedtime and for 20 minutes first thing in the morning [*ibid.*, p. 277]. These dialogues contain "one single idea featuring many themes, the way it [conversation] is in life," with "a lighthearted story running through" and a plot based "on the emotional content of the story," the dialogue roles having "definite character traits" [*ibid.*, p. 278]. The use of such long practice dialogues not for memorization but for listening, reading, and conversation may be the best contribution that Suggestopedia can make toward the elaboration of an ideal eclectic method.

In Suggestopedia there is no analysis but induction [*ibid.*, p. 276]. Errors are not corrected. The attitude of Lozanov is that accuracy will come "in due course" (we know, of course, that this is seldom the case).

Suggestopedia emphasizes the teacher's prestige, "which should create conditions for emotional deblockage" and "free the students of any oppressive factors and stimulate their progress" [*ibid.*, p. 334]. Unfortunately this "prestige" of the teacher is carried to the point of aloofness, for the teacher establishes no personal relationships with his students outside of the lesson.

Another good idea in Lozanov's method, one that should be incorporated in any method, is that of assigning to each student a new name and biography so that he can act out *that* life without fear of embarrassment or of having to reveal details about his real identity [*ibid.*, p. 275].

(It should be noted, however, that even though I have been pointing out good features of several methods that could be incorporated into a good eclectic method, Lozanov, Gattegno, and other dogmatic methodists reject the idea of having selected parts of their methods incorporated into an eclectic method; they insist that their methods --the Silent Way, Suggestopedia, etc.-- are indivisible wholes that should be adopted in every detail.)

As to Lozanov's claims, his book is very impressive, having over 1,000 bibliographical items in English and Bulgarian about neurophysiology and psychiatry --it has at least the trappings of serious research. But when one looks at the claims, which are outrageous, and at the evidence, which does not support them at all, the whole thing collapses like a house of cards. At one point it is said that memorization in Suggestopedia is 25 times [!] faster than with conventional methods [*ibid.*, p. 27]. Elsewhere it is stated, again without any supporting facts, that four times more new words (that is quite a reduction) are given per lesson (and presumably learned) in Suggestopedia than in other methods [*ibid.*, p. 322]. The only experiment reported in some detail [*ibid.*, pp.13-31], however, showed a difference of 21.5 percent in the number of memorized words; but if the unusually low performance of one of the control sections is discounted by comparing medians rather than means, the difference is reduced to 13.6 percent --well within the major Hawthorne effect that must have existed (the Hawthorne effect is the improved performance of subjects that results from the novelty and excitement of knowing they are participating in an experiment). Furthermore, the little experimentation that Lozanov and colleagues have conducted is pseudoscientific. There was no equating of groups according to aptitude and other pre-experimental variables. There is not even a description of the method used by the control classes. Moreover, to be valid, vocabulary retention studies should be tested on nonsense syllables, as Scovel [1979] has pointed out. (We should note, however, that studies in Canada [e.g., Racle 1975] seem to show that good results can be obtained with Suggestopedia.)

Another ridiculous claim made by Lozanov [1978:321-2] is that graduates of his course, with a vocabulary of 2,000 words or less, are able to read "any text." His claims for Suggestopedia extend to the learning of reading and mathematics in first grade [*ibid.*, pp. 323-31] and to all school subjects in the tenth grade [*ibid.*, p. 331]. Suggestopedia is also supposed to help relieve neurotic complaints [*ibid.*, p. 28], increase memory [*ibid.*, pp. 218-9], increase intellectual capacities [*ibid.*, pp. 219-20 and 228-32], decrease suggestibility [*ibid.*, pp. 221-2], improve health [*ibid.*, pp. 222-6], and reduce heart beats per minute and blood pressure [*ibid.*, pp. 226-8]. Of course, all of these may be the result of the (minor) beneficial effect of listening to good music, not much of a discovery.

This modern snake oil, with its outlandish claims that are not at all substantiated even by the "evidence," has justifiedly drawn strong reactions, as for instance that of Scovel [1979:257-8], who wrote that there is "precious little in suggestology which is scientific," for at best it has little to offer to modern eclectic programs, and at worst it is "nothing more than an oversold package of pseudoscientific gobbledygook!" And yet, even Suggestopedia has some things to offer us. While the concert session could not be adopted in most places, in others it could, so there should be research on the effect of good music on learning. The creation of a relaxed, pleasant atmosphere is a good idea. And as we have seen, both the long dialogues for comprehension and the use of new student identities can be made part of an enlightened eclectic method, the identities at the beginning of the program and the long dialogues beginning at the late beginning level (second semester of college).

The Communicative (or Functional) Approach

In Western Europe, and particularly in Great Britain, there has been an extreme swing from form to function in second language teaching, under the influence of Neo-Firthian linguists --Halliday in particular-- and several sociolinguists. This extreme swing is apparently in reaction to a distortion of structural teaching that ignored communication. The movement, which we shall call the Communicative (or Functional) Approach (it has also been called Notional and Notional-Functional), is not directly concerned with how to teach but rather with the content of instruction, in terms of the elaboration of syllabuses. For that reason, it is correct to call it an "approach" instead of a "method."

An analysis of communication is fundamental to this approach. A basic distinction is the difference made by Austin [1962] between the *locutionary force* or *conceptual meaning* of an utterance (e.g., "It's getting late" as a simple reference to lateness) and its *illocutionary force* or *functional meaning* (e.g., "It's getting late" as a suggestion to go home). The emphasis of the Communicative Approach is on illocutionary or functional meanings. In his analysis of communication, Hymes [1972] made a distinction between broad *speech situations* (parties, meals, fights, etc.), *speech events* (face to face conversations, lectures, farewells, etc.), and *speech acts* (making statements, asking questions, approving, regretting, warning, promising, etc.); whether an utterance is one speech act or another may depend on the circumstances in which it is said, on the relationship between speaker and hearer, and so on. Wilkins [1976:25-54] listed many "semantico-grammatical categories" of time, quantity, space, relational meaning, deixis (contextual reference); also "categories of modal meaning" and "categories of communicative function" such as judgement and evaluation, suasion, argument, rational inquiry and exposition, personal emotions, and emotional relations.

The unit of analysis in the Communicative Approach is not the sentence but the *communicative act* (also called "language act," "speech act," or "transaction") in the context of *discourse* or of a *text*. Communicative acts use groups of expressions for agreeing, disagreeing, praising, complaining, promising, apologizing, etc. There is no one-to-one correspondence between form and function. The communicative act of ordering, for example, can be realized by many different forms; conversely, a command form can convey not only an order but also an invitation, advice, an instruction, a prayer, and so forth. Within a given speech situation, moreover, several communicative acts can take place; thus, at the railroad station one may not only buy a ticket but also complain, invite, argue, suggest, deny, express fear or anger, etc.

The Communicative Approach is learner-centered, with the needs of individual students paramount. So the first step in implementing the Communicative Approach is to determine the needs of the learner; then one provides the language to meet those needs. The communicative needs of the learner can be determined on the basis of (1) the typical *situations* in which the learner will find himself, (2) the *roles* he will play, such as student, customer, etc., (3) the *topics* he will need to talk about, and (4) the language *skills* he will need to use[△] (the Communicative Approach is primarily associated with speaking, but some students may not need to learn to speak the language). Somewhat differently, Munby [1978] would base the preparation of a syllabus on a "profile" of communicative needs according to the following criteria: (1) the learner's *purpose*, (2) the *settings* where he will function, (3) the *social relations* he will engage in, and (4) the language *medium* (e.g., spoken), *mode* (e.g., monologue), and *channel* (e.g., via radio). Having obtained this information, Munby would decide on (5) the *dialects* the learner should master, (6) the target *level of command*, (7) the

----

[△] David Wilkins, at a May 12, 1981 lecture in Vancouver, B.C., Canada

communicative events he will need to participate in, each event analyzed into component activities, and (8) the *attitudinal tones* he must express or understand.

The Communicative Approach, as seen from the above, reduces structure to a very secondary role and organizes learning activities according to communicative acts. Among the exercises the students would engage in would be selecting appropriate introductions, forms of address or replies; practicing various ways to start and end a telephone conversation, to complain with various degrees of politeness, to refuse a request, to take leave, to disagree without offending; and so forth. In a limited way, such activities have long been a part of structural-situational methods; but here the emphasis is on style and variety. There is nothing wrong in such instruction --it is necessary-- but it is more suitable for the advanced level. At the beginning and intermediate levels we should be happy if our students can perform such communicative functions correctly in one or at most two ways.

The main problem with the Communicative Approach is that if teaching materials are organized according to communicative acts rather than structure, the students will be structurally quite confused. For example, if the unit deals with "Ways of Requesting Something" and the language is Spanish, the students would have to learn at the same time very different structures, such as:

Deme X, por favor. *(Imperative)*
¿Podría darme X? *(Conditional + Infinitive)*
¿Quiere darme X? *(Present Indicative + Infinitive)*
Quiero que me dé X. *(Present Indicative + Present Subjunctive)*
Me gustaria que me diera X. *(Conditional + Past Subjunctive)*

Teaching all these together is clearly inadvisable. And the only way they can be separated is according to structural criteria. Another example is the number of ways of asking permission to use a telephone which, in English, are at least 57 [Wilkins 1976:60-1], though such a list is not exhaustive. Obviously, all cannot be taught at the same time, especially considering their structural variety; the solution is to teach as models the few patterns involved, one or two at a time, and especially to teach the underlying syntactic rules that will allow the learner to generate them all. Only then, after form has been learned, can the student profit from a systematic consideration of stylistic factors (*ad hoc* stylistic instruction can of course accompany the learning of each pattern).

Another problem is that an accurate and detailed analysis of communicative needs *cannot* be made, despite the functionalists' claim that it can, for even for the individual learner one cannot predict with accuracy the situations, topics, and roles he will deal with. The problem is compounded by the fact that teaching is done in groups and must therefore be geared to the communicative needs of the group. Now groups, other than those having special purposes (to be discussed in the next section), have *general* communicative needs which are underlain by a basic core of structural knowledge. In the face of such general needs, the careful communicative act analysis of the Communicative Approach is rather useless, as much as it may be useful in the case of specific needs. In this, popular wisdom has the last word; when the average student is asked what he wants to learn he says "the language," a simple and perhaps unsophisticated answer that contains a fundamental truth: second language learning is primarily an attempt to satisfy general communicative needs, and particular needs must be grafted onto the tree of basic needs. Basing second language teaching on special needs is justified only when the study is going to be quite limited and there is pressure to use the language immediately for special purposes.

Regarding the relative importance of form and function, it is clear that grammar is what holds sentences together, so it is more basic than any formulation of communicative needs. Both are of course important, and neither should be abandoned or neglected for the sake of the other. The problem with organizing a syllabus according to content rather than form is that content (communicative acts) cannot be pinned down, is infinitely varied, lacks system, and does not lend itself therefore to the principle of gradation --unlike structure, which is fairly regular and systematic and allows careful gradation. As Brumfit [1980:5] pointed out, it is not possible to base a syllabus on an unsystematic, disconnected list; he concluded that "...it is difficult to see how any teaching system other than the grammatical one can be related to learning." Communicative acts, furthermore, cannot generate sentences; only the learner using the grammar can.

The basic problem with the Communicative Approach is then that it offers no valid criteria for selection and gradation, that is, for progression in a second language course or program --the very thing the functional syllabus is supposed to facilitate.

Still, some would make "the use of grammatical features subordinate to the achievement of communicative ends..." [Valdman and Warriner-Burke 1980]. This would be a serious mistake. What is hardly systematic (communication acts) should be based on what is sytematic (the structure of the language) rather than the other way around. Besides, there is a serious practical disadvantage in stressing communication at the expense of structure: learners who from the start are allowed to emphasize communication never quite bother to develop full mastery of the grammar. Rather than abandon the structural-situational syllabus, communicative functions should be added around its core.

Some have expressed many reservations about the structural syllabus. Wilkins, for example, devoted seven pages of a book [1976:7-13] to that. And yet, none of his reservations about the structural syllabus stands the test of even cursory analysis. On the other hand, the communicative syllabus is objectionable because (1) as noted, it presents ungraded structural diversity that is confusing to the learner, (2) there can be no progression from beginning to intermediate to advanced levels (this abandonment of the principle of gradation is perhaps the gravest defect of the communicative syllabus), (3) no objective measurement of proficiency is possible, and (4) there is fragmentation, with little or nothing to link materials with each other.

I have to agree with Widdowson [1978:35] when he said: "The work on notional syllabuses can best be seen I think as a means of *developing* the structural syllabus rather than *replacing* it...." The point for this development has been indicated by K. Johnson [1977] and Kennedy [1978], who recommended that the initial level of instruction should concentrate on establishing a structural and conceptual foundation, with functional factors such as stylistic appropriateness best left for more advanced stages.

The communicative syllabus, then, should be combined with the structural syllabus, with emphasis on structure during the beginning level and the early intermediate level shifting to emphasis on communicative function (stylistics, appropriateness, etc.) during the late intermediate level and especially the advanced level. Throughout, communicative activities should be seen in terms of the cyclical reintroduction of communicative acts and situations around a structural core. After all, it is structure that makes communication acts possible.

The notion of functional as opposed to conceptual meaning and the emphasis on the appropriateness of linguistic behavior are the most useful contributions of the Communicative Approach to second language teaching. Still, it should be kept in mind that educated adult speakers of any language are in possession of most such functional and stylistic skills and need only instruction about the particular ways in which those skills are applied in the second language. Another potential contribution of the Communicative Approach is a better understanding of the communicative process, especially conversation, something that linguists have not managed to do well.

In some quarters, the Communicative Approach, like other "new" approaches in their heyday, is being hailed as the solution to all problems in second language teaching. That it is not. It should be considered a fresh point of view, another contribution to enlightened eclecticism, an eclecticism that should be structurally, situationally, and functionally conceived.

As to objective evaluations, after several years of this movement there aren't any. As Stern and Cummins pointed out [1981:223], the language studies and second language teaching changes brought about under the Council of Europe are not backed by empirical research --indeed, some of their prime movers are contemptuous of research.

Second Languages for Special Purposes

While the communicative needs of school and college students cannot be determined precisely and must therefore remain general, those of specialists in various trades and professions can to a considerable extent be specified, especially in regard to vocabulary and idioms. It is here that the Communicative Approach can make its greatest contribution by providing an analysis of the communicative needs of specific occupations. Special materials for doctors, policemen, social workers, waiters, and accountants would be more motivating for them, as they would be more relevant.

The question is: Should there be separate Special Purpose courses for each occupation or can Special Purpose materials be incorporated into a general program as modules? Both seem to make sense depending on the circumstances. If (1) the amount of time available is *very* limited, and if (2) the group is homogeneous as to occupation, then Special Purpose courses (or minicourses, really) of a limited nature would seem called for. But people of all occupations need to function in the language as a whole; they cannot be restricted to a very narrow list of communicative needs. Even scientists, for example, need to use everyday English if their sojourn in North America is longer than a few days. A Special Purpose course can teach someone to drive a particular linguistic automobile in a particular one-way street and without the inconvenience of traffic signs or even traffic --but is that learning to drive?

Where the time available to the learner is not very limited or where a group is heterogeneous in regard to occupation, the only approach to special purposes that makes sense is to offer Special Purpose materials as modules within a general program. This can be done beginning quite early in the program.

Incidentally, within the Special Purpose movement there is a trend to ask teachers to prepare themselves Special Purpose materials for various occupations. Second language teachers cannot be expected to do this. How can a language teacher prepare special materials in business, medicine, or atomic physics? He is not qualified. Authentic materials already available should be used, adapting them in order to simplify them linguistically.

The Intensive Approach

Along with individualized instruction, minicourses, and the teaching of other subjects in the second language, one of the developments of the seventies was the emphasis on intensive courses. They were not an innovation, only a new emphasis. Intensive courses were proposed in the nineteenth century by Gouin (five hours a day for six months) [L. Kelly 1969], gained favor in the United States during World War II, both under the American Council of Learned Societies and as the Army Specialized Training Program, and have since then been used with considerable success at the Foreign Service Institute, the Defense Language Institute, and certain universities. Intensive courses allow the completion of the equivalent of one semester's college study in as little as three weeks (and unlike the concentrated use of, e.g., alcohol, they don't cause serious negative effects).

Roughly, second language learning goes by the number of hours devoted to it, whether concentrated or spread; but if they are spread, and especially if they are spread too thin, much forgetting can take place that does not occur in intensive courses. The slow program, with its three to five hours a week and its long summer breaks, dilutes the cumulative effect of the study effort.

Intensive programs have several distinct advantages, as follows: (1) there is prompt evidence of achievement, an important advantage with North American students, who want quick results; (2) linguistic data --words and rules-- occur at much closer intervals, this frequency of occurrence and contiguity resulting in better recall and internalization; (3) relationships within the language can be seen more clearly; (4) there is lower program attrition, as students register for longer sequences at one time, and it may also be that a higher percentage goes on to enroll in upper-level courses [Benseler 1976]; and (5) earlier entry into intermediate and advanced courses is made possible, among other things allowing students to major in two fields.

Characteristically, intensive courses have 15-20 hours of class per week plus at least as many hours in lab work and home study. Four semesters can successfully be offered in one [Frank 1973 and my own experience], with results being statistically equivalent to the slower program. Other characteristics of intensive programs are small groups of students, ideally five to nine [Horne 1970], although this is not essential; an emphasis on the spoken language; and team teaching (again, desirable but not essential). A monolingual approach is in no way inherent to intensive study and may in fact retard it. Students should not be allowed to take any other courses concurrently with an intensive second language program [Kalivoda 1975].

Intensive courses demand well-motivated students; they simply do not work well with poorly-motivated ones. Ideally there should be careful selection of the students for intensive courses on the basis of aptitude. If they cannot be screened via an aptitude test, at least there should be self-screening based on explaining to all prospective students how demanding the program is. Success with intensive courses without screening students has been reported [Frank 1972, 1973, and my own experience], but low-aptitude students are bound to have serious difficulties. The solution, when screening is not possible, is to allow the poor students who are not doing well in the intensive course to transfer to a slower program --in that way they would not hinder the progress of the better students and at the same time they would not be forced to drop out, wasting all their efforts up to that point.

Ideally, intensive courses at the intermediate level should be followed by a stay in a second language region or country. Upper-level courses can also be offered on an intensive basis [Hirschmann 1975]. At the advanced level, intensive courses should cover interdisciplinary areas of study.

Materials for intensive courses should not contain very long dialogues or other texts for memorization --there is little time for "digesting" 30-sentence dialogues in an intensive course [Sacks 1967]. Intensive materials should make as much use as possible of recordings, workbooks, and other devices that allow individual study, leaving classtime primarily for communicative activities. (A recent review of intensive second language teaching was done by Conner [1977:97-100].)

Foreign Languages in the Elementary School (FLES)

The teaching of second languages as school subjects in the elementary school (kindergarten to grade six) started in the fifties, saw its greatest popularity in the sixties and declined rather quickly in the seventies. (The reason why FLES is introduced here rather than earlier in this chapter is to allow ready comparison with the Immersion Approach, which is discussed in the next section.)

FLES --of which some programs still flourish-- is based on the premise that second languages are learned better if they are started early, that is, before secondary school, and if they are continued into secondary school and college. There is no quarreling with the value of continuity and articulation; but the early start argument was doubted all along by many. Carroll, for example, wrote in 1960 [p. 13] that except perhaps in the area of pronunciation, it is doubtful that young children are better or faster second language learners than older learners, given the same opportunities and amount of time. Perhaps young children are better at *acquiring* languages than adults, who in turn seem to be better at *learning* languages as school subjects; since FLES is the treatment of the second language as a school subject, it puts young children at a disadvantage. The argument for an early start seems to be based on weak notions such as nativism and child development --acquisition notions misapplied to a learning situation-- and not on solid facts about the second language learning behavior of young children in the classroom.

Since in a learning situation the adult has certain definite advantages, it seems that the second language teaching of children should start when children have begun to exhibit some of the learning characteristics of adults, while still retaining the advantage of greater facility in pronunciation. The characteristics of adult learning begin gradually to manifest themselves at about age 10 and are firmly established by about age 14; within this same period, pronunciation ability (in terms of unguided imitation) begins to deteriorate, so that good imitation ability is rare after age 13. It seems logical, therefore, that the study of a specific second language should begin at the midpoint between these two trends, that is, at about age 12. At that age, children still are reasonably good imitators and have also developed the ability to learn consciously and efficiently; a disadvantage is that at this age children are particularly self-conscious.

But perhaps any discussion of the "ideal" age to start second language teaching is not particularly relevant. As Stern [1963:22] pointed out, FLES does not need to be based on the conclusion that an early age is the optimum age for beginning second language study --it is enough to show that it is a good time to begin, a time that has certain advantages even though it may also have certain disadvantages. With the right kind of program and good teaching, young children in school *can* learn a second language.

Early-age FLES, however, has largely failed. In a large scale British study evaluating ten years of experimental French teaching in the elementary schools, it was found that an early start (age eight) was not cost-effective, as it did not produce better results than a later start (age eleven) [Burstall *et al*. 1974, Burstall 1975]. A still larger survey, the International Educational Achievement Study for French [Carroll 1975], showed that an early start in elementary school was not advisable.

The reasons for the failure of most FLES programs are many, and some of them are behind the failure of other movements as well. We shall list some, not necessarily in their order of importance:

--Failure to define goals and means.

--Shortcomings in the training and certification of teachers; particularly starting programs without qualified teachers.

--Neglect to secure the support of administrators and

parents.

--Unstructured teaching. If attention is not paid to structure and if elementary school classes are just a lot of fun and games, it is no wonder that children are left with a linguistic hodgepodge. There must be careful selection and gradation.

--The abysmal failure of language program articulation. Having several years of school without studying the language they started earlier, or being placed with beginners in secondary school did more damage to FLES students than anything else.

--Insufficient use, misuse, and overuse of technology such as language laboratories.

--Insufficient class time; a second language cannot be learned well on the basis of three 20-minute periods per week.

--Inadequate materials. They should introduce structural teaching, in the form of drill-games if the program starts before age ten; by age ten the materials can be, other than in topics and vocabulary, like secondary school materials in methodology [M.J. Brown 1965].

A viable alternative to FLES would be to offer, beginning in grade three or four, an extended exploratory course. (Exploratory courses have already been discussed in Chapter 10.) There are at least two reasons why this would be desirable. With an exploratory program children could learn the sounds and some vocabulary and expressions in several languages while they can still do this well via imitation. They can also be led to form positive social attitudes toward foreigners at an age when they are still very impressionable about peoples and cultures. Then, beginning in junior secondary school, they could go beyond this general experience to specialize in a particular second language and culture.

The Immersion Approach

For the last fifteen years, especially in Canada but lately also in the United States and elsewhere, there has been much research and activity on the Immersion Approach, according to which a second language is the language of all school activities for several years beginning in kindergarten, with the native language gradually becoming again dominant in the classroom, side by side with the second language.

For a most obvious reason --greater exposure-- immersion programs produce better results than the teaching of the second language as a regular subject in the curriculum [Stern 1976, Schools Council Committee for Wales 1978]. For the same obvious reason, total immersion produces better results than partial immersion [Swain 1978-a] and even a short stay in a second language community can be beneficial.

Parents and educators have questioned the effect of immersion on cognitive development and native language proficiency. But it has been shown that first-grade children taught exclusively in French as a second language show transfer to their native English in reading and have no decrement in their ability to speak English [Lambert and Macnamara 1969]. Furthermore, immersion students quickly catch up with monolingual students in native language skill and may even surpass them by grade five or six; they do as well as monolingual students in the subjects taught in the second language; cognitively, they do as well in IQ tests and may in fact function better in certain cognitive areas, such as creativity [Swain 1978-b]. In addition to this, they have the important benefit of becoming partially bilingual.

There is, however, a fly in the ointment. Although immersion students develop native-like comprehension skills, their productive skills leave much to be desired. They develop a faulty interlanguage [Selinker *et al.* 1975, Spilka 1976]. After six years of immersion their speaking and writing are so defective that serious syntactic errors such as Frenglish **J'ai mangé les* are not infrequent [Harley and Swain 1977, 1978]. Where the second language is more complex than the native language, they simply opt for the pattern found in the more familiar native language [Swain 1978-b]. Their second language contains persistent basic errors, even though they are fluent in it [Politzer 1980].

This is not surprising. When communication is made the only criterion, accuracy almost always goes out the window. Since many errors don't interfere with communication or fluency (and errors are left uncorrected in immersion programs), they become habitual. To make matters worse, immersion students are expected to acquire the second language within learning conditions --the classroom-- which do not resemble acquisition conditions (being surrounded by second language speakers in the environment).

Where a single child is immersed in a classroom made up of native speakers of the second language, he does not develop a pidgin but learns to speak and write accurately

[Macnamara *et al.* 1976]. For that reason, some immersionists have suggested that the solution to the problem of inaccuracy in immersion programs is to bring into the second language classroom some native speaking children. This is wishful thinking. Unless the native speaking peers vastly outnumbered the acquirers, they would tend to accept a pidgin and the result would be substantially the same as now. Others have suggested increasing the opportunities for communication in the second language outside the classroom; but this simply would not be enough to counteract day-long and year-long use of a pidgin.

The Immersion Approach will continue to be defective as long as it relies exclusively on acquisition. The only solution is to combine immersion exposure with formal teaching, a solution proposed by Stern [1976]. Such teaching, starting in grade three, should include structural instruction in the form of drill-games [Cohen 1976], and should in particular include the correction of errors --both techniques designed to counteract interference and overgeneralizations and foster grammatical accuracy.

Total immersion should not be used with older learners, who benefit primarily from a learning, not an acquisition, approach. Being completely surrounded by a second language in an immersion situation can be quite traumatic for a beginning older learner, as he is completely unable to express himself. For older learners, beginning and intermediate second language learning should be via formal teaching, preferably intensive; then, at the advanced level, they can be immersed in the language, preferably in its natural environment.

Is there a "best" method?

Many methods and approaches have been discussed in this chapter and many more, whose acceptance has been only limited, have been left out. Among this myriad methods, is there a "best" one? How is it possible for each method to be the one true and best method, as their proponents claim?

Stevick [1976-a] considered this question and came up with "The Riddle of the Right Method," which in part consists of the fact that very different methods can get good results. Perhaps the answer to this part of the Riddle is that most methods have some good elements, and if these are used to their fullest potential by highly qualified teachers, the results are usually good.

Second language teachers find themselves in a difficult

position. They are asked to commit themselves to methods totally, in a kind of commitment most other mortals reserve for political or religious ideologies. Such a degree of commitment is not reasonable and should be resisted, precisely because in second language teaching there are so many methods, with so many overlapping claims and counter-claims, and especially because there is something good in most methods. This is not to say that teachers should go to the other extreme, be totally uncommitted, and consider second language teaching a field in which "anything goes" and in which one should "do his own thing" --some procedures are more successful than others, and some are even most successful of all for the particular objectives they aim at.

It does not help matters to have certain scholars droolingly approve every new method or approach, nimbly jump to the head of every bandwagon, and irresponsibly claim that older established procedures such as mimicry, minimal pairs, and structural drills are discredited activities that belong to the Middle Ages of second language teaching. Our profession can advance only through careful development and is only hurt by wild faddism.

Given the fact that there are different student and teacher goals, it should be clear that there cannot be a single best method, for all methods must fit specific goals. The best method for any set of goals is then that method which most successfully reaches the agreed-upon goals. Since in general second language programs there are certain things --quite a number in fact-- that all students must learn, that must be learned in a certain way and in a certain order, pluralism, the individualization of goals and means, cannot apply to these. There is such a thing as too much pluralism, which can lead to pluriconfusion and a pluriheadache.

Given general goals, then, and certain general learner characteristics, logic tells us that there must be a best way whereby most students can attain those goals. There may be several good ways, but only one best way, and this best way is most likely to be one that combines the best that other ways have to offer.

Some of the characteristics of good second language teaching have already been discussed throughout this book. Further characteristics that the best method would have to have are the following:

--It would concentrate on practice in the use of the language, from mechanical to creative.

--It would make use of several cognitive strategies, given the fact that students differ in this respect, and it would take into account various student attitudes.

--It would adapt itself to the needs of non-average students.

--It would be unashamedly "artificial." There are no "natural" methods of second language teaching and we should desist from trying to discover them. The very use of the second language in the classroom by speakers of another language is inherently artificial.

--It would try to enlist the students' consent for its procedures. This is not too hard. Fortunately (or unfortunately!) second language students will consent to almost anything.

--It would not emphasize one or two procedures to the exclusion of many other good procedures. If a method does that, a warning flag should go up. There are principled reasons for emphasizing certain procedures and avoiding others at certain times, of course, but the validity of the reasons for emphasizing or avoiding anything should be carefully examined.

--It would not, for example, emphasize fluency at the expense of accuracy or accuracy at the expense of fluency in the program as a whole, as much as it may be necessary to do so at particular points.

--It would concentrate primarily on teaching and learning, and only secondarily on being interesting and entertaining.

--It would be eclectic, incorporating the best from various methods and approaches and combining these elements into a harmonious and effective whole.

--It would combine all three types of syllabus: structural, situational, and functional (communicative).

--It would not require the teacher to sustain on a regular basis a great amount of preparation and a high level of effort; no teacher can do that for more than a few days, considering that he may have to teach as many as five or six classes a day.

--It would make teaching with the method conditional upon the necessary professional training and preparation. Most methods that have seen their heyday and then faded away owed their disappearance to the fact that teachers were hastily trained or re-trained, misused the methods, and brought discredit to them with the poor results they obtained.

Enlightened eclecticism is the only reasonable way out of the present profusion of conflicting methodologies.

We know a great deal about second language teaching/learning, but we have failed to harmonize it and combine it into an effective system. Our failures, then, are not due to a lack of knowledge but to a lack of wisdom [Stevick 1976-a:105]. It is a lack of wisdom which leads some, for the sake of "purity," to remain strictly within one method, and others, for the sake of a misunderstood eclecticism, to practice a "curricular hodgepodge" [Morrow and Strasheim 1977:90]. The wise teacher will avoid either extreme. Rather than settle in Audiolinguia, Cognitia, or Terra Incognita [Stevick 1976-b], the wise teacher will pitch his tent and then build permanent quarters in Eclectica Illuminata. (Some proposals for an eclectic method appear in Chapter 24.)

In the final analysis, the best method is the most effective one in reaching stated goals. Methods should be judged by the end results, not by how they start or how they proceed during the early stages. The test is what percentage of beginning students graduate from the program with the ability to use the second language fluently and accurately, and of course how quickly they get to that point.

Teachers should look objectively at results. They should not let themselves be swayed methodologically by brilliant demonstrations conducted under favorable conditions by prestigious and charismatic advocates of this or that method. If they attend demonstrations, they should observe, not participate themselves, for participants get carried away by the momentum and novelty of it all and lose much of their objectivity.

The ultimate judgment about methods must come from research. Only carefully controlled experiments in which methods are used *at their best* can provide reliable results that can be used for methodological decisions, both in terms of particular procedures and of methods as a whole. Any method whose proponents avoid research or carry out hasty, poorly controlled research should therefore be considered suspect. Whoever develops a really good method will not be afraid to submit it to the impartial verdict of careful experimental research.

13

FROM FORMAL ACCURACY TO FLUENT AND ACCURATE COMMUNICATION

Linguistic competence and communicative competence

Linguistic competence, the ability to use the "machinery" of language both mechanically and creatively, is distinct from communicative competence, the ability to understand and convey comprehensible messages. They are distinct but not independent. Communicative competence largely depends on linguistic competence, as linguistic accuracy greatly facilitates the communication process. That is, linguistic accuracy does not guarantee communication but it is largely what makes it possible.

Communication is concerned with *what* is said, *why, when, to whom,* and *where*. Manipulation (mimicking, drilling, etc.), on the other hand, is concerned with *how* things are said. Effective communication necessarily includes a high degree of linguistic accuracy, but it is not the *mechanical* production of accurate sentences. As Savignon [1972:66] put it, communication "is the sometimes slow, sometimes painful, sometimes non-verbal exchange of thought between human beings."

Many second language teachers have taught mechanically, without attention to communication, perhaps because they did not know how to teach or test communicative skills. In the last decade or so, many scholars have gone to the other extreme, emphasizing communication and saying that mechanical practice and correction are unnecessary [e.g., Jakobovits 1970-b, Holley and King 1971, T. Mueller 1971-a, Oller 1973-c]. But if students are neither drilled nor corrected, how are they going to develop the ready control of structure that is essential to communication?

Anyone, by emphasizing communicative activities, can produce students able to communicate. But how do they communicate? In a very defective interlanguage that is offensive to native speakers and often unintelligible. Is this what we want? The trick is to have communication with accuracy --not communication alone or accuracy alone but *both*. Involvement in communication is a necessary but not sufficient condition for second language learning;

there must also be attention to form. The needs of language teaching in this respect were well expressed by Stanislawczyk and Yavener [1976:49], who said that excessive behavioristic guidance "leads to 'linguistic lockjaw,' while too much freedom brings unauthentic expression."

Accuracy and errors

Accuracy means conforming to a standard, the standard being the way educated native speakers express themselves in the language when not self-conscious, discounting unsystematic performance errors. (When native speakers are self-conscious, as in front of a microphone, they often produce artificial, overcorrect forms.) The standard for accuracy is then systematic performance.

Palmer [1922, 1964:64] enunciated the principle of accuracy, which consists in not allowing opportunities for inaccurate work by restricting the students to those activities in which accurate work can be reasonably expected. Habits of accuracy have to be developed from the start and maintained throughout the program.

There are three main reasons for fostering accuracy in second language teaching/learning. First, any error reduces the redundancy of a message, sometimes drastically, thereby reducing its comprehensibility. Second, most errors are from mildly to strongly offensive to native speakers [Piazza 1978, 1980, Politzer 1978, Guntermann 1978, Chastain 1980]. Since morphological errors seem to be more irritating to them than syntactical ones, it should be clear that inaccuracy causes more negative reactions than incomprehensibility [Guntermann 1980]. Successful communication of an inaccurate kind is highly stigmatized by native speakers, even to the point of social ostracism in certain *milieux*. Even pronunciation errors, which seldom interfere with the conveyance of the message, can cause considerable irritation in the native listener, apparently more so than grammatical errors [Tardif and d'Anglejan 1981]. The third reason for fostering accuracy is that most students want to be accurate and because of that want to be corrected. Most students want to be corrected *all the time;* they especially want correction of their pronunciation and grammatical errors; and they want to be corrected more than their teachers feel they should be [Cathcart and Olsen 1976]. Perhaps the students are trying to tell us something.

Consonant with Palmer's principle of accuracy, we should not allow early free speaking, which results in linguistic monstrosities. Free communication should be a natural outcome of what has preceded it, not an activity for students who lack yet the linguistic skills to perform it. Premature free speaking leads to reliance on the native language, as the student does not know enough of the second language to generate accurate sentences based on it. Premature free communication can, for that reason, be bewildering and frustrating to the student who wants to be accurate. Even when limited free speaking starts within the well-planned program, it should be restricted to the areas under control, refer to familiar ideas, and be kept quite simple in structure.

But many would abandon the principle of accuracy. There are many who say that "It is by making mistakes that we learn not to make them," and that "Only by going into the water can we learn to swim." To these "cheap proverbs" Palmer [1922, 1964:65] would oppose others, such as: "It is by making mistakes that we form the habit of making them"; or, "He who has not learned to swim will drown when thrown into deep water." Students cannot "generate original and meaningful sentences" [Diller 1971:6] from the first day of class without being grossly inaccurate, for the generation of sentences requires a knowledge of structure. This would be going into the water without the least idea of how to swim. Instead, the students should first develop a good degree of mastery over the sound system, and then use in limited communication activities each morphological and syntactical rule and each lexical item after it is learned.

If one starts by forgoing native-like performance, his students will not get anywhere as near to it as if one sets it up as the goal for at least those students who want to reach it. Native-like control of what has been covered is an attainable goal for many students; but usually none reach it when there are no standards of accuracy. These standards cannot be said to exist when the students are told to aim merely at making themselves understood.

Unrehearsed creative speech presupposes considerable language study. Even the practice of having students carefully prepare dialogues and present them to the class is inadvisable unless there can be close supervision for accuracy throughout; otherwise they may say and write incorrect sentences a good number of times before they can be corrected. Students should not be allowed to derive "confidence" from the inaccurate use of the language.

Errors and their correction

In recent years there have been at least four attitudes toward errors. The first one, which we might call *traditional*, holds that errors are bad and show ignorance and lack of application on the part of the student; if he were a good student he would not make errors.

The second attitude, which can be called *structural*, consists in seeing errors as an unavoidable result of the clash of the two language systems; they are unavoidable but not to be "accepted" and left uncorrected. Unavoidable errors, also to be corrected, result from the creative use of the language, which is needed for the internalization of rules. The limitations of these rules may not be learned unless errors are corrected. Perhaps this position was best expressed by Nida [1957:22], who said that learning to speak a second language and to play the piano are similar in that both require practice and both have the making and correcting of errors as an integral part of the process.

The third or *behaviorist* attitude, typified by early programmed materials, places great emphasis on the avoidance of errors; errors are bad, as they lead to bad habits, and therefore they should never be given a chance to occur. This attitude is not only unrealistic, since errors are unavoidable in any relatively free use of the language, but has led to the development of mechanical materials with excessive use of repetition and very simple, mindless drills.

The fourth attitude towards errors can be called *cognitive-communicative*. According to this attitude, errors are not viewed negatively but as evidence of learning and learning strategies, as exponents of the "learner's system." Such an attitude, which would be justified in reference to acquisition but not to learning, has led to the rejection of correction and to the proposal that the second language teacher should stop correcting errors, that is, should discard "the role of *deficiency expert* to assume the less judgmental role of interlocutor" [Galloway 1980].

Three arguments are advanced against correction:

(1) It has negative psychological effects, leading the learner not to risk talking. This is by far the most frequent argument. It is faulty, because if correction is done properly these negative psychological effects do not occur. *Not* correcting errors can have the negative psychological effect that the learner is bewildered because

he does not know when he is speaking correctly and when not; if this is continued it results in loss of confidence in the teacher and the program.

(2) Correction is not a normal part of communication. This can be countered with the obvious point that classroom communication is not normal, natural communication, but at most realistic communication in an artificial, *learning* environment.

(3) The native language acquirer is not corrected for his structural errors. True, but the two situations are very different. The native language acquirer has many models, intensive exposure, and much social pressure to conform linguistically; the second language learner has none of this and therefore needs explicit linguistic feedback if he is going to avoid developing error-laden speech.

Without correction students either feel insecure or develop a false sense of security that leads to the fossilization of a pidgin. Mostly the latter is the case, as lack of correction leads to the belief that one has spoken correctly.

Most students want the teacher to exercise "quality control," that is, to correct errors. Their desire for correction outweighs their desire not to be embarrassed. It is better to put up with the more or less enthusiasm-deadening effect of error correction than let students feel uneasy, without feedback, and eventually feel demoralized with the terminal discouragement of errors that have become habitual.

We should therefore view errors as evidence of failure of some sort, due to either not having learned thoroughly what was taught or having ventured too far out of what is known. Since they are failure, they call for remedial action [Allwright 1975].

Errors will not disappear by themselves under classroom conditions. They must be counteracted. Error-laden interlanguage is characteristic of immigrants but should not be allowed to develop in second language learners, who would have little reason to improve it once it has been accepted as a vehicle for classroom communication. Usually and persistently inaccurate speech is not a necessary prelude to accurate speech, although each rule is likely to be used inaccurately when first used in communicative activities. If accuracy is emphasized from the start, persistently inaccurate speech will not have a chance to develop and become established.

Of course, it is unrealistic to try to correct all

errors, especially during communicative activities --it has been estimated that an error of some kind occurs in the second language classroom every 15 seconds [Fanselow 1977]. Furthermore, overcorrection during communicative activities would indeed result in reluctance to speak, at least for some students. So all errors should be corrected during the presentation and manipulation phases of the teaching cycle, but only major errors during the communication phase. But communication acts riddled with errors should not be rewarded --students will not learn to communicate accurately if they know that during communicative activities "anything goes."

The tendency will be for students to make more errors during the communication phase than during the manipulation phase. (Simultaneous interpreters, for example, cannot work well when they become involved in what they are saying.) If that tendency is not checked by correction, a faulty interlanguage will become established.

Regarding what errors to correct during the communication phase, a possible criterion is comprehensibility. On the basis of this criterion, Burt and Kiparsky [1974] have suggested that *global* errors, which "violate rules involving the overall structure of the sentence" and may greatly affect comprehensibility, should be corrected, while *local* errors, which affect a particular sentence constituent and usually do not interfere with comprehension, should be corrected later or be left uncorrected. It is clear, however, that comprehensibility can be only one of several criteria for correction. For one thing, an indulgent bilingual teacher and a pidgin-speaking class can understand much that sounds very wrong, and at times incomprehensible, to a native speaker. Such speech should not be allowed, even if "understood." Bilingual second language teachers cannot be good judges of comprehensibility, so error correction based on the criterion of teacher's comprehension would be too lax.

A multiple-criterion hierarchy of error correction would include the following criteria:

(1) Errors that interfere with the intelligibility of the message to a monolingual native speaker.

(2) Errors that are unacceptable --irritating-- to native speakers.

(3) Errors involving rules that have already been taught.

(4) Frequent errors of any kind.

(5) Errors resulting from venturing into linguistically unknown territory, especially those showing native language

interference.

If an error is not systematic, that is, if it is a *mistake*, it should be ignored. Native speakers also make mistakes in terms of pauses in the wrong places, repetitiousness, false starts, etc. *Distortions*, errors with what is supposed to have been learned, because it has been taught, should always or nearly always be corrected. *Faults*, errors involving linguistically unknown material, should be corrected sparingly, if at all; here the student is really taking a stab in the dark and cannot be expected to be right. To minimize faults, linguistic adventurism should be actively discouraged, even by penalizing it if necessary, and frequently reminding students that creativity is fine, yes, but within the limits of what they know. Students should not worry about learning how to say what they haven't studied yet; instead, they should concentrate on using to the fullest extent possible what they have learned, and using it accurately.

As to the rare acts of real communication in the second language program, for instance, conversation with a visiting native speaker, such moments are too precious to be interrupted by any correction. The teacher should silently note errors and bring them up later.

Correction should always be done in a kind, matter-of-fact, polite manner that is supportive and not condemnatory. The student should perceive it as clearly applying to the task, not to himself as a person. The tone should be nonthreatening, one of providing information rather than disapproval. There should never be ridicule or embarrassment. If these attitudes prevail on the part of the teacher, no student who wants to be guided in the learning process will resent correction. If the affective feedback is always positive and the communicative feedback is usually positive, there is no reason why negative linguistic feedback, even if fairly frequent, should do any psychological harm [Vigil and Oller 1976].

Many teachers have faulty techniques for error correction. They think that all that is needed is for them to repeat the utterance correctly and for the students to imitate that. But when an error is not clearly isolated from the stream of speech the student may imitate the correct utterance without realizing where or what the error is. Thus, it is more effective, in the case of a student who says incorrectly, in German, **Das war ihres Auto,* to say only "Agreement" or *Auto...?* and let *him* produce the correct *Das war ihr Auto;* if that doesn't work, then only *ihr...* should be given.

Generally, it is better not to provide the corrected utterance for imitation (except perhaps for phonological errors), for the imitation of an utterance is a very passive process. It is better to elicit, by cueing it, the correct utterance from the student; this leads him to internalize the criteria for correct speech rather than depend on the teacher. Whenever possible then, students, who are not Skinnerian rats, should be allowed and enabled to correct their own errors, being provided by the teacher with the correct utterance only when they cannot correct themselves.

Errors during the communication phase can sometimes be corrected by paraphrasing accurately what the student tried to say. Stevick [1980:132] gave as an example the following:

Student: *It's a 12-stories building.
Teacher: Ah, a 12-story building!
or
I'm sorry, did you say a 10-story building or a 12-story building?

While some students may respond to such indirect correction, others will need to be corrected more directly.

Unless for some reason it is not possible to do so, errors should be corrected on the spot, though not interrupting the student in the middle of an utterance --wait until a natural pause at the end of a sentence constituent or at the end of the sentence. Summarizing and reviewing errors at the end of a communicative activity is not very effective --by then the students have forgotten (or filed away for future use) the false hypotheses that led them to make the errors in the first place. If used sparingly, the Community Language Learning technique of recording a brief conversation and then having the students correct the errors themselves is motivationally positive, although because of the time lapse just discussed it may not be very effective.

Teachers should be consistent in correcting errors or their students will become quite confused. The students should have a clear idea of whether the activity they are currently engaged in involves correction of all errors, of only the most important ones, or no correction at all.

A useful teaching/correction technique, if used in moderation, is for the teacher to make errors and have the students correct him. This can be effective in giving the students an awareness of their typical errors. Such an activity should be clearly labelled and conducted as a corrective rather than an imitative one.

Humorous errors occur fairly often. There is nothing wrong in laughing at them, as long as it is clearly understood that you are not laughing *at* the student but *with* him.

It has been shown that students frequently misunderstand corrections of errors by their teachers [Allwright 1975, Chaudron 1977]. This underscores the importance of making corrections quite clear and explicit, as opposed to very indirect.

Frequent errors should be used by the teacher as examples for corrective explanations and remedial drilling in the classroom. It also helps individual students if their frequent errors are noted by the teacher on diagnostic charts.

With respect to who should correct the errors, it should not be only the teacher. In certain activities other students can be encouraged to correct the errors of their peers. But most important of all, the student himself should be trained to notice and correct his own errors. Self-monitoring can be taught, by shifting from (1) teacher correction, to (2) correction of and by peers, to (3) teacher-elicited self-correction, to (4) independent student self-correction.

On the importance of communication in second language learning

Many second language programs make very few communicative demands on the students. This is a serious mistake. We should not be satisfied with mere manipulation, even communication-like manipulation. Our students must have practice in realistic and real communication.

There are four reasons why communication is important to the second language program. First, communicative activities are needed to internalize the rules, to make them unconscious. No one can be said to have learned a rule until he can use it correctly in communication, with his attention on the message. Second, whatever is used in communication is remembered better, whether a rule, a vocabulary item, or a fact, for it becomes integrated into one's cognitive system. Third, there isn't a magic transfer from drills to communication outside the classroom. If there is going to be transfer to situations outside the classroom, there must be communicative activities in the classroom. Fourth, communicative activities are highly motivating.

The method and materials must therefore be such that second language students are exposed to much communication, despite whatever linguistic and personality shortcomings their individual teachers may have. Although communicative activities come logically at the end of each teaching cycle, they should be considered not a side-show but the "main event."

Evidence of the value of communicative practice

That attention to the communicative function of language results in better internalization of rules was shown experimentally some years ago [Oller and Obrecht 1968]. A group of students whose manipulative activities included frequent reference to meaning performed better than a group in which there was little or no awareness of meaning during drilling. (Of course, this compares two extremes; the happy middle consists in starting with mechanical manipulation and then moving on to meaningful manipulation and communicative activities.) In another experiment [Jarvis and Hatfield 1971], practice in which the students had to tell the truth was found superior, in developing first-semester productive skills, to manipulative practice of a mechanical nature. Another study [Joiner 1974-a] showed that real communicative practice in which new information was transmitted yielded superior results than communicative practice based on known facts. In a recent study [Bialystock 1979-b] it was found that functional practice --the use of the language-- was the main factor in second language achievement.

Perhaps the most extensive research of recent years about the teaching of communicative competence and its results is the work of Savignon [1972]. She showed that if 20 percent of instructional time in first-semester French is spent on communicative activities this results in very significant superiority in communicative competence over classes spending the same 20 percent of the time in the language laboratory or in cultural activities in the native language. Of course, this is not very surprising, as what the students practice is generally what they learn. Obviously, if a group engages all semester in communicative activities it will be better at that than a group that does not. There was no difference between the groups in *receptive* linguistic competence or on the course examination. Probably the accuracy of the experimental group's communicative acts was not very good --it doesn't seem to have been considered.

From presentation to communication

Failure in second language teaching is in part due to the tendency of forcing students to use the language too soon for too much. Such early emphasis on free communication is "like teaching a novice climber to ascend Mount Everest by making him climb it before he has practised on any other mountain" [Dodson 1967:58].

Activities that normally require the use of a certain grammatical feature should therefore be postponed until that feature has been learned. Unaided hypothesis testing is undesirable, because the classroom offers two few opportunities for the correction of such hypotheses. In fact, certain basic hypotheses, such as that of general native language-second language equivalence, have to be actively discouraged.

Unlike the young child, who acquires the language as he communicates, the second language student cannot learn well simply by communicating; instead, he communicates with what he has learned.

Progress in second language learning should be measured in terms of an increasing capacity to communicate fluently *and* accurately. Our aim should be freedom within structure, for total freedom in the second language classroom, far from being productive, leads to chaos.

Relevant to this discussion is Rivers' [1975] distinction between "skill-getting" and "skill-using." The first of these refers to learning the mechanics of the language, that is the "forging of the instrument" [Rivers 1968:163-7], and the second refers to the use of the language instrument to express personal meaning. It is like the contrast between learning to play scales on the piano and being able to improvise music, as the two extreme ends of the process. It is *code-oriented learning* versus *message-oriented* activities. (Note, however, that communicative activities can be code-oriented. It depends on the focus of communication. Role-playing is code-oriented if the focus of the activity is not on content. Skill-using can be code-oriented, as when a student "explains" a cartoon to his teacher [Butzkamm and Dodson 1980].) It is as if the student were building, with the teacher's help, a language "machine," except that each part of it is put to use as soon as it is built and added to the partially assembled machine.

Some mimicry, memorization, and mechanical manipulation

is essential, as the point of departure in the sequence that leads to communication. Lower-level tasks such as agreements, paradigm choices, etc. must be automatized if the student is to be free to pay attention to higher-level planning and self-monitoring. Perhaps the biggest problem in second language transfer from form to communication in many programs is that the students have not learned the forms well to begin with.

Learning forms well means that, at least at the beginning of the teaching cycle, rules must be temporarily abstracted from communicative contexts so that they can be fully attended to, without the distraction of message-oriented activities. Then, after some practice, they should be placed again within communicative contexts, as this is necessary for their complete internalization. Many students, however, dislike skill-getting practice and want to substitute cognitive and communicative activity for it. Such activity gives the impression of quick progress, but it is a false impression. It is quick "progress" at the expense of a sound foundation.

Between mechanical skill-getting, during which forms and structures are selected consciously and are the focus of attention, and creative skill-using, with conscious attention to meaning and unconscious attention to form, there is a considerable gap. In this gap there should be bridging activities during which conscious attention is paid to both form *and* meaning, something that is difficult but possible and, moreover, necessary. Without bridging activities of this nature, the sudden shift from structure to communication leads the students to rely on native language habits. The bridge consists of teaching the innovative use of mechanical skills, in the form of increasingly more challenging and freer manipulation.

The gradual shift from conscious attention to form only to conscious attention to meaning only can be described as having five steps, as follows:$^{\triangle}$

(1) *Attention to form only*. This includes pronunciation drills before meaningful work, and the imitation of dialogue sentences and grammatical sample sentences. (This is presentation, followed by understanding.)

(2) *Primary attention to form, secondary attention to meaning (but no communicative function)*. This refers to drills, both mechanical and contextualized. Even in the

---

$^{\triangle}$ Partly based on Littlewood [1980], who proposed only four steps.

case of mechanical drills students should know what they are saying, although no drill is a communicative act. (This is mechanical manipulation.)

(3) *Attention to both form and meaning (about equally)*. Here we find directed communication (cued and patterned response), dialogue variations, meaningful exercises (translation, noncued response and directed discourse), student-generated exercise sentences, and structurally-graded descriptions. "Student-generated sentences" refers to an activity in which the students produce without help sentences similar to those in the preceding drills and exercises, that is, containing the same grammatical rules. It should be clear that this step (3) is the most important one in bridging the gap between structure and communication. (This is communicative manipulation or meaningful exercises.)

(4) *Primary attention to meaning, secondary attention to form*. This includes both guided and free classroom communication situations, free response, free rejoinder, free completion, free association, and conversation. Most of this would be realistic communication, but some real communication is also possible.

(The various activities listed above are discussed in Chapter 17.)

(5) *Attention to meaning only*. This belongs mostly outside and beyond the second language program, as the teacher's functions of control and correction are not exercised. It is all real communication.

Each of these steps builds on the previous one(s): mechanical responses cannot be given correctly without a proper presentation, meaningful exercises cannot be performed correctly without mastering the lower-level mechanical responses, and communicative activities cannot be engaged in accurately without previous successful performance of mechanical drills and meaningful exercises that give automatic control over lower-level rules. Because these steps build up on top of the preceding ones, failure of a class to perform well in any step should mean going back to the preceding one; for example, failure to perform well in meaningful exercises should mean going back to making more choice-making mechanical drills. Merely explaining the rule again is largely useless.

Each teaching cycle --that is, the series of steps followed in teaching each rule-- should include communicative activities at the end. Students should not be expected to practice drills for two or three years in order to eventually communicate. Some communication should occur in every class period, from about one fifth of the time at the early beginning level to about four fifths of the time at the late advanced level (where most of the time should be spent on student discussion of outside reading and writing assignments). When beginning and intermediate students know that they are going to put language to communicative use at the end of each teaching cycle, they are going to be much more willing to patiently go through drills and exercises first.

So it is not a question of meaning rather than form or communicative rather than linguistic competence; it is not a question of "rathers" but a matter of "ands" --both form *and* meaning, both linguistic *and* communicative competence. The trend to eliminate drills is a serious mistake. Drills are essential to efficient rule internalization. The trend to de-emphasize structure as a whole is equally misguided. If structure is emphasized through the early intermediate level (that is, the first three semesters of college), communication can be emphasized from the late intermediate level on, with the advantage that accuracy is by then built in, having been emphasized from the beginning.

As to the teacher's role in all this, it should be clear that he cannot continuously dominate the classroom without repressing self-expression on the part of the students. The solution is for the classroom to be teacher-centered for those activities that emphasize structure and student-centered for communicative activities.

We shall now discuss steps (1) to (4) in a little more detail.

Step 1: Imitation with attention to form only

It is difficult to imitate accurately when one's attention is diverted to the meaning of the utterance. For that reason, in pronunciation drills (during the initial phonological minicourse), in dialogue presentations, and in the presentation of grammatical sample sentences there should be at first, for each utterance, pure mimicry. Then accurate imitation is rewarded by giving the students the meaning of the utterance.

Techniques for facilitating good mimicry will be discussed in Chapter 15 ("Teaching pronunciation") and Chapter 16 ("Dialogues and other presentation devices").

Mimicry, memorization, and modification gradually evolve into the generation of sentences via unconscious rules (habits). There is empirical evidence that dialogue memorization and variation are a good starting point for communication [Veidt 1973]. And of course learning short natural dialogues set in realistic situations has much greater transfer to real-life situations than producing such useless and dull sentences as "This is a pen" or "This rod is blue."

Step 2: Drills with primary attention to form

Drilling can be defined as concentrated manipulation of a grammatical relationship to bring it to the point of automatic use in short-term memory, later to be transferred to automatic use in communication. Drilling usually consists of a series of drills. A *drill* can be defined as a small set of stimuli and response sentences based on a single model and manipulating a single grammatical relationship between the stimuli and the response sentences.

Learning to respond correctly without conscious attention to the rules is the goal of the manipulation phase of the teaching cycle (steps 2 and 3). Drilling is essential to learning a second language --the only option is whether it will be done in the classroom or with recordings. Free communication without previous drill work will be full of errors and lead to the formation of bad habits. Control over language structure must be automatic or it is useless. In the communication act there is simply no time to constantly and consciously look for the right sound, the right form, and the right syntactic rule.

Understanding a rule is only the first step in internalizing it. As Bolinger [1968] put it, "to imagine that drills are to be replaced by rule-giving is to imagine that digestion can be replaced by swallowing." At the same time, we should recognize that drilling without awareness of the rule is of no value unless the rule is so simple that it can be efficiently learned via induction through the drilling.

Some scholars, many teachers, and many students are opposed to drills. Perhaps the main reason for this opposition is that many behaviorally-oriented scholars and teachers have made excessive use --sometimes exclusive use-- of very simple, repetitive drills of the kind that would make learners feel childish and like mindless parrots. Most "pattern practice" fell under this category of types of drills. It is no wonder that "pattern practice" was found not to involve the student, unlike conversation, as shown by measurements of heart rate, galvanic skin response, and breath rate [Brière 1971]. Repetition (and substitution, which isn't much more than repetition) should be minimal in second language teaching. One just cannot ask linguistic adults, who are used to learning by reasoning, to set aside their thinking powers and become passive automatons in order to learn a second language.

Fortunately, there are many types of drills, a good many of which are quite challenging. So the objection of the teacher that he finds drills boring, and the objection of the students who, if given a choice, will say they don't need drills, can be overcome. The students should not have a choice in this matter. This is something they need to do. If they object to drills, all that is needed to convince them of their usefulness is to teach a rule without drilling and then correct them for every error they make in the ensuing communicative activities [Paulston and Bruder 1974:41]. By making successful completion of the drills a condition for freer activities, the likelihood of the former is increased by the desirability of the latter, according to Premack's principle in psychology, which says that "of any pair of responses or activities in which an individual engages, the more probable one will reinforce the less probable one" [Craighead *et al.* 1976:115-6]. It would also help to explain to the students the rationale and importance of drilling.

For the sake of effective learning --and of the sanity of both teachers and students-- it is essential that almost all drills should involve choice-making situations rather than being largely repetitive. With substitution drills, students respond quite well and so teachers congratulate themselves --"Good, they are learning"--, but the students are learning hardly anything. Drills, for example, that deal with only one morphological element are not only boring but they don't teach anything, since for anything to be learned there must be a contrast, a change, a choice. It is far better to start with a choice of two of the morphological elements of a paradigm and then add one or two at a time. To the rather vacuous objection that this involves testing, not teaching, I have three things to say: (1) to be challenging, anything must be a test of something; (2) choice-making is teaching/ learning via closely guided and delimited trial and error, so although the first item or two may be responded to incorrectly, through immediate correction of these and through further trials learning does take place, and rather more quickly and effectively than with simple "pattern practice"; and (3) if the student is going to be able to function in unstructured situations, he must be able to make many choices very quickly, in preparation for which he needs almost exclusively practice in making those choices, not repetition and substitution in which one obviously right response is produced.

Challenging drills include correlation, replacement, four types of transformation, and response drills. (They are discussed in Chapter 17, with further examples given in Appendix B.)

Drills should not be performed without an awareness of the meaning of their sentences. To make sure that the students are paying some attention to meaning, all that is needed is to ask occasionally for an individual translation of a response sentence. This attention to meaning is of course minimal and in no way turns drills into communication. Drills are not intended to be communication. Trying to make drills communicative makes them neither good communication nor good drills. It is better to drill first, then do meaningful exercises, then communicate. In other words, communication should follow mechanics, contextualization, and personalization. (Of course, one or two free responses can be elicited after every drill or two, as this would enhance attention.)

Step 3: Meaningful exercises and other activities with equal attention to form and meaning

In these activities, the students respond or generate sentences while their attention is drawn to meaning rather than mechanically. This means that, while the teacher retains his corrective function, he should somewhat relax his control. Step 3 activities are not free, for they are carefully chosen and conducted so as to elicit repeatedly the rule being learned.

These activities are the true bridge between mechanics and communication. The main possibilities are the following:

--Answering and asking questions, though not freely. These should be questions about what has been studied. Of course, such questions are not *real* interrogatives, for the teacher is not asking the questions in order to learn the answers but in order to find out if the students know the answers [Coulthard 1977:81]. These questions should still be code-oriented, primarily, rather than message-oriented (message-oriented questions and questions relating to students personally belong in step 4). The students should be encouraged to ask a question whenever they answer a question.

--Modifying a dialogue or a text previously learned. This can mean acting out a dialogue with various modifications in content, style, emotional tone, etc.; telling lies about a dialogue or text and having the other students react; retelling a dialogue or text in one's own words; and so forth.

--Direct and indirect translation. Indirect translation would include creating directed dialogues according to instructions in the native language and participating in interpreting situations.

--Generating sentences. This includes free substitution, where a syntactic model is followed; producing additional sentences for drills; producing sentences by providing a missing sentence in a dialogue, creating a whole dialogue role, or creating a whole dialogue to incorporate a given sentence; completing incomplete sentences, with either content words or the end of the sentence missing; producing sentences on the basis of key words from a dialogue or text; producing alternate ways of expressing the same idea; and so forth.

--Describing objects, persons, actions, or visuals. The latter can be anything from famous paintings to photographs to wordless cartoons.

In all of these activities, the rest of the students can be kept alert by being asked, once in a while, "What did he say?"

These activities remain exercises, as they should, as long as attention is on both form and meaning in reference to one or two structures. If attention is allowed to center primarily on meaning, then the exercises become communicative activities, belonging in step 4.

Step 4: Communicative activities with primary attention to meaning

Although most of these activities are fairly free, they are not completely free, for even in this step in the cycle the teacher should make an effort to elicit the latest rule taught --not mechanically, of course, but in the context of communication; he should also offer some correction of errors.

A basic distinction we must make in talking about communication is between *real* communication used to carry out one's own communicative goals, (e.g., asking a question because one does not know the answer, because one wants to know the answer, from someone who may know it), and *realistic* communication, where no particular communication goals are carried out (e.g., asking a question *as if* one didn't know the answer). Within the second language classroom, most communication is realistic rather than real. Realistic communication, however, seems to have a high degree of transfer to real situations, so it is fully defensible.

There should be immediate, short-range, and long-range communication goals in the classroom, as having a variety of goals will prevent discouragement. Most students enroll in second language courses quite unaware of how difficult it is to learn to speak in a second language, for they have forgotten the years of concentrated exposure it took them to acquire their native language. So they should be periodically reminded that they are making good progress within what is a major and lengthy undertaking. The best way to convince them that they are making progress is to turn to earlier material for a while.

In order to foster communicative competence, every bit of material, every exercise, every activity, whether auditory, or oral, or graphic, should result in oral production. Every opportunity should be used for short conversational exchanges. At the beginning these should be kept *very* simple, so as not to lead to inaccurate fluency, but gradually they can increase in complexity and length.

Four things are needed by the students in order to communicate in the second language classroom: (1) motivation, the desire to express oneself, (2) a supportive teacher and classroom atmosphere, (3) the control of needed structures and expressions, and (4) a variety of communicative activities.

With respect to the first of these, one cannot expect too much, considering that some students are uncommunicative and reluctant to speak before a class even in the native language. But most if not all students will express themselves when they have something significant to communicate and if they are listened to. For that reason, it is important to find out where their interests lie, and to allow them considerable input into the communicative process.

Regarding the role of the teacher during communicative activities, it is typical of inexperienced teachers and native paraprofessionals to let the conversation class degenerate into a monologue by themselves, because they don't know how to make the students talk. The teacher should talk little during communicative activities, and gradually less and less. His function is primarily to offer direction, guidance, and correction, not to talk himself. The verbal "noise" in the classroom must come mostly from the students, not from the teacher.

Regarding the classroom atmosphere, it is up to the teacher to create a sense of community, which is necessary, for hermits don't communicate. It helps if the teacher assumes a relaxed, friendly attitude, as if he were talking with friends in his living room. He should show interest in what the students have to say. When he says something himself, he must carefully grade it so that his language will not go beyond the ability of the students to understand it. He should not interrupt the students with corrections but elicit corrected utterances after a natural pause has occurred.

The students must be provided with certain expressions needed for communicative activities, such as "Can you say that again, please?," "Speak slowly, please," "It's my turn," "I'll play the part of X," and expressions for disagreeing, praising, showing enthusiasm or disappointment, and so forth. They should also be taught how to simplify language without using it inaccurately --by means of circumlocution, reliance on gesture and other extralinguistic devices, and the avoidance of difficult optional rules. Paraphrasing is particularly important, as frequently they will draw lexical and grammatical "blanks" both in reception and production.

Limited use of the native language should be allowed during communicative activities. The students should feel free at any time to ask how X (a native language utterance) is expressed in the second language, or even occasionally just insert a native language word in the sentence and go on. Savignon [1972:66-7] found that the intermittent use of the native language contributed to a relaxed relationship between the students and to essential group rapport, thereby predisposing the students to communicate in the second language. She found [*ibid.*, p. 69] that, rather than being damaging, occasional use of the native language saves the train of thought from being interrupted, reduces tension, and allows a floundering discussion to develop a new direction.

Communicative practice should be structured, otherwise only the class extroverts participate. No student should be allowed to develop the "Igor Complex," which we can name after an ESL student at UCLA who dominated class conversation [Allwright 1977]. It is quite demoralizing to the other students.

The person who directs the communicative activities, be it teacher, paraprofessional, or private tutor, needs to be fully aware of what the students have learned so far, to any point in the program, in terms of vocabulary and grammatical structures. For this purpose, it helps greatly to have printed lists of the vocabulary (including idioms), grammatical points, and situations already met by the students. Such lists should also be made available to small conversation group leaders.

Before performing a communicative activity, the students should be given an explanation and if necessary a demonstration of it. In the case of simulations, for example, a sample performance by the teacher and some of the best students would serve to guide the rest of the students in their performances.

Communicative activities require small groups, so classes of more than seven or eight students should be divided into groups. The advantages of splitting the class into small groups are as follows: (1) there is more communication with greater individual participation, as five or six students can talk at once, as opposed to only one in full-class activities; (2) it is highly motivating to the students; (3) the teacher has to divide his attention among five or six units only (the groups), not 30 students, with no loss of control; (4) teacher-student relationships are improved by the fact that the teacher serves as guide and counsellor, not as the only fountain of knowledge; (5) conversation is more natural; (6) everyone has to pay attention, as in a small group it is impossible to doze off; and (7) everyone gets to participate within a reasonably short period of time. There can be problems, of course, such as students who are too shy to participate or students who talk too much; but group pressures usually take care of such problems.

Crucial to the success of small groups is the teacher choice of group leaders. Although for some activities the groups can select their own chairmen, for most communicative activities it is advisable that the leaders be selected by the teacher. (The teacher should also select the members of each group, and change them as needed.) The group leaders should exert both organizational and monitoring leadership, although all students should be encouraged to monitor and correct (according to guidelines) the speakers. The leader's personality is more important than his being the brightest student. This means that the student with the most suitable personality for group leadership may not be the best language student in the group, in which case the group leadership and the monitoring function should be assigned to two different students. The functions of the leader are to get shy students to participate, to limit the participation of extroverts, and to help the weaker students. The functions of the monitor are to correct errors and to provide second language expressions upon request.

If possible, the teacher should meet with the group leaders before each communicative activity, to explain clearly what is expected of everybody. Each activity should also be demonstrated to the class as a whole first, using the best students as model participants. If it is a simulation, for example, the steps would be: (1) division of the class into small groups, (2) description of the simulation (if necessary in the native language, for it must be understood) to the whole class, (3) demonstration of the simulation with some of the best students as participants, (4) performance of the original simulation twice, in the groups, by rotating the roles, and (5) performance of variations of the simulation as suggested by group members.

One problem that can arise is that small groups can, if not closely supervised, settle for what is basically native language conversation with a sprinkling of second language words. This can be avoided by (1) choosing group leaders carefully, (2) sending students around as "reporters," and (3) the teacher himself visiting groups unpredictably.

Some simple activities can be performed in groups quite early. Most activities, however, require a good foundation in the language and should be delayed until the intermediate level and beyond. Teacher flexibility is essential, to change an activity if it is boring or too difficult.

The rest of this section is a listing of communicative activities. They are grouped according to type, not according to level of difficulty.

--Activities for specific structural purposes. These include, for example, activities to practice the use of the past tense, such as telling the events of one's day, describing a trip or vacation, and discussing past events such as news items or historical narratives. Another example is activities designed to practice the asking of questions, such as interviewing a student who plays the part of a famous person, interviewing a student about himself, the game of Twenty Questions, extracting instructions from a student, etc.

--Situations and role-playing (the difference between them is that in situations the students play themselves and in role-playing they play the part of other characters --both are simulations). The situations to be used should be of interest to the students; it will be found that after a while this requirement can best be met by letting the students themselves propose most of the situations. Among the frequently used situations are ordering a meal at a restaurant, shopping, asking for directions, and so forth. An interesting situation is a job interview where a woman is told that she is qualified but would be paid less than a male. Various telephone conversations can also be used effectively. For a challenging situation, have the student as a guest in a Texan home where the main dish is rattlesnake steak [Di Pietro 1978-b]. The possibilities for situations are only limited by the imagination.

Regarding longer-lasting situations and role-playing, some of the possibilities are an imaginary trip through a foreign country [Hollingsworth 1977], converting the classroom into a place of business --with numerous roles-- for a day (it can be a restaurant, a store, a bank, etc.), computer dating, an airplane trip, a country fair, and so on. The key to a successful long-term role-playing activity is to involve as many students as possible in a realistic situation in various types of roles --businessmen, professionals, scientists, politicians, newsmen, etc.-- in which they are to resolve various problems and carry out various tasks. J. Taylor and Walford [1972] offered a treasure of role-playing activities for the classroom. An example is "Front Page," where students are assigned the various reportorial and editorial functions for the publishing of a daily newspaper. The simulated operation of a radio or television station can present the same challenge. The playing of roles assigned to the students at the beginning of the program, as in Lozanov's Suggestopedia, presents many opportunities for communication. The students can also take the roles of ongoing characters in dialogues or the roles of characters in reading selections as the basis for interviews, discussions, etc. Discussions between public figures with opposite views can also generate much communication; for example, think of the possibilities in confrontations between Voltaire and Billy Graham, or Ronald Reagan and Fidel Castro.

--Oral reports. These can start near the end of the beginning level. They should be at first only a few sentences in length. They should be the basis for discussion, otherwise they just give the class listening practice. Questions from the other students may be guided by providing a series of key words, pictures, etc. Meloni and Thompson [1980] have written a good article about oral reports.

--Debates and panel discussions. These can start at the intermediate level. Because few topics hold the interest of most students, the students should be consulted about what topics they wish to discuss. One topic that seems to be of almost universal interest is male-female relations. We have the advantage, over teachers in other subjects, that we can use any topic; but the students should not be asked to discuss in the second language what they could not or would not want to discuss in the native language. The choice of topics is not limited by linguistic considerations (beyond a certain foundation) because "any topic may be treated at any degree of linguistic difficulty" [Stevick 1971:65]. Topics should preferably be assigned in advance, so that the students can be prepared to contribute their ideas.

--Stories. The students can retell a story in their own words or provide variations for stories (alternate endings, etc.). They can also be given just the beginning of a story and be asked to complete it collectively, each student contributing part of the story.

--Visual aids. Comic strips without words can be used, asking the students to vary the lines in successive interpretations. The students can be asked to tell the story of a wordless cartoon or of a photograph or painting that depicts a situation (many of Norman Rockwell's paintings are useful for this). Visuals open to several interpretations stimulate conversation. A visual with a sound track, previously heard, can be played without the sound track, letting the students improvise the narration. Captions can be removed and replaced at will from projected slides if two projectors are used, one for the picture and the other for the caption [Berwald 1977]. The overhead projector can be an excellent device for triggering oral expression [Pond 1963, Carter 1974]. Pairs of students can be given series of pictures, only some of which match, and without seeing each other's pictures be asked to describe them and find out which match [Nation 1977].

To develop fluency, the students can be asked to provide a running commentary for a short film or filmstrip while it is being played (note, however, that this is difficult even for native speakers); the performance can be taped and analyzed. Long readings can successfully be turned into film-making projects at the intermediate or advanced level [Listerman 1973]. A film, by the way, should be viewed several times and made the basis for considerable oral activity --passive exposure to language material is of doubtful value. Video-tape recorders can be used for many communicative activities, such as interviews, dramatizations, everyday situations, off-the-air dubbing, creative dubbing (without the original sound track), self-analysis, field trips, and so forth [Crouse and Noll 1980]. The best skits can be video-taped and a library built over the years, which can be used by all.

--Radio programs. They can be very effective, especially the commercials, which show that the language is not an artificial textbook code but a very real means of communication [Garfinkel 1971-a, 1972-b].

--Recordings. One can have the students listen to a tape recording several times and then talk about its content.

--Use of the telephone. This should be an advanced activity, because telephone speech is difficult to understand due to the loss of sound range. Telephone conversation practice can be made very realistic by the use of the "teleprompter," which consists of two telephones with long cables, a loudspeaker, and a control panel that produces an authentic dial tone, busy signal, and bell [Buscaglia and Holman 1980]. The teleprompter is available from the telephone company. It should be used sparingly so as to preserve its novelty.

--Drama. A drama workshop can be used effectively as an alternative to the language laboratory at the late intermediate level and beyond [Cernyak and Reimer 1980]. From the point of view of a communicative activity, however, memorizing the lines of a play is rather useless; so the students should be allowed to produce the play freely, with their own lines within the general direction of the action (unless, of course, they perform the play in public).

--Games. Many games from television can be adapted for use in the second language classroom. They include such games as Password, What's My Line, Keep Talking, The

20,000 Dollar Pyramid, and I've Got a Secret. Commercial games are sometimes useful, such as *Market: A simulation Game,*[△] *Scrabble* (provided after each word is set on the board each student produces one or two sentences with it), and even *Monopoly* (provided every move is commented upon in the second language). Joiner [1974-b] developed and tested various kinds of guessing games, many of which are suitable at the beginning level --guessing birthdays and other important dates, the prices of objects, the time a student went to bed last night, etc. The game of Gossip can also be adapted to the second language classroom: the teacher reads a narrative to one student, then this student tells it to another, and so on [Gordon 1977]. An oral Jigsaw Puzzle can be devised by giving each student a piece of information which can only be used with other such pieces to put together the puzzle; it can be done with names or pictures of objects whose first letters form a new word, with parts of a story, with cartoon frames, with individual facts about a cultural concept, etc. [Omaggio 1976]. Super Spy is a game in which one member of each group has a secret "mission" that the other members must discover through questions [Paulston and Selekman 1976]. Guilty Party involves a student coming back to the group and discovering what he is guilty of [*ibid.*]. Another successful game activity reported is a treasure hunt using hand-held walkie-talkies, with teams trying to locate and decode a hidden message [Richmond 1980].

--Values and opinions. The expression of values and opinions can be the source of much communicative activity. It is possible for the students to make choices, react to statements, or respond to questions (as well as ask questions), all of this within the context of a discussion of the issues. The students can be asked to list (and discuss) twenty things they want in life or twenty things they like to do [D.E. Wolfe and Howe 1973] --this will encourage the expression of opinions. It should be kept in mind that the main purpose of these activities is self-expression, not the shaping of values, as the latter is not primarily a function of teachers but a function of home and church.

--Controversial statements. Any controversial issue, any event seen from opposite points of view, can be the

----

[△] Available from Benefic Press, Westchester, Illinois.

basis for communicative activities. Controversial statements can be used by the teacher to draw reactions from the students or by the students to draw reactions from each other. Simon *et al.* [1972] published a useful list of controversial statements.

--Props. Communication can be based on teacher-supplied props like a grocery list, a menu, an identification card, a schedule of classes, an application form, etc. [Joiner 1977]. Props can be used in party-type activities too --a "mixer" can be individual lists of information that the students must elicit from each other.

--Confrontations. This is where information given to a student conflicts with that given to another student with whom he must communicate. It can take the form of different intentions --for example, a student "buyer" who is told to walk into a photo shop with the intention of purchasing an inexpensive box camera and a student "salesman" who is told to try to sell him an expensive model.

--List making. Students can be asked to make lists of various things and then discuss their choices and their ranking.

--Readings. A reading can be divided into fragments and then the students should agree (by discussing it in the second language) on the order of the fragments [Freed 1976].

--Student-directed conversation. The Community Language Learning technique of having students tell the teacher what they want to say, in the native language, and having the teacher provide the second language equivalent for student production can be the basis for much conversation.

--Free associations. Various types of stimuli can be used to elicit free associations to maintain a running monologue, either individual or collective.

--Advertisements. Many types of ads can be used to ask the students to assign prices to the items, make comparisons with local prices, and so on. They can also be asked to produce advertisements.

--Sound effects. The students can be asked to tell a story about a sequence of sound effects. Practice materials using sound effects have been developed [e.g., Maley and Duff 1979].

--Objects. The students can be asked to describe and ask questions about and discuss unusual objects [Gordon 1976].

--The "Islamabad Technique." Stevick [1980:139-42]

described a technique whereby with the help of colored rods a student describes a city (the same could be done with a neighborhood, a house, anything for which a plan can be made); then the teacher retells the description; then other students tell what they remember of the description; after that other students ask questions of the first student; and as a possible final step, the rods are piled up and other students are asked to reconstruct the model and talk about it. (Note that drawing a plan on the board and erasing it might do just as well.)

--The "Strip Story." In this technique each student is given a separate written sentence from a story and asked to memorize it; then the students, still without writing anything down, are supposed to find out what the story is like. This means that all students are required to speak at least once, since each is the only source for one sentence. The students should not be allowed to keep the strips with their sentences. The teacher should remain quiet and encourage among the students a party-like communication atmosphere [Gibson 1975].

--Paired communication. This can be done by having students in pairs determine which words in their lists are the same (half of 20 words in each list would be the same), or which sentences in their lists mean the same, without looking at each other's lists. A variation of this is to have students instruct each other on the performance of a task or to have them exchange information needed to solve problems. This can also be used as a testing technique [Byers 1973].

--Fantasy. The use of the imagination can be the source of communicative activities. Students can be asked to imagine they are anything --a rosebush, a rabbit, a drop of rain-- and express what the experience is. They can imagine themselves in any situation or in any role and talk about it [Fasten and Findley 1976].

--Playing with language. The imaginative use of language to create crazy or unusual sentences and word play can be an interesting occasional communicative activity (see Debyser and Laitenberg [1976] for examples).

--Songs. Songs are not particularly useful in teaching the spoken language, because they can be confusing, difficult to understand, and quite different from normal speech. They can be useful, however, if used occasionally for motivation and, if carefully chosen, to teach aspects of the second culture.

On to free, real communication

As interesting as many of the above-listed classroom communicative activities can be, nothing is as motivating as free, real communication with native speakers. Some of the possibilities are listed below.

--Visits by native speakers. They can be interviewed by the students.

--Telephone calls. The teacher arranges with natives to receive telephone calls in which each student is to introduce himself, learn about a particular task he has to perform, and report to the class on the conversation [Paulston 1974].

--Community resources. If the second language is spoken in the community, the students can be given such real communicative tasks to perform as going shopping, cashing a check, visiting restaurants, museums, clubs, the crews of foreign ships, etc.

--Long-distance communication. This can take the form of communicating by letter with pen pals or by means of cassette recordings with tape pals.

--Field trips. A field trip to an area where the language is spoken can be quite motivating. To take full advantage of it, the students should be given a list of practical tasks to perform, such as ask for directions, buy various things, change money, etc.

--Study abroad. This is the ultimate second language experience, one that should come after much instruction at home; another condition for its success is that the students should not stay within native language speaking enclaves but fully associate with the speakers of the second language.

There are many programs in which the possibilities for contact with native speakers are very limited or nonexistent. In such cases, the following list of activities (which can, in fact, be beneficial in all programs) offers possibilities for much realistic and real communication.

--Individual projects.

--Programs for parents.

--Presentation of second language shows, such as puppet shows, for elementary school children, by older students.

--Visits to second language classes in other schools.

--Second language festivals. These are not only a good linguistic experience but can create goodwill in the community and support for second language study.

--Second language camps. These are popular

arrangements whereby a ranch, YMCA camp, lodge, etc. is converted into a second language village for a long weekend [Preller 1974]. Second language teachers and native speakers are invited to attend or visit. Such camps are artificial speech communities, but they are better than nothing.

--Second language weeks. A second language week with the visit of native speakers seems to work quite well for advanced students [Crocker 1973].

At the advanced level, there is no reason for any mechanical activity, which would be found quite boring. One can instead make full use of communicative activities such as debates, round-table discussions, topical discussions, lectures, seminars, films, television, radio, student-produced audiovisual presentations, exchanges with foreign students, historical and literary simulations, and so forth. Beyond the classroom, the advanced student should continue his second language experience by immersing himself in the language and acquiring, rather than formally learning, an extensive vocabulary, further control of style, and idiomatic expression.

Further ideas about communicative activities were provided by Freeman [n.d.], Freeman *et al.* [n.d.],Birckbichler [1977], Moskowitz [1978], Westphal and Joiner [1978], Wattenmaker and Wilson [n.d.], and others. Zelson [1974] gave 29 examples of useful and interesting role-playing activities. Stanislawczyk and Yavener [1976] published a useful list of communicative activities classified according to levels of second language study. Maley and Duff [1978] gave many examples of carefully graded communicative activities ("drama techniques") involving the students both intellectually and emotionally; many of them, however, while fine for children, would not be appropriate for teenagers or adults.

Communicative activities should involve not only the intellect but the emotions as well. If the students are encouraged to express their feelings, their likes and dislikes, their enthusiasm, surprise, and disappointment, the second language course will be much more relevant. (This is especially so in the case of beginners, who cannot converse but could quite early be taught ways of expressing their feelings in the second language.) Affective language activities --such as open-ended sentences that allow the expression of opinions, feelings, values, and humor --increase student attention [Christensen 1977]. At the same time, we should keep in mind that, because feelings are very personal, participation in such activities should be voluntary. We have no right to explore or expose our students' inner beings. Many students resent attempts to expose their personal feelings and values in front of comparative strangers. Students don't come to us to "grow" but to learn a second language, so they justifiably object to "humanistic" snooping by a teacher to try to make them "grow." As a profession, we have no business practicing pseudopsychiatry. So caution is in order when we engage in affective language activities.

One final suggestion about what may be a useful way to practice communication skills. Beginning at the intermediate level, the students should be encouraged to practice pseudocommunication by thinking and talking to themselves often in the second language, producing variations of familiar sentences with everything new they learn. This supplements communicative activities in the classroom, providing considerable practice beyond its walls. It should be continued into the advanced level and indefinitely thereafter.

14

USES OF THE NATIVE LANGUAGE AND OF VISUAL AIDS

A little history

As pointed out in Chapter 12, the Grammar-Translation Method misused and overused the native language, especially in terms of (1) bilingual word lists, the use of which began in the mid-seventeenth century [L. Kelly 1969:25], (2) emphasis on written translation, (3) the translation of sentences and paragraphs containing numerous different grammatical rules, and (4) the constant use of the native language to talk *about* the second language, with the result that graduates could do just that.

The "father" of the reform movement of the late nineteenth century, Viëtor [1882], was not opposed to the use of translation to convey meaning. However, the reformers who carried the day were more extreme, and in their overreaction against the overuse and misuse of translation went to the opposite end, that is, to a rigid prohibition of the use of the native language for any purpose.

Insofar as they were unable to accept that the evil was not translation but its misuse, many of these reformers allowed translation to become the "red herring" [Palmer 1922, 1964:125] of the reform movement. Despite its patent impossibility, they insisted that the native language should be left out not only of the classroom but of the minds of the learners. This is the major emphasis of the Direct Method and of its methodological offspring.

The Structural Method is a bilingual method, with considerable use of the native language, even though it is avoided in many activities.

Two of the three Audiolingual Methods are not Direct Methods but allow the use of the native language in dialogue sentence equivalents, certain exercises, etc. This despite the fact that Brooks, a spokesman for audiolingual teaching, was basically a Direct methodist and was strongly opposed to translation.

The methods that forbid the use of the native language are the Direct Method and the other methods which followed its lead on this principle --the Reading Method, the Audio-Visual Method, the Total Physical Response, the

Silent Way, and the Immersion Approach. The methods that allow the use of the native language are the Grammar-Translation Method, the Structural Method, two of the three Audiolingual Methods, the Cognitive Approach, the Bilingual Method, Community Language Learning, and Suggestopedia. It is evident that in this regard the profession is quite divided.

Five ways of conveying meaning

The most divisive issue with respect to the use of the native language is the question of its use to convey meaning. For that reason, the bulk of this chapter will deal with that matter.

There are in fact, five ways of conveying meaning in second language teaching, which are as follows:

(1) Demonstration, that is, direct association with what the lexical item designates. This has also been called the "ostensive" approach. It may vary from holding up or pointing to an object while repeating its name (e.g., *This is a pen*) to an elaborate audiovisual presentation in which each sentence is heard in a situational context (a dialogue, a story, etc.) and is coordinated with a filmstrip frame or movie scene intended to convey the meaning of the sentence. The acting out, by the teacher, of various actions, emotions or situations also falls under this category.

(2) Definition or paraphrase in the second language. This is used by Direct methodists with more abstract lexical items. But it is virtually impossible to do this, with beginning learners, without having to use a word or words they don't know yet. This is the reason why monolingual dictionaries are so hard to use at the beginning level: in looking up one word one finds others he doesn't know, and in looking those up, still other unknown words appear, and so on.

(3) Illustration, that is, giving a series of contextual examples of the use of the new lexical item, in the second language, so that these contexts may help to make its meaning clear. This, as approaches 1 and 2, is a guessing game. Even when masterfully conducted, such a guessing game will leave some students who --well-- didn't guess. Note also that a guessing game is not an act of communication.

(4) Translation, e.g., giving (or eliciting) the approximate equivalent in the native language and clarifying the extent of that equivalence.

(5) Definition or paraphrase in the native language. This applies to lexical items that have no direct equivalence in the two languages and for which an explanation is therefore necessary, for example, German *Gemütlichkeit* or French *concierge* for English speakers.

Regardless of the approach used, the conveyance of meaning involves equating an expression to something else (the referent or a native language equivalent), differentiating the usage in the two languages, and integrating the new expression with all that is already known of the second language.

Advantages and disadvantages of the monolingual approaches

Three advantages are claimed for the monolingual meaning-conveyance approaches (1, 2, and 3). It is said that these techniques (1) lead to the acquisition of more precise meaning, (2) establish "direct" associations without the intervention of the native language, and (3) result in thinking in the second language from the beginning of the program.

The supposed advantages of monolingual meaning-conveyance are illusory. Approaches 2 and 3 are guessing games, as we have seen. Let us consider the claim that approach 1 --demonstration-- can convey meaning precisely, especially with the help of visual aids. If objects are used, meaning is seldom unambiguous. Without translation, there is no efficient way of conveying the meaning of *blue* in "The blue book is on the table," for unless quite a number of sentences are produced contrasting just the quality of "blue" with other qualities, the sentence can be interpreted as "The large (French, small, teacher's, etc.) book is on the table." And using a large number of sentences to convey the meaning of "blueness" is *indirect*, the roundabout way to do it; the students already know what "blue" means so that only reference to what they know would really be direct.

Monolingual techniques do not prevent the formation of wrong associations. The student who has learned the French word *fenêtre* monolingually is in no way prevented from wrongly saying **une fenêtre de magasin* for a shop-window, rather than the correct *vitrine*, unless the limitations of the equation --an equation he *will* make in his mind-- are pointed out to him. The same applies to the use of French *prendre* in the sense of *carry*, through equation with *take*. The German-speaking student of English, despite monolingual instruction, will match in his mind *let* and *lassen,* and *mean* and *meinen.* A Frenchman who relies on monolingual teaching, without translation, will match the English perfect to his *passé composé* and produce **I have seen him last year* [Palmer 1917, 1968:65].

The problem with the demonstration approach is that, unlike concrete nouns like *un livre, un arbre,* and *un renard,* the great majority of second language sentences cannot be depicted. How, for example, could one portray *J'avais promis d'aller le voir* ("I had promised to go see him") or *Vous allez pouvoir en juger par vous-même* ("You will be able to judge for yourself") [Cole 1976]? Demonstration is very limited when one considers that "much of the language reflects not physical entities in the external environment but mental phenomena, intentions and feelings, personal beliefs and judgements" [*ibid.,* p. 340].

Rather than yielding precise semantization, then, monolingual techniques often establish vague and ambiguous associations and fuzzy concepts as compared with those that can be established via translation [Sweet 1899, 1964: 208]. Both for teaching and testing, "even the clearest pictures tend to elicit a variety of utterances, rather than only the one we want" [Pimsleur 1966-b:198]. A picture has no direct relationship with a word or sentence and can be related to many words or sentences. As Sweet [1899, 1964:198] argued over 80 years ago, the demonstration technique can lead to a narrower or broader conceptualization than the one intended; thus, the picture of a house in connection with the French word *maison* can lead the learner to think that *maison* means the *particular* type of house depicted (*bungalow, split-level,* etc.) or that it means *dwelling in general,* both incorrect conceptualizations.

An experiment I conducted [Hammerly 1974-c] confirmed Sweet's position. Using pictures of five concrete objects, I instructed 100 subjects (university students) via audiovisual demonstration with German and Russian words. Despite the very concrete content of the pictures, the number of subjects misinterpreting the pictures or in doubt about their interpretation ranged from 25 to 60 percent. It has been argued, in regard to this experiment, that "a series of contextualized pictures, rather than pictures in isolation, could reduce the range of speculation" [King *et al.* 1975:191]. Experiments by Dodson and myself, however, provide substantial evidence that meanings are not clearly conveyed even by series of contextualized pictures.

One of the experiments by Dodson [1967:8-9], involving 30 university lecturers, revealed that subjects shown the frames of complete audiovisual lessons (20 frames per lesson) from materials available on the market at the time were able to guess the meaning of only 10-40 percent of the sentences. In my experiment [Hammerly 1978-b], 47 experienced teachers of French, all familiar with recent audiovisual materials, were shown two ten-frame filmstrips from the early dialogues of a fairly recent audiovisual textbook [Capelle and Capelle 1970], filmstrips that included many frames with concrete referents. The filmstrips were presented three times each, one filmstrip with Vietnamese dialogue and the other silently. During the third showing of each filmstrip, the subjects were given ample time to write down their interpretations of each frame (each frame represents one sentence). Even though rough-idea interpretations were accepted and partial credit for partially acceptable interpretations was given, the average comprehension for the group was 48 percent for the dialogue presented with Vietnamese voices and 61 percent for the dialogue presented silently. Individual frames varied considerably in comprehensibility, with a frame with 12 percent at the low end of the range.

Further disadvantages of the monolingual demonstration approach are that visuals are subject to cultural differences, individual differences in ability to interpret the pictures, and technical difficulties in deciding how to represent each word or sentence. Another disadvantage is that with that type of presentation it is not possible to know what meanings are being formed in the minds of the learners; the students can form and maintain for a long time, uncorrected, many wrong conceptualizations. A very serious disadvantage is that the students may be able to "decode" merely the visual message, not the second language, and may therefore be able to imitate well and even to participate in questions and answers without knowing what they are saying [Dodson 1967:10]. We must conclude, therefore, that the first claim made for the monolingual approaches --the conveyance of precise meaning-- is not valid.

The second claim in favor of the monolingual techniques --the production of "direct" associations without the intervention of the native language-- has also been found to be false, both in the case of pictures in isolation in an experimental situation and in the case of the overall monolingual instruction of young children. In the first of my experiments mentioned above [Hammerly 1974-c], 70 of the 100 subjects *immediately* thought of one or more native language equivalents for the foreign word being heard in conjunction with its pictorial representation, and the rest thought of native language equivalents only a brief moment later. (Evidently, second language-native language connections are not indirect at all.) Two recent studies of French immersion in elementary school in Canada [Dumas *et al.* 1974, Day 1977] showed that even in the monolingual instruction of young children the native language plays an important role, as there is considerable evidence of second language-native language interaction and native language lexical interference. As Day [*ibid.*, pp. 59-60] put it, "the distinction between the two languages is not very clear in the minds of the children. Interference from English is frequent...."

What seems to take place with monolingual techniques --whether demonstration, definition or paraphrase, or illustration-- is what Dodson [1967:51] has called "the eureka experience" of the student saying to himself, as Palmer [1917, 1968:63] pointed out long ago, "Ah, *fenêtre* means *window*!" This has been shown experimentally in a study of differential memory for picture and word stimuli [J.R. Jenkins *et al.* 1967], whose authors concluded that, while pictures are more easily remembered than words, people "tend to encode a picture verbally within the native language anyway...." The strength of the native language is such that the beginning second language learner cannot help but use the native language, even if it is never uttered in class, in the process of trying to guess the meaning of a second language expression.

What makes monolingual second language teaching inadvisable is that the inevitable covert second language-native language equations and second language conceptualizations are often wrong but the teacher may not be aware of their incorrectness until much later. What makes monolingual second language teaching inefficient is that the second language-native language equations (the "eureka experiences") may take place soon after the presentation, or many minutes later, or even not at all within the class hour, in which case the students, frustrated at having failed to guess the meanings of various words during class, consult each other, in the native language, after class --a case of the barely informed or misinformed informing the uninformed.

To sum up this point, in regard to "directness" of

association between second language words and reality, the five ways of conveying meaning should be listed as follows: 1, 4, 2 or 5, and 3; but very often because of the guessing factor involved, approach 1 cannot be used. And if by "directness" we mean the quickest way of conveying meaning clearly and precisely, the two translation approaches (4 and 5) are by far the most direct.

The teacher who uses monolingual techniques to convey meaning is relying on the vagaries of his students' minds to form more or less accurate meaning associations now, later, or never, and he cannot know immediately what the associations being formed are nor can he correct them immediately when they are wrong. Would it not be much more sensible to make sure, through the judicious and limited use of the mother tongue and the application of an overt contrastive technique, that the associations formed be as accurate as possible and that they be made immediately?

As to the third claim, that monolingual techniques make the students think in the second language, much depends on how "thinking" is defined. If we define thinking as the cognitive processing of ideas, it should be clear, as noted in Chapter 3 and elsewhere, that we do not think in a particular language but just think, and then express those thoughts in whichever language we are using at the moment --this expression of thought involves mostly unconscious and very rapid processing of language data.
To say that a beginning second language student can be made to think in the second language, then, is nonsensical. Even if we disregarded the important distinction between thoughts and their expression, the mostly imitative, highly primed responses of beginning second language students could not be considered "thinking."

We cannot express our thoughts in a second language until we have a thorough knowledge of it. At the beginning level, cognitive processing in the native language is unavoidable --we can only express our thoughts and feelings in a language we know. Expressing our thoughts in the second language implies direct associations between ideas and their second language expression; this is the reason why it is impossible for beginners, for whom each idea immediately elicits the native language expression of it in their minds.

(Even the "consolidation" of a second language sentence --that is, reaching the point where the students can use it in its context rapidly and apparently without translation-- seems to depend far more on the number of times the sentence is used in communication situations than on whether its initial presentation avoided the native language of the learners [Preibusch and Zander 1971].)

The second language learner cannot ignore what he knows --the native language-- and there is no reason why he should learn to think all over again. Second language learners do not start from zero, so there is no reason for them to go again through the slow childhood steps leading to conceptualization and culminating in abstract thinking. Must they learn all over again what a "brake," a "birthday," and a "bachelor" mean? Obviously not. But monolingual meaning conveyance techniques treat students as if they did not have an elaborate system of concepts, as if they did not know how to think already.

Coordinate bilingualism, the ability to express one's thoughts in each of two languages separately, should be the eventual goal of second language instruction, to be reached gradually over a period of several years. It is quite unrealistic to expect to have coordinate bilingualism from the start of instruction. It is far more realistic, and quite possible, to gradually develop an increasing ability to express one's thoughts in the second language during communicative activities, while at the same time making use of translation during presentation and manipulative activities.

In addition to the uncertainty of conveying the right meaning, monolingual techniques are inadvisable because they are very inefficient. Even their advocates [e.g., Corder 1966-b:27] admit that these techniques are very slow. Some would say that time is not wasted during this roundabout putting of the meaning across because the learners are listening to the second language; but such listening is not listening with understanding, so it is *not* communicative listening but a guessing game. After the teacher has tried all kinds of tricks and maneuvers to teach the Spanish word *vaca,* when the students finally guess it they are inclined to say "Oh, you mean *cow!* Why didn't you tell us?" Efficiency and directness dictates that if a student asks "What does *bateau* mean?" it would be unnecessarily time-consuming to draw a ship on the blackboard, make a paper boat, or cruise about blowing an imaginary foghorn, when in a very small fraction of the time one can tell the student "Cela veut dire *boat*" and *then* immediately use the time thus saved to make the students aware of the limitations of the equivalence and to have them use the word several times in different statements and questions in the second language. The point is, the use of native language equivalents to convey meaning saves time that can be used for meaningful manipulation and communication.

Professional versus natural translation

Many consider translation a specialized skill that can be developed only after one has a thorough knowledge of the two languages involved. This attitude is typified by Moulton's [1966:116] statement to the effect that the beginning language student who thinks he can indulge in the "high art" of translation "is suffering from delusions of grandeur." Such arguments about the specialized nature of translation have been used by some to support monolingual second language teaching.

The problem with such a view is that it fails to differentiate between professional translation and natural translation [Harris 1978]. Professional translation is indeed an advanced skill that even bilinguals have great difficulty in developing. It is a difficult skill, usually possible in one direction only, and literary translation in particular is subject to demanding artistic criteria. Obviously, since few bilinguals can do this, beginning second language learners haven't the slightest hope of doing it.

But there is also natural translation, the much simpler activity of providing across-language conceptual equivalents of everyday sentences. This all bilinguals can readily do. In fact, bilingual infants translate naturally from the age of about two [Ronjat 1913, Harris and Sherwood 1978]. They do not produce nonsense mistranslations, for they are very conscious of meaning and of the need for "COMAL" --"Conservation of Meaning Across Languages" [Harris 1978:420]. The fact that all bilinguals can do natural translation and very few can be trained as professional translators proves that these are two different types of translation. Natural translation is oral and informal; professional translation is usually written (interpretation constitutes only five percent of the total), formal, accurate in every detail, and quite deliberate.

It is not professional translation but natural translation that is used in the second language class, by teachers and learners, during teaching/learning activities and for testing purposes. As already pointed out, such translation occurs even if the native language is avoided in the classroom.

On translatability

Some say that many things cannot be translated. But this is what Butzkamm [1973:120] called "the myth of the missing equivalent." It is true that poems are largely untranslatable in terms of their structure, rhythm, etc., though not of their ideas and feelings. It is also true that word-by-word translation does not work, producing linguistic monstrosities, and that certain words reflecting different customs and institutions --"high school," "college," "drugstore"-- require a paraphrase or explanation. But, by and large, what can be expressed in one language can also be expressed in another, without much difficulty.

Second language words have native language equivalents of one sort or another when they refer to shared cultural features. The two languages frequently fail to correspond exactly at the word level, but they correspond almost always at the sentence level. This has been found to have psychological reality in that short simple sentences can be translated faster than isolated words [Macnamara 1967].

Everybody translates

All persons exposed to more than one language translate. Converting a second language utterance into his native language is as unavoidable for the beginning second language student as converting foreign prices to prices in his own country's currency is for the tourist [Dodson 1967: 54]. When shown a new object, the student can't help but say to himself, "Aha, a necktie" --the native language equation is inextricably tied to the acquisition of word meaning. We can go farther and say that the second language student does not know exactly what a noun, verb, adjective, etc. means until he has satisfied himself that he has found the right native language equivalence for it.

Many have stated the reality of the tendency of second language students to translate all new items [e.g., Carroll 1966-a, Kirstein 1972, C. Anderson 1974, Hosenfeld 1976]. That the students need to translate is evident from the fact that beginning and intermediate students buy bilingual, not monolingual dictionaries. With a monolingual dictionary, one wastes much time looking up words to explain other words to explain still other words, ad infinitum. If you were a beginning or intermediate student of, say, Russian, would you want to use a Russian/Russian dictionary or a Russian/English one?

Coordinate bilinguals very often translate. They also

switch languages quickly and easily. This shows that thought is not in any particular language and that bilinguals store the two languages together. Evidence for this comes from a series of experiments by Kolers [1963, 1966-a, 1966-b, 1968]; one of them [1968], for example, showed that bilinguals exposed to mixed sentences did not remember which language the sentences were in. This suggests strongly a single thought system making use of grammars and lexicons located close together in the central nervous system, probably with bilingual equivalents for the same concept located in adjacent neurons. The readiness with which bilinguals translate can be seen in the fact that, if a bilingual learns the names of certain plants and trees in one language and wants to know what to call them in the other language, he does not take a monolingual or bilingual friend to the woods but asks for the word equivalents or finds them in a bilingual dictionary.

As Palmer [1917, 1968:57] observed, even fervent partisans of the Direct Method translate --if one of them is reading a chemistry book in German and comes across the unknown word *Wasserstoff,* he may not use a bilingual dictionary, true, but the moment he finally understands the word he says to himself: "Ach so, *Wasserstoff* bedeutet *hydrogen*!" So, if even Direct methodists translate, we must come to the conclusion that everybody translates. This being the case, we have another reason why second language learners should be allowed to translate.

It is impossible to leave the native language out of the second language learning situation. As Palmer [*ibid.*, p. 63] pointed out, regardless of our efforts to eliminate the native language, "we do not and cannot prevent the student from forming bilingual associations if he wishes to do so." Since we cannot hush up the native language, since it continues to speak quite loudly in the minds of our students even if it is not used in our classrooms and even if it does not appear in our textbooks, we might as well be reasonable, accept the inevitable, and use the native language to our advantage to the extent that this is possible.

Advantages of translation

One advantage of the use of natural translation in second language teaching is that it saves a great deal of time without doing any harm. It is the surest, most direct, most economical, easiest, and most precise way of conveying meaning. Avoiding it would be uneconomical and unnatural. Using it increases efficiency, for it frees much time for real communicative activities, as a few seconds in the native language can save many minutes of pantomime and prevent serious misconceptions.

Another advantage of translation is that it makes knowledge more precise. There may not be absolute equivalents across languages but there are approximate equivalents which, if supplemented as needed with brief pointers, can give a fairly precise idea of the meaning of second language words. (The exact semantic boundaries of a word are learned over a period of time, of course, as in the native language.) Thus, while the exact meaning of a word is learned gradually through observation of its use and one can seldom convey all of its meaning at once, the use of native language equivalents comes closest to that, much closer than demonstration, definition or paraphrase, and illustration in the second language.

Sweet pointed this out [1899, 1964:198]:

> ...to a German the word *Hut* and the idea "hat" are so intimately connected that the one suggests the other instantaneously and without effort. Again, the picture gives us only part of the ideas associated with the word *chapeau*....the greatest advantage of a word as opposed to a picture is that it is practically an epitome of this whole group of ideas, and the equation *chapeau* = *Hut* enables a German to transfer bodily such a group of ideas from his own to the foreign word. This the picture cannot do....

Sometimes only translation will give the learner awareness of the correct usage of a second language expression. Thus, without the translation *I wonder*... an English speaker will assume that French *Je me demande*... is a strong form equivalent to *I ask myself (ibid.,* pp.200-1). Without knowledge that the correct equivalent is *at present,* the English speaker will assume that French *actuellement* means *actually*. Without guidance in the form of a brief explanation with native language equivalents, he will assume that French *prendre* is the equivalent of *take* in all its contexts, and say things like **Je vais prendre ces livres à la bibliothèque*.

By withholding translation, then, we may fail to prevent serious misconceptions. The native language does, in conveying meaning, what visual aids could do if they could be unambiguous (which they cannot be) --cue meaning. Furthermore it gives the learners reassurance and allows them to perform various essential cognitive operations.

Natural interpretation and translation are, furthermore, among the principal uses that a second language can be put to. They also open the door to a great variety of presentation, practice, communicative, and testing activities that would not otherwise be possible.

Therefore, when ESL teachers feel proud in saying that they haven't allowed a single word of Spanish, French, Arabic, etc. in their classrooms, this is completely misplaced pride. What succeeds --the use of the native language to, among other things, convey meanings-- must be allowed, even encouraged. As Palmer noted long ago [1922, 1964:126] the "comparatively innocent process of translation" should be rehabilitated, as it allows language teachers to "proceed naturally enough from the known to the unknown." Many scholars in more recent times have agreed that translation performs a useful role in second language teaching/learning. Among them are Politzer [1965], Marty [1965], Belasco [1967], Rivers [1968], and Ney [1968]. So there is no reason at all to have guilt feelings or to feel shame or fear of ridicule about the use of translation in the second language classroom.

Translation and transfer

The error of most structural methods has been in not counteracting interference overtly. No amount of practice in which the native language is avoided will be as effective in overcoming native language interference as exposure to overt contrasts. The best way to make interference disappear is to learn different responses *in the presence* of the cause of interference, that is, in the presence of the native language.

Since monolingual mechanical practice does not directly counteract interference, beginning and intermediate students revert to the native language in their minds as soon as the use of the second language is meaningful; so we should proceed with most rules by having first bilingual mechanical practice, then monolingual mechanical practice with some attention on meaning, then bilingual and monolingual meaningful exercises, and finally and only then monolingual communicative activities.

The value of overt contrastive techniques is that they allow the learners to see the similarities and differences between the two codes and they enable the teacher to make sure that those differences have been perceived. There are definite advantages in this. Lim [1970], for example, found that students who were aware of native language-second language contrasts had significantly fewer interference errors in a translation test, and no more errors in monolingual activities than students who had been taught monolingually. Of course, the advantages of the contrastive presentation of meaning are lost when the native language is "adapted" to "facilitate translation," as when French *On dit qu'il est riche* is rendered as "One says that he is rich" rather than "They say he's rich"; correct natural translation matches sentences stylistically rather than being as close as possible to word-by-word translation.

To conclude this section, the overt and explicit use of the native language introduces contrastive analysis in the area of meaning, "the oldest form of contrastive study" [Mills 1977:739]. Such contrastive use of the native language facilitates positive transfer when the two languages correspond; it forestalls the pre-emptive effect of the native language, both in terms of preclusive and intrusive interference, when the two languages differ partially; and it makes clear the situations where the two languages are quite different. To enable us to have all these advantages, second language teaching methods must be bilingual.

How not to use and how to use translation

The misuse and overuse of translation in the Traditional Method takes six forms, as follows:

(1) One-to-one word lists and word-by-word translation.

One-to-one word lists do not offer the learner either a linguistic or a nonlinguistic context, both of which are essential to correct vocabulary usage. Such lists, as well as single-word vocabulary cards, lead to such ridiculous translations as **Canadien cheddar fromage avec pétards* for *Canadian cheddar cheese with crackers,* seen on a menu, and many other such monstrosities. In the enlightened use of translation, whole sentences within a broader context are translated, not words. Furthermore, it is the concepts that are related rather than the forms that express them. In other words, the native language is related indirectly to the second language response via the concept. So natural translation is the translation of ideas, not of words, conceptualization intervening between the forms of the two languages. The native language cannot have a detrimental effect when it is used to cue concepts, for it is the concept, not the native language words, that stimulates the second language response.

(2) Emphasis on written translation.

Written translation is very inefficient, for in the time it takes a student to translate a sentence in writing, he can say and translate several sentences orally. Another problem with written translation is that it tends to foster word-by-word equations, while with oral translation the fleeting nature of the cue leads to emphasizing the concept rather than the words. Written translation also gives the learners time to edit and re-edit the sentences, hardly preparation for the give and take of oral communication. Furthermore, while written translation is followed by delayed correction, which is not very effective, oral translation in class or the laboratory can be followed by more effective immediate correction. For all these reasons, second language translation should nearly always be oral.

(3) Emphasis on similarities.

In the Traditional Method the mistake is made of emphasizing the similarities between the two languages. As we have seen, the enlightened use of translation should be contrastive, that is, emphasizing differences and disabusing students of the incorrect hypothesis of isomorphism.

(4) The translation of paragraphs containing numerous different grammatical rules.

The Grammar-Translation Method makes use of interlingual grammatical puzzles. Such puzzles may be challenging for a few students with high IQ's, but they are frustrating, time-consuming, and counterproductive for all others. Such grammatical puzzles naturally result in many errors; but the purpose of second language practice should be to facilitate the learning of correct responses through controlled exposure to limited choices, not to put the students constantly in situations where they face an unmanageable number of choices and consequently keep on making many errors. In modern translation exercises, short sentences containing only one or two grammatical operations are used.

(5) The use of the native language to generate sentences.

In Traditional Method teaching, native language sentences are the point of departure for the generation of second language sentences. Without second language models for reference, the students produce "sentences" which are not natural translations but have the structure of the native language and the vocabulary of the second language.

There is nothing wrong in providing native language cues to the concepts as long as the resulting sentences are generated on the basis of second language models. If the learner knows quite well the necessary second language sentence patterns, in the form of model sentences he has thoroughly learned, there is no reason for native language cues to cause him to construct second language sentences according to native language patterns.

(6) Excessive use of the native language.

In the Traditional Method the native language is used almost all the time. An enlightened use of translation makes use of the native language for certain specific purposes and part of the time, with a gradual phasing out of translation and phasing in of monolingual instruction.

Research evidence

There is some research evidence of the advantages of the use of the native language. Several scholars have found a bilingual method of instruction more effective than a monolingual one; among them are Mishima [1967], Dodson [1967], Lim [1968, 1970], Sastri [1970], and Butzkamm [1973]. Dodson [1967:15] found that the worst of three groups, in comprehension, pronunciation, and fluency, was the one given the second language sentences and pictures only. He found that for best results, the presentation should be (1) second language sentence orally, (2) native language equivalent of the sentence for the *acquisition* of meaning, (3) visuals for the *retention* of meaning, and (4) printed second language sentence made available. Sastri [*op. cit.*] found that Bilingual Method students were superior to Direct Method students in all tests at the end of the second year of ESL (unfortunately, no statistical analysis of significance is reported). Butzkamm's [*op. cit.*] is the most thorough treatment of the issue of monolingual versus bilingual language teaching to date; it discusses the literature on the subject as well as a number of significant studies.

Preibusch and Zander [1971] found that monolingual instruction did not significantly help fifth graders, the avoidance of the native language not being a significant factor. Dodson [1967:4-8] found that even the best pictures in certain audiovisual courses were not understood by ten percent of the students. And while a number of psychological experiments have shown that picture-word pairs are retained better than word-word pairs, it should be evident that best comprehension and retention is achieved by using sentence-sentence-picture triads, taking full advantage of the comprehension-ensuring use of the native language and of the retention-enhancing use of pictures.

Even such largely unrelated studies as the brain research by Wilder Penfield and other neurologists would seem to support the use of a bilingual method. They showed that two languages are located in the same part of the brain. Thus Franke [1884] is contradicted: neurologically, translation is more direct than monolingual reference to pictures, etc., as the visual data is on the other brain hemisphere.

Meaningful practice following the conveyance of meaning

The ability to associate directly a second language expression and its meaning is, according to Dodson [*ibid.*, p. 51], the result of sufficient use of the second language expression in meaningful practice, not of how the meaning was originally conveyed. And the more time is devoted to conveying meaning, the less time there is for meaningful practice in the second language.

When the Direct Method succeeds --slow as this may be--, it is because the learner *has* connected the second language expressions to the native language expressions, despite the avoidance of the native language in the method. So it makes sense to convey the meaning of a new word as quickly as possible, in the native language, thus ensuring *comprehension,* and then spend the time thus saved to use it meaningfully in the second language, thus facilitating *internalization.*

When the meaning is first conveyed, the native language expression will be in the conscious awareness of the learner, but through meaningful practice it will drop out from consciousness and become unconscious. During that practice, the phasing out of awareness of the native language equivalent is accomplished by giving the learner less and less time to translate in his mind, until he simply has no time to translate and must respond directly in the second language.

Thus *the use of the native language can improve second language production,* as it results in immediate certainty of the meaning and frees more time for meaningful practice. The paradox --first noted by Otto [1921]-- is that *through translation the native language is eliminated;* that is, the student doesn't have to spend any time searching for native language equivalents (as he has been given the meaning), but can instead concentrate on using the word meaningfully in the second language.

Gradation in the use of the native language and the second language

The second language can only slowly and gradually become the language of instruction. This gradual development starts with the native language as the foundation and eventually reaches the point where there is understanding and production without translation. In other words, we learn the second language through the native language, for we reason and conceptualize subvocally in the language in which we have conscious awareness, and that, at the beginning and for a long time, is the native language; only after considerable exposure to the second language does it become possible to do either of these things in the second language.

While there should be no hesitation or misgivings about using the native language when necessary for understanding, the native language should not be overused. If it is, the learners get into the habit of translating every word. They also come to think that the second language is just a class game and that whenever there is something important to be said it is said in the native language.

The second language should be used whenever it can be understood. The students must be asked to do as much as possible in the second language; they must be steeped in it. As Carroll *et al.* [1967] concluded in their study of the second language attainment of college majors, the extent to which the second language is used in the classroom is "a possible favorable influence" --logic tells us that this is undoubtedly a very important factor in second language learning.

The native language should be used primarily in the presentation of material; there is less need for it in practice activities, in which it can be gradually eliminated. Much use of the native language can be avoided by teaching, as needed, those expressions used in the conduct of the class. (But an early lesson on classroom expressions is almost useless, as those that are not used immediately are forgotten.)

At the early beginning level, no more than 20 percent of the time (more in the first 15-20 hours) should be taken up by native language production. Gradually the native language should be used less and less, so that by the late intermediate level it should take no more than eight to ten percent of the time, and at the advanced level no more than about five percent of class time, just the time needed to present and consolidate the meaning of new lexical items. At the advanced level there is no reason to discuss anything in the native language, though it would still be used in glossing new lexical items in readings.

Conclusion

In conclusion, between techniques that work well, the most economical should be used, that is, the most direct, the one using the least effort, the least time, and the simplest means. This is the use of the native language to convey meaning and for several other specific purposes. Efficient second language teaching is bilingual, without losing any quality in the process. This is close to what Butzkamm [1973:190, my translation] called "enlightened monolingualism," which he defined as "the systematic, purposeful and strictly controlled introduction of the native language within a mainly monolingual methodology."

To make bilingual teaching possible, the teacher has to know the language of his students. Without that knowledge he cannot understand many of their errors or help them to overcome them. It is disappointing to see that many second language materials --especially ESL materials-- do not take into account the language of the students nor make use of it. Even when the teacher does not or cannot know the languages of his students, as in heterogeneous classes, he can and should use materials that provide the sentence equivalents in the various languages represented in the classroom. By distributing such printed materials and teaching bilingually, much time can be saved and the conveyance of precise meaning can be ensured.

Other uses of the native language

In addition to the conveyance of meaning, the native language can and should be used for the following:

--In the introduction to the program, to get acquainted, to explain the nature of the course, to instruct the students on how to learn a second language, to introduce the second culture, to introduce linguistic concepts and terms, and to pre-test the students (motivation, background questionnaires, etc.)

--In teaching pronunciation, to give articulatory explanations, to conduct phonetic differentiation drills, to carry out the "shaping" technique, and to correct errors contrastively. (See Chapter 15.)

--In teaching grammar, to explain rules deductively and to guide the discovery of rules, to contrast second language and native language sentences that illustrate a rule, and to practice difficult contrasts or determine whether interference has been overcome, by means of translation exercises. (See Chapter 17.)

--To ascertain whether the students are paying attention to the meaning of what they are saying, especially in grammatical drills.

--To answer questions or clarify matters whenever the students seem "lost."

--To give early cultural comments.

--To give directions to any new activity or technique, in the classroom or the laboratory.

--To simulate conversation on tape.

--In early listening comprehension activities, to allow the students to show what they have understood.

--In reading materials, to provide glosses of words at the bottom of the page or a running text in two columns.

--In test instructions and certain types of test items (for example, to elicit use of specific rules in speaking tests).

--In giving homework assignments.

--In announcing anything that would not be understood in the second language (of course, for any repeated announcements, the second language expressions should be taught and used).

This long list does *not* mean that the native language is to be used all the time. Far from it. It should not be used readily on each and every occasion someone wants it used. It should be used readily --especially at the beginning of the program-- for the specific purposes listed above, reluctantly and sparingly for others, and not at all in many activities.

Uses of visual aids

Visual aids are at their weakest at conveying meaning, something they do imprecisely and unreliably. They are at their strongest as aids to recall. Excluding their use to convey meaning, which is quite inadvisable, the following are advantageous uses of visual aids:

--As mnemonic aids, that is, to help retain and recall utterances. For this purpose they need not be complete representations of sentence ideas (which they can seldom be anyway), but just reminders of some salient feature of the sentence.

--As conversation stimuli. Much conversation can be based on printed or projected images.

--To help explain linguistic features. Examples of this are face diagrams for the teaching of sounds and the charts used to teach certain grammatical rules.

--To enhance comprehension of a passage. G. Mueller [1980] found that seeing a visual representation before hearing a passage significantly enhances comprehension. In other words, visuals seem to enhance attention and guide expectations.

--As attention-getting devices. Care must be exerted, however, that they don't detract from attention to something more important. For example, presenting a visual aid along with a new sentence for imitation means that, to the extent that the attention is drawn to the visual aid rather than the teacher and how he is saying the sentence, imitation will suffer.

--To give cultural insights. Here the ideal media are film and television, which can bring the second culture into the classroom in living color and sound.

--For motivational purposes. A number of studies have proved the motivational effectiveness of visual aids. Mollica [1976], for example, showed that cartoons can be highly motivating and can be used in a variety of ways.

--For certain types of test items, such as *free* speaking based on telling a story in pictures. But as a testing technique, free speaking is too subjective and very hard to evaluate. Note, moreover, that visual aids cannot be used reliably to elicit particular responses, as most pictures will elicit a variety of responses. Visual aids have often been misused in this respect.

15

TEACHING PRONUNCIATION[△]

Different approaches, different results

At X University the French majors cannot pronounce differently *rue* and *roue* or *sans* and *son*. When they want to say *abbé* they say *abbaye*. They make *beau* rhyme with English *go*. And although they are as reasonable as anybody, they seem stubborn, for instance, in their persistence in curling their tongues toward their palates when producing an *r*. These and other errors characterize their pronunciation of French as poor. Unfortunately that is the case with students of French and other second languages at most universities, colleges, and schools.

At Y University, instead, after about four weeks of instruction most students in the Beginning French classes make clear distinctions between the pairs of sounds listed above and other such pairs. When they want to say something, what they say sounds like what they want to say. Among other things, they have learned to cut their final *o*'s short of glides and to raise the back and keep the front of their tongues low and flat when pronouncing an *r*. In brief, the pronunciation of some *beginning* students at Y University and at a few other institutions equals, and that of many other students approximates, French native standards, something that few if any *advanced* students at X University and most other institutions achieve.

While they describe two extremes, the situations just discussed are not exaggerated. Despite the emphasis given to the spoken language in recent years, advanced second language classes where most of the students have poor pronunciation seem to be still numerous enough to constitute the norm. Yet beginning classes in which the majority of the students develop and retain good pronunciation skills, though in the minority, do exist.

[△] Portions of this chapter are from my article "The Correction of Pronunciation Errors," *The Modern Language Journal,* Vol. LVII, No. 3 (© 1973 by the Regents of the University of Wisconsin), pp. 106-10;used by permission.

To the question, why is there so much poor pronunciation among second language program graduates, there is a multiple answer. First, the Traditional Method, because of its background of classical language teaching, considers pronunciation unimportant, an attitude that has spread to teachers using other methods. The result is that "pronunciation has been the Cinderella of language teaching" [L. Kelly 1969:87], obscure and neglected, still waiting for her Fairy Godmother. Second, only a minority of second language teachers are good pronunciation models. When the poor ones serve as models, their students learn their poor pronunciation habits. If, aware of their deficiencies, they don't teach pronunciation, their students suffer from the lack of such instruction. Few, unfortunately, will use recordings as models. Third, few among the minority who are good models know *how* to teach second language pronunciation.

This last point brings us to the main reason why the beginning students at Y University have a far better pronunciation than the advanced students at X University. Marked differences among students at the same school level cannot be attributed to age. Intelligence is an unlikely variable for large groups. It would be reasonable to expect the motivation of advanced students to be higher than that of beginners. The ability to imitate accurately varies from person to person but cannot account for large group differences. Thus, it seems logical to conclude that pedagogical considerations explain the differences. That is, other factors being equal, results depend primarily on how pronunciation is taught.

For pronunciation must be taught. Pronunciation "does not take care of itself except with preschool children" [Lado 1964:74]. Without instruction in pronunciation, students will naturally use native language sounds instead of second language sounds, with only the exceptional good mimic doing better. (Fortunately most languages have no more than eight or ten difficult sounds, so the teaching of second language pronunciation can indeed be successful.) That pronunciation is to be taught does not of course mean that one has to choose between pronunciation and communication --the goal should be good communication with good pronunciation.

Six major pedagogical considerations account in the aggregate for the differences in results in the teaching of second language pronunciation. They are *emphasis, gradation, standards, the basis of presentation, guidance,* and *practice*. Each of them will now be discussed in turn.

Emphasis

If pronunciation is not given emphasis at the right time it will never be learned well except perhaps by young children and the rare superior mimic. Pronunciation can be emphasized at various points in the second language program, including early, evenly throughout, or late in the program. Since pronunciation habits --good, not-so-good, or bad-- are formed early in the program, it seems obvious that it is at that point that the development of a good pronunciation should be emphasized, for in a few weeks the beginner will pronounce or mispronounce every sound in the language many times.

An emphasis on pronunciation during the first weeks of the program does not mean an exclusive emphasis. Even the best-motivated students would become restless after hours of nothing but pronunciation work. So, almost from the start, work on pronunciation must alternate with meaningful use of language samples and with other meaningful activities (orientational, cultural, and so forth). At the same time, during some of the work on pronunciation greater efficiency and better results will be achieved if meaning and grammar are temporarily excluded. As the beginning course progresses, the periods of concentration on pronunciation can become shorter and less frequent, while the periods of concentration on other language activities can increase in length and frequency.

Probably the best way to emphasize pronunciation at the beginning of the program would be by means of a semi-programmed pronunciation minicourse covering the first 15 to 20 hours of instruction. Such a course is discussed later in this chapter.

Gradation

The students should be introduced to the sound system of the language step by step, starting as a base with those sounds the two sound systems have in common and then adding the sounds that are different one or two at a time. This means that the first hour of class, instead of being presented with a full-fledged dialogue or a series of sentences containing about all the sounds in the second language, the students should be taught three or four new sounds and a few short phrases containing only the sounds mastered up to that point. It is unreasonable to expect good results when beginners are plunged, from the first day, into the numerous complexities of a fully developed dialogue, or into the phonological complexities of learning their names in the second language, or phonologically difficult greetings.

Standards

When a program aims almost exclusively at producing graduates who can read and only seldom speak, it is only natural, though regrettable, that many teachers will settle for bare intelligibility. When, on the other hand, the goals are more encompassing and spoken communication is a primary goal, higher standards are necessary.

A basic aim should be not to speak the second language with native language sounds. What may of necessity be adequate for phrase books for tourists (coh MONT ah LAY VOO?) is completely unacceptable in the second language classroom. Second language students should aim much higher.

The problem is how high to aim. Native-like performance is a valid ideal goal, and not just for those who desire to adopt a new identity and become part of the second culture --a good accent helps intelligibility immensely and speaks of how seriously the learner has taken the second language; it is appreciated by native speakers. I have known a good number of adult learners who have developed a native accent as a result of instruction, so perhaps many adults *can* learn (though probably extremely few can acquire) perfect pronunciation. Other than the rare cases of neural or muscular atrophy, all adults are equipped for the task. And yet, as desirable as native-like pronunciation sounds, and as true as it is that the students should be given a chance to reach it, it is too demanding as a standard for a class as a whole. With proper instruction and practice some students, perhaps many, can attain such a demanding standard; but there will be many who, for a variety of reasons, cannot. Such students should not be held back from further progress in the language because of their imperfect pronunciation.

A phonetic standard, then, where every sound should be exactly right in all details, is obviously too demanding. A phonemic[△] standard, where only the sound contrasts are

----

[△] A phoneme is the smallest unit of sound that has the potential of changing one word into another. It functions in contrast with all other sound units. An example is English /p/ and /b/, which contrast in many word pairs and sentences, such as *Let's put the pin here* and *Let's put the bin here*. Phonemes and their use in second language

controlled, is much too loose, as the students may control the contrasts but do so in many ways which are quite different from the native speaker's. While "the smallest phonic system in any language is the system of sounds abstracted by the *listener* and not the one realized by the speaker" [Léon 1966:60], lack of control over the main allophones☆ of phonemes will result in an objectionable accent and in occasional misunderstandings. Phonemic disdrimination is adequate for listening, but speaking cannot be in phonemes --it must be in phones of one sort or another. If attention is given first to phonemes, with the intention of attending to allophones weeks later, the results are poor, for major phonetic inaccuracies become habitual and speech remains inelegant to the point of unacceptability.

The best solution is to establish, as a class standard, control of all the phonemes with their major allophones, that is, contrastive sound units plus their major variants in their respective phonic environments. This would not be as demanding as perfect phonetic accuracy but would go a long way towards eliminating foreign accent and misunderstandings. At the same time, those students who want to attain native-like performance should be assisted in every way toward that goal.

In establishing a standard, care should be exerted not to demand the maintenance of sound distinctions that even native speakers ignore. For example, in French few native speakers distinguish between the [œ̃] of *brun* and the [ɛ̃] of *brin,* the former having been replaced by the latter; similarly, in rapid colloquial speech French speakers do not have a phonemic distinction in vowel length between the long /ɛ:/ of *maître* and the short /ɛ/ of *mettre,* for both are short. Care should also be exerted to exclude from the classroom such spelling pronunciations that natives may indulge in, especially when asked about their pronunciation, reading aloud or making a recording; for example, many speakers of Spanish have the mistaken notion that the word *vaca* should be pronounced with a [v], and do so when paying special attention to pronunciation, although at all other times they naturally pronounce it

---

teaching are discussed later in this chapter.

☆ An allophone is a noncontrastive variant of a phoneme. English /p/, for example, has three main allophones: aspirated [pʿ] as in *pin,* unaspirated [p¯] as in *spin,* and unreleased [p’] as in *nip.*

['ƀaka] or ['baka], depending on the preceding phonic context.

Once determined and made clear to the students, pronunciation standards must be maintained continuously and consistently, even into the advanced level, otherwise there will be deterioration of the initially established good pronunciation. To ensure that students continue to pay attention to pronunciation and intonation, these should remain part of exam grades through most of the program, at the beginning and intermediate levels in particular.

The objectives of individual students should be taken into account, though this does not mean that teaching must proceed strictly on the basis of their initial goals. Some students may need to be persuaded to modify their objectives, either to rise above minimal intelligibility, or to broaden linguistically exclusive standards (e.g., academic Parisian French), or to be more realistic about their possibilities and expectations. All, of course, should be encouraged to aim as high as they can reach.

Different goals also involve different durations: the first, short-term goal (first 20 hours or so) is for everyone to develop good pronunciation initially; a medium-term goal is to make this initial good pronunciation habitual; a long-term goal is to maintain it at a high level throughout.

Basis of presentation

Where the basis of presentation is graphemic,[△] there are inevitable distortions, for, as seen in Figure 15.1, such a presentation is *three* steps removed from the pronunciation of the second language. As an example of this situation, the Traditional Method practice of telling English-speaking learners of French or Spanish that the *é* of French *allé* or Spanish *hablé* is "pronounced"[☆] like the *a* in English *fate* leads through several mental steps to the final distortions shown in Figure 15.1. Following such instructions, sounds are processed indirectly through three unnecessary codes, as opposed to the single-step

----

△ A grapheme is a unit of the written code. The English grapheme ≪ a ≫, for example, consists of the various manifestations of the letter *a*, such as a, ɑ, A, Á, etc.

☆ Strictly speaking, letters are not pronounced. Letters represent sounds, and it is the sounds that are pronounced.

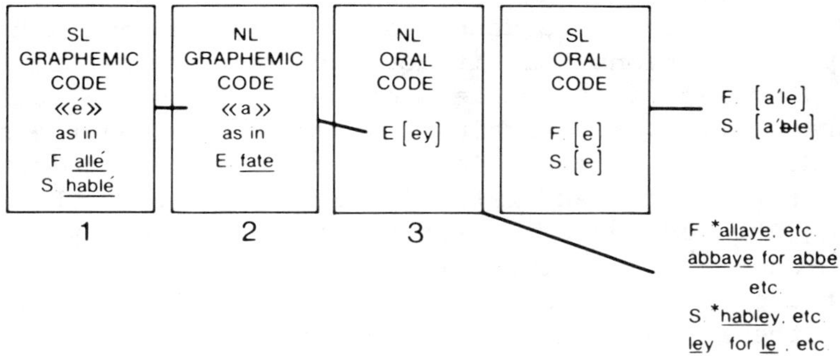

Figure 15.1

approach of basing pronunciation on the second language oral code.

It should be noted that basing the pronunciation of a second language sound on the second language written code (thereby eliminating steps 2 and 3) does not improve things much, for the students still process second language graphemic data, mentally, through the two native language codes. We have already seen, in Chapter 10, that the imitation of utterances is hindered when the standard written form intervenes, either before or along with the oral form. Basing pronunciation on the written language will lead to mistakenly following graphemic rather than auditory stimuli when the stimuli conflict, which is often.

This leaves direct basis on the second language *oral* code as the only possibility likely to result in successful development of accurate pronunciation habits. Even when the learner's goal is just to read the second language, he must (mentally) pronounce it *some* way; if he learns to pronounce it correctly, his perception and recall of grammatical and lexical units will be much improved. Even dead languages could be learned more easily if the students learned to pronounce them acceptably and consistently --then the visual input would be reinforced by auditory input and correct subvocal speech.

Guidance

Programs, such as Direct Method programs, that rely on unguided imitation seldom produce good results (other than with unusually good mimics), for the learning of the sound system of another language is a complex task requiring considerable guidance. There are many problems that the students will simply not realize on their own.

One of the forms guidance takes is the use of articulatory explanations, but it does not have to be limited to that. Indirect guidance is provided by presentations that encourage discovery procedures (such as letting the students discover the conditioning environment of allophones), by a careful order and rate of presentation, by the use of an adequate pedagogical transcription and other visual aids, by the choice of suitable pronunciation drills, by the prompt and efficient correction of pronunciation errors, and by the administration of diagnostic pronunciation tests.

Some of the criteria that can be used in determining the order of presentation are the role of the sound or group of sounds within the structure of the sound system, the commonness of its occurrence in the language, the relative difficulty it presents to the learners, and so forth.

Two of the criteria for choosing a rate of presentation are the learners' attention, which is limited to an x average number of details at any one time, and their ability to develop and retain control over those details, which is a function of the amount and frequency of practice within a given time.

Certain visual aids can be very effective. It is possible to show the articulation of many sounds (more easily for consonants than for vowels) by means of face diagrams, models of the vocal apparatus, photographs, or caricatures (exaggerating visible articulations), with or without the use of audiovisual equipment. Some kinds of charts serve to display clearly native language-second language differences in intonation, stress, and rhythm; other kinds give the learners an idea of the relationship between elements in the sound system, such as vowel charts (or vowel "triangles") and consonant charts. Individual student charts where the sounds and patterns the student controls are checked by the teacher or laboratory monitor can be very informative for the student and helpful in his language practice. Second language pronunciation can also be improved considerably through the analysis of video-tape recordings [Ecklund and Weise 1981]. An adequate pedagogical transcription can be quite useful and will be discussed in a later section in this chapter.

The teacher can also guide the students by choosing carefully the types of pronunciation drills that will best highlight each problem. Different drills are needed, for example, in presenting second language sounds that are unlike any native language sounds, such as Spanish [r̃] as in *perro* for speakers of English, and second language sounds that are partly similar to a native language sound such as the [t̄] in Spanish *tío* for English-speaking learners. (A later section in this chapter will treat the various types of pronunciation drills and how to teach them. The correction of pronunciation errors is similarly discussed in a later section. Pronunciation tests are discussed in Chapter 21.)

Practice

Every time the learner listens to or speaks the second language, he is, of course, practicing sound discrimination or production. In the context of this book, however, "practice" (in this case, "pronunciation practice") will refer to those receptive and productive activities in the performance of which primary attention is given to certain (e.g., pronunciation) problems to be mastered (freer "practice" can be referred to as "communicative activities" or simply "conversation"). In the case of pronunciation, such systematic practice starts with mostly mechanical drills, which are essential to the development of good pronunciation because this is the one area of second language performance in which habitual, unconscious control is far more important than intellectual selection.

But practice does not stop with mechanical drills --it extends to include at least some meaningful activity in which the newly learned sounds are involved. When a method is partially cognitive (as in the case of the "enlightened" eclectic method I propose), habit formation can start with (1) the performance of an action with conscious understanding, move from there to (2) repetition of the action frequently and consciously, and through this practice, which moves from the mechanical to the semi-free, to the (3) attainment of the ability to perform the action automatically --that is, without conscious attention-- whenever the action is called for. As applied to the formation of correct pronunciation habits in a second language, this would mean that a mental grasp of what is involved would not hinder but help the initial accurate production of the new sounds; it would also mean, however, that the learner's initial production would not become habitual unless he went *beyond* that original mental grasp and achieved, through frequent and appropriate practice, automatic control over the sounds.

The classroom does not offer sufficient opportunity

for the individual practice of sounds that is necessary for the development of phonological habits. It has to be supplemented by practice in the language laboratory or at least with tape recordings (which could be studied anywhere with portable cassette machines). In a number of ways, though, recordings have been widely misused. One example is the question of guidance. In most colleges and universities students have to carry out pronunciation practice in the laboratory without any guidance. This can be quite ineffective, as many students listen to their own errors, do not detect them, and think everything is just wonderful. Laboratory monitoring has been touted as the solution to this problem, both at the college and secondary school levels, and it is heavily relied upon by many. But the value of teacher monitoring is mostly illusory, since the average "monitored" student is still on his own all the time except for a very small part of the laboratory session, totalling about one and a half minutes in a 30-student class [Hammerly 1974-b]. The road to effective pronunciation practice with recordings lies instead in giving the students the necessary linguistic sophistication --differentiation, discrimination, and distribution training, and an awareness of the nature of the difficulties they will face-- *before* they start their work with any particular recorded material. Given such training, students *can* both perform and be informed critics of their own performance, whether they are "monitored" or not.

As for activities bridging the gap between pronunciation practice and communication, especially during the first 15 to 20 hours of the program, some of the possibilities are the following: idioms, sayings, brief quotations, minidialogues (about four short sentences in length), choral speaking, certain games, the names of the students in the second language, and competitions (e.g., who can perform a minidialogue or recite a short poem best from the phonological point of view). All of these activities would of course be phonologically graded. Such meaningful activities are essential, for we cannot say that a phonetic differentiation, a phonemic discrimination, or an allophonic distribution has been mastered until it can be used correctly when it is not being highlighted, that is, when the attention is primarily on meaning.

Major approaches

Based on the six major pedagogical considerations and

subfactors discussed so far, it is now possible to characterize five major approaches to the teaching of second language pronunciation.

(1) *The traditional approach:* This approach has typically little or no emphasis on pronunciation throughout most of the program, followed by optional late emphasis in the form of an advanced pronunciation course. It lacks gradation of any kind. This approach is associated with a literary second language goal resulting in low pronunciation standards not influenced by linguistic concepts. It uses a native language-second language graphemic basis and little or no guidance or practice, except in the advanced pronunciation course, which comes too late to effect any major improvements on poor early habits. This approach is found especially in traditionally-oriented university departments where second language programs are designed primarily to develop literary scholarship. It is also found, minus the advanced course in pronunciation, in many secondary schools.

(2) *The direct approach:* In this approach the emphasis on pronunciation varies from little to adequate and is usually distributed throughout the program. There is no gradation. The approach is associated with communication as the main if not the only second language goal. Standards are quite variable and no linguistic concepts are used. There is an oral basis without a prereading period and with avoidance of any reference to the native language. There is heavy reliance on unguided imitation, with little or no guidance and without explanations. There is little or no pronunciation practice as such. Many commercial language schools use this approach; it can also be observed in many elementary and secondary schools. It is widely used in Europe.

(3) *The phonetic approach:* Phonetics and phonology have existed for thousands of years, from the time of Panini in India (400 B.C.). As applied to second language teaching, the phonetic approach to pronunciation started in the late nineteenth century and saw its golden age during the 1920s and '30s, although it is still practiced by some. In this approach, the emphasis on pronunciation is excessive and given throughout the program. There is usually some form of gradation. The standards are meticulous. There is an oral basis, with occasional use of a prereading period. Guidance is generally adequate, but some of the procedures --much *active* use of the International Phonetic Alphabet (IPA), for example-- are

ineffective. Pronunciation practice (of sorts) tends to be excessive. Few schools now use the phonetic approach in North America, although there has been a resurgence in the use of the IPA in second language teaching in recent years, resulting from the rejection of phonemic and phonemic-allophonic transcriptions.

If analyzed in all its phonetic detail, the stream of speech is a constantly changing continuum and phones are only brief points that can be isolated within that continuum. In minute detail all phones are different from one another in some way and the same word is not pronounced exactly the same way twice. But excessive detail --Navarro Tomás [1932], for example, proposed a 20-vowel system for Spanish!-- is self-defeating when it comes to second language teaching, for the learner cannot possibly control so many phones or be aware, e.g., of the number of millimeters that his mouth is open or other such minor phonetic detail. Besides, many allophones are the automatic result of their phonetic environment and need not be taught in order to be used correctly.

In terms of broad articulatory phonetics or functional phonetics a word is almost always pronounced the same way and minute differences between phones having no functional role whatever can be ignored. (This would bring us into phonemics.) And yet, certain phonetic characteristics of languages are very important if one wishes to have an acceptable accent and even, occasionally, for comprehension. For example, foreign accent can be markedly reduced by adopting the *basis of articulation* of the second language (for instance, in North American English the face muscles are relaxed, the throat muscles tense, and the hesitation vowel is a mid-central [ʌ]; on the other hand, in the Romance languages the face muscles are tense, the throat muscles relaxed, and the hesitation vowel is [ɛ], as the tongue position is higher and fronter when not speaking). So students should have some training in holding the characteristic mouth position of the second language. Certain phonetic features are important because they affect a good number of phonemes --an example of this is palatalization in Russian.

While some phonetic differences across languages are not important from the point of view of perception --whether an [n] is dental or alveolar, for instance, makes little difference--, others are. Hall [1966:90] reported that his pronunciation of German *Filme* as ['fɪɫmə], that is, with an English "dark *l*" (with the surface of the tongue hollowed), was occasionally misunderstood as *Firma* ("business firm"). The voicing of an initial /b/ is shortest in German, and short in English, but longer in French, Spanish, and Russian --the result is that the phonetic error of not fully voicing an initial /b/ can result, in Spanish, in *van* being misunderstood as *pan*. The most offensive sounds, to native speakers of other languages, that a North American English speaker can produce are probably a retroflex palatal [ɹ] and the diphthongization of /e/ and /o/ into [ey] and [ow], and these can all be considered phonetic errors.

We see then that phonetics is very useful. Although the systematic study of phonetics has no place in the second language classroom, the teacher needs a good knowledge of phonetics if he is going to be able to help his students with their problems.

(4) *The structural approaches:* There are two such approaches, (a) the phonemic one, and (b) the phonemic-allophonic one. They both use adequate emphasis, some gradation, an oral basis, and adequate guidance and practice. The only differences between these two approaches are in the standards used and the procedures derived from them. The phonemic approach (1940 on) is characterized by minimal standards, as all that matters is that the student make the contrasts in the language, regardless of how he goes about it. The problem is that the phonemic contrasts of a language can be observed with sounds that deviate markedly from native second language sounds. The phonemic-allophonic approach (1956 on) adds to the standards the important refinement that all the major allophones must be controlled, and this according to their phonetic characteristics.

The notion of the phoneme as a functionally significant sound has been around in modern times since the late nineteenth century and is very useful in second language teaching, despite its rejection by more recent linguistic theorists. What native speakers perceive as the "same" or "different" --in other words, what contrasts or does not contrast for them-- is obviously of importance to the second language learner. It is the only way of determining the degree of functional importance of sounds and the only way to reduce the infinite number of sounds to a manageable inventory. Without phonemics, it is impossible to tell which differences in sound are most important for the native speaker. Without phonemics, the Spanish speaker will think that the difference between [ɪ] and [iy] is not important, and fail to distinguish between *bit* and *beat*; the English speaker learning Hindi will fail to differentiate between aspirated and unaspirated [p], [t], and [k], and thereby be frequently misunderstood; learners of French may fail to distinguish between *roue* and *rue*; learners of Chinese may misuse tone phonemes, so that "chicken" and "wife" become the same and the cook may be told to "Kill your wife and cook her" [Hall 1966:11]. The potential importance of phonemic control is seen in the fact that Japanese soldiers during World War II got killed at night because of their inability to say the password "Lollobrigida"; similarly, it is recorded in ancient times that the Gileadites killed 42,000 fleeing Ephraimites who mispronounced the word "Shibboleth" [Judges 12:4-6].

One of the problems with phonemics was the insistence of many structural linguists in dealing with phonemes as unanalyzable units. This tendency to divorce phonemics from phonetics, rather than think of phonemes as bundles of articulatory features to be compared, led to such problems, in second language teaching, as transcriptions that underdifferentiate phonemes --for example, using the same symbol for the [ɛ] in English *bet* (/bet/) and the [e] in *bait* (/beyt/); or using the same symbol for the [a] in German *Stadt* (/štat/) and the [ɑ] in *Staat* (/šta:t/). But for the second language learner no clearly noticeable phonetic difference is redundant, so a reminder of it should appear in the transcription. Another difficulty with phonemics is that it has not dealt adequately with certain phonological processes such as the nasal vowel [ɛ̃] in North American English *twenty* and the voiced flapped allophone of /t/ and /d/ as in *latter* and *ladder*.

Despite these and other shortcomings, phonemics remains essential to second language teaching, provided it is supplemented by allophonic and articulatory phonetic data. The importance of phonemic contrasts can be easily demonstrated to second language classes. All it takes is a few sentences in which native language phonemes are confused. (My favorite one is of the Chinese diplomat who goes to a high-class restaurant and orders "chicken with lice.")

But to be anywhere near accurate, second language pronunciation must go beyond phonemics to the control of all important allophones. It is precisely these allophonic (phonetic) details that a native speaker can ignore which pose the biggest problem for the second language learner who wants to speak the language without a marked accent.

He too can ignore "intrinsic" allophones, that is, those allophones that are unavoidably and automatically determined by their phonic environment, following general articulatory "rules" (like a fronter [k$^{<}$] before a front vowel and a backer [k$^{>}$] before a back vowel), for he will automatically produce them. But he cannot ignore and must learn the "extrinsic" allophones, those that are largely arbitrary phonetically, that is, that don't follow unavoidable articulatory "rules" (like fricative [ƀ], [ð], and [ǥ] in Spanish). If misused, the latter contribute to a marked accent and to occasional misunderstanding --for example, if Spanish *de todos modos* ("anyway") is pronounced with the English allophone of /d/, it is heard as *de toros moros* ("of Moorish bulls").

(5) *The generative approach:* Emphasis on pronunciation with an approach following generative principles tends to be quite inadequate, for generativists are concerned primarily with syntax. Still, some generativists see considerable value in generative phonology for the teaching of second language pronunciation --among them are Scott [1966], Schane [1970], Wardhaugh [1970-a], Kreidler [1972], Dickerson [1975, 1977], and C. Hill and Rittershofer [1976].

There are several problems with generative phonology which make it inapplicable for the crucial first few weeks of second language instruction. It relates pronunciation to syntax, and many generative phonological rules reflect this relationship, but beginners know little or no syntax. Most generative phonological rules are either graphemically based or state graphemic-phonological relationships, but the beginner needs to stay away from the interference of spelling while he is developing his pronunciation habits. The beginner should not nor does he need to base his pronunciation on the way words are spelled; he should rely instead on guided imitation of a good model. Even the native speaker of English who is learning to read or, who later, comes across a new word, is better off if he does not base his pronunciation of the word on its spelling (except for certain regularities) or on generative rules but consults someone or checks the pronunciation in a dictionary. A few simple spelling-to-sound rules may be useful when reading is started at the intermediate level; but these are simple rules known long before generative phonology (such as the school rule for so-called short and long vowels in English). A further problem is that generative phonological rules are highly mentalistic, complex, antibehavioristic, computer-like, and abstract, all qualities that make them unsuitable for use in the second language classroom [Hammerly 1973-b].

At the *advanced* level, certain generative rules relating such pairs of words as *capacity* and *capacious, sign* and *signify, paradigm* and *paradigmatic, courage* and *courageous, pale* and *pallid, face* and *facial,* and *deduce* and *deduction* may be useful *provided* the rules apply to more than two or three pairs of words. But it should be clear that learning to contrast *bit* and *beat* should come at the very beginning of the program and learning to pronounce such words as *face* and *sign* should come rather early, but learning the rules that relate *face* to *facial* and *sign* to *signal* can wait until the intermediate or advanced level, not to speak of the other words listed in the literature, most of which are learnèd words to be added at the very advanced level only.

Chomsky and Halle [1968:49] were right in admitting that for an actor speaking a language he doesn't understand (a situation very similar to that of the beginning second language learner), or more generally, for someone "who wishes to produce tolerable speech without knowing the language," a phonemic transcription would be superior to their generative phonological representations.

To the question: *Which of these approaches is best?* the answer must be, then, that the best approach is phonemic-allophonic-phonetic, with some use of generative rules at the advanced level. The approach should be phonemic in that all contrasts in the sound system of the second language are attended to (*not* in the use of a phonemic transcription, which lacks adequacy of detail); it should be allophonic in that all important extrinsic variants of phonemes are attended to also; it should be phonetic in that phonetic features are the basis for comparison across languages, and, for certain features, the only way to understand certain phenomena within either language.

Phases in the teaching of a pronunciation problem

The teaching of a second language pronunciation problem should follow three major steps: auditory discrimination, awareness and understanding, and production, ending in integration.

(1) *Auditory discrimination*

Must a student learn to hear a distinction before he can produce it? Generally this is the case, and we can say with Léon [1966:59] that "[a]s long as the sound has not been heard correctly, it cannot be reproduced correctly except by chance." As Pimsleur [1959:12] put it, "hearing a distinction is certainly the first step toward learning to imitate it."

Auditory discrimination is usually ahead of production. This is especially evident in the child, in whom receptive control can exist even without production [Diebold 1965: 249]. An example is the following exchange reported by W. Miller [1963:863]: "Recently a three year old child told me her name was Litha. I answered 'Li*th*a?' 'No, Litha.' 'Oh, Lisa.' 'Yes, Litha.'" This does not mean, of course, that there has to be any lengthy period of time, in the case of linguistically adult learners, between the perception of a distinction and its production.

Auditory discrimination/differentiation training has been found to significantly improve sound discrimination even under white noise conditions [Dreher and Larkins 1972]. Many studies have shown its significant beneficial effect on sound production, among them experimental research studies by Pimsleur [1963], T. Mueller and Niedzielski [1968-b], and Dreher and Larkins [1972].

On the other hand, there is evidence that improvement also works in the opposite direction, that is, that learning to articulate a sound improves one's ability to perceive it. In other words, perception has a kinesthetic component, through muscular feedback [Anisfeld 1966:118]. Thus, phonological instruction improves sound discrimination.

It is even possible to learn to produce a sound without having heard it first. Obrecht [1956-57] found that, with the help of a visual representation of the speech apparatus, his students of Spanish could produce new sounds before they heard them. This is not to say that we should give up auditory discrimination training and rely instead on visual representations of articulation. For best results, both should be used.

It seems to be the case that perception facilitates production *and* viceversa. That is, whether the initial act is one of perception or production, each act of perception seems to facilitate production and each act of production seems to facilitate perception, in a sort of gradually closing mutual feedback loop.

Perception of sound distinctions is markedly affected by the native language of the learner. As Lado [1964:72] pointed out for stress, speakers of French, Persian, and Spanish hear a three-syllable word with equal stress on all three syllables as if it were stressed, respectively, on the last, first, and middle syllable. We hear sounds according to our expectations, and without sound discrimination training our expectations will be based on the native language. So auditory training should emphasize the differences between the two languages that might otherwise be disregarded; the best and most efficient way of doing this is to have the students tell apart (given previous cognitive awareness of the problems) second language words pronounced correctly from those pronounced with a native language sound.

Second language sounds must be discriminated in all frequencies of the human voice. Despite claims to that effect, there is no evidence that each sound has an ideal range of frequencies in which it should be taught (although different sounds have greater or lesser acoustic activity at different points in the spectrum). There is no particular advantage in postponing the time when the students must perceive a sound from the unsynthesized, broad range spectrum of the natural human voice.

It is the function of the auditory discrimination phase to make sure that the students learn to hear the differences between two (occasionally three) sounds. For each pronunciation problem, this phase need not last longer than two minutes or so. Given one or more pairs of words (or word parts) containing the two sounds, all four possibilities --X/Y, Y/X, X/X, and Y/Y-- should be used, although the pairs in which the two sounds are the same should be used sparingly. Furthermore, the four possibilities should be used in unpredictable order.

There is no need for very involved drills in this phase. Starting with "same" or "different" responses (if necessary with some initial exaggeration of the difference), the teacher can quickly make sure that the students hear the difference and move on to another type of discrimination drill, such as "No. 1" for sound X and "No. 2" for sound Y, or "the English sound" and "the German sound." All that the students need to do during the discrimination phase is raise one or two fingers, or raise their hands or not raise them. In conjunction with these two techniques, the students may be helped in their choice by two transcription symbols. If there seems to be hesitation, a discrimination test can be quickly administered before moving on to the second phase; of course, if the test shows poor discrimination, further discrimination practice, perhaps with the help of an articulatory explanation, should be given.

For an example of auditory discrimination training, let us suppose that the problem to be taught to English speakers is the fact that /o/ is not diphthongized into /ow/ in Spanish. The teacher could start by asking the students to raise their right hands when the two utterances are different.

The students hear:

(to)mó, mow....... and they should raise their hands, whereupon the teacher says "Different"

dough, (Span.) do... and they should raise their hands, whereupon the teacher says "Different"

mow, mow.......... and they should not raise their hands, the teacher then saying, "Same"

(pe)só, sew....... and they should raise their hands, whereupon the teacher says "Different"

(Sp.) no,(Sp.) no.. and they should not raise their hands, the teacher then saying, "Same"

know, (Sp.) no..... and they should raise their hands, the teacher then saying, "Different"

and so on, but only with pairs in which the only difference is between English /ow/ and Spanish /o/. To teach and test such interlingual differences, few natural pairs are useful, as almost all have more than one difference. The solution is to (1) use the natural pairs that can be used, if any, (2) use word parts, as above for Spanish *(to)mó* and *(pe)só*, (3) make up words, provided they follow the phonological rules of the language(s), and (4) use second language words with or without a native language sound (or viceversa: native language words with or without a second language sound). Note that while reference has been made, in the drill above, to "the students," individual students should also be called upon to respond, in an unpredictable manner; this greatly enhances attention.

To go on with our drill on /o/ versus /ow/, at this point --earlier if many responses were wrong-- two pedagogical transcription symbols can be shown or written on the blackboard, as in Figure 15.2. Then discrimination drills can be done in which only one utterance is given and the students are to raise their right hands only when the utterance has "Sound No. 2" or "the Spanish sound." After they have done this successfully, they are

$\bigcirc^{w}$	$\bigcirc^{\not w}$
English	Spanish

Figure 15.2

ready for phase 2.

(2) *Awareness and understanding*

This means helping the students to become aware of the nature of the problem and understand what is involved in the articulation of the new sound(s). Some awareness and understanding is in fact brought about during the auditory training phase, as the attention of the students may have been overtly drawn during phase 1 to certain observable characteristics of the sounds (in the example given, the relative closing of the lips for /ow/). But in phase 2 the teacher makes sure that every student is clearly aware of the differences between the sounds and explains as necessary their articulation in order to facilitate the production of the second language sound(s) --production which constitutes phase 3.

If the difference was clearly demonstrated in phase 1, with the help of adequate pictorial transcription symbols, the explanation of the difference can come from the students themselves. Exaggerated articulations, brief articulatory pointers (including, if necessary, blackboard aids), and the right questions can lead the students to discover by themselves the differences between two sounds. If the students' explanation is inadequate, the teacher needs to reword it or even give the entire explanation himself. This articulatory explanation need not be technical, although some members of our profession [e.g., Matluck 1957] believe, with some justification, that the process of learning the pronunciation of a second language can be made more efficient by teaching the students a few articulatory terms (after all, don't they have to learn to talk about "molecules" and "atomic weights" in chemistry, etc.?) My personal experience has been that phonetic terminology is useful but can be avoided without any serious disadvantage if the teacher has the requisite knowledge and the ability to translate it into brief and simple articulatory explanations, with demonstrations and face diagrams as needed.

Thus, it is not necessary to teach words like "retroflex," "uvular," and "fricative" in order to describe the differences between a North American English [ɹ] and a European French [ʀ]. For the [ʀ], it is enough to ask the students "not to curl the tongue backwards but keep the tip tight against the lower teeth and raise the back of the tongue" and, if this with its accompanying demonstration is not enough, hand signals and the presentation of the two face diagrams and transcription symbols in

Figure 15.3 should make everything clear.

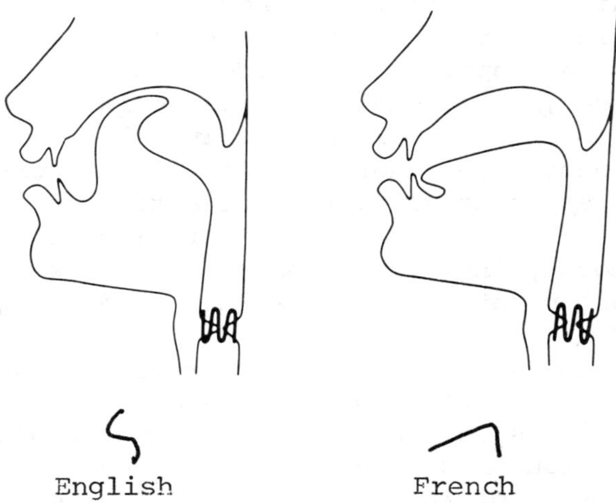

Figure 15.3

It should be obvious that unless the students understand the differences in articulation between two sounds, only the few good mimics among them will be able to produce them close to native standards during the production phase. This is why the process of discovery/explanation is so important. Discovery/explanation procedures can be used for the various types of pronunciation problems, including allophonic ones --in these, examples are given of utterances containing two or three different allophones and the students are asked to try to define the phonic environment in which each occurs.

(3) *Production*

This includes production with attention on the problem gradually shifting to practice with attention on communication, the result being integration of each new sound into the growing system. Production with attention on the problem should first consist of guided imitation of a model, then guided production without a model, and finally unguided production. In dealing with any problem, it is best to first differentiate the new sound from those native sounds with which it is usually confused, and after that to contrast it with other second language sounds; in other words, the overcoming of interference should come before the integration of the new sound into the second language sound system.

Production should start with very short utterances and

then go on to longer ones (phrases and sentences, phonologically graded of course). As in the auditory discrimination training phase, there should be alternation between individual students and the class and this should be always in an unpredictable order. In the production phase, however, individual sound articulation has to be evaluated, so there should be mostly reliance on individual responses, for choral responses hide errors, while individual responses allow the correction of errors for the benefit of the whole class. Normally, then, there should be mostly individual responses followed occasionally by choral imitations, so that all students get to participate.

In the example of Spanish /o/ versus English /ow/, since we are not dealing with pairs of second language utterances, it is only necessary for the students to imitate the Spanish ones (there would not be any point in their production of the English words). The early practice would proceed approximately as follows:

Teacher: *(to)mó*

Student 1: [mow]

Teacher: *No* [mow], [mo] (accompanying the latter with a scissor-like hand signal indicating that the glide [w] is supposed to be cut off)

Student 1: [mo]

Teacher signals to the class to repeat [mo] as said correctly by Student 1.

Class: Mostly [mo], some [mow]

Teacher: *No* [mow], [mo]

Teacher: (Spanish) *do*

Student 2: [do]

Student 3: [dow]

Teacher (exaggerating articulations): *No* [dow], [do]

Student 3: [do]

Teacher signals to the class to repeat [do] as said correctly by Student 3.

Etc. --the same procedure for *(pe)só*, (Span.) *no*, and so forth.

Then a similar procedure is followed with longer utterances (long words, phrases, sentences) incorporating Spanish /o/ plus sounds in common between English and Spanish plus any other Spanish sounds that have already been learned. Then activities bridging the gap between form and meaning are performed, such as learning by heart a minidialogue, a saying, one or more names, etc.

Incidentally, during the production phase it is very

useful --for later reference-- for the students to memorize one utterance pair for each problem; they can be referred to later in the course when the more usual correction procedures fail.

All three phases for the teaching of a pronunciation problem should take no more than ten to fifteen minutes, after which some other activity can be performed for another ten minutes before going on to another pronunciation problem (that is, during the initial 15 to 20 hour pronunciation minicourse).

Only phonetic differentiation has been illustrated. The section on drills later in this chapter gives examples of types of drills intended to deal with other phonological problems, such as phonemic discrimination and allophonic distribution.

A pedagogical transcription

Like the standards for the teaching of second language pronunciation, transcriptions may be phonetic, phonemic, phonemic-allophonic, or pedagogical transcriptions incorporating the best of those three approaches as well as articulatory and corrective reminders.

Many second language teachers are opposed to the use of transcriptions of any kind. Among the reasons for this opposition are the following:

(1) "Learning a transcription first and then learning spelling is unnecessarily learning two things." To this I can say that whenever spelling and pronunciation differ, two things have to be learned anyway, and a transcription facilitates the learning of one or both of them. (The transcription I shall propose leads by a series of steps to spelling, thereby helping to learn both pronunciation and spelling as associated systems, not as two unrelated things.)

(2) "The use of a transcription results in confusion and in more spelling errors." For this reason, only transcription should be used for a while and then phased out, step by step, in favor of spelling. One should lead to the other. Of course, if the transcription symbols are not systematically related to spelling, spelling errors will later occur. But even with the use of the IPA, which does *not* provide a smooth transition to spelling, Palmer [1922, 1964:63] found that exclusive use of it in the early stages led to greater *accuracy* in spelling later. My transcription [Hammerly 1965, 1974-a], the Articulatory Pictorial Transcription (APT) facilitated

spelling to the extent that after one school year of Spanish my students could spell unknown dictated Spanish words better than a fourth-year class of Spanish majors.

(3) "Transcription has been overused." In some cases this is true. Some teachers have taught IPA rather than pronunciation. I remember having engaged in the useless task of transcribing into IPA French sentences from a written text containing words that I had never pronounced. Such active use of transcriptions, even in the more justifiable activity of taking dictation, is quite unnecessary. All that is needed is a passive control of the transcription as an aid to perception and recall. Such a passive control is not difficult to attain, considering that students learning Greek and Russian must master many new letters and yet do so with relative ease.

(4) "There is no evidence that transcriptions help." In addition to the two items of evidence given under (2) above, the relevance of transcriptions is further supported by the fact [Robinson 1969] that adult ESL students have been found to improve their pronunciation very significantly ($p < .001$) with the use of Pitman's Initial Teaching Alphabet (ITA). This with a transcription not specifically designed for learners of English as a second language!

Phonetic transcriptions date back to the Renaissance [L. Kelly 1969:73]. However, phonetic transcriptions that try to be all things to all people --that is, that aim at universal use-- are unsuitable for second language teaching because they cannot take into account the particular problems of a learner of a particular native language learning a particular second language. Furthermore, in their attempt to use familiar letters as much as possible they often elicit, through force of habit, native language responses to those letters. Another disadvantage of the transcriptions used so far is that they make it impossible to have a smooth transition between transcription symbols and spelling.

Pedagogically, then, the main *weakness* of the transcriptions used so far is that they are based on linguistic rather than pedagogical principles. The principle of bidirectional one-to-one co-respondence between symbol and sound, for example, is a sound principle for international phonetics, but in second language teaching it makes it impossible to relate a sound to a variety of spellings or a spelling to a variety of sounds. All that is needed, in a pedagogically-based transcription, is a *unidirectional* fit between symbols and sounds. Phonetic and phonemic transcriptions also use arbitrary symbols that in no way remind the learner of the articulation involved. They also use symbols that foster mispronunciations, such as, for example, representing the various different kinds of *r* sounds with some kind of *r* letter, which will invariably elicit the sound(s) it represents in the native language.

Specifically, the IPA has the following additional shortcomings, from a pedagogical point of view:

--It requires the learner to differentiate between symbols which he automatically considers free variants of each other, such as [a] and [ɑ], and [e] and [ɛ].

--It requires the student to learn new symbols for sounds for which he already has a perfectly good graphic representation in the native language; examples for speakers of English are [ʃ] for ≪sh≫ as in *ship,* [tʃ] for ≪ch≫ as in *cheer,* and [j] for ≪y≫ as in *boy*.

--Certain strange new symbols have to be learned, symbols which in no way remind the student of the corresponding articulations, as for example [ø].

The Articulatory Pictorial Transcription [Hammerly 1974-a] is based, instead, on the following pedagogical principles:

(1) A separate transcription should be devised for each pair of languages, as the problems of pronunciation are to a great extent particular to one target language and one native language. This does not mean that all symbols are going to be different for each pair of languages, but that certain symbols must be different. For example, the problems that native speakers of French, Spanish, and German have with a final English /b/ as in *cab* are quite different. The French speaker will tend to release it with a short [ə], so for him the symbol should include a reminder that the final /b/ is not to be released, such as  or . The Spanish speaker will tend to produce a fricative, so he should be reminded that in this environment (as in all environments) the English /b/ is a stop; this can be done by the use of the symbol , the vertical line indicating interruption of the air stream, a convention which of course has to be taught (the Spanish speaker needs this reminder in some environments only). The German speaker will tend to devoice it, so the reminder for him should be an indication of the vibrations

of the vocal cords such as b̰ . The same sound, but three symbols (or one symbol with three adaptations). The English-speaking learner of Spanish has another problem with the corresponding Spanish phoneme: he will tend to make it a stop when it should be a fricative; for him the reminder of the pronunciation of Spanish /ƀ/ as in *caballo* should be [symbol], the space between the double line representing the opening for the continuous release of the air stream.

(2) Whenever the sound-spelling correlations are the same in the two languages, the standard spelling symbols should be used. Thus Spanish speakers learning English do not need a new symbol for ≪ch≫ as in *cheer,* since that combination of letters has precisely that value in Spanish (although of course they need a different representation for the /š/ of *charlatan* and the /k/ of *chemistry*).

(3) The symbols should offer visual cues to the articulation of the corresponding sounds. It is only by following this principle that a transcription can directly remind the learners of the pronunciation of sounds. Examples given so far in the text include ◯ for [o], [symbol] for the English [ɹ], and [symbol] for the French (and in many contexts German) [ʀ]. Two examples from Spanish are ⋀ , which when initially taught can be described as the movement up and down of the tip of the tongue against the alveolar ridge, for the flapped [ř], as in *caro,* and [symbol] , a representation of the trilled [r̃] as in *carro.* For the vowels of many languages, examples are [symbol] for the high-front spread [i], [symbol] for the mid-front spread [e], and ▯ for the low-central [a].

(4) The articulatory instructions that are given by the teacher when teaching the sound at the beginning of the course should be included, if possible, in the symbol for that sound. An example of this is [symbol] , which reminds the English-speaking learner of the original instruction not to aspirate initial Spanish (or French) [t].

(5) The symbols should not only represent the sounds but also counteract the unwanted tendencies of the native

language. Examples of this have already been given in regard to the Spanish /o/, that is, the APT symbol ◯, and in reference to the various reminders about final English /b/ for speakers of French, b or b, German, b, and Spanish, b. These reminders should be used only as long as needed to establish habits.

(6) There should be a gradual, step by step transition between pronunciation and spelling. This transition is in four steps, which are illustrated in Figure 15.4 for the Spanish [ř] and the French (or Spanish) [a]:

A.P.T. SIGN-TO-SPELLING PROGRESSION

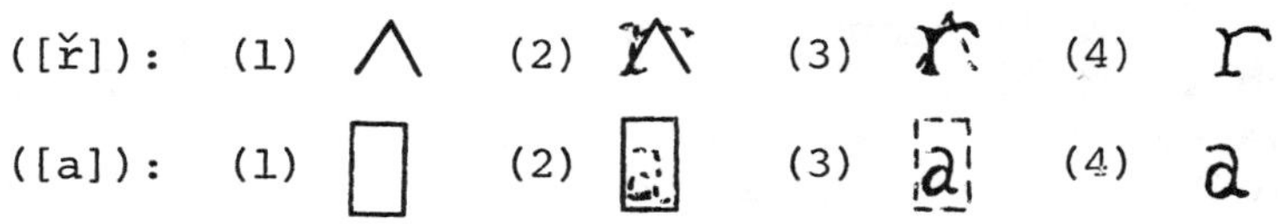

([ř]): (1) ∧ (2) (3) (4) r

([a]): (1) ▯ (2) (3) (4) a

Figure 15.4

Step (1) uses the APT symbol alone; step (2) adds to the APT symbol the spelling symbol in dotted lines or in a different light color; in step (3) the APT symbol appears in light dotted lines and the graphemic symbol appears in normal print; and in step (4) only the spelling appears, the APT symbol having been phased out and the standard spelling phased in. The four steps may be completed within the first 10 to 15 hours of the program for the easier problems, but the complete transition requires several months for the more stubborn problems.

(7) Finally, whenever possible what is known about the mechanics of reading should be incorporated into the transcription. For example, it is known that readers concentrate their vision on the top half of the line, so more information whould be provided in that area. It also helps to separate syllables with a space.

Note that while the APT is a contrastive phonetic-graphemic transcription, not a phonemic one, it can and should be used to support phonemic-allophonic instruction.

My book about the APT presents symbols based on the above principles for Spanish, French, and German for speakers of English and for English for speakers of Spanish, French, and German. These principles can be used for any two languages, although of course there cannot be a smooth transition to the written language in the case of nonalphabetic languages.

Research is needed on many aspects of the use of the APTs, although its value was demonstrated in the Ohio State University experiment [Hammerly 1965]. Matters that need to be worked out include the question of whether all symbols should be introduced in the first step of the APT or some directly in the second step (APT symbol plus dotted spelling), how long each step should last for various types of problems, and so on. As regards the APTs for English as a second language, it seems evident now that the difficulties in representing English vowels in conjunction with their spellings are such (in particular due to discontinuous representations) that in steps 2 and 3 the transcription and the spelling should appear on parallel lines, as it would be impossible to have them combined in one line and retain easy readability.

It should be noted that the APT has a number of definite advantages over previous transcriptions. In addition to some of the advantages already made evident, note that it helps both those who learn through the ear and those who learn through the eye; it helps both to learn new sounds and to remind the learners of their articulation; it corrects both articulatory and spelling-based tendencies to errors; and it makes use of motor memory, which is the most effective and long-lasting type of memory.

But no matter how good a transcription the APT may be, it remains an aid within an overall phonemic-allophonic-phonetic-graphemic pronunciation program. It does not do away with any of the other pronunciation teaching devices, such as auditory discrimination training, discovery and explanations, and practice by means of drills, minidialogues, and so on. Pronunciation has to be taught, and no transcription can change that.

The important thing to remember is that, without a transcription, most students develop a very faulty pronunciation based on native language spelling and articulation habits; or they may develop their own deficient transcriptions, which are usually worse than nothing. A good transcription such as the APT, however, can support the learning process, satisfy the need to have something in writing for the visually-dependent, and serve as a reminder of what a high standard of pronunciation should be like.

More on imitation

Some structuralists, among them Bloomfield, have

advocated an excessive amount of repetition. This may be what led to the reaction of opposing any repetition as unnecessary, mindless, parrot-like behavior. Uttering without understanding is anathema to some teachers, and yet it is a very necessary first step in learning to pronounce a second language with native-like accuracy and fluency.

As a first step, mimicry necessarily involves a good part of the time --as much as 50 percent or so-- during the earliest part of the program, to be soon reduced to no more than 20 percent during the rest of the beginning level and 10 percent later. Other than in dialogues and pronunciation drills, the amount of repetition should be minimal, usually limited to repeating examples of grammatical rules. Being only the first step, mimicry should soon yield to several other steps leading to manipulation and free production. Linguistic habits, i.e., the unconscious and accurate use of rules, are not learned by simple repetition but by the more challenging forms of manipulation, as the rules involve choice-making.

Imitation is not simple. It involves (1) perception of the model, (2) reproduction of the model, (3) perception of one's own production, and (4) evaluation of one's own production in relation to the model. In second language learning this is far more difficult than in the native language, for everything is unfamiliar, that is, there is no basis for a "grammar of expectations." Mimicry should not be broad and careless but should involve conscious attention to the articulation of the segmentals (consonants, vowels, and semivowels), pitch (if any) and intonation, stress, rhythm, gestures --all of this at normal speed.

In imitation, the learner is rewarded for sameness and criticized for difference. The result of this discriminative feedback is that the learner develops discrimination himself and thereby the capacity to be his own monitor and critic. This is essential if he is to retain high pronunciation standards while working on his own or mostly on his own, as in the language laboratory.

To conduct mimicry effectively, the teacher needs to have native-like pronunciation himself; otherwise he should not act as a model but rely on recordings by natives. These recordings can easily be used in class by means of a tape recorder and a foot pedal. In order to help the students articulate sounds correctly, the teacher needs also to know how both the second language sounds and their closest native language sounds are articulated, and know how to lead the students from the latter to the former. Without such guidance there can only be mostly inaccurate imitation.

Some specific pointers to improve the imitation process follow.

--Do not ask a student to imitate an utterance more than two or three times in a row. It has been found [Locke 1970] that more than two repetitions do not significantly improve the imitation of unfamiliar sounds by children between the ages of four and twelve. It seems that excessive repetition triggers a rejection mechanism. And of course, too much repetition leads to boredom.

--Speak at normal speed. Very few native speakers, even after considerable training, can speak very slowly while retaining the phonetic characteristics of connected speech. The great majority distort speech when they slow it down, going to single word articulation which, when speeded up by the students to normal speed, sounds quite strange. It is much easier for the students to learn connected, normal-speed speech from the start, and then learn the changes that are made when speech is slowed down. When speech is slowed down by the model, it is impossible to give it correct intonation. So speech should be maintained at a normal speed throughout (about four or five syllables per second). There is of course a range of normal speed, and within this range the slower (slow-normal) speed can be used. If the students have difficulty with an utterance, rather than slow it down abnormally (and introduce the corresponding distortions) it should be segmented, with pauses between the segments but normal speed within each segment.

--Choral response should not be used for imitation when the purpose is to practice accurate pronunciation. It hides errors within the torrent of sound, as the responses of students with softer voices get lost under the volume of the louder voices. Rewarding successive approximations works with individual learners but not with a group, for in rewarding the whole class one is also rewarding many poor approximations, thereby lowering the standards for the whole class. When the better students see the poorer students being rewarded for poor approximations, they lose their motivation to excell and become satisfied with mediocre performance themselves. Choral repetition should be used only after successful individual repetition and for nonpronunciation purposes, such as the imitation of examples before grammatical drills.

--To help the imitation of longer utterances, start them from the end. It seems that this is the best way to learn a long chain. (More on this in the next chapter.)

Finally, it was found [J. Brown *et al.* 1972] that students using the "Tok-Bak," an audio-active voice reflector (an acoustic shell that reflects the student's voice toward his ear), scored significantly higher ($p < .05$) in a pronunciation mimicry test than those not using it.

Pronunciation drills and techniques

There are many types of pronunciation drills and techniques, each suitable for particular types of pronunciation problems.

(1) *Phonetic differentiation drills*

These drills have as their purpose learning to differentiate between a second language sound and a native language sound with which it tends to be confused and which the students are likely to substitute. These drills require, at least on the part of the teacher, the use of native language utterances in order to bring the difference clearly to the attention of the students. It has also been suggested that at the beginning of the production phase the students should produce both utterances too, so that they may become better aware, articulatorily, of the differences involved (only experimentation will show whether there is an advantage in this).

This type of drill can be said to have "the pedagogical value of the minimal [phonemic] pair on an interlingual basis" [Politzer and Staubach 1961:49]. Our English/Spanish example, including pairs such as *mow ≠ (to)mó*, *know ≠ no*, etc. illustrates this type of drill. Examples of English/French pairs are *say ≠ ses* and *nay ≠ né*, and *sell ≠ sel* and *bell ≠ belle*. An English/German example would be *fell ≠ Fell*.

It has been suggested that one can also use words with and without a native language sound, for instance, two words correctly pronounced and one with a native language sound [*ibid.*, p. 50]. There is nothing wrong with this, provided the native language accent affects only one sound in the word, so that the differentiation is still minimal. There should also be only one difference in the case of pairs of actual words. Thus, as Léon [1966:70-1] observed, a pair like French *note* versus English *nut* (or *note*) would be inadequate to differentiate between French [o] and English [ʌ] (or English [ow]) because there would be at least one additional noticeable difference, the release of the final [t] in the French word (plus a perhaps not-so-noticeable difference in the point of articulation of the [n]'s).

It should be realized that at least in the initial phase of a drill we are dealing with one sound as opposed to another, not with meaningful utterances as such. The items in differentiation pairs may have nothing in common, or even be empty, semantically and yet they are very useful for the comparison of sounds.

(2) *Phonemic discrimination drills*

These are drills that present phonemic contrasts in the second language, without overt reference to the native language.

English-speaking students can be made aware of the importance of phonemic contrasts by being exposed to such English learners' phonemic errors as *I travelled by sheep* (for *I travelled by ship*), and being told that phonemic errors in the language they are learning can be just as serious.

Examples of minimal pairs that could be part of phonemic discrimination drills include English *cut* ≠ *cot* and *pup* ≠ *pop* for the phonemic contrast /ə/ ≠ /ɑ/; Spanish *pasito* ≠ *pesito* and *inglesas* ≠ *ingleses* for unstressed /ă/ ≠ /ĕ/; French *chat* ≠ *chant* and *va* ≠ *vent* for the contrast /a/ ≠ /ɑ̃/; and German *Stadt* ≠ *Staat* and *Wall* ≠ *Wahl* for the contrast in quality and length between /a/ and /ɑ:/.

It should be observed that in teaching phonemic discrimination drills, both items in each pair should be presented together, without a student imitation between them, for otherwise the nature of the contrast does not come clearly to the attention of the students. The four possibilities --X/Y, Y/X, X/X, and Y/Y-- should be used, in unpredictable order, both in the discrimination and the production phases. Note too that both utterances in the pair should have the same intonation.

Phonemic discrimination drills are very important, as our students must control all the sound contrasts in the language. But while phonemic discrimination drills are crucial, they are far from enough. A common mistake in second language teaching is to limit pronunciation drills to the phonemic discrimination type. Learning the pronunciation of a second language requires several types of drills for the various types of problems, depending of course on the structure of the two sound systems involved.

Also to be noted is the fact that many suprasegmental features (stress, pitch, intonation, etc.) can be taught by means of phonemic discrimination drills. To give some examples, English primary versus weak stress can be practiced phonemically by contrasting such pairs of words as *import* (noun) and *import* (verb); English sentence stress can be practiced by contrasting stress on the different words of a sentence like *I didn't tell Lucie you were nasty*, with the corresponding changes in meaning; and Spanish word stress can be drilled with such minimal pairs as *esta* ≠ *está* and *tomo* ≠ *tomó*.

(3) *Allophonic distribution drills*

These are designed to bring awareness of and to practice the distribution of allophones of a given second language phoneme. (Phonemic distribution drills will be treated separately.)

In the case of allophonic distribution drills, minimal pairs are not possible, as allophones are not in contrast but must be accompanied by various conditioning phonic environments.

Some examples of items that can be used in allophonic distribution drills are: English *pin, nip* and *pal, lap* for the distribution of the aspirated [pʿ] and the unreleased [p'] allophones of /p/; Spanish *oda, onda* and *toda, dato* for the fricative [ð] and occlusive [d] allophones of /ð/;[△] French *cadre, quatre* and *ogre, ocre* for the voiced [ʀ] and voiceless [ʀ̥] allophones of /ʀ/; and German *ich, ach* for the front [ç] versus the back [χ] allophones of /χ/ (if not analyzed as separate phonemes).

From the examples just given it is clear that allophonic drills can be of several subtypes: *sound substitution*, as in French *cadre, quatre* and German *ich, ach; sound addition or subtraction*, where the addition or deletion of a phoneme results in an allophonic change, as in Spanish *oda, onda* or the opposite; and *sound reordering*, by either inverting the phonemes in the whole word, as in English *pin, nip* or reordering the syllables, as in Spanish *toda, dato*.

Allophonic drills have no discrimination phase, as there are at least two differences between the utterances.

[△] Since the fricative allophones [ƀ], [ð], and [ǥ] are the norm rather than the exception in connected Spanish speech, they should be used as symbols for the respective phonemes.

Instead, examples are given for repetition, and from them the students should become aware of the phonic environment in which each allophone occurs, "discovering" it and stating it in their own words. The production phase can be done in the same way as phonemic discrimination drills, that is, by asking the students to repeat the pair of words. However, it is far more effective, in order to better bring the conditioning phonic environment to the attention of the students, to teach these drills, in much the same way as grammatical correlation or transformation drills are taught, by telling the students to repeat one word and then say it again after substituting, adding, dropping, or reordering specific phonemes in the word. In other words, allophonic distribution lends itself to fairly cognitive teaching, from discovering and stating the environmental rules to applying them in drills.

(4) *Phonemic distribution drills*

These drills, which can also be called *phonotactic,* allow practice in the production of second language phonemes in positions or sequences in which they do not occur in the learner's native language. They have no discrimination phase.

Languages differ markedly in the phoneme positions and sequences they allow. Spanish, for example, allows very few final consonants and no final consonant clusters; French allows two-consonant final clusters; and English allows up to four consonants in final position (e.g., *glimpsed*). A Spanish speaker learning English needs to practice the production of such sequences as initial /sp-/, /st-/, and /sk-/. An English speaker needs to practice sequences such as /žl-/ (*Je la vois*) and /-lml-/ (*Il me la donne*) for French; /pf-/ (*Pfennig*) and /-tst/ (*jetzt*) for German; /dv-/ (*dva,* "two"), /kt-/ (*kto,* "who"), and /mn-/ (*mnógo,* "much") for Russian; and /ŋ-/ and /-h/ for several Oriental languages.

This type of drill is taught basically in a productive manner, with help as needed. The help that is most useful takes the form of the "shaping technique," which is discussed below.

(5) *Shaping technique*

This is a productive technique that consists in starting with a sound or sequence of sounds that the student can pronounce (usually native language sounds) and moving, by steps, to the desired second language sound or sound sequence. It should be noted that, unlike other drills that use the principle of contrast, the shaping technique relies on positive transfer from the native to the second language via successive approximations.

An example of shaping a sequence is that of English /sp-/ as in _speak_ for the Spanish speaker; this can start with something like _Es pícaro_, and then the student can be led to drop the /e/ and then the ending; or he could get started by producing a long [s::] followed by the rest of the English word, with the shaping consisting of gradually shortening that [s] to normal length; or a short [e] can be added between the /s/ and the /p/ and then dropped in steps. Another example of shaping a sequence would be that of the English speaker learning German /pf-/, as in _Pfennig_, who could get started with a slow rendition of the word _cupful_, then speed it up, then say the nonce word *_cupfennig_, and then drop the initial phonemes /kə-/.

The shaping technique can be used not only to teach the production of difficult sequences; it can also be used to teach individual new sounds. Thus, as several authors have noted, the Spanish flapped [ř] may be derived for English-speaking students from the flapped /t/'s and /d/'s that occur in such English words as _totter_, _Betty_, _ladder_, and _caddy_. Hayes [1965:292] suggested that German speakers (and this applies to French speakers as well) can learn to produce the retroflex English [ɹ] of _roast_ in three steps: (1) [zo:st], something the speakers can say, as German has the word _so_ (and French the word _zoo_); (2) "run the tip of the tongue back along the roof of the mouth to about the middle and try to say [zo:st]"; and (3) "keep the tongue in the same curled-back position but lower it until there is no audible friction or buzzing sound." Moulton [1962:29] suggested three alternative ways of teaching the German [ç] by shaping: (1) start with the initial /h/ in English words like _hue_ and _human (human_ → *_me-human_ → German _mich);_ (2) start with a long [y::] as in _y-y-yes_ and unvoice it; or (3) whistle the highest note you can reach with lips spread. According to Bowen and Stockwell [1960:51, 54, 55], English speakers can learn to produce Spanish [ƀ], [ð], and [ǥ] rather easily by producing a "slightly inebriated" rendition of such English words as _rubber_, _mother_, and _sugar_. Alternatively, the same effect can be attained with those three sounds by asking the students to breathe deeply and say such English words without any interruption in the flow of air.

Two subtypes of the shaping technique are the

sound-range technique and the *sound-bracketing technique*. In the sound-range technique, students are asked to produce slowly a range of sounds, such as, for example, the continuum of front vowels from [i] to [æ], and then they are asked to stop at a particular point in the continuum where a second language sound occurs. In the sound-bracketing technique, two known points of reference are used, and the point between them is the goal to be reached. Thus, an English speaker trying to learn Spanish, French or German [a] can be led to its production by starting with the two English vowels [æ] and [ɑ], saying them several times, and then placing the tongue in a position midway between those two known vowels. Another example is the learning, by an English speaker, of French or German [ü], which can be accomplished by starting with [i] and [u] and then producing a sound with the tongue position of [i] and the lip protrusion of [u] (in this case, it seems that holding the lip position of [u] and then moving the tongue as if to try to say [i] produces the best results).

(6) *Phonic distribution drills*

These drills serve to practice the distribution of related sounds --not allophones, as they belong to two or more phonemes-- whose occurrence is predictable in certain environments.

An example is the automatic distribution of final nasal consonants in Spanish. While phonemically a word like *sin* can be said to end in an /n/, a final /n/ undergoes a whole range of assimilations from [m] to [N͕], depending on the consonant that follows it, as can be seen in Figure 15.5.

sin papel......[m]......bilabial
sin falta......[ɱ]......labiodental
sin nada.......[n]......dental
sin cheques....[n͕]......alveopalatal
sin ñapa.......[ñ]......palatal
sin casa.......[ŋ]......velar
sin gente......[N͕]......pharyngeal

Figure 15.5

These drills can be taught like allophonic distribution drills.

(7) *Suprasegmental drills*

These have as their purpose the practice, sometimes in contrast with native language patterns, of second language patterns of stress, intonation, and other suprasegmental features that cannot be dealt with under the other types of drills.

For example, a speaker of North American English learning Spanish might be asked to imitate a series of sentences contrasting intralingually the intonation of "yes-or-no" questions (as in *¿Trabaja bien?*, ending in intonation /2↑/) and "interrogative-word" questions (e.g., *¿Por qué trabaja bien?*, ending in /1↓/). Or he might be asked to contrast interlingually Spanish intonation in greetings (as in *Buenos días, señora,* ending in /11↓/) with its English counterparts (as in *Good morning, madam,* ending in /22↑/).

Unfortunately, suprasegmentals are often neglected in the teaching of second languages, probably because they are the features with which the non-native second language teacher makes most of *his* errors in pronunciation and because it is the aspect of pronunciation of which the *native* second language teacher has the least conscious awareness. Attention to stress, intonation, and rhythm should be given from the beginning of the second language program and should continue throughout it.

At the very beginning of the program, while the segmentals (vowels, consonants, and semivowels) are being learned, the suprasegmentals cannot be practiced without asking the students to produce segmentals that they do not control as yet. For that reason, the order of presentation of suprasegmentals *vis à vis* segmentals should be as follows: (1) have the students listen to the voices of second language speakers speaking the students' native language with foreign suprasegmental patterns, since this is the most effective way of impressing upon them the need for suprasegmental accuracy; (2) practice a few of the most common second language suprasegmental patterns while (a) giving the students the native language meaning and (b) asking them to produce a vowel, e.g., [e], [a] or [ə], or to produce native language sentences with second language suprasegmentals; (3) simply correct major suprasegmental errors while the segmentals are being learned; and (4) follow this with a systematic study and practice of second language suprasegmental patterns after the segmentals have been learned.

As with other features of sound systems, the important thing is to concentrate on suprasegmental *differences* between the two languages. The English speaker does not need, for example, to study the whole system of intonation of Spanish, French, or German, as much is the same as in

English.

In teaching and correcting suprasegmentals, gestures by the teacher can be very useful. Thus, stress can be effectively indicated by clapping the hands or knocking on the table or wall, and a horizontal movement of the hand or hands rising or dropping at various levels can indicate intonation levels almost as well as a transcription (of course, both visual aids and transcriptions can also be quite useful in the teaching of suprasegmentals).

(8) *Unison speaking technique*

Schwartz [1967:169] suggested the use of a unison speaking technique when other types of guidance and exercises fail. (Unison speaking consists of the student imitating the teacher as he speaks --naturally there is a delay of a fraction of a second). Schwartz wrote of an Italian girl learning English with whom nothing seemed to work in breaking her habit of adding syllables to English sentences, but unison speaking was successful. This technique is particularly useful in teaching second language rhythm and syllabification, but it could also be helpful with other suprasegmental features. Research is needed on this technique.

(9) *Articulatory tricks*

Tricks or gimmicks make use of simple material aids or actions to make the students aware of the articulatory processes needed in the production of certain second language sounds. Voicing versus the lack thereof can be demonstrated by (a) placing the palm of the hand on the head, (b) stopping an ear, or (c) placing two or three fingers on the voice box. A narrow strip of paper or a lighted match near the mouth can help bring awareness of the difference between the aspirated allophones of English /p/, /t/, and /k/ versus the lack of aspiration that the equivalent Spanish or French phonemes have in the same environments. The sharp point of a pencil placed on the lower lip can help to ensure that there is no lip closure in the production of Spanish [ƀ] (that is, the upper lip must not touch the pencil point during the articulation of the [ƀ]). These are all examples of articulatory tricks or gimmicks.

(10) *Unacceptable drills*

Such drills, unacceptable from the point of view of teaching or practicing second language sound discrimination or production, include dictation and "saturation" drills.

During the initial teaching of pronunciation, dictation

would involve the undesirable introduction of writing, thus requiring the students to pay attention to two different and often conflicting codes. The way it is usually done, one or two words at a time, dictation involves only recall of previously learned graphemic material, not sound discrimination (for which the various techniques of phase one are far better) nor listening comprehension (which can be practiced without any need to write anything). Dictation can be useful in only two ways: as a test of spelling skill and, at the very advanced level and in full sentences, as an integrative test of overall auditory comprehension and linguistic competence.

"Saturation" drills make use of sentences in which a newly learned sound occurs a great number of times. Examples are: in English, *She sells sea shells by the seashore* (for /s/ vs. /š/); in Spanish, *Rápido ruedan las ruedas del ferrocarril* (for /ř/); and in French *Le curé a su ce qu'il a lu sur les murs de la cure* (/ü/) [Mackey 1965:264]. Such sentences containing numerous occurrences of a sound or two do not show what the student will do when not so guided, that is, in unguided production. Such sentences are so highly improbable that they likely have very little transfer to everyday conversation. Furthermore, they are difficult for native speakers, so it seems rather unreasonable to expect beginning second language students to produce them --the practice can only generate frustration.

Some second language specialists also object to the teaching of sounds in isolation. It is clear that stops, flaps, affricates, and semivowels cannot be produced in isolation, as they would need a vowel to accompany them. In the case of vowels and continuant consonants, however, the sound can be articulated in isolation; so, if necessary for the teaching of the sound or for error correction, this can be done. There is nothing wrong with isolating isolatable sounds as long as the students are not left with the sounds in isolation but with longer utterances in which the sounds occur in the context of other sounds.

More on suprasegmentals

Problems with stress, intonation, juncture, and rhythm (suprasegmentals) should be practiced early, as all utterances of two or more syllables have them. An awareness of syllabification should also be developed early.

Stress is not phonemic in French, but it is in English (*import* as noun vs. *import* as verb), in Spanish (*hablo*

"I speak" vs. *habló* "he spoke"), and in German (*unterhalten* "to hold under" vs. *unterhalten* "to keep up"). A list of second language surnames can be an effective means of teaching stress discrimination at the beginning of the program.

Intonation can keep many sentences from being ambiguous. For example, *I didn't leave because he arrived,* with falling intonation, means "I stayed because of his arrival," while with rising intonation it means "I left for some other reason." While English, German, and Spanish have definite intonation levels, a small number of significant intonation levels has not been established for French. If intonation patterns are not learned properly in the early part of the program, bad intonation habits will set in that will be very difficult to correct. It is not uncommon to observe students who have mastered all aspects of the phonology of a second language but the intonation.

Rhythm is syllabic (with little difference in duration between stressed and unstressed syllables) in Spanish and French, but it is stress-timed in English and German, with primary stress counting as one unit and weak stress counting hardly at all. Thus, the sentence *John is a student* has two units of rhythm, but so do the sentences *John is a good student* and *John is a very good student*. A Spanish or French speaker will tend to mark the first of these three sentences with five "beats" and the third with eight.

The great majority of syllables in English and German end in a consonant, unlike French and Spanish, in which the great majority end in a vowel. Using English syllabification in French or Spanish will result in a noticeable accent.

In terms of a visual representation for suprasegmentals, one of the best ones is the system of dots on a scale developed by Kenneth L. Croft [Lado 1964:81], as in Figure 15.6. The size of the dot indicates the degree of stress, the height of the dot the intonation level, and

Johnny went home.

Figure 15.6

the line from the final dot the juncture. Another representation, developed by myself in conjunction with the APT, would use a line of varying thickness at various heights, as in Figure 15.7.

Figure 15.7

Research is needed on the best way to represent suprasegmentals.

Lane and Buiten [1966] reported on the successful use of a computer-based display of intonation, stress, and rhythm. Yet the time has not yet come when computers are economically feasible in more than a few second language programs. An oscilloscope can help with suprasegmentals (and it is relatively inexpensive) by converting speech into visual patterns [Richmond 1973]. It has also been shown that early exposure to suprasegmentals in electromechanically-generated form helps their discrimination [Feldman 1973]. A recent finding has been that Spanish suprasegmentals can be taught successfully with self-instructional materials [Mantini 1980]; this is important, considering that many teachers cannot handle the teaching of suprasegmentals too well.

Pronunciation errors and their correction

A careful introduction to the sound system of the second language during the first three weeks or so of the program can reduce greatly the incidence of errors later on. Errors *will* occur, however, both during the introduction and, hopefully less frequently, in the rest of the course.

Some specialists believe that by simply not rewarding the errors they will disappear. I have observed, on the contrary, that errors tend to remain unless corrected and that they disappear much faster when they are corrected. For the second language student to learn pronunciation, his phonological behavior must make a difference in his environment, in terms of feedback from the teacher.

Most errors in pronunciation, though unavoidable despite the best efforts of the teacher, can at least be often predicted, on the basis of contrastive analysis. Some pronunciation errors, however, are not due to native language interference but to causes such as false analogies, wild guesses, vagueness in remembering forms, and general lack of accuracy [Mackey 1965:369]. The latter can result in great instability in pronunciation, with some sounds produced in many different ways [Walz 1980].

The errors of second language learners (or, incidentally, acquirers) differ markedly from those of native language acquirers. While the native language acquirer tends to simplify consonant clusters by reduction (*blue* as *bue*), second language acquirers tend to insert a vowel (*tree* as *tuhree*); the same thing --deletion vs. epenthesis-- may happen with final consonants; children acquiring their native language often delete weak syllables, but adult second language acquirers seldom do [D. Oller 1974]. Note also that the strategies of phonological simplification among second language acquirers differ according to their native language [Tarone 1980].

Among adult English-speaking second language learners, the most noticeable errors, characteristic of a North American English accent, are the diphthongization of [e] and [o] into [ey] and [ow], the use of the retroflex palatal [ɹ], the use of [ə] for other vowels in unstressed position, the use of the dark [ɫ], the intrusion of glottal stops, and the use of emphatic stress out of place. (Some second languages have one or more of these pronunciation features.) Note that of these errors all but one can be considered phonetic in nature. Furthermore, they are all easily overcome *if caught early*.

The nature of the language task affects the production of errors. From the point of view of pronunciation errors, it is easiest to be accurate in pronunciation drills, somewhat less easy in dialogue presentations, a little less easy in dialogue performance, more difficult in grammatical drills, still more difficult in guided communicative activities, and most difficult in free conversation. Ensuring accuracy in the easier activities facilitates the development of accuracy in the more difficult ones. As attention shifts away from pronunciation to meaning, fewer errors should need to be corrected if the groundwork has been properly laid. Normally all pronunciation errors should be corrected during pronunciation drills and dialogue presentations and performances, and only major errors during grammatical drills and communicative activities, provided high standards are maintained from the start and not allowed to deteriorate. An experimental study showed that if initial attention to pronunciation is subsequently neglected, initial accuracy can quickly decline [Walz 1980].

There are unfortunately certain practices in our profession that encourage pronunciation errors. One of them is the reliance on choral responses, something that has already been discussed. The problem is that with choral responses the errors cannot be picked out --even if the teacher moves around the classroom, he can at best hear at the same time the general rhythm and intonation of the whole group plus the specific pronunciation errors of the three or four students closest to him or with the loudest voices. No, there must be reliance on *individual* responses in any sound production work, with only occasional group imitations *after* the item has been responded to correctly by an individual student.

Another unfortunate practice is the frequently-given advice that imitation should begin with several repetitions by the whole class, then by sections, then by rows, and finally by individuals. Such a practice means that by the time the individual is reached, he may have mispronounced the utterance six or seven times, developed "confidence" (what a misused word) in doing so, and thereby gone a long way toward making that pronunciation habitual. The solution is to rely primarily on individual responses from the start. This has the advantage of letting everyone in the class know what errors they have to avoid, since they would hear, in addition to correct models, typical incorrect individual renditions that would be corrected on the spot. Having heard someone corrected for making a certain error, it is less likely that the rest of the students will proceed to make the same error.

The question is: How should pronunciation errors be corrected? Some answers are obvious. Correction should be immediate though not to the point of interrupting free conversation in midsentence. Only the linguistic feedback should be negative; the affective and the communicative feedback should remain positive. If correction can be elicited rather than just given, it should be elicited, although the possibility of elicitation applies mostly to allophonic errors.

Less obvious is the answer to the question: What specific techniques should be used in the correction of pronunciation errors? The technique advocated at the Northeast Conference [Eddy 1959:15 and G. Jones 1964:11], was the simple repetition of the utterance or word mispronounced. This is also the technique shown in several films for teacher training. But the success of the repetition technique depends entirely on the student's ability to imitate, which may be quite poor. What does the teacher do if, as a result of perceptual or articulatory interference, the student cannot imitate correctly, even after several repetitions, as is frequently the case? Continue to model the utterance repeatedly and pointlessly? It would be much better to let the student know from the start exactly *where* the error is and *what* the error is, two bits of essential information that the repetition technique denies the learner.

Thus, the effective correction of pronunciation errors should (1) *isolate the error* from the longer utterance as a whole, so that the student will know *where* the error is, and (2) *differentiate the error,* through a contrastive technique, from the correct pronunciation, so that the student will know *what* the error is and what he is expected to say instead. To illustrate, if an English-speaking student hears the Spanish phrase *Buenas noches* ("Good evening/night") and mispronounces it as *['bwenəz "nočεs] the error can be isolated and differentiated in one step by the teacher saying "*No* [-nəz-], [-naz-]," and then, after the student says correctly [-naz-], adding more of the utterance for imitation, e.g., "['bwenaz-]," and finally the whole phrase again, "['bwenaz "nočεs]."

Care should be taken, however, when isolating the mispronounced segment, not to separate it from its phonically conditioning environment. Thus, if a student mispronounces Spanish *la vacuna* ("the vaccination") as *[la ƀə'kuna], it would not do to isolate the second syllable, for this would mean that the [ƀ] would change to [b], since it would then be in initial position; the result would be that one error would be exchanged for another, with the student saying [la ba'kuna]; the shortest segment that can be isolated in this case without creating additional problems is [-aƀa-], and, in practice (since this [l] should cause no problems), [laƀa-].

Another distortion that should be avoided is a change in stress during correction. The corrected item should retain its original stress rather than have it shifted for emphasis. For example, if an English speaker mispronounces Spanish *señorita* [seño'řita] as *[siño'řita], it is wrong to say "*No* *['siñořita], *['señořita]," for this means that the erring student will change a vowel error for a stress error and end up saying *['señořita].

Examples of the isolation and differentiation technique for the correction of pronunciation errors in several languages follow ("T" stands for "teacher" and "S" for "student").

Spanish

T: ['ay"třɛs'čikosa'ki] *(Hay tres chicos aquí)*
S: *['ay"tɹɛs'čikosa'ki] (an English *r*)
T: *No* [-tɹɛs-], [-třɛs-]
S: [-třɛs-]
T: [-"třɛs'čikos-]
S: [-"třɛs'čikos-]
T: ['ay"třɛs'čikosa'ki]
S: ['ay"třɛs'čikosa'ki]

French

T: [e'kutlamü"zik] *(Écoute la musique)*
S: *[e'kutlamyu"zik] ([yu] for [ü])
T: *Pas* [-myu-], [-mü-]
S: [-mü-]
T: [-mü'zik]
S: [-mü'zik]
T: [-lamü'zik]
S: [-lamü'zik]
T: [e'kutlamü"zik]
S: [e'kutlamü"zik]

German

T: ['dasʔɪstʔɑyn"špi:gl] *(Das ist ein Spiegel)*
S: *['dasʔɪstʔɑyn"spi:g̍l] ([s] for [š])
T: *Nicht* [-spi:-], [-špi̍:-]
S: [-špi:-]
T: [-'špi:gl]
S: [-'špi:gl̍]
T: [-ʔɑyn'šp̍i:gl]
S: [-ʔɑyn'špi:gl̍]
T: ['dasʔɪstʔɑyn̍"špi:gl]
S: ['dasʔɪstʔɑyn"špi:gl̍]

English for Spanish speakers

T: ['hiyz"pʿowlɪš] *(He's Polish)*
S: *['hiyz"pʿolɪš] ([o] for [ow])
T: *Not* [-pʿo-], [-pʿow-]
S: [-pʿow-]
T: [-'pʿowlɪš]
S: [-'pʿowlɪš]
T: ['hiyz"pʿowlɪš]
S: ['hiyz"pʿowlɪš]

Note that whenever a correction is made the student is not left with a corrected segment but the whole phrase is built up again for repetition.

Often pronunciation errors cannot be corrected on the first try. In those cases, it helps to refer to the pair of words or utterances used in initially teaching that problem (herein the advantage of memorizing one pair of words, with their meanings, for each problem). If that doesn't work, it may be necessary to very briefly teach the problem again, making use as needed of articulatory pointers, transcription reminders, visual aids, etc. (since all this has been done before, only brief reminders are needed in the later correction of stubborn errors). It may also be necessary to resort to the shaping technique described earlier in this chapter.

In the correction of suprasegmental errors, gestures can be very helpful. An intonation pattern can be shown with hand movements. Rhythm and stress can be indicated by tapping. As a last resort, suprasegmental features can be represented graphically on the blackboard --I remember the case of a student who kept mispronouncing Spanish *a propósito* [apřo'posito] ("by the way") as *[apřopo'si̲to] and resisted all attempts at correction until

*a-pro-*PO*-si-to*

was written on the blackboard.

If the error persists after several attempts at correction, it may be that a psychological point of diminishing returns has been reached; that is, after three or four various attempts at correcting an error, most students become frustrated and less receptive to correction and may even begin to produce *more* errors in the utterance. If that point is reached, it means that the teacher has pressed the student too hard. It is better to observe the reactions of the student carefully and, before that point is reached, leave the student alone for a while (although *not* rewarding him with "Very good" or its equivalent) and then come back to him later when he is again receptive to correction.

Frequently there will be more than one error in an utterance. Some students can handle the correction of more than one error at the same time, but most need to be corrected one error at a time. Thus it is necessary to establish a hierarchy of error correction. This can be based on intelligibility or offensiveness. According to the criterion of intelligibility, Stockwell and Bowen [1965:121-2] recommended that the order of correction of segmentals, *after* the suprasegmentals, should be (1) segments that cause misunderstanding, (2) segments that produce obvious accent, and (3) all others. The criterion of offensiveness means that priority should be given to those pronunciation errors which are most offensive to the ears of native speakers. These, we know, are more often phonetic than phonemic [Hayes 1965:287-8] --for example, an English [ɹ] for a Spanish [ř] or [r̃] or for French or German [ʀ] would certainly rank high as contributing to "a horrible American accent" [Moulton 1966:54-5]. It seems that, ideally, the two types of hierarchies of correction should be combined in the correction process, as they are complementary rather than mutually exclusive.

When several students consistently make a certain pronunciation error, a temporary group for remedial activities can be formed. Such groups, which are disbanded as soon as the problem has been overcome, can be formed not only for pronunciation but also for grammatical difficulties that might be found to persist.

It is important that, especially early in the language program, pronunciation errors be corrected "immediately and insistently" [Bowen and Stockwell 1960:1], for otherwise there can be no hope of having the students develop the best control over the sound system of which they are capable. This will reduce considerably the need for correction at the intermediate or advanced levels of the program, at which point the correction of pronunciation errors is basically remedial and usually not very effective. It is also important that the teacher should consistently maintain high standards of pronunciation in the class, for if he becomes lax in this respect excellence can erode very quickly and the class can all too easily revert to native language habits of pronunciation. To help maintain high standards, perhaps nothing contributes as much as correction and making pronunciation a significant part of course grades.

Correlates of success in second language pronunciation

Several factors have been found to relate to success with pronunciation.

(1) *Age*

It is a commonplace that young children acquire better second language pronunciation than adults. Not frequently realized, however, is that with proper instruction adults can do better than young children under classroom learning conditions.

In classroom language learning (as opposed to acquisition) children do not necessarily do well; proof of that is that they differ greatly in their ability to learn the formal variety of the native language taught in school. Children seem to retain until age 12 or 13 the ability to acquire second language pronunciation perfectly, although by the age of 10 this ability begins to deteriorate. Asher and Garcia [1969], for example, found that the quality of English pronunciation of Cuban children was in inverse relationship to the age of their arrival in the United States. But Politzer and Weiss [1969] showed that in school instruction the quality of pronunciation is positively correlated with age. Olson and Samuels [1973] found that junior high and college students did significantly better than elementary children in German pronunciation after two weeks of instruction that included ten 15 to 25-minute sessions of pronunciation practice.

Young children may be helped in the acquisition process by the fact that they have more fluid ego boundaries and are more likely to identify with second language speakers than adults; they are also subject to greater pressure to conform. Adults are helped in the learning process by their greater cognitive and learning skills and by their ability to concentrate consciously on pronunciation problems.

(2) *Sociolinguistic and cultural factors*

It may be that the reason for the failure of many adults to develop a perfect accent is sociolinguistic and cultural rather than physiological [J.H. Hill 1970]. Many adults think of their native language as *the* way in which people should speak. Many do not want to be identified with second language speakers. I remember, for instance, a girl in Texas who could speak with perfect Spanish pronunciation inside the classroom but whose pronunciation deteriorated markedly as soon as she left the classroom; upon questioning her, I found out that she did not want to be identified as a Spanish speaker, apparently because of the lower socioeconomic status of Spanish speakers in Texas.

(3) *Personality variables*

Pronunciation is more related to personality variables than any other aspect of second language learning and use. It may be that to a great extent pronunciation difficulties are psychological rather than physiological. Pronunciation runs deeper into personality makeup, especially identity, than anything else in a second language. L. Taylor *et al*. [1969] found that accurate pronunciation of Japanese after four hours of instruction correlated with a test of empathy. In another study [1971], they found that high empathy correlated with correct pronunciation in spontaneous speech and intuition correlated with accuracy of imitation. Guiora *et al.*[1972-a] determined that reducing inhibitions with a small amount of alcohol --enough to lower inhibitions but not enough to interfere with cognitive activity or muscular control-- significantly improved pronunciation; they attributed this to an increase in empathy, although H.D. Brown [1980:106] pointed out that it could just as well be the muscle-relaxing effect of the alcohol.

(4) *Musical ability*

It has been claimed by several authors that musical ability correlates positively with good second language pronunciation. The question is far from settled. If such a correlation is definitely confirmed, it will likely be found to apply to acquisition but not to learning.

(5) *Predictive value of factors*

Purcell and Suter [1980] found that the four most useful predictors of pronunciation accuracy were: (1) the native language, accounting for nearly 42 percent of the variance; (2) aptitude for oral mimicry; (3) residency in an English --the second language-- environment; and (4) strength of concern for pronunciation. Together these factors accounted for 67.3 percent of the variance. Note that factor 3 (residency) applies to an environmental second language learning situation but not to a remote one.

The introductory pronunciation minicourse

Pronunciation is best taught by an introductory minicourse of 15 to 20 hours plus follow up. A pronunciation course any time later is too late, and without early pronunciation instruction pronunciation is not learned well. With proper early training in pronunciation, when the students reach the advanced level they will have no marked foreign accent to contend with. The students should not therefore proceed in earnest to a study of the grammar and vocabulary of the language until they have developed a good degree of mastery over the sound system.

The pronunciation minicourse should introduce the students to the sound system of the second language gradually, one or two sounds at a time. The teaching of most sound-spelling correlations (step 2 of the APT) should come near the end of the minicourse. (In the far-from-ideal situation in which the students are handed a textbook with standard spelling on day one, the relationship betwen letters and sounds should of course be taught from the start.)

On the first day of class the students should be given individual pronunciation charts/checklists which they are to use from then on. The teacher and student would mark these charts according to individual needs and accomplishments. Some basic articulatory training --Palmer [1922, 1964:46] called it "mouth gymnastics"-- should be done during the first few hours. Phonetic concepts can be taught nontechnically and always should be used with reference to the two languages in the classroom. Training in articulatory phonetics has been found significantly helpful in the learning of second language pronunciation [Catford and Pisoni 1970]. Required equipment during the minicourse, in terms of articulatory phonetics, would be individual handheld mirrors for the students --a mirror is effective for watching the articulation of several vowel features and some consonant features.

With regard to the order of presentation of sounds, the minicourse should start with all those sounds in common between the two languages, which usually means several consonants and possibly some vowels, and should then present the other sounds, one or two at a time. The choice of problems to be taught should be based on both contrastive analysis and past observation of errors. Normally vowels should be taught first, as they constitute the core of syllables and are more common; they should be taught first in stressed position, where they are more noticeable, and then in unstressed position. Less common and more difficult sounds can be left for the latter part of the minicourse.

It is better not to use meaning during pronunciation drills, for meaning leads to associations with previous knowledge and this results in interference. All new sounds, whether completely or partly different from native language sounds, should be treated as something new, not associated with but *differentiated* from known sounds with which they might be confused. At the same time, it is very useful for later reference if the students learn one word pair for each sound with the word meanings, in translation, both as isolated words and as words in sentences (again, translated).

A lively pace should be maintained in the minicourse, never letting the students get tired or bored with any activity. Very few students are willing to do pronunciation drills for hours, and even these soon get tired. Since pronunciation work must necessarily be mostly meaning-free, it is essential that it be alternated with meaningful activities of the type listed in the "Practice" section earlier in this chapter. All pronunciation errors should be corrected during the pronunciation minicourse, and each time several new problems have been taught there should be a brief test on them.

The teaching of much in second language pronunciation can be fairly cognitive, since many of its features are systematic [Rochet 1978]. It also is, fortunately (since many second language teachers are poor models or don't know how to teach pronunciation or both), largely programmable, which means that pronunciation minicourses could be developed for the various native language-second language combinations and put into use before the regular course begins.

(For a comprehensive treatment of the teaching of second language pronunciation to about 1968, see Hammerly 1970-b.)

16

DIALOGUES AND OTHER PRESENTATION DEVICES

Advantages and disadvantages of using dialogues

The use of dialogues in second language teaching goes back at least to St. Augustine in the fourth century A.D. [L. Kelly 1969:35]. But while a number of modern methods use dialogues, others do not. Among the advantages of dialogues are the following:

(1) Dialogues, if well-written, provide the students with samples of the spoken language, that is, frequently-used vocabulary, idioms, grammatical patterns or rules, and types of constructions used in speech.

(2) Dialogues present every new item in both linguistic and situational context, the natural context of everyday conversation. Contextualized sentences are more meaningful and easier to learn and remember than isolated sentences [J. Oller and Obrecht 1969]. It is easier to memorize a sentence than to memorize the six or seven words that make it up. Word isolation is a convenience for dictionary making only, not a good basis for language learning. The basic unit of beginning second language learning is not the word or even the isolated sentence, but sentences in a situational context.

(3) Dialogues provide the opportunity for further practice (beyond the introductory pronunciation minicourse) in the perception and production of sounds. Dialogue memorization develops the memory span for second language sounds; since a native-like memory span is essential to communication, this is an important advantage. The repetition of sentences after a model, at normal speed, also helps develop fluency --even at the advanced level there should be some repetition of fairly complex sentences for comprehension and fluency development.

(4) Dialogue sentences provide the most practical basis for early sentence generation through analogy and combination. They save the learners from having to build sentences from scratch, which inevitably leads to reliance on native language rules. For a learner who is not yet competent, being able to rely on memorized sentences and their manipulation for sentence generation is a great

advantage --incidentally, there is some evidence that young native and second language acquirers rely on the memorization of fixed phrases too [Hakuta 1974, 1976, Gallagher 1976]. So dialogues, if properly exploited, allow the learners to go from the verbatim to the creative.

(5) Dialogues can be the starting point, the "linguistic beachhead" [Lado 1964:61], for many activities. Drills, questions and answers, communicative activities, and conversation cannot be done with beginners out of nothing. The language cannot be invented. Samples must be learned in order to have something to manipulate and communicate about. For example, drills out of nowhere --that is, based on isolated sentences-- are not as meaningful as those based on sentences taken from a communicative event. Dialogues provide quick access to communicative activities.

(6) Dialogues are valuable from a motivational point of view, for their mastery gives students the satisfaction of being able to perform with segments of the language in a short time. The attainment of such initial goals gives a sense of accomplishment at a time when the learners cannot yet have such a feeling in other aspects of language use, such as free communication.

(7) Dialogues provide an opportunity to teach the students to act out second cultural behavior. Inhibitions about acting like a foreigner are lost in role-playing.

(8) With the use of dialogues it is easier to stay within carefully graded materials, going from easy to difficult one step at a time and keeping practice systematic and thorough. Dialogues allow a smoother transition to communication, reading, and writing. Thus, playing roles, in which the students express the meaning conveyed by the characters they are playing, should naturally come before, not after embarking on the free use of the language.

Note that there is some empirical evidence of the value of dialogues. Veidt [1973] found that dialogue memorization and variation provide a better basis for communication than dialogue-less instruction.

Dialogues have, however, several potential shortcomings that must be kept in mind in their preparation, teaching, and use. They are listed and discussed below.

(1) If not carefully written, dialogues can easily be linguistically and situationally artificial. To give an example, many ESL books offer informal dialogues in which

"How are you?" and "Goodbye" are used, when in fact the natural informal greeting and leave-taking in North America are "Hi" and "See you" or "Bye." As to the fact that learning dialogues is not natural language behavior but "language-like" behavior similar to that of parrots, we should keep in mind that parrots do not know what they are saying while our students should, and that very few of the procedures in the classroom are natural language behavior anyway. Artificial procedures are perfectly justified if they facilitate learning and communication. Linguistic artificiality in dialogues, however, is not justified.

(2) Many dialogues contain useless sentences. True, this is a potential shortcoming. Dialogues must contain really basic patterns and elements; for the less frequent ones, other means of instruction such as narrations and readings are more efficient.

(3) Even for the basic patterns and elements, dialogues are only one way of introducing them. We shall mention others later in this chapter.

(4) Dialogues can easily be made an end in themselves, especially by teachers who are linguistically insecure and would prefer to avoid communicative activities. As stated earlier, dialogues are only a point of departure and should be followed by many other activities, in particular communicative activities.

(5) It is hard to memorize in the second language, harder than in the native language. For that reason, memorization should be kept to a minimum. Probably no more than about 80-100 well-chosen sentences need to be memorized in a second language program. Memorization for any one lesson should not include more than six to eight short sentences, either as a separate dialogue or as part of a longer comprehension dialogue. And there should be no need to memorize the *sequence* of sentences of any dialogue, but only the individual sentences and their meaning (this is discussed further later in this chapter).

(6) The motivational effect of early dialogue mastery begins to disappear after three months or so. Again, true, and a reason why dialogue memorization should be used for a short while only.

On memorization

Some memorization is unavoidable in second language learning, but it should be the kind that has carry-over to communication and not the meaningless memorization of rules, paradigms, and word lists. If a method emphasizes the memorization of words, the students will construct sentences with numerous errors, based on native language rules. Sentence construction should be based on the memorization of sentences that are illustrative of sentence types and transformational rules, not on putting together isolated words.

By analysis only, that is, without a stock of sentences and sentence parts in one's memory from which one can proceed largely by analogy, one would have to recall numerous rules in order to produce even a fairly short second language sentence. Second language learners have difficulty in communicating in the second language because, unlike native speakers, they rely too much on analysis and too little on memorization and analogy.

Memorization of samples of the language allows their full exploitation. It would not be possible, for example, to fully exploit a dialogue for the various adaptation, personalization, and creative activities that should be based on its study unless its sentences are thoroughly memorized verbatim in the first place.

Every sentence produced --in the second language or in the native language-- has either been memorized or is a combination of parts that have been memorized. Many of the simple short sentences that a competent native speaker uses are memorized matter. There is evidence that in the native language "formula speech" (memorized phrases and sentences) accumulates until a rule is formed on the basis of analogy [Braine 1963, Huang 1972]. Hakuta [1974, 1976] observed that a Japanese child learning English used fixed phrases, both in English and, earlier, in his native Japanese. These phrases were mastered and used many times before the structures were known. Such phrases make it "possible for the children to express functions which they are yet unable to construct from their linguistic system, simply storing them in a sense like large lexical items" [Hakuta 1976:333]. So, for the young child there seems to be a two-stage acquisition process, with memorization preceding rule formation for each rule in turn [Gallagher 1976]. Memorization performs the same function in second language learning, with the difference that the process is greatly condensed.

Second language memorization, however, should not be rote learning. Rote learning or parroting is mechanical and non-meaningful. Dialogue memorization is mechanical too, but it is meaningful. Furthermore, psychologists determined long ago that sheer repetition does not necessarily lead to retention; what is important is practice in retrieval. So what is needed with dialogues, more than sheer repetition, is practice in their meaningful performance.

As necessary and useful as memorization is in second language learning, it has certain shortcomings and should be used with caution. The shortcomings are:

(1) Memorized sentences can seldom be used verbatim in communication situations. We all know of students who went to Paris (or Mexico City, or Bonn) and were disheartened to discover that the natives did not know their half of the dialogues. Dialogue memorization is a sound basis for the development of communication skills but the memorized sentences cannot be applied directly to a communication situation.

(2) Excessive emphasis on sequence memorization and failure to fully manipulate each memorized sentence mean that even when a memorized sentence can be used verbatim, the learner has to run through most of the dialogue in his mind before he can say it.

(3) Memorization is boring; for that reason, it should be kept to the necessary minimum.

(4) Memorization is difficult. Think of the time it takes to memorize a sonnet (14 lines) in the *native* language! For that reason, the dialogues or sections of dialogues to be memorized should be no longer than six or eight sentences each, and the total number of sentences to be memorized in the program should not exceed 80-100. There is absolutely no theoretical justification for, and many practical grounds to object to, numerous long dialogues for memorization, with long sentences. (It has been found, for example, that it takes double the time to learn a 20-word list than two 10-word lists [Stevick 1976-a: 29].) Above all, there is no reason to memorize the sequence of sentences in dialogues, probably the most time-consuming and unnecessary practice --unnecessary because very few sentences will ever again occur in that order and because it is very easy to remind students of the sequence by means of a special script.

(5) Much that is memorized is redundant, containing very little new grammar or vocabulary. The answer to this objection is to require selective memorization. The only sentences that are worth memorizing are those that (a) present frequent fixed sequences, such as greetings, (b) illustrate each grammatical rule, (c) illustrate each sentence type, and (d) contain common idioms, which are

handled as extended lexical units. There is no further need for memorization. From these carefully-chosen 80-100 sentences, plus other, non-memorized presentation material, an infinite number of sentences can be produced via analogy (substitution) and transformation.

(6) Memorization is not necessary at the advanced level, except for words and idioms. The more advanced the level the greater the memory span and the lesser the need to memorize dialogues. (The repetition of increasingly longer and more complex sentences is necessary, however, at the advanced level, to further develop comprehension and lengthen the memory span.)

I cannot end this section on memorization without reiterating that memorization is not an end in itself but a point of departure. It allows quick access to samples of the language which illustrate the rules and allow their understanding, thereby facilitating the internalization of rules on the basis of which the learner can generate his own sentences.

Types of dialogues according to function

A basic distinction in dialogue function is between *presentation* dialogues and *practice* dialogues. Presentation dialogues are usually taught at the beginning of a course unit, practice dialogues are normally used at or near the end of a unit. All dialogues have the function of facilitating conversation and should therefore contain useful expressions and be conversationally oriented. In addition to that, presentation dialogues for memorization should be structurally oriented, that is, should demonstrate grammatical rules. Presentation dialogues for comprehension, which are not memorized, need not illustrate grammatical rules but serve as the basis for passive vocabulary expansion (which is turned into active vocabulary through practice).

Practice dialogues include directed dialogues and dialogue-like conversational stimuli. Either by following directions or by taking a situational dialogue as a rough model, the students can generate many sentences of their own at the end of each course unit.

Types of presentation dialogues for memorization according to linguistic content

There are two basic types of memorization dialogues according to linguistic content --strictly graded and "seeded." In strictly graded dialogues, no examples of grammatical patterns or rules appear in the dialogue that have not appeared before or will not be practiced in that same unit. This means that strictly graded dialogues must contain several examples of each new grammatical pattern or rule and nothing that will be studied in future units. The problem with such dialogues is that, under those restrictions, it is seldom possible to write dialogues that sound like natural samples of conversation. The result usually gives the impression that, for example, "Frenchmen must be strictly systematical beings, who one day speak merely in futures, another day in passé définis, and who say the most disconnected things only for the sake of being able to use all the persons in the tense which for the time being happens to be the subject for conversation, while they carefully postpone the use of the subjunctive until next year" [Jespersen 1904:17-8].

Seeded dialogues may contain examples of grammatical patterns and rules that will not be studied for a while. Thus, the dialogue for Unit 3 could contain, in addition to the examples of the grammatical points to be studied in that unit, examples of grammatical patterns and rules to be studied in Units 4, 6, 9, and 20. These examples are handled, by the teacher and the students, as unanalyzed wholes, that is, as if they were idioms (much as many greetings, which contain difficult grammatical rules, are handled); this is always possible when native language equivalents of the dialogue sentences are given. At the same time, these early examples of patterns and rules to be studied in the future perform the function of structural "seeds" in the sense that they give a preview of those grammatical points and serve for reference, as examples that can be recalled when those patterns and rules are studied.

Other aspects of the content of dialogues

Dialogues should be realistic and authentic in their linguistic, cultural, and communicative aspects.

Early dialogues should have very simple sentences, with independent clauses predominating or used exclusively. But simple sentences does not mean SAADs or the "kernel" sentences of generative-transformational grammar --sentences can be quite simple and still contain several transformations.

A well-written dialogue spreads the phonological, grammatical, and lexical learning problems among several sentences rather than concentrating them at a few points.

A good dialogue will not try to present all the forms of a paradigm if in so doing artificiality is introduced; it is better to present only some of the forms of the paradigm in the dialogue and the rest immediately before the grammatical drilling.

Culturally, many situations are neutral, and for that reason it is perfectly all right to have culturally neutral dialogues. Perhaps, to facilitate a gradual introduction to the second culture, the early dialogues should refer to foreigners in the native cultural setting, that is, on culturally familiar ground; then the students can embark on the unfamiliar by having the dialogue situations set abroad.

How to teach a dialogue

There are several approaches to the teaching of dialogues. A basic difference is the way meaning is handled, even when native language equivalents are used. (The advantages of natural translation were discussed in Chapter 14.) Some teachers believe that a dialogue should be taught without alternating between the two languages in the teaching process. As a result, they will give a native language summary of the dialogue or the sentence equivalents before or after the presentation of the dialogue, or ask the students to read them ahead of class. The problem with making the students aware of the meaning before the dialogue presentation is that then the students, during the teaching of the dialogue, will devote almost all their attention to semantic matching and much less attention to *how* the second language words and sentences are uttered. Delaying the conveyance of meaning until after the dialogue has been presented means that the presentation is frustrating and boring to the students, for they have to spend 20, 30 or more minutes practicing sentences that they do not understand. The students very much want to know what they are saying; on the other hand, once they know the meaning of a sentence they want to move on to the next one without having necessarily mastered the pronunciation, intonation, etc. of the preceding one.

It seems that the best solution to this dilemma is to withhold the meaning of each sentence until it has been produced fairly accurately, and then give the meaning (what the students most want) as a reward for accurate production. When the students know that they will not be given the meaning of a word or sentence until they have produced it with acceptable accuracy, accurate production becomes much more important to them, as a way of obtaining from the teacher the meaning of the utterance. (Such conditioning of a pleasant reward on the previous performance of an unpleasant activity has been clearly demonstrated to be effective in psychological studies.)

Having tried various ways of teaching dialogues, I have found that the one most conducive to accurate production, understanding and recall of meaning, and the maintenance of high motivation consists of the following major steps: (1) teach *how* to say the word, phrase, or sentence; (2) reward fairly accurate production in step 1 with *what*, that is, the meaning of the utterance, and practice the awareness of its meaning; and (3) teach the sequence of sentences, though not for memorization, and the roles --that is, *who* and *when*-- with the help of a script (to be described); this third step is normally part of the homework of the students.

This breaks the teaching/learning of words and sentences in dialogues into distinct tasks that the students can pay attention to one at a time --a pedagogically sound principle. This differs markedly from other types of dialogue presentation, such as some audiovisual ones, where the student is expected to pay attention simultaneously to many things: who is speaking, what he is saying (that is, if it can be guessed), to whom he is saying it, how he is saying it, and even what culturally different features the pictures show. It is simply far too much to attend to at the same time. (As we shall see, the type of presentation I propose can also make use of visual aids, but in a very different manner.)

Step No. 1 (*how*) can be subdivided, for each sentence part and sentence, into (a) imitation of the teacher (or of a recording) as a model, and (b) repetition of the utterance without a model, in both cases with correction as needed, though this would be particularly needed in substep 1-a. This imitation should be completely new and fresh --if the students are exposed to a dialogue in any form before it is presented, this will negatively affect their imitation. Correct imitation is not a simple parrot-like activity (parrots take a long time to learn to imitate anything and of course they are not aware of meaning) but takes intense concentration. The teacher should not be inflexible in the number of repetitions; for many utterances, two repetitions are enough, but many require more and some utterances are so easy that one repetition is adequate. The disadvantages of relying on choral imitation were discussed in Chapter 15. Choral repetition may protect some students from embarrassment but it frees the student from the need to imitate accurately through individual effort. Occasionally the class rather than individual students can imitate the teacher, and occasionally individual students who produce a perfect rendition of an utterance can have the satisfaction of having the class imitate them.

Beginning second language students can imitate accurately about three or four syllables, so most sentences for imitation will have to be broken down into manageable segments. Such breaks should occur, if possible, where there is a break in thought; but more important than that, for imitation purposes, is that the break points should be chosen so as to retain the normal sentence pronunciation of the sounds adjacent to them --in other words, a break should not change the allophones of the sentence.

When a sentence is longer than the students can handle or when a certain difficult sound or sequence of sounds occurs somewhere in the middle of it, it can be predicted that there will be imitation problems; such sentences require special handling. If a sentence is short, there should be no problem in teaching it in its natural order, that is, beginning with the first word and going on to the end of the sentence. When a sentence is long but presents more of a memory problem than particular phonological difficulties, a useful technique is the *backward buildup*. This consists of having the students repeat first the last word or two of the sentence, then the preceding word or two plus the last one(s), etc., until the students are repeating the whole sentence. For example, the following would be a backward buildup for the sentence *Tomorrow we're going downtown to see a movie:*

a movie.
to see a movie.
downtown to see a movie.
we're going downtown to see a movie.
Tomorrow we're going downtown to see a movie.

Some people have ridiculed this technique, but it is a technique based on solid principles --it is known that the end of a long utterance tends to be remembered less well than the beginning [R.L. Johnson and Friedman 1971] and that long chains are remembered better when learned starting from the end. By using the backward buildup the student (1) remembers well the end of the sentence because he has repeated it most times, and (2) remembers well the beginning because he has repeated it most recently. In the natural order, the last part of the sentence would be said the fewest times and would be easily forgotten. Teachers who are not too sure of their intonation patterns can control intonation better with the backward buildup, although with a little practice it is possible to learn to retain the intonation of the sentence as a whole even when proceeding by sentence parts in the natural order. (Of course, the backward buildup should not be used with natural series such as numbers or the days of the week.)

When experience --or, the first time through, awareness of contrastive problems-- indicates that most students are going to have a phonological difficulty somewhere in the middle of the sentence, an *outward buildup* technique is better. Instead of proceeding in the normal order, or the backward order, and then getting stuck where the difficulty lies, it is more efficient to start with the segment(s) where the difficulty exists and then build the rest of the sentence outwards, that is toward the beginning and the end.

Finally, with shorter sentences the normal order can be used, if necessary breaking the sentence up into two or three parts and thereby implementing a *forward buildup*. However, it is important with these and all segments in sentence buildups that each segment should not end with a closing intonation pattern but with whatever intonation pattern that segment has in the sentence as a whole.

What constitutes a short or a long sentence will vary with time. At the beginning of the program about six syllables or longer makes a sentence fairly long for the students. Gradually they learn how to handle longer sentences and soon six syllables become a short sentence, unless they are all new words or forms. The ratio of new to known words will of course affect the difficulty that a sentence will present to the students at later stages of the program.

Before asking the students to produce a sentence, whether in parts or in its totality, the new items in the sentence should be taught, in both step 1 (imitation) and step 2 (conveyance of meaning). Not only that, but if a word appears for the first time in a dialogue and it is not in its basic form or with its basic meaning, as it often happens, the basic form or meaning of the word should be taught first, and only then the particular derived form or unusual meaning with which the word appears in the dialogue sentence. For example, suppose that the subjunctive form *tenga* appears in a Spanish dialogue before the infinitive *tener* has been learned: the right thing to do is to teach *tener* before the sentence in which *tenga* appears, and to relate the latter to the former. Or suppose a Spanish dialogue has the sentence *No me tomes el pelo* ("Don't pull my leg") before the word *pelo* has been taught: the latter should be taught first, with its usual meaning ("hair"), for otherwise the students will think that *pelo* is the general equivalent of "leg." The importance of teaching these basic forms and meanings first lies in the fact that they are far more useful, in generating sentences, than any derived forms or special meanings.

Imitation should be at normal or slow-normal speed. Students who learn to use the language haltingly in an overprecise style find it extremely difficult to switch into a smooth conversational style later in the program; for that reason an informal conversational speech style at normal speed, with its typical junctures and assimilations, should be learned from the start. Slowing down speech distorts it. If there is a need to slow down a sentence, therefore, what should be done is have longer pauses *between* segments while retaining normal speed *within* segments.

Step No. 2 (*what,* the ascertaining of meaning) does not follow step 1 *(how,* imitation of the utterance) for all dialogue sentences at the same time but for *each* new word and for *each* sentence. For each new word and each sentence, in turn, after it has been imitated accurately, the meaning is elicited or given. If there is any reason to think that the students can guess the meaning correctly and without much difficulty, they should be allowed to produce the native language equivalent --being able to occasionally guess the meaning of a word or sentence is both challenging and motivating. If it is believed that the students cannot guess the meaning (as it will be the case with most new utterances), or if they try to guess and fail after one or two tries, the native language equivalent should be provided by the teacher. Note again that it is not enough to translate whole sentences; the meaning of the new component words should also be known, for otherwise the students will not be able to extract the words and phrases from the sentences for the generation of other sentences. Of course the students need to be told, if necessary repeatedly, that native language equivalence is "in this context" and should not be assumed to apply to all contexts.

The point is that the meaning of new words and of sentences should be made clear during the dialogue presentation. Semantic clarity is assured by the use of native language equivalents. With other approaches, such as the audiovisual one, the students can "learn" the sentences, learn their sequence, and play the roles without knowing what the sentences mean!

That attention to meaning should be separate from imitation has some support. Dodson [1967:10] found that the average elementary and secondary student could not cope efficiently with the two different processes --imitation and acquisition of meaning-- at the same time.

Step No. 2 is divided into (a) the ascertaining of meaning, and (b) consolidation of the awareness of meaning. Substep 2-a has already been discussed. Substep 2-b consists of alternating between repetition of the sentence and occasional translation into its native language equivalent. The purpose of this substep is to establish a strong bond between the sentence and its meaning. It is better not to do this substep with isolated words, as this would tend to strengthen the incorrect assumption that the equivalence is general, applying to all contexts.

(With linguistically heterogeneous classes, as many English as a Second Language classes are, step 2 obviously cannot proceed as described. What should be done is distribute, before beginning the presentation of a dialogue, native language scripts in the various languages. Then as each new word and as each sentence reaches the point of satisfactory imitation, the students can be referred by *number* to its contextual equivalent, for each student in his own language.)

At this point, having ended with step No. 2 for at least four sentences, visual aids can optionally be shown or projected for each sentence showing a salient feature of its meaning. (We could call this substep 2-c.) Here visual aids can help the students to become aware of the sequence of sentences and serve later as mnemonic devices to recall the sentence sequence during future dialogue performance. Step No. 3, which can be done as homework, consists in learning the sequence and continuity of the conversation and of the roles in it, with the help of a study script.

After having gone through four or so sentences with steps 1 and 2, the monotony of dialogue presentation can be broken very effectively by asking a few personalized questions based on new words in those four sentences. Then the teacher can go back to teaching more of the dialogue.

Sample of dialogue teaching

In this sample, it must be remembered that the number of repetitions is much smaller than that required in a real situation. The number of student errors is also smaller than normal. The teacher should keep in mind that he will tend to get bored with a dialogue before the students have had a chance to master it. For the students, learning a dialogue well is a challenging and difficult task. Rather than speed it up because he feels bored, the teacher should observe the students for signs of fatigue and vary the activities when they appear.

The dialogue is in Spanish, for English-speaking learners. Frequently used instructions are signalled, but some are given in Spanish. They are *repita* ("repeat," singular), *repitan* ("repeat," plural), *no* ("not"), *o* ("or"), *inglés* ("English"), *castellano* ("Spanish"), *traduzca* ("translate," singular), *sí* ("yes"), and *todos* ("everybody").

Teacher: *Repita:* Hola Juan[△]
Student 1: Hola Juan[☆]
T: Hola Juan[△]
S 2: Hol[ə] Juan
T: *No* -l[ə]-, -la-[△]
S 2: -la-[☆]
T: Hola[△]
S 2: Hola[☆]
T: Hola Juan[△]
S 2: Hola Juan[☆]

△ The teacher signals an individual student. The signal can consist in pointing to the student with a pencil or even with the forefinger. During the orientation to the course, the teacher should explain that, although pointing is not polite in conversation, he will have to do it in class in order to save much time. Another important reason for pointing or signalling of various kinds is that it avoids verbal intrusions between the modelling of an utterance and its imitation. Different signals are used to elicit an imitation and a translation.

☆ The teacher nods approval of this accurate response.

T: Hola Juan◇
Class: Hola Juan☆
T: "Hi John"
T: ir△
S 3: ir☆
T: ir◇
C: ir☆
T: "to go"
T: vas△
S 4: vas☆ △
S 5: vas☆ ◇
C: vas☆
T: "you go" *o* "you're going"
T: ¿vas a clase?△
S 6: ¿vas a clase?☆
T: ¿vas a clase?△
S 7: ¿vas a clase?☆ ◇
C: ¿vas a clase?☆
T (to no one in particular): *¿Inglés?*
S 4: "are you going to class?"☆
T: *¿Castellano?*△
S 8: ¿vas a clase?☆
T: Hola Juan, ¿vas a clase?△
S 9: Hola Juan, ¿vas a clase?☆
T: Hola Juan, ¿vas a clase?◇
C: Hola Juan, ¿vas a clase?☆
T: *Traduzca*△
S 10: Hi John, are you going to class?☆
T (referring to the last utterance): *Traduzca*△ (checking up on student 2)
S 2: Hola Juan, ¿vas a clase?☆
T: *Todos*◇
C: Hola Juan, ¿vas a clase?☆
T: matemáticas△ (partial backward buildup)
S 6: ma[θ]emáticas
T: *No* ma[θ]e-, mate-△
S 6: mate-☆
T: matemáticas△
S 6: matemáticas☆
T: matemáticas△
S 4: matemáticas☆ ◇.

◇ The teacher signals the class. An effective way of signalling a response by the whole class is with a sweeping motion of the open hand.

C: matemáticas☆
T: clase de matemáticas△
S 7: clase de matemáticas☆
T: *Repitan:* clase de matemáticas◇
C: clase de matemáticas
T: *¿Inglés?*△
S 8: "math class"☆
T: Hola Juan, ¿vas a clase? *Traduzca*△
S 3: "Hi John, are you going to class?"☆
T: *Repita:* Sí, de matemáticas△
S 5: Sí, de matemáticas☆ ◇
C: Sí, de matemáticas☆
T: Sí, de matemáticas△ (checking up on student 6)
S 6: Sí, de matemáticas☆
T: "Yes, to math class"
T: ¿y tú?△
S 2: ¿y tú?☆
T: ¿y tú?◇
C: ¿y tú?☆
T: "and you?"
T: *Traduzca:* Hola Juan, ¿vas a clase?△
S 7: "Hi John, are you going to class?"☆
T: *Traduzca:* Sí, de matemáticas, ¿y tú?△
S 1: "Yes, to math class, and you?"☆
T: *Repita:* examen△ (outward buildup in anticipation of difficulties with *e<u>x</u>amen*)
S 9: e[gz]amen
T: *No* e[gz]a-, e[~~g~~s]a-△
S 9: e[~~g~~s]a-☆
T: e[~~g~~s]amen△
S 9: e[~~g~~s]amen☆
T: *Traduzca*△
S 4: "exam"☆
T: *Castellano*△
S 5: examen☆
T: *Repitan:* inglés◇
C: inglés☆
T: *Traduzca*△
S 3: English☆
T: un examen de inglés△
S 7: un examen de inglés☆
T: un examen de inglés◇
C: un examen de inglés☆
T: *Traduzca*△
S 1: "an English exam"☆
T: *¿Castellano?*△

S 6: un examen de inglés☆
T: Voy△
S 3: Voy☆ ◇
C: Voy☆
T: "I go" *o* "I'm going"
T: Voy a un examen de inglés△
S 5: Voy a un examen de inglés☆ ◇
C: Voy a un examen de inglés☆
T: *Traduzca*△
S 8: "I'm going to an English exam"☆
T: ver△
S 7: ver☆ ◇
C: ver☆
T: "to see"
T: vemos△
S 2: vemos☆ ◇
C: vemos☆
T: "we see" *o* "we'll see"
T: nos vemos△
S 5: [noz'bemos]
T: *No* [noz'be-], [noz'ƀe-]△
S 5: [noz'ƀe-]☆
T: [noz'ƀemos]△
S 5: nos vemos☆
T: nos vemos△
S 8: nos vemos☆ ◇
C: nos vemos☆
T: "we'll see each other" *o* "see you"
T: Bueno, nos vemos◇
C: Bueno, nos vemos☆
T: *¿Inglés?*△ (they had the word *bueno* earlier in the course)
S 3: "OK, see you"☆
T: *¿Castellano?*△
S 9: Bueno, nos vemos☆
T: *Repitan:* ir◇
C: ir☆
T: *¿Inglés?*△ (it appeared in sentence 1)
S 4: "to go"☆
T: vaya◇
C: vaya☆
T: "it may go"
T: bien◇
C: bien☆
T: "well"
T: *Repita:* Que te vaya bien△

S 1: Que te vaya [b]ien

T: *No* ...ya[b]ien, ...ya[ƀ]ien△ (starting with *vaya* would lead to the production of the wrong allophone)

S 1: ...ya bien☆

T: ...te vaya bien△

S 1: ...te vaya bien☆

T: Que te vaya bien△

S 1: Que te vaya bien☆ △

S 4: Que te vaya bien☆

T: Que te vaya bien◇

C: Que te vaya bien☆

T: Literally, "That it may go well with you," but what would you really say in such a situation in English?

S 6: "Good luck!"☆

T: *Sí, ¿y en castellano?*

S 5: Que te vaya bien☆

T: Bueno, nos vemos. Que te vaya bien.△

S 3: Bueno, nos vemos. Que te vaya bien.☆ △

S 9: Bueno, nos vemos. Que te vaya bien.☆ ◇

C: Bueno, nos vemos. Que te vaya bien.

T: *Traduzca.*△

S 10: "OK, see you. Good luck!"☆

At this point, as substep 2-c, a picture can optionally be shown for each sentence as they are repeated in sequence:

Carlos: Hola Juan, ¿vas a clase?

Juan: Sí, de matemáticas, ¿y tú?

Carlos: Voy a un examen de inglés.

Juan: Bueno, nos vemos. Que te vaya bien.

After this has been done two or three times for the sequence of four sentences, with pictures and modelling, it is done two or three times with pictures only, plus the first word of each sentence as an additional help if needed. Then role-playing starts, first by having the teacher play one role and the whole class the other, then by switching these roles, then by having the roles played by class halves, and finally by individuals. Then, before moving on to the next section of the dialogue, simple personalized questions based on these four sentences can be asked for two or three minutes, thus providing a change of pace as well as an idea of the importance and relevance of the dialogue.

As can be seen from the sample dialogue teaching above, this is an *abbreviated* and *simplified* presentation, as usually there are more errors and it is necessary to have more imitations. Teaching a dialogue properly is not just a matter of having the class repeat each sentence two or three times. It is a rather involved and lengthy task, one that the teacher in a hurry will not do well. It is a great opportunity, which should not be neglected, to reinforce high standards of pronunciation and intonation and to make sure that each new word and sentence is solidly related to its meaning. The earliest dialogues need the slowest and most careful presentation; later the students will make fewer errors and be more adept at guessing meanings, so dialogue presentation can be faster. Note also that dialogues should be presented at a fast tempo and that students should be called to participate unpredictably, for otherwise the presentation becomes very boring.

The study of a dialogue

After a dialogue has been presented in class, that is, after steps 1 and 2 plus the use of one picture per sentence, step 3 --the thorough learning of the dialogue plus an awareness of the nature of each role in it-- is normally handled as individual study. This study would ideally be done with tape recordings and a script. (This script would be distributed at the end of step 2.) If tape recordings cannot be used, the students would have to rely on the *study script* alone.

The earliest study scripts should consist of (1) a picture for each sentence, the same one introduced in substep 2-c during the dialogue presentation, (2) each sentence in pedagogical transcription, to remind the students of its pronunciation, intonation, etc., and (3) the native language equivalent of each sentence. Preferably the script should also have, before each sentence, the new words that appear in it in their basic form and also in two columns for (a) each word in transcription and (b) its native language equivalent in the context of the sentence in which it appears. Note that standard spelling should not be used in the early dialogue scripts, as it causes the pronunciation to deteriorate markedly. Even when given as just a third column, that is, alongside a transcription, the students tend to ignore the transcription and base their pronunciation, with disastrous results, on the standard spelling.

One of the worst things that can be done, in terms of accuracy, for a dialogue, is to let the students study it with a textbook with standard spelling. The excellent pronunciation attained in class at the cost of so much effort is ruined when the students memorize the sentences on the basis of spelling, which they interpret with native language sounds. In the unfortunate situation in which the students *have* to use a textbook (as when its use is compulsory), a step 2-d should be included in the dialogue presentation, which should consist of reading the sentences aloud several times, with strict correction of the resulting errors.

Dialogue performance

When the students come next time to class to perform the dialogue, they should be handed out *performance scripts*. These can have two forms: (a) a picture plus the first word (in transcription) for each sentence, if pictures have been used in the presentation, or (b) indirect "directed dialogue" instructions in the native language as to what to say, followed by the first word of each sentence.

The picture-plus-word performance script requires no explanation. The indirect-instruction performance script can be illustrated as follows, on the basis of the sample dialogue given above:

1) Carlos, greet Juan and ask him if he's going to class. *Hola... (in transcription)*
2) Juan, answer that yes, you're going to math class, and ask Carlos where *he*'s going. *Sí, de...*
3) Carlos, reply that you're going to an English exam. *Voy...*
4) Juan, tell Carlos OK, that you'll see him. Wish him well. *Bueno...*

Full native language sentence equivalents would encourage word-by-word translation. But indirect instructions such as those above convey the idea of the message but cannot be translated word by word from the native to the second language. Therefore, rather than encouraging incorrect word-by-word translation, they counteract it.

The use of performance scripts saves the students from the very time-consuming task of memorizing the sequences of sentences in dialogues, a rather useless endeavor anyway, since extremely few sentences will occur in that order ever again. These scripts then free the students to concentrate on saying the sentences right and on their meaning, which are the really valuable objectives of dialogue learning. It is only in this sense that I would recommend the memorization of 80-100 sentences.

Dialogue exploitation

There is nothing wrong in memorizing a number of sample sentences provided that the teacher and students realize that they should be far from satisfied with just rattling them off. Well conceived oral programs go beyond memorization to the creation of novel sentences through analogy and combination. Some of the activities that can be used to fully exploit a dialogue are listed below.

--A student gives a known word from a dialogue and names another student; the second student is expected to give the whole sentence in which the word occurs.

--The teacher asks personalized questions using words and phrases in the dialogue.

--The students ask each other and the teacher personalized questions.

--Dialogue sentences or parts of them are used as the first (model) sentences in drills of various kinds.

--The dialogue can be told as a story, by the students, in their own words, in the third person. At the beginning this can be done in the present tense (*Carlos dice "Hola" a Juan y le pregunta si va a clase)*, later in the past *(Carlos saludó a Juan y le preguntó si iba a clase)*, with different attitudes toward the reality of the story, etc. The story should be told by several students each time, called at random, each telling what refers to one or two sentences.

--The dialogue can be acted out with various modifications and adaptations of the situation, first according to teacher specifications, then letting the students propose their own adaptations; this calls for considerable ingenuity and much sentence generation.

--The students can be asked to divide into small groups and prepare dialogue variations covering a situation similar to the original dialogue but with different words. Note that they should not be asked to create original dialogues, something few *natives* can do well, but to adapt creatively a known dialogue according to carefully specified guidelines.

The teacher's imagination is the only limit to what can be done to vary, adapt, and expand a dialogue in order to effect the transfer from its sentences to free communication. Activities based on each dialogue should go on for several weeks, and use of its vocabulary and structures indefinitely thereafter.

The Monostructural Method

A variety of the Structural Method, the Monostructural Method, differs from the other varieties in that it does not make use of dialogues. Instead, each new grammatical structure is presented by means of isolated sentences, and the students are not exposed to more than one new rule at a time.

We have already seen that sentences in context are learned and remembered better than isolated sentences [J. Oller and Obrecht 1969]. Another problem is that, without dialogues, the students have to spend several weeks at the beginning of the program in the rather irrelevant and boring discussion of classroom objects.

Most significantly, the dialogue approach and the Monostructural Method have been compared experimentally, and it was found that dialogue students were superior to monostructural students in eight of ten posttests. Their superiority was most marked in writing, reading, vocabulary, and grammar [Blickenstaff and Woerdehoff 1967].

Other presentation devices

Other devices in addition to dialogues can be used to introduce language material in the classroom.

--Speaking material can be introduced in the form of very short narrations, which can be divided into sentences and taught like a dialogue.

--For listening comprehension and speaking practice, a good procedure is the presentation of brief teacher monologues --"microtexts"-- of about 20-30 seconds' duration (they can be based on written texts of no more than 50 words). They can deal with just about any topic. They can be especially prepared or can be excerpts from radio, television, newspapers, etc. Stevick [1971:365-80] recommended the following procedures with these monologues: (1) the students listen to the text several times, (2) they ask questions in the second language about the meaning of words in the text, (3) the teacher asks questions about the text, (4) the students in turn say what they remember, (5) the students retell the text, and (6) the students write the text or discuss it or relate it to comparable experiences or role-play it.

--Television commercials can be used as the basis for oral work [Skirble 1975].

--At the intermediate level, cartoons and comic strips are effective presentation devices. They can be used in conjunction with reading.

--At the intermediate and especially at the advanced level, readings from any source can be used (their presentation is discussed in Chapter 19). So can advertisements, films, radio and television excerpts, simple poems, and songs.

--Humorous anecdotes can be used from the late beginning level and are particularly effective. A drawback is that such material can only be funny once; with repetition humorous anecdotes become stale and tiresome. So they are more suitable for comprehension practice than for the presentation of material that is to be repeated, manipulated, and exploited in various ways.

17

TEACHING GRAMMAR[△]

On the importance of grammar

Chapter 15, and to a lesser extent Chapter 16, have underscored the importance of developing a good control over the sound system of the second language. But even with an excellent pronunciation, if a second language learner makes serious grammatical errors he will be misunderstood quite often.

A good control over the morphology and syntax of the second language is therefore essential. Grammar is the skeleton of language, that which holds a language together and allows it to function. If the grammar of a second language is not learned properly, the tendency is for the damage to be permanent, for it is far easier to expand one's second language vocabulary than to correct grammatical errors that have become habitual.

We should not go any further without trying to define "grammar" for our purposes. The word "grammar" has been used in many ways. Generative-transformationalists define grammar broadly as a set of rules for the generation of sentences, a set which includes phonological and lexical rules; it is in this broad sense, that is, in reference to a description of systematic performance, that I have already used the term "grammar" elsewhere in this book, as when talking about "languistic grammars." But because, for teaching purposes, it is quite useful to deal with the phonology and lexicon separately, this chapter shall avoid such a broad definition but mostly restrict the use of the term *grammar* to the rules governing the morphology (word formation) and syntax (word order) of the language. Note that this excludes many uses of the word "grammar," such (a) a set of prescriptions, (b) a set of rules to be memorized, (c) something which only

----

[△] Portions of this chapter are from my article "The Deduction/Induction Controversy," *The Modern Language Journal*, Vol. LIX, Nos. 1-2 (© 1975 by the Regents of the University of Wisconsin), pp. 15-8; used by permission.

the written language has, or (d) a book [Pelosi 1973]. Grammar is, instead, the actual morphological and syntactic structure of the language, the structured way in which people speak, discounting slips of the tongue, unfinished sentences, etc.

It is the grammar of the language, not the meanings of words, that allows the speaker in English to conclude that in Lewis Carroll's poem "Jabberwocky" [in *Through the Looking Glass*]:

'Twas brillig and the slithy toves
(1) (2) (3)
Did gyre and gimble in the wabe;
(4) (5) (6)
All mimsy were the borogoves,
(7) (8)
And the mome raths outgrabe.
(9) (10) (11)

....

(1) must be a noun or adjective, (2) an adjective, (3) a noun, (4) and (5) verbs, (6) a noun, and so forth. An analysis of the language based on meaning would not throw any light on the structure of these lines. This shows the importance of grammar to comprehension.

Popular grammar, traditional grammar, and languistic grammar

The differences between linguistic (generative-transformational) and languistic grammars have already been discussed in Chapter 4. As a reminder, a languistic grammar is pragmatic, concrete, nontechnical, follows no particular theory, makes use of rules-of-thumb, and so on. As an indication of the inapplicability of certain linguistic grammars, note that in generative-transformational grammar tense forms, inflections, and agreements --all of which are very important early concerns of the beginning second language learner-- are not basic but "late" rules.

Popular grammar is what the average native speaker consciously knows or thinks he knows about the structure of the language. This is mostly based on traditional grammar. Most native speakers have a number of misconceptions, although all grammars contain some misconceptions. The importance of popular grammar in languistics is that popular notions about the language must be taken into consideration as a point of departure from which to lead learners toward correct ideas about the structure of the language.

Traditional grammar has shortcomings but the importance of these has been exaggerated. It is true that its definition of parts of speech on the basis of meaning is inadequate (for example, a *yawn* and a *homerun* are nouns but are not "names of persons, places, or things," and *wait* and *procrastinate* are verbs even though they are not "words denoting action"); but lists of parts of speech based on meaning would be nearly identical to those based on form and function --ideally form, function, context, *and* meaning should be incorporated in these definitions. It is true too that the prescriptivism of many traditional grammars is undesirable; there is no reason to condemn *It's me, If I was you,* and *Who did you see?* if that is the way the great majority of English-speaking people speak --a languistic grammar should be based on what people actually say, not on what a self-appointed elite says they should say. It is also true, finally, that the written basis of traditional grammar is undesirable --a languistic grammar should be based on the spoken language.

Despite these three important shortcomings, there is little conflict between traditional grammar and modern linguistics. It is mostly the simplified traditional grammars for use in the schools that have objectionable features. A *modified traditional grammar* which has been adapted to make it nonprescriptive, based on the spoken language, without Latinate (or other) universal categories, and with word classes defined not only on the basis of meaning would be suitable as a languistic grammar (assuming it meets the other specifications given for a languistic grammar in Chapter 4). After all, there is little in modern linguistic formulations that is new --roughly the same facts have been known for a long time, and the main thing that has changed is the formulations, not the facts.

A *languistic grammar* should have both form and content determined by languistic, not linguistic, principles. For example, it should show an obvious relation to the data, even if it means some redundancy; it should also distinguish between morphology and syntax ("grammar" in the narrow sense), its main area of concern, and pronunciation and vocabulary, to be dealt with separately.

The morphology/syntax part of a languistic grammar should have three types of rules: (1) morphological rules, (2) formulations of "sentence patterns" or basic sentence types, in slot-and-filler form, and (3) transformation rules describing operations to be made on surface structures in order to modify and combine basic sentence types. Rules of types (2) and (3) in particular should take into account the characteristics of the native language of the learner. Note that such a slot-and-filler, surface structure-plus-transformations model is generative, as it allows the creation of an infinite number of sentences. (Note also that the use of slots and fillers and of transformations in languistics preceded the development of tagmemic and generative-transformational linguistic theories by many decades --the former pedagogical rules and exercises are *not* based on the latter linguistic theories, nor is there any reason to let linguists stake out for their own exclusive use the corresponding terminology.)

Languistic rules, which often differ from linguistic rules, are the rules that second language learners need to learn in a second language program. They should be, among other things:

(1) as concrete as possible, that is, based on actual sentences and the relationships between them;

(2) as simple as possible;

(3) as nontechnical as possible (if calling verbs "polka dotted elephants" helps learners to learn them, do so);

(4) cumulative, to be learned one at a time and integrated with those rules learned up to that point;

(5) as close as possible to popular grammar and traditional grammar without distorting the facts and with refinements on traditional grammar drawn from various linguistic schools as needed; and

(6) limited to what can be learned at any one time, that is, in the form of a rule-of-thumb, leaving exceptions and fine points until later.

A rule-of-thumb is defined by Webster as "a general principle regarded as roughly correct and helpful but not intended to be scientifically accurate." To that I would add that in second language teaching a rule-of-thumb is useful if, as a general guideline, it covers a minimum of 80 percent of cases, the remaining 20 percent to be accounted for by further rules in the future or as individual exceptions. In other words, there is a movement from rules-of-thumb to accurate linguistic rules as the second language program progresses.

Rules-of-thumb should be accurate as far as they go. There is no justification for rules in second language textbooks to be "linguistically inadequate, difficult to decode, sometimes utterly meaningless and, with a surprising frequency, just plain wrong" [Bull and Lamadrid 1971], as at least 50 percent of the rules in Spanish textbooks seems to be.

Languistic rules are of three types in regard to the relationship between the two languages: (1) *bilingual rules,* which are identical in the two languages and need not be taught (an example is the normal order Subject + Verb + Object of declarative sentences in English and other European languages); (2) *monolingual rules,* which are quite unrelated across languages and therefore cause no interference, although of course they have to be taught; and (3) *contrastive rules* differing partially across languages, causing considerable interference, and requiring intensive instruction. The student needs to learn to combine all rules, even those that need not be taught, in order to generate sentences.

Contrastive languistic rules, which are particular to a given native language and a given second language, can be expressed monolingually and statically, e.g., "In the Spanish noun phrase most adjectives follow the noun" or bilingually and dynamically, as follows:

(*English)* Det + Adj + Noun → Det + Noun + Adj (*Spanish)*

Morphological languistic rules should be expressed statically, transformational languistic rules dynamically; the syntactical make-up of basic phrase and sentence types can be expressed (as in the example just given) statically or dynamically, depending on whether it is done monolingually or contrastively.

A languistic grammar need not have anywhere near the completeness of a linguistic grammar, for only the frequently used rules will be taught, the others being *acquired* concurrently or later. As long as a languistic grammar covers 80-90 percent of the facts about the morphological/syntactic structure of the second language it is quite adequate. Total or 99 percent coverage would make it far longer and too unwieldy for pedagogical use.

Grammatical gradation

The order of presentation of grammatical patterns and rules in the second language program should be based on the following criteria:

(1) *Simplicity*. Whenever possible, the simple should come before the complex, the easy before the difficult. No grammatical point needs to be difficult, for if it is complex it can be divided into a number of simpler subpoints. Difficulty depends on (a) the degree of

difference between the two languages and (b) the intrinsic characteristics of the second language pattern or rule. (Particular sentences are more or less difficult depending on the number of words and the number of transformations they have.) Within a grammatical point, sometimes considerable simplification is possible; for example, by teaching their *sandhi* variations (automatic consonant/vowel endings), French possessive adjectives can be reduced from 25 forms to 15 basic forms (*me*^{z} for /me/ and /mez/, *lœʀ*^{z} for /lœʀ/ and /lœʀz/, etc.).

(2) *Regularity*. Whenever possible, we should proceed from regular to irregular. Thus, regular English past tense forms and regular English noun plural allomorphs should be taught before the irregular ones, and regular Spanish present tense verbs should be taught before the ones showing stem irregularities.

(3) *Frequency and utility*. What is more frequent and useful should be taught before what is less so. This criterion is often in conflict with the criterion of regularity, for certain irregular forms are very frequent (because, being so frequent in use, they resist the regularization process). So there is a need to compromise between criteria (2) and (3). For example, the highly irregular English verb *to be* has to be taught very early because it is so common in use. Uncommon irregular forms can of course be delayed or not taught at all. Because of their frequency, contracted forms (such as *I'll* and *isn't*) should be taught quite early and should be taught not only for comprehension but also for production. Where because of communication needs an advanced form has to be introduced early, it should be presented on an *ad hoc* basis, without analysis or manipulation, delaying its formal teaching until the right point in the program.

(4) *Linguistic independence*. Whenever possible, what is linguistically independent should be taught before what is linguistically concomitant. For example, a good many verbs have to be taught before object pronouns are taught, since the latter cannot be used without verbs. Another example: the subjunctive cannot be learned without learning considerable vocabulary first.

(5) *Interlingual similarity*. What is interlingually similar should be presented before what is dissimilar. For example, for English speakers learning French or Spanish, uses of the article that the two languages have in common should be taught and used in communication before such uses as exemplified in *Les canadiens sont grands*

("Canadians are tall") and *Me gustan las papas* ("I like potatoes") are taught. At the same time, it would be a mistake to delay much the presentation of contrasting structures, for the learners would get the wrong idea that the two languages do not differ very much. Note also that what makes many divergent relations across languages so difficult (like Spanish *por/para, ser/estar,* and the two past tenses for English speakers) is that they involve semantic as well as syntactic differences across languages.

In addition to these five criteria, there are three additional ordering criteria that apply *within* grammatical points.

(6) *Linguistically basic first.* Whenever other forms can be derived from a basic form, teach the basic form first. For instance, the basic form for many adjectives in spoken French is the feminine form, from which the masculine form can be derived by dropping the final consonant sound. This makes sense, for if one were to go in the opposite direction he would have to know, for each adjective, not only the masculine form but which particular consonant to add to it to form the feminine. On the other hand, when the feminine is taken as the basic form, as recommended, the feminine includes the masculine, which can be easily derived from the feminine. Another example is two-stem French verbs like *finir* and *vendre*. By learning the long stem (the plural stem) as the basic form --/finis/ and /vɑ̃d/-- the short (singular) stem can be derived from it by dropping the last consonant from the long stem.

(7) *The restricted before the pervasive.* Certain rules involving a limited number of choices are best handled by teaching first the alternative(s) having restricted contexts and then letting the students know that the other alternative is used everywhere else. For example, the few uses of Spanish *estar* can be taught and then the students can be told that for everything else they should use *ser*. Students of French can be told when *être* is used as an auxiliary and then informed that for all other verbs *avoir* is used. Note that this is not a question of norm before exceptions, as both alternatives are part of the norm, nor of basic before derived, as one alternative is not formally derived from the other.

(8) *Form before usage.* Normally, forms should be learned first, then the various ways in which they can be used. The exception to this is where usage determines

the choice of form, in which case usage should be learned first. Examples of the latter are the two past tenses and the subjunctive of French and Spanish, which for English speakers present primarily a usage, not a form, problem. If the students learned these forms first, they would immediately start misusing them, with detrimental effects on performance which would be difficult to correct. It is far better to make them fully aware of the reasons for the choices first, and then teach them the forms that go with those choices.

There are only certain linguistic rules that must be taught in a particular sequence. The number of these is small. Everything else can be organized according to communication needs. Only the rules that are most productive need to be taught systematically. The learner can (and generally does) go beyond these rules to acquire many of the less frequent ones. Highly literary structures can be handled simply on the basis of *ad hoc* footnotes in readings. Infrequent spoken structures do not need to be taught systematically but can be explained briefly as they appear. Simplification can be attained by eliminating the teaching of optional rules; but simplification for pedagogical purposes should never go against correctness and naturalness.

Teaching morphology

What one language may express syntactically, i.e., by means of word order, another language may express morphologically, i.e., by means of affixes. An example of a syntactically-based language is Chinese; an example of a morphologically-based language is Latin; English lies somewhere in between. A language with many inflections is not necessarily difficult and a language without inflections, such as Chinese, is not necessarily easy. In fact, a language with numerous cases but high regularity in their use, such as Finnish, with its 15 cases, may be easier to learn than a language with few cases but complex rules for their use, such as German, with four cases.

In speaking a language one must make high-level choices, such as semantic and syntactic choices that affect whole sentences, and lower-level choices, such as morphological agreements. For effective production, the lower-level structures should be mastered first to the point of automatism, so as to free the attention for the higher-level choices.

Lower-level rules include all morphological rules

--gender, person, number, verb endings, etc.-- plus many simple rules of word order. It is impossible to communicate effectively if attention must be paid to these lower-level rules. They are simply too many. Here is where drilling is most useful.

The types of drills most suitable for the teaching of morphological rules are correlation drills and replacement drills (examples of drills appear later in this chapter and in Appendix B). Morphemes should not be practiced in isolation but as part of words in sentences, which exhibit syntactical rules.

A set of related morphemes --the endings of a tense, for example-- should not be learned in a fixed order, because they will not occur in a fixed order in speech. They should be learned and practiced in random order. And they should be learned and manipulated in sentences, for an isolated little "poem" of verb forms does not transfer to communicative use of the language. The ability to recite paradigms is almost totally unrelated to the ability to speak; in fact it interferes with it, because in order to use a form near the end of the paradigm one has to recite to himself first the forms preceding it in the paradigm. Paradigms are not functional, they do not translate readily into the generation of sentences. Thus, all I remember from two years of high school Latin is *amo, amas, amat* and *bonus, bona, bonum* (those paradigms do stick in the mind!), but I could not understand nor produce a Latin sentence even under penalty of death. Paradigm learning involves memorizing forms without thinking and without knowing how to use them. As Sweet [1899, 1964:130] put it, students learning paradigms by heart are "taught the names of tools without being taught their uses." It is much better to use correlation drills, starting with two forms and, once the contrast between these has been mastered, adding one or two forms at a time and using them in unpredictable order until the whole set of forms is under control.

Some second language teaching is virtually restricted to morphology. This is a mistake. Second language teaching should give adequate attention to syntax and semantics as well. At the other extreme, it is also unsound to emphasize syntax and semantics to the point where morphology is neglected.

Teaching sentence patterns

A "sentence pattern" is a particular structural string,

that is, the formal properties of a sentence type when all the content morphemes have been removed. A sentence pattern can therefore have very many lexical manifestations. Perhaps it will be clearer if we speak of *abstract sentences,* composed of grammatical functions such as Pronoun + Verb + Noun Phrase and *concrete sentences* that are actually uttered, such as, for the abstract sentence just given, *He read the book, I compose songs,* or *They sold the house.* Sentence patterns are then abstract sentences, (actual) sentences are concrete sentences. Through vocabulary selection, each abstract sentence or sentence pattern can be the basis for a very large number of different concrete sentences.

The number of types of sentence patterns in any language is fairly small, and an infinite number of sentences can be produced from them via substitution and transformation. Sentence patterns are most easily made evident by means of substitution drills. When they differ significantly from native language patterns, however, it is best to bring the contrast out by means of translation drills.

"Pattern practice" is simple, usually inductive, manipulation of a sentence pattern. It has limited application, more cognitively-oriented drills being more useful. "Pattern drills" are drills limited to one sentence pattern, as most drills should be in order to avoid confusion.

Teaching transformations

A transformation modifies a sentence pattern or combines two sentence patterns into a more complex one.

In linguistics, transformation rules are bidirectional and operate on the surface structure realizations of sentence patterns, changing one surface structure to another. They need to be bidirectional because changing a sentence, e.g., from the negative to the affirmative or from the passive to the active is just as important as the other direction, even though the initial presentation of the transformation would likely be in the other direction. Transformations need to be performed on the concrete realizations of sentence patterns because of the need for concreteness in second language teaching.

Transformations are taught by means of transformation drills, both simple, one-sentence transformation drills involving expansion, reduction, or transposition, and complex, two-sentence transformation drills involving the combination of two sentences.

Politzer [1972:100-14] suggested a number of principles

for the teaching of transformations. For example, he recommended that those transformation rules that are parallel in the two languages, such as (1) (a) and (b) below, need not be emphasized at all, while those that are nonparallel, such as (2) (a) and (b) below, need to be drilled intensively.

(1)	(a) Ute kann Latein lesen.	Kann Ute Latein lesen?
	(b) Ute can read Latin.	Can Ute read Latin?
(2)	(a) Ute liest Latein.	Liest Ute Latein?
	(b) Ute reads Latin.	Does Ute read Latin?

Analysis or analogy?

"Analysis" can be defined as dividing a whole into its parts and determining their nature, function, and so forth. "Analogy" is comparison on the basis of partial resemblance.

Analysis is not sufficient in second language learning. One does not learn to perform in a language through the study of its grammar, although such study is necessary and useful at the right time and place. Grammatical analysis cannot substitute for practice. It is unfortunate that there is a tendency to analyze and move on, without driving the rule to the unconscious through practice.

If there is no overt understanding of a grammatical pattern, the students will develop their own covert understanding, which may be quite wrong --this is one reason why some analysis is necessary. But classroom analysis need not have a high degree of abstractness; in fact, for the average class much abstractness is undesirable, as it only leads to confusion and hesitation. In order to drive a car we don't need to know the principles of the internal combustion engine, but only how to operate the pedals, the gear shift, and so forth. On the other hand, a driving instructor would be foolish if he merely said: "Imitate me."

Another reason why analysis is necessary is that without an understanding of the functions of words and their relationships it is difficult to transfer sentence patterns to other situations in order to generate novel sentences. (Drills should be on these relationships, not imitations without understanding.) To put it another way, some analysis facilitates analogy, for in order to produce new sentences by analogy the student needs to know what to base his analogy on, and that requires some elementary analysis, whether overt or covert, of the sentence pattern. It is better to make that analysis overt and thereby ensure its correctness.

A third reason for the use of analysis is that the students want to understand what they are doing. But some students would go to extremes and would want to spend all the time on analysis; any tendency to that should of course be rejected.

Since analysis facilitates learning, it should either precede or accompany it; the claim that analysis should follow learning becomes therefore logically untenable.

Many of the rules we apply when we speak a language are based on unconscious analogy. By analogy, a learner of English who has been exposed to *in there* and *up here* can say *down there* even though he has never heard it. But analogies should be based on what is known, or false analogies can result. The use of analysis can help prevent false analogies.

It is clear that we should not rely on analogy only, but make use of contrast (especially in the examples at the beginning of a grammatical point), questions, explanations, and practice. Exclusive reliance on analogy can lead to "undergeneralizations," where a rule is assumed to apply to known items only and not to other items of the same kind. For example, a learner who relies on analogy only may undergeneralize the endings of Spanish *-er* verbs to the *-er* verbs he knows only and not to all the other *-er* verbs. The reason for undergeneralization is failure to state the rule, that is, to make an overt generalization and state the extent of its application.

We conclude then that both analysis and analogy are necessary, and neither is by itself sufficient for efficient and effective second language teaching. We can produce an infinite number of novel sentences by analogy to a limited number of sentence patterns only if we understand their structure (best done through analysis) so that we can modify them and combine them via transformation rules.

Deduction, induction, and guided discovery

"Deduction" in second language teaching refers to a process whereby instruction goes from the general to the particular, that is, from a rule statement to the application of the rule in specific cases. "Induction" refers to going from the particular to the general, that is, from examples to a generalization based on them; this generalization, however, is usually left unstated, so that the rule is supposed to be learned through practice, without analysis. In "guided discovery" the students "discover" and state the rule themselves on the basis of examples plus questions from the teacher.

Deduction is typically associated with the Grammar-Translation Method. In that method, an excessive use is made of deductive explanations, and as a reaction to that some second language teachers reject deduction in any form. But there is great value in conscious reasoning, at least for the more complex rules that cannot easily be remembered if induction only is used. Many habits, such as piano playing, typing, driving, swimming, start consciously. They are complex habits that cannot easily be picked up without deductive guidance. In a second language, although most morphological patterns can be learned mechanically, certain syntactical patterns in particular (e.g., the two past tenses and the subjunctive in French and Spanish) benefit greatly from a deductive cognitive approach. There is nothing wrong in rule statements provided the students understand they must also internalize them through practice.

But that is precisely the danger with deduction. As soon as something is understood, or after very little practice, many teachers, conscious of the impatience of the students, move on to the next rule without bothering to do the mechanical drills, meaningful exercises, and communicative activities necessary for the rule to become an internalized linguistic habit. Of course, if such learning activities were fully performed, the initial deductive presentation could do no harm, but teachers erroneously assume performative knowledge from cognitive knowledge. No piano teacher will assume that a pupil can play the piano because he can explain sheet music or the movement of his fingers on the keyboard --and yet many second language teachers are satisfied with an intellectual demonstration of proficiency.

Reasoning can be perfectly adequate as a starting point (for certain rules), but teaching should never stop there. Practice must change cognitive knowledge into performative knowledge, or the learner will be like the piano player who can't play because he has to explain to himself every movement of his fingers. Rote memorization of rules, without performative internalization, does not work --proof of that is the fact that English-speaking children repeat, and teachers repeat, till they are blue in the face, the "rules" about "I" vs. "me," "will" vs. "shall," and double negation to no effect [Grittner 1977:

135]. The problem is that it is not possible to perform fluently and at the same time review numerous rules mentally. Another difficulty with the excessive use of deduction is that predigested rules are uninteresting; but letting the students discover complex rules by themselves without guidance, while more interesting, is too time-consuming. The solution, for most rules, is guided discovery.

Induction is particularly associated with the Natural Method and the Direct Method, both of which are opposed to the learning of rule statements. Many modern methodologists, some structuralists among them, advocate induction; but there is no proof that induction is more effective and much reason to believe that it is a slow and uncertain process.

In induction, the students are left to "formulate" rules by themselves, as best they can. There is no overt eliciting of generalizations, nor are these corrected or reformulated. The result is that the covert, unguided generalizations that the students form are often wrong. It would be much better to lead the students, from the start, to the formulation of correct generalizations.

Certain simple rules can be taught inductively, as differential feedback will make the rule clear in the students' minds in just a few minutes. But the great majority of rules benefit from the overt use of reason. Infrequent rules that are not the object of teaching and subtle rules that have not yet been formulated must also be acquired inductively.

Guided discovery combines features of deduction and induction. As in induction, examples are given first. Then, with the help of questions, the *students* analyze the examples and try to formulate the corresponding generalization. The students' generalization is corrected as needed, by eliciting corrections through questions. Then the rule arrived at by the students is used as a guide for their responses in mechanical drills, meaningful exercises, and communicative activities.

An advantage of guided discovery is that it is challenging and motivating. The students like to rely on their own abilities and act as mini-field linguists, as opposed to just being given predigested rules. Furthermore, it seems that they remember better what they discover than what they are given, although this claim requires research.

Which of these --deduction, induction, or guided discovery-- should be used? Induction can be used with simple rules with which the learners can arrive at the right hypothesis within a fairly short time, otherwise it becomes quite inefficient. But it would be an oversimplification to say that an inductive approach should be used only when the second language rule is simpler than the native language rule. There are many second language rules that are more complex than their native language counterparts and yet can be learned quickly without a rule statement. An example is article-noun agreement in Spanish, which, although not present in English, can be learned inductively in a few minutes. It seems that if the rule consists of a mechanical difference between the two languages involving no new concepts (in the example given, both gender and number agreement exist elsewhere in English), efficient inductive learning is possible. About 20-30 percent of the grammatical points of commonly-taught Western European languages represent such (minor) mechanical differences and could be taught inductively.

Certain grammatical points are difficult enough that an explanation is essential and that the necessary explanation cannot quickly be arrived at by the students themselves. They are rules based on semantic distinctions lacking or expressed very differently in the native language, such as Spanish *ser* vs. *estar,* French *passé composé* vs. *imparfait,* the use (not the morphology) of *cases* in German and Russian, the system of Japanese *honorifics,* etc. for English-speaking learners. That knowing the rule in such cases seems to help performance was demonstrated in my experiment with *ser/estar* [Hammerly 1977], in which the ability of the subjects to state the rule correlated significantly ($p < .01$) with performance. About 20 percent of the structures of Western European languages seem to require a deductive approach if teaching is going to maintain a reasonable level of efficiency.

That leaves 50-60 percent of the rules as neither simple enough to be handled by induction nor difficult enough to require deduction. This majority of medium-difficulty rules is best handled by guided discovery.

Criteria to help determine the teaching procedure for individual rules are charted in Figure 17.1.

Example of a guided discovery presentation --a lesson in Spikian

Instructions to the reader: Cover each line below until you have performed the operation requested by the teacher ("T"). ("S" stands for "student(s)," who except

CHART FOR THE DETERMINATION OF TEACHING PROCEDURE FOR INDIVIDUAL RULES

Presence or absence of a difference	SL rule = NL rule	Second language rule ≠ native language rule			
Nature and degree of the difference	None	Mechanical (minor)	Mechanical (major)	Semantic (minor)	Semantic (major)
Teaching procedure to be used	No teaching necessary. Just introduce, point out identity, and use	Induction	Guided discovery		Deduction
Statement of rule	None		By students, after examples		By teacher, at the beginning
Use of NL equivalents of SL examples	Not necessary but may optionally be used		Necessary for contrast and in order to counteract overtly the tendency to negative transfer		

Figure 17.1

for repetitions would reply individually; the directions "Repeat" and "Translate," although written out in the lesson below, can be effected by hand signals.)

T: (Repeat) *Spikian spiki.*
S: *Spikian spiki.*
T: "I speak Spikian."
T: (Repeat) *Enco spiki.*
S: *Enco spiki.*
T: "I speak English."
T: (Repeat) *Franco spiki.*
S: *Franco spiki.*
T: "I speak French."
T: "What is the position of the verb in these Spikian sentences?"
S: "The verb comes last."
T: "Fine. Now let's practice this in drills and exercises." (Mechanical drills, meaningful exercises, and communicative activities follow.)
T: (Repeat) *Spikian spiki.*
S: *Spikian spiki.*
T: (Translate)
S: "I speak Spikian."
T: (Repeat) *Spikian spiku.*
S: *Spikian spiku.*
T: "You speak Spikian."
T: (Repeat) *Enco spiki, Spikian spiku.*
S: *Enco spiki, Spikian spiku.*
T: (Translate)
S: "I speak English, you speak Spikian."
T: (Repeat and translate) *Franco spiku.*
S: *Franco spiku* = "You speak French."
T: "How do you indicate personal subjects in Spikian?"
S: "You put them at the end of the verb."
T: "Yes, they are verb endings. What verb ending stands for *I*?"
S: *-i.*
T: "Yes. What verb ending stands for *you*?"
S: *-u.*
T: "Very well. Let's now practice using them." (Drills, exercises, and activities follow.)
T: (Repeat) *Spikian spiki e?*
S: *Spikian spiki e?*
T: "Do I speak Spikian?"
T: (Repeat) *Ai, Spikian spiku.*
S: *Ai, Spikian spiku.*
T: "Yes, you speak Spikian."

T: (Repeat) *Franco spiku e?*

S: *Franco spiku e?*

T: "Do you speak French?"

T: (Repeat) *Ai, Franco spiki.*

S: *Ai, Franco spiki.*

T: "Yes, I speak French."

T: "How do you ask a question in Spikian?"

S: "You raise the pitch of your voice at the end."

T: "Yes, but is that all?"

S: "You add the syllable *e* at the end."

T: "Yes, the particle *e*, a separate word, is added at the end."

T: "And how do you answer a question affirmatively in Spikian?"

S: "You say *Ai*."

T: "Where does *Ai* go?"

S: "At the beginning of the sentence."

T: "OK, let's practice this now."

(Practice follows on asking questions and answering them affirmatively. Negative replies are studied later, as they are more complex.)

This gives an idea of a guided discovery presentation. Of course, for each of the rules, if the students are confused and cannot answer correctly the simple structural questions, the teacher should ask simpler questions and/or go back to giving more examples. It is clear that in this type of presentation the students (and you, the reader) have learned several things about the grammatical structure of Spikian by relying on analogy and contrast within Spikian, and comparison with English. There was no need to ask you to memorize for example, "In Spikian the word order of declarative sentences is object plus verb" or "The verb subject in Spikian is a suffix, *-i* for the first person singular and *-u* for the second person singular," etc. You and many students would have understood these and other rule statements, I am sure; but I doubt that they would have speeded up very much the learning process if given deductively, and I am sure they would have made that process less interesting. In any event, in the case of high school students and even of many college students, most rule statements are so much gobbledygook --they don't understand them because, if they have ever been introduced to grammatical terminology in their English classes (and most of them have not), they have soon forgotten it as something quite unnecessary for them as native speakers of English. (Keep in mind too that even if a grammatical explanation pacifies some students, there is no assurance that they have understood it.)

Guided discovery presents the grammar of the second language as a series of interesting little problems to solve. But it does not stop at solving the problems --it follows their solution with intensive practice designed to internalize the rules, to make them habitual.

Incidentally, the approach shown with the Spikian lesson differs considerably from the techniques used in much "audiolingual" teaching ca. 1960. Three major differences are (1) the use of the native language, quite consciously, to bring out overtly the differences between the two languages, (2) the use of intralingual contrasts from the start, and (3) the use of cognition throughout the presentation, involving the student's mind in the learning process, both in terms of structures and sentence meanings.

This approach has the further advantage that it helps develop linguistic sophistication in the students. They will need grammatical sensitivity if they are going to be able to acquire intuitively the many minor rules that are not overtly taught in the second language program. Bialystok [1979-a] showed that the learner's linguistic intuition must and can be developed.

Guided discovery was already proposed by Jespersen [1904:127-8], who called it an "inventional grammar," referring by that to the fact that in discovery procedures the students themselves (with some help) "write" their own "grammars" of the second language as they go through the program.

Rather than being given a series of correct responses to learn, in guided discovery the students are provided with problem-solving situations and then have practice based on the student-determined solutions. They solve *intralingual* problems on the basis of contrast and distribution considerations. To solve each possible *interlingual* problem, they have to ask themselves the question: Is the rule different in the two languages, and if so, how does it differ?

When the student works something out by himself, he has a sense of discovery and satisfaction in his achievement. He does not feel dependency but freedom and power. Both initial learning and recall seem to be better under those conditions.

Steps in the teaching of a grammatical point

The steps in the teaching of a grammatical rule can

then be listed, for most rules, as follows:

(1) *Exemplification,* where examples are considered, repeated, and understood.

(2) *Formulation,* where the rule generalization is expressed, if possible by eliciting it from the students.

(3) *Practice,* starting with *manipulation* with attention on the problem and leading gradually to freer practice with attention on *communication.*

Inductive teaching omits step 2 (*formulation*). Deductive teaching puts step 2 before or along with step 1 and is limited to formulations expressed by the teacher.

Grammatical exemplification

A good case can be made for introducing examples of a rule over a period of several weeks before it is studied. This "seeding" gives familiarity with the rule and fosters inductive processes that prepare the ground for the formal presentation of the rule later in the course.

All rules should be taught in the context of sentences and these preferably drawn from a dialogue or text. What occurs in a certain context should be taught in that context. For example, French *ne* does not occur as an isolated word but only with a verb; the same thing is true of *je.* As Jespersen [1904:116] put it, "what usage has joined together, let no grammar put asunder."

Rules must be fully illustrated by examples, otherwise many students will not understand them. The abstract --the rule-- should be taught through the concrete --the examples. That rules are not as useful to understanding as examples is seen in the fact that whenever linguists discuss grammar they illustrate every new grammatical insight with examples. If linguists need them, students need them much more.

Examples should be drawn from dialogues, readings, narrations, and the various other presentation devices discussed in Chapter 16. For certain rules, particular types of material are useful; for example, advertisements are an effective way of teaching the imperative.

The examples should never be artificial sentences that are communicatively highly improbable if not impossible, even if they can illustrate a grammatical rule. Traditional textbooks have been seriously at fault in this, using such sentences as "The philosopher pulled the lower jaw of the hen," quoted by Sweet [1899, 1964:73] from a Greek course, and "La plume de ma tante est plus belle que le tablier du boulanger," parodied from many such sentences. The examples must be likely communicative acts, if not drawn from real conversation.

The examples can be equated literally first, but should then be translated into authentic sentences in the native language. "The pen of my aunt" syndrome [James 1980:164] should be avoided, for that is not English, and neither is "Classical music is pleasing to me" for Spanish "Me gusta la música clásica," nor many other such "translations." Besides, such translations obscure the usual contrasts.

The examples should be organized for the learners into the necessary contrastive and comparison pairs. Beginners especially have sufficient difficulty without having to arrange the examples themselves.

It is useful to have the students memorize one example --that is, a contrastive or comparative pair-- as a reminder of the rule. This has the advantage that it can be used for reference when errors occur in the future.

Grammatical formulation

As already explained, for most rules the grammatical formulation can and should be elicited from the students. In this section, however, we will discuss primarily those formulations given by the teacher, as in deductive presentations --that is, we shall discuss the nature and use of explanations.

Some second language specialists believe that all explanations should be avoided. But without official explanations, the students make their own, and these may be very faulty. Explanations are useful because they can help guide future linguistic behavior. Furthermore, adult second language learners *want* to know the rules, so this fact should be exploited, if nothing else for its motivating value.

It is then not a matter of choosing between drills and explanations. Explanations facilitate linguistic behavior. Too, since we do not know how each student learns, we should use *both* drills and explanations, so that each student may benefit from his preferred combination of them.

This does not mean that a great deal of class time should be spent on explanations. Even in the deductive grammar lesson, explanations should not take up more than about 5-10 percent of the time devoted to a new rule.

Rule statements do not answer the question "Why?" --that would require going back in time, and we would have to stop at Proto-Indo-European or some such protolanguage without fully answering the question. But explanations do provide a systematic answer to the question "How is it done in language X?" Such knowledge reassures learners and gives them guidance about how to behave in the second language.

During the formulation stage in the teaching of a grammatical point the students should feel free to ask questions as needed. The responses to these questions, as the explanations themselves, should be brief and to the point, should take into account what the students know, and should be followed by examples, concluding with the opportunity for the students to provide examples in order to show that they have understood. Teachers often omit this last step, which is crucial.

Where should the explanation of the rule come? If it comes in the form of a "summary of behavior" following the drills, it comes too late to serve any purpose. If the students can already use the rule correctly, the generalization is superfluous; if they cannot, they probably would have been helped by having it earlier, for now they will need further drills anyway. So the explanation should come before the practice starts, as it will make the students more aware of the crucial aspects of that practice and will give them a better chance to internalize the explanation through that practice. J.C. Jenkins [1970] found experimentally that explanations *preceding* Spanish drills resulted in significantly better performance.

There is value in explanations (preferably student-formulated) even in the case of inductive teaching. When the students start responding correctly, having covertly discovered the rule, it helps the weaker students greatly to state the rule overtly for them.

Seliger [1979] found no correlation between post-test subjective "rules" about the use of English *a* vs. *an* and performance with this rule; he concluded that conscious rules do not function as monitors. This may be true with *acquired* simple, mechanical morphological rules, for at no time in this experiment had the actual rule been overtly formulated. But the evidence from my experiment with *ser* and *estar* [Hammerly 1977] supports the view that in second language teaching/learning a *taught/learned* rule *is* used to monitor performance.

Despite the evident value of rule formulations, it should not be thought that they should take up much of the time in the classroom. Explanations should be kept to the minimum, practice extended to the maximum. If the students want to learn minor details of a rule, they should be directed to reference materials.

Languistic explanations have to explain (a) form, that is, present a morphological or syntactical analysis, and (b) usage, that is, the communicative function of the structure. Explanations are clues that aid second language learners to understand, internalize, and remember aspects of the structure of the second language.

How should an explanation be formulated? The following should prove to be useful guidelines.

(1) Explanations should be short and to the point. No explanation should last longer than two or three minutes. Exceptions to the rule and minor points of usage can be considered later, so only their existence needs to be acknowledged in the initial explanation.

(2) Explanations should be as simple as possible. Going over all the parts of a complex rule at once is pedagogically very unsound, for it is too much for the students to absorb. Instead, when a rule is complex, give partial, simplified, interim rules, to be amplified and modified later.

(3) Explanations should be in the students' native language (unless, of course, the students have reached the point where they can understand them easily in the second language). No purpose is served, and much harm is done, by trying to explain something difficult via something more difficult. A brief explanation in the native language is much more effective than repeated or lengthy explanations in the second language, also leaving more time for manipulative and communicative practice.

(4) Explanations should incorporate, whenever possible, visual aids such as charts, lines showing changes in word order, colors, shapes, etc.

(5) Explanations should be, as much as possible, devoid of technical language. Technical language is the reason why most explanations are not understood. North American students simply lack grammatical terminology, as they either have not studied it for English or have quickly forgotten it. (This can to a certain extent be remedied.[△]) Language students are not linguists. With younger students, it may be far better to refer to the gender of

----

[△] Books that offer a quick survey of English grammar for second language learners are available; see, for example, Spinelli 1979 and J. Morton 1979.

nouns as "*le* words" and "*la* words," or as "boy words" and "girl words," rather than refer to them with terms like "masculine" and "feminine." With older students, some terms --such as "noun," "adjective," "determiner," "pronoun," etc.-- can be taught, for they may not only save time but add precision. But whenever possible the more familiar terminology of traditional Latinate grammars should be used, adapting it as needed.

(6) Each explanation should be immediately followed by intensive practice. If practice does not follow immediately, the relevance of the explanation is lost on the students and they fail to internalize it, since it becomes a cold intellectual fact rather than a guide to performance.

Grammatical practice

In step 3 (practice) manipulation should continue, if necessary with other intervening activities, until the response to the structural cues is automatic, i.e., below the level of consciousness, for without automatic control the students will fall back on native language habits. This means that it may be necessary to reintroduce manipulation of a rule cyclically, as we cannot expect our students to fully master all rules upon first encounter. Some rules are difficult enough that they require coming back to them several times. On first encounter with a difficult rule, approximately 80 percent mastery by 80 percent of the students should be the guideline to move on (to come back to it later, of course). But even after several "shots" at it, 100 percent mastery by all students may not be possible. In that case, the weak students should be referred to remedial study with recordings, workbooks, and so on.

Grammatical drills should be only the first step in the practice phase. They should be followed by increasingly freer activities incorporating the rule under consideration. Changing gradually from mechanical drills to free communication is the only way of ensuring that the initial mechanical skill is generalized and transferred to the unconscious competence of the learner.

Like all items in the second language, grammatical rules must be reintroduced frequently or they will be forgotten. It is not enough to "teach and get out of the way," except perhaps for the most common rules that will recur every few sentences anyway.

Unacceptable exercises

Before discussing the various types of acceptable

drills and exercises and how they should be written and presented in class, we need to consider briefly certain unacceptable exercises and why they are unacceptable.

Exercises containing sentences that are extremely unlikely to be used in communication should not be used, as already mentioned.

Exercises in which sentences have blanks to be filled (e.g., *La fille ____ professeur est partie*) should be used sparingly if at all. The normal use of language is in sentences, not in isolated words. Furthermore, it has been found that students can complete these exercises without even reading the whole sentence.

Even more unacceptable are exercises that mix the two languages within each sentence by presenting words in the native language in parentheses (e.g., *La fille (of the) _____ professeur est partie*). This destroys the continuity of the sentence, not to speak of what it does to its communicative function.

Perhaps most unacceptable of all are those exercises in which the students are supposed to produce word parts, either in the form of declensions or conjugations or following instructions such as "write the second person plural present indicative of the verb X."

The traditional type of translation exercise, which does use full sentences but in which each sentence has a different pattern and contains numerous different grammatical rules is also unacceptable for teaching purposes, as useful as it might at times be as part of the testing process.

Similarly unacceptable for teaching grammar but often acceptable for testing it are multiple-choice and matching exercises.

Finally, it should be obvious that *written* exercises in general are no efficient way to develop the ability to use grammatical structures in primarily audiolingual communication. Not only do written exercises give the student an opportunity to slowly edit and re-edit his answers which is not available in speech, but most written exercises can be completed without *any* attention to meaning, since the answers are largely predictable [Hosenfeld 1975:157-60]. Textbook authors even "help" the students by italicizing key words, which allows them to ignore completely the rest of the sentence! A third, and perhaps most important reason for maximizing oral drills and minimizing written ones is that oral drills performed at a quick tempo allow far more practice than written drills within a given period of time. Oral drills also permit immediate reinforcement, which is much more effective than the delayed reinforcement of written exercises.

Grammatical drills and exercises

Our modern grammatical drills are derived from Palmer, with numerous improvements produced by the U.S. structural school of applied linguistics. Most, however, have been in use in various forms for centuries. This means that, despite surface similarities drills are not based on linguistic theories, e.g., substitution drills are not based on tagmemics (or on Palmer's "ergonics" [1917, 1968:199-223]) and transformation drills are not based on generative-transformational grammar. The drills preceded the linguistic theories by many, many years.

To clarify some terms, we can say that *structure drills* include both *grammatical drills* and *pronunciation drills*, the latter having been discussed in Chapter 15. The difference between *drills* and *exercises* is that drills are mechanical, that is, do not allow a constructed response and have only one acceptable answer, while exercises imply emphasis on the conscious application of knowledge to construct responses and often have more than one acceptable answer. In other words, drills are more mechanical and exercises more creative, although neither drills nor exercises constitute communication. Drills do not involve word selection or pattern construction skills --both of these are provided. Neither drills nor exercises involve sentence generation --they are not the improvisation of music but the playing of piano scales. Being able to perform within the closely controlled structure of drills, then, does not mean that those same rules can be used in unstructured situations, only that the foundation for such unstructured use of the rules has been laid.

Neither drills nor exercises are communication nor do they pretend to be. Attempts to make them resemble communication results in practice materials which are neither good communication nor good drills. Drills require no personal commitment and make no pretense of being interesting or emotionally fulfilling. They are simply meant to give dexterity in the use of grammar rules, a dexterity that effective communication requires. Their "meaning" consists in that --that is, they are structurally meaningful, not communicatively meaningful, although their sentences should be communicatively acceptable. This means that, if we do not go beyond drills to develop communication skills, our students may have excellent performance within the limitations of drills and still be quite unable to communicate.

Some --Lado, for example [1964:106]-- have suggested that drills should divert the attention of the students from the point being taught. I recommend precisely the opposite: drills should enlist the cognitive ability of the students in the learning task, between each stimulus and each response, and they should drive this grammatical awareness into the unconscious through practice.

If drills are too easy, they can be performed without understanding a word of the drill sentences. While during drills attention to meaning should be secondary, it should be ensured by occasionally asking a student, at random, for a translation of a drill sentence. This should especially be done whenever the students' attention seems to wander away from meaning. Attention to meaning during drill practice enhances student interest and motivation. So the students should know what they are saying at all times, with the possible exception of the initial imitation of sample sentences and of the informal testing of structural control, at the end of a drill session, by using unknown words.

Drills should encourage students to respond intelligently, each frame representing a miniproblem to be solved between the stimulus and the response. The students must also know *why* they are supposed to respond in a particular way. The miniproblem to be solved is based on the formula:

$$\frac{\text{Model sentence } a}{\text{Model sentence } b} : \frac{\text{Cue}}{\text{Response sentence}}$$

The miniproblem is thus posed by the teacher; then the student should consider it; then the student produces his solution to the problem (his response); next the teacher evaluates the student's solution; then the teacher provides the student with feedback; and finally the student evaluates the teacher's feedback and determines whether his own solution was correct or not. If the feedback is negative --that is, if the student's solution was incorrect-- the student should reconsider the miniproblem.

Feedback or reinforcement during drills can take several forms. Positive feedback can be a *reward* (something tangible), *approval* (a nod, a smile, words such as "Yes" or "Good"), or *confirmation* (the teacher giving the correct response). Of these, rewards are seldom practicable in educational contexts, and confirmation is quite unnecessary --if the student has responded correctly there is no need at all for the teacher to repeat the correct response. That leaves approval as the only positive feedback that makes sense. Negative feedback includes *nonreinforcement* (ignoring the incorrect response) and *correction*. We have already seen in earlier chapters that nonreinforcement is generally disconcerting and ineffective. That leaves correction as the recommended alternative, as correction is effective in eliminating erroneous responses. (It should be noted that many rules can be learned fairly quickly through the differential reinforcement of drill responses, even without a careful presentation of the rule --this is, however, not recommended, for psychological reasons, as trial and error can be an emotionally painful process.)

Grammatical drills and exercises can be classified on the basis of several criteria. Most have a model, and most have, in each frame, a cue and a response. One of the criteria for the classification that follows is what the learner has to do between the cue and the response. A second criterion is the degree of difficulty of the operation, which goes, in this classification, from generally easiest to generally most difficult. The third criterion is the degree of freedom of the response; in this respect the classification goes from most controlled to freest. A further criterion is the general function that the drill or exercise can perform --does it serve to introduce, to practice, or to test the grammatical point being taught?

The drills and exercises will be illustrated whenever possible with examples from English for Spanish speakers, although some require the use of other languages. (Examples from several languages for the main drill and exercise types appear in Appendix B.) Several conventions are followed in the presentation of these sample drills: when two columns are used, the column on the left represents the teacher's stimuli and the column on the right the students' responses; only the first few frames of each drill are given.

I. *Introductory drills:* These involve no grammatical change from cue to response.

1. *Repetition:* These involve no change whatever from cue to response; only phonological knowledge is needed by the student.

1-A. *Simple repetition:* This consists in repeating a series of sentences that illustrate just one feature of a grammatical rule, without any contrasts.

Example (formation of the past):

I walked to the store.

The bus stopped at the corner.

Mr. Jones cashed a check.

Here all sentences have the /-t/ allomorph[△] of the English past tense. There is no contrast. And because there is no contrast, nothing is really being learned, since, for all the student knows, *all* English verbs may form their past in this way. Simple repetition should not be used.

1-B. *Contrastive repetition:* This consists in repeating sentences that contrast two structures, or two features of a rule, or a secong language versus a native language construction.

Example (still formation of the past):

I walked to the bookstore and ordered a book.

The driver stopped the car and raised the window.

After he cashed the check, he called a cab.

Here each sentence illustrates the /-t/ and the /-d/ allomorphs of the English past tense. Because there is this contrast, these sentences can be used as the basis for teaching when each of these two allomorphs is used; the third regular allomorph and the irregular forms can then be added. Contrastive repetition can be used effectively to bring grammatical awareness about many types of structures, even considerably complex ones.

2. *Substitution:* No grammatical change is involved from cue to response; only knowledge of the function of words to be substituted is needed by the student. A cue is substituted for a word or words in the previous sentence; no further changes are necessary.

2-A. *Single-slot substitution:* The substitutions always occur in the same place in the sentence.

Example (/-t/ allomorph of the English past tense):

We talked downtown.	We talked downtown.
worked	We worked downtown.
danced	We danced downtown.

2-B. *Multiple-slot substitution:* The substitutions occur in different places in the sentence, but still

----

[△] An allomorph is a variant of a morpheme. Grammatical morphemes (there are also lexical morphemes) are the minimal sequences expressing a grammatical function.

without choice-making correlations.

Example (same grammatical feature):

We talked downtown.	We talked downtown.
at home.	We talked at home.
John	John talked at home.
worked	John worked at home.

It is clear that, from the point of view of learning a grammatical rule, substitution without choice-making correlation, whether single- or multiple-slot, is no better than simple repetition --no grammatical rule is being manipulated, no grammatical choices are being made, therefore no grammatical learning results from it. Yet some materials have an overabundance of such mindless drills.

Some would say, for example, that in teaching a set of morphemes, such as a verb tense set, there should be several substitution drills on each form separately, and then one or two combining them all. But the correlation between the various subjects and verb forms should be the key activity, for learning to make the choices fast and accurately ought to be the goal. For that reason, the emphasis should be from the start on contrasts (two forms at a time) and choice-making practice, not on mindless repetition or substitution with only one form at a time.

Simple repetition and substitution drills are indeed guilty of the charge that "pattern practice is parroting." Parroting is grammatically worthless, as useful as it may be in developing articulatory dexterity. Emphasis should be instead on the intelligent and ever faster making of choices. More challenging, choice-making drills are more interesting to the students and force them to pay attention. They require the students to "be there" in order to perform. Drills are more challenging if they always offer the possibility of being in error, without which they cannot establish in the students' minds the limits of the rule. Maintaining a chance that the answer will not be right is not "testing" the students, it is teaching them to make choices and to internalize the underlying choice-making criteria.

Substitution drills are worthless as a way of teaching active control over grammatical rules.

<u>II. *Practice drills*:</u> In these drills, a choice is made between the cue and the response; some cognitive knowledge precedes, or develops with, the practice, and performative knowledge is the outcome. These choice-making mechanical drills are called "practice drills" for the very specific reason that I believe they should constitute the bulk of

the grammatical practice. Because of the fact that choices are involved, some second language teaching specialists call them "testing" drills, with the unfortunate result that many textbook authors tend to avoid them and use instead, as the bulk of their drills, the so-called "learning drills" (here called "introductory") which in fact teach very little or nothing and offer such little challenge to the students that they find them tedious. Choice-making drills ("practice" drills) do not really "test" (except in an irrelevant technical sense) *if* they are preceded by "seeded" material, the presentation of contrastive examples for repetition and translation, and, where needed, overt formulation of the rule.

3. *Correlation:* The knowledge required by these drills is awareness of the dependent correlated forms. The cue is substituted for a word or words in the previous sentence and necessary agreements in form are made elsewhere in the sentence.

3-A. *Single-slot correlation:* Correlations occur in only one place in the sentence.

Example 1 (English tense construction agreement with time reference):

We walk a lot.	We walk a lot.
Yesterday	Yesterday we walked a lot.
Tomorrow	Tomorrow we'll walk a lot.

Example 2 (Spanish present indicative verbs in *-ar*, agreement of endings with subjects):

Yo trabajo en el centro.[1]	Yo trabajo en el centro.
Usted	Usted trabaja en el centro.
Nosotros	Nosotros trabajamos en el centro.

Note that before a correlation drill with all the forms of a tense can be done successfully --without many errors-- there should be contrastive repetition drills and correlation drills teaching and adding forms one or two at a time.

3-B. *Multiple-slot correlation:* Correlations occur in two or more places in the sentence.

Example (English tense construction agreement with time reference):

We first talk and then play.	We first talk and then play.

---

[1] "I work downtown."

Yesterday	Yesterday we first talked and then played.
Tomorrow	Tomorrow we'll first talk and then play.

In practice, correlation is often combined with substitution, that is, a drill may contain mostly correlation (C) frames with some substitution (S) frames, as in the example below.

Example of *multiple-slot correlation-substitution* (English present tense subject-ending agreement):

	Cue	Response
	We study English every day.	We study English every day.
(C)	John	John studies English every day.
(S)	in school.	John studies English in school.
(C)	Our friends	Our friends study English in school.
(S)	Spanish	Our friends study Spanish in school.
(C)	Louise	Louise studies Spanish in school.

Correlation drills differ from traditional conjugations in that (1) full sentences are used, (2) the forms are not practiced in a fixed order, and (3) there is a much greater number of responses. Correlation drills lend themselves particularly well to the practice of gender agreement, number agreement, subject-verb ending agreement, time reference-verb tense matching, case agreement, and preposition-noun matching --in other words, they are useful whenever a number of forms have to match other forms or contexts.

4. *Replacement:* The knowledge required for these drills is awareness of the forms to be replaced. After the teacher gives two pairs of model sentences showing the operation involved, the student, *without further cues*, substitutes one grammatical form for another in the successive model sentences. The nature of the operation is explained before the replacement drill starts.

Example (English for Spanish speakers, replacement of present tense forms with past tense forms):

Cambien los verbos en las siguientes oraciones del presente al pasado.[2]

----

[2] "Change the verbs in the following sentences from the present to the past."

Ejemplo[3] 1:
Si yo digo...[4]
I walk to school. I walk to school.
Ustedes dicen...[5]
I walked to school. I walked to school.
Ejemplo 2:
Si yo digo...
I have breakfast at eight. I have breakfast at eight.
Ustedes dicen...
I had breakfast at eight. I had breakfast at eight.
Ahora, cambien:[6]
I take the bus home. I took the bus home.
I eat dinner at six. I ate dinner at six.

We have seen then that substitution, correlation, and replacement all have a morpheme, word, or phrase replaced by another. But in substitution there is a cue and no change elsewhere in the sentence, in correlation there is a cue plus change elsewhere, and in replacement there is change in the sentence without a cue.

5. *Transformation:* The knowledge required for these drills is awareness of the operation to be performed and of the words involved in and affected by the operation.

5-A. *Simple transformation:* Only one sentence at a time is involved.

5-A-i. *Expansion:* One or more words are added to a sentence.

5-A-i-a. *Single expansion:* A single utterance is added to each sentence.

Example (English affirmative to negative):
Cambien las siguientes oraciones
del afirmativo al negativo.[7]
Ejemplo:
Si yo digo...
I like Chinese food. I like Chinese food.
Ustedes dicen...
I don't like Chinese food. I don't like Chinese food.
Ahora, cambien:
I eat lunch at home. I don't eat lunch at home.

---

[3] "Example"
[4] "If I say..."
[5] "You say..."
[6] "Now change:"
[7] "Change the following sentences from affirmative to negative."

She's studying English.	She's not studying English.
We play tennis.	We don't play tennis.

5-A-i-b. *Progressive expansion:* More than one utterance is added to each sentence, one by one, progressively.

Example (position of noun modifiers):

Agreguen a las oraciones, una tras otra, las palabras que les daré.[8]

Repitan:[9]

He's a student.	He's a student.
Ahora, añadan:[10]	
Canadian	He's a Canadian student.
tall	He's a tall Canadian student.
handsome	He's a tall handsome Canadian student.
gum-chewing	He's a tall handsome gum-chewing Canadian student.
Repitan:	
We like cars.	We like cars.
Ahora, añadan:	
new	We like new cars.
American	We like new American cars.
fast	We like fast new American cars.
four-door	We like fast new four-door American cars.

5-A-ii. *Reduction:* One or more words are dropped from each sentence.

Example (Spanish nominalization of adjectives):

Change the following sentences by dropping the noun (and changing the pronoun if necessary)

Example:

If I say...

Quiero una pluma buena.[11]	Quiero una pluma buena.
You say...	
Quiero una buena.[12]	Quiero una buena.

Now change:

---

[8] "Add to the sentences, one by one, the words I will give you."

[9] "Repeat:"

[10] "Now add:"

[11] "I want a good pen."

[12] "I want a good one."

Deme un problema fácil.[13] Deme uno fácil.
Es una compañía importante.[14] Es una importante.
Perdí un reloj caro.[15] Perdí uno caro.

(Note that in English the corresponding rule would involve a replacement, not a reduction transformation.)

5-A-iii. *Transposition:* The word order of a sentence is changed.

Example (English statements with modals to questions):
Cambien las oraciones siguientes de declaraciones a preguntas.[16]
Ejemplo:
Si yo digo...

John can sing well.	John can sing well.
Ustedes dicen...	
Can John sing well?	Can John sing well?
Ahora, cambien:	
We must buy a newspaper.	Must we buy a newspaper?
I should write a letter.	Should I write a letter?
We can drive fast on this street.	Can we drive fast on this street?

5-B. *Complex transformation or sentence combination:* Two sentences are combined into a more complex one, usually with some other operation involved too.

Example (English subordination):
Combinen los siguientes pares de oraciones como en los ejemplos.[17]
Ejemplo 1:
Si yo digo...

This is the man.	This is the man.
y[18]	
We wanted to see him.	We wanted to see him.
Ustedes dicen...	
This is the man we wanted to see.	This is the man we wanted to see.

Ejemplo 2:
Si yo digo...

---

[13] "Give me an easy problem."

[14] "It is an important company."

[15] "I lost an expensive watch."

[16] "Change the following sentences from statements to questions."

[17] "Combine the following pairs of sentences as in the examples."

[18] "and"

These are the things. — These are the things.
y
We argued about them. — We argued about them.

Ustedes dicen...

These are the things we argued about. — These are the things we argued about.

Ahora, combinen:[19]

This is the boy.
You wanted to meet him. — This is the boy you wanted to meet.

These are the cars.
You asked about them. — These are the cars you asked about.

III. *Directed communication drills:* These are drills that are choice-making, in the sense that a response is constructed, and mechanical, but they differ from the preceding practice drills in that each frame resembles a miniature conversation, with a question and a response.

6. *Response:* The knowledge required of the student is how to construct a reply to a question.

6-A. *Cued response*: The response to the question is based on a cue or cues given by the teacher.

6-A-i. *Single-cue response*: A single cue is given (usually in a soft voice) by the teacher.

Example:

Contesten las preguntas siguientes usando las respuestas que yo les sugiera.[20]

Does he want to go? (Yes) — Yes, he does.
Is the window open? (No) — No, it isn't.
Can we speak English? (Yes) — Yes, we can.

6-A-ii. *Multiple-cue response*: Two or more cues are given and the student chooses one of them. Multiple cues do not need to be given in a different tone of voice.

Example:

Contesten las preguntas siguientes escogiendo una de las posibles respuestas que yo les sugiera.[21]

Does he want to go or to stay? — He wants to go. *or* He wants to stay.

---

[19] "Now combine:"

[20] "Answer the following questions by using the answers I'll suggest."

[21] "Answer the following questions by choosing one of the possible answers I'll suggest."

Is the window open or closed?	It's open. *or* It's closed.
Can we speak English or read it?	We can speak it. *or* We can read it.

6-B. *Patterned response*: The student answers questions according to a pre-set pattern.

Example:

Contesten las preguntas siguientes
de acuerdo con el formato ilustrado
en el ejemplo.[22]

Si yo digo...

Are they from New York?	Are they from New York?

Ustedes dicen...

Yes, they are, and so is their sister.	Yes, they are, and so is their sister.

Ahora, contesten:[23]

Is she from New York?	Yes, she is, and so is her sister.
Is he from New York?	Yes, he is, and so is his sister.
Are you from New York?	Yes, I am, and so is my sister.

6-C. *Inverted response*: The knowledge required of the student is an awareness of how questions are asked. The operation consists of the teacher providing an answer to an unexpressed question and the student trying to ask the question that would result in such an answer.

Example:

Hagan las preguntas que correspondan
a las respuestas que les daré.
Basen cada pregunta en la última
parte de cada respuesta.[24]

He wants to go.	What does he want to do?
The window is open.	Is the window open?
We can speak English.	What (language) can we speak?

It is a little artificial to move from statements to questions, but it is good manipulative practice, as the

---

[22] "Answer the following questions according to the format illustrated by the example."

[23] "Now answer:"

[24] "Ask the questions that correspond to the answers I will give you. Base each question on the last part of each answer."

students do need formal practice in asking questions.

In response drills of all three types (plus freer exercises to be discussed later), if the student does not reply immediately the teacher should wait --the student is processing his response while keeping the cue in short-term memory.

The so-called "Cummings device" recommended by some authors combines substitution and response drills. It has two parts: (1) a *presentation* for mimicry and manipulation like a substitution frame, and (2) *exploitation* in the form of a two-utterance response frame [Stevick 1971: 310-14]. As a presentation device, the Cummings device should be used with restraint --a two-line "conversation" is neither real nor realistic. As a grammatical device it doesn't provide adequate mechanical practice.

<u>IV. *Meaningful exercises*</u>: These are not mechanical but allow for a constructed response. While there is basically only one response to each frame, this response can vary within limits.

7. *Translation or interpretation*: These exercises consist in the oral translation of sentences based on a second language model and native language semantic cues.

Many language teachers object strenuously to the use of translation exercises in modern methods. But, as Rivers [1975:137-40] pointed out in an excellent discussion on the subject, modern translation exercises are very different from the traditional, Grammar-Translation Method type. In the first place, one or more model sentences are given, and these are sentences in the second language, not the native language. The native language serves only to provide a semantic cue for the production of the next sentence on the basis of the second language model. As Dodson [1967:91, 96] put it, in these exercises the native language only cues the concepts in the learner's mind, not the actual second language words; the stimulus is then the concept, and as there is no direct link between the native language cue and the second language response, there can be no detrimental effects. Secondly, modern translation exercises are oral, not written. Thirdly, the sentences are short but complete, without blanks. In the fourth place, the exercise concentrates on only one grammatical point, unlike the complex sentences of the old-type translation exercises, which combine many rules. Modern translation exercises follow a pattern, all of the sentences in each exercise being of the same type. Fifth, thoroughly familiar vocabulary is used, so that the stimuli in the native language are not semantic puzzles. Sixth, idiomatic equivalents rather than artificial word-by-word equivalents are used. Seventh, they are performed at a fast tempo rather than slowly constructed; by demanding immediate responses, word-by-word translation is prevented. Eighth and finally, natural translation rather than professional translation is involved, that is, the simple matching of structural patterns and lexical items rather than the use of literary or technical skill.

Besides being markedly different from traditional translation exercises, modern translation exercises are also different from *monolingual* drills in several respects [Butzkamm 1973:94-7], in addition to the obvious fact that they make use of the native language. Bilingual exercises consciously activate lexical meaning; they force the students to process the sentences cognitively, for responses cannot be produced without thinking. Another difference is that they are more flexible and after a few sentences need not retain the structure of the first sentence in the exercise (the native language can lead translation exercise sentences in any direction). A third difference is that bilingual exercises can deal better with difficulties found through contrastive analysis, by focusing attention on them. They thus counteract tendencies to isomorphism. What best way to deal with areas where grammatical interference is strong than overcoming it by exposing the students to that interference under controlled, guided conditions? Deconditioning can only be accomplished effectively in the presence of the old habit, so native language interference can best be overcome by practicing language contrasts (by means of translation exercises) to the point where the native language rule is no longer used in producing second language sentences. A fourth difference is that, unlike response drills, translation exercises cannot simulate a conversation; however, they can simulate an interpreting situation.

Translation exercises are excellent to practice the production of idiomatic phrases, for consolidation or quick review of any grammatical point, and for testing. They are particularly useful in the areas where the grammatical interference of the native language is strong. They can also be a good supplement to a presentation of new material --Dodson [1967:88-9] found that an eight-sentence story could be reproduced far better when the presentation included an "interpretation exercise" as opposed to imitation only.

Students find translation exercises more challenging than monolingual drills. T. Mueller and Harris [1966], for example, reported that in learning structures many of their first-year college French students preferred to do bilingual exercises first, because they felt that contrastive drills best brought the essential structural element to awareness.

Of course, translation is perfectly all right as long as it is a means to practice and not an end in itself. It is natural to translate in many situations, but students must not be allowed to form the habit of translating everything they hear --this hinders communication.

Example of a translation exercise (Spanish agreement of *gustar* with the surface object):

Repitan:

Me gustan las papas.	Me gustan las papas.
"I like potatoes."	

Traduzcan:[25]

I like rice.	Me gusta el arroz.
We like rice.	Nos gusta el arroz.
He likes tomatoes.	Le gustan los tomates.
They like potatoes.	Les gustan las papas.

Note that translation exercises can be grammatical or lexical in orientation, or both; as lexical activities, they are discussed in Chapter 18.

8. *Non-cued response*: Questions are asked, without cueing the responses, about things for which the students know only one answer, as would be the case for factual questions about a reading, or about what can be seen in the classroom, etc.

9. *Directed discourse*: In this kind of exercise the students speak about what someone else has said or are asked to say definite things to each other.

9-A. *Speech reporting*: Here students take turns in reporting, in the third person, present or past, what other students say. The latter may be conversing freely or following instructions.

9-B. *Directed dialogue*: In this variety of directed discourse the students are told what to say to each other. My experience has been that if the instructions are given in the second language then the performance of the students can be quite mechanical (as almost everything is

----

[25] "Translate:"

being given away and they don't really have to generate sentences) and therefore quite boring. Far more interesting and more challenging is to give the instructions in the native language, in which case directed dialogue becomes, in effect, indirect consecutive (natural) interpretation.

V. *Communicative activities*: While these are not free conversation, for a grammatical rule is still being emphasized, the students have considerable freedom in choosing what to say, and their responses are largely unpredictable, as they may contain new information. (Some of these activities can also be used for lexical practice.)

10. *Sentence generation*: The students are asked to produce a series of short sentences incorporating the rule being studied. As a variation, they may be asked to cue other students, monolingually or bilingually, to produce such sentences.

11. *Free completion*: The teacher lets his voice trail off, leaving sentences incomplete, and the students complete them as they want to.

12. *Free response*: The teacher asks questions designed to elicit a certain grammatical structure but otherwise leaves the students free to say what they want. For example, "What did you do during the weekend?" elicits past tense responses.

A subtype of free response is *chained response*, which consists of a series of questions eliciting true, preferably autobiographical answers [Chastain 1976:350]. Note that yes/no questions are much easier to answer than questions requiring an explanation for an answer. With either type, early in the program the students should answer with full sentences, then they can be allowed to reduce them (it is useless for them to reply *Oui, madame* or *Non, madame*: while it reveals comprehension it gives no practice in production).

13. *Free rejoinder*: The teacher makes statements and the students reply with comments about them.

14. *Free association*: Various visual and verbal stimuli are used to keep a student monologue or conversation going. The stimuli should present one item only --a picture of a person or thing, or a word.

15. *Description*: The students are asked to describe someone or something in the classroom or in a picture. Particularly effective for this is the use of wordless cartoons.

16. *Situation or role-playing*: A situation is

described and the students are asked to play themselves in it; or they may be asked to play various roles. Usually a demonstration is helpful. Then the students perform in the situation, with a considerable degree of freedom, introducing their own variations.

VI. *Testing exercises*: At any point, a drill with unknown lexical items will reveal whether the grammatical generalization has been successfully made or the students are able to use the rule correctly only with the vocabulary they know. This is then a type of informal test. So is in fact a more difficult, freer type of drill with respect to the preceding ones --if the students can't do the more challenging drill or exercise, it means they need more practice with easier ones. Practice drills can be used for testing purposes. Translation can also be used as a testing device, for just about anything. A special type of drill that can be used in informal testing is the distractor drill.

17. *Distractor drills*: These are choice-making mechanical drills containing a distractor. A good indication of whether a grammatical point has been mastered is the ability of the students to use it correctly when their attention is drawn to something else. This is the principle behind distractor drills. The distraction can be lexical or grammatical in nature.

17-A. *Lexical distractor*: The students are expected to produce the new grammatical point correctly while paying attention, at the same time, to lexical changes in the sentences.

Example (English past tense forms for speakers of Spanish):

Cambien las oraciones siguientes
del presente al pasado, haciendo
también los cambios de vocabulario
indicados por las figuras.[26]

Mary sees the book (shows picture of a car)	Mary saw the car.
They are looking for a house (shows picture of a letter)	They were looking for a letter.
I am buying a newspaper (shows	

---

[26] "Change the following sentences from the present to the past, making also the changes in vocabulary indicated by the pictures."

picture of a book) I bought a book.

17-B. *Grammatical distractor*: The students are expected to produce the new grammatical rule correctly while paying attention, at the same time, to another grammatical change based on a previously learned grammatical point.

Example (English past tense forms):
Cambien las oraciones siguientes del presente al pasado, al mismo tiempo cambiando el sujeto dado del singular al plural o del plural al singular.[27]

He walks fast, doesn't he?	They walked fast, didn't they?
We are busy, aren't we?	I was busy, wasn't I?
She speaks slowly, doesn't she?	They spoke slowly, didn't they?

It should be obvious that distractor drills are difficult enough that they must be preceded by considerable practice with the new grammatical structure. The time to use them is at the end of the practice drills and before going on to directed communication and to the meaningful exercises. It is at that point that the teacher thinks that perhaps the class has already learned well the mechanics of the new structure; he needs therefore to test the validity of that assumption, and distractor drills allow him to do it before going on to more meaningful activities.

How to write drills and exercises

The characteristics of drills largely determine how they should be written. Some of the pointers to be kept in mind for the writing of drills and exercises are the following:

(1) The drill or exercise should fit the structure. For example, transformation drills should be used to teach changes in word order, not to teach morphological structures.

(2) Drills should have about seven frames. Fewer frames do not fully exploit the sentence pattern. More can mean boredom.

----

[27] "Change the following sentences from the present to the past, changing at the same time the subject given from the singular to the plural or from the plural to the singular."

(3) Make sure that each drill cue can generate only one sentence. Nothing can slow down and destroy the effectiveness of a drill session more than ambiguous cues.

(4) Every sentence should be a meaningful, plausible sentence. *La plume de ma tante* and *The Englishman's cane* deserve the oblivion they have been getting.

(5) Drill sentences should be short.

(6) Drill sentences should not include any new phonological or lexical items.

(7) Drill sentences should be as simple as possible.

(8) In practice there is nothing wrong in combining drill types. The nature of the grammatical rule often makes this necessary.

How to teach drills and exercises

(1) Drill sessions should be done with books closed. If students refer to the printed page they will think they know the rule before they really control it orally.

(2) Instructions should be clear as to what the students are supposed to do in each frame.

(3) At least two examples of each new operation should be given. (Note that the examples of drills given in this chapter contain fewer sample sentences than normally required.) Once the students are familiar with the various types of drills, these can be identified by name and fewer examples will be needed.

(4) Maintain a fast tempo. If a student does not answer fairly soon, call on another, better student. Nothing is more boring than d-r-a-g-g-i-n-g drills.

(5) Use group responses, by the whole class, for the introductory drills only --repetition and substitution-- and individual responses occasionally followed by choral repetition of correct answers for the other drills and exercises, in which more than one answer or a constructed answer is possible. If choral response is used in drills and exercises in which more than one answer or a constructed response is possible, the class will produce an indistinct jumble of noise as different students give different answers at different speeds. Not only will the teacher be unable to hear the students distinctly, but if he rewards an apparently correct general response he will also be rewarding many incorrect individual responses, something totally counterproductive. Furthermore, choral responses prevent the active construction of sentences.

(6) Call on the students in unpredictable order; otherwise student No. 10 will take a little nap while students

1 to 9 respond to their cues.

(7) First give the cue, then point to the student who should respond. This helps to make the whole class more attentive. Furthermore, all students should be encouraged to answer all cues, mentally when not called to respond aloud. Certain attention-enhancing tricks can also be used when calling on students, such as raising the right hand and then pointing with the left, or looking at one student and pointing to another.

(8) Fairly frequently ask for the native language equivalents of drill sentences. This will ensure that the students will pay attention to the meaning of what they are saying.

(9) Do not require students to respond immediately from the beginning of a drill session. In the early part of the practice phase they need a little time to think. As the practice phase progresses, faster responses can be required.

(10) Do not present a particular drill more than twice in a row. It is better to have additional drills on the same point than to do the same drills over and over, as in the latter case correct responses may come from memory rather than from attention to the crucial feature(s) of the rule.

(11) Have a variety of activities. Any one type of drill or exercise should not be used for more than five minutes.

(12) Move as soon as possible into choice-making, response construction types of drills and exercises. They should constitute at least 80 percent of a drill session.

(13) Correct essential errors --errors having to do with the point being practiced or with anything studied earlier. (Grammatical errors and their correction are discussed briefly later in this chapter.)

(14) Move on to the next drill or exercise or to the next step in your lesson when about 80 percent of the class can answer correctly and quickly. You cannot gear your speed to that of the slowest students. If you do that, you will induce boredom in the majority of the class.

(15) Do not make a drill/exercise session too short or too long. Teachers tire of a drill session before the students do, as they already know the grammar and may have taught those drills several times before. So teachers must take care that they don't make a drill session shorter than the students need to internalize the rule. At the other extreme, very long drill sessions result in

fatigue and boredom and rather little learning. A session with drills and exercises of various types should not last longer than 15-20 minutes.

(16) Alternate drill sessions with personalized, semi-free conversation. This will do much to enhance motivation and prevent boredom.

(17) Always build bridges between mechanical practice and communication. Practice drills are not enough. They should always be followed by directed communication, meaningful exercises, and communicative activities.

Many drills and exercises can be cued with pictures rather than orally. There should be considerable use of multi-tense drills, exercises, and communicative activities, as controlling the tense system is crucial.

In those programs that employ native instructors, it is really a waste of human potential to put them to teach drills, as if they were machines. All drills, and most exercises, can be done by the students, individually, with tape recordings, and that is how they should be done, leaving the classroom for the more challenging types of exercises and for communicative activities.

Grammatical errors and their correction

You will recall that when we discussed pronunciation errors we noted that lower-level phonetic errors are more offensive than higher-level phonemic errors. A parallel situation exists with respect to grammatical errors: morphological errors are generally more offensive than syntactic ones. Thus, a Spanish speaker who hears an English speaker say **Estoy yendo a Seattle mañana,* with *Estoy yendo...* instead of *Voy...* ("I'm going to Seattle tomorrow") or **Dudo que Juan llega a tiempo,* with *llega* instead of *llegue* ("I doubt John will arrive on time"), is far less bothered than if the English speaker says **Me gusta el cocina francesa,* an error in article-noun gender agreement. This in spite of the fact that higher-level syntactic errors have a much greater potential to interfere with the communication of the message.

We should not have the attitude that everything must be done to prevent the occurrence of errors in the classroom. It is by making errors that the learners receive essential differential feedback and learn the limits of the rule. Besides, exposure to errors by others does not lead to the incorporation of those errors in one's own speech if they are identified as errors and corrected --it will lead, instead, to their avoidance.

Errors during the repetition of examples of a rule should be handled like any imitation errors, as already discussed previously, that is, basically by the twin processes of isolation and differentiation.

On the other hand, grammatical errors, especially after some practice, should be corrected by eliciting the correct response (and in the process making indirect appeal to the rule), *not* by giving the correct response to imitate, from which the students learn little or nothing. It is the faulty generalization that must be tackled, not the errors that result from it. More than accuracy in a particular sentence, correction must aim at perfecting the knowledge of the rule the imperfect knowledge of which resulted in the error.

By eliciting the correct response through the right questions, the knowledge of the student is brought into play and corrected if necessary. The student is led to discover the correct response by himself, with help as needed.

First an indication that an error has occurred should be made, preferably non-verbally (such as a head shake), to give the student a chance to correct himself. The teacher should know the students well enough to know which can and which cannot respond to indirect correction; for those who cannot, more direct correction is needed. As a second step, the student can be informed of which type of rule he has violated --this can be done verbally or by means of some sort of signal [Schachter 1981]. As a third and still more direct form of correction, the student can be reminded in a variety of ways of the rule he has violated. Suppose, for example, that a student of English as a second language says **The cars runs*. The correction can be elicited, reminding the learner of the rule, in the following alternate ways:

(1) "runs...?"
(2) "The cars..."
(3) "Plural."
(4) "The car runs," but "The cars..."?

If all of this fails, as a final step the correct response can be given, but always in reference to the rule: "The car runs" (accompanied by the raising of one finger) "but 'The cars run'" (accompanied by the raising of two fingers).

To further emphasize that the important thing is to both understand and internalize each rule, it helps if occasionally the teacher says, especially to an erring student who should know better: "Think, please!"

As a shock treatment, especially for students who are being just careless, it helps to let other students correct them. This should be done with caution, as some students will feel inferior to their classmates if these correct them.

Further thoughts on practice

All learners need conditioning practice if they are going to be able to internalize the rules. Drills are not just for *some* types of learners. Even the best students need considerable practice beyond the point where they understand a rule if they are going to develop linguistic habits based on it. Practice must continue to the point of internalization of the rule regardless of how quickly bright students may want to move on to other rules.

Textbooks and workbooks could provide much grammatical practice if publishers were not so determined to save space that they omit the responses to the drills and exercises. Textbook drills in which the responses are not provided are less than totally useless --they are definitely harmful, for the student often responds incorrectly and, because he gets no feedback, assumes that he responded correctly. It would be better for textbook publishers to publish half the drills with responses than twice the drills without them. It should be an unbreakable principle that any drill or exercise must be printed with the responses in two columns or interlinearly. If provided with the right kind of instructions, format, and encouragement, students will say each response aloud, or write it, before uncovering it.

Knowing the grammar of a second language

Many people think that "knowing grammar" means the ability to recite paradigms and rules. Knowing grammar is, instead, the ability to use a language fluently without making morphological or syntactic errors. That is, as much as cognition may help to get there, knowing grammar is not intellectual, cognitive knowledge but applied, performative knowledge.

When a student uses a rule correctly every time it is called for, we can say he knows it, i.e., he has internalized it. This does not mean that he needed necessarily to be consciously aware of it as a statement of linguistic description, since some rules can be learned inductively.

Once a structure has been properly presented, drilled,

and practiced in communicative activities, there is no reason why the student could not have a control of that rule that approximates native control. Mastery can be nearly total, rule by rule. Second language rules are additive and combinatory. There is no valid reason why a second language should be learned globally rather than rule by rule. A frequent result of proceeding globally is the loss of accuracy (or its nondevelopment), leading to the early fossilization of a very defective interlanguage. When we proceed rule by rule, combining each new rule with what has been learned to that point, the learner, rather than very defectively approximating the second language grammar as a whole, learns to come very close to matching native performance for each rule within an increasingly comprehensive control of the grammar. In this way, rather than a superficial and inaccurate knowledge of the whole grammar, we can impart to second language learners a thorough knowledge, rule by rule, of more and more of the grammar.

18

TEACHING VOCABULARY[△]

The importance of vocabulary learning

The importance of vocabulary learning was indicated by Wilkins [1972:111], who said that "while without grammar very little can be conveyed, without vocabulary *nothing* can be conveyed." However, vocabulary does not need to be controlled to the same degree as phonology or grammar. All native speakers of a language know 100 percent of the phonology and 99 percent plus of the morphology and syntax, but very few know as much as 50 percent of the vocabulary. So knowledge of a *second* language involves control of as close as possible to 100 percent of the phonology, about 80-90 percent of the grammar (all major and most minor grammatical rules), but only 5 percent or less of the total vocabulary --about 10,000 words are needed for literary reading, 7,000 words for general reading, less for listening, and even less for speaking or writing.

Learning a second language is not, therefore, a matter of either learning its grammar or accumulating vocabulary. One could know a large number of words and still neither understand, nor be able to communicate, in a second language. Both extremes --too much emphasis on structure or excessive emphasis on learning words-- are to be avoided.

When to teach vocabulary

It has been argued by languists of a strong structuralist orientation that the language classroom is an artificial environment and that therefore there is nothing wrong --and certain advantages-- in strictly limiting the vocabulary in the early stages to that needed to exemplify phonological and grammatical patterns. Among the arguments for not emphasizing vocabulary early in the program are

----

[△] Portions of this chapter are reprinted from my article "Conveying Lexical Meanings in Second Language Teaching," *The Canadian Modern Language Review/La Revue canadienne des langues vivantes* 35, 4 (May 1979):567-80. By permission of the Editor, Anthony S. Mollica.

the easily ascertainable facts that early vocabulary emphasis leads to (1) a disregard for structural control, (2) the false impression that words are functionally meaningful in isolation rather than in context, and (3) the development of bad habits as the students are rewarded, through communication acts, for utterances that are lexically correct but phonologically and grammatically inaccurate. This process of premature lexicalization whereby a second language learner concentrates on vocabulary before passing through a stage of phonological and grammatical categorization results inevitably in a very faulty pidgin. It is much better to have the students master the system of the language first, then concentrate on vocabulary expansion.

At the same time, an extreme restriction on vocabulary as recommended by some structuralists is inadvisable. A language classroom is a social environment in which the students wish to communicate with the teacher and with each other, so frustrating this desire to communicate would hurt their motivation. Consequently, while early second language learning is not primarily a matter of learning vocabulary, sufficient vocabulary should be taught to make some conversation possible in the classroom, within narrow limits at first, but gradually on more and more topics of interest to the students.

Once the basic structure of the language is under control and can be used with ease, vocabulary learning can proceed without hindrance. This will constitute the major task of the late intermediate and advanced levels, and beyond, as this most time-consuming endeavor is never finished. It is not that learning vocabulary is harder than learning structure, but there is far more to learn.

While much advanced vocabulary can be self-taught, basic vocabulary is not easily acquired, so *it must be taught,* contextually, in graded materials. And the meanings of the basic vocabulary must be formally provided, as it is quixotic to expect that second language students will derive all the meanings of words from the situations in which they are used.

Meaning

Each meaning of a lexical item consists of a denotation (what it refers to) and its cultural connotations (the ideas society associates with it). These can be determined by observing all the contexts in which the word is used and eliciting associations from the speakers of the language. On such a basis a *lexigram* [Ramsey 1981] can be established for each item, something that allows interlingual comparison.

Some contexts and associations are personal rather than cultural. We can refer to these as experiential connotations. For example, *wine* means something very different to a Baptist minister and to a wino. But we cannot take experiential connotations into account in second language teaching.

Words differ across languages mostly in their cultural connotations and to a much lesser extent in their denotations, most of which have perfect interlingual equivalents. A denotation is what a word refers to, either factually or conceptually. Connotations are largely emotional in nature --thus *escargot* and *snail* have the same denotation but very different connotations. Each of the distinguishable meanings of a word must be considered a separate denotation; thus we can speak of $head_1$ (the part of the body containing the brain), $head_2$ (the director of an organization), $head_3$ (the foam in a glass of beer), and so forth. Given specific contexts, there are denotational equivalents across languages for the great majority of words; of course, the limitations of each denotation must be explicitly provided, via a very brief native language remark; providing a whole network of second language associations and restrictions would be incredibly inefficient.

Much of word meaning is subjective. Osgood and Suci [1955] showed that as much as 70 percent of the meaning words have is on a subjective, evaluative (good/bad) dimension.

Linguistics has fostered the establishment of a clear distinction between meaning and form, keeping them apart. Meaning is related to structure but differs from it. Thus the same statement can be a warning, an order, an act of persuasion, even an inquiry depending on the intention of the speaker and his relation to his interlocutor. Conversely, the same meaning may be expressed by many different sentences.

Generative semantics, which organizes meaning into distinctive features, cannot solve entirely the question of meaning because the same object may be described in several ways depending on what it is being contrasted with. Thus, a black, round, plastic object near the speaker can be described, in relation to other objects in his presence, as "the black one," "the round one," "the plastic one," or "the near one" --in other words, the relationship object-word is not quite stable.

In the use of language, the speaker does not transfer meanings to the mind of the listener, in spite of the fact that we talk about "conveying meaning." The meanings are already in the mind of the listener, so all the speaker can really do is arouse them and sometimes reorganize them.

It should be kept in mind that structural linguists did not study meaning much, although they did pay some attention to it by recording what forms meant and transmitting that information to other linguists and to second language learners in the form of glosses. It remained for generative semanticists to make a serious and concentrated effort in the study of meaning. Still, linguists in general, and languists as well, have tended to neglect vocabulary studies.

Learning the full meaning of any word is a gradual and complex process. J. Richards [1976] explained well the fact that the knowledge of a word by a native speaker is very complex, so the task for the second language learner is long-term and difficult. Exposure to the word in many contexts, through extensive listening and reading, is necessary in order to learn its full meaning, and such exposure should be accompanied and followed by much use of the word in conversation if it is to be part of one's active vocabulary.

Active and passive vocabulary

Active vocabulary is the vocabulary one can produce, in speech particularly but also in unaided writing. Passive vocabulary is the vocabulary one can understand in listening or reading. In any language that one knows well, the passive vocabulary is larger than the active vocabulary; this is in part due to the fact that active vocabulary items are frequent in use and carry a heavy functional load.

Following our division of second language learning into a beginning, an intermediate, and an advanced level, it seems advisable to concentrate on active vocabulary goals during the beginning level, as this would facilitate communication, active plus some passive during the intermediate level, and a greater percentage of passive vocabulary during the advanced level. This is represented pictorially in Figure 18.1.

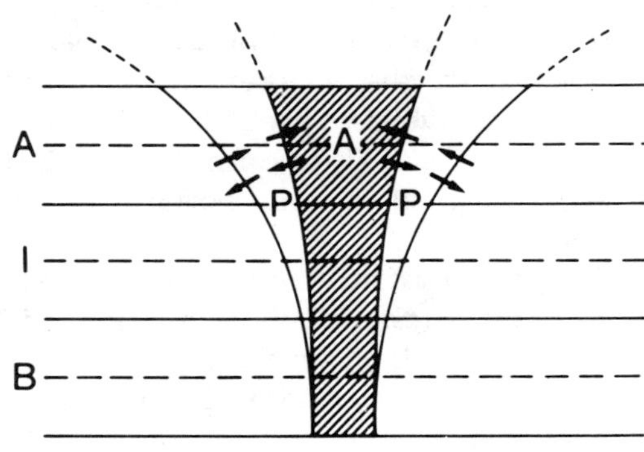

Figure 18.1

The small arrows indicate that what is not known can become passive vocabulary through exposure and what is passive can become active through practice; in the opposite direction, lack of practice can turn active vocabulary into passive, and through lack of exposure passive vocabulary is forgotten. Every effort should be made to convert passive vocabulary to active, and to keep it active.

Reading, no matter how extensive, results only in passive vocabulary. In fact, literary vocabulary and the ability to communicate in the spoken language are largely unrelated. As an example, Mackey [1965:161] referred to the French author André Gide, who produced excellent translations of Shakespeare and Conrad but could not ask a London bus driver where to get off. To have vocabulary readily available for recall, it must be used systematically in speech. Note also that most (maybe 95 percent) of the vocabulary that becomes passively acquired through graded reading in second language programs should be active vocabulary, as it is active for the native speaker.

In closely related languages, of course, the learners *start* with a large potential passive vocabulary composed of cognate words.

Words within a language

The vocabulary of a language is composed of content words (nouns, verbs, adjectives, and adverbs), certain phrases, and idioms. Function words such as pronouns, auxiliary verbs, determiners, prepositions, conjunctions, etc. (words such as *he, any, to, the, not, with,* the auxiliary *do*, and so forth) are part of the grammar, as they express mostly, if not exclusively, grammatical meaning.

Function words constitute a small list of words that occur very frequently, so unlike the content words they should be completely under control by the end of the beginning level. We have to learn all the function words, but no one can learn all the content words. So content words, which carry most of the referential and emotional meaning, are necessary but not sufficient, and function words, which carry the structural meaning, are essential.

About 80 percent of the content words in English are borrowed from other languages, the biggest contributor being Latin, via French. More than 10,000 French words entered English following the Norman conquest. All these borrowings make it easier for English speakers to learn Romance languages, particularly French, as the English speaker can guess about 30 percent of French vocabulary without any study.

Collocations, the combinations in which words occur in a given language, are largely arbitrary. For example, while *big* and *large* are roughly synonyms, it is not possible to say **a large lie*. We can say *mother tongue* and *native language*, but not **mother language* [Wilkins 1974: 22]. English uses *black and white* but Spanish expresses the same idea with *blanco y negro* ("white and black"). Collocation is a frequent source of error for the second language learner; he sounds foreign because he either uses the wrong collocations or fails to use second language collocations altogether. Being rather capricious, collocations must be learned by trial and error.

Note that there seem to be no exact synonyms within a language. When one considers all the contexts and associations of a pair of "synonyms," it seems that there are always differences. Some such differences are rather subtle. For example, French *an* is used after cardinal numbers and when emphasizing a unit of time, while *année* is used after ordinal numbers and when emphasizing the duration of an action --distinctions which English speakers find hard to make.

There are phrases that must be considered single lexical units --not only verbs, like *get up* and *block off* but nouns like *Statue of Liberty, merry-go-round,* and *inches-per-second.*

Idioms are phrases or sentences whose meaning cannot be derived from the added meaning of the parts. They are quite capricious and many do not make any sense if taken literally. For example, it makes no sense for someone to say *I'm up now* --meaning "I'm awake now"-- while lying horizontally in bed. Another example is *How do you do?*, which if taken literally invites the response *How do I do what? True idioms* or simply *idioms* are those that are idiomatic from a monolingual point of view, such as French *tout à l'heure* ("a few minutes ago, in a few minutes") and Spanish *dar la lata* ("to make a nuisance of oneself"); that is, in the case of true idioms the native speaker cannot rely on the meaning of the parts. These would be referred to as English idioms, French idioms, Spanish idioms, etc. *Second language idioms* or *pseudoidioms* are those second language expressions which, because they lack parallelism with the native language, present particular difficulties for the second language learner; but natives have no trouble deriving their meaning from their parts. Examples are French *avoir faim* ("to be hungry") and Spanish *hacerse el tonto* ("to play dumb"). Second language idioms should be described in terms of the two languages involved. Thus, we can speak of *avoir faim* as an English-to-French pseudoidiom, but not a Spanish-to-French pseudoidiom, since the two expressions correspond exactly in Spanish and French.

Words across languages

There seem to be no exact one-word equivalents across languages. Lexigrams [Ramsey 1981] show that when all important associations are considered, there can be subtle differences across languages between words assumed to be equivalents. For example, English *hospital* is only a partial cognate of Spanish *hospital*, as in Spain the non-poor go to a *clínica*. There are words without equivalents. For example, there are no Spanish single-word equivalents of English *pet* or *afford*, no English single-word equivalent of German *Gemütlichkeit* or Spanish *compadre*, and no French single-word equivalent of English *shallow*. Often meaning is split differently across languages. The two-way split *savoir/connaître* in French represents a different view of reality than that of English *to know*; similarly reality is being classified differently when English has a two-way split between *wholesale* and *retail* and French has a three-way split for the same reality --*gross*, *demi-gros*, and *détail*.

We must therefore guard the students against the assumption that vocabulary is on a one-to-one relationship across languages. They should be trained to take advantage of the native language concepts they have but at the same time not be over-ready to accept correspondences.

Equivalences are *valid*, but their validity can be guaranteed only for the contexts in which they have been taught; the more different the situation in which a word is used, the more the equivalence should be distrusted.

Very common words can have many denotations with different equivalences across languages. An example is *head;* the equivalent of its most common denotation in French is *tête*, but other denotations have the equivalents *chevet, face, pomme, bout, haut bout, directeur, mousse, rubrique*, and so on [Mackey 1965:95]. Another example is the equivalence between English *go* and at least six German verbs: *gehen, fahren, laufen, reiten, rudern*, and *fliegen*. So it should be clear that different equivalences may have to be learned for each of the denotations of a second language word. Learning second language vocabulary consists in part in learning the contexts in which equivalences apply.

The reason for all these differences is that languages are social phenomena, with different cultures organizing reality differently. But languages conceptualize only *some* things differently. Very noticeable differences --such as those mentioned by Whorf and others-- can be found by comparing languages whose speakers have very different cultural outlooks, such as English-speaking Americans and speakers of Amer-Indian languages. But in the Western Indo-European languages, reality is classified in very similar ways, as the cultures and the experiences are very similar. So in going from one to another of these languages, it isn't necessary to learn a whole new system of concepts in learning the vocabulary. Almost all concepts have more or less precise equivalents. And when a single-word equivalent is not available, equivalence is possible with a phrase.

The lexical structure of their native language predisposes its speakers to see some things in a certain way and makes it difficult for them to see them differently. Making second language learners aware of the lack of logic in their own language will make them more receptive to different ways of categorizing reality and to illogical expressions in the second language.

Denotations and connotations across languages

We need to consider denotations, connotations, and special uses of words. As an example, let's take the word *milk* and its equivalents. The main denotation or basic meaning of the noun *milk* is approximately "a liquid produced by mammals to feed their young; some animal milk (usually cow's or goat's) is used for human consumption." It is clear that this denotation of *milk* is identical with the basic denotation of Spanish *leche*, French *lait*, German *Milch*, etc. Numerous such comparisons have led me to conclude that *denotations are very often the same across languages*. If such equivalence did not exist, it would be impossible to produce bilingual dictionaries!

Connotations, continuing with the example of *milk*, would be what a given culture (cultural connotations) or individual (experiential connotations) associates with *milk* or its denotative equivalent. Leaving aside experiential connotations, about which very little can be done in the second language program, it is clear that *cultural connotations are frequently different across languages*. To pursue the example of *milk* (in almost all of North America) and *leche* (in much of Latin America and Spain), the following are some of the differences in cultural connotations: (1) *milk* is sold mostly in cartons or bottles (and, more recently, in plastic containers), *leche* is often sold by pouring it from pitchers; (2) *milk* is pure and unadulterated, *leche* usually reaches the customer with considerable water added; (3) *milk* is clean, usually extracted by machine and untouched by human hands, but *leche* is mostly extracted by hand in rather unclean places; (4) people drink *milk* several times a day, *leche* is drunk only at breakfast time and occasionally with snacks; (5) people drink *milk* alone, *leche* is often mixed half-and-half with coffee (*café con leche*); (6) *milk* is drunk cold, *leche* is mostly drunk warm; and (7) just about everybody drinks *milk*, while it is mostly children who drink *leche* and some *muy macho* men would never touch it.[△]

Special uses of a word include its appearance in idioms and other set phrases. Examples with *milk* include *milk run*, *the milk of human kindness*, and *milk-livered*; examples with *leche* include *estar (algo) en leche*, *un tipo de mala leche*, and *lo que en leche se mama, en la mortaja se derrama*. From such uses of *leche* and other words, it is clear that *special uses of a word, in set phrases, are very frequently different across languages*.

[△] Example developed from a similar presentation by Robert Lado in a lecture some years ago.

The relationship between a given denotation of a word, the connotations of that meaning, and the special uses of the word, in idioms and other set phrases, related to that denotation can be represented graphically as in Figure 18.2.

Figure 18.2

In accordance with the preceding discussion, a particular denotation appears at the center of the diagram, since it constitutes the basic meaning to which other elements are related. The connotations are shown surrounding the denotation and constitute the sum of cultural concepts related to that denotation. Finally, the special uses of the word related to that denotation and often to one or more connotations of the word are depicted as lines extending outwards from the basic meaning. (Of course, a set phrase may in turn be surrounded by connotations of its own.)

Order of presentation of meanings

It follows from the above that whenever possible denotations, the basic meanings of words, should be presented first, followed by connotations and then by special uses of the words. Furthermore, when a word has several denotations (e.g., the English verb *run* in *Let's run to the bus stop, We'll run an ad in the paper, He'll run for class president,* etc.) the most basic and useful denotation for communication --usually the most concrete one, from which the others are derived--should be presented first. To take the example of Spanish *pelo* ("hair"), the basic, concrete denotation of *pelo* should be introduced first, in sentences such as *Córteme el pelo* ("Cut my hair"); cultural connotations, such as that expressed by *En la frontera mexicana les cortan el pelo a los hombres que lo llevan muy largo* ("At the Mexican border men with long hair are given a hair cut") would come next, along with information about other attitudes and customs (all insights that can be presented in brief native language cultural notes if so desired); and special uses of the word like *No me tomes el pelo* ("Don't pull my leg") and *No tiene un pelo de tonto* ("He's no fool") would come last. Derived words such as *peluquero* ("barber"), with their denotations and connotations, can of course be taught soon after the basic word (in this case, *pelo*) has been learned.

The size of second language vocabulary

The size of the vocabulary of native speakers is considerable. A first grader controls approximately 17,000 basic words plus derived words for a total of about 30,000; a twelfth grader knows about 50,000 basic words plus 30,000 derived ones, for a total of 80,000 words; and educated adults know a total of about 200,000 words. It should be clear that the vocabulary of a second language learner can never hope to approach the corresponding native figures; but neither does it have to, for a second language learner can attend to all his basic communication needs with a much smaller vocabulary.

As mentioned in Chapter 10, a reasonable goal is to teach about 1,000 basic lexical items in the first year of college language instruction (beginning level), 1,500 in the second year (intermediate level), 2,000 in the third year (advanced level), and 2,500 in the fourth year (very advanced level). A total of 1,000 words corresponds to what the Council of Europe calls the "threshold" or "survival" level, 2,500 words (the end of our intermediate level) corresponds to their "basic" level, and 7,000 words (our very advanced level) corresponds to their "advanced" level.

The important thing to remember is what can be done with vocabularies of various sizes. An active vocabulary of 1,000 well-chosen words allows the generation of a very large number of sentences, so it would meet the requirements of elementary communication. For basic speaking of more than the bare essentials, a vocabulary of 2,500 words is needed. This is also adequate for simple writing. Because the generator of sentences controls his language, speaking and writing can proceed with a considerably smaller vocabulary than listening and reading. For listening, a vocabulary of at least 4,500 words is essential, as the listener cannot be selective. For *general* reading, a vocabulary of 7,000 words is minimal, since written materials are richer in vocabulary than speech. For *literary* reading, which is richer in lexical variety and creativity than general reading, a still larger vocabulary of at least 10,000 words is necessary. Keep in mind that the reader has no choice of vocabulary.

Where does this leave the second language program and its students? It is patently clear that second language students cannot start to read literature after one year of college study, when their vocabulary is only 1,000 words. What they would do, given that vocabulary, is not read but painstakingly decode. A *normal speed* program would require four years of college study before the students have a vocabulary of 7,000 words and can do *general* reading and, marginally, read literature. This points to the need of speeding up the timetable by at least doubling courses, so that four years (or eight semesters) of second language study can be completed in two years, thereby enabling college students to *really* read, and enjoy reading, writings in the second language beginning in the junior year (fifth semester). For the same reasons, intensiveness is desirable in the schools.

Vocabulary selection

Given the fact that the vocabulary of second language students must necessarily be fairly small, it becomes very important to select it carefully. A discussion of criteria of selection follows.

(1) *Frequency.* This refers to the number of times the word occurs in running texts or speech. 95-97 percent of what we say uses the 10,000 most frequent words; yet many of the others are quite important for their heavy semantic load. Most frequent words have several meanings, some of which may not be frequent. Frequency lists

(unlike what has been done) should be based on meanings, not forms, for as it is now each word on a frequency list is just "the tip of a learning iceberg" [Howatt 1974:9]. It may be that none of the meanings of a word is frequent, but it comes out as frequent when all its uses are added up indiscriminately. The vocabulary for oral courses should be based on frequency lists derived from the *spoken* language, such as *Le Français elementaire*, not on lists based on literary texts.

(2) *Range*. This refers to the number of different texts or speech samples in which the word appears.

(3) *Availability*. This has to do with the situational usefulness of the word, that is, whether it is necessary in certain situations. Thus, words that are useful in the classroom include low-frequency *blackboard* and *desk*; in various other situations *fork, soap, post office,* and *Thursday*, also low in frequency, are quite useful. Availability, which could be called "situational frequency," is an important complement to the criterion of frequency.

(4) *Coverage*. This refers to the number of things one can say with the word. For example, the word *bag* includes, and has more coverage than, the words *suitcase, valise, handbag, sack,* etc. Coverage also refers to the capacity the word has to combine with other words to say different things. An example of a high coverage word is English *get*. Coverage includes too the ability of a word root to serve in the formation of derived words. An example is German *kaufen*, with its derivate words *einkaufen, verkaufen, Kaufhaus, Kaufman,* etc. Coverage is the principle of selection that was used in choosing the vocabulary for Basic English, which has only 850 words but allows, with some circumlocution, the expression of almost any idea.

(5) *Familiarity*. This refers to how often the word is listed by speakers when asked to list words on various topics.

(6) *Classroom communication usefulness*. This is determined by asking students to list the topics they want to talk about and the words they want to be able to use. (This is done in the native language.)

(7) *Learnability*. This refers to ease of learning, which depends on similarity between the two languages. For example, for a German speaker *hound* is easier to learn than *dog*, for it is a cognate of German *Hund*. Of course, as this example and many others show, cognates are not always the most useful, frequent, available, etc. words.

These seven criteria are often in conflict, so considerable wisdom is required in balancing them off against each other and reaching valid decisions in vocabulary selection.

Galisson [1979] proposed that basic vocabulary be expanded via selection based on "instrumental lexicology." This consists in deriving everyday vocabulary from the specialized vocabularies of various disciplines such as politics, law, medicine, economics, and so forth. It seems a valid approach to lexical expansion.

Through the use of selection procedures we can arrive at a basic, core vocabulary which all second language students in a general program should learn. But the students need to go individually beyond that, to "basic-plus" vocabulary whose selection is largely up to them. To help them in this vocabulary expansion, advanced courses should be in more areas than just conversation and literature --a sampling of all areas of experience and knowledge is necessary, with particular emphasis on student interests.

What vocabulary to teach and when

Early vocabulary instruction should concentrate on familiar concepts, as second language learners, like native speakers, have difficulty with unfamiliar concepts. With young children, concrete vocabulary should be taught before abstract vocabulary.

The low-frequency vocabulary of difficult prose and most poetry does not belong within the second language program per se. It is uncommon and it overloads the memory, preventing the second language learner from concentrating on learning common vocabulary, which should come first. Difficult prose and most poetry should be considered very advanced reading material to be given after the students have learned a very advanced vocabulary of at least 10,000 words.

The presentation of new vocabulary

New vocabulary should be presented within linguistic and nonlinguistic contexts. This is normally done in dialogues, narrations, readings, dramatizations, and with the help of pictures or realia. Some vocabulary, such as the days of the week, the months, and so on, is presented in series; this is valid as long as the vocabulary has to be stored in memory in a series. Supplementary vocabulary can be taught with vocabulary drills, to be discussed later in this chapter.

The following steps should be followed in vocabulary presentation:

(1) *Perception.* Make sure the students hear the word properly.

(2) *Imitation.* Make sure the students can repeat the word accurately. Perception and imitation combined ensure the learning of the *form.*

(3) *Conveyance of meaning.* Provide or elicit the native language equivalent of the word, within the context of a sentence, stating briefly any contextual limitations of the equivalence. This will enable the learner to learn the *meaning* and *function* of the word in that context.

(4) *Meaningful practice.* By means of meaningful practice, first in meaningful exercises and then in communicative activities, the learner can internalize the *relationship between form, meaning, and function.* This fourth step is the most time-consuming one, but it is essential.

On conveying meaning

This was discussed in detail in Chapter 14, so only a few additional comments will be presented here.

Conveying meaning in the native language should not be a matter of last resort but should be done regularly as the most efficient and precise way to do it, provided any contextual limitations of equivalences are very briefly pointed out to the students. This is precisely one of the main problems with monolingual demonstration techniques --they do not make clear what the word *cannot* refer to, that is, its contextual limitations, so undesirable one-to-one equivalences are made in the mind. Lengthy paraphrases in the second language in no way avoid the same one-to-one equation problem.

When the native language is used to convey or ascertain meaning, the native equivalent serves as the door to the ground floor of meaning. Above this ground floor the two languages provide two different superstructures on the same foundation. Full acquisition of the meaning of a word requires climbing to and exploring its superstructure; how entrance to the ground floor of the building is accomplished is largely irrelevant, so the most efficient way --*contextually delimited interlingual equivalence*-- should be used.

Beginning second language learners semanticize according to native language categories and only gradually develop second language categories. If native language-second language differences are pointed out, this can only help speed up the process of development of second language categories in the minds of the learners. This does not mean, of course, that the students should come to depend on comparisons with the native language for all their insights into word meaning --they should gradually learn to depend less and less on the native language and more and more on their growing ability to perceive relationships and categories in the second language.

For the presentation of new word meaning, semantic features and semantic primitives such as those used in generative semantics cannot be used directly. For example, the semantic primitives of *uncle* are "brother of father or mother." Such a presentation of the meaning of *uncle* would be justified only in a heterogeneous class in which (1) the teacher does not know the languages of the students and (2) no printed native equivalents for each language are available. Whenever one of those disadvantages is eliminated, the students can be given, or referred to, the equivalent word, that is *oncle, tío, Onkel, zio,* and so forth.

The mediation of associations

It seems that if associations are used in learning words, the words are retained quite well [Cohen and Aphek 1981]. The more meaningful an item is --the more associations between it and others-- the more easily it can be learned. Teachers can provide useful associations, but it seems that mediators that are created by the learners are more effective than those imposed on them [Bruner 1961]. Examples of such mediators or associations are *blank* for Spanish *blanco* ("white"), as most blank paper is white, and *donate* for French *donner* ("to give"), as donating is a form of giving. Learner-generated associations seem to be effective even when they are rather "wild."

It has been found that second language learners make many different types of associations. Cohen and Aphek [1981] found eleven different types among their 13 students of Hebrew. Associations were made between words or parts of words and native language words or phrases, with other second language words, with names, with words in a third language, with letters, with objects or places, etc.

Words perceived as more pleasant result in more successful associations [Pollio 1966]. My own impression is that the more emotionally-laden associations, within reason, produce the best results. Research is needed in order to find out what is the best use of associations, which types of associations are most effective, and much more.

There is no reason to fear that by making associations the learners will always be forced to recall the association in order to produce the word. Gradually, through active use of the words, the mediators are phased out and the second language words become directly accessible.

Vocabulary exercises and activities

In addition to the presentation devices already discussed, several types of exercises, bilingual and monolingual, can be used for vocabulary presentation and expansion.

Vocabulary expansion exercises have three phases: (1) *presentation* of each word in a sentence, with each sentence repeated several times with knowledge of its meaning (all but the new word should be known); (2) *practice* with the new words, after four or so have been presented, by means of communicative activities (questions and answers, comments, student-generated sentences, etc.); and (3) *testing*, again after four or so words have been presented and practiced, in order to determine if they have been learned.

In bilingual vocabulary expansion exercises a known second language model sentence is used, the sentence pattern is held constant, lexical items are substituted one at a time, and the sentence equivalents are given. For example, for English-speaking learners of French who know the sentence *J'aime les frites* ("I like French fries"), the following exercise can be done to teach the names of additional food items:

J'aime les frites.	J'aime les frites.
J'aime la laitue. "I like lettuce."	J'aime la laitue.
J'aime les haricots. "I like green beans."	J'aime les haricots.
J'aime les champignons. "I like mushrooms."	J'aime les champignons.

At this point the words *laitue, haricots,* and *champignons* would be used in a number of personalized questions and answers, comments, and student-generated sentences. Then the testing phase would come, in which the order would be reversed, still using a constant pattern --the teacher gives simple English sentences and the students provide the French equivalent.

Monolingual vocabulary expansion exercises require a basic knowledge of the language, so generally they cannot be used until the intermediate level and beyond. These exercises take advantage of the various relationships between words, such as synonymy, antonymy, hyponymy,[△] rough definitions, and completions. The same three phases --presentation, practice, and testing-- are followed, in about the same manner, except that everything is done in the second language.

Example of synonym exercise sentences:[☆]

Another way of saying "very small" is *minute*.

Another way of saying "fast" is *rapid*.

Another way of saying "smart" is *bright*.

Example of antonym exercise sentences:

The opposite of "sweet" is *bitter*.

or

Sugar is sweet, but coffee is *bitter*.

The opposite of "heavy set" is *slender*.

or

Jackie Gleason is heavy set, but Cher is *slender*.

Example of hyponym exercise sentences:

Cars, trucks, and trains are *vehicles*.

Milk, coffee, and Coca-Cola are *beverages*.

Books, magazines, and newspapers are *publications*.

Example of rough definition[◇] *or completion sentences:*

A heavy storm with strong winds is a *hurricane*.

Someone who sells meat is a *butcher*.

A contract for the use of a building is a *lease*.

For further relations between words that can be used to convey their meanings see Scherer and Wertheimer [1964: 100-1].

A further type of vocabulary expansion activity is the teaching of word families, such as, from Spanish *nación*,

----

△ Hyponymy is a relationship of inclusion; the co-hyponyms (the included words) are mutually exclusive. See the example.

☆ There is, of course, no absolute synonymy (or antonymy), so these presentations have to be supplemented by contextual instruction and practice that make the allowed collocations evident.

◇ Pedagogical definitions, unlike dictionary definitions, do not have to be very precise. Note that whether these sentences constitute definitions or completions depends on the presentation.

the derived words *nacional, nacionalidad, internacional,* etc.

Exercises for vocabulary practice are designed for student production. They include variation exercises, paraphrasing, association, word games and puzzles, analogies, and guessing games.

Variation exercises are bilingual. They start with a model sentence and then the teacher introduces, by means of native language sentences, successive variations in content words and, sometimes, structure.

Example of a variation exercise (English to Spanish):

Quiero leer un libro.	Quiero leer un libro.
¿Inglés?	"I want to read a book."
"I want to write a letter."	Quiero escribir una carta.
"We want to read the paper."	Queremos leer el periódico.
"Who wants to buy a novel?"	¿Quién quiere comprar una novela?

Paraphrasing consists in the students first choosing alternate ways of expressing the ideas of words and idioms from multiple-choice questions, and then providing their own paraphrases for each new word and phrase. Paraphrasing has the advantage that it trains the students in circumlocution techniques, an ability which they will need during communication acts whenever they can't think of the precise word to say.

Association exercises consist in giving the students a word and asking them to provide all the related words they can think of. For example, to the stimulus *car*, they might respond with *tire, gasoline, travel, steering-wheel*, etc. It is also possible to elicit chain associations, such that each new word produced is related to the immediately preceding one. For example, the word *class* could start the following chain: *professor, bad memory, number, two, three, trio*, etc.

Word games should be used with caution, because only some make efficient use of practice time. Games in which a long time is needed to produce a few words --such as *Scrabble* and crossword puzzles-- are best avoided or modified so that more communication is involved in their use. Some word games are very productive; for example, saying or writing as many words as one can think of, within a given time limit, by using the letters of a written word can lead to the production of a large number of words within a short period of time. Puzzles can also be quite useful if the time-use factor is kept in mind.

Analogies can be used effectively to practice

vocabulary, listening comprehension, and reasoning [Plaister 1981]. This is provided the analogies are discussed in the second language, not just completed.

Guessing games can be used for many purposes [Joiner 1974-b]. For example, if the vocabulary of dates needs to be practiced, the students can be asked to guess --with the help of feedback-- each other's birthdays rather than merely be drilled on the expressions.

Teaching cognates and false cognates

The presentation of cognates --they don't need to be taught as such-- should be delayed for a while, for at least two reasons. Their introduction *en masse* early in the program (1) contributes to difficulties in pronunciation, as they tend to be pronounced with native language sounds, and (2) creates the false impression that the two languages have a general vocabulary similarity, when in fact the similarity may apply mostly to infrequent and learned words. Thus, the use of many cognates early in the program leads to erroneous cognatization on the part of the students --for example, saying **huilo* for Spanish *rueda* ("wheel").

I would recommend waiting until the early intermediate level, when more time begins to be devoted to reading, for the introduction of many cognates. At that time, the students should be made aware of both phonemic-graphemic and morphological correspondences across languages.

Examples of phonemic-graphemic correspondences follow:

German	*English*
≪*f*≫ or ≪*ff*≫	≪*p*≫
helfen	help
Schiff	ship
≪*s*≫,≪*ss*≫ or ≪*ß*≫	≪*t*≫ or ≪*tt*≫
das	that
besser	better
Fuß	foot
≪*ch*≫	≪*k*≫ or ≪*ch*≫
machen	make
Kirche	church

For these and many other such German-English correspondences see Banta [1981].

Examples of morphological correspondences follow:

English	*French*	*Spanish*
/-šən/ or /-žən/	/-syõ/ or /-zyõ/	/-syón/ (/-θyón/)
nation	nation	nación
vision	vision	visión

English	*French*	*Spanish*
/-tĭy/	/-te/	/-ðáð/ (/-ðáθ/)
facility	facilité	facilidad
city	cité	ciudad
/-ə̆r/ or /-ɔ̀r/	/-œR/	/-ór/
color	couleur	color
senator	senateur	senador
/-ĭy/	/-i/	/-ía/
company	compagnie	compañía
philosophy	philosophie	filosofía

By teaching students the affixes of the second language and how they relate to those of the native language, we can give them a powerful vocabulary-learning tool.

False cognates, words similar in form but different in meaning, should be taught in a restrictive environment that excludes misinterpretations. For example, a French word like *librairie* ("bookstore," not "library") should be first introduced and learned by English speakers in a sentence like *J'ai acheté deux livres à la librairie* ("I bought two books at the bookstore"), which makes its meaning clear, and not in a sentence like *Je vais à la librairie* ("I am going to the __?__"), which will very likely be misinterpreted by the student who doesn't know the word. Similarly, Spanish *lectura* ("reading," not "lecture") should be first introduced in a sentence like *Leo mucho porque me gusta la lectura* ("I read a lot because I like reading"), not in simply *Me gusta la lectura*, which is interlingually ambiguous.

Visual aids and realia can also be used effectively, in presenting false cognates, to help establish in the minds of the learners the necessary contextual specifications. The students also need essential practice in rejecting the native language interpretation, so they should be exposed to choice-making exercises, especially in the form of translation.

Teaching true idioms and second language idioms (pseudo-idioms)

Students should be aware of idioms and their nature. The best way to accomplish this is with examples of native language idioms, which can be shown to be very seldom directly translatable into the second language. Sugano [1981] wrote an excellent article on idioms and their teaching. She classified idioms into (1) expressions of politeness or greeting, (2) idioms that are reasonably alike in the two languages, (3) idioms that differ in one or two significant content words, (4) idioms that can be understood figuratively, (5) idioms with little or no resemblance or with misleading resemblance, and (6) proverbs. According to Sugano, types (1) and (2) do not need to be formally taught, as they are learned from their contextual use; type (3) should start later in the first year; type (4) still later; type (5), which causes the greatest difficulties, should not come before the second year of study; and type (6) should be introduced as a "spice" from the beginning of the program (but we should be careful not to introduce proverbs that reflect an earlier stage of the language, as many do).

Idioms from types (3) to (5) should be formally taught with appropriate exercises. (Sugano found the treatment of idioms in many Spanish textbooks quite inadequate.) The technique I have found most effective in the teaching of idioms consists in (1) giving rough native language equivalents, which in most cases will not be literal translations, (2) explaining the idioms if necessary, and (3) practicing their use. (For idioms that are equivalent across languages no explanation is necessary, of course.) Among the practice activities for idioms, Sugano recommended having the students (1) recognize the idioms in context, (2) prepare illustrations and let the other students guess the idioms they refer to, (3) participate in idiom translation exercises, (4) come up with the idiom called for by a situation, and (5) write humorous dialogues in which a second language speaker uses idioms and another speaker takes them literally.

Idioms must be practiced until they are learned by heart. They are not amenable to a cognitive approach, for they don't make sense from the meaning of their parts.

Expressions such as English *I've just* plus perfect form of the verb, Spanish *Acabo de* plus infinitive and French *Je viens de* plus infinitive are not true idioms, as within each language the meaning of the parts adds up to the meaning of the whole. These are examples of second language idioms (as opposed to English, French or Spanish idioms) or pseudoidioms. Because *Acabo de* plus infinitive does not match the English equivalent, it presents a serious learning problem --the English speaker will tend to say in Spanish (Spanglish, really) **Justamente he* plus the perfect form of the verb, and in French **J'ai justement* plus the perfect form of the verb. What is needed with pseudoidioms, as with any problem causing serious interference, is for the students to practice the second language idiom in the presence of its interfering native language counterpart so many times that the second language expression will acquire inevitability and the native language expression will lose its power to interfere. What is necessary, then, is frequent translation drills on such problems. Of course, the idiom should then be internalized in the *second* language.

Many students --and even some textbooks!-- treat such phrases as *get out, get off, get in,* etc. as "idioms." These are not idioms in any sense, but two-word lexical items, although subject to some manipulation. They should simply be taught and learned as units, that is, handled as any other lexical item.

The need for vocabulary recurrence

Contiguity learning (in lexical learning, form and meaning need to be contiguous) requires frequent presentation of the two stimuli. If words do not recur, they are quickly forgotten. From the first presentation to the thorough learning of a word, it normally takes many uses of the word. During the first several days it should be used often, otherwise it will not establish itself in memory.

After initial learning of the word, it needs to recur at certain intervals, and the students need to be somehow reminded of its meaning, or it will become gradually weaker in memory and then disappear. The question of how frequent the intervals should be for retention to be maintained has not been settled and deserves careful research. It is clear that regular intervals are not necessary, that progressively longer intervals will suffice. Lado [1964:45] suggested time interval factors of two (2, 4, 8, 16, 32, etc.) or three (3, 9, 27, 81, etc.), but this requires experimentation.

Some do's and don't's

In intensive presentation devices and readings, which are going to be virtually memorized, do allow a high concentration of new vocabulary, as much as one word in three.

In extensive readings, which are going to be read just once or twice for enjoyment and vocabulary expansion, don't present more than one new word per 20 (or better yet 30) words of running text. It is very frustrating to have to stop a reading every few seconds to look up words.

When you introduce a new word in a reading or narration, do use it several times in several contexts, not just once or twice.

Don't teach words in isolation, as in word lists. As Jespersen [1904:114] put it, words in isolation are "only ghosts or corpses of words." To be remembered, words must be associated with both linguistic and nonlinguistic contexts, as meaning is a sociolinguistic phenomenon. Vocabulary lists and cards matching second language and native language words one to one are therefore not only inadvisable but clearly harmful, as they lack either type of context and lead therefore to the "generation" by simple concatenation of linguistically terrible native language-based sentences.

So do teach each new word accompanied by such other words that will make its nature and functions clear. For example, the gender of each noun should be learned as part of the vocabulary learning process, not as a separate grammatical task. Thus, the French word *nez* ("nose") should be initially presented with an article, *le* or *un*, not as "*nez* (m.)," and the two words learned as one unit, so that the gender can always be recalled when the word comes to mind.

Flash cards are very useful, as they end the problem of vocabulary appearing in a fixed order. So do use them, but *not* the ordinary flashcards with one second language word on one side and its native language equivalent on the other, both out of context. Words in flash cards should appear in sentences, which should be used in both languages, one language on each side. Each card should contain *several* short sentences, illustrating the use of the new word in several contexts. The presentation of several sentences would be particularly useful in bringing out different important denotations of the new word and their various native language equivalents. Such cards would serve a useful practice function, although of course for full vocabulary learning what is needed most is oral communication practice and the use of *abundant recombination materials*, which unfortunately no program that I know of supplies.

Do teach quite early the vocabulary and expressions needed for functioning in the second language classroom. Examples of this are such expressions as *Again, please, What does X mean?, How do you say X in German (English, etc.)? I'm sorry, I don't understand (remember, etc.)*, and so on. Note, however, that memorizing a dialogue or list of sentences containing all these expressions is not very effective --they should be taught one at a time, as needed.

Do provide a different context for each new lexical item. Teaching "related" words such as the parts of the face or the body, names of fruits or vegetables, or the names of the various animals at the zoo or circus is little different from teaching word lists, for the situational context is invariable and there is no significant change in linguistic context. The names of the parts of the face, for example, are *not* closely related linguistically or situationally. The word *eye* is much more frequently used in connection with eye color, with *glasses, looking,* etc. than with words like *nose, mouth*, and so forth; similarly, the word *mouth* is much more closely related to the size and shape of someone's mouth and to verbs like *talking, kissing,* etc. than to names of the other parts of the head or face. The physical relationship between parts of the face or of the body may be of interest to doctors, nurses, and artists, but for the student such an approach to vocabulary teaching is as dull and ineffective (it hinders situational recall) as the use of lists.

Do teach awareness of the morphological rules governing word families, i.e., how from *general* one can derive *generalize, generally, generalization,* etc. Such awareness of word family derivation is a powerful vocabulary recognition and expansion tool.

If two or more second language words are similar in meaning, don't teach them in similar contexts, as this will increase the likelihood of confusion. Minimal pairs should be avoided in the area of vocabulary, except where experience shows that confusion will definitely arise. As the second new item is learned, it can be contrasted *later* with the previously learned item with which it might be confused [Paulston and Bruder 1974:27]. I remember being confused for a long time between *Korb* ("basket") and *Eimer* ("bucket") in German; this was the result of learning them together in a reading in which both were used in exactly the same contexts, as containers in which to put pieces of coal; it was not until I learned the word *Korbball* ("basketball") that the confusion was finally cleared, many lessons later; it would have been much better to present them separately in mutually exclusive contexts.

Words having close similarity in form (while different in meaning) can also cause confusion. For speakers of non-Indo-European languages, for example, there can be much confusion between *get out* and *get off* or *ascend* and *descend* if they are taught together.

Hadlich [1965] found experimentally that comparison with English for such pairs as Spanish *saber/conocer* ("to know"), *ser/estar* ("to be"), and *dejar/salir* ("to leave") caused more difficulty for the students than teaching each word separately. Others [D.L. Wolfe 1967, J. Richards 1974] support the view that a contrastive approach is undesirable, that it is what renders "problem pairs" problematical. But studying a second language --or any problem in a second language-- without reference to the native language is quite unwise, for if the interference of the native language is not counteracted it will manifest itself in errors. The language learner, at least at the beginning level, does not operate cognitively just within the second language. These studies may not show that the contrastive approach is not valid, but maybe only that words in problem pairs should be presented first separately, and only then contrasted between themselves and in reference to the native language. Clearly more research is needed in this area.

Do encourage students to keep vocabulary notebooks, entering in two columns, in sentences, the words they have learned with their meanings. However, it is not necessary to enter all words in the notebook, as many are learned rather easily and don't require frequent review. The ones that should be entered are those that the student keeps on forgetting and looking up over and over again, that is to say, the "nuisance words" [Moulton 1966:18].

Do encourage the guessing of the meanings of new words in readings, provided they are reasonably easy to guess. To be fairly easy to guess, the word must be surrounded by few or no unknown words, the topic and the context must be clear, and the word must occur several times in quick succession in different contexts. This is very rarely the case in second language readings; almost all of them present very many unknown words in high concentration, and typically the new words do not occur several times in reasonably quick succession --in fact, such a repetition of a word would be considered bad style in general writing and literature, as much as it is desirable in second language texts. Given the right kind of specially-prepared texts, the ability of the students to guess can be practiced systematically; but with almost all ungraded readings, the students must be *provided* with the meanings of new words --asking them to "guess" under such unfavorable conditions is asking them to do something that it is nearly impossible for them to do well.

Do enlist the participation of the students in the vocabulary learning process. By teaching vocabulary to other students, the students not only learn what they are taught but also learn better what they teach [Feeny 1976].

By the late intermediate level, and especially at the advanced level, do let the students choose, with your help, an *individual vocabulary development program*. In this the students should have considerable leeway as to the fields and topics in which they want to acquire vocabulary. Such an individual program would consist primarily of extensive reading, followed --and this is essential for active vocabulary development-- by conversation based on it.

Degree of difficulty of vocabulary items

Not much is known about this. It seems that more concrete vocabulary is easier to learn than less concrete words. For example, it was found that native speakers learned nouns (more concrete) more easily than verbs [Marshall *et al.* 1975]. In terms of second language learners, it was found, using a mnemonic approach (sounds plus image), that English-speaking learners of Spanish were more successful in recalling nouns than verbs or adjectives [Raugh and Atkinson 1975].

This is an area in which considerable experimental research could and should be conducted.

Vocabulary errors and their correction

Vocabulary errors consist in using a word with the wrong form, or the wrong collocation, or the wrong meaning.

Formal errors may consist in using wrong phonemes in the word. If the sound system is under control, these cannot be considered pronunciation errors --the student could perfectly well pronounce the correct sounds of the word if he knew which sounds go into it. These are formal vocabulary errors with a phonological basis. An example is my pronunciation of the English word *demon,* which for many years was /dɛ́mən/, not /díymən/, possibly under the combined influence of Spanish *demonio* and English *lemon*. This was not a phonological error, as I controlled that sound contrast without any problem. The problem was not knowing the form of the word. Correction of such an error consists simply in pointing out what the form is, as opposed to how the student is producing it --in the example given, "Not /dɛ́mən/, /díymən/."

Other formal errors are morphological in nature, again not because the student does not know the morphemes but because he does not know which to use or whether to use one or not. Transfer from the native language is quite common. Thus, the speaker of French who is aware of the cognate relationship French *certain*/English *certain* will tend to transfer his *incertain* from French to English rather than use English *uncertain*. Or he may use in the second language a prefix that exists only in the native language, such as saying **de-advise* in English by transferring /de-/ from French *déconseiller* ("to advise against"). The lack of a word in the native language can also lead to not using a second language word that is morphologically related to a known second language word; for example, the native speaker of French may not use English *inexpensive*, even though he does use *expensive*, because in French *coûteux* has no negative counterpart. In correcting morphologically-based vocabulary errors, a more cognitive approach should be used, one making intralingual contrasts and interlingual comparisons. Meaning is not involved.

Syntactically-based vocabulary errors such as those involving collocations and idioms should simply be corrected by reminding students of the correct expression. There is no logic involved.

Semantic vocabulary errors can be due to various intralingual and interlingual causes. Probably most semantic vocabulary errors are the result of the student assuming complete equivalence across languages, when the equivalence applies to certain contexts only. The correction of semantically-based vocabulary errors should deal with the causes of the errors, not with the surface errors themselves. The wrong criteria the student is using for his choice of words is what has to be corrected, so it would be quite inadequate to simply give the correct word.

All types of vocabulary errors may be corrected by the student himself if the teacher, without providing the correct word, simply reminds the student of the context in which the word first appeared; of course, this would work only for words whose initial contexts were thoroughly learned to the point of near-memorization.

The treatment of vocabulary in textbooks

Most second language textbooks offer very little help for the vocabulary learning task of the student. The following textbook features would facilitate that task:

--New words should be given in dark type (or some other typographical emphasis device). This facilitates not only noticing the new words upon first encounter but also reviewing them later.

--False cognates should be specially marked.

--Cognates should also be marked. Unless they are marked, many students will not make a particular effort to guess their meanings by reference to similar native language words.

--Equivalences, plus when necessary major contextual limitations, should be marked with small numerals and appear in small type at the bottom of the page. (The reasons for this arrangement will be discussed in the next chapter.)

--To give practice with the verbal form of numbers, Arabic numbers should not be used until the intermediate level; before then, they should be written out in full.

--The vocabulary sections at the end of textbooks should not have only a second language-native language list. A native language-second language list is quite important. It is needed when the student can't remember a word when constructing his own sentences. Without a native language-second language list what can he possibly do? Try to remember where in a dialogue or reading --and in which lesson-- a second language word occurred and then look it up?! The vocabulary sections of textbooks should also indicate, for each word, the page and line in the main body of the text where the word can be seen in context, that is, one such reference for the first time each denotation occurred.

The use of dictionaries

Since the beginning and intermediate second language student does not know enough of the second language to understand the definitions in a monolingual dictionary, it follows that if he needs to use a dictionary it should be a bilingual one. Unfortunately, most inexpensive bilingual dictionaries limit themselves to providing a list of equivalences without giving their contextual restrictions or examples of their use. Since in the early stages of the program the students are usually unwilling to buy anything more expensive than a small or medium-size dictionary, and since such dictionaries do more harm than good, some second language specialists object to the use of any dictionary. The solution --again between the two extremes-- is to have beginning and intermediate students rely primarily on (good) vocabulary sections of textbooks, with a good, large bilingual dictionary available to them in a readily accessible reference area, which can be a corner of the classroom.

After the students have acquired a basic knowledge of the language, that is, by the end of the intermediate level, they can make increasing use of monolingual dictionaries. The first monolingual dictionary should be a learners' dictionary with a controlled vocabulary in the definitions. In the meantime, use of a good bilingual dictionary would continue, but gradually it would be used less and less. Of course, the same *caveat* given for pocket-size bilingual dictionaries applies to small monolingual ones.

The need for research

Even more than in the areas of phonology and grammar, there is great need for research in the area of vocabulary. Some of the questions --among a very large number-- that need to be investigated are:

--What is the relative effectiveness of memorizing new vocabulary versus just using it in communication?

--Does it help to write the new words, one or several times?

--What is the best arrangement for the presentation of native language equivalents?

--Which associations are most effective? Logical ones? Emotional ones? Phonological ones? Configurational ones?

--What is the best pattern of recurrence?

--How helpful is it to "act out" words?

There is need for both "one-shot" and longitudinal studies of these and many other questions.

19

TEACHING LISTENING COMPREHENSION, READING, AND WRITING

Throughout this book the speaking skill has been emphasized. This is as it should be, for it is the central skill --we say to ourselves what we hear and read, and we can only write, without the help of dictionaries and grammars, what we can say. However, the other three intralingual skills are also quite important. In this chapter, which is divided into three parts, we shall discuss the nature and the teaching of listening comprehension, reading, and writing.

PART I: LISTENING COMPREHENSION

Listening and the other skills

Listening comprehension does not develop automatically from the other skills. For instance, Belasco [1970] found that many teachers of French could not understand native speakers; he concluded that "it is possible to develop so-called 'speaking' ability (vocalizing) and yet be virtually incompetent in understanding spoken language." That is, normally the learner can understand what he can say if it is produced, like his speech, slowly and in a formal style; but practice is needed if he is to understand rapid colloquial speech by natives. Receptive exposure to classroom language is not enough --there should be systematic listening practice with native voices.

Perhaps of all the intralingual skills, listening comprehension has received the least attention. It should be as highly developed as reading skill if one is to be a successful communicator. Rather than as a by-product of other practice, it should be seen as a primary skill in its own right, to be given more emphasis both in the classroom and in the laboratory [Pimsleur 1971, Dickinson 1971] and via the home study of cassette tapes or records.

Listening and reading need to be more wide-ranging in scope than the productive skills, for in real communication the listener and reader is exposed to the language in ungraded fashion, that is, he can neither control nor simplify the material. Many of the clues to meaning given to aid reading comprehension can also be given to aid listening comprehension. Like reading activities, listening activities can proceed largely on an individual basis if the necessary facilities (recordings and equipment) are made available to the students.

The process of listening comprehension

Listening, rather than being a passive process, is mentally a very active process. According to Rivers [1971:126-9], speech perception proceeds in three stages all forming a single complex operation: (1) "sensing" rapid, roughly defined impressions, a relatively passive stage; (2) "identification through segmentation and grouping," applying to the collocation rules of the language, an active stage; and (3) "rehearsal and recoding" (going on simultaneously with the other two stages), whereby material is recoded for long-term storage. A "sunburn" model --intensive exposure to ungraded listening materials-- is ineffective because, although given control of the sound system one can segment unknown words into their phonemes, one cannot segment such words into morphemes, group the words, or recode them [*ibid.*, p. 130].

Reorganization of material for long-term storage consists in simplifying sentences into a more easily recoverable form, detransforming them while retaining transformational semantic markers. The result is that sentences are basically stored as SAADs or kernel sentences. Note that if, as claimed, we compare what we hear with covertly reconstructed messages, then speech perception is a form of speech production, definitely an active process [*ibid.*, p. 123].

Familiarity with the probabilities of occurrence of sounds and words enhances listening comprehension. This familiarity will normally develop through exposure to the language, but learners can be helped greatly by being taught what to expect, that is, by being provided with a grammar of phonological and grammatical expectations. This can take the form of early training emphasizing rapid recognition of indicators of phonological and grammatical structure [*ibid.*, p. 131].

Characteristics of good listening materials

Most listening materials should be carefully graded

so as to introduce a bare minimum of unfamiliar words, although as we shall see ungraded materials can also be put to some limited uses.

Listening passages should use normal speed from the start, as slowed-down speech is distorted and leads the learner to rely on auditory cues that will not be present in normal speech. The transition from slow speech to normal-speed speech is very difficult. Even beginners can understand familiar material at normal speed, provided it is presented in short sentences and with pauses between them for mental processing of the material, pauses that can be gradually shortened, with the sentences gradually lengthened. Normal speed is essential because the listener should not constantly interrupt a speaker in face-to-face communication and cannot do so in lectures, broadcasts, and so on. That slowing down speech offers no advantage was shown in a pilot study by Philip D. Smith [1980]. He found that the use of 20 percent electronically slowed speech had a negative effect on listening comprehension in second semester college French as measured at the end of the term by the MLA Cooperative Listening Comprehension Test. This despite the fact that through the semester speech was gradually speeded up to normal.

Speech in listening comprehension passages should be natural --not letter perfect but having the usual redundancies of informal speech, including pauses, repetitions, saying the same thing in two different ways, and expressing oneself in sentences which are not perfectly formed. Letter-perfect recordings, lacking in redundancy, are much more difficult to follow. Much use should be made of recordings of actual conversations between native speakers.

At the advanced level, listening passages should include different regional and social accents. Although our learners do not have to control actively more than one dialect, or a hybrid dialect, they need to understand speakers from various regions and social strata.

Percentage of time devoted to listening

The time devoted to listening in the classroom --that is, to listening as such, as opposed to listening as part of oral activities-- should gradually increase from about 5 minutes per class period at the early beginning level, to about 8 minutes at the late beginning level, 10 minutes at the intermediate level, and 15 minutes at the advanced level. This of course should be supplemented, beginning at the intermediate level, with much individual listening in the laboratory or with take-home cassettes or records.

But no listening activity should go on uninterruptedly for more than two or three minutes at any level, because the effort the students have to put in is great and after a few minutes fatigue sets in and listening comprehension suffers.

Stages in teaching listening comprehension

The first stage in training the students in listening comprehension is sound discrimination training. This starts during the first hour of instruction and extends for 15-20 hours, in alternation, of course, with sound production and other activities.

Stage 2 is listening to dialogues and other presentation devices, first verbatim and then with variations.

Stage 3 is listening to recombinations of known materials, that is, brief narrations combining in new ways what is already known.

Stage 4 consists of recombinations that include some new vocabulary items that can be easily guessed from their context. The use of cognates can be increased.

Stage 5 is listening to graded new materials, with very few new items.

Stage 6 consists of listening to ungraded materials. Other than their use for early selective listening, ungraded materials belong at the advanced level.

The progression through these six stages must be quite gradual. At all times, a listening presentation can be aided by gestures, pantomime, visuals, and so forth.

Intensive listening

Most of the listening time --almost all of it at the beginning and intermediate levels-- should be spent in listening intensively to graded materials. What is meant by intensive listening is listening several times, with considerable care, to a rather short passage.

For intensive listening, the students should be able to understand almost everything. Studying a listening passage and getting only a vague idea of its content is frustrating and serves no purpose. Advance helps (native language equivalents, etc.) should be provided for anything new in the passage. Much use should be made of recombination of known materials.

What is said above about passages applies to the

teacher as well. The teacher should not do a lot of free talking --listening comprehension must be developed systematically. Frequently surrounding beginning or intermediate students with ungraded language is inefficient and ineffective. (If it were such a good idea, all immigrants would have very good listening comprehension, which many don't.)

Graded extensive listening

Extensive listening consists in listening to a fairly lengthy passage only once. Graded extensive listening passages have no new words or maybe very few new words (like 1:60 to 1:30 or so). If new words are used, they are practiced and their meaning provided, in advance (as in the case of intensive listening).

The advantage of graded extensive listening is that it gives much useful practice in listening to the familiar in new combinations. It also offers the students the opportunity of listening for enjoyment, as less effort than in other forms of listening is involved. Some materials for extensive listening could even be made available for optional use, with the students completing a comprehension questionnaire based on them.

Graded extensive materials, like intensive ones, have to be specially written, either originally or by adapting material for native speakers.

Ungraded extensive listening

In addition to graded listening, there is a role in the second language program for ungraded listening. It permits the students to develop (1) the ability to notice certain details about the language, and (2) the skill to follow the main ideas in spoken communication, a useful skill.

Years ago Nida wrote about the advantages of "selective listening" [1957:30-8] --listening first to intonation features, noting contours on paper, then to "strange sounds," then to "similar sounds," then to words and phrases, and finally to grammatical forms. Minn [1976], Gomes de Matos [1980], and Harvey Taylor [1981] have endorsed such a use of ungraded materials. Minn would use them for such specific tasks as reporting how many words of a certain type are used (e.g., definite articles), isolating from their context certain lexical items whose native language equivalents are given in advance, and finding out which information was missing in the native language introduction to the passage.

Of course, ungraded extensive listening passages should not be used for the detailed comprehension of ideas until the advanced level. When used, they should offer quite a variety of topics, kinds of language, levels of formality, and so on.

Some listening activities

Among the listening activities, some of the most useful are listed below, in approximate order of increasing difficulty.

(1) Recombination narratives, providing a new context for known elements and rules. This should be done quite often.

(2) Indicating whether statements in a series are true or false.

(3) Responding physically to increasingly complex commands.

(4) Giving, in the native language, the gist of a passage.

(5) Participating in a variety of laboratory exercises, including general knowledge quizzes, arithmetic problems, etc.

(6) Answering, in the native language, questions about a passage.

(7) Listening to a short dialogue and telling the teacher who the speakers were, what they said, and where they were.

(8) Listening to a monologue about a person and filling out a questionnaire on the person.

(9) Listening to broadcasts. Certain items, such as weather reports, can be used early [Sawyer 1977].

(10) Listening to informal conversations between native speakers; Dickinson [1971] found this quite effective.

(11) Listening to an ongoing story on male-female relations; Wierenga [1979] found this a good way to sustain interest.

(12) Listening to jokes; if very simple, these could be used early, but normally they cannot be used until the late intermediate or advanced level, for having to explain a joke deprives it of its humor.

(13) Listening to recordings from pen pals.

(14) At the advanced level, second language students should have practice in listening to the language under conditions of noise or reduced redundancy, such as talking on the phone or at a cocktail party, situations that can

be simulated. As Spolsky [1973:170] put it, in addition to knowing the items in the language, knowledge of a language "also involves being able to supply these items when they are missing, or being able to do without them." Native speakers can do this, and all speakers need this ability, so it should be practiced.

For listening practice, all dialogues and other presentation devices, including readings, should at some point be heard in full. In the case of long readings, this can be done by means of recordings.

Second language students should not be asked to listen to conversations prepared by other students. They should listen to natives.

Dictation will not teach listening comprehension to someone who doesn't have it. Dictation by full sentences at normal speed can be a good way of testing overall listening comprehension, but not of teaching it. There are better ways of practicing listening comprehension. The only function word or phrase dictation can have is that of practicing the relationship between sounds and letters and the conventions of the writing system. After the students know how to spell all the sounds of the language and have mastered all the written conventions, dictation ceases to have any useful pedagogical function. Since the teaching of the written language should be delayed until the intermediate level, there is no reason at all to use dictation before then.

Steps in the presentation and exploitation of a listening passage

In preparation for the presentation of a listening passage, the students should be made familiar with the general context of the passage. A brief summary and a series of carefully selected prequestions can serve as "advance organizers" [Ausubel 1960, Barnes and Clawson 1975] which make learning easier, as they relate the unfamiliar to the familiar. But to be effective, advance organizers must present information of greater inclusiveness and abstraction than the material to be learned.

The second step is to teach the key new words needed in order to understand the passage. This can best be done by putting the new words within a short series of sentences and teaching them bilingually, as any dialogue sentences.

Step No. 3 is to have the students listen to the passage, followed by postquestions, twice, and have them answer the questions the second time they hear them. This has the advantage of further focusing the listening attention of the students during the second presentation of the text.

The fourth step is to have the students listen to the selection a third time.

As a fifth step, the students try to retell the passage collectively (one sentence each) in their own words.

These five steps apply to intensive listening passages. For extensive listening passages, the students are also provided with advance organizers and other aids (such as a bilingual series of sentences containing the new words, if the passage is graded), but they listen to these longer passages only once, completing at the end an appropriate task showing what they have understood.

Broadcasts should be taped and a native language script prepared. Then the presentation should consist of (1) listening to the selection trying to guess the new words, (2) reading the native language script, (3) listening to the selection a second time, (4) answering questions about it, and (5) listening to the selection a third time, to fill in some of the details missed earlier.

At a more advanced level --perhaps the late advanced level and beyond-- the students should have practice in listening to new material "cold," without any advance preparation. This is important practice, for they need to develop their ability to guess more new words from context, something they will frequently need to do in real communication situations.

To connect listening activities with speaking, it would be desirable to break up one of the readings of the listening passage by the teacher (maybe the second one) into phrases and ask the students to repeat them. Listening tapes for laboratory or home study could similarly have pauses for repetition. However, not all listening presentations and recordings need to have pauses built into them. Another way of connecting listening to speaking is for the students to answer questions on the listening passage in the second language, rather than just answering multiple-choice questions or answering questions in the native language.

Some suggestions on how to listen

In listening to difficult material, it helps to eliminate all distractions. Visual images, even looking at the inside of a booth, can be distracting. Closing one's eyes can help with recordings and radio broadcasts.

With listening material having a visual impact, such as personal presentations, television broadcasts, and films, full advantage should be taken of visual clues, such as those offered by gestures and facial expressions.

For any type of material, second language students need to listen far more attentively than in classes in other subjects, taught in the native language. It enhances student attention to intersperse frequent questions throughout the listening materials.

Creating visual images about the content of the selection will help the listener to remember it much better (the same thing applies to readings). But the key is self-elaborated images, which seem to have much greater impact than images provided by the teacher.

Need for testing

Listening comprehension should be checked every step of the way. There is no use for a stage in which students listen to material and are not asked to demonstrate their comprehension.

In testing listening comprehension (and in much of its teaching) an effort should be made to avoid too much reliance on translation. The attention of the learner should be on the interconnection between words and phrases in the second language and on direct comprehension, not on finding native language equivalents for every word.

On retention of auditory material

Listeners retain only 20-30 percent of information contained in spoken messages in the native language, so it is unfair to expect more than that in the second language, even with concentrated attention. During the early use of listening texts, just recognizing the words and following the main idea is such a difficult task that there is no chance to retain much. Gradually, first with short sentences and then with longer ones, short-term retention and then long-term retention becomes possible.

(For further reading on listening comprehension, see what Rivers has written [1968:135-57, 1971, 1975:58-104, and elsewhere].)

PART II: READING

Reading and the other skills

The written language is two steps removed from reality, as it is based on the spoken language and it is the latter that refers to reality.

When we read, especially when we read unfamiliar material (which everything in the second language initially is), we say what we read to ourselves and listen to ourselves say it. This is true until the very advanced level, when rapid reading becomes possible, and even then we say to ourselves the new words. That silent speech occurs during reading has been thoroughly demonstrated [Edfeldt 1960, many others]. Silent speech may in fact aid comprehension and facilitate the development of reading proficiency [McGuignan 1973].

Thus, reading is related to the spoken language. The importance of oral control for reading was shown experimentally by Hatch [1974], who found that while non-natives crossed out all specified vowels in a text, natives crossed them out in content words and stressed syllables only --this shows that only oral control allows approaching native reading patterns. (Incidentally, non-natives make better proofreaders.)

Consequently, it is essential to establish an oral foundation in the second language before reading starts, so as to ensure that silent speech while reading will be based on second rather than native language speech patterns. Herein lies the importance of the students reading the early readings aloud the first time through, so as to ensure that later subvocal echoing will be accurate.

Despite its being based on audiolingual skills, reading should not be considered an appendage to them. As Politzer [1964:133] put it, "reading is not merely an automatic extension of audiolingual knowledge." The students must be taught how to read, especially in terms of sound/spelling correlations, syllabification, and the recognition of grammatical morphemes.

From the extreme of the Traditional Method, in which reading was the be-all and end-all, some have gone to the other extreme, in the Audiolingual and Audiovisual Methods, the extreme of not emphasizing reading enough. Even those programs that emphasize reading are obviously not being very successful, as indicated by the paucity of second language reading material available in bookstores and newstands [Grittner 1977:256-8].

That reading is not being sufficiently emphasized is a pity, for it greatly helps long-term retention of vocabulary and structure. Furthermore, it seems to enhance listening comprehension significantly, at least among bright children learning Spanish [Lipton 1969].

The process of reading

Reading has three stages: recognition, structuring, and interpretation. The first stage, recognition, is mostly an activity for intermediate-level students who are starting to read, and interpretation is mostly an activity for very advanced students; but the reader can't help but engage in all three stages during the reading of any text. While reading we also pay attention to three different kinds of meaning: lexical, grammatical, and cultural.

Literacy should come after oral competence has been established. As Moulton [1966:131] expressed it, "normal writing systems are intended only for those who already know the language" and "they were not designed to meet the needs of those who are *learning* the language." But the fact that writing is two steps removed from reality and derived from speech should in no way detract from its great importance as a means of communication and medium of culture.

In many countries, especially in those in which literacy is a major concern, second language teachers and students may feel that they are not learning anything unless they are studying the written form of the language. Such an attitude should be counteracted. The use of a pedagogical transcription is of much help in this regard, as it satisfies the desire to study printed language.

Probably we learn the mechanics of reading only once, in the native language, and then tend to transfer that facility into the second language. The problem with that transfer is that the sound/spelling correlations of the native language may be all wrong for the second language. That is the reason for introducing students to the sound/spelling correlations of the second language gradually, over a period of several weeks or even months, so that they will *not* transfer unsuitable native language reading habits to the second language. In other words, to a large extent learning to read a second language means learning to read all over again; if this is not recognized, there will be serious problems in the reading comprehension and speech of the students.

There are several differences between learning to read the native language and learning to read a second language. Interference has already been mentioned. Another major difference is that the native language learner has spoken the language for several years, controls its sounds and structures, and has a vocabulary of many thousands of words. Yet, it takes him years to learn how to read. This being so, why should we expect that learning to read a second language should take only a few hours?

Varieties of written language

There are three systems of writing in use in the world· *alphabetic*, which represents consonants and vowels, as in the Roman, Greek, Cyrillic, and Korean alphabets; *syllabic*, which represents syllables, as in the Japanese *hiragana* and *katakana* syllabaries; and *logographic*, which represents morphemes and words, as in the Chinese writing system, also used in Japanese.

All writing systems, having been designed for people who already know the language, are poor reminders of how the language is pronounced (logographic systems don't remind of that at all). So it is a serious mistake and a hindrance to success to take the writing system of a second language as the point of departure for learning it.

Alphabetic systems have the disadvantage of not representing regional differences in pronunciation, but the marked advantage that only a small number of symbols needs to be learned. Logographic systems have the advantage that they can serve several very different languages, but the great disadvantage that many thousands of different complex symbols have to be learned, a task that unnecessarily consumes a large proportion of school time.

Although the value of written symbols is relatively independent and must be learned for each language, there is no need, for example, to be unduly frightened by the "enormous" task of learning a new alphabet like Cyrillic or Greek. The task is relatively easy, infinitely easier than learning a logographic system.

Still, the writing systems of some languages are easier to learn than others. Thus, children learn to read languages that have a good sound/spelling fit, such as Dutch, Turkish, or Spanish, quite easily, without having to spend years on intricacies. Poor sound/spelling fit results from (1) the alphabet not having enough letters, (2) borrowings with foreign spellings, and (3) changes in the sound system not reflected in the writing system [Moulton 1966]. These conditions describe a language like English, whose writing system has a very poor sound/spelling fit. English spelling is morphophonemic. It differentiates homophonous words like *sew* and *sow* or *no* and *know*. It does not show the differences in pronunciation in the roots of words like *Canada* and *Canadian* or *photograph, photographic,* and *photographer*. This might marginally facilitate reading comprehension, but it causes the serious problem that often the reader doesn't know how to pronounce an unfamiliar word or even a word whose meaning he understands.

To a lesser extent, French is also morphophonemic; but what makes the French writing system most difficult is the fact that, as is the case with English, many sounds are represented by several letters or letter combinations, and certain letters and letter combinations represent more than one sound. Thus in languages like English and French what may be easy to say is not necessarily easy to read, and viceversa. So just exposing the students to the written language, with these and, to a lesser extent, all languages, is not enough. There must be systematic instruction to overcome the various problems presented by the learning task.

In certain minor respects, the written language can be more explicit than the spoken language. For example, German makes the identification of nouns in the written language quite easy by requiring that they be capitalized.

It may be necessary, in learning to read (and write) certain languages, to learn new mechanics for the reading process. Thus Arabic is written from right to left; Chinese logographs are written in columns, from top to bottom, and the columns from right to left; and an alphabet may present quite a number of new symbols.

Since logographic systems provide no information about how the words are pronounced, it is essential that they should be alphabetized through the late intermediate level, with only very slow and gradual introduction, at the advanced level, of logographs for which the words are thoroughly known. Any new words should always be presented alphabetically and used alphabetically for quite a while, regardless of the level of instruction. I still remember my utter frustration, after a few weeks of spoken Japanese, at being handed out the dialogues in the logographic *kanji* system --there was no way to practice the spoken sentences, to review them, or to relate them to the written language; there was no way to learn.

Characteristics of good reading materials

Second language reading materials, through the advanced level (third year of college, or third semester in a double-concentration program), should be simple in vocabulary and structure but interesting in their ideas. If one is forced to choose between level of difficulty and topical interest, the right level of difficulty should have priority.

As if this were not enough to differentiate them from almost all creative written materials, second language reading materials have to have much repetition, something that is anathema to the creative writer. We must necessarily conclude that second language reading materials should be specially written or substantially adapted from what is available for other purposes.

Even natural texts such as transcribed conversations should not be used early without much adaptation, for early exposure to "the bewildering mass of details which constitute the actual rumble of speech" [Fries 1945:5] can only be confusing and frustrating. Much more so for literature. Going very slowly through a literary text and looking up in a dictionary several words per line is not reading, it is laborious decoding that serves no useful purpose. Since all reading materials should be adapted until the very advanced level (fourth double-speed semester), if literature is going to be used within the second language program --not within a literature program, which is another matter-- it *must* be simplified. There is nothing wrong in drastically simplifying literary texts *for the purpose of second language learning* as long as the students are made aware of the simplification and told that they are expected to read the original work much later. It is better, at the intermediate and advanced levels, to expose the students to literature in a simplified but enjoyable form, than to force them to read, without enjoyment, original literature they cannot possibly understand.

Control over the function words is essential to reading. For that reason, Politzer's [1964:134] suggestion that grammatically significant symbols be printed in special color or special type in the early readings seems very valid.

As to the level of difficulty of reading material, a reading difficulty formula for second language texts is not yet a reality, but certain observations can be made. Many second language textbooks have very difficult readings, not systematically graduated in difficulty [J.C. Brooks and Jerrolds 1980]. Readability formulas for second language texts should not be based at all on word length, for, especially between Western European languages, the longer words (which by the formulas are supposed to be more difficult) are easier than the shorter words, for the longer words are frequently cognates. A valid readability formula for second languages would have to take into account the contrasts and similarities between the two languages. New word density and syntactic complexity would also seem valid criteria, as would less crucial criteria like format, style of expression, plot, organization, and idea density; Chapman [1975] found that the greater the number of these factors were favorable, the greater was the ease of comprehension for second-semester Spanish and German college students. Marks *et al.* [1974:262] found that "slight increases in word frequency of a small percentage of words in reading materials can produce sizable increases in story comprehension." As to the difficulty in assigning meaning from context it is lesser for nouns (more concrete) than for verbs or adjectives.

New word density is a crucial gradation factor. Although Holley [1973] found no difference in vocabulary learning of German reading materials whether density was 1:100 or as high as 1:15, this does not mean that density makes little difference. Her experiment did not explore the effect of very high density materials (1:5 or higher) on vocabulary learning. Such densities are frequent in second language readings. The constant interruption of looking up words with texts with very high new-word density not only is time-wasting and frustrating but does not even allow the reader to follow the ideas he's reading.

Early second language reading requires books about nature and man, richly illustrated, printed in fairly large type, with authentic stories and information adapted to the students' mental age [Kellermann 1981:11]. Such reading materials could be produced in "practice-centered" workshops [Politzer 1966] where native speakers who can write creatively and understand children and young people could team up with second language teachers, languists, and illustrators. In these workshops, the teams could write and adapt much reading material, including games and other activities, and tests based on it. Such team production would largely solve the problem of having enough interesting and simple reading materials for second language programs [Kellermann 1981].

Percentage of time devoted to reading

As already stated, the beginning level should present

the language audiolingually only, with the help of a pedagogical transcription like the APT. By the early intermediate level, students can be introduced to the reading of orally-familiar recombinations of known words, in the form of very short readings done aloud in the classroom, and then the reading of carefully graded texts can begin. During the early intermediate level, presentation and practice with readings should take no more than about 20 percent of class time, as they should be studied mostly at home. This percentage would increase to about 30 percent during the late intermediate level and 40 percent during the advanced and very advanced levels. (Note that these percentages include listening, speaking, and writing activities based on the texts.) At no time, however, should most of class time be devoted to dealing with readings; more active control of the language results from audiolingual activities.

Stages in teaching reading

Generally students, especially the orally-weaker ones, will want to start to read too early. Premature second language literacy should be avoided, as it has disastrous effects on speech.

Preconditions for starting to read are the development of good sound discrimination, good listening comprehension for simple material, good pronunciation, and fluency and accuracy in the basic audiolingual use of the language.

The first stage in teaching reading should be going from sounds to spellings, by reading aloud material previously learned orally, even memorized.

The second stage consists in going from spellings to sounds, by reading aloud, first, recombinations of material previously learned orally, but with no new words; then unfamiliar words and short texts.

Stages one and two --the relationships between pronunciation and spelling-- can be handled very smoothly by the several steps of the Articulatory Pictorial Transcription. Without thorough knowledge of sound/spelling correlations, reading in a second language becomes a hit-or-miss affair. But that thorough knowledge *can* be given, gradually, by phasing out the transcription and phasing in the spelling, starting with the correlations presenting the least difficulty, and moving on to those where there is the greatest interference or inconsistency. It should be mentioned that neither second language learners nor children learning to read their native language can bypass these two stages involving the perception of sound/spelling correlations --one cannot learn to read in underlying abstract lexical forms which have no psychological reality. These two stages would normally be completed by the end of the beginning level.

The third stage involves reading specially written or edited short texts that are graded in their vocabulary content so as not to include more than about 1:20 new to known words. This reading should be on a wide range of topics. Editing should include reducing or eliminating slang expressions, unusual constructions, regionalisms, and archaisms. The third stage begins in the early intermediate level and goes on through the advanced level.

In the fourth stage the students read controlled unedited materials. They are unedited but they are controlled in the sense that they are selected with care according to the criteria of linguistic (not conceptual) simplicity and relevance to the second language program. The fourth stage begins at the late advanced level.

Finally, in the fifth stage we have free ungraded autonomous reading based on an individual reading program to suit the interests of each student, although of course he reports orally about what he has read and this is made the basis for class discussion. The fifth stage begins at the very advanced level.

Unedited materials, incidentally, can be used for selective reading, in a manner very similar to selective listening.

Within ungraded materials, there is a progression in difficulty, with comic books being the easiest, and in progressively more difficult order letters, newspapers, magazines, "simple" literature, and, hardest, difficult literature.

Intensive reading

Intensive reading consists in the detailed classroom study of short texts, less than one page per class hour. Intensive readings should be varied and carefully graded to the level of the learners; this and the use of repetition is more important than making the readings titillatingly interesting. Intensive readings should be read several times and should be fully exploited in class.

It is best to have several degrees of intensiveness of readings alternating in the program --very short readings that will be studied very thoroughly, to the point of near memorization; those that will be read two or three times; and extensive readings, with little new vocabulary, that will be read once. That is to say, the program should offer both intensive and extensive reading at the same time, in alternation. It is possible, of course, to do intensive reading of key paragraphs or sections of an extended text.

Extensive reading

This consists of longer assignments, of several pages, to be read outside of class. Throughout the intermediate level and into the advanced level, extensive reading should be carefully graded, so as to avoid a laborious decoding situation. Such carefully graded texts were the mainstay of the Reading Method and should be revived for teaching the reading skill with more modern methods. New second language words are more easily learned if spread over a good number of pages than if concentrated in a few lines, and the time spent reading the longer text is in no sense wasted.

Extensive reading material should be considerably easier than intensive material. For that reason, it cannot be unadapted material written for natives, but must be prepared with the second language learner in mind.

Graded extensive readers should present no difficulty and, if possible, should be enjoyable. The readers should be progressive, bringing in some new vocabulary. Not only is writing "plateau" readers with no new vocabulary nearly impossible, but the plateau reader serves no useful pedagogical function, only a review function. To facilitate comprehension, early readings (extensive or intensive) should not have culturally unusual content and should relate closely to the other content of the course.

The use of graded extensive readings should be continued until the point is reached where the students can start reading native materials comfortably, with only occasional use of a dictionary. One of the distinct advantages of extensive reading is that it helps to establish accurate semantic fields based on the second language as opposed to the native language.

By the late intermediate level, extensive reading should take up about half of all reading time; by the advanced level, there should be no need for intensive reading, and all reading should be of the extensive kind, first graded, then ungraded.

With ungraded, unedited materials written for natives, if the students have not been gradually brought to the point where they can handle them, they will have the frustrating experience of finding uncertainties pile up on top of uncertainties. There must be a slow and gradual preparation before language in all its literary complexity can be handled.

Ungraded extensive reading would normally start with reading for the main ideas or for general information, then for general comprehension, and finally --after much practice-- for detailed comprehension.

Extensive reading, whether graded or ungraded, should be followed, preferably by sections, by multiple-choice comprehension tests, most of them for self-testing but some for a grade. (Beginning in the late intermediate level, reading comprehension tests should also involve constructed responses.) If the completion of the reading task is not recorded and if a grade is not given, many students will become lax about their reading assignments. Furthermore, the content of all readings, short and long, intensive and extensive, should be the basis for audiolingual work in class, otherwise the vocabulary in the readings will remain passive and may be quickly forgotten.

Some reading activities

The content of readings should be related to the mental age of the students, their interests, their competence in the second language, and their attitudes toward the second culture and toward reading in general. The variety of interests of second language learners is quite large: they are interested in most things about nature, man, and their relationships. The best way to determine their specific interests is to ask them, by means of a questionnaire.

Among the reading activities that can be successfully carried out within the second language program are the following, in approximate order of increasing difficulty:

(1) Unscrambling of dialogue sentences, a good exercise in both comprehension and awareness of discourse [Flynn and Trott 1972]. The same can be done with the sentences of a reading, although it is harder.

(2) Word games, which can provide considerable enjoyment [Bennett 1975].

(3) Matching of pictures and caption lines [Flynn and Trott 1972].

(4) Comic strips.

(5) Light verse.

(6) Magazine fillers, such as brief quotations, maxims,

and short jokes.

(7) Advertisements.

(8) Letters.

(9) Stylistically simple diaries.

(10) Plays, if modern and conversational (in many plays the characters don't converse the way people do).

(11) Children's literature; most second language students don't mind the simple topics and plots, as they find reading children's literature good language practice and even enjoyable.

(12) News stories.

(13) Magazine articles.

(14) Short stories.

(15) Easy longer prose literary works.

(16) Fables; although their ideas may be simple, they contain much unfamiliar, often archaic, vocabulary.

(17) Difficult longer prose literary works.

(18) Poems. Many poems may be easy to read, but almost all contain unusual constructions quite different from everyday language. Second language students should be absolutely sure of their knowledge of the language before they are exposed to its unusual forms, otherwise they will assume that what is poetic license is part of the standard language.

Note that, as far as the second *language* program is concerned, reading materials can come from any source, that is, they can be materials originally written in the language being learned or translated into it from any other language --of course, only the former would give insights into the second culture.

On literature

In regard to literature, perhaps nothing leads students to drop from second language programs more than the frustration produced by having to read literature without the prerequisite skills. As Dodson [1967] said, literature is the Mount Everest of every language, and one should not try to scale Mount Everest before having accumulated extensive experience climbing lesser mountains. Literature has been written for native speakers with vocabularies of at least 100,000 words, not for second language learners having a shaky control of 1,000 words or less!

Literature cannot even be appreciated without a thorough knowledge of the everyday language, for literature is the esthetic use of language and therefore its esthetic effect is lost on those who don't know the difference between everyday language and esthetically superior language.

Consequently, unedited literature should not be introduced until the very advanced level --i.e., the fourth semester of a double-speed (10 hours per week) program. And then, simpler, easier literature should be read first, only gradually switching to more difficult literature. Before that point in the program, if literature is used it should be adapted to the level of the learners or read in translation (although the latter option offers no language practice, only cultural insights).

A literature program (as opposed to a second *language* program) that would start before the very advanced level of the language program should therefore rely on adaptations or translations. More appreciation of literature can be attained by using good adaptations or translations than by forcing students to decipher second language literature before they are ready to read it. One has to know a second language extremely well to get more out of reading literature in the original language than in a good translation or adaptation.

Adapting literature for use in the second language program, far from being a "crime," is a desirable way of providing interesting graded readings to the students. If properly adapted, any work of literature can be used from the late intermediate level on. It has even been found that medieval literature like *La Chanson de Roland*, if properly simplified and modernized, can interest elementary students [Petry 1981]. Literature from all ages, *all languages,* and all styles can be adapted for use in any second language program.

Steps in the presentation and exploitation of a reading passage

Before actually presenting a short reading for intensive study, several preparatory steps are necessary. These, and the steps that follow them, appear below.

(1) Give a summary of the main ideas contained in the reading. During early reading this summary may need to be given in the native language. It has been found that giving the learners the theme of a story before they read it results in their remembering more --18 percent more words in one particular experiment [Dooling and Lachman 1971].

(2) Teach the new vocabulary, at least the most

important or most difficult words, in a series of basic sentences, bilingually. Also explain any grammatical difficult item (there *shouldn't* be any in graded readings).

(3) Ask and distribute prequestions. These are questions that help further focus the attention of the learner during the reading. They should deal with general comprehension, not details. These questions should stimulate the students' thinking about the topic of the reading. Some discussion can precede the reading, but obviously the questions cannot be answered in reference to the specific reading before reading it.

(4) Read the selection aloud (or play a recording), with appropriate pauses, while the students follow it with their books open. This gives rather limited listening comprehension practice, but it helps to strengthen in the students' minds the relationships between sounds and letters. Reading comprehension has been shown to improve significantly when the act of reading is accompanied by an auditory presentation [Fahmy 1979].

(5) Have the students read the selection aloud, one sentence each, and correct any spelling pronunciation errors. During reading aloud, reading comprehension suffers, as attention is on form, not meaning. However, this step is essential during the first months of reading if correct sound/spelling correlations are to become firmly established. As soon as good sound/spelling correlation habits have been formed, reading aloud should be phased out, since it is rather boring to all students except the one reading. Reading aloud should be in meaningful word groups, not word by word, and with appropriate intonation. Reading aloud has the advantage of giving additional oral practice to the shy students. Furthermore, it has communicative functions, such as reading messages over the phone, reading to children and the disabled, reading papers at conferences, etc. [Greenewald 1980].

(6) Assign the reading to be read silently several times at home.

(7) The following day, ask comprehension postquestions, not identical but along the same lines of thought as the prequestions.

(8) Personalize the reading by asking personal questions using the vocabulary and concepts in the reading. These questions can wander far afield from the reading without any harm being done.

(9) Have the students retell the reading in their own

words, one sentence each. This can be varied as to time reference, attitude, and so forth.

(10) Have a general discussion based on the reading and its implications.

Other postreading activities, some of a testing nature, would be multiple-choice questions, fill-ins, completions, summary writing, and so on.

In the case of extensive readings several pages in length, steps (4) --the teacher reading aloud-- and (5) --the students reading aloud-- should apply to selected paragraphs, not to the whole reading; also note that step (6) would normally involve reading the selection at home only once.

On conveying meaning in readings

If the native language equivalents are provided in word lists before the reading, there is no opportunity to guess meanings, a useful skill that should be developed, and there is constant reference back to the list rather than trying to grasp meaning directly. These disadvantages are over and beyond the already-discussed fact that word lists provide neither linguistic nor nonlinguistic contexts.

The teaching of basic sentences before the reading is better, for at least the words have a linguistic context. However, only key words, not all words can be efficiently presented this way. Also, to avoid constant reference back to the basic sentences it is necessary to provide glosses (native language equivalents) in the readings.

Two options are to provide glosses interlinearly or to provide a bilingual text in two columns. Two problems with the interlineal presentation are that (1) native language word order would be very strange, so only glosses for individual new words can reasonably be provided, and (2) even with the use of a plastic shield with transparent and dark horizontal stripes the temptation to always look at the native language word, resulting in a hopelessly mixed reading, is too strong. A system of two columns makes the temptation to constantly refer to the native language less powerful, as finding the exact location of the equivalent word in the native language column is not always easy. Belasco [1967] proposed the two column approach on the grounds that it makes precise concepts clear and does not make the native language unintelligible through the reordering of words, as in interlineal translation. Parent and Belasco [1970] found that students who read in parallel columns developed better reading comprehension than those who read monolingually; particularly helped were the lower-ability students, without the higher-ability students suffering any hindrance.

Another option --one very frequently used in second language textbooks-- is to present the glosses on the margin. This is not a good approach, because it makes the glosses too readily available, resulting, as with interlineal translation, in the student doing much mixed reading.

To foster the habit of trying to guess meanings and reading second language texts without constant reference to the native language equivalents, the glosses should be accessible, yes, but not too readily so. A good way of arranging this --one that a few textbooks use-- is to have all the glosses in small type at the bottom of the page, related to the text by small raised numbers. This glossing is sufficiently inconvenient that one wants to read as much as possible without referring to it, but at the same time it's there if needed.

Beginners cannot be expected to guess many words in a reading. They could guess intelligently provided (1) only an occasional word is new, and (2) the word reappears several times in different contexts within a short time, although some words can be guessed correctly on first occurrence. When several words in the context of the new word are unknown, it is hopeless. Perhaps that's why only advanced students can frequently guess words from context --they understand most contexts. Practice in guessing from context can be done systematically, by means of the cloze procedure (see Chapter 21) [Plaister 1973], perhaps beginning at the early advanced level. Guessing the meaning of a new word can be greatly facilitated by mentally translating into the native language the sentence(s) that provide the relevant context.

More on questions about readings

Prequestions facilitate reading comprehension. They should not deal with unimportant details but with basic content in terms of who, what, when, where, why, and how.

Postquestions can be of several types, which are listed approximately from easiest to most difficult as follows:

(1) *Repetitive*. These ask for a repetition of what is in the text.

(2) *Restative*. These ask the student to tell what is in the text in his own words.

(3) *Inferential*. In this case the student is asked to draw a contextual inference from two or more items in the text.

(4) *Implicational*. These call for situational suppositions about text items.

(5) *Experiential*. In this case the student is asked to relate something in the text to his own personal experience.

(6) *Evaluative*. These call for value judgments about ideas in the text or about the text itself and its effectiveness; the latter involve some literary sophistication, so they should be reserved for very advanced students.

(The above list is partly based on Dacanay [1963:270-6] and Davies and Widdowson [1974:167-75].)

Many students need to be asked questions, for they are too shy to volunteer comments about readings. After a homework reading assignment, discussion could start by letting students ask other students any questions they may have.

Motivation in reading

Most people are not reading-oriented, so the teacher must make efforts to motivate them. They can be encouraged to read by enthusiasm on the part of the teacher, evidence of satisfaction on the part of students who have been reading, immediate goals, and immediate informal feedback and testing.

Reading efforts should be tangibly rewarded. But perhaps the best source of motivation is satisfaction resulting from acts of discovery, growing self-reliance, appreciation of what one reads, and awareness of one's own progress in reading. In regard to the latter, I remember, for example, the considerable satisfaction I felt when I was first able to read a short book chapter in German while looking up only six words --it was gratifying evidence that all the previous efforts were beginning to pay off.

Motivation to read is also related to personality. Introverted students, who tend to be weak in speaking, generally have good motivation to read, as reading becomes an outlet and an opportunity for the development of an alternate skill. Extroverts, on the other hand, may not be too inclined to read; they should be shown that reading has the advantage of providing them with more material to talk about.

Allowing student participation in the process of

developing reading skill can be highly motivating. The most important type of student participation comes in the form of letting them express their (reading) interests and ensuring that appropriate readers are provided according to their interests. In some programs, it is possible to enlist the help of talented students to prepare readers for younger students. A project in Malaysia, where older students wrote (with teacher guidance and editing) and illustrated story books, using younger students as the central characters in the stories, was quite successful --the young children were enthusiastic about listening to, reading, and owning books about themselves written by older students [Rodgers 1978].

Some suggestions on how to read

For intensive reading, after listening to it the students should read the text aloud, to establish the pronunciation and intonation of the words and to get a preliminary notion of the meaning of the text. On the next reading, they should read silently, concentrating on meaning and noting the glosses of new words or underlining them and glossing them at the bottom of the page if they are not glossed. On subsequent readings (there should be at least four readings in all), they should also read silently, concentrating on the new words in particular, but trying to avoid if possible looking at their glosses. At the end of the third and further readings, the students should try to answer questions about the reading. In the final reading, they should stop after each paragraph and, without looking at it, try to summarize it aloud in their own words. If they follow these steps, the students will be relating reading to speaking, at the beginning in terms of a very simple oral activity and at the end in terms of a fairly creative one.

For extensive reading, more attempts at guessing should be tried. Thus, with ungraded extensive readings, the students should not look up every word but only crucial ones, such as nouns or verbs; they should try to read at a faster tempo than for intensive reading; and they should not translate everything but underline a few essential new words and write their glosses at the bottom of the page, separated by slant lines or hyphens --equivalents should *not* be written between the lines, as that makes them too accessible, so that the context is not even attended to in order to recall the meaning of the word. Extensive readings should not have to be read more than once. However, the new vocabulary, underlined in the text and glossed at the bottom of the page, should be studied at least three additional times over the week following first encounter. This can best be done by gradually adding and dropping text sections for vocabulary study.

Dictionaries should be used only after trying to guess the meaning of a word from context and failing to do so. Advanced readers characteristically rely more on context than beginning readers. Dictionaries, whether bilingual or monolingual, should provide contextual examples --at least one-- of each meaning of a word.

Forming visual images as one reads and when possible even responding physically to the words read seems to facilitate recall of words and phrases. This is what is meant by *active* reading. It is possible also to read *creatively,* by making use of the imagination before, while, and after reading a text to see the story from another point of view, to imagine what one would say to the characters or to the author, to imagine a different setting or how a segment could be acted out, etc.; instructions for such modifications should precede the reading.

Literature should not be read within the second language program on the basis of literary analysis, but for general reading and enjoyment. Thus, such concerns as the structure of plots, underlying themes, psychological characterizations, and so forth are not relevant to a second language program --they belong in a literature program.

As to reading speed, there is some evidence [Ferguson 1974] that through rapid reading second language learners can grasp main ideas better, by disregarding unfamiliar vocabulary, with the result that overall reading comprehension is higher; this could alternate occasionally with the more careful reading that should constitute almost all of the reading program. James [1970] even suggested that various devices used in speeding up native language reading rates, such as the tachistoscope, be used in second language reading. More research is needed on the relationship between reading speed and the comprehension of second language reading materials.

On the retention of written material

George [1973] experimented with several aspects of second language reading retention and reached the following conclusions, which are relevant to the reading process:

--"There is persistent interference from previous

knowledge."

--Some insignificant details are remembered better than important points.

--A challenging single-reading memory task results in better retention than any one of a number of indefinite repetitions.

--"It is not repetition which conduces to learning, but repetition of *effort*."

--Cross-associations affect learning.

--There must be separate contexts for each new item.

--"Remembering is *reconstruction*."

--Analogy is constantly at work.

Individual reading

Reading lends itself better than any other skill to individually paced study without supervision. Within a college library there should be a room, and within the school classroom an area, devoted to second language reading. Within that room or area there should be, easily accessible, "at eye level and at arm's length" [Kellermann 1981:10], a great variety of readers on different topics and at different levels of difficulty, popular magazines, newspapers, even comics. The students should be able to read in the second language about anything they are interested in; wide topical choice is needed for motivation enhancement. The students should want to read extensively for pleasure; if they don't want to, something is wrong with the options being offered them.

At the very advanced level, there should be some reading in common, but mostly there should be individually-tailored reading programs, with the students presenting in class a summary of what they have read, after they themselves teach their classmates the minimal vocabulary required to discuss the readings. Most reading, at the very advanced level, consists then of different students reading on different topics and getting together to discuss what they have read. In this ungraded extensive reading of magazines, books, etc. the students will benefit from keeping a notebook where they note important new vocabulary and set phrases such as proverbs, and reviewing the notebook entries often.

In the case of young children, readers should be made available but they should not be required to read them. They should be able to take them home to read *if they wish to do so* [Kellermann 1981].

(A useful additional discussion on second language reading is King *et al* [1975].)

PART III: WRITING

Writing and the other skills

Communicative writing is putting down on paper what we can say and would say in the presence of a listener. It is therefore directly based on speaking: before or as we write something, we say it subvocally to ourselves. In its creative form, however, it has further and rather stringent requirements, which is the reason why only a minute minority of the speakers of any language are good creative writers.

As far as second language teaching/learning is concerned, writing is the most difficult and the least useful skill --two reasons not to emphasize it and to delay it until a listening-speaking-reading foundation has been established. Since the basis for writing is speech, there must be a good control of speech before writing is attempted.

Without good control over the spoken language, the student "writer," unable to draw from his second language experience, will produce, with the help of dictionaries and grammars, texts that are grossly inaccurate translations from the native language. It should be an inviolable principle that second language students will not be asked to write what they cannot say. When asked to go beyond their knowledge, the students become "unguided linguistic missiles."

What the students are asked to write should also be of lesser difficulty than what they are asked to read. There should be extensive reading before any generative writing is attempted. (Writing exercises can start earlier.) That extensive reading facilitates writing is seen in the fact that most good authors were voracious readers in their youthful years. But note also that writing seems to facilitate reading, for it strengthens visual impressions.

A writing manual, starting with simple exercises and gradually moving on to the generation of sentences, paragraphs, and longer texts, should be a standard teaching/learning tool from the late intermediate level on.

The emphasis on writing, as in the other skills, should be on useful communicative functions. What will the students need to write? At most they will need to write letters and fill out applications and other forms.

They certainly won't need to write creatively in the language. So fancy literary writing that has no practical communicative functions serves no purpose in the second language program. We cannot expect our students, who barely know the second language, to write creatively *and accurately* in it.

Native versus second language writing

Native speakers, who *already know* the language, can pay attention to forming novel ideas, organizing them, and expressing them well then they write (and yet so few can do it!), but the second language learner is not in that position at all. How can we expect the second language student, then, to write good compositions when very few natives, who know their language thoroughly, can do it?

Our problem is that the emphasis on literacy and writing skill of the native language school situation (and the parental and even student attitudes on the value of writing associated with it) has been inappropriately transferred to the second language learning situation, where it is quite out of place. Second language teachers, school administrators, students, and parents should recognize that second languages are very different from the other school subjects, and that the basic type of homework with second languages should be to study cassettes or records, only much later to read and, very infrequently, to write.

Stages in teaching writing

The teaching of writing should proceed according to the following stages:

(1) Learning new graphemes, if any. At first, they should just be traced, then copied, and then they can be produced without help from dictation. To learn Chinese characters, character sheets requiring the step-by-step addition of strokes in the right order can be of great help.

(2) Learning sound-spelling correlations. For languages using the Roman alphabet, this would be the first stage. It is accomplished by copying material learned orally, by the use of spot dictation (letter or word blanks) or full dictation, which can be done in the laboratory, and by writing words and sentences from memory. Song lyrics can also be used for spot dictation [P.C. Smith 1980].

(3) Sentence drills and exercises. These are exercises using a model sentence and an operation such as correlation, replacement, transformation, i.e., the various drill types discussed in Chapter 17. Transformation writing exercises combining, breaking down, and varying sentences by making use of kernel sentences have been found [Cooper 1981] to result in significantly better --more mature and more complex-- writing and, as a bonus, significantly better speaking.

(4) Aided sentence generation. Here rather than follow a model the students are expected to generate a sentence, with various degrees of help. They may be provided with most of the sentence (completion), with the key words --in their basic form-- of the sentence (dehydrated sentences), with the native language equivalent (sentence translation), with a picture or cartoon for which they have to write a sentence or caption (visually cued sentences), or they may simply be asked a question that they should answer in writing (response).

(5) Paraphrasing. Given a model, the students write, with various substitutions and other changes, sentences, paragraphs, dialogues, letters and messages, and longer texts of various kinds. The model may be written or auditory. The imitation of the style of one or more authors is another form of paraphrasing. As paraphrasing is rather difficult, it should be delayed until the advanced level.

(6) Summarizing and note-taking. This is somewhat more difficult than stage 5, for the emphasis is on the students themselves carefully organizing the ideas.

(7) Guided text generation. This ranges from closely controlled to semi-free communicative and self-expressive writing. Without a model, but with all the necessary directions, the students generate paragraphs, picture narrations and descriptions, translated texts, letters and messages, guided individual or collective composition, etc.

(8) Free text generation. This is for the very advanced level. The activities here may be the same as in stage 7, although there are some activities particularly suited to stage 8. What differs from stage 7 is the degree of control. While in stage 7 prewriting directions are given, in stage 8 there is only postwriting monitoring by the teacher, and student rewriting as needed. Some of the activities particularly suited for stage 8 are exchanges of correspondence with natives, or, if these cannot be arranged, with other students; writing and

answering letters for a "Lonely Hearts" newspaper column; writing diaries or, twice a week, a short paragraph for a journal (which is passed back and forth between the student and the teacher, who adds his comments in writing); writing a journal about a hypothetical situation, such as life in a foreign country or a trip around the world; providing an ending to a story, and then reading the original ending; preparing and posting materials for a bulletin board, like the horoscope, historical vignettes, even graffiti; writing free-form minipoems, rather disjointed free verse without rhyme or meter [Knorre 1975]; writing alternate lyrics for songs; and writing essays, term-papers, and book reports, either individually or collectively.

As letter writing is likely to be the only kind of second language writing the students will do beyond the program, they need to experience the writing of many types of letters.

Compositions should be guided --without some guidance, the students can write compositions while avoiding all the structures they find difficult, and the teacher may not be aware of their problems. Collective writing of a fairly long project like "a day in our lives" [F. Schumann 1975] or a story of male-female relations can be very effective.

At the right time --the very advanced level-- there should be much writing practice, outside of class, of course. Brière [1966-b] found that sheer practice did more to improve the fluency and quality of writing than traditional practice with correction --this matter, however, remains debatable.

There is no stage 9. If there were one, it would be entitled "free creative writing." But free, belletristically oriented creative writing has no place in the second language program. It cannot be done without numerous errors until the language is fully mastered, after several years of residence in the second language environment. It requires drawing from a very vast knowledge of the language, and when this vast knowledge does not exist, it can only result in linguistic monstrosities. As done by the students in our second language programs, free creative writing is not writing but doing jigsaw puzzles incorrectly on paper. And very little of these laboriously constructed creative endeavors seems to "stick" anyway, except, unfortunately, the errors.

Writing, by the way, should be done without a

dictionary. If a student needs to check a dictionary it is because he doesn't know how to say something. And if he doesn't know how to say it, he shouldn't even be trying to write it. (The use of the dictionary to check spellings is of course another matter.)

Steps in writing activities

Many writing activities follow a reading activity and consist of the students writing the letter, story, news item, etc. in their own words, after the reading has been subjected to the usual steps of comprehension questions, personalization, variation, discussion, and so forth.

In the case of dictation, it helps to (1) read the text at normal speed, for general comprehension, (2) read the text broken into phrases, each read twice for the students to write, and (3) read the text at normal speed again, to let the students check their work. Then the students can switch papers, the text is distributed or displayed, and the papers are marked by circling or underlining errors. The papers are then collected and the following day, after having reviewed the papers, the teacher can comment on frequent errors and perhaps do some drilling based on them.

In the case of free text generation (stage 8), especially topical essays (or "compositions"), the students' ability to write will be much improved if they are given general guidance in the form of questions such as:

--Answer: What? Who? Where? When? Why? How?

--Give an example

--How do you feel about it? [Colman 1977]

Without such or preferably more specific guidance, many students are too inhibited about writing.

At the very advanced level, literary models can be imitated [Olstad 1964]. The steps required in this case are (1) reading for comprehension, (2) discussing the style of the author, (3) orienting the students, in class, about writing topics, (4) writing, outside of class, and (5) reading of essays in class, each followed by discussion.

Written errors and their correction

To reiterate, second language students should be asked to write only what the teacher is reasonably sure they can say to themselves correctly. If the students make many errors in their writing, it is a clear indication that they are not ready for that stage of writing and should be doing simpler, more basic things, especially audiolingual work. The situation will be helped by frequently reminding the students that they should not try to write at their native language level of written expression, that the key word in writing is "simplify" [Rivers 1968:253].

One problem with the correction of written work is that this correction is not immediate and can therefore be ineffective. The result is that the errors continue to be repeated in successive essays. The problem is exacerbated by the fact that most teachers (as with oral errors) correct at the surface level, by just providing the correct form, not by dealing with the cause of the error. What should be aimed at (again, as with oral errors) is the incorrect generalization and its related decision process that led to the error. That decision, not the surface error, is what needs to be countermanded.

Thus, returning compositions full of red surface corrections to the students is not only discouraging but also quite ineffective. It is much better to select a section of the composition at random and to indicate on it, by using a code, not what specifically should have been written but only the fact than an error of a certain type has been made. Then the students are asked to find out what errors they have made (and why) and present a corrected version of that section of the composition. (Of course, the complete composition is graded, on general criteria.) It is essential that the student correct his own errors, from the coded instructions --underlinings, code numbers referring to grammar rules, question marks, carets, etc. or oral instructions on a cassette recording. If he doesn't figure his own errors out he is unlikely to learn anything from the whole endeavor.

Grading of writing should take into account several factors, to be weighed approximately as follows:

--Grammatical accuracy (morphology and syntax)...40%
--Vocabulary (words and idioms)..................30%
--Spelling and punctuation.......................10%
--Content and organization of the ideas..........20%

While only a section of the composition would be corrected for the benefit of the student, all of it would be evaluated according to the four criteria just listed. Linguistic and communicative competence should be weighed about equally.

It is possible to correct compositions by means of cassette tapes. According to R. Phillips [1968] and Sawyer [1977], the correction of compositions is more effective if taped by the teacher, with explanations as needed; with a little practice this takes no longer than the conventional marking method. It is a more personal method of marking. Also, by giving the grade at the end of the recording attention is greater --in conventional marking, many students look at the grade at the top of the paper and largely ignore corrections.

As stated earlier, Brière [1966-b] found experimentally that frequent and plentiful practice in writing resulted in major improvement in fluency and quality even though errors were not corrected; that is, according to his experiment what counts is quantity, not quality. However, other studies (with natives) show that frequency of practice without instruction does not improve quality and may be detrimental [Dressel *et al.* 1952, Hunting 1967]. Most languists seem to favor the position that writing must be corrected by the teacher and rewritten by the student to be of any pedagogical value, and that it is better to have less writing and exploit it fully than very frequent writing without pedagogical exploitation. The issue has not been settled; more research is needed, including controls of the different ways of correcting written work. In the meantime, the suggestions for correcting written work given in this section seem to be the ones that make best sense.

Multiskill activities

The second language program should start with only two skills, listening and speaking. After reading has been introduced and practiced for a while, there can be three-skill activities, such as (1) listening to a passage, (2) reading it, and (3) talking about it. After writing has been practiced for some time, four-skill activities become possible. Anything that has been heard, read, and talked about can be written about. Conversely, something originally written by the students can be heard, read aloud, and discussed. After the four skills have come into use in the program, only the imagination of the teacher and the students limits the possibilities of skill use --almost any item can be introduced via any skill and practiced in all the others.

20

TOWARD CULTURAL COMPETENCE

As stated in earlier chapters, *second language competence* is composed of *linguistic competence,* which allows the exercise of *communicative competence* within the framework provided by *cultural competence.* All three types of competence are interrelated and are essential to the second language learner who wishes to communicate effectively in a socially acceptable manner.

Cultural competence is the ability to relate a second language to the psycho-socio-cultural reality in which it functions [Trescases 1981]. It is not something the students develop through occasional cultural activities added haphazardly to the program for the sake of variety --cultural competence must be systematically and continuously developed by showing our students how everything we teach relates to the second culture.

Toward a definition of culture

A novel, ground-breaking definition of culture should not be expected in this book. Suffice it to say that Kroeber and Kluckhohn [1954] examined over *300* definitions of culture and were unable to find a precise common denominator. Obviously what is needed is a broad definition. As Seelye [1974:22] put it, culture is widely understood as "a broad concept that embraces all aspects of the life of man, from folktales to carved whales." In other words, culture is the total way of life of a people.

For languistic purposes, we can divide culture into three types: *informational (or factual) culture, behavioral culture,* and *achievement (or accomplishment) culture.*

Informational culture

This refers to the information or facts that the average educated native knows about his society, the geography and history of his country, its heroes and villains, and so on. While such facts are the least important type of culture and should not be overemphasized (as they often are), they are nevertheless important. Since people in a second culture are proud of their history and of other facts about their society, second language learners who are ignorant about such important facts will be resented for not having bothered to learn them. Second language learners should learn whatever the members of the second culture cherish or consider very important.

Behavioral culture

This refers to the sum of everyday life. Murdock *et al.* [1964] listed almost 100 areas of behavior, subdivided into 900 subcategories. Nostrand [1967] proposed a model of sociocultural systems which he called the "Emergent Model"; it lists a total of 30 main headings under four parts: the culture, the society, the individual, and the ecology.

How the people in a society behave is a function of basic human needs (physical and psychological), the environment (geographical, economic, political, etc.), and tradition. This is shown in figure 20.1 (this refers to the behavior of a society; for individual behavior, a box labelled "WILL" would appear immediately below "BEHAVIOR").

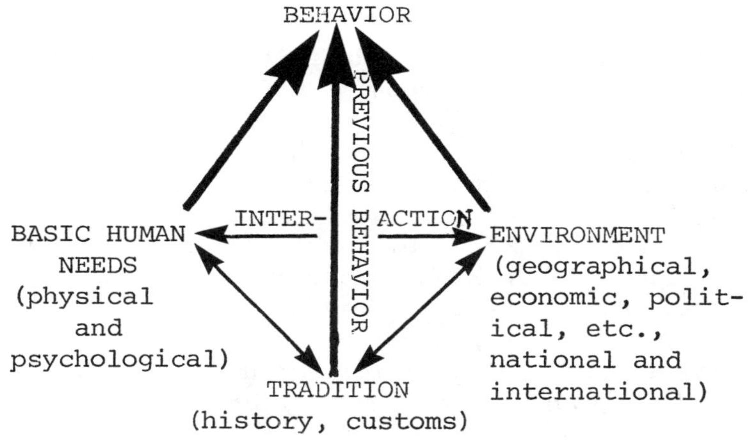

Figure 20.1

In the study of behavioral culture, we are interested far more in behavior that is typical than in peculiarly individual behavior. That is, we are interested in customs, not in personal quirks.

The physical and psychological needs of people are universal. What differs is the way in which these needs are satisfied in different societies. The priority given to the various needs also differs from one society to another. Of course the individual chooses a unique combination among the myriad options. [Seelye 1974:25-7]

The emphasis in second language programs should be on behavioral culture. Behavioral culture --especially conversation formulas and kinesics-- is the form of culture most important to successful communication. Understanding patterns of behavior --actual behavior plus attitudes, values, etc.-- is not only essential to communication but very necessary to an understanding of literature and other forms of achievement culture. So behavioral culture should be emphasized throughout the second language program, at the beginning and intermediate levels in particular.

Note also that it is not enough to acquire a cognitive knowledge of behavioral culture. The learner should know how to behave in the second culture, that is, he should develop a performative knowledge of its behavior patterns.

Achievement culture

For a long time emphasis in the study of culture was placed --and in some institutions still is-- on the artistic and literary accomplishments of a society. These accomplishments in letters, arts, and music *are* important, and educated second language learners should be cognizant of them. However, their study has tended, unfortunately, to preempt the more basic study of behavioral culture. This situation fortunately has been changing in recent years.

Culture in the second language program

Next to pronunciation, culture is the weakest aspect of second language teaching. It will simply not take care of itself by means of occasional *ad-hoc* remarks. The cultural aspect of second language instruction should be carefully planned, taught, and tested, as carefully as the language itself. It should be a significant part of the course grade, giving the students the idea that it is important and giving the linguistically weaker students the opportunity to do well in something.

Ideally, cultural instruction should be offered first in an exploratory course (see Chapter 10) in which the patterns of behavior of people around the world would be considered, in the native language of course. Students would like this, as for most of them the second language program constitutes the only exposure they will have to other cultures. Detailed attention to a specific culture can come later, in connection with the study of its language.

Knowing the pronunciation, grammar, and vocabulary of a language is not enough to prevent breakdowns in communication --a study of the culture associated with it is essential. Many scholars have stated this fact. According to Fries [1955:14], culture is not just an adjunct of the second language program, "something alien and apart from its main purpose, to be added or not as time and convenience may allow, but an essential feature of every stage of language learning...." Nostrand [1966:2] wrote that a language "is not self-dependent," that is, it "cannot be wholly understood without reference to the culture of which it is a part and the social relations which it mediates."

Culture is necessary to an effective understanding of language and language is necessary to an effective understanding of culture. So it is not desirable to have language without culture --it reduces motivation-- or culture without language --it creates frustration about being unable to communicate. Culture should be taught *as* the language is learned [Tucker and Lambert 1973].

This does not mean that culture and language are inseparable in every respect. Separate mental processes are involved in learning a second language and learning about its culture, so in pedagogical practice, although language and culture are interrelated, they can be taught often as distinct things. Proof of this is that much about a second culture can be taught in the native language.

Culture in the second language program should not have only a foreign setting. To a reasonable extent the culture component should give attention, especially in the early stages, to the ethnic minorities within the country of the learners. It should be kept in mind, however, that the study of life in foreign countries is more likely to be motivating than the study of the life of ethnic minorities, with which one is likely to be largely familiar; ethnic minorities may also be viewed with a certain amount of antagonism.

Cultural instruction and activities can make the study of a second language stimulating and highly motivating to our students, also performing the useful social function of reducing ethnocentrism and xenophobia.

The teaching of culture cannot wait until the advanced

level, for only ten percent or so of our students reach that level. Some cultural instruction --at first incidental to language learning, then more and more on its own merits-- should take place in the second language program from the first day of class. Our students need to have a basic understanding of the second culture before they start reading clippings from the foreign press, stories, and other writings, otherwise such bits and fragments will be misinterpreted. Learning about a second culture, like language learning itself, goes on throughout life beyond the second language program.

Language and culture

Certain aspects of the grammatical structure of a language may be culturally related. The use of the subject pronouns *tú* and *usted* (Spanish), *tu* and *vous* (French), and *du* and *Sie* (German), and their related object pronouns and possessives, for example, have definite patterns of behavior related to them.

One has to be cautious, however, in relating language structure and behavior. The Spanish speaker who places himself as the indirect recipient of the action in *Se me cayó el plato* (literally "The dish fell itself to me") feels no less guilty than the English speaker who says *I dropped the dish*. He does not see himself as a passive pawn of nature. Very little about attitudes can be induced from grammar.

More can be learned about the attitudes of a people from the expressions they use. For instance, in North American English there are many expressions dealing with money, such as:

He is worth a million dollars
Another day, another dollar
A million-dollar baby
The 64,000-dollar question
Put your money where your mouth is
A two-bit punk
A penny saved is a penny earned
I feel like a million dollars

In the aggregate, these and other money-related expressions give a valid impression of the great importance of money in our society.

Attitudes toward other cultures

Tucker and Lambert [1973:248] pointed out that before the age of ten, children perceive foreigners as "different but interesting" while later they are seen as "different and bad." Something is wrong with our educational system when it allows the formation of such negative attitudes. (Not that ethnocentrism is all bad. A certain degree of ethnocentrism is desirable, for it provides a sense of identity.)

But positive attitudes are not a *sine qua non* of successful second language learning. I have known a number of very successful learners of Spanish who had rather negative attitudes toward Hispanic people. I have been able to observe the same situation with respect to learners of other languages.

Stereotypes

Americans are materialistic, informal, and crazy about sports.
Englishmen are reserved and polite.
Hispanics are emotional, impulsive, and lazy.
Germans are industrious, disciplined, and stubborn.
Frenchmen are intellectual, suave, and sexy.
Orientals are inscrutable.

These and other popular generalizations --intercultural stereotypes-- may be reasonably on the mark for broadly defined segments of each culture; but they obscure the great variety that exists in each culture within the context of general trends.

As applied to any particular segment of the population, and especially to any individual, stereotypes can be quite wrong. Stereotypes are the tools of lazy minds. They are blunt axes for a task --understanding other peoples-- for which a surgeon's knife is needed. So cultural materials in the second language program should have as one of their earliest objectives the discrediting of stereotypes. Without dispelling stereotypes there cannot be progress toward cultural competence.

This does not mean that we should emphasize the unusual in the second culture. The unusual should be seen against the backdrop of the typical and obviously it is the tapestry of the typical that the second language student must become very familiar with first.

That North Americans tend to lump all foreigners, in particular all foreigners of a given language background, into one pigeonhole, is seen in the "Principle of Homogeneous Hispanicity" [Lusky 1981], according to which all Spanish speakers are seen uniformly. Even Spanish textbook authors and teachers, who should know better, often talk of "Latin Americans" doing this or thinking that, when in fact there are great differences between the various Spanish-speaking peoples.

To help students see the distorting effect of generalizations, Lusky [1981] found it very effective to have the students write about a "North American stereotype" from the point of view of a foreigner. Seeing ourselves as others see us makes us aware of the unfairness of stereotypes and helps us to see others in a better light.

Intracultural stereotypes --those established by a culture about itself-- are equally to be avoided and discredited. The very favorable images that Intourist creates for the Soviet Union or that the Alliance Française promotes for the culture and civilization of France are hardly balanced, real pictures of the respective cultures. Cultural self-images are, of course, part of the total cultural manifestation.

Cultural relativism

The attitude we need to develop towards other cultures is one of cultural relativism. Cultural relativism, however, can be carried too far. We cannot approve of ritual murder and cannibalism, for example. The important thing is to lead our students to understand behavior, not necessarily to approve it. (I don't approve of bullfighting, for example, although I think I understand it.) Cultural relativism, then, is not an attitude of "anything goes" but a realization that there is nothing intrinsically better about our patterns of behavior, that they too may look picturesque to others [Nostrand 1966:5-6].

Cultural relativism will prevent us from ridiculing foreign customs in order to feel superior or for any other reason. But cultural relativism should not lead us to lose our perspective --while we must try to penetrate the foreign mentality, we should take full advantage of the fact that, as outsiders, we can be more objective [Nostrand 1966:6].

The cultural connotations of words

While the denotations of most words are the same across languages, so that most words can be understood without a knowledge of their cultural connotations, few words are the same across languages in all their cultural connotations. This is because experience, values, etc. differ across cultures.

Examples abound. In addition to *leche* and *milk*,

discussed in Chapter 18, we can mention French *pain* vs. *bread*, different in most respects, and French *pharmacie* vs. *drugstore*. If the cultural connotations of second language words are not learned by our students, we cannot really say that they understand the meanings of the words.

Even within a language there are sociocultural connotations to many words. Thus, a Frenchman would never refer to a stranger's parents as his *papa* and *maman*. And the sexual cultural connotations of apparent synonyms in English can be seen clearly in such pairs of words as *figure* and *physique*, *shriek* and *roar*, and *glow* and *perspire* [Barrutia 1967-b].

Kinesics

Communication is accompanied by body movements, facial expressions, gestures, the observation of distance norms, etc., all of which come under the name of kinesics.

In regard to posture and movement, different peoples may not only assume different postures but even walk differently. Putting your hands on your hips is a sign of anger among the Chinese. Americans consider placing their feet on the desk something casual and folksy, but it is frowned upon as boorish and disgusting in many other countries; among the Moslems, it is very impolite to even point the soles of your feet or shoes towards others.

Facial expressions for certain emotions --fear, anger, happiness, and so forth-- seem to be universal. However, the display of emotions is differently regulated by each society.

Eye management can differ across cultures. For example, in Japan eye contact is considered rude, so the Japanese seldom engage in it --they tend to look instead at other people's necks.

Gestures can differ markedly, as they too are culture-bound. Even the most familiar gestures can be misunderstood. Thus, in Eskimo and Greek, head nodding means "No." Whistling in public shows approval in North America, disapproval in Spanish-speaking countries. The North American gesture for "Come here" is understood as "Good bye!" in many other cultures. In India, waiters are summoned by snapping the fingers, something unacceptable in North America and used to call a dog in some Latin American countries. Even within one general linguistic area there may be marked differences in gestures; thus, most Spanish speakers have just one gesture to indicate height, but Mexicans have three: one for a person, another for an animal, still another for inanimate objects.

According to Edward T. Hall [1966:117-25] middle-class Americans use four distances for various situations: intimate, personal, social, and public. The personal distance used in informal contacts between friends is about two to three feet. Intimate distance is 18 inches or closer. The problem arises when members of another culture have a closer personal distance and invade the American's intimate distance. I have seen several times, for example, a Latin American and a North American start a conversation at one end of the room and gradually move all the way to the other end as the North American retreated to protect his "bubble" of intimate space. Presumably the Latin Americans thought the North Americans were cold and distant. Generally North Americans and northern Europeans stand farther apart than Latin Americans, Arabs, Greeks, Turks, and certain other peoples, who tend to stand close.

Not only do North Americans keep their distance, they do not touch. People in many cultures, when talking with a casual acquaintance, touch each other, pat each other on the elbow or arm or shoulder, even on the back. In many cultures, people of the same sex touch, hold hands, embrace, even kiss without there being any sexual connotations as in North America.

The significance of kinesics to second language teaching lies in the fact that authentic speech is accompanied by culturally authentic gestures, etc. So whenever the second language is spoken in the classroom, both teacher and students should use authentic gestures and other kinetic features of the second culture.

Taking advantage of student interests

Most of our students are already curious about how foreigners live, so it is a matter of channeling that curiosity into rewarding and interesting directions. Perhaps the best point of departure is to show them how foreign people of their same age and circumstances live, and later expand this rapport to people of other ages and circumstances.

Students who lack much interest in second languages may become interested through exposure to their cultures. But the nature of students' cultural interests should be determined in advance. Part of the activities of the first day or two of class should be the administration of a student background and interest questionnaire, and an important part of that questionnaire should deal with what the students want to learn about the second culture.

Goals and levels in the teaching of second cultures

Cultural instruction should not be haphazard; it should have definite goals. As general objectives, Nostrand [1966:4] proposed (1) crosscultural communication and (2) crosscultural understanding. Lafayette and Schulz [1975: 108-9] reduced testable goals --from the numerous ones proposed by Nostrand and Seelye-- to three, for secondary schools: "1. *Knowledge*. The ability to *recognize* cultural information or pattern.... 2. *Understanding*. The ability to *explain* cultural information or pattern.... 3. *Behavior*. The ability to *use* cultural information or pattern." These seem valid overall goals.

Broad cultural goals are important, but more specific goals are also necessary. One way of describing them is in relation to the three types of culture discussed previously. Goals for informational culture include recognizing and interpreting major geographical features, historical events, and institutional characteristics of the second culture. Goals for behavioral culture include understanding and being able to carry out the common behavior patterns of the second culture. Goals for achievement culture include being familiar with and appreciating the outstanding literary and artistic achievements of the second culture.

More specifically, cultural goals for the classroom can be ordered in an approximate progression of both time and difficulty according to the following ten steps (partly based on proposals by Nostrand and Seelye):

(1) Knowledge of the cultural connotations of words and phrases. It would be conveyed by means of very brief cultural connotation comments, and where necessary visuals and realia. This would be done from the beginning of the program. Note however that throughout the beginning level cultural insights should be incidental to the development of the language skills. Only once in a while, maybe once a week, a cultural point could be developed in greater length, in the form of a cultural aside or even a culture capsule. (Types of cultural activities are discussed later in this chapter.)

At the beginning level, students have quite a task just learning the basics of the language, so their job should not be made more difficult by adding heavy cultural content. Whatever cultural instruction takes place, has to be done in the native language at this level, thereby taking time away from language instruction. Systematic cultural contrasts and the systematic study of the second culture in the second language have to be left until the intermediate level and beyond.

(2) Knowledge of how to behave in common situations. These are such frequent situations as greetings, introductions, leave-taking, eating, and so on. This knowledge involves both understanding "strange" behavior and being able to perform it. It refers to those aspects of behavior that are essential, that must be complied with; minor breaches will normally be excused by the members of the second culture [Nostrand 1966:4].

Step 2 would also start at the beginning of the program and, like step 1, would extend throughout the program.

(3) The development of interest and understanding toward the second culture. This goal is best accomplished by outside-of-class readings in the native language, until the late intermediate level, when the readings can be done in the second language. The beginning student should be handed, at the beginning of the program, a bibliography of interesting readings about the second culture. Some of these readings could be given as occasional assignments, for *brief* discussion (in the native language) in class.

(4) Understanding of crosscultural differences. Here the basic technique is contrasting behavior patterns in the two cultures. This can be handled in the form of culture assimilators, capsules, clusters, minidramas, etc. Since more knowledge of the second language is needed for this, it is a goal for the intermediate level and beyond, although some very simple culture assimilators could be handled in the second language during the late beginning level.

(5) Understanding of intracultural institutions and differences. This goal, which involves giving insight into such second culture institutions as the family, the school system, government, etc. and the way various groups and individuals relate to them and differ among themselves, should be a goal for the late intermediate and advanced levels.

(6) Research-like projects. At the advanced level and beyond, students can carry out research-like projects in which they investigate --primarily in second language

sources-- some aspect of the second culture of particular interest to them. This research-like activity should be distinguished from serious academic research of the kind graduate students and university professors conduct.

(7) Development of an integrated view of the second culture. According to Nostrand [1974:274], an understanding of a second culture as a whole "is unlikely to occur to a student through his own trial and error, even if he had years for the purpose." So such an integrated view of a second sociocultural system should be *provided* to the students. This should take place preferably at the late advanced level or at the very advanced level, when the students have had sufficient exposure to the patterns of the second culture to be able to participate intelligently in a synthesis.

(8) Ability to evaluate statements about the second culture. Again, this, generally speaking, has to come after much cultural instruction, and preferably after step 7.

(9) Development of empathy toward a second culture and its people. The reason this is placed here, as an advanced step, is that empathy normally develops from direct contact with members of the second culture, and this usually takes place at the advanced level or even beyond the program. Occasional visits by native speakers to the classroom may not be enough to develop empathy --the language learner usually needs to live for a while among the natives. So the best way to develop empathy toward the members of a second culture is to experience their culture first-hand by living among them, preferably after much language and culture instruction at home. (Of course, in a limited way any sympathetic insight into the second culture throughout the second language program contributes to the development of empathy.)

(10) Academic research on second cultures. This is clearly something beyond the second language program.

For most of the ten goals given above there are not only verbal but also nonverbal activities involved.

The overall goal cannot reasonably be biculturalism, but enabling our students to function as "welcome strangers" in the second culture. The emphasis should be on understanding the second culture, not on securing commitment to it. Understanding a second culture is not only worthwhile in itself but allows the learner to understand better his own culture. (The reverse is also true: an understanding of one's own culture can help to understand another culture.)

Strictly speaking, people can be bilingual but not bicultural. One can be superficially bicultural, but in things that really matter one cannot behave in two, often opposite ways without developing emotional problems. Of course a person can be acultural while he does not choose among conflicting cultural values demanding his allegiance. But aculturalism is emotionally uncomfortable, and soon the person must choose among the options. The choice may consist of a combination integrating selected values and behavior patterns of the two cultures so as to satisfy the person's needs, but values and patterns in conflict cannot long coexist without considerable emotional upheaval.

The use of crosscultural contrasts

Like the sound system, like the grammar, a grasp of second culture is a question of understanding differences and similarities, both inter- and intraculturally, and of course of integrating the intracultural elements into a system. It is impossible for second language students to leave the mentality of their own culture at the classroom door; it is impossible for them not to make comparisons. We might as well accept this fact and overtly direct these comparisons, to make sure they will be enlightening and not misleading.

Systematic cultural comparisons can be done from the late beginning level on, in the native language if necessary. But there should not be exclusive emphasis either on differences or similarities --we should aim at a balanced medium. It is quite possible that excessive emphasis on contrasts reinforces ethnocentricity and stereotypes [Lusky 1981]. As Seelye [1974:121] put it, contrasts can be a motivating point of entry to the second culture, but once inside it the students should be helped to realize that, when seen in its cultural context and in reference to universal needs, "even seemingly bizarre behavior usually makes perfect sense." Isolated features of a second culture, seen apart from its overall structure, can result in erroneous impressions and stereotypes. As Cornfield [1966:126] pointed out, it is only when they are attached to a common base that particular cultural features cease being just patches and "their designs and shapes blend and relate to one another to make a recognizable whole."

The use of the native language

Whatever can be taught in the second language should be so taught. However, we cannot wait to start cultural instruction until there is a very good command of the second language. Concentrated cultural instruction should be delayed until there is a sound linguistic basis and it can be done in the second language, at the advanced level; but at the beginning and intermediate levels it is necessary to give some cultural insights in the native language, phasing it out gradually in favor of the second language.

Nevertheless, there is no reason why most activities --culture assimilators, for example-- could not be conducted in a simple form of the second language. If so done, the desire to participate in cultural activities will serve as a motivation to learn the language.

Cultural activities and techniques

Basic to successful cultural instruction is the creation of the right atmosphere. The classroom and the laboratory should surround the students with a multisensory second language and culture environment, rich in visuals, realia, and music. A cultural island should be created and its details frequently changed. As Morain [1976:31] put it: "Eyes that have seen the far side of the moon will not focus for long on three square feet of static bulletin board." Bulletin board displays should be changed every week or two, with teams of students assigned to prepare each display, which can consist of pictures, news, cartoons, art, ads, proverbs, poems, song lyrics, kitchen recipes, etc. Posters and other classroom decorations should be changed every few weeks. Care should be exerted that pictures portray the typical, not the unusual or quaint, and that they not reinforce stereotypes. Cultural authenticity in all teaching materials contributes to the creation of the right atmosphere. For greater cultural impact, visuals, preferably film, should be used in conjunction with all presentation material, dialogues in particular [Nostrand 1966:22].

The cultural activities to be listed and discussed in this section should, whenever possible, be done in the second language. They are listed in approximate chronological order and order of difficulty, although of course there is much overlap.

(1) *Cultural asides* are brief cultural comments made during other class activities. Examples are the cultural connotation comments made upon presentation of new words

and phrases (including clichés) whose connotations differ from those in the native language.

(2) *Foreign elements survey.* One of the earliest if not *the* earliest cultural activity for the students can be looking for evidence of second culture elements in their midst: place names, foods, films, music, imported objects, historical events and figures, paintings, dances, and so forth.

(3) *Realia exchange.* As a cultural experience, an exchange of boxes containing objects typical to each culture can be enlightening and lead to much second language conversation [Green 1972:11].

(4) *Culture cartoons* can be drawn about various aspects of second culture customs, such as dining or tipping in France, school activities in Mexico, or boy-girl relations in Brazil.

(5) *Classroom calendar.* All dates that are important in the second culture --holidays, important events, birthdays of the famous-- should be entered in the classroom calendar and briefly commented on.

(6) *Bicultural timeline.* Allen and Valette [1972:252] suggested using two colors of ribbon to fasten a double timeline around the classroom walls; on these ribbons the most important events in the two countries through the centuries can be marked.

(7) *Culture games.* These are best suited to deal with facts in informational culture, such as the recognition or production of the names of important people, places, monuments, and so forth.

(8) *Audiomotor units* can be used to teach second culture behavior, by instructing students to act as if they were in the second culture [Elkins *et al.* 1972; Meade and Morain 1973]. Items particularly suitable for such units would be restaurant visits, shopping, anything where the students can learn by doing.

(9) *Culture samples* or "slices of life" [Morain 1976: 36]. These are items from the second culture presented in the classroom and used for brief cultural instruction. Examples are clippings from the foreign press, advertisements, very brief taped broadcasts, jokes, or the latest hit song.

(10) *Culture assimilators.* A technique developed by Fiedler *et al.* [1971], the culture assimilator presents a single crosscultural situation that causes puzzlement or conflict. The learner then chooses a response from four explanations of the behavior and receives feedback

when he reads the comments about his response (each feedback response appears on a different page). Culture assimilators can be programmed, with the advantages of active involvement and the possibility of study outside of class. Seelye [1974:101] claimed that culture assimilators "have been shown to be more effective in controlled experiments" but offered no data.

(11) *Culture capsules* are a technique developed by H.D. Taylor and Sorenson [1961]. They consist of a short text dealing with a minimal cultural phenomenon or difference plus supporting pictures and realia. They can be taught in 5-10 minutes. For examples of culture assimilators or capsules, refer to the teaching materials prepared by J. Dale Miller and Anthony Papalia.

(12) *Culture clusters,* developed by Meade and Morain [1973] consist of three or four related culture capsules presented on successive days followed by a half-hour minidrama or simulation. The whole class participates in the dramatic activity culminating the cluster. Examples of suitable themes for culture clusters are a French country wedding [Meade and Morain 1973], a family dinner [Seelye 1974:114-9], a bullfight, or a Christmas celebration.

(13) *Cultural minidramas* were developed by Raymond L. Gorden, a sociologist from Antioch College [Seelye 1974: 91]. Of course, skits have been in use for a long time, and have been found to be effective [Behmer 1972]. A cultural minidrama consists of three to five brief episodes, each illustrating miscommunication. The cause of the whole misunderstanding becomes evident only in the last episode. Discussion follows each episode; during the discussions the teacher should be nonjudgmental and should encourage the students to talk by asking them questions that require an explanation, rather than "yes" or "no," for an answer.

According to Seelye [1974:93], not more than one or two minidramas can be performed effectively in a language program, for after that they lose the "emotional sensation of self-confrontation."

(14) *Situations*. Here the students play themselves in one event. Several such events can be combined into a situational series. Only the imagination limits the possibilities.

(15) *Role-playing*. Here the students assume other identities for one event or for ongoing role-playing covering many events. For example, students could, for a whole semester, play the parts of small businessmen, labor

leaders, landowners, military officers, university students and various other roles in a Latin American country [Seelye 1968:64-5]. Or a whole term could be used to simulate travel through a foreign country. Or a village in the second culture could be created in the classroom, with students playing the various roles in it [Reinert 1974-a:292].

Decaroli [1972] warned, however, that as interesting as role-playing may be it tends to result in less retention of information than traditional methods.

(16) *Discussions and debates*. Cultural discussions and debates can be held on numerous topics such as school and university life, work habits, economic conditions, the role of technology, human relations, government, religion, attitudes, and the role of women in society. Advance preparation based on readings from the foreign press is desirable. Key new vocabulary should be included in simple sentences and distributed to the class for study before the discussion or debate.

(17) *Humor*. Much can be learned about another culture from what makes its people laugh. Note that this is mostly an advanced activity, for the subtleties of humor are lost on those who don't have a good control of the language, and having to repeat jokes because of poor comprehension deprives them of all interest for those who have understood them.

(18) *Proverbs*. There are mixed feelings about the use of proverbs to teach cultural patterns. On the one hand, Zenner [1970] claimed that proverbs reveal the attitudes and thinking patterns of people, and several methods authors recommend their use in the form of signs to be posted around the classroom. On the other hand, Nostrand [1974:286-7] observed that proverbs have limited cultural value because they rarely reveal culturally peculiar wisdom and they often contradict each other --as a result they can be misleading.

(19) *Songs*. Damoiseau and Marc [1967] claimed that songs provide a good basis for illustrating aspects of the daily life in a second culture. Balanced against this possible advantage is the fact that in North America young people and adults don't like to sing in public, only young children do, so at least on this continent the possibilities for exploiting songs are rather limited.

(20) *Folklore*. Morain [1968] argued that folklore presents the attitudes of a society much more clearly than literature. Among the advantages she saw in folklore are

the fact that folk tales are usually short and in conversational style.

(21) *Films.* Foreign films are an excellent source of cultural insights. But before recommending a film to his students, the teacher should see it both to make sure it is suitable and to be able to suggest to them what to look for from a cultural point of view. A useful exercise with films is for the students to see only two-thirds of a movie and then predict its ending on the basis of cultural assumptions.

(22) *Cultural readings.* These should start, in the native language, early in the program. Then, as soon as it is in harmony with other program objectives, simple readings in the second language can start. The culturally most-revealing readings are found in magazines, newspapers, advertisements, social science books, and statistical abstracts. The students can be assigned short readings for the primary purpose of discovering cultural concepts, not just for general comprehension; in this case prequestions are needed.

(23) *Literature.* This is discussed in the following section.

(24) *Culture-oriented writing.* Soon after the students start writing, some of their writing assignments can be culturally oriented. They can be asked to write a short essay on a cultural contrast, either from the native or the foreign point of view. They can be asked to complete an incomplete narrative of a cultural nature. Many forms of writing can have cultural content.

(25) *Cultural projects.* As cultural projects, school students can construct a mural or a diorama, prepare posters, build replicas, and organize various programs. Older students can research a topic and report to the class. For example, they can use Brooks' [1969] "inquiry technique" and draw out from the teacher and from (other) native speakers a list of the items that are important in a foreign youth's life. Or they can read up and report on each of the various cities and regions in the foreign country.

Brooks [1964:82-96] suggested a long series of challenging questions that can be used as the point of departure for cultural projects. Seelye [1976:125] suggested that the initial cultural hypotheses in such projects could be considerably refined by the students asking themselves how their generalizations are affected by age, sex, social class, and place of residence of the natives on which the generalizations are based.

(26) *Culture minicourses.* These are limited-credit courses extending over several weeks or even a whole term. They should not be offered until the late intermediate level, when the students can handle most material in the second language; otherwise the culture minicourses are not supportive of the objectives of the second language program as a whole.

(27) *Contact with natives.* This is essential to the development of empathy. (a) *Visitors.* Seelye [1974:81] suggested that at least one native speaker should be invited into the classroom each month. Most foreign visitors, and parents who speak the second language, are flattered to be invited to talk with the students. But visitors should be interviewed by the teacher in advance; as Allen and Valette [1972:269] pointed out, if the visitor does not articulate well, is not receptive to questions about his country, and has difficulty in meeting people, it would be a waste of time to invite him. The class should be prepared for a visitor by reading and discussing about his background and country of origin, by practicing the vocabulary likely to be needed in the interview, and by thinking of a series of questions to ask him. (b) *Letter-writing.* Once letter-writing has been practiced for a while, each student should send real letters abroad, asking for brochures, information, samples, etc. [Allen and Valette 1972:256]. This correspondence is then shared with the whole class. (c) *Pen and tape pals.* Pen and tape exchanges between students are highly motivating. They too should be shared with the whole class and become largely class projects. (d) *Short-wave radio.* Via amateur short-wave radio, classes can be paired internationally, resulting in a greatly enriched communicative and cultural exchange.

(28) *Cultural community resources.* Outside the classroom, the community may offer numerous cultural resources. Field trips or individual outings can be organized to visit native speakers, ethnic community activities, exhibits, restaurants, etc.

(29) *Language club activities.* The school second language club --and if your school doesn't have one, you should urgently encourage its establishment-- can organize various cultural activities, with participation of all club members and invited guests (other second language people in universities, schools, and the community). Among the activities could be a "foreign culture day," a

second language fair or festival, a concert, an exhibition, a Christmas program, an international variety show, or an international banquet [Cornfield 1966:133-7]. A series of cultural programs can also be prepared and presented by parents of foreign backgrounds, which would be a successful way of involving them and their children in the second language program [Green 1972:22].

(30) *A trip to the second culture area.* The ultimate cultural activity is a visit to the country or region where the second language is spoken. If at all possible, such a trip should be a regular offering of the second language program, a credit-bearing option at the advanced level. If possible it should last at least a month, preferably one semester. The motivating effect of looking forward to such an experience is tremendous.

Among programs that are suitable for longer experiences of this nature are the junior year abroad, student exchange programs, summer camps abroad, and the Experiment in International Living; many programs also bring foreign students to North America.

(For examples of cultural techniques and activities see Seelye [1974], Lafayette [1978], and Hendon [1980].)

Literature and cultural instruction

Great literature has appeal because of its style or philosophy, or because it deals with topics of universal interest. It rarely presents the usual, everyday life of a society. Characters in much fiction tend to be stereotypes and their interaction is seldom representative of real patterns of behavior. Furthermore, great literature tends to be several decades old, so it can give an erroneous impression of the current cultural (and linguistic) situation [Cornfield 1966:137].

Literature is very restricted as a source of information about second cultures. Not only that, but it can be quite misleading, whether intentionally so used or not. Russians reading such American novels as *Babbitt* form the wrong impression about the role of businessmen in the United States [Nostrand 1966:16]. Students of Spanish who read mostly Latin American political protest literature get the false impression that Latin Americans in general are itching to destroy the established order and to welcome a Marxist form of government.

Literature cannot be understood properly without a good knowledge of the second culture, so a thorough cultural orientation should be a prerequisite for its study.

As Seelye [1968:41] expressed it: "Social science as source, literature as example"; in other words, we should first identify cultural patterns with the help of the social sciences and only then see how those patterns are illustrated in literature.

At the very advanced level --where literature can be introduced in the language program-- literature should be one of several options. Many second language students are more interested in cultural patterns, history, drama, art, films, politics, and many other areas of life. Note that in the uncommonly taught languages, where there are no established literature faculties, cultural study is not just literary but includes everything that constitutes culture, with literature being a small part of it. We should follow this example in the commonly taught languages as well, offering our students advanced cultural instruction based primarily on current magazines and newspapers and current popular literature, selections from books on various topics, and interdisciplinary studies.

Interdisciplinary studies

Ideally interdisciplinary studies combine second language learning with the study of other subjects, with the result that knowledge of both improves. In practice, however, many interdisciplinary programs have the serious shortcoming that they make minimal linguistic demands on their students, as minimal as the completion of just two college semesters in the second language. In some programs, fewer than ten percent of the courses require second language knowledge [R.D. Lambert 1973]. Under those circumstances, the second language program and interdisciplinary studies are not mutually supportive.

Most courses in interdisciplinary studies should be taught in the second language. This means that an advanced knowledge of the language should be required. If this condition is met, interdisciplinary studies can be an ideal way of penetrating the second culture and understanding the mentality of its people.

When a full interdisciplinary program cannot be mounted, at least certain subjects in the curriculum could be offered in the second language. This has the advantage of resulting in higher enrollments, although it has the disadvantages that there may be animosity from colleagues in other departments and that most second language teachers are so specialized that they couldn't teach other subjects [Burelli 1975].

(On interdisciplinary studies, see T.E. Kelly [1974] and Conner [1977:100-4].)

Travelling and living abroad

Beyond the second language program (recall that travelling abroad as part of the language program is also desirable), living abroad is linguistically and culturally most illuminating. Knowledge of the second language and culture can best be increased by teacher efforts "to inspire, cajole, threaten, or bribe the student into spending some time abroad" [Seelye 1968:66].

Before going abroad, the right attitudes should be formed at home. Gezi [1965] found that among Middle-Eastern students in California there was a highly significant correlation ($p < .001$) between pre-arrival attitudes and subsequent adjustment. Their adjustment, which correlated significantly with interaction with Americans, also correlated highly significantly with success in college. So development of the right attitudes is essential to success in a sojourn abroad.

Also before going abroad, second language students should be familiar, both cognitively and performatively, with everyday behavior in the second culture, as detailed earlier in this chapter.

Travel abroad should involve definite objectives and activities, planned in advance, to explore the foreign way of life. Allen and Valette [1972:271] suggested seven such miniprojects.

Reactions to cultural immersion

Acculturation in the foreign environment has been described [H.D. Brown 1980:132] in terms of four stages: (1) excitement and euphoria, (2) culture shock, (3) gradual recovery, with anomie, and (4) full recovery, with assimilation or adaptation. These are stages that occur *in the environment*, not in the second language program. The second language program, as we shall see, can speed up these stages upon arrival in the foreign country, and even nearly eliminate one of the stages.

The excitement and euphoria stage lasts a few days. Everything seems new and interesting, a joy to behold. Then suddenly comes the realization that most values and behavior are incompatible with one's own, and culture shock sets in. Culture shock is "a somewhat psychotic state" [Nostrand 1966:6] which can be largely prevented by an attitude of imperturbability resulting from the administration of "little doses of culture shock" in the classroom [Nostrand 1966:7]. Culture shock is "a form of anxiety that results from the loss of commonly perceived and understood signs and symbols of social intercourse" [Adler 1972:8]. It has also been described as presenting "a rather severe picture of an unwitting and helpless victim of an illness, and an illness for which there is no clearcut cure" [H.D. Brown 1980:134]. Not a small element of culture shock is the realization that we may not be wanted wherever we go. To help overcome culture shock, much contact with the common man is needed, contact such as can be had in local travel. The important thing is not to withdraw but rather to immerse oneself in the second culture.

Graduates from a good second language program of which cultural instruction is an important part need not go through a full-fledged stage 2 (culture shock); at most they would suffer from "crosscultural fatigue" [Seelye 1974:85], a much milder symptom of the difficulties in the process of acculturation. Crosscultural fatigue is partly due to the fact that in a second culture we don't know what to look at and what to ignore (as the natives do), so we are forced to pay attention to everything, and this is tiring. Our ethnocentric attitude to what is different is what causes most of the problem; to see our values and our standards rejected is shocking.

Early during the third stage (gradual recovery), feelings of anomie develop. Anomie consists in not feeling oneself to be a member of either culture but rather acultural. To integrate with another people tends to reduce one's integration with one's own. The result is that for a while one feels he doesn't belong in either culture. Having an integrative orientation does not help but rather aggravates the feelings of anomie.

Anomie can also happen to advanced students in the second language program even if they have not visited the other culture. As stronger ties are established with the values of the second culture, advanced language students may feel that their ties with their native culture have become weaker. A common reaction to these feelings is that, in order to regain their sense of identity, such students allow their linguistic and cultural proficiency in the second language to deteriorate. To prevent this, they need to be reassured that they are not expected to become bicultural, only bilingual with a knowledge and understanding of, and empathy toward, the second culture.

The fourth stage (full recovery) involves either becoming in every respect a member of the second culture (assimilation) or adapting oneself to it by integrating certain of its patterns of behavior with one's own. Note that it is possible to have full assimilation or "tossed salad" integration but not biculturalism --cultural conflicts must be solved one way or another.

Evaluating the results of cultural instruction

Testing will be discussed in the next chapter. Here broader results are being considered. Biculturalism in our students is not a viable goal. What can we expect from cultural instruction? We should be pleased if we can develop in our students (1) an understanding attitude toward "strange" behavior, (2) performative knowledge of how to behave in common situations, (3) cognitive knowledge of commonly-known facts about the second culture, (4) appreciation of the literary and artistic achievements of the second culture, and (5) positive attitudes towards the second culture and its people.

In regard to the development of positive attitudes, the evidence so far is mixed. Savignon [1972:58-9] stated that language study seems to result in a marked decrease in ethnocentrism. Perhaps positive attitudes are correlated with higher second language proficiency. Perhaps negative attitudes such as excessive ethnocentrism or bias against foreigners can be overcome through favorable exposure. However, Cooke [1969] and Bals [1971] found that cultural instruction does not change attitudes significantly. This deserves much further study. It seems difficult to believe that cultural instruction of the right content and nature would not have a positive effect.

Teachers and culture

Second language teachers need to understand both cultures if they are to convey effectively the concepts and behavior patterns of the second culture. For that purpose, their training should include courses in sociology, history, geography, politics, economics, etc. in reference to both cultures.

An integral part of the preparation of the second language teacher should be living at least one year in the country or region whose language he wants to teach, and revisiting that country from time to time throughout his career, bringing back objects, pictures, books and other materials he can use in the language program.

Second language teachers should regularly read second culture periodicals, especially those dealing with popular culture and current events. They should also cultivate friendships with native speakers of the language --this would give them not only the opportunity to practice using the language but also of inviting these friends and acquaintances as visitors to their classrooms.

Research

Advanced students should not only learn about a culture but acquire the tools of crosscultural research [Jenks 1974-a, 1974-b], which they can use in investigating various cultural questions.

Serious cultural research, however, is an academic pursuit followed best at the graduate and professional levels. To facilitate it, Nostrand [1974:317] has proposed the formation of "survey teams, on the model of the ACTFL bibliographical teams, to carry out continuing 'working syntheses'" of cultures, under the direction of a coordinating center.

For either research-like projects or serious research, recent information is needed, as the various cultures change in their manifestations. For this one cannot rely heavily on native speakers in the community, for they may have stopped behaving according to their culture as a result of their residence abroad; furthermore, they may not be able to answer questions about those patterns of behavior which they still practice, because their behavior is largely unconscious.

(Among those who have written extensively about the teaching of culture we can mention Robert Lado, William Marquardt, Nelson Brooks, Howard Nostrand, Ned Seelye and, more recently, Howard B. Altman, Victor E. Hanzeli, Genelle Morain and Robert Lafayette. Particularly relevant are Seelye [1974] and Nostrand [1974].)

21

TESTING

The place of testing and evaluation in the second language program

Although some teachers, and probably many students, find testing distasteful and may consider it unnecessary, testing is a very necessary part of the process of continually evaluating teaching and learning. Because of this close connection between testing and teaching, second language teaching cannot be much better than the tests used to evaluate it. This does not mean, however, that testing is a form of teaching: teaching is *imparting* knowledge, testing is *evaluating* it; it is important to keep this distinction in mind.

Tests perform several very useful functions in the second language program. First of all, they help set objectives, letting students know what they should know by any point in the program. Of course, most comprehensive tests can only sample knowledge, and if the teacher teaches to the test sample, he defeats its purpose, as it no longer serves as a sample. Preparing tests can help clarify the objectives in the teacher's mind. It is essential, however, that the objectives stated to the students should agree with the content of the tests. The students study for the content of the tests, not for some other objective, however often stated --it is useless, for example, to insist that the course has as its main objective audiolingual skill if all tests are paper-and-pencil tests.

Tests are also a major source of extrinsic motivation for most students. That they motivate students to put in extra effort is enough of a reason to use them.

Tests are not learning devices in the sense that they teach language, but they can help the students learn what it is they don't know yet (that they should have learned), so they fulfill an important diagnostic function. And the pattern of responses of the class as a whole can tell the teacher which elements and rules need to be taught again. Of course, for this diagnostic function to benefit the students, the results of each test should be given out as soon as possible. For reinforcement purposes, the teacher should go over the test orally as soon as the test is over (the reading and writing parts can be projected).

Tests seldom cause anxiety if the objectives of the program are made clear and the tests contain no surprises either in content or format. Tests must test what has been taught and learned. To avoid surprises, whenever a new type of test item is to be used, it should be explained and illustrated with examples before the test. The first taped test, whether to be given in class or the language laboratory, should be preceded two or three days earlier by a student self-test of a format parallel to the official test. All tests other than quizzes should be announced in advance, so that there are no surprises regarding time of administration. Regarding quizzes, Valette [1977] suggested the students should be told to expect a quiz every period, although on some days it will not be given.

Second language tests should measure performative, not cognitive knowledge --we can usually tell what a student knows by what he does. Abstract knowledge, on the contrary, in no way guarantees performative knowledge.

Testing must be frequent, so as not to allow the accumulation of undigested knowledge, which leads to cramming and quick forgetting. However, not too much time should be devoted to testing --perhaps no more than about ten percent of total class time.

Testing also serves to evaluate the effectiveness of teaching and of the teacher. In addition to tests, student questionnaires also provide feedback about the course. Without student input, second language programs cannot adapt to student needs and interests and thereby reduce attrition. All students who stop taking a second language at any point should be given a questionnaire to find out the reasons. Furthermore, about one third- to halfway through all second language courses, much can be learned (in time to apply it) by asking the students simply to list and rank what they like best, what they like least, and what they would do differently if they were the teacher.

Some testing terminology

Measurement is the comparison of a performance with a standard. *Testing* is formal measurement, primarily of an objective type; it is not only the observation but the quantification of student performance. *Evaluation* is informal measurement, largely subjective in nature.

In *objective* measurement, there can be only one correct answer to each question. In *subjective* measurement, it is impossible to predict the answers to questions; typical subjective items are questions requiring self-expression, as in speaking and writing.

The differences between a *quiz*, a *test*, and an *exam* are in duration and comprehensiveness. A quiz lasts about five minutes, or at most ten minutes, and covers current material. A test may last from half an hour to one hour and covers one or more units. An exam may last two hours or longer and covers at least half the content of the course.

There are four types of scales of measurement: *nominal, ordinal, interval,* and *ratio*. A nominal scale classifies data into categories such as male/female, native/foreign, etc. An ordinal scale merely ranks. It is the interval scale which is most useful in testing, for it places all scores within a range of equal intervals. Equal interval scales also lend themselves to powerful parametric statistics. (Statistical formulas, however, will not be given in this book, as they are available in many sources.) The fourth type of scale, the ratio scale, is found in the physical sciences; ratio scales have true zero values, permitting direct comparison of different points on the scale (for example, four ohms is twice as much electrical resistance as two ohms).

A *speed* test is one in which the testees are competing against a time limit; they may not all answer all items. On the other hand, in a *power* test all answer all items, as adequate time for that is given.

Formative tests are given during a course or program, *summative* tests at the end of the course or program. A formative test can be *partial*, covering the last unit or two, or *cumulative*, covering everything learned up to that point in the program. Note that if all tests are cumulative, there is no need for a final exam at the end of the course.

Tests can be *norm-referenced* or *criterion-referenced* in regard to the analysis of their results. In norm-referenced tests, each student's score is compared to those of the other students. In criterion-referenced tests, passing depends on mastering a certain percentage of what must be learned, regardless of how other students are doing.

With respect to their content, tests can be *discrete-*

point or *integrative* (also "global"). Discrete-point tests measure knowledge of specific elements of the language, while integrative tests attempt to measure overall communication skills and underlying competence.

Pure tests measure one language skill only, via the same skill. *Hybrid* tests make use of two or more language skills and therefore do not measure one skill only. Particularly questionable is the validity of tests that claim to measure a language skill by making use of both audiolingual and graphic skills. Listening and speaking, on the other hand, quite naturally go together.

In a multiple-choice item the question is introduced by the *lead* (or "stem"), which is followed by the *options* (or "alternatives"). The options include a correct response and several incorrect responses or *distractors*.

Types of tests

There are four main types of tests: *aptitude, progress, achievement,* and *proficiency* tests.

Aptitude (or "prognostic") tests attempt to predict success in second language learning; their predictive validity is rather rough, as several factors other than aptitude enter into second language learning success.

Progress tests measure what the student has learned up to any point within a specific program with specific materials and conditions. Teacher-prepared tests are progress tests. The bulk of this chapter will deal with progress tests.

Achievement tests measure progress in second language learning but without reference to any particular program or set of materials. They permit therefore comparisons across programs. A good testing program combines teacher-prepared progress tests with standardized achievement tests at key points in the program, such as at the end of each level.

Proficiency tests measure what any person (not just a student) knows of the second language in reference to a particular use of the language --e.g., does this student know enough English to enter graduate studies at an American university? Does this foreign service officer know enough Spanish to handle consular work in Spain? Proficiency tests measure language knowledge regardless of how it has been acquired.

Two uses of some of these tests are the *diagnostic* function and the *placement* function. A test is performing a diagnostic function when it is used to determine the weaknesses of the students, that is, what it is they have not yet learned and must still learn. Then further instruction can be provided or the students can be directed to remedial work. Both progress and achievement tests can be used for this purpose. Diagnostic tests can be norm-referenced but are nearly always criterion-referenced. More emphasis should be placed on the diagnostic function of tests than on testing to grade or rank students.

A test is performing a placement function when it is used to determine the place of entry of a student in the program. Placement in beginning streams can be effected by means of aptitude tests. Placement somewhere in a program in progress can be effected by means of progress, achievement, or even proficiency tests.

Note that generally speaking proficiency tests are inadequate as a measure of progress. This is because, while overall language proficiency may be normally distributed, within a program there cannot be such marked differences between students at the same level, i.e., having completed the same materials. There are of course considerable differences, but not such that would show clearly in an overall proficiency test. If all students are more or less at the 0+ or 1 F.S.I. level (see Appendix C), a proficiency test cannot differentiate between them. For that reason, such proficiency tests as the F.S.I. interview and the cloze technique should be adapted if they are going to be used as progress tests.

Requirements for a good test

For a test to be acceptable, it must meet requirements of *reliability, validity,* and *practicality.*

Reliability refers to the stability of the scores. If students are given the same test again without any intervening learning, for the test to be reliable they should obtain approximately the same scores (some variation due to moods, attention, or circumstances makes perfect 1.0 reliability impossible). This is the *test-retest* approach to determining reliability. Another approach is to give *alternate forms* of a test and then correlate the ranks. A third approach, perhaps the most practical one, is the *split-half* technique, according to which the score ranks on odd-numbered items are correlated with those on even-numbered items. Lado [1961:335-8] provided step-by-step directions for the calculation of a split-half coefficient of reliability.

Unreliability may result from (1) differences in time

and circumstances, (2) limitations and imperfections of the test, and (3) scorer or examiner fluctuation [Lado 1961:330-1]. Reliability coefficients vary with the language component or skill being tested. Vocabulary, grammar, and reading have the highest reliability, then listening comprehension, then, lowest, writing and speaking. Thus, a reliability coefficient of .85 would be high for a speaking test but low for a reading test [Lado 1961:332].

Realistic forms of testing speaking and writing may have high face validity but low reliability. Examiner fluctuation is a particular problem with speaking tests. Scorer fluctuation is a serious problem with such writing tests as essays; for example, Finlayson [1951], after having six experienced teachers mark 200 children's essays on a scale of 0-20, found that there was a discrepancy of 20 percent between the *average* marks of the most lenient and the strictest markers. Others have found that the same marker may fluctuate considerably in marking the same essays at different times.

The reliability of a test can be increased by (1) asking more questions (the average of many quizzes *is* reliable), (2) increasing the number of options and the effectiveness of the distractors in multiple-choice items, and (3) having questions with a wide spread of difficulty, thus resulting in a greater spread of scores.

The importance of reliability lies in the fact that if a test is not reliable it cannot be valid. With wild fluctuations, nothing is being measured.

Validity refers to whether a test measures what it claims to measure and nothing else. *Face* validity refers to the impression one has upon inspection of the test. *Predictive* validity has to do with whether scores predict future performance (a correlation is established with an accepted criterion). *Concurrent* validity estimates the measurement of present performance (again, via correlation with an established criterion). *Content* validity has to do with how well the test samples the content of what is to be learned. *Construct* validity is based on an analysis of the psychological and linguistic factors involved in performance; aptitude tests, for example, claim construct validity. *Criterion* validity or simply *validity* refers to the basic question: Does the test test what it claims to test?

Some tests, such as the Rorschach inkblot tests, have little face or content validity but have good criterion validity. Certain language tests, such as the cloze test and textual dictation, seem to have little face or content validity but may be high in construct validity, as performing those tasks seems to call for the use of competence.

Regarding face validity, we should accept the fact that naturalness is no guarantee of validity. All tests are artificial, but no less valid because of that. If a test taps the right cognitive processes and performative knowledge, it does not matter if it is "artificial," that is, if its procedures do not resemble language use.

Practicality in a test refers to its scorability, administrability, and cost. An objective test that can be scored by machine is practically speaking preferable to one that requires elaborate human scoring. A test that is easy to administer and makes few time and manpower demands is preferable to one that requires much time or personnel. When many students have to be tested, cost becomes an important factor.

Another desirable feature of language tests is that they should limit themselves to linguistic and communicative competence. Test items that ask for interpretation, for example, are going beyond what a second language test should test.

Objective tests

What makes a test objective or subjective is the scoring. Objective test items have only one correct answer and many can be scored mechanically. Subjective tests rely on constructed answers that require human, and often quite difficult, scoring.

Objective tests were developed around the turn of the century. They have limited face validity, as they look artificial, while subjective tests are outwardly valid. However, objective tests are superior in other types of validity; they allow, for example, a much better sampling of the body of knowledge.

Objective tests take a long time to prepare, but much time is saved in their scoring. This allows for frequent testing, which is highly desirable. Objective tests give students a fairly precise idea of their progress. So not only should the teacher give such tests greater weight, but the students also tend to do so.

Objective tests are most useful with the receptive skills. Some objective items are possible for writing and speaking tests, and objectivity can be added to subjective scoring by predetermining quantified criteria, but for the productive skills it is necessary to use, occasionally, more subjective devices such as directed writing and interviews.

Objective test items include multiple-choice, true/false, matching, and open-ended items (fill-in or completion). Because of their high guess factor (50 percent), true/false items should be avoided. Pictures can be very ambiguous and should therefore be avoided as cues for objective items. Matching questions are acceptable, provided the lists are of unequal length; unless one list contains four or five options more than the other, the students can guess some of the answers by the process of elimination. With open-ended items, there is no guess factor and no need to present wrong options. They are particularly suited to the testing of productive skills; but care must be exerted not to make it possible for the testees to fill in blanks or complete incomplete sentences without reading and understanding the whole sentence.

Preparing a good multiple-choice item is difficult. It is particularly important to make sure that the distractors represent likely errors the student would have produced by himself, for if the wrong answers are unlikely, the item is a giveaway, a gift. The best way to obtain likely distractors is to give the test first as an open-ended test, and then select the distractors from the most common errors made by the students [Ingram 1974:323].

There is nothing wrong in using wrongly-formed answers as distractors: the students do not come to a test in order to *learn* what is presented to them but in order to *discriminate* between correct and incorrect [Ingram *ibid.*]. But the students should be informed in which particular sections of a test they will be exposed to wrong forms. Used judiciously, incorrect forms can be quite useful in determining whether interference and overgeneralizations have indeed been overcome. Morphologically and syntactically wrong options are no more wrong than lexically and contextually wrong options.

According to Lado [1961:191-2], multiple-choice items should: deal with learning problems; have clear short leads (the long ones test memory) in simple language, with sufficient but not excessive context; have only one right or best option; be independent of each other; have options that are as brief as possible; and make it impossible to choose the best option except through knowledge, i.e., provide no extraneous clues to the right answer. A common mistake is to write multiple-choice items that can be answered without considering all the options.

Note that multiple-choice items are not necessarily discrete-point items. They can be integrative in nature. For example, most of the questions in the listening comprehension and reading comprehension sections of the MLA Cooperative Foreign Language tests are integrative, they don't deal with individual elements.

Multiple-choice item analysis

To be useful, a multiple-choice item (1) must not be too difficult or too easy and (2) must discriminate between good students and poor students. These two criteria can be determined by means of two arithmetical formulas, the index of difficulty and the index of discrimination. These formulas are applied after a test has been given and there is multiple-choice data to analyze.

The index of difficulty is simply:

$$\frac{\text{Number of incorrect responses}}{\text{Number of examinees}}$$

Thus, if there are 40 students and 30 answer an item incorrectly, this would be a difficult item with an index of .75. On the other hand, if 10 answer an item incorrectly, this would be a rather easy item with a difficulty index of .25.

The ideal point of difficulty lies at the midpoint between chance (in the case of four-option items, .25) and a perfect response (1.0), that is, .625 for four-option items. Of course in practice a range below and above the ideal point is acceptable, for example .4 - .85 in the case of four-option items.

The index of discrimination is determined by comparing the number of correct answers among the best fourth of the students (according to raw score) with the number of correct answers among the worst fourth of the students (again according to raw score), for any particular item. (According to some statistical oddity, 27 percent of the students should constitute each group, but for all practical purposes 25 percent is quite adequate.)

The formula for item discrimination is therefore:

$$\frac{\text{No. correct in best fourth - No. correct in worst fourth}}{\frac{\text{No. of students in class}}{4}}$$

Thus, if 8 students in the best fourth of a 40-student class answered the item correctly, and 4 students in the worst fourth did, the index is .4 (8 - 4 / 10). If the same number from each fourth answered correctly, the index is 0. If more in the worst fourth answered correctly than in the best fourth, the index of discrimination for that item is negative. The index of discrimination should be .2 (positive) or higher --if it isn't, something is probably wrong with the item.

A tally of responses for each option will indicate whether an item is ambiguous and whether some of the distractors are useless in that they do not attract any students --for all practical purposes a four-option item with an unattractive distractor becomes a three-option item. In addition to ambiguity, an item may fail to discriminate because it tests something not taught or poorly taught (very few students answering correctly in the best fourth) or because it tests something learned by all the students (all answering correctly).

A good test will result in a good spread of scores, so that, for example, the best and the average scores will not be separated by only a few points. Item analysis can contribute to the development of a good test. According to the results of the item analysis, particular items can be modified or even replaced, with the result that the test is much improved.

Translation in testing

Translation items validly answer the question: Has interference on this point been overcome? Translation items can be used effectively with the four skills. As Lado pointed out [1961:243] in regard to speaking tests, the use of the native language as a stimulus allows us to give precise information without giving away clues to the response we want to elicit. Sewell [1974/75] made a strong case for the use of translation in testing reading comprehension. Oral translation is used in the reading part of the F.S.I. interview. In regard to writing, Matthews-Břeský [1972] considered translation a perfectly valid approach, the one that can best test certain aspects. Nickel [1975] strongly supported translation as one valid type of test.

When translation is used, however, there should be a delay between stimulus and response to process the idea; otherwise translation may proceed from language A surface to language B surface, resulting in many errors. Too, translation sentences should not contain a high concentration of grammatical and lexical problems, for this also increases greatly the difficulty level and the number of errors.

Stages in the history of language testing

Spolsky [1978-a] differentiated between three periods in second language testing: (1) "pre-scientific," prior to World War II; (2) "psychometric-structuralist," beginning in the 1950s; and (3) "integrative-sociolinguistic," characteristic of recent developments.

In fact, there is an overlap, and no testing specialist can be associated with one stage only. Even Lado, who is usually associated with the second stage and who emphasized isolated elements and contrastive analysis to excessive lengths, did not follow an exclusively psychometric approach. He called for global tests. He talked about the validation of test items on the basis of native speaker performance [1961:346] --this is criterion-referencing. He allowed the inclusion of too easy or too difficult items if the problems were part of the skills to be tested [*ibid.*, 349] and talked about basing test content on a sample of what is to be learned [*ibid.*, 20] --these are domain-referencing ideas.

Note that the forerunner of stage 3 was Carroll, who in 1961 first presented misgivings about discrete-point testing and called for integrative testing.

On aptitude tests

In Carroll's model of learning [1962], five factors account for success in school learning. Two instructional factors are adequacy of presentation (quality of instruction) and opportunity for learning (time allowed to learn). Three student factors are general intelligence, motivation (shown in perseverance, i.e., time devoted to learning), and aptitude (time needed to learn a task). Note that three of the five factors are related to time. Observe also that aptitude is only one of five factors.

The two standardized aptitude tests available today are Carroll and Sapon's Language Aptitude Test --MLAT-- [1959], with an Elementary version --EMLAT-- [1967], and the Pimsleur Language Aptitude Battery --LAB-- [1966-a]. They emphasize sound discrimination and sensitivity to structure. The LAB, by including verbal intelligence, grade-point-average, and interest in language study, attains higher predictive validity than the MLAT. But the LAB is suitable only for grades 7-9. For the lower grades (3-6) and the higher grades (10-adult) the EMLAT and the MLAT respectively should be used.

Pimsleur's LAB emphasizes auditory ability, as he concluded that the three major components of second language aptitude are verbal intelligence, motivation to learn, and auditory ability [1966-b:182]. In an earlier study [1964] he and others found that the main factor in underachievement in second languages (doing poorly in second languages while doing well in other subjects), a problem for 10-20 percent of students, was poor auditory ability.

It seems that both aptitude tests predict student success in inductive oral language study reasonably well. They are probably poor predictors of success in deductive courses. Gardner and Lambert [1972], Racle [1975:166], and Krashen [1978:8-10] all claimed that one or both of the current aptitude tests relate to formal learning but not to the *acquisition* of communication skills, for which motivation and attitudinal factors seem to be more important, as they would determine the degree of contact with native speakers. Is it the case that aptitude tests reflect only ability for formal linguistic operations? Savignon [1972:63] apparently disagreed. She found that MLAT scores correlated highly (.80) with scores for the French communicative competence of students who had had communicative activities throughout the term.

It should be noted that the current aptitude tests can only mean anything if administered to educated native speakers of English. Sections 2 and 4 of the MLAT (section 4 is even difficult for native speakers) and sections 3 and 6 of the LAB are not valid for non-native speakers of English. For use by the latter, the tests would have to be translated.

According to Politzer and Weiss [1966] language aptitude can be increased by second language learning or by study skills classes. Aptitude also increases with age but decreases during maturity.

How can aptitude test scores be used? The first thing to realize is that second language aptitude is not a special gift only some have. All have some aptitude, and with adequate motivation and time, all normal people can learn a second language. Using aptitude test scores to exclude students from a program can only be justified in such special programs where selection is essential, in which case aptitude test scores can drastically reduce the cost of the selection process. But aptitude test scores should not be used to exclude students from regular programs. After all, aptitude is only one of at least five factors of success. Besides, as Sandstrom and Pimsleur [1970] pointed out, we cannot know whom to exclude, for we do not know who will need a second language later in life, who will travel abroad, or whose future educational and career opportunities will require a second language.

In programs where students are placed in fast, average, and slow classes, however, aptitude test scores would be quite useful for initial placement. Aptitude test scores are also quite useful in research in second language learning. By measuring their aptitude, we can make sure that there is no major difference in this respect between experimental and control students, a difference that would invalidate the results of an experiment.

Discrete-point and integrative (global) tests

Discrete-point test items are independent (they can be answered in isolation) and test control over particular rules and elements. Oller [1976-b] defined discrete-point tests as requiring isolated skills, aspects of skills, components of skills, and discrete elements of skills. Integrative tests, on the other hand, measure overall language proficiency. As already mentioned, Carroll [1961] first called for tests of total communicative ability. Such integrative tests include the cloze technique, textual dictation, oral interviews, tests of listening and reading comprehension, and free, unaided composition.

Extreme statements have been made against discrete-point tests and in favor of integrative tests. Oller [1972-b], for example, said that a sampling of 50,000 discrete points would still not constitute a test of language competence. But linguistic competence seems to be composed of (1) control over rules and elements, whose attainment constitutes the bulk of language learning, and (2) the integration of those rules and elements into a working whole --so discrete-point tests measure most of language competence. Farhady [1978] in fact found a correlation of .87 between the discrete-point and the integrative subsections of a standardized ESL test (from Farhady [1979-a:352]). It is possible to conclude then that discrete-point tests and integrative tests provide very similar results rather than being opposite ends of a continuum. They don't test the same thing, but obviously there is much overlap, so that perhaps both types of test measure a general second language proficiency factor [Oller 1976-a:166]. Farhady's conclusion [1979-a:354] was that there seems to be "virtually no difference between discrete-point and integrative tests in what they measure or their results."

Both types of tests are needed, as they correspond to the two aspects of linguistic competence specified above. Progress tests should rely primarily on discrete-point items, both because second language teaching is done point by point and because the testing of particular rules and elements can be more objective. But at least one section of each progress test should be integrative in nature, since rules and elements need to be interrelated in the mind of the successful learner. Test sections should also be used that combine the best of discrete-point and integrative testing --an example is "rational multiple-choice cloze," to be discussed in the section on the testing of reading; another example is progress interviews, to be discussed under the testing of speaking. Perhaps the earliest progress tests in the program, however, should be limited to discrete-point items, as the integration of rules has not yet taken effect.

Proficiency tests can consist primarily of integrative techniques, as these are an economic way to obtain a fairly accurate measurement of general proficiency. However, discrete-point sections should also be included. This is because students from different cultural backgrounds score differently in discrete-point and integrative subtests [Farhady 1979-c]. It is also because certain integrative techniques do not measure language ability with sufficient specificity, as may be the case for essays and interviews.

With the debate about the merits of these two types of tests and what they measure still going on, the conviction has emerged that the reason that cloze tests, textual dictation, oral interviews, essays, etc. correlate strongly with each other is that they tap the same ability --a general language ability or general language proficiency factor [Oller 1976-a]. The problem is that they also correlate highly with general intelligence. So we are left with the possibility that integrative tests may not really be second language tests after all, for as long as second language proficiency is not separated from general ability factors second language testing cannot be said to exist.

Norm-referenced and criterion-referenced tests

Cziko [1981] discussed the differences between

psychometric and *edumetric* tests. Psychometric tests differentiate examinees maximally and compare them --typical is the *norm-referenced* test, which ranks students. Edumetric tests yield scores without reference to other examinees. They include *domain-referenced* tests, concerned with ensuring that course content adequately represents what needs to be learned, and *criterion-referenced* tests, concerned with the degree of mastery over the course material. (But note that maximally-differentiating items can also represent domains of knowledge.)

Whether a test is norm-referenced or criterion-referenced depends on the use that is made of its scores, not necessarily on the content of the test. Usually, however, the content differs in that norm-referenced tests include high discriminating items and do not include items that everyone can answer correctly. So norm-referenced tests may not accurately reflect what the student *does* know [Jorstad 1974:230].

The norms of norm-referenced tests are scores of groups of examinees whose characteristics are known, thereby allowing a valid comparison. From the point of view of the examinee, the problem with norm-referenced tests is that he is not competing against the subject matter but against other examinees, so that a poor score can lead to feelings of inferiority and therefore to a dislike for the second language program and a desire to leave it.

Criterion-referenced tests, related to mastery learning, were the major language test development of the late '60s and the '70s, corresponding to the individualization movement. The criterion of performance is what the bilingual native speaker of the second language would do, that is, 100 percent, and lower criteria are related to that (e.g., 80 percent of that), not to what other examinees may do. Good criterion-referenced tests require very specific learning objectives, representative of the performance of the native speaker and chosen for their validity and appropriateness. The student's performance is measured against criteria for the mastery of such objectives. Either he knows what he was told to learn and moves on in the program or he goes back to review in order to take an alternate version of the test later. (Obviously this requires a self-paced learning program.)

Testing grid

The testing possibilities discussed in the remaining sections of this chapter, both discrete-point and integrative, can be represented by a testing grid as shown in Figure 21.1. (Culture has been left out.) The boxes in Figure 21.1 have been filled with only one or two of the various possible testing activities.

Testing linguistic competence and communicative competence

In testing, it helps to keep in mind the distinction between linguistic and communicative competence. It is a distinction between formal performance and expressive performance [Valette 1977:18-9].

All term or major tests should test both linguistic and communicative competence. Partial formative tests, however, should concentrate on linguistic competence. Testing linguistic competence alone is valid, for it does not lead to errors in communication. Testing communicative competence alone, however, whether as a separate test or as part of a larger test, is not desirable if it is done with disregard for linguistic accuracy --this encourages linguistic carelessness.

Testing the elements

Despite the current trend toward integrative testing techniques, the fact remains that the elements need to be tested in the second language program. Progress tests must test the elements. As Lado noted [1961:27], success in a situational test does not guarantee knowledge of the language, for situational tests have "only the outward appearance of validity."

But while progress tests must test the elements, proficiency tests can concentrate on global proficiency with relatively little attention to elements. Elements should be tested nonsituationally, overall proficiency situationally. Elements and skills need not be tested separately from each other: it is possible to test a sampling of elements within each skill.

Testing the components

To avoid overloading the student's attention with many different things at the same time, progress tests should test the components of phonology, graphemics, grammar, and vocabulary separately. That is, one thing should be tested at a time. Well-known lexical items should be used in the grammar sections of tests, and well-known grammar in their vocabulary sections. In scoring tests --other than their integrative sections--, pronunciation, grammar, and vocabulary should be evaluated separately, that is, in separate subsections, concentrating on one

TESTING GRID

	LISTENING	SPEAKING	READING	WRITING
PHONOLOGY	Sound discrimination	Sound production	Reading aloud Rhyme	-----
GRAPHEMICS	Dictation	-----	Grapheme identification	Grapheme production
GRAMMAR	Sensitivity to deviance	Drills Directed dialogue	Sensitivity to deviance	Drills Directed writing
VOCABULARY	Visually-cued vocabulary Auditory multiple-choice	Lexical translation drills	Graphic multiple-choice	Lexical translation drills
INTEGRATIVE	LISTENING TEST	SPEAKING TEST	READING TEST	WRITING TEST
	SL to NL interpretation	NL to SL interpretation	SL to NL translation	NL to SL translation
	ORAL INTERVIEW		CLOZE TECHNIQUE	
	NOISE TEST			
	TEXTUAL DICTATION			

Figure 21.1

and ignoring the others in each subsection.

Basic to testing the components is the concept of interference. Component testing should be largely directed at finding out whether interference has been overcome in sounds, suprasegmentals, grammar, and vocabulary.

Testing phonology

The testing of phonology involves three aspects: (1) sound discrimination, (2) sound production, and (3) sounds relative to graphemes.

(1) *Testing discrimination*. Testing discrimination with "same" or "different" minimal pairs is much too easy. It is better to ask the student to match an utterance with one of three options, with "none" giving a fourth option.

Example (French /ü/ vs. /u/ and /i/):

The student hears:

vu A. *vit* B. *vous* C. *vu* D. *None*

He sees:

A B C D

and circles his choice.

Suprasegmentals can also be tested via multiple choice, by asking the students to circle the number corresponding to the stressed syllable (preferably they should have a text with numbers written above each syllable) or by choosing between lines representing various possible intonations for a phrase, which they hear.

(2) *Testing production*. While there can be year-round informal evaluation of pronunciation in the classroom, phonological production should also be tested formally.

"Pronunciation" items matching words by spelling, such as some proposed by Lado [1961], do not really test pronunciation, for they say nothing about how the students pronounce the words.

The most convenient way to test pronunciation is by asking the students to record their imitation of a number of short phrases. Imitation is a valid test of pronunciation: whatever sounds a student can't imitate he cannot produce by himself either; what he can imitate he can produce when speaking carefully. (Careful pronunciation is hindered by attention to meaning and by the fluency of the communication process; but don't we want to measure the students' pronunciation at its best?)

In each phrase to be imitated no more than two or three sounds should be scored. An evaluation of individual sounds is far more reliable than a global pronunciation score.

I have found that it's best to score each key sound on a 1-0 basis. Either it is right, the way (or one of the ways) a native would say it, or it is wrong, containing one or more deviations from the native norm. There is no logically defensible 5-point or even 3-point scale for sounds --besides, such scales make scoring very difficult and subjective.

Imitation tests should include not only familiar words but also unfamiliar ones, about half and half. Using only familiar words would make it much too easy.

To test the production of intonation, perhaps the best technique is to ask the students to record a simple dialogue for which native language cues are given. The dialogue should not contain anything new, just a recombination of known rules and elements.

Note that when we test production we are also testing discrimination, as the students presumably can hear any distinction they can produce.

(3) *Testing the relationship of sounds to letters*. The students can demonstrate their awareness of the relationship of sounds to letters by reading aloud and (in English) by identifying words that rhyme. Since cognates may present pronunciation problems due to the misinterpretation of spelling, G. Wilkins and Hoffman [1964] recommended that they be used in pronunciation tests of the reading-aloud type; they found them to be reliable indicators of level of achievement in pronunciation.

Testing graphemics

For the identification of graphemes, one can use an oral word to be matched to written multiple choices. Thus, for students whose native language does not use the Roman alphabet, the potential problem of confusing ≪b≫, ≪d≫, and ≪h≫ can be tested by their hearing the word *bay* and choosing among the printed options *bay, day, hay,* and *None*.

For the production of graphemes, testing can take the form of word dictation, either with letter blanks or with no help on the students' papers. The teaching and testing of sound/spelling patterns is, by the way, the only function of word dictation.

Testing grammar

Testing grammar through listening, one can use multiple-choice items whose distractors include (1) common student errors or (2) correct words inappropriate to their context. There is nothing wrong in using common student errors, and much valid about it, provided that the students are told that in that section of the test they will hear incorrect language.

Testing grammar through speaking, one can use most of the drills and exercises discussed in Chapter 17. It is also possible to have directed dialogue, with instructions in the native language so as not to give away much of the answers.

Written multiple-choice grammar items can, like listening items, test the students' sensitivity to deviance.

For writing, various types of drills and exercises can be used, as well as a variety of forms of directed writing.

Testing vocabulary

Auditory multiple-choice items can be used, calling for synonyms, antonyms, answers to brief definitions, or the word that best completes a sentence. Auditory input can be aided by means of visual cues.

In speaking, vocabulary can be elicited by means of lexical translation drills, that is, what we referred to in Chapter 18 as "bilingual vocabulary expansion exercises," except that here only their testing phase would be used.

In reading, the multiple-choice items are presented in written form. Written words can also be matched to pictures.

In writing, vocabulary is elicited from the student monolingually, in the form of sentence completions, or bilingually, in the form of lexical translation exercises.

In the case of idioms, the students can be asked to paraphrase them or translate them.

Testing appropriateness

Second language students should not only know how to say something but also when to say it. At the late intermediate and advanced levels, awareness of appropriateness can be tested via multiple-choice items. Farhady [1979-b] developed a multiple-choice ESL test of appropriateness ("Functional Test for English as a Second Language at UCLA"). As an example of an appropriateness question, testees can be asked whether a student should say to a professor:

1. I'd appreciate it if you could give me some advice.
2. I want you to give me some advice.
3. I wonder if you could give some advice for me.
4. Hey, give me some advice.
5. *None of the above.*

Testing the skills

All the skills taught should be tested, in proportion to the emphasis given to them in the teaching program. The receptive skills are not easy to evaluate informally but easy to test formally. On the other hand, the productive skills are easier to evaluate informally but difficult to test formally, especially because of the time involved in grading such tests. For that reason, the receptive skills should be tested frequently, the productive skills only on major tests. But it is essential that they be tested.

In addition to emphasizing the receptive skills and occasionally testing the productive skills, there is a natural progression from testing the mechanical aspects of skills to testing their meaningful aspects. The two factors give us the testing progression shown in Figure 21.2.

TESTING PROGRESSION

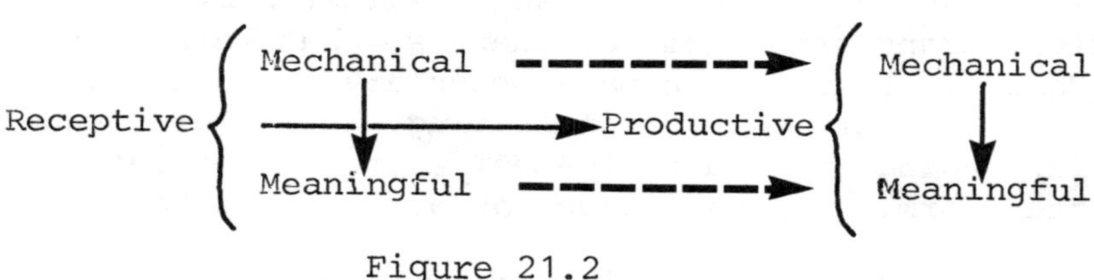

Figure 21.2

A skill should be tested, whenever possible, through that skill only. Thus written answers are of doubtful validity in tests of listening, speaking, or reading. The important thing, especially early in the program, is to keep the spoken and the written language apart. So it is acceptable for a speaking test to combine listening and speaking, since it is the way they occur in real communication; but combining listening and reading, or speaking and writing reduces the validity of a test as a *skill* progress test, as much as it may be a valid procedure in an overall proficiency test.

Testing listening

The testing of the various components via listening has already been discussed. Here we shall concentrate on the global testing of listening comprehension.

It is important that integrative tests of listening comprehension (and this applies also to reading comprehension) should not measure knowledge of particular words or rules but general understanding. There is a tendency in particular to test vocabulary rather than comprehension.

Among the procedures that can be used to test listening comprehension (cf. Valette [1977:102-10]) are the following:

--Measuring understanding of the gist of a story, narration, news item, description, etc.; here just the main idea is involved.

--Asking multiple-choice questions on the content of an audio passage; here more detailed questions are involved.

--Asking the students to obtain information from an audio passage or follow instructions given in it.

--Asking the students to relay oral messages, such as telephone messages.

--At the intermediate and advanced levels, textual dictation, sentence by sentence, of recombination materials.

--At the advanced level, having the students take notes from lectures.

--Also at the advanced level, measuring comprehension under adverse conditions: on the telephone, with background noise, or at very rapid speed (normal speed should be used from the beginning, although with pauses between sentences at first).

Some suggestions for listening test item presentation follow:

--Listening items of the multiple-choice type should be read twice. This reduces or eliminates the factor of auditory memory. Without two readings, it is easy to miss or forget an option or even part of the lead.

--If pictures are used, there should be at least four. Questions with only two or three pictures are too easy.

--Where rapid speech, with its deletions and assimilations, is normal in a given context, it should be used, even early. Of course, such speech should be used in teaching.

Testing speaking

First of all let me emphasize the importance of testing speaking. As Lado wrote in 1961 [p. 239], "...testing the ability to speak a foreign language is perhaps the least developed and the least practiced in the language testing field." The main reason speaking should be tested is that it increases student motivation to learn to speak. As Pimsleur [1966-b:206] pointed out, students mostly put forth effort into what affects their grades, so it is "absolutely essential" to test speaking if we want to teach the speaking skill.

Informal evaluations of speaking ability, however frequent, are not enough: the students give more importance to grades that are based on formal tests. So if the students are to take oral goals seriously, the speaking skill must be tested formally, at least two or three times per term.

The neglect of oral testing observed by Lado is still present today, despite rather frequent pleas that communication be included in second language tests. Tests of global listening/speaking ability (or of communicative competence, which is the same) continue to be the stepchild of second language testing.

Of course, many second language teachers cannot test speaking skill formally. They have no language laboratories for lab tests and have too many students for interviews. The solution for them is to announce that a considerable part of the term grade (at least one third) will be based on the evaluation of speaking ability in the classroom. Then they can mark a few students each day; it isn't possible to give every student a daily speaking mark. At the end of the term, they should have several speaking marks for each student, the average of which is his speaking grade for the term. Speaking grades should be handed out every month or two. This system is not ideal --for one thing, it is rather subjective--, but the results that can be obtained with it are far better than if the speaking skill is not graded.

Many speaking test techniques have been suggested, but only a few lend themselves to regular programs lacking an overabundance of personnel and time. J. Clark [1972-a] distinguished two types of speaking tests: *monologue* and *conversational*. The problem with monologue techniques, such as asking a student to talk about a topic or to tell a story represented by a series of pictures, is that its evaluation is very difficult, for some students will make a few correct but very simple remarks while more adventurous students may talk at length and in the process make many errors. That leaves conversational techniques as the more useful ones; several will be discussed in this section.

Further on the use of pictures, note that pictorial stimuli very often fail to elicit many of the responses we want, so their use should be generally avoided in formal speaking tests. Besides, talking about pictures is some steps removed from a conversational exchange, which is basically what integrative speaking tests should have.

From the start the students should be told that they are to try to speak accurately, that linguistic accuracy will be an important part of the speaking grade. If this is not done, inaccurate extroverts will get the best grades. We should remember that in schools we are not teaching merely linguistic survival but educated second language performance.

The scoring of speaking tests should be agreed upon in advance. Scorers can be trained and given quantified criteria, the result being considerable interscorer reliability.

A very useful speaking test technique is directed dialogue with instructions in the native language. It combines directed response, role-playing, and interpretation. It has been in some use at least since 1947, when it was used as Part III (Conversation) of the achievement test in the Investigation of Second Language Teaching [Agard and Dunkel 1948:56-60]. It is especially suitable for lab speaking tests.

Another useful technique is straight oral translation or interpretation. By using the native language in this manner, previously learned second language items can be elicited and these can in turn be graded objectively. About oral translation in testing, Pimsleur [1966-b:200] said that it is more reliable than pictures and that giving oral native language stimuli is not really translation in the traditional sense --the native language sentences "merely provide an input of information to be transmitted in [the second language] by the student," who simply cannot use word-by-word translation.

Still another useful technique is to describe a number of situations and ask the student to say the one line that fits those situations [Fabian 1973].

The use of the language laboratory to give speaking tests has its advocates and its opponents. The popularity of language laboratories has come and (at least for the time being) gone, but even during their heyday they were seldom used to test speaking. Even in institutions that have excellent laboratory facilities, these are seldom used to give speaking tests.

One objection to the labs is their artificiality --but what *isn't* artificial in a second language program? Real conversation is only possible outside the second language program, in the real world where the second language is not being learned but is used exclusively for communicative purposes. Another objection is that the equipment makes the students nervous --but if the lab has been used extensively as part of the learning process, the students will not find it threatening at all. It is true that in the lab the students do not benefit from gestures and facial expressions, but neither would they on the telephone. A further objection is that, because lab tests are very time-consuming to prepare, the answers cannot be given out as feedback --this is true, but neither is detailed feedback given for a face-to-face interview; furthermore, much feedback can be given for a lab test, in terms of points for each skill, each grammatical subsection, pronunciation, vocabulary, and simulated conversation.

Oral testing in the laboratory has certain definite advantages. It allows for objectivity in scoring. It provides the same testing conditions for everybody. It makes mass oral testing possible, no doubt the greatest advantage. It also makes it possible to provide the students with self-administered practice tests of the listening and speaking skills; before major tests they could have previews of their formats.

For the efficient scoring of lab tests, only the student answers should be recorded, leaving out all instructions, examples, and pauses, so that the resulting cassette would have just student answers, one right after the other. This is best done by means of remote-control student equipment, via a silent-track controlling relay. However, remote-control equipment is not essential; the students can operate the "record" and "stop" controls manually, and if necessary all instructions and questions can be read aloud by the teacher. Voice-operated relays are not desirable, as they usually cut off the first sound or two of each utterance. In order to avoid pauses on the final tape, the students should be directed to start recording all together (after an appropriate pause to think of the answer) and to stop the tape as soon as they have completed their answers. The master tape pauses for the student answers should be long enough that even slow students can answer but not so long that poor students can listen to the better students and imitate their responses. The students should answer each item only once --answering twice brings on serious grading complications; furthermore, it makes it possible for poor students to imitate good students. Directions (in the native language) and examples for each section should be clear and should be read twice.

The ideal laboratory progress speaking test for the beginning level (after that, phonology need not be tested as it should be fully under control) would take about 15-18 minutes to administer and three to four minutes to score each student's cassette, and it would consist of four parts: pronunciation, grammar, vocabulary, and simulated conversation. The pronunciation part would consist of the imitation of five short phrases, each containing two key sounds or suprasegmental features, for a total of 10 points (of course the students would not know which sounds are being tested, nor could they read anything). In this part, everything would be recorded, without pauses to think. The grammar section would have three drills of five sentences each, each drill dealing with one grammatical rule, for a total of 15 points. In this section, there would be instructions and examples preceding each drill (read twice); the sentences would be short and simple, and for each there would be a 10-second pause to think (not recorded) and then seven seconds to record the answer. The vocabulary part would consist of five short sentences for oral translation, containing a total of 10 lexical items being tested. Each sentence would be read twice, followed by the usual pause to think and a shorter time to record the answer. Finally, there would be a simulated conversation, with native speakers participating in some of the roles and the student being told (in the native language, twice) what to say, which he would record in his own words, each time after a pause to think. The length of the simulated conversation and the length of the sentences the students should say would increase as the program progresses; at the early beginning level a simulated conversation of five short sentences (at three points each, for a total of 15) seems to work out very well. The point totals for this early speaking test would therefore be: 10 for pronunciation, 15 for grammar, 10 for vocabulary, and 15 for the simulated conversation, for a total of 50 points.

As the program progresses, the emphasis given to each section of this basic speaking test would change. There would be no pronunciation section beyond the late beginning level. At the intermediate level, more emphasis would be placed (and scoring weight given to) grammar and vocabulary. At the advanced level, most of the grammar should have been mastered, so emphasis would shift to vocabulary and to longer and more complex simulated conversations.

I used speaking tests such as the one described above for many years, with very satisfactory results. Not the least of their advantages is that native assistants can easily be trained as scorers. Another advantage is that they permit giving the students considerable feedback in the form of points per section and subsection.

If the number of students is small enough to permit it, progress interviews can be given, in alternation with lab tests or as the only type of oral test if there is no lab. Unlike overall proficiency interviews, which take 15 minutes or longer, progress interviews can be conducted in about five minutes. But even five-minute interviews require an inordinate amount of time if given regularly to large classes; the solution is not to give them frequently but perhaps only about twice per term if lab tests cannot be given, and maybe only once per term if they can.

Unlike a proficiency interview, a progress interview covers specific material that has been studied, so it is possible to prepare in advance a short list of fairly specific questions. These questions should be on a series of cards, one set per interviewer, and each card should have four or five alternate questions of similar difficulty using the same structure, so that different students can be asked parallel questions. Preparation in advance should include possible "ice-breakers" and closings. The questions on which the students will be evaluated should get them to talk a little within what they know or should know by that point in the program. They should not ask for the verbatim or near-verbatim reproduction or summary of something learned in class.

Scoring an interview is not as difficult as it might seem. I have found the scale in Figure 21.3 quite useful. In addition to using five scoring points for each criterion, it is also possible to give each criterion numerical values, but then the weight given each criterion would have to be changed depending on the level of the program at which the interview is given. For example, pronunciation should have considerable weight at the early beginning level but not at the advanced level, and fluency should have the reverse emphasis. Other criteria have been suggested in the literature: comprehensibility, amount of communication, effort to communicate, and so forth. Comprehensibility has the difficulty that a bilingual teacher cannot judge this quality as a monolingual native would. Amount of communication rewards extroverts,

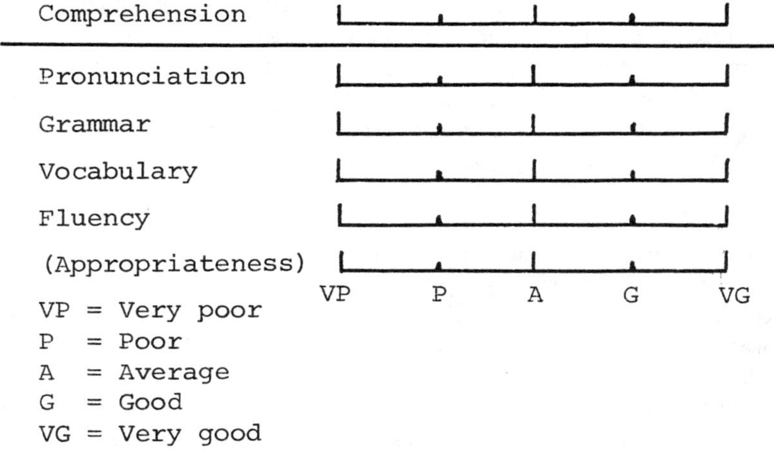

Figure 21.3

that is, it is more a measure of personality than of linguistic and communicative competence. I fail to see how the criterion "effort to communicate" can be evaluated objectively. The criterion "appropriateness" appears in parentheses in Figure 21.3 because it is a criterion that should be applied mostly at the advanced level --beginning and intermediate students have too much difficulty getting simply understood to worry much about appropriateness.

The use of the rating scale suggested above, plus the use of checklists, plus the training of interviewers can bring much objectivity and considerable reliability to the process of scoring interviews. During the interview it is quite possible to score a student simultaneously on the four or five criteria being used, as well as mark a checklist.

Although it is possible for only one person to conduct the interviews, ideally it should be done by two people. In the latter case, one person mostly asks the questions and the other mostly observes, although both can mark printed scales as the interview progresses. At the end of the interview, after the student has left, the two examiners put the final marks on their scales and calculate the average of the two evaluations as the final grade. During the interview, both examiners should face the student, keeping their printed scales behind open books or clipboards. Nothing makes an interviewee more nervous than having someone sit behind his back to score him.

As feedback, each student should be given, after all the interviews in a given testing session are over, a copy of his marked scales and checklist.

To train interviewers, the best method is to play and discuss video-tapes or recordings of previous interviews and then have them grade such previous interviews as supervised practice.

Testing reading

Reading tests can measure control of grammar, vocabulary, and global reading comprehension. All three can be measured by means of multiple-choice items. In the case of grammar, in a separate section clearly so labelled, distractors with incorrect morphology and syntax representing typical student errors can be used. In the case of vocabulary, the lead can ask for a synonym, an antonym, a hyponym, or the best completion. For global reading comprehension, texts of various kinds can be used, including signs, schedules, advertisements, menus, and other texts present in the second culture.

The global comprehension section of reading tests should have a time limit, for otherwise the text will be checked many times, thereby making the test too easy. There should be specially prepared reading tests; just using auditory materials in printed form is not adequate, as reading differs from speaking in style and range of vocabulary.

Preparing a good reading test is time-consuming. For that reason, reading tests should be kept secure. Rather than distribute them after grading, the feedback given should be limited to posting a detailed distribution of scores per subsection.

It does not seem valid to test reading comprehension through translation. The students may lack the productive control of the *native* language needed to convey all the nuances of the second language text, even though they may understand the text quite well.

A possible substitute for long reading tests with numerous passages and questions is the "rational multiple-choice cloze" technique. This consists of a single continuous passage in which certain words are blanked out --not every *n*th word but rationally, by choosing "points of difficulty"-- and below each blank four options are given, three words or phrases and "None" for option "D." As the students read the passage, they circle the best option for each blank. This type of test combines the advantages of discrete-point tests with the advantages of integrative tests --it can test knowledge of any grammatical or lexical point and at the same time requires overall awareness of meaning and context for successful completion. Preliminary studies with this type of test have shown that the same passage can discriminate between students at the end of two, three, or four semesters of college Spanish. A study of concurrent validity is in progress as of this writing.

Testing writing

Second language tests should not have a heavy emphasis on writing, for this draws student effort away from the audiolingual skills. Especially to be avoided is constant written translation, a legacy of the Grammar-Translation Method which has done our students a great deal of harm (although certain limited uses of translation in testing writing may be desirable).

The main reason why writing should not be emphasized is that it is the least useful and the most artificial of the four intralingual skills, evidence of which is the fact that many native speakers of English never master the art of writing in their native language. Whatever writing is taught and tested in the second language program, then, should be everyday writing, not creative writing of which very few people are capable even *after* thoroughly learning their native language.

To test punctuation, spelling or morphology, test texts can be handed out in which punctuation marks, letters or morphemes have been omitted. Grammar (both morphology and syntax) can be tested by means of the various types of drills discussed in Chapter 17, and also by several forms of directed writing. Dehydrated sentences such as *John / Mary / go / restaurant / dinner* or *Hier / mon / tante / aller / église* can serve to test agreement and the use of function words. (Incidentally, in many languages the use of infinitives as cue words is perfectly justified --the infinitive is a basic form from which other forms can be derived, it occurs in several common constructions, and it is the dictionary entry form of verbs.) Vocabulary can also be tested in writing tests by means of completions or by means of bilingual lexical drills (as you will recall, these are translation drills with a second language model sentence and a fixed pattern). Completion items, however, should not be bilingual, as this makes thinking in either language impossible. The two languages should never be mixed within the same sentence --only ideas can be successfully transferred from one language to another.

Where there is known to be potential interference, testing should be via translation, in order to determine if the interference has been overcome. This applies especially to certain grammatical rules, but also to other aspects of the language.

As writing tests, free compositions or essays provide neither an adequate sample --the students can avoid most problem areas-- nor the opportunity for objective scoring. Compositions are not real acts of communication --what is being communicated by whom to whom? They are an artifice of the school situation. The billions of hours that have been spent by language students writing compositions and by teachers grading them could have been used much more profitably on audiolingual skills, reading, and everyday writing. Several of the criteria used in marking compositions --style, originality of ideas, and the imaginative use of language, for example-- are in no sense part of linguistic or communicative competence.

It is far better to test global writing ability through more limited, less ambitious activities such as various forms of directed writing --rewriting texts using another subject or tense, or from another point of view, taking messages, writing letters, summarizing passages, writing dialogues from dehydrated sentence cues, taking notes, answering advertisements, applying for various things, and so forth.

Testing knowledge of the second culture

If a knowledge of the second culture is considered an important goal --and I think it should be--, it should be tested.

Both informational and achievement culture can be easily tested by means of objective paper-and-pencil techniques --multiple-choice, matching, fill-in. In testing these two types of cultural knowledge, however, one should be careful not to test items of questionable authenticity and relevancy, especially those that "can be correctly answered by a superficial familiarity with geographical and historical facts" [Seelye 1968:69-70].

Behavioral culture testing should not only concentrate on how people in the second culture behave but also on their views about themselves and others. Individual testing could involve actually behaving as in the second culture, but few classes are small enough to allow such testing --in the vast majority of cases, what is needed is mass testing techniques. Here the culture assimilator, minus the feedback, seems the most suitable testing device. Pictorial cueing is also possible.

The fact that most behavioral culture statements are "probability statements" rather than uncontestable truths [Nostrand 1974] should not be a barrier to testing. Multiple-choice items can deal quite well with probability statements.

Measuring attitudes

At certain points, especially at the beginning of the second language program, it is useful to determine student attitudes. Attitudes can be measured in many ways, but two useful questionnaires are the Jakobovits Foreign Language Attitude Questionnaire [Jakobovits 1970-a] and the Dufort Foreign Language Attitude Scale [Dufort 1962]. Jorstad [1974:262], however, noted that the Jakobovits FLAQ has difficult language that makes it unsuitable for the schools and that the Dufort FLAS seems to be too general, so perhaps better questionnaires need to be developed.

Evaluating learning styles

Lepke [1978] reviewed five instruments used to measure individual learning styles. These were also discussed by Valette and Linder [1979:206-8]. They are the following: Dunn *et al.* [1975], J.E. Hill [n.d.], Hunt [n.d.], Papalia [1976:16-7], and Reinert [1977]. They variously use responses to words, scales, answers to questions, paragraph completions, etc. The development of a valid and reliable standardized test of learning styles seems to be still in the future.

Integrative proficiency tests: the cloze technique

Cloze tests were first used by W.L. Taylor [1953] to measure the readability of native language texts; they have been the object of much research in second language testing since the late '60s. In a cloze test, every nth word (usually every fifth or seventh word) is blanked and the testee is expected to fill these gaps. Cloze tests can be scored by the exact word method, in which case not even natives get close to 100 percent correct responses, or by the acceptable word method, which is more valid but poses serious complications in scoring.

Since many educated natives are not good at completing cloze tests, Carroll *et al.* [1959] concluded that what cloze tests measure is somewhat independent of competence. Cloze tests give scores that allow a general separation of the proficient from the nonproficient, or the natives from the non-natives [J. Oller and Conrad 1971, J. Oller 1973-a, Stubbs and Tucker 1974, Hinofotis 1976, many others]; however, they do not do this consistently [Alderson 1980]. In some settings, they have been found to discriminate between several levels of proficiency within second language programs [Cziko *et al.* 1977, Brière *et al.* 1978], so they have at least the potential of being used as progress tests, especially if modified as will be discussed below.

Scores on cloze tests have been found to correlate highly with other tests. Darnell [1970] found a correlation of .84 between a cloze test and total scores on the Test of English as a Foreign Language. Alderson [1979] concluded that cloze tests correlate better with tests of grammar and vocabulary than tests of reading comprehension; they also seem to relate more closely to low-order core proficiency tests than to higher-order tests. Caulfield and Smith [1981] found a correlation of .90 between either a cloze test or a noise test and the total MLA score at the end of level II high school Spanish.

In regard to the frequency of the blanks, Alderson [1980] found that the mere amount of context was not a crucial factor among non-native speakers. As to scoring methods, the semantically-acceptable procedure results in better discrimination between natives and non-natives than the exact word procedure, as it enables natives to fill correctly close to 100 percent of the blanks [J.C. Anderson 1979]. The acceptable word method also reduces the probability of "gyps" (the examinee losing a point for something he knows --Cziko [1981]) and makes the test more sensitive to differences in proficiency [J. Oller 1972-a, Alderson 1979]. "Clozentropy," a scoring method that weights acceptable answers according to their frequency of use by native speakers in a pretest [Darnell 1970, Reilly 1971] seems to be the most valid procedure. But note that scoring by the acceptable word procedure is quite cumbersome, and clozentropy could only be done efficiently with a computer.

Certain misgivings have been raised about cloze tests. Carroll [1973] noted that cloze tests have little or no diagnostic power and so could only be used as summative tests. Garcia-Zamor and Krowitz [1974] pointed out that cloze tests do not test communicative ability and that, furthermore, scores are affected by the irritation this type of test causes in some examinees.

Porter [1976] correctly claimed that the cloze test is not a valid test of reading comprehension, as language production is involved. He suggested adapting the cloze test for receptive purposes by turning every blank into a multiple-choice item. Using multiple-choice cloze procedures, Jonz [1976] found a correlation of .66 with a college ESL placement test. Huser [1979] found correlations of .86 (N 47) and .77 (N 107) between a multiple-choice cloze test and much longer ESL entrance exams at two Brazilian universities. The options for a multiple-choice cloze test can be chosen from the wrong responses in a standard cloze test administration. Multiple-choice cloze tests offer a tremendous time saving in scoring over standard cloze tests.

Another modification of cloze tests --one that, together with the use of multiple choices, may make cloze tests very useful within second language programs-- is the use of rationally as opposed to randomly chosen blanks. By the rational selection of blanks it is possible to test the particular grammatical and lexical problems the students may have at any level, in addition to testing their global comprehension and competence. Thus, rationally-blanked, multiple-choice cloze tests could be used at any level of the second language program after the introduction of reading. They would combine the best of discrete-point tests with the characteristics of integrative tests.

A further development in cloze testing is the "reverse cloze" technique or "editing task" developed by Davies [1975] and also proposed by Bowen [1978]. It consists in the random introduction of extraneous words in a text, which the examinees are expected to circle or cross out within a limited time. Mullen [1979] found that the editing task correlated more highly than standard cloze tests with direct integrative tests such as oral interviews and writing.

Integrative proficiency tests: textual dictation

Textual dictation differs from word dictation in that, while in textual dictation whole sentences from whole passages are dictated at normal speed, in word dictation only isolated words or phrases are dictated. Word dictation, which has a function only when the students are being introduced to writing, hardly tests sound discrimination --there are far better techniques for that-- and in no way tests listening comprehension, since many words can be written without even understanding them.

In textual dictation, the passage is read three times at normal speed, the first time without pauses, the second time with a pause after each sentence for the students to write, and the third time with a shorter pause after each sentence for the students to correct their work. (Dictation segments should not be longer than about 12 words.) Under these conditions --conversational speed and fragment length that challenges short-term memory-- textual dictation can be a good measure of overall proficiency [J. Oller 1973-b:194-5], for it forces the examinee to process each sentence cognitively and make use of his competence.

J. Oller [*ibid.*] found textual dictation not only to be a good indicator of overall proficiency but also to yield much information that is diagnostically useful. Textual dictation is "a device which measures the efficiency of *grammar-based expectancies*" [J. Oller and Streiff 1975:77]. If the examinee's grammar of expectancies is incomplete, his response will deviate from the actual sequences. Natives, on the other hand, can fill gaps from context.

J. Oller [1971] found that textual dictation correlated at .86 with the total score of the UCLA ESL Placement Examination. Several other studies [S. Johansson 1973-b, Whitaker 1976, and others] have found high correlations between textual dictation and other tests. Furthermore, high correlations have been achieved between textual dictation and other integrative tests. So such tests, concluded J. Oller and Streiff [1975:77] must be "tapping an underlying *competence*."

In scoring dictation, it is recommended that one point be taken off for each misspelled but recognizable word, and two points off for each unrecognizable or omitted word. But perhaps those spelling errors that do not affect pronunciation should not be counted off --for example, **shagrin* is not only a perfectly clear spelling for *chagrin* but is in fact a *better* way to spell it.

It seems that the spread of scores (variance) is higher for textual dictation than for more traditional tests. It also seems that the validity of textual dictation changes with the particular sound-spelling fit of each language; thus, Stansfield [1977] showed that it is easier to perform on a dictation test in a language which, like Spanish, has a close fit between sounds and spelling.

To be valid as a measure of proficiency for placement purposes, a passage for textual dictation should be unknown to all examinees. To be valid as a measure of progress in a language program, a passage for dictation should be a new recombination of what is known to the students.

Valette [1964] found that when students are not exposed to frequent dictation throughout the course, a final textual dictation test correlates highly with a full-length examination of the listening, reading, and writing skills (the language involved was French). If done right, especially if the sentences are long enough to require cognitive processing, textual dictation could be a useful way of measuring the overall linguistic competence of intermediate and advanced second language students.

Textual dictation has certain disadvantages too. First of all, it does not really test sound discrimination, as claimed, because the context helps in guessing most of the words whose sounds are not heard properly. Another problem is that it is a hybrid rather than a pure test. Moreover, it tells us nothing about the speaking skill of the examinees. There is abnormal repetition and pauses not found in speech. But the most serious disadvantage of the dictation test is that scoring is slow and cumbersome, taking an inordinate amount of time.

A modification that is possible is to hand out a printed text with carefully selected, frequent blanks, and read each sentence only once. This "textual spot dictation" would be rather time-consuming to prepare but quick to administer and score, and the scoring would be very objective. Textual spot dictation would also allow testing specific problems rather than wasting time with what all examinees know.

Integrative proficiency tests: the noise test

The noise test is a textual dictation test in which white noise is added to cover up every nth word. (White noise consists of random frequencies like those heard in the background of radio broadcasts; it has a "sh/sh/sh" quality.) Spolsky *et al.* [1968], Spolsky [1969-b], and Gradman and Spolsky [1975] concluded that the noise test is a good indication of overall proficiency, highly correlated to the TOEFL test. But Gaies *et al.* [1977] found the rankings without noise to be about the same; and Johansson [1973-a] concluded that noise tests correlate well with other measures only in the case of students who are close to natives, so they cannot be recommended as tests of overall proficiency.

From the point of view of the second language program, noise tests may not be useful, as they seem to discriminate between natives and non-natives but not to be discriminative enough to distinguish among non-natives at the same level of the program. Native-like ability to make use of redundancy under adverse conditions is not needed by second language students until they are very advanced. Another disadvantage --a serious one-- of noise tests is that they can be quite irritating and can arouse emotional reactions in some examinees, thereby invalidating the results.

Integrative proficiency tests: the proficiency interview

In the proficiency interview, as pioneered by the Foreign Service Institute of the U.S. Department of State, each examinee is interviewed by a team of two interviewers of which the junior member, a native speaker, conducts the interview while the senior member, a linguist, observes and takes notes. On the basis of the answers to earlier questions, further questions are asked. An interpreting situation may be created to elicit what the examinee has apparently avoided.

The use of two judges scoring the examinee independently increases considerably the reliability of the final rating. As Wilds [1975:34] put it, "one examiner testing alone is likely to lose both his skills as an interviewer and his perceptiveness as an observer to a degree that cannot be justified on grounds of economy."

While the basic rating of most examinees can be roughly determined by an experienced interviewing team in about five minutes, more time --a total of about 15 minutes-- is needed to pinpoint the exact S (speaking) rating when plusses are used (F.S.I. ratings go from 0 to 5, with intermediate plusses; see Appendix C). In addition to this, another five to ten minutes may be spent establishing the R (reading) rating (same numbers), for which texts of various degrees of difficulty are given to the examinee to read and translate orally. Progress interviews in language courses, on the other hand, can be much shorter (about five minutes), for they are aimed at specific knowledge and presumably several will be given per term, thereby increasing total reliability.

Note that at F.S.I. there are numerical scales

available for use after each interview; but they are seldom calculated, i.e., only when there is doubt or disagreement. Since in progress interviews the differences being evaluated are much smaller, the scoring scales should always be used during the interviews.

To reduce the nervousness of the examinee during an interview, the first couple of questions should be easy ones. Most examinees are only nervous at the beginning, although a few are nervous throughout and can't therefore really show what they know. After all, as realistic as an interview may be, "both participants know perfectly well that it is a test and not a tea-party..." [Perren 1967:26].

Wilds [1975] claimed that the oral interview system works --it gives valid and dependable ratings that are extremely useful in making job decisions [*ibid.*, p. 35]. J. Clark [1972-b] reported on a study showing correlation coefficients ranging from .82 to .92 for F.S.I. proficiency interview scores and a series of discrete-point tests on vocabulary and grammar administered to 44 Peace Corps trainees.

Despite its definite advantages, the proficiency interview cannot be used as a progress interview in the schools without major adaptation; it is "not ideal for the normal academic situation..." [Wilds 1975:35]. F.S.I. ratings are more suitable for the evaluation of proficiency after completion of an advanced intensive program, or after considerable exposure to the language in the environment, than for the evaluation of growing competence within a program.

The proficiency interview has certain potential disadvantages. Much time can be wasted as the examinee repeatedly uses similar structures and topics. He may have nothing to say about certain topics. Certain types of structures --questions, for example-- seldom if ever come up. There can be personality problems. And scoring can suffer from the halo effect (scoring down an examinee who follows a very good examinee) or the "shadow" effect (scoring up an examinee who follows a very bad examinee). But by and large these disadvantages are minor and can be compensated for with corrective measures.

Integrative proficiency tests: elicited imitation

Swain *et al.* [1974] found elicited imitation to be a good testing alternative to spontaneous speech. The technique consists in the examinee repeating sentences containing specific grammatical difficulties and exceeding short-term memory capacity, so they require processing (decoding and re-encoding). It is a promising technique, one that perhaps could also be adapted for use in progress tests in the classroom.

A general language proficiency factor?

Strong correlations have been found among very different tests, such as nonverbal IQ and TOEFL [Flahive 1977], native language proficiency and second language proficiency tests [Johansson 1973-a, 1973-b, Bezanson and Hawkes 1976, others], tests of different skills, and discrete-point and integrative tests. All of this seems to point to the existence of a "general language proficiency factor" [J. Oller 1976-a] which may be strongly correlated with general intelligence.

If this is so, we have come full circle, from the time when we could not test language skills separately, to the separate testing of all aspects of language proficiency, to the conclusion that language proficiency does not differ much, after all, from general intelligence. One can't help but think that we lost our bearings somewhere along the way.

Some suggestions about test preparation

(1) It is very important to know what will be tested and why. Validity enters into the former, the definition of objectives into the latter.

(2) Testing should concentrate on what most bilingual native speakers can do well, not on what very few can do well.

(3) The sampling for language tests should not be random. This is not difficult with progress tests but can be quite difficult with proficiency tests.

(4) Tests can have any number of points, not just 100.

(5) The fact that a monolingual native speaker fails an item is not evidence that it is not valid. Lado [1961: 76] noted that monolingual natives would not understand instructions in the language of the learners, might be confused by their lack of experience in second language learning, might follow certain artificial rules of correctness, and might not take a language test seriously enough to do their best; but none of these conditions would invalidate an item for a second language test.

(6) All instructions for tests should be in the native language. Instructions should be crystal-clear. The

students are supposed to demonstrate their knowledge through their answers to the test items, not by guessing the meaning of the instructions. Either the task is self-evident, in which case no instructions are needed, or it requires an explanation, in which case we should not run the risk that some students will not know what to do [Pimsleur 1966-b:187].

(7) Any new type of item should be illustrated with sample items and their answers.

(8) A test should include some items that are more difficult, so as to discriminate between the weaker and the stronger students.

(9) The items should be organized so that the easier ones, or at least a few easy ones, come first. This reduces the anxiety of the weaker students at the start of the test, allowing them to relax and do their best.

(10) Test items should be independent of each other. Otherwise missing one can lead to missing others, or answering one correctly can lead to guessing others.

(11) Each item should have only the minimal conditioning context necessary to answer it. Thus, the word "yesterday" or the phrase "last night" are sufficient cues for items requiring the past; there is no need to present a story as a lead. A series of items does not have to refer to the same context to be valid; in fact, a common context may make guessing possible.

(12) The test paper and answer key should be prepared with ease of scoring in mind. Fractional credits --half points or quarter points(!)-- should be avoided. If an answer requires partial credit, the scoring should be planned so that the smallest partial credit is worth one point.

(13) For more efficient test construction, an item file should be kept. On 4"x6" cards each item can be written on one side and a cumulative tally of test data on the other. This facilitates the selection and revision of test items.

Grading

Grades, good and bad, encourage students to work harder; that is, if they are not too generous or too stingy. This is the main reason why grades should be used beyond the early elementary grades. Another reason is that the great majority of both students and parents want grades, especially if they are based on tests rather than subjective evaluations of classroom performance. Evaluation in reference to impersonal norms is both wanted and needed. Nesset [1973] found that in Minneapolis senior high schools, where alternate evaluation systems were allowed, 90 percent of grades were letter grades. E. Jenkins [1974] determined that, when given a choice, less than 10 percent of college students choose an alternative to traditional grades.

Kirschenbaum *et al.* [1971] have suggested eight alternatives to traditional grading, including such indefensible practices as self-evaluation and blanket grading for the whole class. Of the eight alternatives, probably the most widely used are mastery learning (to be discussed in Chapter 23) and pass/fail.

The problem with the pass/fail system is that achievement tends to decline under it [Gold *et al.* 1971]. It seems that students on the pass/fail system do not reach the level of achievement of those on the grade system and that they are also absent more often. Grades evaluate and provide a standard to work for; pass/fail (or pass/no credit) neither evaluates nor motivates. In a pass/fail system, the student tends to work just to pass.

It has been suggested that pass/fail or pass/no credit should be an option for the first second language course taken by a student in a program. The reasoning is that he may not know whether he will like the language or that he may find the methodology in the new program very different from what he is used to. But if students want to find out whether they like a subject or how it is taught, they should be able to see video-taped lectures and classes, read reading lists or examine the language textbook, borrow recordings, or do independent study. There is no reason why they should ruin a course by doing it without much motivation and erratic attendance under pass/fail or pass/no credit. Regular courses should be for serious study, and everything should be done to prevent serious students from being demoralized by the attitudes and behavior of unmotivated students.

Grading has to be done on a tentative basis until norms for a test are established. Only norms --what percentage of examinees get what-- make scores meaningful, except of course for criterion-referenced tests, for which norms are not needed.

Until norms for a test have been determined, we have to make do with one of several less-than-satisfactory systems. One of them is the curve. The normal curve (see Figure 21.4) tells us what percentage of scores occur between the mean (average) and various numbers of standard

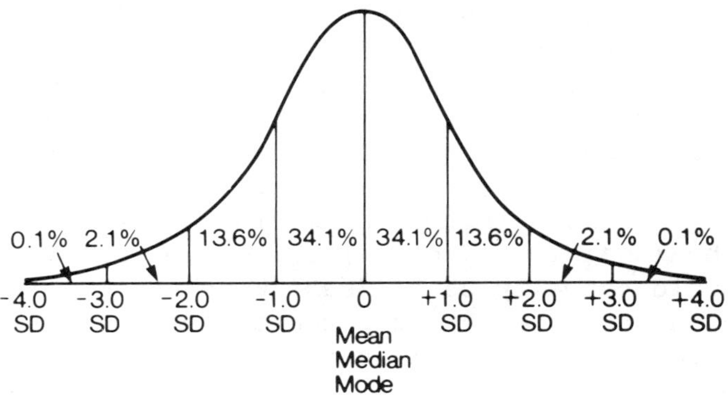

Figure 21.4

deviations from the mean (the standard deviation is a measure of score spread). Thus, 34.1 percent of scores fall between the mean and one standard deviation, that is, 68.2 percent between plus or minus one standard deviation. The problem is that such information is largely useless with a relatively small class, whose scores seldom form a normal curve. A class may be better than average or poorer than average, in either of which cases scoring by the curve is meaningless. Moreover, the value of the mean cannot be fixed for all courses at all levels --while in beginning courses the mean might be a C or C+, it should be obvious that in advanced courses the students constitute a select group for which the mean should be a B or B+, and at the graduate level, anything below an A- is a low grade. The decision of which letter grade value the mean of a test will have, even with a perfectly normal curve, is an entirely subjective decision the teacher must make in consultation with his conscience and his philosophy of education.

The common practice of basing grades on the percentage of correct answers (90 percent for an A, 80 percent for a B, etc.) is the most meaningless and unfair of all grading systems. If a test is very difficult, A students may get only 70 percent or even less of the answers right. And if a test is extremely easy, 90 percent for an A would be far too generous, as two thirds of the class might get 90 percent. How an otherwise reasonable teacher expects to be able to write tests that are exactly right in degree of difficulty for percentage grades to be valid and fair is something I have never understood.

The third alternative --of all tentative grading systems the least objectionable-- is the modified curve. In a modified curve, the basis for grading is not the mean, which can be seriously affected by a few very high or very low scores, but the median, that is, the middle score. A value is assigned to the median, according to the level of the course (let's say, for example, C), and grades above and below the group around the median are assigned according to the (again, subjective) criterion that at this level there should normally be *at least* W percent A's and X percent B's and *no more than* Y percent D's and Z percent F's. These percentages, as well as the percentage of C's, should of course change with the level of the course.

The grading system to be used in the course should be explained in some detail at the beginning of the course. It should be made clear that the highest grades will go to those students who best meet the criteria established for the course.

Grades should be given for daily activities such as the study of assigned material, e.g., dialogue performance, even though only a few students may be thus graded each day. Quizzes should be graded. Although the grade of individual students on any one quiz is not important, there should be an important cumulative quiz grade.

If a student gets so nervous during tests (as a few do) that he performs below his competence, obviously his test score is not a reliable indication of what he can do. In such cases, test scores should be supplemented, in establishing the final grade, by informal evaluation. This need not apply to more than an occasional student.

A course grade in a second language program should give about equal emphasis to communication and structure, although in the early courses structure should receive greater emphasis and in the advanced courses the emphasis should be primarily on communication, structure having presumably been mastered already.

In composition-type tests --which, to repeat, I do not recommend-- the practice of taking one point off per mistake unfairly penalizes the student who writes much creatively and makes mistakes and rewards the student who writes little mechanically and avoids structures and words of which he is not sure. Instructions as to what risks not to take should precede free writing items.

Although second language learning is cumulative, so that one might be tempted to use the last test mark as the course mark, it is not advisable to do so. Giving all or most of the weight to the later tests or last exam militates against the students putting on a steady effort throughout the course. In languages, steady effort is essential, for there really is no way to catch up by cramming.

Standardized tests and their uses

A test becomes a standardized test through a series of steps. First, the level of difficulty or of study is decided upon. Then the sample of knowledge to be measured is determined. Then test items are written, edited, and organized. Next comes a preliminary administration of the test. Following this is a statistical analysis of the results of the preliminary test. The items are then edited. The test with revised items is administered again. Norms for the test are established. Finally, if alternate forms of the test have been written, the two or more forms are equated (having, of course, been administered, analyzed, etc.).

Standardized test results are most easily interpreted in terms of percentiles, that is, the percentage of examinees that a particular score outperforms. Some tests provide standard scores. These give a round number as the mean (e.g., 50, 100, 500) and have a standard deviation equal to one fifth of the mean (e.g., 10, 20, 100); so standard scores make quite clear the relationship to the mean and the standard deviation. Some tests also provide stanines, which divide raw scores into nine segments, each (except for stanines 1 and 9, which are open-ended) corresponding to half a standard deviation. Another figure some tests give is the standard error, whose importance lies in the fact that it shows that a given score is not precise but represents a small range.

Standardized language proficiency tests correlate highly with other measures of success such as grades and conversational ability, so they *are* valid, although as Brière [1973] noted, they tend to be biased against any sociolinguistic group other than the norming population of, in the United States, middle-class, white, native speakers of English. (Ideally standardized tests should have norms for various socioeconomic groups.)

Strictly speaking, only standardized tests are true tests --all others must be considered tentative.

Most standardized language tests are not just discrete-point tests, for many of their questions require overall skills to answer. However, being able to do well in standardized tests does not necessarily mean ability to function in the second language (for instance, I have done very well in some advanced standardized tests in French and yet my ability to understand spoken French in real life leaves much to be desired). Norm-referenced tests, which are relative, should be supplemented by criterion-referenced tests, which are absolute.

The greatest weakness of standardized language tests like the MLA Cooperative Foreign Language Tests and the Pimsleur Proficiency Tests is in testing the speaking skill. They rely too much on pictures, which are haphazard in eliciting production and which result in a free type of production that cannot be graded objectively. Pimsleur wanted to use oral translation in his tests, but was forced to rely on pictures because of the polemic about the use of translation. The MLA speaking tests put far too much weight on pronunciation (more than half the points) and do not elicit specific structures.

Standardized listening comprehension tests should include sections on sound discrimination and differentiation, which most don't. Their reading sections should be better fitted to the levels for which they are intended; in the case of the two tests mentioned, the reading sections are too difficult for the levels indicated. Carroll [1966-a] pointed out that the MLA tests are inadequate in evaluating communication and grammar, as high scores can be attained through knowledge of vocabulary only. In a word, much can be done to improve standardized second language tests. Furthermore, their norms should be re-established every ten years or so.

In addition to their use in second language teaching research, standardized tests can be used for advanced placement purposes and to evaluate programs, courses, teaching materials, and teachers. By using course-independent tests, it is possible to evaluate programs and courses. Tests that measure only the content of a specific course are as valid or invalid as the course itself, so they might not be measuring real language proficiency. On the other hand, a standardized test, given at the end of a course or program, allows us to evaluate its results and to make objective comparisons with other schools, with other methods, and with several other variables. To that end, standardized tests can be given as part of the final examination or by promising extra points to those students who do particularly well in them if they are not part of the regular grade. (Some motivation has to be provided for students to try to do well in these tests.)

There is much merit in the proposal that teachers' performance, and consequently salaries and advancement, should be judged on the basis of the ongoing performance of their students in standardized achievement tests [K. Mueller 1972]. This would be one form of accountability, perhaps the most important one. Of course, no teacher should be judged on the basis of the standardized test scores of any one class in particular, but on the performance of many groups of students over a period of years. Note also that alternate forms of the tests would have to be changed frequently, so that teachers could not teach *for* the tests.

There should be, throughout North America, a program of standardized second language testing with national standards and tests for each level of the various programs. This, more than anything, would enable us to reach and maintain high standards and to conduct solid ongoing research on methods and other variables. To help facilitate this, J. Clark's [1972-b] proposal for the establishment of a computerized test item pool would be excellent. Such a pool can be used to generate test items which can be scrambled to produce many alternate tests, free from errors or security problems [Jorstad 1974:276], even adapted to the native language background of the students.

(Much has been written about second language testing, with a considerable amount of repetition. For further reading, perhaps the most worthwhile books are Lado [1961], Jones and Spolsky [1975], Valette [1977], and J. Oller [1979].)

22

THE LANGUAGE LABORATORY AND THE USE OF MEDIA[△]

PART I: THE LANGUAGE LABORATORY

Definition

We can define the language laboratory as an area containing equipment designed to facilitate second language learning (cf. Hayes [1968:1]). This definition is broad enough to encompass all types of installations and yet demanding enough (the laboratory must facilitate learning) to support high technical and pedagogical standards.

Some historical comments

Parker [1962:67] noted that the use of audio equipment in language teaching goes back to 1904, when a French course was produced in England on an Edison cylinder. "Talking machines" were in use at Yale University as early as 1906 [Clarke 1918]. The precursors of the modern language laboratory were phonetic laboratories built by several universities, at first having only headphones connected to a single source. The first elaborate installation that can be referred to as a modern language laboratory was opened at Louisiana State University in 1947, soon followed by other such installations at Georgetown University, Yale University, the Foreign Service Institute, the University of Michigan, the University of Iowa, and Wayne State University [E. Hocking 1967].

For a decade, only a minority of colleges and universities built language laboratories. Then beginning in 1958 and supported by the National Defense Education Act came a laboratory explosion in the United States, during which many thousands of laboratories were installed in schools and universities throughout the country. This "golden age" of the language laboratory in America lasted about a decade, coming to an abrupt end in 1969 with the

---

△ Portions of this chapter are from my article "The Myth of Language Laboratory Monitoring," *The Modern Language Journal*, Vol. LVIII, No. 7 (© 1974 by the Regents of the University of Wisconsin), pp. 336-9; used by permission.

cutoff of federal funds. Now the situation is almost back to the pre-NDEA era: it is mostly colleges and universities, plus a very few scools, that have laboratories in working order.

Advantages and disadvantages of the language laboratory

The language laboratory has many advantages, among them the following:

(1) It provides the students with individualized audio-lingual practice. For this practice to be individualized in speed and content, however, the students must have control over their individual recordings.

(2) It offers greater exposure to the second language.

(3) It frees the teacher from the more mechanical aspects of second language teaching, such as most drills, reading aloud, and dictation. The creative teacher will never be replaced; he should accept, however, the use of machines and paraprofessionals for the functions they can perform. The machine frees the good teacher to have more time to discuss stimulating subjects and to provide his students with individual advice and help. The unimaginative teacher who devotes most of his time to mechanical drills *can* and *should* be replaced by a machine.

(4) The laboratory brings to the second language program the voices of many native speakers.

(5) Model voices can be heard clearly, as many times as necessary; they do not change or get tired.

(6) The headphones provide isolation and privacy, allowing for better concentration. The booth also does this, but in the schools it is not such a good idea to have booths --partially hidden from the teacher's sight, certain students do not study and do damage to the equipment.

(7) The teacher can give students individual attention through the intercom, without interrupting the whole group.

(8) Whatever individual correction can be offered by the teacher in the laboratory has the advantages of being immediate and private.

(9) If the laboratory has individual recorders, student self-evaluation is possible.

(10) The library-type laboratory can substitute, in languages, for the use of home or library study in other subjects.

(11) The library-type laboratory can also be used for remedial work.

(12) Laboratories facilitate listening comprehension

testing, and if they have individual recorders they make efficient oral testing possible.

(13) The laboratory is a flexible facility that can serve many purposes, not only practice with drills; there can be a variety of listening comprehension materials, simulated conversation, tests, and even the presentation of some types of new material.

(14) With an electronic classroom (see below), it is possible to have half the class work under the direction of the teacher and the other half under the direction of a laboratory program.

(15) With older students and special materials, the whole course can be largely self-instructional, that is, centered around the laboratory and a conversation group activity area. This is especially useful for courses and languages having low enrollments insufficient to justify classroom teaching.

(16) The language laboratory offers teachers an opportunity to improve their own audiolingual skills.

Most of the advantages listed above were pointed out by Hayes [1968:15-6]. The value of the language laboratory hardly needs to be proved. As E. Hocking [1967:61-2] noted, having to prove the value of machine practice "is a little like having to prove that on the average, airplanes travel faster than automobiles...." But then an inexperienced pilot using the wrong kind of gas and a plane that hasn't been overhauled in a long time *could*, on a short run, lose a race with an automobile driver. In many places, that is precisely what happened. The laboratories were fed the wrong software, were improperly used and inadequately maintained, and the automobile beat the airplane.

A disadvantage of the language laboratory is that it involves a commitment to continued costs, continual maintenance, an overhaul every year, and total replacement of booth equipment every ten years or so; this is a major commitment that rather few institutions can make.

Other disadvantages are more potential than real. For example, one such "disadvantage" is the fact that one cannot "talk" to a machine, that at most one can have simulated conversation with it. But the language laboratory was never intended to provide conversation.

The language laboratory fell into disuse in the early seventies for a number of reasons, among them the following:

(1) Many teachers did not want to use the lab, as they

were afraid it would replace them.

(2) Equipment was often poorly designed and poorly maintained.

(3) The people who directed lab work (teachers or lab assistants) were frequently poorly trained.

(4) There was lack of coordination between the classroom program and the laboratory program.

(5) Perhaps the main reason for failure was the lack of adequate materials. Most tapes contained unimaginative, boring drills that tried to elicit automatic rather than thoughtful responses. As Grittner [1977:313] put it, "...people can be bored to death as readily with technological devices as with live human presentations." Recordings would have been much better if they had relied primarily on challenging drills making use of the students' minds, if they had offered considerable variety, and if they had made occasional use of the unexpected, including humor.

(6) The laboratory was used too little and poorly. One or two 20-minute sessions per week, for example, can have no effect on learning, especially if they replace classroom work. Among the many misuses of the lab was using it too mechanically.

(7) Frequently students were not adequately oriented for the use of the lab.

(8) Another problem was that often the laboratory was not available for review or remedial work.

(9) Finally, due to the financial problems already mentioned, old equipment that was no longer usable was not replaced.

All this added up to formidable odds against the success of the language laboratory in the schools. But the soundness of the idea that the laboratory can be a valuable aid remains intact.

Types of language laboratories

Laboratories can be classified according to four criteria: functions, access to the materials, controls, and location.

1) *Functions*. With respect to functions, that is, what the equipment can do, language laboratories can be *audio-passive, audio-active,* and *audio-active-comparative*.

Audio-passive equipment consists just of earphones; only listening activities can be performed effectively with such equipment. The student's voice is not picked up, amplified or directed to his ears. If he responds orally, he can't hear himself very well, and what he *can* hear is distorted by bone conduction.

Audio-active equipment, which provides each student with a headset with a microphone so he can hear himself clearly, is a substantial improvement over the audio-passive situation. And yet, it is far from providing all the necessary laboratory functions. The student cannot, for example, go over what he finds difficult, nor compare his imitation to the model. Frankly, having an audio-active laboratory is little better than having no laboratory at all --just about everything that can be done in an audio-active laboratory can be done as well in the classroom.

The audio-active-comparative laboratory provides each student with an individual recorder, thereby allowing him to listen, record his responses, and play his recorded responses for comparison with the model. Only by recording can the student objectively compare his pronunciation and intonation with that of the model, provided, of course, he has had the necessary discrimination training. Ideally, his recorded responses should be available on immediate playback by pressing a button controlling a mechanism that automatically rewinds the tape and plays back the last few seconds of it. The recording function is particularly important for the early phonological work, for each new dialogue to be studied during the beginning level, and for speaking tests throughout the program.

Note that there is nothing inherently audio-active-comparative about the library-type lab, which can have just tape players. Similarly, there is nothing inherently audio-active about the electronic classroom or the mobile lab, both of which can have recorders.

2) *Access to the materials*. In this regard, laboratories can be of three types: *library*, *broadcast*, from a console or a dial system, and *broadcast-record*, a combination of the first two.

In the library access, individual students have access to individual copies of the recorded materials. By having their own cassettes, the students can progress at their own pace, replaying difficult parts as needed; pedagogically, this is the only sound type of access. Ideally, the student should use the facilities as he needs them and be in control of them. The laboratory should be used for individual study *in addition* to class, not as a substitute for classroom activities (except, of course, in self-instructional programs). The cassette has maximized access, making it possible to assign oral exercises as homework, as many students have cassette machines and the others could be provided with them through a rental or loan system. Beginning students need to have a recorder, intermediate and advanced students can manage very well with a cassette player, as they should have mastered, by then, the perception and production of sounds. For certain materials --those requiring no responses-- take-home records should be made available.

In the broadcast access, only the teacher has the materials and makes them available by broadcasting them either from the console or through a dial system. This destroys much of the flexibility of the language laboratory. Dial access makes access itself most flexible, as programs can be dialed from anywhere; but it has the serious disadvantages that the student cannot replay parts of the tape, cannot progress at his own pace, and must first hear the program wherever it is, in progress, unless he is the first to dial it.

In broadcast-record access, the program is first broadcast into the booths and recorded onto individual cassettes. After this recording, the students can work in the library mode. It is, however, a waste of time for the students to have to just listen (and maybe respond, without recording) while the program is being copied, without being able to stop it the first time through, the time they most need to stop it. To prevent this waste of time on a "dry run," it is very desirable that the individual copies be made before the lab session.

3) *Controls*. The control of a lab program can be by the *student, remote,* or *combination* (student with remote override).

Student control is essential. It is what allows individualized use of the language laboratory. Remote control by itself would be undesirable --the students *must* be able to control their individual cassettes. Thus, an automatic laboratory program is pedagogically undesirable and quite dehumanizing. Remote control, however, is very useful for laboratory testing of the speaking skill, so the most desirable type of control is student control with remote override.

4) *Location*. With respect to location, laboratories can be *conventional, mobile,* or *electronic classrooms*.

The conventional laboratory is a special room used for laboratory practice only. It is quite useful in colleges and universities, where students do not all have a similar schedule and can therefore come to a conventional lab during their free hours. In the schools, however, the conventional laboratory is not very convenient, as moving whole classes to and from it causes considerable disruption and waste of time.

The mobile lab --equipment that is rolled into the classroom, with individual sets distributed to the students--has the advantage of low cost but the disadvantages that (1) it is inconvenient and time-consuming to set up, and (2) the equipment, being light, is not sturdy enough for heavy long-term use.

In the elementary and secondary schools, the best solution to the location variable is to have electronic classrooms with cassette recorders. If the electronic classrooms have no recorders, there should also be a conventional, library, audio-active-comparative laboratory. Electronic classroom equipment may be in booths around the walls of the classroom or, better yet, in convertible desks --desks that convert into laboratory booths by having their tops turn into dividers. With recorders, the electronic classroom is the ideal setup, for no special room is needed and the equipment can be used at any time with minimal disruption; the students can work with recordings when ready for them, not according to a rigid lab schedule.

Physical characteristics of the conventional laboratory

With regard to its size, the conventional laboratory should accommodate the largest class that will use it as a group, for such activities as oral tests. If it is to be used as a library lab only, it should accommodate peak demand hours. In all cases, a ten percent allowance should be made for mechanical failure.

Student space, per booth, including aisle space, should be a minimum of 3 by 5 feet. Booths should be used only with responsible older students. Having the booths face away from the teacher may be a solution to the problem of younger student misbehavior, but it has the serious disadvantage that it eliminates eye contact, which is essential for certain instructions (e.g., "Put on the headsets"), for correction, for testing, etc. Booths are not really necessary --modern headsets provide adequate sound insulation. If a school is to have booths anyway, they should have transparent front panels.

Most consoles are far too elaborate. They should provide program broadcast (preferably three channels), two-way communication with an annunciator (a device which attracts the attention of the teacher when a student needs help), an all-call button to talk to the whole group, and (very useful but not essential) remote control of all the student booth functions. Other fancy functions are probably not worth their cost.

In the lab or adjoining it there should be maintenance, editing, and copying facilities.

The audio quality needed in language laboratories

The most sensitive human ears can hear a range of 15-20,000 Hz (Hertz or cycles per second), but for most people it is less than that. For language laboratories, the important thing is to cover the range where significant sound distinctions are made. This range must be much wider than that used for native speech, for the second language learner can guess few or no sounds from context and needs therefore to hear every sound clearly.

Phonetic cues, according to Hayes [1968:56-7], begin to appear at 150 Hz, but significant distinctions appear at about 250 Hz. In fact, the lowest frequencies should be eliminated, as they tend to mask the higher frequencies. Most linguistically significant phonetic features are audible from 250-6,000 Hz, although a number of fricative consonants are located primarily above 6,000, e.g., the contrast between /f/ and /θ/ [K. Harris 1958].

LeBel [1950] showed that wide frequency is needed for speech therapy, and this is in the native language. In the second language, Buka *et al*. [1962] found that reduction of high frequencies below 7,300 Hz, and especially below 5,000 Hz, made it impossible for many English speaking boys and girls to perceive a number of phonemic contrasts in German and French. They concluded that the range needed for language laboratories is 250-8,500 Hz ± 3 dB (decibels, a measure of relative sound loudness).

Because the second language learner has little or no redundancy available to him, he must hear *everything* clearly. The fidelity of the equipment he uses needs to be second only to high fidelity, and far better than that of dictating machines and telephones, which have a range of only 300-3,000 Hz [Hayes 1968:41]. And yet some would teach second languages via telephone! Hayes' [1968:63-4] conclusions were that as a minimum laboratory equipment should cover the range of 250-6,000 Hz at ± 2 dB and 6,000-8,500 Hz at ± 5 dB, and that very low frequencies and high frequencies (above 10,000 Hz) should be eliminated. Elsewhere in his useful book, Hayes gave specifications for the various kinds of lab equipment, suggestions for the nontechnical testing of equipment, and guidelines for simple service and maintenance.

The higher the speed of the tape, the better the fidelity. Because of this, it is preferable to obtain masters at 7½ inches per second (ips), which has better fidelity than 3 3/4 ips. Student copies can be at 3 3/4 ips or (in cassettes) at 1 7/8 ips. The wider the recording, the better the fidelity. For that reason, masters should be at least at half-track, preferably at full track. Wire systems, being very narrow in width, have low fidelity and should not be used.

Wireless systems that rely on radio signals also have low fidelity, unless they make use of the FM band and have FM receivers --but that would make them rather expensive.

Note that all components of the lab system must meet the fidelity specifications as given by Hayes. It serves no purpose to have a good recorder if the earphones, or the microphone, or any other component is of low quality. Like the weakest link in a chain, the poorest component determines the sound quality of a whole laboratory system.

Certain desirable features of language equipment

The ideal laboratory recorder would have an easily controlled pause button so that pauseless tapes can be used. With a pauseless tape, each student determines, according to his needs, the length of the pause he needs to respond; the tape has only a uniformly brief pause for the operation of the pause button. Fixed pauses do not quite suit anyone.

Also very desirable would be a device allowing the indefinite replaying of a tape segment of any length. If this is not possible, at least the last few seconds should be easily replayable by pressing a single button.

A feature student machines should also have is an outlet that allows students to make their own copies for home study. Of course, to do this one must first make sure it would be allowed by the publisher, i.e., that it would not be a copyright violation.

The advent of the cassette meant an end to the tape threading, breakage, and stretching problems. Cassette machines offer great flexibility, allowing students to work with recordings just about anywhere, even in their cars. They mean also greatly reduced costs. Cassette consumer products, however, are machines of relatively poor quality, made to be thrown away rather than fixed.

Such machines have poor sound quality and should not be used in language learning. Cheap cassette tapes are also a misguided form of savings, because they damage the recorders' heads.

Agatstein [1971] reported considerable success and very favorable student attitudes in a program in which all students were required to buy a cassette recorder and given homework assignments on cassette. Perhaps the best solution would be a combination of machine purchase by those who can afford it, rental from the school by those who cannot buy one, and a library lab for use by all, including those who cannot afford renting a machine. In any event, cassettes for home use should avoid presenting new material, for most home machines do not have the fidelity to permit hearing unfamiliar material with adequate clarity.

Recordings: their form, content, and use

Commercial laboratory materials became available around 1960, before which time teachers had to prepare their own. Since some commercial materials are not very good and all need to be supplemented at certain points, language teachers need to know how to make tape recordings. There should be a recording studio in every college and university and in every school district.

To make a recording it is necessary first to make a detailed tapescript, as good recorded materials cannot be improvised, except of course for impromptu conversations. Instructions in laboratory tapes should be in the native language, only gradually to be replaced by second language instructions. Speech should be at normal speed with pauses for cognitive processing as needed. The only way to slow down speech without distorting it is by recording it at normal speed and then expanding it by means of a speech compressor/expander, which electronically introduces inaudible interruptions. But such time-expanded speech, as we have seen in Chapter 19, can have a negative effect on listening comprehension. Within normal speed there is a range, and recordings should be at the slower end of this range.

Taped drills should not exceed seven or eight frames. Each frame should consist of two to four phases. In repetition activities, two phases --model and imitation-- are enough. In very simple drills, such as simple substitution without correlation, there should be three phases --cue, response, and confirmation--, for there is a slight possibility of error and therefore the correct response should be provided. In more challenging drills, where there is greater likelihood of error, there should be four phases --cue, response, confirmation, and repetition of the correct response. Some have suggested a fifth phase --reconfirmation-- in order to leave the native model in the mind of the learner; but this does not seem necessary, as imitation of the correct response normally leaves the native model in the student's mind anyway.

The pauses for the student phases should be based on a unit that we can call SNSA, for "*s*low-*n*ormal *s*ubvocal *a*rticulation" --the time it takes to articulate the response subvocally at slow-normal speed. Note that this is not just thinking of the answer --thinking is too fast-- but consciously articulating it subvocally. On that basis, repetitive responses require 1½ - 2 SNSAs, constructed responses to simple drills 2 SNSAs, and constructed responses to more difficult drills 2½, 3 or even 4 SNSAs (4 would be reserved for very difficult multi-sentence transformation drills). Pauses in listening passages for which repetition is desired should be uniformly long and just long enough to permit stopping the tape to imitate the sentence, after which the "pause" button is released and the playing of the recording goes on.

The total length of laboratory tapes need not be limited to the usually recommended 20 minutes. Tapes should last about 70 percent of the duration of the lab period, to allow repetition of the difficult parts. The lab period would be about 25 minutes long in high school and 50 minutes long for college students and adults. Thus the ideal duration of a tape for a 50-minute lab period would be about 35 minutes.

In making master recordings one should avoid polyester tape, which can stretch, altering the sounds, a condition that cannot be corrected. Acetate tape is better, as it breaks clean and can therefore be repaired by splicing.

The master tapes should be kept apart and used only to make master copies or program tapes. If used in the laboratory, the master tapes could be accidentally erased. Even proximity to an electric motor can damage them.

The number of tape copies to be used in a library system depends on the number of students that attend during peak hours. Roughly, one fourth of all students in a college course may attend the library lab at the same time. So if a course has 80 students, 20 copies of tapes of the current lesson should be available. As new lessons are studied, a reduced number of copies of the older lessons needs to be kept, as shown in the following schedule for a class of 80:

Copies of current lesson....................20
Copies of preceding lessons:
30% of peak number....................... 6
(To be kept until the test covering that lesson)
Copies of lessons preceding the last test:
10% of peak number....................... 2

Of course this assumes that the students are strongly encouraged to use the lab, not only in word but in deed (a good percentage of the grade being assigned to oral lab tests).

Regarding the content of the tapes, most of the drills discussed in Chapter 17 can be made into oral drills for the language lab. It is important, however, that choice-making drills dealing with contrasts should be emphasized over repetition and substitution. What has made many materials unimaginative and dull is the lack of linguistic choice in them, the fact that they present series of examples of single structural features. Each tape should have a progressive variety of drills, not rely on drills of the same or similar types. Not only that: lab tapes should not consist just of unrelieved drills but should have quite a variety of content making use of several skills. A little humor, a little diversion in the lab is highly desirable.

There is no need, as some have suggested, for three alternate sets of tapes for average, slow, and better students. If provided with a pause control, all students can use the same tapes, the slow students doing some drills again, the fast students responding faster and skipping some drills. Self-tests at key points would tell the students what to skip or what to repeat.

The library lab should also have several copies of a set of "general" tapes, designed to practice basic structures with any textbook. Such tapes serve review and remedial functions, as it is better to perform those functions with different tapes rather than go again over a familiar program.

Lab materials should not be the same as those in the book. If something is available in written form in or out of the classroom, the students will not be interested in listening to it in the lab. The lab should be a place for oral work without written materials. Lab manuals that put all tape contents in writing destroy the purpose of lab practice.

The laboratory and the classroom

The orientation at the beginning of the program should include an orientation to the use of the laboratory and how to study in it --all in the native language, of course. A very important function of the orientation is to convince the students of the importance of studying in the laboratory several times a week, preferably every day. Nothing will do this more effectively than making clear that oral drills will be an important part of speaking tests to be given in the lab, tests which will make up a large part of the course grade. Demanding good audiolingual performance in class at all times will also contribute to lab attendance. The students should be told too that their main concern, especially at the beginning level, is learning correct responses, something to which lab work can contribute much. Providing cassettes for home study will underline the importance given to recordings in the program.

Should the language laboratory be used to introduce and teach new material or only to reinforce and expand what is presented in class? It depends on whether the lab is used in coordination with class work or for self-directed independent study. When the lab is used as an adjunct to the class, it does not teach but complements the teacher and the text; it only gives further practice with oral materials and allows oral testing; it cannot provide conversation, which is to be had in class. Ideally, the lab should be used for all the mechanical practice; but because of the difficulty in coordinating this (except in the electronic classroom), it is necessary to have some mechanical work in the classroom and use the laboratory for extra practice.

The laboratory and the classroom have thus different, complementary functions. The laboratory should be used primarily for skill-getting and the classroom primarily for skill-using. When the two are coordinated, it makes little sense to have the students study something in the lab first and afterwards use it in class; by following this order the students may form bad habits that the teacher is then forced to try to undo, which is very uneconomical. Imitation, for example, is best done face-to-face, because visual observation of the teacher facilitates it, equipment has fidelity limitations, and the teacher, unlike the machine, can provide adequate feedback.

Generally speaking, coordination between the classroom and the laboratory is best achieved by having (1) class presentation, followed by (2) laboratory practice, mostly of a mechanical nature, and then (3) class communicative activities. That is, in class a point of familiarity with the new material is reached, further practice with the material is done in the lab, and then what has been mastered there is applied creatively in the classroom. A class-lab grammar lesson, then, would have the following five substeps: (1) examples would be provided in class, most from previously learned material, some new; (2) a generalization would be arrived at by the students, with help as needed from the teacher; (3) some simple drills would be done in the classroom; (4) the bulk of drills would be done in the lab, including in particular challenging ones; and (5) the students would participate in classroom conversation incorporating the new rule.

In self-instructional programs new material is learned in the lab. Here the lab forms, in conjunction with printed materials and small conversation groups, a complete teaching program. When it comes to conversation, the self-instructional program has to rely on human interaction --the lab can only provide simulated conversation. Kalivoda [1972] reported that advanced oral training can be provided on an individual, intensive basis by a combination of taped program, dictionary, and tape recorder; but it would be far better to combine this with conversation in small groups. Such self-instructional programs would be suitable for well-motivated college or adult students.

Monitoring

Monitoring, the act of listening in to students working in the lab without their awareness and then evaluating or correcting them or diagnosing their difficulties, has been hailed by some as very desirable, even essential to laboratory work. Yet not only is it not essential, but it tends to be ineffective and counterproductive. (Unlike monitoring, having someone at the console to help the students when they want to be helped is of course desirable.)

In the first place, monitored students are on their own 95 percent of the time in a class of 20 and 97 percent of the time in a class of 30. Secondly, few teachers possess enough knowledge of the phonetics of both languages and of the techniques of error correction to be able to detect and correct errors efficiently. Third, errors could not be detected efficiently even by a star teacher, for while he is listening to someone who may not be making any serious errors at the moment, a number of other students may be making major errors that go undetected; in the classroom, in choral repetition, an experienced teacher can hear the errors of several students at once, not just one student.

In the fourth place, error correction in the laboratory is inefficient because only one student can benefit from it, as opposed to the classroom, where all students benefit from seeing an error corrected. Fifth, the avoidance of embarrassment in error correction is a poor argument for monitoring: classroom correction, properly handled, is not embarrassing, especially if the students are convinced that errors are an unavoidable part of learning. Sixth, the "confidence" the students develop in the privacy of their lab booths is *false* confidence, as they assume wrongly that, with the teacher at the controls, if they make any error they will be corrected, when in fact this will hardly ever (three percent of the time?) be the case.

Seventh, monitoring does not ensure discipline with young learners any better than the presence of any credible authority figure in the lab; this authority figure would usually be the teacher, who can be on call rather than monitoring. Eighth, monitoring can be annoying and disruptive; many students do not like to be interrupted while studying tapes, as it causes them to lose track of the program. Ninth, the practice of assigning grades via monitoring is hardly defensible. The grading system should not invade study time. No one would think of grading study in the library or at home before it is over, so why do it in the lab while it is in progress? Also, monitoring grades are essentially unfair, as some students are graded on easier responses than others. Too, a cumulative monitoring grade does not represent overall proficiency, as each lab program is usually confined to one pattern or rule. A final disadvantage of monitoring is that it very likely retards the development of self-critical ability, an essential ability that the students must develop, since they are going to be on their own almost all the time anyway.

If evaluation is deemed desirable in the laboratory --other than in speaking tests-- then the students should be asked to prepare a segment of the recording --one or two drills or three or four sentences-- and produce it upon request. This allows diagnostic evaluation of their difficulties and assignment, if necessary, of remedial tapes. The successes or failures of the students with various items can then be entered on individual charts, on which information can also be entered in or after class.

For all the reasons given above, it seems that laboratory monitoring can be dispensed with. All that is needed is a two-way communication capability so that the student can ask the teacher for help when he needs it and requests it.

Self-evaluation

Many doubt the value of allowing students to judge their own pronunciation and intonation. They think the students will listen enraptured to the sound of their own voices and fail to detect any errors. But if given sufficient linguistic sophistication beforehand, almost all students can judge fairly well the differences between their recorded imitations and the articulations of the model.

Since the students' ability to detect their own errors will depend on their previous discrimination training in class, it is essential that this training be given and that it be thorough. What is needed is a process of discrimination and articulation training. This process would require a phonologically competent and knowledgeable teacher, adequate materials, and recorders for individual student practice. The process would be mostly self-instructional but would involve teacher evaluation of selected performances; it would result in considerable skill in self-evaluation.

Some pointers on the use of recordings

During phonological practice, when students record and listen to their own voices, they should do so for short stretches of no longer than one minute. The delayed feedback of later listening to a long recording is ineffective.

Few recorded materials need to be played more than once. Instead of playing the entire tape and then going back to play the entire tape again or the sections that caused difficulty, it is better to master each section before going on to the next. Self-tests at the end of each section let the students evaluate their control and determine whether they need further work with that problem; this further work is better done with a supplementary cassette rather than by going through a familiar recording again. When a recording is replayed, it is possible for many students to answer certain stimuli from memory rather than by paying attention to the crucial feature(s) and making the corresponding linguistic choices.

Misuses of the laboratory

The most common misuse of the laboratory is requiring students to work with recordings that are not suitable --the exercises are too easy or too difficult, there is an insufficient variety of activities, or the quality of the recordings is poor.

Another common misuse of the laboratory is to have students work as a group, all responding at the same time to a rigid program which they in no way control. Better work than that can be done in the classroom.

Putting the lab to do what it cannot do --e.g., offer opportunities for conversation-- is another misuse.

If the program coordinates class and lab work, a further misuse of the laboratory is to use it for the initial presentation of material.

Another misuse of the laboratory is to play the same recordings over and over, allowing responses through recall rather than construction.

Perhaps there is no greater misuse of the laboratory than using it to present literary works to students who are not linguistically ready for them. Yet some excellent laboratories are being used that way, forgetting that the lab's purpose is to give audiolingual practice.

If misused, the language laboratory is worse than useless --it is a harmful waste of time.

The laboratory as a listening library

Any material for listening can of course be brought to and presented in class. But it is highly motivating and pedagogically useful to enable students to listen to a variety of materials any time they want. That is the function of the listening library.

The listening library consists in a collection of recordings of a cultural nature, such as plays, poems, songs, lectures, as well as less culturally-oriented materials such as radio programs, the sound tracks of television programs and movies, telephone conversations, social party conversations, talks of all kinds --in a word, a sample of anything and everything spoken in the second language.

News broadcasts in particular have been found to be highly motivating to second language students [W.F. Smith and Woerdehoff 1970]. Short-wave broadcasts could be taped for listening practice too.

A caution about recordings by professional actors: they often use an artificial pronunciation and intonation, making them unsuitable for language students.

For advanced students, listening materials could be recorded with brief pauses after every sentence and content questions after every six to eight sentences, to which the students have to either record a response, on a separate cassette, or (at the advanced level) reply in writing. This greatly increases the pedagogical value of the listening experience.

Research on laboratory effectiveness

There have been several studies of the effectiveness of language laboratories, which have yielded contradictory results.

The Keating Report [1963] concluded that the laboratory was ineffective. However, this study lacked proper controls. No record was kept of how the laboratories were actually used. The listening test was based on written texts. The "speech production" test was not a full-fledged speaking test but consisted merely of the imitation of ten words and the reading aloud of ten short sentences. The study was conducted at a time (1961-62) when there were few or no commercial tapes available for the higher levels. In this study, the non-lab students had 25 percent more class time. Except for two schools, the lab students had just one lab session per week (!). At most, what the Keating study shows is that conditions for the use of the lab in 1961 were far from desirable and that laboratory improvisation by inexperienced teachers does not work.

Lorge [1964] conducted a series of experiments that showed that daily 20-minute use of an audio-active-comparative laboratory resulted in better achievement than other lab conditions, including no lab. One lab session per week did not have any effect. Daily use of the audio-active-comparative lab made that lab condition first or second in 13 out of 14 variables measured. Furthermore, it resulted in a much higher percentage of students going on to advanced courses.

W.F. Smith [1969] concluded after studying two laboratory conditions, electronic classrooms, and a no-lab situation, that laboratory or electronic classroom practice has only a marginal effect on learning when used twice a week for choral response and that beginners benefit if part of their practice includes record-playback responses. He also concluded that the best equipment for schools is a combination of electronic classrooms and laboratories.

One of the objectives of the Pennsylvania Project [P.D. Smith 1970] was to study the effectiveness of laboratories. The results showed that, as it could be expected, 20 unimaginative minutes of laboratory work in lieu of classwork twice a week have no effect. The laboratory classes used the lab with considerable rigidity and quite mechanically: a 10-minute tape run twice in each lab session. This exposed the "lab" students to only 20 minutes of recordings per week, while the "no-lab" students had a tape-recorder in the classroom that was played 10 minutes a day (for a total exposure of 50 minutes of recordings per week). The labs were used in lockstep fashion, all students doing the same thing at the same time (no wonder they were no better than a tape recorder in the classroom). Teacher adherence regarding the use of the equipment was not measured or evaluated. The grading of lab work was inconsistent. No adequate provisions were made for maintenance, with the result that half of the labs were out of order ten percent or more of the school year. Such research does nothing to answer basic questions about the laboratories and their use and effectiveness.

Some conclusions

There can be no doubt that the right study of the right kind of recordings enhances second language learning. The problem is that too often laboratory work has consisted of lockstep practice with mindless drills, two defects that invalidate any lab work.

The audio-active lab is worse than nothing, as it does not allow responses according to individual needs or individual review of difficult sections or objective comparison of responses with the model. At least in the classroom the teacher can introduce a certain amount of individualization.

Cassette machines have resulted in such a reduction in costs that there no longer is any justification for not providing all of our students with individual audio-active-comparative facilities. Only such facilities can really foster the learning of the speaking skill. (The laboratory is not needed expressly to train students in listening comprehension, although of course an existing laboratory can be used for that purpose.) Audio-active-comparative equipment in every booth means of course early discrimination and articulation training.

A serious error of the sixties was to extend to the schools the type of laboratory --a conventional lab--suitable for colleges and universities. Apparently this happened because the consultants on labs during the sixties were college people. Electronic classrooms fit school needs much better than conventional labs. The electronic classroom can be used at any time with minimal disruption. The conventional lab requires disruptive group treks back and forth or individual study during free hours, which school schedules normally do not allow.

As Dodson [1967:2] pointed out, education has moved from the cottage industry of private tutoring to the factory system and specialized labor, but unlike industry it has only begun to use mechanization and barely started to use computer controls. The rational use of recordings and laboratory facilities can do much to bring second language teaching in line with industry in the 1980s.

(Books on the language laboratory are rather dated. They include Hocking [1967], Hayes [1968], and Stack [1971], although the last of these, while technically good, is pedagogically unsound.)

PART II: SOME SUGGESTIONS ON THE USE OF MEDIA

Media include (1) *audio* (records, tapes, radio, and the telephone); (2) *visual* (blackboard, posters, charts, maps, flashcards, books, photographs, the overhead projector, the opaque projector, silent film, slides, filmstrips, duplicated materials, the computer screen, and the teaching machine); (3) *audiovisual* (sound film, television, video-tapes, and video-discs, plus coordinated audio and visual presentations; and (4) *objects* (realia, puppets, games, and kits).

Different media are especially suitable for different aspects of the second language teaching/learning process. However, because language is basically an audiolingual phenomenon which is also written, auditory media and the printed word are enough for most needs, with the exception of the conveyance of significant cultural differences, for which visual media and objects are especially useful.

1) *Audio*. Radio broadcasts can be used quite

effectively in the laboratory [Boyd and Wolfe 1973]. Garfinkel [1972-a, 1972-b] reported on the successful use of live radio broadcasts designed for second year high school students of Spanish and containing carefully selected proverbs, jokes, songs, interviews, commercials, etc. Ideally, all second language programs offering advanced level studies should have a high quality short-wave receiver capable of picking up broadcasts in all the second languages taught in the program.

Telephones have reduced frequencies, so they should not be used to introduce new second language material. However, at the advanced level practice under reduced frequencies is desirable, so there should be some use of telephone conversations.

2) *Visual*. The blackboard can be used, among other things, to memorize a text, first by reading it through two or three times, then by continuing to "read" it in its entirety as more and more words are erased.

Flashcards should not match one second language word to one native language word, but should instead be sentence-to-sentence.

There are many ways in which the overhead projector can be used in the second language classroom, some of which were suggested by Pond [1963]. The overhead projector has the advantage over the blackboard that materials can be prepared in advance and shown when wanted; over the opaque projector it has the advantage of not needing darkness, producing less heat and no noise, and being less bulky and heavy. The overhead projector should be used for structurally oriented materials, not just semantic or contextual materials [Carter 1974].

Slides have over filmstrips the advantage of greater flexibility, as they can be combined in any order and mixed with older ones, thus allowing creativity in presentation --inexperienced teachers, however, may feel more secure using filmstrips [Wright 1974:269].

The students can contribute to the gathering and preparation of visuals. They can make line drawings for the overhead projector, collect pictures, design and letter posters, etc. It is a motivating experience.

3) *Audiovisual*. Very useful are flashcards with a magnetic strip, allowing audiovisual practice. Two machines designed to read them are the Audio-Flashcard Reader (Electronic Futures Inc.) and the Language Master (Bell and Howell).

Sound films are not particularly suited to second

language learning unless especially prepared for that purpose. Even second language teaching films may not be suitable --they are too expensive to produce and tend to emphasize entertainment rather than teaching. At best, films can provide a supplementary listening and cultural experience. They are not really needed in order to have a good second language program. Films prepared for natives will lead to incomprehension and frustration except in the case of very advanced students. Even these should receive copies of the scripts and listen to the sound tracks in advance of viewing the films.

Individual cartridge-loading 8-mm sound-film projectors could be used to considerable advantage, especially during the early phonological minicourse. As an advanced activity, a second language class could produce a short 8-mm film as a project --Fearing [1969] reported that such a project results in much second language production and peer correction.

The advantages of television are that it makes for lively teaching and that it can convey much cultural information. But it is a passive medium, offering listening and seeing but no speaking, either manipulative or communicative. So by itself it cannot support a second language program; it can only supplement the activities of a live teacher. It is better than nothing where there are no schools or qualified teachers, but in regular programs it can only provide cultural and motivational enrichment. As Corder [1966-a:239] put it: "Television teaching suffers from one very serious defect: it is a vehicle of *one-way communication*." To make matters worse, those who have dominated second language teaching via television insist on using monolingual techniques that make progress very slow because programs are difficult to understand.

When video-tapes or video-discs reach a low price (if ever), they will be useful general tools in second language teaching. In the meantime, due to high cost, video-tape remains a medium for special uses, such as the display of certain cultural materials and teacher training. That video-tapes can be effective has been amply demonstrated. Sisk [1975], for example, showed that the discussion of video-taped student dialogue performance significantly improved the students' performance. Huberman and Medish [1975] reported that a two-semester university Spanish course with video-tapes resulted in markedly better listening comprehension, recall, and grammatical and lexical accuracy in speaking and writing; the video-tapes were also found to be highly motivating, lowering attrition. Video-discs have similarly great potential; especially convenient is their capability to carry all other media forms, even books. Yet most of these audiovisual media do not allow a record-compare function, which is essential to second language learning.

4) *Objects*. Certain realia --a model of a house, a model of part of a town, etc.-- could be constructed and used not only in second language teaching but also in other subjects. An exchange of boxes containing objects typical of each culture can be arranged with a foreign school. Another useful proposal [Garfinkel 1972-c] is collecting discarded or inexpensive materials for use in second language activities, something the whole class can contribute to.

23

SELF-INSTRUCTION AND INDIVIDUALIZED INSTRUCTION

Self-instruction and its advantages

Self-instruction, which includes programmed instruction and computer-assisted instruction and which is an element of individualized instruction, is an approach, not a method, as self-instructional language programs could follow various methods.

Among the advantages of self-instruction are that it frees the teacher to help students on an individual basis, it permits the students to pace themselves according to ability and time available, and it allows more active participation by the individual student, as he has to respond to every item.

In self-instructional programs, the students are given detailed directions, clear learning objectives, and ample feedback. Interaction with a machine or programmed textbook is not necessary, as learning can proceed effectively by means of recordings and workbooks. The correct response to each stimulus can be on cards or on a two-column workbook arrangement.

Results can be quite good, as shown by the experience of Boyd-Bowman [1966, 1972] with up to 30 critical ("neglected") languages. As Morehouse put it (in Boyd-Bowman [1973:v]), "self-instruction is not a cut-rate method which produces shoddy results."

Of course, to be successful, self-instruction requires well-motivated students and some interaction with native speakers, as total self-instruction would not do for learning pronunciation or developing conversational ability.

Student reaction to self-instructional programs is quite favorable. A survey mentioned by Boyd-Bowman [1972] showed that 90 percent of students considered such programs very successful or moderately successful; 32 percent found not having formal instruction and actual *advantage*.

Adult students in particular find self-instructional programs advantageous, as their schedules make class attendance difficult, they may live far from where the classes are held, and they like independence, preferring to be self-reliant rather than to follow orders.

Programmed instruction and its advantages

Programmed instruction was first proposed in 1926 by S.L. Pressey, an educational psychologist at Ohio State University who devised "a simple apparatus which gives tests and scores --and teaches."

It should be noted that a machine is not essential to programmed instruction, although it is desirable. Education should be ahead of industry in automating what can be automated, but unfortunately the reverse is true --industry has far outstripped education [Barrutia 1969:21]. As Barrutia put it: "...we should give the machine the task of teaching habitual behavior and the teacher that of teaching creative behavior" [*ibid.*, p. 15]. Using the teacher to do the mechanical aspects of language teaching is "the mechanization of the teacher" [*ibid.*, p. 16], which should be avoided. The teacher who refuses to use the machine for the mechanical aspects of language teaching is "even less efficient than a carpenter who refuses to use power tools in his trade" [Ornstein *et al.* 1971: 159]. It should be clear that *what a machine can do well, a machine should do.*

Using teaching machines has all the advantages of self-instruction plus the advantage, with computer equipment, that the student cannot move on to the next item until he has answered the preceding item correctly.

Characteristics and types of programmed instruction

The first essential characteristic of programmed instruction is that terminal behavior is carefully specified. The problem, as Valdman [1968-a] pointed out, is that terminal behavior cannot be specified for something as infinite and complex as language. We must conclude that only the mechanical aspects of second language learning can be described in terms of terminal behavior. But if important components of language skill can be described and ways of learning them can be devised, perhaps it is not too important that language skill itself cannot be described in detail.

The second essential characteristic of programmed learning is the division of the learning task into a series of small steps leading from the entry behavior to the terminal behavior. These steps consist of a cue, a response, and immediate feedback. In early programs, the steps were very small, but these proved to be too boring to the brighter students; later programs have used somewhat larger steps.

Thirdly, active student responses are required at every step. It is rather useless not to respond. As E. Hocking [1967:107] put it: "Trying to beat the machine is like cheating at solitaire."

Fourthly, at every step the student is provided with knowledge of the accuracy of his response. This feedback reinforces correct responses and rejects incorrect ones.

We can thus say that every step combines teaching and testing, so that a program can be said to be composed of hundreds of small lessons and small tests. In addition to that, it is desirable to have longer progress tests at crucial points in the program.

Early programs tried to make each step so simple that there was virtually no possibility of error. Later programs have allowed a margin of error, partly on the ground that this makes the steps more challenging.

A desirable feature of programs is their adaptation to individual learners through branching (see below).

There are three types of programs: *linear* (or "single-track"), *cyclical* (or "circular"), and *branching*.

Linear programming, based on the theories of B.F. Skinner, forces every student to complete the same series of very small steps. It is inherently boring to the above-average and even, in some cases, to the average students. It was rejected by the generativists, who, unfortunately, rejected all programming along with it --another example of overreaction.

Cyclical programming represents a minor improvement over linear programming in that it requires the students to repeat material cyclically until they meet a criterion for going on. But this doesn't help the bright students.

Branching programs were developed by N.L. Crowder (who called them "intrinsic"). In branching programs, the students are treated differently according to their responses. Thus bright students are allowed to skip certain parts of the main program, while slow students are directed to remedial frames. The basic type of item is the multiple-choice question, with the learners profiting from the mistakes made through trial and error. Thus, all practice to the point of internalization and not beyond that.

Early programs relied on mechanical conditioning

without explanations. But explanations can save many programming steps. So programming should follow the principles of cognitive habit formation, according to which rules are applied consciously until they are mastered and can be applied automatically.

If we want the machine to be in charge and control the progress of the learner, then branching programs require a computer. But this is not necessary with well-motivated students, who can be put in charge and allowed to control all the materials and teaching devices themselves. Thus, some programmers have gone to great lengths to hide the answers from the students so that they won't have access to them until they have produced the appropriate responses. This is unnecessary with well-motivated students, who can cover the answers with a cardboard or plastic card. Index cards can also be used [Chardkoff 1981] to put a sentence and cue on one side and the response on the other.

Some desiderata for programmed language materials

Presentations in programmed language materials should be both auditory and visual. Few of the early programs used recordings.

Meaning should be introduced early, though not necessarily from the start. A case can be made for some structural learning without reference to meaning, but F. Rand Morton's Spanish program, in which the students had to spend about 280 hours working without reference to meaning, was extreme to the point of absurdity.

Laboratory facilities should be used, so that there can be active oral responses. Morton [1961] was right in saying that the language laboratory can be a teaching machine. The fact that the lab tape goes on regardless of student responses does not disqualify the laboratory as a teaching machine: it is simply a teaching machine of which the student is in charge --responsible students will attend to auditory feedback, review segments of the recordings they find difficult, and generally use the recordings as a linear program.

During beginning and intermediate programs, meaning should be conveyed and explanations given in the native language.

Branching is highly desirable in language programs. While low-aptitude students can do well with linear programs [T. Mueller 1968-b, Joiner 1974-a], bright students can find them dehumanizing and an insult to their intelligence.

A linear/branching program

Barrutia [1969, 1970] experimented with a Spanish program combining linear and branching characteristics. All students had to answer the same multiple-choice questions, but while those who answered correctly went on to the next question, a small computer directed the recorded tape of those who answered incorrectly to corrective tracks (reverse and forward on two of eight tape tracks for each incorrect response), and then back to the original question until it was answered correctly.

This was one of the earliest attempts to use branching in second language programming. The program ("Program L") taught only listening and understanding, but the other skills were practiced separately. Program L students were found to do as well as classroom-taught audiolingual students in writing and better than them in listening, speaking, and reading. However, it was found that some students did not do well with automated self-instruction.

Barrutia's original assumption was that total automated self-instruction would be equal to or better than classroom instruction. Later he adopted the view that programmed instruction should be supplemented by personal interaction in small supervised groups.

Possibilities and limitations of programmed instruction

What programmed instruction is best suited for is the teaching of reading skills and the development of vocabulary. It is also quite capable of providing auditory training (poor auditory ability is the cause of much failure), but it has been estimated [Ornstein *et al.* 1971: 115-6] that auditory conditioning takes, at the college level, about half a semester, during which little other instruction can take place.

Programmed instruction is weakest for the productive skills. There is little question that free speaking and free writing will never be programmable. The more mechanical aspects of speech, however, can be programmed to a considerable extent, especially if the students are trained in evaluating utterances as correctly or incorrectly pronounced [Ornstein *et al.* 1971:119].

Due to the impossibility of programming conversation, attempts at total self-instruction are a serious mistake. But most aspects of early second language learning are programmable, and if this is combined with conversation in small groups with native paraprofessionals, better results may be obtained than with the regular teacher-led classroom program.

Still, certain potential disadvantages should be kept in mind. Some students don't do well in self-instruction. Work with programmed materials can be fatiguing. The introduction of a programmed course or courses --equipment, materials-- can be costly.

Partially programmed instruction

Theodore H. Mueller promoted with his French programs the use of "display sessions" (a term coined by Valdman) where the students demonstrated what they had learned in directed conversation with a teacher and two or three other students. The problem with this is its high cost.

Perhaps the solution to having partially programmed instruction is to use programming for only certain functions within a broader program of "guided learning" [Valdman 1968-b]. This means that programming could be combined with conventional instruction by using programming (1) for certain components, (2) remedially, (3) as review or catch-up materials, and (4) for supplementary materials, in all these cases for aspects that cause particular difficulty.

Partial programming enables second language learning to remain a social experience, not just an individual one. In class group work, the students can put to meaningful, creative use what they have been learning via the program. The program would thus be combined with personalized, face-to-face work of various kinds. Whether the student works alone or with others would depend on the nature of the activity. Memorizing a dialogue, for example, is best done in pairs. Conversation is best done in groups of about four to eight. Cultural activities can be done in fairly large groups.

Thus, programmed learning cannot replace the teacher, at least in his function as conversation leader. Of course, he normally performs other functions in partially programmed courses: manager of the learning process, diagnostician, motivator, and evaluator, both of the learner's progress and of the program itself.

Partially programmed courses have proven successful at special schools such as the Foreign Service Institute. In their "programmatic" courses, available so far in Spanish, German, and Portuguese, four hours a day are spent with the programs and two hours a day in class in the introductory courses. The first 100 hours of the Spanish program, for example, cover the sound system, basic grammar and expressions, and a vocabulary of 420 words.

On the effectiveness of self- and programmed instruction

As it has happened with other trends, some saw in this new approach --programmed instruction-- an opportunity for a "quick buck," and rushed to publish extremely defective programs, some of which simply presented clumsily what a good classroom teacher could present far more effectively [Ornstein *et al.* 1971:4].

Such a trend was fortunately largely counteracted by serious efforts and research at a few educational institutions. In a 1967 study at the University of Kentucky [Ornstein *et al.* 1971:161-2], T. Mueller found that a programmed course benefited particularly the average and below-average students and resulted in significantly lower attrition; he found that attrition in first-semester French was reduced from 40 percent to 15 percent [T. Mueller 1968-c]; achievement was superior to national norms [Ornstein *et al.* 1971:19]. Banathy and Jordan [1969] reported that a partially programmed approach combining programmed exercises with classroom-laboratory instruction produced superior results over conventional instruction. In 1969 and 1970, the Language Bureau of the Public Service Commission of Canada tried T. Mueller and Niedzielski's *Basic French, a programmed course* [1968-a] and obtained good results; the self-instructional aspect of the course was found to contribute to motivation among civil servants. Estarellas [1970] reported success with and favorable reactions to a linear program using videotapes, audio-tapes, and books, with motivation the only problem. Prince and Casey [1972] found linear programming effective in teaching several aspects of Spanish grammar. Boyd-Bowman [1973] showed that a supervised independent study class using mastery learning scored about the same as conventional and team-taught classes after a year of Spanish; there were no significant differences in the results.

All of these studies and others prove that partial self-instruction can produce as good or better results than conventional instruction, and at much lower cost, as such programs are machine-intensive rather than personnel-intensive. Programming works not despite an unsound theory but because a theory of induced learning through intelligent conditioning is valid. The language-like behavior that programmed materials can teach underlies creative linguistic behavior and is essential to it. What works should not be rejected on questionable theoretical grounds.

Computer-assisted instruction

As the programmed instruction movement was losing much of its steam in the early seventies, its energy was transferred to computer-assisted instruction, which allows branching programming. Apparently the first computer-assisted instructional program in second languages was the German program established by Adams *et al*. [1968].

Computer-assisted instruction has the following advantages over earlier programming:

--It facilitates branching; this permits skipping and remedial work.

--Larger steps are possible, as errors can be corrected in the branches.

--More than just pace can be individualized.

--The content of the next stimulus can be made to depend on the previous response.

--Partial prompts to a correct response can be provided.

--There can be close supervision of student progress, with the computer keeping a record of student errors and of what each student has learned and prescribing his work accordingly, thus encouraging the practice needed to prevent the formation of wrong habits.

--Although creative language cannot be handled and the computer cannot evaluate speech, dialogue-like activity between the student and the computer is possible.

--In readings, a computer can provide glosses as needed [Henning 1976] and can be programmed to give each gloss a maximum number of times, to gradually shorten its display of the gloss, and to provide various lexical hints rather than the gloss.

--Interactive meaningful practice can be provided in the form of "semantic drills" using blanks and multiple choices [Schaeffer 1981].

Regarding results, it should be noted that at the University of Illinois there has been, for a long time, successful use of computer-assisted language instruction in a good number of languages via PLATO (*P*rogrammed *L*ogic for *A*utomatic *T*eaching *O*perations) programs. Specific studies include that reported by Adams *et al*. [1968] and Morrison and Adams [1968], according to which by the end of one year of computer-assisted instruction in German, combined with classroom activities, the students were significantly superior in writing to an audiolingual group using the laboratory; there were no significant differences in the other skills; the dropout rate of the computer group was 23 percent as opposed to 40 percent for the control group; the computer was especially effective in teaching grammatical rules and vocabulary. At the State University of New York-Stony Brook, Rosenbaum [1969] found that students in a German computer-assisted program performed about as well as an audiolingual group in listening and speaking and significantly better in reading and writing, with gains larger for the average and below-average students. Turner [1970] found that Spanish students who worked with a computer program ("CARLOS") emphasizing grammar and the written language averaged 36 fewer errors on a final written test and scored significantly higher on the CEEB Spanish Reading Examination. Not a small element in the success of computer-assisted programs is that in them the students can respond individually about ten times more than in the conventional classroom [Rosenbaum 1969]. Student attitude toward computer-assisted language instruction is quite favorable; Scanlan [1971] found that 90 percent of students would recommend computer-assisted courses to others; Olsen [1980] found students quite enthusiastic.

Some potential drawbacks of computer-assisted language instruction are the following:

--Hardware and computer time are very expensive. Yet Scanlan [1971] claimed that if many students make use of the system the cost becomes quite low; he estimated the cost of the PLATO system at the University of Illinois-Urbana as 35 cents a student hour, lower than language laboratories.

--Programming can be poor; this is due to the fact that programmers are not trained in second languages and second language teachers and authors are not trained in computer programming. This can be remedied.

--The systems available are incompatible; this again is a problem that could be minimized in time.

--There is a need for constant updating of programs, something very expensive; but the problem could be reduced by making computer language programs independent of current events.

--Many people think that computer-assisted instruction is dehumanizing. Those who try it, soon change their attitudes as they realize the computer gives them far greater freedom of choice. Generally public attitude toward computers is becoming more positive, as programmable calculators and computer-based games are being used more and more.

Of course, it would be a serious mistake to try to provide full second language instruction via computers. They are suitable for the cognitive and mechanical aspects of reading and writing, not for creative writing or for the audiolingual skills; voice synthesizers have been connected to computers, but the sound quality is far from adequate for second language work.

Conclusions about self-, programmed, and computer-assisted instruction

In the euphoria of the sixties, leaders of the programmed instruction movement expected mass demand for second language instruction of such proportions that programmed instruction would be the only solution. When instead of larger enrollments there was a drastic drop in the number of second language students, language teachers saw themselves fighting to protect their jobs and with no desire whatsoever to turn to teaching machines.

Today probably no more than five percent of all schools use programmed or computer-assisted second language instruction, and even in these few schools they are used to a very limited extent. Not surprisingly, there is little interest on the part of publishers.

Perhaps programmed and computer-assisted instruction will be first accepted in the form of short programs for specific purposes rather than longer programs to cover the bulk of instruction. Self-instruction, without special machines, is gaining acceptance as a way of offering "neglected" or "critical" languages on a regular basis when small enrollments make conventional courses uneconomical.

The self-instruction movement --if it can be called that, as it isn't large-- resulted in the establishment in 1972 of the National Association of Self-Instructional Language Programs (NASILP). This association provides member institutions with information about and evaluation of self-instructional programs, as well as access to master tapes and many other services.[△]

[△] The current address of the National Association of Self-Instructional Language Programs is Humanities Building, Box 38, Temple University, Philadelphia, PA 19122.

In conclusion, teachers, media, language laboratories, self-instruction, programmed instruction, and computer-assisted instruction all have important roles to play in second language teaching. Perhaps what is needed is *variable partially self-instructional programs*, variable in the sense that most materials come with instructions for use in the classroom or via independent study or in different combinations of both. In connection with such materials, most audiolingual practice could take place in the language laboratory, most graphic practice with teaching machines or computers, and all creative, free use of the language by means of personal interaction in a classroom or conversation lounge.

Individualized instruction --what it is

The individualized instruction movement of the seventies was a reaction to lockstep instruction, which takes little account of individual differences. Individualized instruction is an approach --not a method-- that maximizes attention to individual student differences.

Individualized instruction has a long history in North America. It was the mode of instruction in the one-room schoolhouse. It is widely used in the teaching of mathematics and reading, as each student studies these subjects at his level of competence. There was a major individualization movement in the United States from the 1890s to the 1920s. Furthermore, many teachers have long adapted to the individual needs of their students, which is a form of individualization.

Individualized instruction is based on the idea that there are important differences between students and that treating all students alike is quite undemocratic, for it fills the needs of only a minority of the students. It is a mistake to speak to 30 or 40 bodies as if they had only one mind, for as Benardo [1972] put it, in a class "there are 30 or 40 minds ticking away, appearing to listen to you, appearing to be enthralled, but very often on their own wavelengths, far, far away from you." In lockstep instruction, the bright students can get bored and the slow students fail --hardly a desirable situation.

In individualized instruction it is possible to individualize pace, goals, means, and content. Other characteristics of individualized instruction (adapted mostly from Gougher [1972:2-5]) are the following:

--The students are tested often, preferably when ready to be tested; tests are used both to diagnose difficulties and evaluate progress.

--Tests are criterion-referenced.

--Mastery learning is a condition for going on; a minimum 80 percent accuracy (usually higher) is required in order to proceed to the next unit.

--Failure will still occur, as some students simply will not do the work.

--Each student helps plan his own curriculum; he has a considerable number of choices open to him.

--Variable credits are essential.

--Flexibility in scheduling is desirable.

It should not be assumed from the above that individualized instruction has no structure and that the student, in a very permissive atmosphere, is allowed to do "his own thing."

--Good individualized programs are closely and carefully structured and students in such programs do more, not less work.

--The students are given detailed instructions, in the form of learning activity packets (or "LAPs"); these are discussed below.

--A core is essential; additional material should also be available.

It should be clear that at the beginning level, when all students have to acquire the basics of the language, the only thing that can be individualized is pace. At the intermediate level goals, means, and to a certain extent (in the form of supplementary materials) content can also be individualized. At the advanced level, individualization takes especially the form of content choice, mostly in terms of minicourses.

Self-pacing

The importance of self-pacing is seen in the fact that in Carroll's [1963] model of school learning three of the five principles are related to time. In lockstep instruction, such time constraints mean that only a small minority achieve mastery of the subject of instruction.

Students learn at different rates of speed, so individualization means first of all self-pacing. Without individualization of pace, some students score very high and others repeatedly score very low, as they cannot get a good mark within the time allotted. The unfairness of this, as Shuell and Lee [1976:122-3] have noted, is that it is like comparing the running abilities of individuals on the basis of their reaching or not a specified location, without considering how far they have had to run.

Even students of low ability and below-average intelligence can master such complex tasks as learning a second language if they know what to do and are given adequate time to do it. This does not mean that 100 students will be at 100 different points in the program. Their progress will naturally form a normal curve, allowing for small group activities; in fact, the fastest student should not be allowed to go faster than two or three other students, and the slowest student should not be allowed to proceed slower than two or three other students, thus guaranteeing small groups at the two extremes of the curve.

To ensure that there is some progress by all students, a certain minimum speed should be established. Perhaps one third to one half the normal lockstep speed would be suitable. Without a minimum speed, some students may not make any progress at all. Besides, if progress is too slow, elements of the language that should be related in the mind remain unrelated.

Goals and learning strategies

It is desirable to allow students a choice of goals. A frequent choice of goals is whether they want to learn to just read the language or learn primarily how to speak it.

Once a goal is chosen, however, there is a best way to reach it that is inherent to the nature of the goal. Thus, one does not learn to speak a language by reading it. Having chosen an audiolingual goal, the student has to be willing to study in ways conducive to audiolingual attainment.

For that reason, it is a serious mistake to try to individualize means to the same goal in terms of learning strategies. We cannot shirk responsibility for student learning by saying it depends on personal learning strategies over which we have no control. It is the duty of the teacher to guide the student into the adoption of the learning strategies most suitable to his particular goal. This may involve teaching him how to learn and offering him certain preliminary forms of training, such as auditory discrimination and differentiation training. But it is the teacher who knows (or should know) how languages are best learned and who should determine and implement the procedures for the attainment of any goal.

Mastery learning

Mastery learning --the requirement that each student should master a task before proceeding to the next one--is an important part of individualized instruction. It is particularly important for second language programs, because these programs have a cumulative effect --if something is not mastered, it will affect all future performance.

It is up to the teacher to maintain high standards in an individualized program. The minimum mastery level should be 80 percent for just passing, higher for good marks.

Performance objectives

In individualized instruction, the student is told what he should be able to do at the end of a unit of study, the conditions for this performance, and the performance criterion (such as percentage of correct responses). This statement to the student is a performance objective.

Performance objectives respond to the demand for accountability. They also answer students' questions about what is expected of them and why. They could be the basis for regional, national, and even international articulation. They could be used to reward not only excellence in learning but also excellence in teaching.

While only the mechanical aspects of second language learning can be specified in detail in performance objectives, this is very useful, as far as it goes. The basic rules and elements of the language must be mastered by all students and here performance objectives can play a very important role.

Performance objectives ensure that all students will study what is necessary for the attainment of their goals --left to themselves, some students may not feel even important needs. At the same time, performance objectives don't limit the students, since they are free to learn anything else they want.

(Two good books on performance objectives are Valette and Disick [1972] and Steiner [1975].)

Learning activity packets (LAPs)

To guide individual and small group study in an individualized program, many recommend the use of learning activity packets. These consist of the following seven parts:

1) Title or topic, for filing purposes.

2) Rationale --the why of the packet, important for motivational reasons.

3) Performance objectives.

4) Self-administered pre-test, similar in format to the official post-test. Students who do very well in the pre-test can skip the LAP.

5) Learning activities. There should be a variety of these --oral and graphic, receptive and productive, individual and in small groups, with or without the use of equipment and media.

6) Self-administered post-test, similar in format to the official post-test. Students who do well in this go on to take the official post-test. Those who do poorly are directed to further learning activities.

7) Official post-test, which is administered to the students by the teaching staff, with marks recorded.

Teichert [1972] found that "learning packages" significantly ($p < .01$) improved learning and reduced the number of dropouts. This doesn't mean that LAPs are imperative in self-paced programs --in most cases checklists are adequate. Of course, if there is enough time available to prepare them, LAPs should be written. Part of the problem is that writing good LAPs is not easy, even when the necessary time is available.

LAPs have been misused by making them the basis for much individual study. Learning a second language is largely a social activity. Useful as they are, LAPs are harmful if they turn social interaction into a situation where numerous individual students work by themselves.

Testing in individualized instruction

From the discussion of LAPs above, it is clear that at least four alternate forms of each test are needed for each unit --one for the self-administered pre-test, one for the self-administered post-test, and at least two for the official post-test.

That these many tests are needed is evident from their purposes and the philosophy of individualized instruction. The pre-test is necessary to orient the students to the key features of what they are to learn and to permit LAP skipping. The self-administered post-test lets them know if they have really mastered the unit and if they are ready for the official post-test. Since the official post-test will have to be administered several times, as groups of students and individual students complete the unit, it is obvious that it should be available in several alternate forms.

Perhaps groups of teachers can work on the preparation of alternate forms of tests. Paraprofessionals can help in administering and scoring the numerous tests needed. Alternate forms of tests can be provided for by picking and shuffling 4 x 6 cards each containing a test item; about two or three times the number needed for each test must be prepared [Reinert 1972].

Group and individual work in individualized instruction

At the beginning of the individualized program and for several weeks students should meet as a class. The purpose of this is to enable the teacher to (1) give general instructions, (2) give pointers about second language learning, (3) teach the elements of pronunciation and intonation, something the students cannot do very well by themselves, (4) provide a brief cultural orientation, and (5) establish the necessary *esprit de corps*. Not the least reason for starting with lockstep instruction is that many students themselves prefer such a start [Morrey 1971].

After pace individualization has started, the *esprit de corps* can be maintained by having some whole-class activities on a regular basis. These can be all the activities that are not geared to specific levels of language skill, such as cultural activities, language games, visits by native speakers, slide lectures, singing and dancing, and so forth.

Pace individualization means the formation of streamed groups. Membership in these groups is not permanent but is subject to change as the students reach various points in the program. For conversation practice, the number of students in small groups should be four to eight, ideally five or six. Occasionally, temporary groupings by interest rather than position in the program can be formed.

The topics of conversation for small groups should be carefully chosen by the teacher, taking student suggestions into account. Leaving each group to its own devices does not produce good results. Controversial topics should not be used with beginners, as their linguistic limitations will make their attempts at discussion very frustrating.

Papalia and Zampogna [1972] found that a third-year French class that worked mostly in small groups outperformed ($p < .05$) a conventional class in the four language skills and had much larger enrollment into the fourth year (63 percent vs. 35 percent).

For some activities, such as practicing dialogues, drills, and questions and answers, pairs of students work better than small groups. For many activities, individual study is possible.

The teacher in individualized instruction

In lockstep instruction the teacher is at center stage, the fountain of knowledge for his class, all-powerful and omnipresent, sure that no learning is taking place unless he is being listened to. For some teachers, who are "hams" at heart, it is difficult to change from such a role to a less central one. But such a change is necessary, especially when one considers individual student needs and the fact that the lockstep class teacher spends as much as two-thirds of class time on things that a non-teacher (including a machine) can do.

In individualized programs, the teacher is a manager of the learning process. This involves planning it, guiding it, motivating learners, helping them and evaluating their work, being counselor and partner, and having neither paternalistic and autocratic nor *laissez faire* attitudes. The teacher no longer does everything, certainly not what machines or less specialized personnel can do. And yet he *is* very important, and on his attitudes and behavior depends the success or failure of the program.

The relationship between the teacher and the students is also changed. He gets to know them better on a one-to-one basis. Because of that he can help them better and he can determine which students are sufficiently responsible to be in charge of their own learning. The teacher does not assume, toward any student, the attitude of "take it or leave it" --no matter how much self-pacing there may be, the teacher is responsible for ensuring that learning does take place.

The student in individualized instruction

Since students learn what is important for them as individuals, an effort must be made to convince them of the advantages of learning a second language. Beyond the whys, the students need to be told what to learn, how, and even by what date (there must be a minimum speed).

Students may misunderstand their role in individualized instruction, and interpret freedom as laxity. Excessive freedom is counterproductive. We cannot base our procedures on the frequently confused vagaries of student feelings. In some individualized programs instruction has been excessively centered around student wishes. We do know better than children what needs to be learned and how, and there is nothing wrong in making such knowledge part of the individualized program.

A minimum speed is particularly important. I remember visiting an individualized program directed by one of the leaders of the individualization movement and learning that near the end of the term 40 percent (!) of the students had not done anything. Even with college students, we cannot refuse to be at least partially *in loco parentis*. Given absolute freedom, some students may spread a day's work into two weeks, two months, or the whole year.

In individualized instruction each student is seen as a different person who moves at his own speed (within limits), who is at the level determined by his own performance (and not his age), who largely motivates himself and can be responsible for his own learning, who can behave as an adult (within limits) if given the opportunity to do so, and who will use (with some exceptions) the opportunity to learn and do the necessary work.

Peer teaching in individualized instruction

Some peer teaching occurs in any program, whenever a student helps another with a learning difficulty. In individualized instruction, this can be encouraged and systematized. Students in advanced courses can be used as tutors and monitors for students in the early courses, especially for the slow students. This reportedly works quite well, as the more advanced students take pride in doing it and the younger students look up to the older ones. Reportedly the tutors learn a great deal from the experience, as maybe it is true that one doesn't really learn something until he has to teach it.

Semke [1975] found that a tutoring program where second-year German students led small groups of first-year students was a success. At the end of the year first-year students voted overwhelmingly to keep the program, and second-year students asserted they learned more than the beginners.

To facilitate such peer-teaching programs, perhaps the advanced students should be given partial credit toward their own courses for the time and effort spent in tutoring.

Peer teaching could be used in partially individualized instruction where all students have to be at the same point in the program on given dates (i.e., where pace is not individualized). In that case, the better students in the same course, who have already mastered the unit, would help the poorer students until all have met the criterion for going on to the next unit.

Grading, credits, and scheduling in individualized instruction

A system of lockstep instruction fails hard-working students of below average ability, for they cannot get a passing grade within the time allotted.

In individualized instruction, grades are not based on comparisons between students but are assigned on the basis of mastery over the material. Teetor [1972] added to letter grades the categories shown in Figure 23.1.

		Passive Knowledge	Active Knowledge
"5"	"Superior"	90%	90%
"4"	"Outstanding"	80%	80%
"3"	"Good"	80%	50%
"2"	"Fair"	80%	30%
"1"	"Passing"	80%	10%

Figure 23.1

It seems to me that, contrary to Teetor's figures, minimum active knowledge (for a "Passing" grade) should be 50 percent, as language knowledge, if not made active, tends to be forgotten. Another system proposed for individualized programs is Reinert's [1972], which consists in giving an A to those who pass with 80 percent the first time they take the test, a B for those who reach 80 percent the second time, and a C for those who need to take the test three or more times to reach that criterion. (This has the added advantage that it discourages excessive test taking.)

Whatever system is adopted, administrators, parents, and students all want and deserve accurate student progress evaluation and specific grades. Grades have the useful additional function of inducing poorly motivated students to work, if nothing else to avoid a failure. Grades should be supplemented by frequent reports to parents --every month, for example-- telling them where their children are in the program and where they should be by that date.

The use of failing marks should not be eliminated altogether. The knowledge that they are occasionally used does wonders to prevent procrastination. There should be a minimum speed and a minimum level of mastery below which there is failure. Failure is, after all, a part of life, and language students can learn important lessons from it.

For some students, it may be necessary to use signed, formal "contracts" according to which they agree to cover a certain amount of material and to learn it to a certain level of mastery by a given date. Well-motivated students don't need this.

Regarding credits, there is no reason why they should be awarded on the same date, and on the basis of whole courses, to everybody. Units of credit can be awarded at any time during the school year. Alternatively, fractional credits can be awarded at the end of the term for whatever the student has completed. It is the rigidity of administrators who do not allow variable credits to be granted that has made X years of a second language meaningless, as without variable credits no mastery criterion can be applied.

As to scheduling, the easiest way out of many possible problems is to have all levels of each language offered every period of every day, although the teacher will be available only on certain hours.

Minicourses

After the students have completed the basic-skills courses and have reached the advanced level, they should be allowed to pursue personal interests, further develop certain skills, or meet career needs. This individualization of content is best accomplished by means of minicourses, limited-credit courses lasting from a few weeks to a whole semester and offered on a largely self-instructional basis.

Since minicourses are electives, the students should have a voice in their preparation, especially in terms of suggesting topics. These topics will normally fall into three categories: language skills, culture, and special interests.

Minicourses are an ideal form of enrichment for those who are taking a regular advanced course, and of skill maintenance for those who are not. They have the additional advantage that no single minicourse is long enough to be boring.

Through the offering of many minicourses, an individualized program can serve the interests of all students.

Logan [1973] showed the large variety of long- and short-term courses that it is possible to offer in an individualized high school second language (German) program.

Materials for individualized instruction

Local preparation of all-new materials is much too time-consuming and expensive, and it normally needs to be done by a team. So most individualized programs adapt existing materials. Specialists can prepare materials for widespread adoption. But publishers cannot be expected to produce the great number of alternate programs needed to individualize goals, content, learning strategies, personality characteristics, etc., so at best we can expect the production of materials that individualize pace plus possibly some goals. A step forward would be the production of many small modules that a teacher can put together in different combinations to provide for greater individualization [Logan 1970:141-2].

On the effectiveness of individualized second language instruction

Reports from many individualized programs indicate that attrition is greatly reduced through individualization.

M. Smith [1968] found that classes that progressed according to the criterion of mastery (90 percent of the students responding correctly at least 80 percent of the time) scored markedly higher in the final test than those that progressed at the teacher's option, usually after finishing each unit. Teichert [1972] found that the use of learning activity packets (one per week) in beginning college German resulted in significantly higher ($p < .01$) scores in the midterm and final exams and in the MLA-Cooperative Listening and Speaking tests. Papalia and Zampogna [1972] showed that individualized high school French level III classes with learning activity packets and emphasis on small group work scored higher ($p < .05$) in all four skills of the MLA-Cooperative tests. Students in a self-paced class in beginning college Spanish achieved as well or better in the MLA-Cooperative Listening and Reading tests than those in a lockstep course [Hartley 1972, Hartley and Dannerbeck 1974]; it was also found in this study that a conventional textbook with carefully prepared performance objectives is quite adequate for self-paced instruction. Students in individualized German did as well or better than regular course students in final tests at the University of California, Berkeley [Clausing *et al.* 1972]. At the University of Colorado, enrollment in Spanish doubled after 1972 as a result of the establishment of an individualized program; informal observation also indicated noticeably higher achievement, especially in the productive skills [Walker 1976:143]. A three-year experiment at Ohio State University, involving six languages, showed that individualized instruction based on the self-paced study of tapes and written materials at home or in learning centers halted the decline in enrollments; however, lack of a minimum speed meant much procrastination and many students not earning a single credit [Scully 1980].

We see from the above that individualized instruction can be quite effective, but also that its effectiveness can be drastically reduced by not taking a few simple preventive measures.

Potential disadvantages of individualized instruction

Some of the problems in establishing and running an individualized program are the following:

--Administrators, parents, and students may be unwilling to change. This is a problem with any innovation, and the solution is to do the necessary public relations work.

--It is very time-consuming to set up. True, but once established it need not take more time than a lockstep program. Besides, the availability of appropriate materials with numerous tests would greatly reduce the time needed to set it up.

--It is very time-consuming to maintain. This need not be so; the use of self-tests and peer teaching greatly reduces administration time.

--It takes much careful planning, far more so than a lockstep program. True, but it is worth the effort.

--Individualizing a program is too time-consuming for the individual teacher to do by himself. True; although some have done it, without adequate materials it is not recommended.

--Individualized instruction requires team teaching, something few schools can afford. This is not true --the one-room rural schoolhouse is proof of it.

--Individualized programs are too dependent on two key people: an enthusiastic teacher and a supportive administrator; if either leaves or cools off to the idea, the program disappears [Sutton 1972:113]. This is true; however, a successful individualized program will naturally attract the support of other people on a continuing basis.

--Individualization requires special facilities. This is not true. A regular classroom can be easily adapted to it; for individual study all that is needed is a way to provide the correct answers to the various drills and exercises.

--Articulation with schools higher up is very difficult. As long as most colleges go by years of study rather than mastery in their admission requirements, articulation will continue to be difficult regardless of the nature of the lower language programs. Individualization does not particularly add to the problem.

--Some teachers cannot teach in individualized programs. True: teachers who cannot function with a high noise level (although the quiet of the lockstep classroom only hides boredom and frustration) or who are unwilling to delegate much of the responsibility for learning to their students find individualized instruction to be "against the grain."

--Not all students do well in individualized instruction. True: immature students cannot embark on a program of self-directed learning; many students prefer lockstep instruction. Zampogna *et al.* [1976] found that, given a semester of each type of instruction, 40 percent of the students preferred individualization, 40 percent preferred a traditional environment, and 15 percent preferred individualization but felt they needed a structured classroom (it can be inferred that the kind of individualization that was being proffered was rather unstructured). Twarog and Walters' [1981] report on individualization at Ohio State University confirms that many students cannot be left to study on their own without any structure or deadlines; they listed student procrastination and "no shows" as problems. Individualization should extend to the type of class --individualized or lockstep-- preferred by the learner.

--There is a tendency to do away with structure in individualized programs. This introduces overall permissiveness, with disastrous results. There is no reason why individualized programs could not be nearly as structured as lockstep programs.

--There is a problem with test security, as faster students can convey to slower students the content of the tests they have taken. This problem can be solved by producing a good number of alternate forms of tests by choosing test items from a large test item pool as suggested by Reinert [1972].

--Students can go too slow or too fast. True, but this is easy to solve: bright students should not be allowed to go faster than the fastest small group, slow students should maintain a minimum speed or suffer penalties and in any event should not be allowed to go slower than the slowest small group.

--Individualized instruction can easily become mechanical individual study excluding social interaction. This is true only if communicative activities are not promoted.

--There is a danger of trying to individualize too much. This is true. It would be wonderful if each learner could freely choose his goals, ways to reach them that suit his personality, the content of instruction, and his pace --but it would be totally unwieldy. It is impossible to accomodate instruction to "the entire spectrum of individuality" [Chastain 1976:229] --choices must necessarily be restricted. The need to guide the student as closely as necessary should not be sacrificed on the altar of individual differences.

Conclusions about individualized instruction

Individualized instruction, especially in regard to pace and major goals, is highly desirable, as there is no such thing as an "average" student --each student is an individual with particular characteristics, abilities, wants, and needs.

As we have seen in the preceding section, almost all of the possible difficulties in individualizing instruction *can* be overcome. It is therefore to be regretted that individualized instruction has not been adopted by all secondary and postsecondary institutions offering second languages. It is to be hoped that despite the receding of the individualization movement from the forefront of second language teaching more such institutions will "see the light" and adopt at least pace and major goal individualization for the benefit of their students.

For those that do not want to fully commit themselves to individualization, perhaps the compromise solution would be partially individualized instruction, where all are tested together, those attaining mastery going on to side enrichment work, those not attaining mastery doing extra work and *then* being tested for a grade --this combines mastery learning, the elimination of failures, enrichment, etc. within conventional class treatment

[Chastain 1976:225-8].

Of course, many teachers have long used a sort of individualization by the simple device of asking the harder or earlier questions from the bright students and the easier or later questions from the slow ones; but this lacks several of the advantages of the Chastain proposal just described and many of the advantages of full individualization. It is also possible to individualize instruction for some students or for some parts of the program.

(Three good books on the individualization of second language instruction are Altman [1972], Gougher [1972], and Logan [1973].)

24

A RESEARCH BASIS; CONCLUSIONS

PART I: A RESEARCH BASIS

The need for research

Research can be defined as a careful search for the truth. It was defined by Good [1945] as "the careful, unbiased investigation of a problem, based insofar as possible upon demonstrable facts and involving refined distinctions, interpretation, and usually some generalization." Recently H.D. Brown [1980:219] referred to research as "explicit answers to carefully framed questions."

Tentative answers, such as most of the proposals in this book, do not become scientifically explicit until they are subjected to the rigors of experimental research. Languistics is an empirical science, and its only hard data come from the careful observation of variables. Intuition and logic can be a good source of hypotheses, but only empirical research can test the hypotheses.

Without a research basis, we shall always be the slaves of fashion in the feeder disciplines --linguistics, psychology, education, etc.--; we shall always follow mere opinions and fads, be unable to resolve controversies or resist bandwagons, and remain very much without a sense of direction.

With a research basis and a systematic program of experimentation such as exists in the exact sciences, languistics can assure the accumulation of knowledge rather than continue to unsystematically probe this and that [Butzkamm 1973:171]. The data thus obtained would have value as empirical knowledge quite apart from any theories and would contribute to languistics developing its own theory. The principles and procedures originating from any particular source would then be widely applied only after they have proven effective, that is, after they have been empirically validated.

Attitudes toward research

One should neither be enamored with research nor be cynically skeptical about it. The best attitude to have is one of informed, selective appreciation. This means, among other things, not accepting uncritically the results of those experiments that confirm prevalent beliefs or rejecting unquestioningly those that don't.

It seems strange, but many people in our profession would rather accept emotion-laden subjective views than facts painfully culled from empirical study. This distrust of and aversion toward research has several causes, among them the following:

(1) Research can yield apparently contradictory results. The solution to that consists in learning to read and interpret research. For example, a few studies seem to contradict much evidence that early exposure to spelling has a negative effect on pronunciation; however, a careful reading of those few studies shows that they introduced other variables favorable to the reading groups and unfavorable to the oral groups.

(2) Teachers know little about research. Here the answer is to include a research component in their training.

(3) Many teachers react negatively to research because they have often been asked to implement research findings in a hurry. Here the solution is to make administrators aware of the practical limitations of research.

(4) Much research is irrelevant to the classroom. The participation of teachers in *classroom* research would increase the applicability of research.

(5) Research is very expensive. This is true of large-scale studies. But small-scale studies need not be expensive. In fact, good teachers are always conducting informal experiments, that is, trying out something with a certain group of students and observing whether it works; with some training, they could turn some such informal observations into formal observations and thus not only satisfy their curiosity and improve their teaching but also contribute to knowledge in languistics.

(6) Research cannot be implemented because of the reluctance of the "establishment" to change. But if one cannot succeed in obtaining implementation locally, one can at least report his findings to the profession, in the hope that others will find themselves in a position to implement them.

Teachers can learn much from research and can be trained to conduct some research themselves, and researchers can learn much from teachers --it is a mutual feedback situation.

Types of languistic research

In addition to theoretical inquiries dealing with ideas, and in order to validate such ideas, three types of research are needed in languistics: descriptive studies, small-scope experiments, and large-scope experiments.

Descriptive studies include such things as surveys, case studies, questionnaires, diaries, interviews, and observational studies; they constitute about 70 percent of languistic research [Frechette 1976].

Small-scope experiments deal with only one or at most a few variables and involve comparison under controlled conditions; they are usually though not necessarily small in scale.

Large-scope experiments deal with many variables; they are usually but not necessarily large in scale. (Partly based on Stern and Cummins [1981:237-40].)

Some difficulties in languistic research

The main difficulty with research in languistics is that which haunts research in all the social sciences --unlike the physical sciences, where everything can be controlled, it is quite difficult to maintain controls on people. Among the people variables that are hard to control are the attitudes and behavior of teachers and students, the attitudes of parents and peers toward second language study or toward a particular language and culture, and the social environment in the school and the community.

A solution that is sometimes proposed is that experiments be carried out under teaching laboratory conditions. The problem with that is that the less conditions are like the classroom situation, the less validity teaching experiments have. Thus, in methodological comparisons there is no guarantee that teachers will adhere to their assigned methods; using recorded lessons rather than live teaching would solve that problem but would greatly reduce validity. It is possible, however, to video-tape all teacher-taught lessons and spot-check them immediately to ensure that each teacher follows his assigned method.

What the student actually does can obscure the effect of experimental treatments; thus, monolingual method students cannot be stopped from translating often, traditional method students can engage in much audiolingual activity, etc. [Carroll 1966-b].

Statistical calculations can be misleading --class means, for instance, can obscure such variables as the relationship between procedures and learner characteristics. Even time of instruction can be a significant variable, as Politzer [1972:146] found in an experiment.

Additional problems are that few studies are comparable, since they differ in more than one variable [Asher 1972:179]. Furthermore, isolated experiments with non-comparable control groups remain isolated; they do not add up to a body of knowledge.

The gravest fault of most languistic research is the lack of sufficient controls. And the pity of it is not so much that certain things cannot be fully controlled, but that much that *can* be controlled has not been controlled.

Experimental research is our only hope for significant progress. Despite its potential shortcomings, it is all we have. It may be impossible to be totally objective in languistic research, but that doesn't mean we should not try. Not trying would be like a surgeon not washing his hands because some patients will die anyway.

Some methodological research studies

Delattre [1947] conducted, in the school year 1946-47, an experiment at Oklahoma State University involving the study of French with records vs. traditional instruction. The record class had a 12-week pre-reading period. At the end of the school year, the record class was evaluated by Delattre as being superior in all skills except spelling. Unfortunately, there was no pre-test and there were very few controls.

Agard and Dunkel [1948] conducted an investigation of the effectiveness of the "Army" method. Theirs was not an attempt at experimentation but a survey. They were able to determine the apparent superiority of the structural method for the development of oral skills, especially pronunciation. However, they also concluded that relentless drill can result in much boredom.

The first major experiment conducted with serious attempts at controls was that of Scherer and Wertheimer [1964] at the University of Colorado, in German, for the school years 1960-62. It was not, as frequently described, a two-year experiment but a one-year experiment with follow-up testing, for during the second year there were no separate groups in terms of instruction. The methods compared were a direct (monolingual), inductive audiolingual method --not the main type of audiolingual method-- and the traditional, grammar-translation method, with pre-reading for the audiolingual group. There was extensive pre- and post-testing. Needed laboratory facilities were not available in time, so the traditional students, who needed no special facilities, were able to do about three times the amount of study of the audiolingual students. Despite this, the audiolingual students were markedly superior in listening and speaking at the end of one year (and managed to retain superiority in speaking at the end of a second year of undifferentiated teaching). Basically what this study showed is that what is emphasized is learned best, as the traditional students were superior in reading and writing (and translation).

In my 1964-65 experiment at Ohio State University, I compared a group taught according to a 12-week pre-reading, structural, bilingual, audiolingual method with randomly selected students from classes taught traditionally with a method emphasizing reading and dictation. No pretest was given; the only student data were their IQ scores, which were similar across groups. At the end of the school year, the audiolingual students were vastly superior in listening and speaking and had scores similar to the control students in a relatively easy reading task; writing ability was not measured, but the audiolingual group, which had had no dictation whatsoever during the year, was superior in spelling *unknown* words from dictation, although the traditional group had had daily dictation practice.

Chastain and Woerdehoff [1968] reported that after one year of instruction in Spanish at Purdue University, audiolingual students (exposed inductively to drills and to the four skills one at a time) were better in the repetition of phrases but significantly poorer in reading than students exposed to deductive cognitive exercises and to all four skills from the start. After two years [Chastain 1970] there were no significant differences. Probst [1970], on the other hand, found an audiolingual-visual method superior to a cognitive-code method for teaching Spanish to university students.

It was thought that the study that would settle most questions in the audiolingual vs. traditional ("cognitive") controversy would be the Pennsylvania Project [P.D. Smith 1970]. It compared three methods: "second-generation" traditional, "first-generation" audiolingual, and modified audiolingual ("audiolingual plus grammar"). This terminology already shows the difficulty. The methods were never adequately defined: Why can't "audiolingual" be also "cognitive"? What, if anything, is "audiolingual" *without* grammar?!

The study was very ambitious. It included 58 secondary schools and 104 second language teachers of French and German. It covered a four-year span (1965-69). The project had six leaders of the profession as consultants, including Lado and Valdman. It made use of numerous pretests and post-tests and sophisticated statistics.

And yet, the results were disappointing to those who expected the superiority of the audiolingual method to emerge. At the end of four years, the only significant differences were superiority of the traditional classes in reading and writing (the traditional classes had also been superior in listening at the end of two years). No significant advantage was found in the use of the language laboratory as used in the study.

Here, again, one can evaluate research better by reading between the lines. To take the use of laboratories, no significant advantage was found in their use. But how were they used? Very unimaginatively, on the basis of two 10-minute tapes per week, played twice --hardly a use conducive to much learning.

The main finding, about the relative merits of the methods, is faulty for several reasons. To begin with, classes were assigned to methods on the basis of which textbooks they used, not on the basis of how they were used. What did the teachers really do? Observers knew the method of each class and used separate scales for each method; but even with this faulty observation system it became clear that traditional teachers spoke far more than expected and audiolingual teachers spoke less than expected. Thus there was a convergence of the methods towards a common teaching practice. The amount of audiolingual work done by a teacher seems to have depended on his oral ability, not on the textbook/method to which he was assigned (proof of this was the correlation between teachers' scores in speaking proficiency and student scores in listening comprehension).

Another problem resulted from the assignment of teachers to methods. Most teachers had been trained traditionally and preferred to teach according to that training, so many of the audiolingual teachers were teaching against their preference. Related to this is the fact that, although training in audiolingual teaching was provided, it was pitifully inadequate --a total of just 13 hours! My experience has been that someone who has been taught and trained traditionally needs many months of retraining before he can barely teach audiolingually, and years of audiolingual teaching experience before he can do a really good job. This may have been the greatest weakness of the Pennsylvania Project.

A further weakness is that in the first year the audiolingual classes covered only 10-15 units with 525-650 words while the traditional classes covered 28-30 units with 1,400-1,500 words [Valette 1969]. It is no wonder, therefore, that at the end of two years the traditional classes were ahead in the receptive skills of reading and listening; yet the difference in mean points was small, which may indicate better retention for the audiolingual classes.

Basically the problem with the Pennsylvania Project is that, instead of showing what *can* be done with different methods under reasonably favorable conditions, it showed what *was* being done under conditions that were unfavorable to the audiolingual method and favorable to the traditional method. Thus, it did not answer any of the important questions of second language teaching methodology.

A program of research

It seems clear from the preceding that large-scale, large-scope experiments consume much energy but shed little light. The reason they are not very enlightening is that there is little agreement on goals and procedures and that a high level of control is impossible. The only possibility for fruitful research in our field lies in small-scale --small-scope or large-scope-- experiments.

This problem was discussed by Carroll long ago [1953]; he concluded that large-scale studies comparing methods were unlikely to yield useful information. Lado [1961: 378-80] also discussed this and concluded that experiments of single variables are preferable to large-scope and large-scale methodological experiments. He recommended smaller, highly controlled experiments.

A program of languistic research should consist therefore of a large number of interrelated small-scale (initially small-scope) experiments. They should be carried out under classroom conditions, so as to retain their validity for the classroom.

Ideally these small-scale experiments should be coordinated and should be conducted at a few educational institutions especially interested in second language teaching and research. Once many small-scope experiments have indicated the value of various procedures, large-scope (but still small-scale) experiments can be attempted. Such large-scope comparisons of methods on a small scale, conducted with great care at a few institutions, would show what *can* be done by combining demonstrably good procedures in various ways under attainable favorable conditions.

Idealistically, Asher [1972:180-2] proposed that all language classes curriculum-wide and nationwide could be part of a research program. All would be administered aptitude tests, biographic questionnaires, pre-tests, and criterion-referenced post-tests. Computers would score the listening and reading tests, teachers the speaking and writing tests. The computers would then analyze results in and across groups, matching groups and making findings. The problem with this proposal is that, while it would solve the problems of research design, it would totally lack controls in terms of what is actually done in each class.

More realistic perhaps is to hope that in the not too distant future a few regional centers for second language teaching and research could be established, perhaps within existing universities. At such centers, teams of languists, linguists, psychologists, educators, statisticians, and language teachers could cooperate to carry out systematic experimentation designed to answer basic questions about second language teaching and learning. It would not take many years for research in such centers to answer most questions, and the answers can then be translated into a much higher level of success in our practical endeavors.

(On the planning and conduct of educational research, see Tuckman [1978]. On research in second language teaching, see Green [1973].)

PART II: CONCLUSIONS

Our profession and new ideas

Our profession can be compared to a vast stony ground. It is not propitious to the growth of new ideas. Here and there there are spots with good earth, where new plants can grow and from where, when conditions are favorable, they can propagate to the rest of the field. But because the ground is so stony, the new plants soon shrivel and die, leaving only traces of their existence in the impoverished crops.

This is what has happened, for example, to such good

ideas as the Audiolingual Method, language laboratories, programmed instruction, and individualized instruction. Once they spread from their original grounds to the broad field they became distorted beyond recognition and soon disappeared, for, having been hopelessly distorted, they were not found to be particularly fruitful. And all of these trends left only small traces in the ongoing, business-as-usual second language teaching enterprise.

To the concerned second language teacher, all of this can be very confusing and disheartening. A multitude of voices claim his allegiance. Trends come and go with almost clockwork regularity. Often he is asked to reject an idea *in toto* because of some defect that could be easily remedied. And to top things off, he is even urged to abandon practices he has found to be successful, on the ground that they are no longer modern or no longer agree with accepted theory.

Good second language teachers, like good farmers, have always been interested in the development of a better plant with better yield. They have always engaged in synthesis, in enlightened eclecticism, resisting in the process the pressures to follow blindly this or that new trend and at the same time being willing to incorporate into their teaching the good things that any new trend has to offer.

That we must improve our methods there is no question. Carroll [1967], for example, found that second language majors have "limited working proficiency" in listening comprehension and speaking. I would estimate that few go beyond a 1+ on the F.S.I. scale. A new enlightened eclecticism --a new combination of successful elements-- is needed if we are going to change this situation.

Unfortunately few teachers are in a position to develop new methods. The better varieties of plants can seldom be developed in the field --they should be carefully crossbred and cultivated in special greenhouses, and *then* distributed for widespread use, after their characteristics, yield, etc. have been carefully studied.

The C.A.B. Method: a proposal

It is in the light of the above discussion that I would like to propose a new method --new not so much in its elements but in the fact that it represents a new combination of known elements plus one or two new elements of its own.

I call it the C.A.B. Method, the *C* standing for

"Cognitive," the *A* for "Audiolingual," and the *B* for "Bilingual," these being *not* all the characteristics of the method but just the main ones. In fact, the *C* stands for more than "Cognitive" --it represents "Cognitive habit formation." Similarly the *A* should be understood as representing "Audiolingual-visual," that is, audiolingual emphasis with visual support. The *B* does represent only "Bilingual."

Since this is an eclectic method, it includes every type of good teaching that is not in conflict with its basic principles. It is thus the opposite of special or exclusive methods that attempt to teach second languages by relying primarily on a single procedure. As an eclectic method, the C.A.B. Method is an organic, developing system, with room for new procedures and improvements as they prove themselves effective. At all times, however, its elements must be in harmony, or much effort will be wasted and there will be much loss in effectiveness; the concept of enlightened eclecticism excludes the haphazard putting together of any group of procedures that do not harmonize.

Among the characteristics of the C.A.B. Method are the following:

(1) The program should start with a phonological introduction of 15-20 hours duration. This introduction is not devoted exclusively to phonological work but alternates such work with a certain amount of meaningful activity, especially in the form of phonologically graded minidialogues. The articulatory explanations given and the discrimination and production drills used should be supplemented by the use of a pedagogical transcription such as the Articulatory Pictorial Transcription. (Chapter 15 dealt with the teaching of pronunciation.)

(2) Structural patterns (rules) should be grasped whenever possible through guided discovery, consolidated by teacher explanations as needed. Each new rule is to be introduced in class with examples, followed by the understanding of the rule (or of a "rule of thumb" if necessary) and a few drills, but the bulk of the structural practice is to be done afterwards by the students with cassette tapes, workbooks, or both. Emphasis should be on mastery learning, that is, not moving on to the next rule until the previous one has been mastered, not just mechanically but also in (at first very limited) communication. Mastery learning is ideally used within a self-

paced program, although it is also possible within a lockstep program. There should be no rush to cover all the important rules of the language in two semesters of college or two years of secondary school --covering them more slowly, once but with thorough learning, is preferable. There should be reviews every five units or so; furthermore, knowledge should be built up in such a way that everything learned up to any point is re-used frequently in communicative activities. (Chapter 17 dealt with the teaching of grammar.)

(3) There should be emphasis, early in the program and throughout it, on spoken communication (hence "Audiolingual") with overt structural understanding (hence "Cognitive"). Semantic understanding should be initially through the native language (hence "Bilingual"), gradually shifting to monolingual second language teaching. When needed to practice conversation, large classes should be divided into small groups which are led either by teacher's aides or paraprofessionals, by more advanced students, or by some of the best students in the same class. Communicative activities are in the second language, with the student allowed to obtain, in the native language, second language help from the teacher as needed. There is a gradual shift from controlled practice to semi-free and free conversation.

(4) Vocabulary is not to be emphasized early, as this is detrimental to the development of structural control; but certainly more vocabulary should be taught than in the audiolingual materials of the '50s and '60s, so as to make more communicative activity possible. (Chapter 18 discussed the teaching of vocabulary.)

(5) There should be correction of student errors, although not at all times, since it can disrupt certain communicative activities. The teacher should, during those activities, note serious errors and discuss them at the end. There should be a gradual shift from teacher monitoring of errors to student self-monitoring, paralleling the shift from emphasis on accuracy to emphasis on fluency with accuracy.

(6) It is at the beginning of the program that the students need most the support of the native language. It should be used as little as possible but as much as necessary for the teacher to help the students and for the students to obtain help from the teacher. Early in the program it should be used, for example, for explanations, to present semantic equivalents of words and

sentences, to give directions, and in certain types of drills. The native language can be gradually phased out as it is needed less and less. (Uses of the native language were discussed in Chapter 14.)

(7) Visual aids should be used, not as ways of conveying meaning, which they don't do well, nor as the center around which the whole lesson turns, but as the useful adjuncts they can be. Visual aids can serve, for example, as mnemonic devices, conversation stimuli, and to give structural insights.

(8) Dialogues can be used as one of several means to introduce new material for thorough learning, and as the primary way to do it at the beginning level. A few short dialogues can illustrate the main types of sentences in the language and should be learned very well for future reference. Except for social formulas, however, there is no point in memorizing the sequence of sentences in dialogues, so dialogue scripts should be used that will enable the students to act out the dialogues without having to memorize their sentence sequences. Dialogues lend themselves to various structural manipulations that can be quite helpful in developing competence in the language. (Dialogues, their teaching and exploitation were the subject of Chapter 16.)

(9) Listening comprehension should be systematically taught, as it does not develop automatically from the various activities already listed; but a long period of only listening is not recommended, as it fosters inaccurate subvocal speech. Reading and writing should be introduced gradually after an audiolingual foundation has been established. (These three skills were discussed in Chapter 19.)

(10) In addition to linguistic and communicative competence, second language teaching should aim at developing cultural competence. Cultural activities in the second language can begin, in a simple way and in reference to the language, quite early. A more systematic study, in the second language, of culturally different aspects of life should follow the establishment of a good language foundation in which the cultural content is primarily that which the two cultures have in common --it is a sound pedagogical principle to go generally from the familiar to the unfamiliar. (The teaching of second culture was considered in Chapter 20.)

Although I have tried most of the elements of the C.A.B. Method in combination, with considerable success,

I must say that the total package is, for the time being, just a proposal. Although materials currently available can be adapted to cover most of the C.A.B. Method, some new materials --especially for the introductory phonological minicourse-- would have to be developed. The C.A.B. Method is not therefore proposed as something ready-made and available, but rather in the hope that at least some members of our profession will want to fully develop it and try it. Experimental research would of course be particularly welcome.

A final word on languistics

As Stern [1981] noted, most university language departments have a scholarly approach to literature and linguistics and an unscholarly, unsophisticated approach to language teaching. This need not be so. There is a growing body of knowledge --languistics-- about which serious research is possible, for its theories and procedures are scientifically testable.

Languistics is an empirical science distinct from other disciplines, for its theories can only emerge, not from the concerns of linguists, psychologists, educators, and others, but from a careful analysis of the concerns of languists.

Languistics is empirical despite the anti-empiricism currently characteristic of certain of its feeder disciplines. Every second language program can and should become an empirical study in second language teaching/learning. Every second language class can and should be an opportunity to test languistic hypotheses.

In fact second language teaching may be one of the best testing grounds for linguistic and psychological theories. It is nearly ideal for testing the laws of learning --where else can one find grown or growing learners who start with virtually zero knowledge, where else can transfer effects be studied so definitely within a real situation, where else can input data and activities be so closely controlled, where else can much of the terminal behavior be measured with such relative ease?

Being empirical, languistics bases its progress on the testing of hypotheses against carefully collected data. Relevant data in languistics are (1) all significant information about the second language and the native language and their cultures, about the learner, the teacher, the method, the teaching materials, and the learning environment, and (2) all the responses of second language learners, in relation to what the corresponding native language responses are and what the second language responses should be. We should concentrate our efforts on collecting and analyzing such data, for the improvement of the efficiency and effectiveness of our professional endeavors.

We thus come to the end of this book. Someone once stated that theories are extended definitions. In that sense, this book has very much been concerned with theory, for it has been an extended definition of the science of linguistics. It is hoped that it will encourage further linguistic research and development and, in consequence, lead to significant improvements in the quality of second language teaching and learning.

THE END

T.G.B.T.G.

APPENDIX A

PHONETIC SYMBOLS

THIS BOOK	*IPA (if different)*	*EXAMPLES*
CONSONANTS		
p		E. paper, F. poche, G. passieren, S. peso
t		E. take, F. tendre, G. toll, S. techo
k		E. cake, F. colis, G. kaufen, S. cosa
?		E. aye[?]aye, G. [?]ein[?]andere
b		E. band, F. barbe, G. bieten, S. ambos
d		E. dime, F. dire, G. drei, S. andar
g		E. get, F. gourmet, G. ganz, S. tengo
f		E. fine, F. faim, G. feiern, S. fiesta
θ		E. thin, Castilian Spanish cero
s		E. say, F. cinq, G. lassen, S. sopa
š	ʃ	E. shin, F. chaud, G. sprechen
ç		G. recht (E. human)
χ		G. acht, Castilian Spanish jota
h		E. hat, G. hoch, Caribbean Spanish hijo
ƀ	β	S. haba, uva (E. tubful)
v		E. vest, F. venir, G. weinen
ð		E. that, S. todo
z		E. lazy, F. rasoir, G. sehr, S. desde
ž	ʒ	E. leisure, F. jour, River Plate Spanish calle
ǥ	ɣ	S. lago
ʀ		F. rue, G. raten
č	tʃ	E. chin, F. tchèque, G. Tscheche, S. chico
ǰ	dʒ	E. jet, F. Cambodge, River Plate Spanish sin lluvia
m		E. make, F. mois, G. malen, S. meter
ɱ		E. inform, F. viennent voir, G. infolge, S. enfermo
n		E. night, F. nez, G. nicht, S. noche
ñ	ɲ	F. agneau, S. año
ŋ		E. sing, G. links, S. cinco
ř	ɾ	S. cara, (American English letter, ladder)
r̃	r	S. ropa, perro
l		E. leave, F. sel, G. viel, S. leal
ł	ɫ	E. hotel
y	j	E. yes, F. chandail, G. jetzt, S. seis
ɹ		American English road, arrow, bear
w		E. widow, F. oui, S. bueno
ʻ		indicates aspiration
¯		" unaspirated release
ʼ		" non-release
<		" front articulation
>		" back articulation
ˬ		" voicedness
˳		" voicelessness
ˇ		" flapped articulation
ˌ		" a syllabic consonant
ː		" long duration (consonants or vowels)
VOWELS		
i		E. beat ([biyt']), F. lit, G. sie ([zi:]), S. sí
ɪ		E. bit, G. bitten
e		E. bait ([beyt']), F. baie, G. beten (['be:tn̩]), S. ve
ɛ		E. bet, F. mettre, G. Bett, S. verdad
æ		E. bat

THIS BOOK	IPA (if different)	EXAMPLES
VOWELS (cont.)		
ɨ		E. children, uses
ə		E. about, F. leçon, G. gefallen
ʌ		E. cut
a		F. patte, G. alt, S. casa
ɑ		E. father, F. pâté, G. baden (['bɑ:dn̩])
u		E. lose ([luwz]), F. doux, G. suchen (['zu:χn̩]), S. tú
ʊ		E. look, G. rund
o		E. go ([gow]), F. eau, G. holen (['ho:ln̩]), S. oso
ɔ		E. horn, F. donner, G. noch, S. corto
ü	y	F. juste, G. lügen (['lü:gn̩])
ø		F. feu, G. hören (['hø:ʀn̩])
œ		F. seul, G. können
ɛ̃		F. pain (American English twenty)
œ̃		F. un, brun (often replaced by [ɛ̃])
ɑ̃		F. sans (American English haunted, Monty)
'		precedes a stressed syllable (or a syllable with secondary stress when indicated)
"		precedes a syllable with primary stress (when indicated)
͜		is used under a semivowel

APPENDIX B

SUPPLEMENTARY GRAMMATICAL DRILLS

This appendix provides certain sample drills to supplement those given in Chapter 17. The languages involved are English for speakers of Spanish, and Spanish, French, and German for speakers of English. Only the more complex drills are illustrated. Although not given below, examples of the operation involved should always precede a drill. The convention is followed of listing the teacher's stimuli on the left and the students' responses on the right side of the page. Only the first three frames of each drill are given.

3-A) Single-slot correlation

Example 3 (French agreement with noun):

Ce fauteuil est vieux.	Ce fauteuil est vieux.
Cette chaise	Cette chaise est vieille.
Ces monsieurs	Ces monsieurs sont vieux.
Ces dames	Ces dames sont vieilles.

Example 4 (German dative forms of definite article):

Wir gehen aus dem Haus.	Wir gehen aus dem Haus.
Geschäft.	Wir gehen aus dem Geschäft.
Kirche.	Wir gehen aus der Kirche.
Laden.	Wir gehen aus dem Laden.

3-B) Multiple-slot correlation (-substitution)

Example 2 (Spanish agreement with noun):

Estos cuadernos son míos.	Estos cuadernos son míos.
Este	Este cuaderno es mío.
goma	Esta goma es mía.
mías.	Estas gomas son mías.

Example 3 (French: several types of agreement):

Nous attendons nos amis à la gare.	Nous attendons nos amis à la gare.
Vous	Vous attendez vos amis à la gare.
cinéma.	Vous attendez vos amis au cinéma.
Mes soeurs	Mes soeurs attendent leurs amis au cinéma.

Example 4 (German tense agreement with time reference):

Heute essen wir früh und gehen dann ins Theater.	Heute essen wir früh und gehen dann ins Theater.
Gestern	Gestern assen wir früh und gingen dann ins Theater.
die Oper.	Gestern assen wir früh un gingen dann in die Oper.
Morgen	Morgen werden wir früh essen und dann in die Oper gehen.

4) Replacement

Example 2 (Spanish indicative to subjunctive when expressing doubt):

Sabe hablar francés.	Dudo que sepa hablar francés.
Espera salir premiado.	Dudo que espere salir premiado.
Hay un apartamento vacío.	Dudo que haya un apartamento vacío.

Example 3 (French present to *passé composé* with *être*):

Je pars pour Paris.	Je suis parti pour Paris.
Vous sortez de la gare?	Vous êtes sorti(s) de la gare?

Nous venons du marché.	Nous sommes venus du marché.

Example 4 (German present to present perfect):

Sie hat immer Zeit.	Sie hat immer Zeit gehabt.
Ihr sprecht zu schnell.	Ihr habt zu schnell gesprochen.
Er redet viel zu viel.	Er hat viel zu viel geredet.

5) Transformation

5-A) Simple transformation

5-A-i) Expansion

5-A-i-a) Single expansion

Example 2 (Spanish adjective addition):

Ahí está la cuenta. Otra.	Ahí está la otra cuenta.
¿Dónde está mi cuaderno? Azul.	¿Dónde está mi cuaderno azul?
Ese es el auto que vimos. Segundo.	Ese es el segundo auto que vimos.

Example 3 (French adjective addition):

Brigitte sort avec un docteur.	Brigitte sort avec un docteur.
jeune	Brigitte sort avec un jeune docteur.
allemand	Brigitte sort avec un docteur allemand.
petit	Brigitte sort avec un petit docteur.

Example 4 (German negation of sentences with prepositional phrases):

Wir fahren dieses Jahr nach Deutschland.	Wir fahren dieses Jahr nicht nach Deutschland.
Ihr geht heute abend ins Kino.	Ihr geht heute abend nicht ins Kino.
Sie assen gestern im Restaurant.	Sie assen gestern nicht im Restaurant.

5-A-ii) Reduction

Example from French (transposition is involved):

Je veux t'accompagner à la gare.	Je le veux.
Il peut obtenir des informations.	Il le peut.
Nous savons nager.	Nous le savons.

Example from German (omission of dependent infinitive with modals):

Ich muss noch in die Bibliothek gehen.	Ich muss noch in die Bibliothek.
Müssen wir jetzt schon nach Hause fahren?	Müssen wir jetzt schon nach Hause?
Wir können schon sehr gut Deutsch sprechen.	Wir können schon sehr gut Deutsch.

5-A-iii) Transposition

Example 2 (Spanish transposition of subject pronouns and adverbs of place):

Nosotros estudiamos aquí.	Aquí estudiamos nosotros.
Yo vivo ahí.	Ahí vivo yo.
Ustedes trabajan allá.	Allá trabajan ustedes.

Example 3 (French question formation):

Il parle allemand.	Parle-t-il allemand?
Nous sommes arrivés en retard.	Sommes-nous arrivés en retard?
C'est la voiture de Janine.	Est-ce la voiture de Janine?

Example 4 (German question formation):

Du gehst jetzt nach Hause.	Gehst du jetzt nach Hause?
Wir schreiben heute eine Klausur.	Schreiben wir heute eine Klausur?
Sie kaufen sich ein neues Haus.	Kaufen sie sich ein neues Haus?

5-B) Complex transformation or Sentence combination

Example 2 (Spanish):

Este es el hombre. Lo vimos.	Este es el hombre que vimos.
Dame la pinza. La necesito.	Dame la pinza que necesito.

Son agentes. Venden casas.	Son agentes que venden casas.

Example 3 (French):

Paul a une soeur. Elle est timide.	Paul a une soeur qui est timide.
Paul a un frère. Il est bête.	Paul a un frère qui est bête.
Paul a une tante. Elle est jeune.	Paul a une tante qui est jeune.

Example 4 (German):

Ich weiss es. Sabine studiert Englisch.	Ich weiss, dass Sabine Englisch studiert.
Wir glauben es. Diese Geschichte ist wahr.	Wir glauben, dass diese Geschichte wahr ist.
Er fühlt es. Hier stimmt etwas nicht.	Er fühlt, dass hier etwas nicht stimmt.

7) Translation

Example from Spanish to English:

We took a liking to him.	We took a liking to him.
"Nos cayó en gracia."	
Nos cayeron en gracia.	We took a liking to them.
Ella me cayó en gracia.	I took a liking to her.
Le caí en gracia a Juan.	John took a liking to me.

Example 3 (English to French):

Je viens de rentrer.	Je viens de rentrer.
"I just got home."	
I just finished the letter.	Je viens de finir la lettre.
She just bought a dress.	Elle vient d'acheter un robe.
They've just arrived.	Ils viennent d'arriver.

Example 4 (English to German):

Das Theaterstück gefällt uns.	Das Theaterstück gefällt uns.
"We like the play."	
I like the concert.	Das Konzert gefällt mir.
He likes Switzerland.	Die Schweiz gefällt ihm.
We like these cars.	Diese Autos gefallen uns.

17) Distractor drills

17-A) Lexical distractor

Example 2 (Spanish imperfect tense forms):

Queremos leer un libro.	
(Picture of a letter.)	Queríamos leer una carta.
Compra una camisa.	
(Picture of a suit.)	Compraba un traje.
Conozco a esos señores.	
(Picture of a young girl.)	Conocía a esa niña (chica).

Example 3 (French *aller* plus infinitive):

Michel achète une chemise.	
(Picture of a car.)	Michel va acheter une voiture (auto).
Paul et Marie regardent un avion.	
(Picture of a house.)	Paul et Marie vont regarder une maison.
Nous lisons des romans.	
(Picture of a letter.)	Nous allons lire une lettre.

Example 4 (German present perfect):

Ich sehe ein Buch.	
(Picture of a newspaper.)	Ich habe eine Zeitung gesehen.
Sie gehen ins Theater.	
(Picture of the opera.)	Sie sind in die Oper gegangen.
Wir fahren an den Strand.	
(Picture of the mountains.)	Wir sind in die Berge gefahren.

17-B) Grammatical distractor

Example 2 (Spanish imperfect tense forms; distractor: number):

Queremos leer un libro.	Quería leer unos libros.
Compra unas camisas.	Compraban una camisa.
Conozco a esos señores.	Conocíamos a ese señor.

Example 3 (French *passé composé* with *avoir*; distractor: interrogation):

Il mange tout le riz.	A-t-il mangé tout le riz?
Nous fermons le bureau.	Avons-nous fermé le bureau?
Vous trouvez mon frère.	Avez-vous trouvé mon frère?

Example 4 (German present perfect; distractor: subject pronoun number):

Wir kaufen Kaffee und Kuchen.	Ich habe Kaffee und Kuchen gekauft.
Ich laufe heute 5 km.	Wir sind heute 5 km gelaufen.
Am Abend trinkt er Milch.	Am Abend haben sie Milch getrunken.

APPENDIX C

FOREIGN SERVICE INSTITUTE RATINGS

At the F.S.I. proficiency interviews, all examinees are given two ratings, an "S" rating for speaking and an "R" rating for reading. Both ratings go from 1 to 5, with intermediate plus signs, although 0 and 0+ may also be assigned.
Following are the definitions of absolute ratings [Wilds 1975:36-8]:

Elementary proficiency

S-1 Able to satisfy routine travel needs and minimum courtesy requirements.
R-1 Able to read some personal and place names, street signs, office and shop designations, numbers, and isolated words and phrases.

Limited working proficiency

S-2 Able to satisfy routine social demands and limited work requirements.
R-2 Able to read simple prose, in a form equivalent to typescript or printing, on subjects within a familiar context.

Minimum professional proficiency

S-3 Able to speak the language with sufficient structural accuracy and vocabulary to participate effectively in most formal and informal conversations on practical, social, and professional topics.
R-3 Able to read standard newspaper items addressed to the general reader, routine correspondence, reports and technical material in his special field.

Full professional proficiency

S-4 Able to use the language fluently and accurately on all levels normally pertinent to professional needs.
R-4 Able to read all styles and forms of the language pertinent to professional needs.

Native or bilingual proficiency

S-5 Speaking proficiency equivalent to that of an educated native speaker.
R-5 Reading proficiency equivalent to that of an educated native.

The above ratings are absolute and thus apply to any language. Of course, "the amount of time and training required to reach a certain level will vary widely from language to language" [Wilds 1975:36].

APPENDIX D

A GRADUATE PROGRAM IN LANGUISTICS

The need for a separate discipline of languistics was discussed in Chapter 1. It should be clear that literary scholars, linguists, and educators have neither the academic background nor the interests to be in a good position to direct the process of second language teaching or the training of second language specialists and researchers. Second language teaching will continue to suffer, in terms of attention, quality of staffing, etc., as long as it is secondary to literature or linguistics or general educational concerns.

What is needed, at the head of and in every area of the field of second language teaching, is languists, people highly trained at the graduate level in all aspects of languistics and in theory and research in particular. Such training would differ from what is offered in a number of North American universities under the name "foreign language education." In a graduate program in languistics, no general courses in education --with useless generalities on curriculum development, the history of education, evaluation, etc.-- would be offered or allowed. Instead, after satisfactory completion of a clearly defined multidisciplinary undergraduate program, graduate students in languistics would take courses just in languistics, with the possible exception of certain linguistics and psychology courses that might be particularly relevant to their individual interests and research goals.

The emphasis in graduate studies in languistics should be about equally divided between theories and their practical consequences. Theories have a marked effect on our professional endeavors; we can ignore theories only at our own risk. Languistic studies should concentrate primarily on languistic theories (theories in the science of second language teaching/learning) but should also pay attention to theories in linguistics (the science of language), psychology (among other things, the science of learning), education (the science and art of teaching), and to some extent the socio-cultural disciplines (sociology, anthropology, etc.). Throughout, an enlightened eclectic approach to the discipline is in order --it isn't a question of the future languist following the latest proclamations but of his questioning all assumptions and procedures, retaining only what is sound and effective and "believing" only in that.

What follows is an annotated list of what should be the requirements for an M.A. and a Ph.D. in languistics.

Prerequisites

(1) An acceptable grade point average.
(2) Adequate Graduate Record Examination scores (verbal and mathematical).
(3) Adequate knowledge of the language of instruction. This can be measured, when applicable, by such tests as the Test of English as a Foreign Language.
(4) Advanced four-skill (listening, speaking, reading, and writing) knowledge of a language other than the language of instruction. This can be measured, when applicable, by such tests as the MLA-Cooperative Foreign Language Tests.
(5) Ability to read professional publications in a third language. This can be measured by such tests as the Graduate School FL Test (Educational Testing Service), which is given in French, German, Russian, and Spanish. If the language of instruction is English, one of (4) and (5) should be French or German.
(6) Successful completion of two semesters of a non-Indo-European language. The study of a non-Indo-European language broadens experience and gives numerous insights on language and language learning not otherwise available.
(7) Undergraduate linguistics courses to include introduction to linguistics, phonetics, phonemics, generative phonology, morphology, and syntax.
(8) Undergraduate courses in psychology to include introduction to psychology,

learning, perception, motivation, memory, and personality.

(9) Undergraduate courses in education to include pedagogical theory and educational psychology.

(10) Two undergraduate courses in statistics. A basic knowledge of statistics --most North American universities offer statistics courses for non-mathematics majors-- is essential if the languist-to-be is to interpret adequately much published research and especially if he is to conduct any empirical studies himself.

(11) Several culture-related courses, to include an introduction to sociology, an introduction to anthropology, and at least one course on the history, geography, economy, politics, arts, etc. of the second culture(s) with which the candidate will be concerned. These requirements are intended to enable the future languist to deal effectively with the teaching of cultural competence, an integral part of any modern approach to second language teaching.

(12) It is also desirable, but not essential, that the future languist take one or two undergraduate second language "methods" courses, preferably two --one general and one with particular reference to the language with whose teaching he will be concerned.

Graduate languistics courses

All of the courses listed below are 3-hour courses.

(1) Research in languistics (required in the first semester as a graduate student)
(2) Languistic implications and applications of linguistics and psychology (required)
(3) Methods and approaches in languistics (required)
(4) Contrastive analysis and error analysis
(5) The teaching of second language pronunciation, grammar, and vocabulary
(6) Languistic evaluation and testing
(7) Languistic technology
(8) The teaching of second cultures
(9) History of languistics
(10) Native language acquisition
(11) Bilingualism
(12) Social aspects of languistics
(13) Practicum I: supervised second language teaching (this might be required, depending on the student's career plans); graduate students in languistics should give learning to be good language teachers as much or more priority as learning to be good scholars
(14) Practicum II: supervised second language materials preparation (this might also be required of some students).

In addition to these 14 courses, there should be courses on the teaching/learning of specific second languages (e.g., ESL, French as a SL, Spanish as a SL, etc.) and there could be a number of languistics seminars and reading courses studying specific topics in depth. Moreover, the students should be urged, if not required, to take linguistics courses of the types "Structure of X," "Structure of Y," and "Contrastive structures of X and Y," Beyond relevant linguistics courses, other courses outside languistics could be allowed when they make a relevant contribution to a student's program.

Credit and thesis requirements

For the M.A. in languistics, 24 hours (8 courses) would be required, of which up to 9 hours (3 courses) can be outside languistics, plus a 6-hour thesis.

For the Ph.D., the candidate would complete an M.A. in languistics (or its equivalent) plus 24 hours in graduate courses (8 courses), of which up to 18 hours total (6 courses) can be outside languistics, plus a 6-hour dissertation.

I believe that graduate programs in languistics such as those described above would go a long way toward solving pedagogical and research needs in our discipline.

BIBLIOGRAPHY

ABBREVIATIONS

AACTFL........*Accent on ACTFL*
ACTFL.........American Council on the Teaching of Foreign Languages
ADFLB.........*Association of Departments of Foreign Languages Bulletin*
AFLT..........*American Foreign Language Teacher*
AL............*Applied Linguistics*
BCAAL.........*Bulletin of the Canadian Association of Applied Linguistics*
CMLR..........*The Canadian Modern Language Review/La Revue canadienne des langues vivantes*
ELT...........*English Language Teaching*
FdM...........*Le Français dans le Monde*
FLA...........*Foreign Language Annals*
FR............*French Review*
H.............*Hispania*
IRAL..........*International Review of Applied Linguistics in Language Teaching*
J.............Journal
JEP...........*Journal of Educational Psychology*
JVLVB.........*Journal of Verbal Learning and Verbal Behavior*
L.............*Language*
LL............*Language Learning*
LR............*The Linguistic Reporter*
MLJ...........*The Modern Language Journal*
NALLDJ........*National Association of Learning Laboratory Directors Journal*
PNCFL.........Pacific Northwest Council on Foreign Languages
RWCNECTFL.....Reports of the Working Committees, Northeast Conference on the Teaching of Foreign Languages
SSLA..........*Studies in Second Language Acquisition*
TESOLQ........*TESOL Quarterly*
U.............*Die Unterrichtspraxis*
WPB...........*Working Papers on Bilingualism*

Abbott, Gerry. 1980. Towards a More Rigorous Analysis of Foreign Language Errors. *IRAL* 18:121-34.

Ackerman, Thomas J. 1972. Teacher Attitude, Aptitude, and Motivation. In D. Lange and C. James, eds. 1972:35-59.

Acton, William. 1979. Second Language Learning and Perception of Difference in Attitude. Unpublished doctoral dissertation, University of Michigan.

Adams, E.N., H. W. Morrison, and J.M. Reddy. 1968. Conversation with a Computer as a Technique of Language Instruction. *MLJ* 52-3-16.

Adcock, Dwayne. 1976. Foreign Languages in Elementary and Emerging Adolescent Education. In G. Jarvis, ed. 1976:289-325.

Adiv, Ellen. 1980-a. An Analysis of Second Language Performance in Two Types of Immersion Programs. *BCAAL* 2,2:139-54.

----------. 1980-b. L1 and L2: Same or Different? *BCAAL* 2,2:73-83.

Adler, Peter S. 1972. Culture Shock and the Cross Cultural Learning Experience. In Davis S. Hoopes, ed., *Readings in International Communication*, vol. 2 (Pittsburgh: University of Pittsburgh Press), 6-21.

Agard, Frederick B. and Harold B. Dunkel. 1948. *An Investigation of Second-Language Teaching* (Boston: Ginn).

Agatstein, Michael. 1971. Individualization of Language Learning Through the Cassette Recorder. *NALLDJ* 6:22-6.

Aguas, E. Floro. 1964. English Composition Errors of Tagalog Speakers and Implications for Analytical Theory. Unpublished doctoral dissertation, UCLA.

Alderson, J. Charles. 1979. The Cloze Procedure and Proficiency in English as a Foreign Language. *TESOLQ* 13:219-27.

----------. 1980. Native and Nonnative Speaker Performance on Cloze Tests. *LL* 30:59-76.

Allen, Edward D. and Rebecca M. Valette. 1972. *Modern Language Classroom Techniques --A Handbook* (New York: Harcourt Brace Jovanovich).

---------- and Rebecca M. Valette. 1977. *Classroom Techniques: Foreign Languages and English as a Second Language* (New York: Harcourt Brace Jovanovich)

Allen, J.P.B. 1974. Pedagogic Grammar. In J.P.B. Allen and S.P. Corder, eds. 1974:59-92.

---------- and S. Pit Corder. 1974. *Techniques in Applied Linguistics,* Edinburgh Course in Applied Linguistics, vol. 3 (London: Oxford University Press)

---------- and S. Pit Corder. 1975. *Papers in Applied Linguistics,* Edinburgh Course in Applied Linguistics, vol. 2 (London: Oxford University Press).

---------- and H.G. Widdowson. 1975. Grammar and Language Teaching. In J.P.B. Allen and S.P. Corder, eds. 1975:45-97.

Allouche, Edith K. and Gerard L. Ervin. 1976. Expanding the Options: Curricula in Many Languages. In G. Jarvis, ed. 1976:245-87.

Allwright, Richard L. 1975. Problems in the Study of the Language Teacher's Treatment of Learner Error. In M. Burt and H. Dulay, eds. 1975:96-109.

----------. 1980. Turns, Topics, and Tasks: Patterns of Participation in Language Learning and Teaching. In Diane Larsen-Freeman, ed., *Discourse Analysis in Second Language Research* (Rowley, Mass.: Newbury House), 165-87.

Altman, Howard B., ed. 1972. *Individualizing the Foreign Language Classroom: Perspectives for Teachers* (Rowley, Mass.: Newbury House).

---------- and Victor E. Hanzeli, eds. 1974. *Essays on the Teaching of Culture* (Detroit: Advancement Press). Reprinted in 1979 by Heinle and Heinle (Concord, Mass.).

---------- and Robert L. Politzer, eds. 1971. *Individualizing Foreign Language Instruction* (Rowley, Mass.: Newbury House).

Anderson, Charlotte. 1974. Reaching the Student. *ADFLB* 5,iii:5-7.

Anderson, J. Charles. 1979. Scoring Procedures for Use on Cloze Tests. In C. Yorio *et al.*, eds. 1979:193-205.

Andersson, Theodore. 1969. *Foreign Languages in the Elementary School: A Struggle Against Mediocrity* (Austin: University of Texas Press).

Anisfeld, Moshe. 1966. Psycholinguistic Perspectives on Language Learning. In A. Valdman, ed. 1966:107-19.

Anthony, Edward M. 1963. Approach, Method and Technique. *ELT* 17:63-7.

Applbaum, Ronald L., Edward M. Bodaken, Kenneth K. Sereno, and Karl W.E. Anatol. 1974. *The Process of Group Communication* (Chicago: Science Research Associates).

Arendt, Jermaine D. 1970. Media in Foreign Language Teaching. In D. Lange, ed. 1970:157-89.

Asher, James J. 1972. Implications of Psychological Research for Second Language Learning. In D. Lange and C. James, eds. 1972:157-86.

----------. 1977. *Learning Another Language Through Actions: The Complete Teacher's Guidebook* (Los Gatos, California: Sky Oaks Productions).

---------- and Ramiro García. 1969. The Optimal Age to Learn a Foreign Language. *MLJ* 53:334-41.

Austin, John L. 1962. *How to Do Things with Words* (Oxford, England: Clarendon Press).

Ausubel, David P. 1960. The Use of Advance Organizers in the Learning and Retention of Meaningful Verbal Material. *JEP* 51:267-72.

----------. 1963. *The Psychology of Meaningful Verbal Learning* (New York: Grune and Stratton).

----------. 1967. *Learning Theory and Classroom Practice* (Toronto: The Ontario Institute for Studies in Education).

----------. 1968. *Educational Psychology: A Cognitive View* (New York: Holt, Rinehart and Winston).

Axelrod, Joseph. 1966. *The Education of the Modern Foreign Language Teacher for American Schools* (New York: Modern Language Association of America).

Bailey, Nathalie, Carolyn Madden, and Stephen D. Krashen. 1974. Is There a "Natural Sequence" of Adult Second Language Learning? *LL* 24:235-43.

Bals, Hildegard. 1971. The Effects of Adding Content in Culture to the German Curriculum: A Method of Study. Unpublished doctoral dissertation, University of Georgia.

Banathy, Bela H. 1967. The Systems Approach. *MLJ* 51:281-9.

---------- and Boris Jordan. 1969. A Classroom Laboratory Instructional

System (CLIS). *FLA* 2:466-73.

Bandura, Albert. 1970. Vicarious and Self-Reinforcement Processes. In Robert Glaser, ed., *The Nature of Reinforcement,* Part II (Washington, D.C.: Office of Naval Research), 51-129.

Banta, Frank G. 1981. Teaching German Vocabulary: The Use of English Cognates and Common Loan Words. *MLJ* 65:129-36.

Barnes, Buckley R. and Elmer U. Clawson. 1975. Do Advance Organizers Facilitate Learning? Recommendations for Further Research Based on an Analysis of 32 Studies. *Review of Educational Research* 45:637-59.

Barrutia, Richard. 1967-a. Dispelling the Myth. *MLJ* 51:23-8.

----------. 1967-b. Overcoming Cultural Barriers (ERIC microfiche ED 019 901).

----------. 1969. *Language Learning and Machine Teaching* (Philadelphia: Center for Curriculum Development).

----------. 1970. Computerized Foreign Language Instruction. *H* 53:361-71.

Bartlett, Barrie E. 1979. Pedagogic Grammar and Applied Linguistics. In Gertrud S. Mazur, ed., *Proceedings of the 30th Annual Meeting of the PNCFL,* Part 2 (Corvallis, Oregon: Oregon State University) 186-9.

Bartz, Walter H. 1974. A Study of the Relationship of Certain Learner Factors with the Ability to Communicate in a Second Language (German) for the Development of Measures of Communicative Competence. Unpublished doctoral dissertation, Ohio State University.

Beach, Jo L. 1973. FLES Via Peer Teaching. *AACTFL* 4,ii:5.

Behmer, Daniel E. 1972. Cultural Mini-Skits Evaluated. *AFLT* 2,iii:37,43,48.

Belasco, Simon. 1967. The Plateau; or The Case for Comprehension: The 'Concept' Approach. *MLJ* 51:82-8.

----------. 1970. C'est la guerre? Or Can Cognition and Verbal Behavior Co-Exist in Second-Language Learning. *MLJ* 54:395-412.

Bellugi, Ursula and Roger Brown, eds. 1964. *The Acquisition of Language.* Monographs of the Society for Research in Child Development 29 (Serial No. 92).

Benardo, Leo. 1972. The Old Way Is Good Enough --Or Is It? Lecture given at a pre-conference workshop at the 1972 meeting of the American Council on the Teaching of Foreign Languages (Atlanta, Georgia, November 1972).

Bennett, Ruth L. 1975. Individualizing Instruction with Word Games. *H* 58:124-5.

Benseler, David P. 1976. Intensive Foreign Language Courses: Theory, Practice, Unrealized Potential. Paper presented at the November 1976 meeting of the American Council on the Teaching of Foreign Languages, in New Orleans. Referred to by Conner 1977:100.

Berne, Eric. 1964. *Games People Play* (New York: Grove Press).

Berwald, Jean-Pierre. 1977. Teaching Foreign Languages with Mass Media. Paper presented at the November 1977 meeting of the American Council on the Teaching of Foreign Languages, in San Francisco. Referred to by Westphal 1979:129.

Bezanson, Keith A. and Nicolas Hawkes. 1976. Bilingual Reading Skills of Primary School Children in Ghana. *WPB* 11:44-73.

Bialystok, Ellen. 1979-a. Explicit and Implicit Judgments of L2 Grammaticality. *LL* 29:81-103.

----------. 1979-b. The Role of Conscious Strategies in Second Language Proficiency. *CMLR* 35:372-94.

Bierce, Ambrose. n.d. *The Devil's Dictionary* (Garden City, New York: Dolphin Books).

Birckbichler, Diane W. 1977. Communication and Beyond. In J. Phillips, ed. 1977:53-94.

Birkmaier, Emma M., ed. 1968. *Britannica Review of Foreign Language Education,* vol. 1 (Chicago: Encyclopaedia Britannica).

Blatchford, Charles H. and Jacquelyn Schachter, eds. 1978. *On TESOL '78 --EFL Policies, Programs, Practices* (Washington, D.C.: Teachers of English to Speakers of Other Languages).

Blickenstaff, Channing B. and Frank J. Woerdehoff. 1967. A Comparison of the Monostructural and Dialogue Approaches to the Teaching of College Spanish. *MLJ* 51:14-23.

Bloom, Lois, Lois Hood, and Patsy Lightbown. 1974. Imitation in Language Development: If, When and Why. *Cognitive Psychology* 6:380-420.

Bloomfield, Leonard. 1942. *Outline Guide for the Practical Study of Foreign Languages* (Baltimore: Linguistic Society of America).

Bolinger, Dwight. 1967. The Foreign Language Teacher and Linguistics. In Joseph Michel, ed., *Foreign Language Teaching: An Anthology* (New York:

Macmillan), 285-96.
Bolinger, Dwight. 1968. The Theorist and the Language Teacher. *FLA* 2:30-41.
----------. 1972. The Influence of Linguistics: Plus and Minus. *TESOLQ* 6: 107-20.
---------- *et al.* 1960. *Modern Spanish,* a project of the Modern Language Association of America; third edition, 1973 (New York: Harcourt Brace Jovanovich).
Boswell, Richard E. 1972. Toward a New Eclecticism in Modern-Language Teaching. *FLA* 6:237-46.
Bourque, Jane M. 1974. Study Abroad and Intercultural Communication. In G. Jarvis, ed. 1974-b:329-51.
---------- and Linda Chehy. 1976. Exploratory Language and Culture: A Unique Program. *FLA* 9:10-6.
Bouton, Charles P. 1969. *Les mécanismes d'acquisition du français: langue étrangère chez l'adulte* (Paris: Klincksiek).
Bowen, J. Donald. 1975. *Patterns of English Pronunciation* (Rowley, Mass.: Newbury House).
----------. 1978. The Identification of Irrelevant Lexical Distration: An Editing Task. *TESL Reporter* 12,1:1-3,14-6.
---------- and Robert P. Stockwell. 1957. Orthography and Respelling in Teaching Spanish. *H* 40:200-5.
---------- and Robert P. Stockwell. 1960. *Patterns of Spanish Pronunciation --A Drillbook* (Chicago: University of Chicago Press).
Boyd, Margery M. and David E. Wolfe. 1973. The Effect of Radio on Motivating a Fourth Year German Class. *U* 6:118-20.
Boyd-Bowman, Peter. 1966. Self-Instruction in the "Neglected" Languages --A Progress Report from Kalamazoo College. *MLJ* 50:21-3.
----------. 1972. National Self-Instructional Program in Critical Languages. *MLJ* 56:163-7.
----------. 1973. *Self-Instructional Language Programs --A Handbook for Faculty and Students*. Occasional publication No. 20, The University of the State of New York, The State Education Department, Foreign Area Materials Center and Council for Intercultural Studies and Programs in cooperation with the National Association of Self-Instructional Language Programs.
Braine, Martin D.S. 1963. The Ontogeny of English Phrase Structure: The First Phase. *L* 39:1-13.
----------. 1971. On Two Types of Models of the Internalization of Grammars. In Dan I. Slobin, ed., *The Ontogenesis of Grammar: Theoretical Symposium* (New York: Academic Press), 153-86.
Brannon, R. Marshall and David E. Cox. 1976. Coping with the Real Problems in the Secondary Schools. In G. Jarvis, ed. 1976:151-99.
Brière, Eugene J. 1966-a. An Investigation of Phonological Interference. *L* 42:768-96.
----------. 1966-b. Quantity Before Quality in Second Language Composition. *LL* 16:141-51.
----------. 1971. Discrete versus Non-Discrete Testing in English Proficiency. In Roy Cherrier, ed., *English Language Testing: Report of the RELC Fifth Regional Seminar, Bangkok, 25-30 May 1970* (Singapore: Regional English Language Center), 133-9.
----------. 1973. Cross-Cultural Biases in Language Testing. In J. Oller and J. Richards, eds. 1973:214-27.
----------, Gerhard Clausing, Donna Senko, and Edward Purcell. 1978. A Look at Cloze Testing Across Languages and Levels. *MLJ* 62:23-6.
Brooks, J. Carroll and Bob W. Jerrolds. 1980. The "Lecture" --But They Can't Read It! *FLA* 13:359-63.
Brooks, Nelson. 1964. *Language and Language Learning: Theory and Practice,* second edition (New York: Harcourt Brace and World).
----------. 1969. Teaching Culture Abroad: From Concept to Classroom Techniques. *MLJ* 53:320-4.
----------. 1975. The Meaning of "Audiolingual." In H. Hammerly and I. Sawyer, eds. 1975:1-11.
Brown, Charles T. 1974. Communication and the Foreign Language Teacher. In G. Jarvis, ed. 1974-b:5-35.
Brown, H. Douglas. 1977. Some Limitations of C-L/CLL Models of Second Language Teaching. *TESOLQ* 11:365-72.

Brown, H. Douglas. 1980. *Principles of Language Learning and Teaching* (Englewood Cliffs, N.J.: Prentice-Hall).
Brown, James W. *et al*. 1972. A Testing of the Audio-Active Voice Reflector in the Foreign Language Classroom. *MLJ* 56:144-7.
Brown, Margaret J. 1965. A FLES Research and Experimental Project. *H* 48:890-4.
Brown, Roger W. 1973. *A First Language: The Early Stages* (Cambridge, Mass.: Harvard University Press).
---------- and Camille Hanlon. 1970. Derivational Complexity and Order of Acquisition in Child Speech. In John R. Hayes, ed., *Cognition and the Development of Language* (New York: Wiley), 11-53.
Bruder, Mary N. 1978. Evaluation of Foreign Language Textbooks: A Simplified Procedure. Appendix 2 in H. Madsen and J.D. Bowen, 1978:209-18.
Brumfit, Christopher. 1980. From Defining to Designing: Communicative Specifications versus Communicative Methodology in Foreign Language Teaching. *SSLA* 3:1-9.
Bruner, Jerome S. 1961. The Act of Discovery. *Harvard Educational Review* 31:21-32.
----------. 1966. *Toward a Theory of Instruction* (Cambridge, Mass.: Harvard University Press).
Buka, M., M.A. Freeman, and William N. Locke. 1962. Language Learning and Frequency Response. In E. Najam, ed. 1962:62-79.
Bull, William and Enrique E. Lamadrid. 1971. Our Grammar Rules Are Hurting Us. *MLJ* 55:449-54.
Bureau of the Census, U.S. Department of Commerce. 1976. *Current Population Reports* (Washington, D.C.: U.S. Government Printing Office).
Burling, Robbins. 1968. Some Outlandish Proposals for the Teaching of Foreign Languages. *LL* 18:61-75.
Buros, Oscar K., ed. 1975. *Foreign Language Tests and Reviews* (Highland Park, N.J.: Gryphon Press).
Burelli, Louise F. 1975. Building an Interdisciplinary Program. *MLJ* 59:28-31.
Burstall, Clare. 1975. French in the Primary School: The British Experiment. *CMLR* 31:388-402.
----------, Monika Jamieson, Susan Cohen, and Margaret Hargreaves. 1974. *Primary French in the Balance* (Windsor, England: National Foundation for Educational Research).
Burt, Marina and Heidi C. Dulay, eds. 1975. *New Directions in Second Language Learning, Teaching and Bilingual Education (On TESOL '75)* (Washington, D.C.: Teachers of English to Speakers of Other Languages).
---------- and Carol Kiparsky. 1974. Global and Local Mistakes. In J. Schumann and N. Stenson, eds. 1974:71-80.
Buscaglia, Michael J. and William L. Holman. 1980. The Teleprompter: A Simulating Device for Developing Communicative Competence. *MLJ* 64:451-4.
Buteau, Magdelhayne F. 1970. Students' Errors and the Learning of French as a Second Language: A Pilot Study. *IRAL* 8:133-45.
Butzkamm, Wolfgang. 1973. *Aufgeklärte Einsprachigkeit: zur Entdogmatisierung der Methode im Fremdsprachenunterricht* (Heidelberg: Quelle und Meyer).
---------- and Carl J. Dodson. 1980. The Teaching of Communication: From Theory to Practice. *IRAL* 18:289-309.
Byers, Burton H. 1973. Testing Proficiency in Interpersonal Communication: Experimentation at RELC. *RELC J* 4,ii:39-47.
Canale, Michael, Raymond Mougeon, and Edouard Beniak. 1978. Acquisition of Some Grammatical Elements in English and French by Monolingual and Bilingual Canadian Students. *CMLR* 34:505-24.
Capelle, Janine and Guy Capelle. 1970. *La France en direct* (Waltham, Mass.: Ginn).
Carroll, John B. 1953. *The Study of Language* (Cambridge, Mass.: Harvard University Press).
----------. 1960. Foreign Languages for Children: What Research Says. *National Elementary Principal* 39:12-5.
----------. 1961. *Testing*. (Washington, D.C.: Center for Applied Linguistics).
----------. 1962. The Prediction of Success in Intensive Foreign Language Training. In Robert Glaser, ed., *Training Research and Education* (Pittsburgh: University of Pittsburgh Press), 87-136.
----------. 1963. A Model of School Learning. *Teachers College Record* 64:723-33.

Carroll, John B. 1966-a. The Contributions of Psychological Theory and Educational Research to the Teaching of Foreign Languages. In A. Valdman, ed. 1966:93-106. Also in *MLJ* 49 (1965):273-81.

----------. 1966-b. Psychology --Research in Foreign Language Teaching: The Last Five Years. In R. Mead, ed. 1966:12-42.

----------. 1967. Foreign Language Proficiency Levels Attained by Language Majors Near Graduation from College. *FLA* 1:131-51.

----------. 1971. Current Issues in Psycholinguistics and Second Language Teaching. *TESOLQ* 5:101-14.

----------. 1973. Foreign Language Testing: Will the Persistent Problems Persist? Paper presented at the First International Conference of ATESOL, Dublin, Ireland, June 1973. Available as ERIC microfiche ED 079 432.

----------. 1974-a. Aptitude in Second Language Learning. In Gilbert Taggart, ed., *Proceedings of the Fifth Symposium of the Canadian Association of Applied Linguistics,* 8-23.

----------. 1974-b. Learning Theory for the Classroom Teacher. In G. Jarvis, ed. 1974-b:113-49.

----------. 1975. *The Teaching of French as a Foreign Language in Eight Countries* (New York: Wiley).

----------. 1981-a. Conscious and Automatic Processes in Language Learning. *CMLR* 37:462-74.

----------. 1981-b. Twenty-five Years of Research on Foreign Language Aptitude. In Karl C. Diller, ed., *Individual Differences and Universals in Language Learning Aptitude* (Rowley, Mass.: Newbury House), 83-118.

----------, A.S. Carton, and Claudia P. Wilds. 1959. *An Investigation of Cloze Items in the Measurement of Achievement in Foreign Languages.* (Cambridge, Mass.: Laboratory for Research in Instruction, Graduate School of Education, Harvard University).

----------, John L.D. Clark, Thomas M. Edwards, and Fannie A. Handrick 1967. *The Foreign Language Attainments of Language Majors in the Senior Year: A Survey Conducted in U.S. Colleges and Universities* (Cambridge, Mass.: Laboratory for Research in Instruction, Graduate School of Education, Harvard University). Available as ERIC microfiche ED 013 343.

---------- and Stanley Sapon. 1959. *Modern Language Aptitude Test* (New York: The Psychological Corporation).

---------- and Stanley Sapon. 1967. *Elementary Modern Language Aptitude Test.* (New York: The Psychological Corporation).

Carter, Thomas P. 1974. The Imaginative Use of Projected Visuals. *FLA* 7: 314-24.

Cartier, Francis A. 1968. Criterion-Referenced Testing of Language Skills. *TESOLQ* 2:27-32.

Catford, John C. 1969. Learning a Language in the Field: Problems of Linguistic Relativity. In S. Rosenberg and A.P. van Teslaar, eds., *Studies in Language and Language Behavior,* vol. 8 (Ann Arbor, Mich.: Center for Research on Language and Language Behavior), 7-14.

---------- and David B. Pisoni. 1970. Auditory vs. Articulatory Training in Exotic Sounds. *MLJ* 54:477-81.

Cathcart, Ruth L. and Judy E.W.B. Olsen. 1976. Teachers' and Students' Preferences for Correction of Classroom Conversation Errors. In J. Fanselow and R. Crymes, eds. 1976:41-53.

Caulfield, Joan and William C. Smith. 1981. The Reduced Redundancy Test and the Cloze Procedure as Measures of Global Language Proficiency. *MLJ* 65:54-8.

Cernyak, Susan E. and Robert C. Reimer. 1980. The Drama Workshop: A Lab Alternative. *FLA* 13:395-7.

Chapman, Helen G.C. 1975. Criteria for the Selection of Short Prose Fiction to Be Used in Level II (Intermediate) Foreign Language Classes. Unpublished doctoral dissertation, University of Texas at Austin.

Chardkoff, Joan C. 1981. Index Cards: Computer-Assisted Instruction For Financially Deprived Schools. *FLA* 14:213-6.

Chastain, Kenneth D. 1970. A Methodological Study Comparing the Audio-Lingual Habit Theory and the Cognitive Code-Learning Theory: A Continuation. *MLJ* 54:257-66.

----------. 1976. *Developing Second-Language Skills: Theory to Practice,* second edition (Chicago: Rand McNally).

----------. 1980. Native Speaker Reaction to Instructor-Identified Student

Second Language Errors. *MLJ* 64:210-6.
Chastain, Kenneth D. and Frank J. Woerdehoff. 1968. A Methodological Study Comparing the Audio-Lingual Habit Theory and the Cognitive Code-Learning Theory. *MLJ* 52:268-79.
Chatagnier, Louis J. and Gilbert Taggart, eds. 1971. *Language Laboratory Learning: New Directions* (Montreal: Aquila).
Chaudron, Craig. 1977. A Descriptive Model of Discourse in the Corrective Treatment of Learners' Errors. *LL* 27:29-46.
Chomsky, Noam. 1959. Review of B.F. Skinner's *Verbal Behavior*. *L* 35:26-58.
----------. 1965. *Aspects of the Theory of Syntax* (Cambridge, Mass.: MIT Press).
----------. 1966. Linguistic Theory. In R. Mead, ed. 1966:43-9.
----------. 1968. *Language and Mind* (New York: Harcourt Brace Jovanovich).
---------- and Morris Halle. 1968. *The Sound Pattern of English* (New York: Harper and Row).
Christensen, Clay B. 1977. Achieving Language Competence with Affective Learning Activities. *FLA* 10:157-67.
----------. 1979. Beyond the Desk. In J. Phillips, ed. 1979:93-117.
Chun, Judith. 1980. A Survey of Research in Second Language Acquisition. *MLJ* 64:287-96.
Clark, John L.D. 1972-a. *Foreign Language Testing: Theory and Practice* (Philadelphia: Center for Curriculum Development).
----------. 1972-b. Measurement Implications of Recent Trends in Foreign Language Teaching. In D. Lange and C. James, eds. 1972:219-57.
Clark, Ruth. 1975. Adult Theories, Child Strategies and Their Implications for the Language Teacher. In J.P.B. Allen and S.P. Corder, eds. 1975:291-347.
Clarke, Charles C. 1918. The Phonograph in Modern Language Teaching. *MLJ* 3:116-22.
Clausing, Gerhard, Klaus A. Mueller, and Wilfried M. Voge. 1972. Individualized German Instruction at the College Level --A First Appraisal. *FLA* 6:73-87.
Cloos, Robert I. 1971. In-Service Programs in Foreign Languages at Elementary and Secondary Levels. In D. Lange, ed. 1971:247-77.
Cohen, Andrew D. 1976. The Acquisition of Spanish Grammar Through Immersion: Some Findings After Four Years. *CMLR* 35:562-74.
---------- and Edna Aphek. 1981. Easifying Second Language Learning. *SSLA* 3:221-36.
Cole, Leo R. 1976. Relationships Between Visual Presentations and Linguistic Items in Second-Language Teaching. *IRAL* 14:339-50.
Coleman, Algernon. 1929. *The Teaching of Modern Foreign Languages in the United States* (New York: Macmillan).
----------. 1931. A New Approach to Practice in Reading a Modern Language. *MLJ* 15:101-18.
Colman, Lee. 1977. Is There a Magic Formula for Teaching Original Composition in French? *FR* 50:412-6.
Comenius, Johann A. 1648. *Orbis sensualium pictus* (Sidney: Sidney University Press, 1967).
Conner, Maurice W. 1977. New Curricular Connections. In J. Phillips, ed. 1977:95-121.
Cook, H. Robert. 1967. *The Relationship of Comprehension to Speech Production in Second Language Instruction; Proportion and Sequence* (Bloomington: Indiana University). Available as ERIC microfiche ED 014 927.
Cook, Vivian J. 1969. The Analogy Between First and Second Language Learning. *IRAL* 7:207-16.
Cook, Walter A.S.J. 1969. *Introduction to Tagmemic Analysis* (New York: Holt, Rinehart and Winston).
Cooke, Madeline A. 1969. A Study of the Development of Positive Attitudes Toward Native Speakers of Spanish. Unpublished doctoral dissertation, Ohio State University.
Cooper, Thomas C. 1981. Sentence Combining: An Experiment in Teaching Writing. *MLJ* 65:158-65.
Corder, S. Pit. 1966-a. Modern Foreign Language Teaching by Television. In A. Valdman, ed. 1966:235-51.
----------. 1966-b. *The Visual Element in Language Teaching* (London: Longman).
----------. 1967. The Significance of Learner's Errors. *IRAL* 5:161-70.
----------. 1968. Advanced Study and the Experienced Teacher. In George E. Perren, ed., *Teachers of English as a Second Language* (Cambridge, England:

Cambridge University Press), 67-94.
Corder, S. Pit. 1971. Idiosyncratic Dialects and Error Analysis. *IRAL* 9:147-60.
----------. 1973. *Introducing Applied Linguistics* (Hamondsworth, England: Penguin Books).
----------. 1974. Error Analysis, In J.P.B. Allen and S.P. Corder, eds. 1974:122-54.
Cornfield, Ruth R. 1966. *Foreign Language Instruction --Dimensions and Horizons* (New York: Appleton-Century-Crofts).
Coulthard, Richard M. 1977. *An Introduction to Discourse Analysis* (London: Longman).
Craighead, W. Edward, Alan E. Kazdin, and Michael J. Mahoney. 1976. *Behavior Modification: Principles, Issues, and Applications* (Boston: Houghton Mifflin).
Crocker, Renate. 1973. A German Week in High School. *U* 6:19-21.
Crouse, Gale and Bruce A. Noll. 1980. Using Videotape to Teach Foreign Languages. *FLA* 13:391-3.
Cummins, Jim. 1979. Cognitive/Academic Language Proficiency, Linguistic Interdependence, the Optimum Age Question and Some Other Matters. *WPB* 19:197-205.
Curran, Charles A. 1976. *Counseling-Learning in Second Languages* (Apple River, Ill.: Apple River Press).
Cziko, Gary A. 1981. Psychometric and Edumetric Approaches to Language Testing: Implications and Applications. *AL* 2:27-44.
----------, N.E. Holobow, and Wallace E. Lambert. 1977. A Comparison of Three Elementary School Alternatives for Learning French: Children at Grades 4 and 5. Unpublished manuscript, Department of Psychology, McGill University. Referred to by Cziko 1981:38.
Dacanay, Fe R. 1963. *Techniques and Procedures in Second-Language Teaching* (Quezon City, Philippines: Phoenix Press; reprinted by Oceana Press, Dobbs Ferry, New York).
Dalbor, John B. 1972. A Simplified Tagmemic Approach for Teaching Spanish Syntax. *H* 55:490-7.
Damoiseau, R. and E. Marc. 1967. La chanson moderne: étude de civilisation et de langue. *FdM* 47:40-4.
Darnell, Donald K. 1970. Clozentropy: A Procedure for Testing the English Language Proficiency of Foreign Students. *Speech Monographs* 37:36-46.
Davies, Alan. 1975. Two Tests of Speeded Reading. In R. Jones and B. Spolsky, eds. 1975:119-30.
---------- and Henry G. Widdowson. 1974. Reading and Writing. In J.P.B. Allen and S.P. Corder, eds. 1974:155-201.
Day, Elaine M. 1977. The Development of French in Eight Anglophone Children Enrolled in an Immersion Program in Coquitlam, British Columbia. Unpublished M.A. thesis, Simon Fraser University.
Debyser, Francis and Heide Laitenberger. 1976. Le crocodile et le moulin à vent. *FdM* 123:14-9.
Decaroli, Joseph. 1972. What Research Says to the Classroom Teacher: Simulation Games. *Social Education* 36:541-3.
Delattre, Pierre. 1947. A Technique of Aural-Oral Approach. *FR* 20:238-50 and 311-24.
----------. 1962. Une technique "audio-linguale" d'initiation au français. *FdM* 13:15-7.
Desberg, Dan *et al.* 1960. *French Basic Course* (Washington, D.C.: Foreign Service Institute, U.S. Department of State).
---------- and Lucette R. Kenan. 1964. *Modern French* (New York: Harcourt Brace and World).
DeVilliers, Jill and Peter DeVilliers. 1973. A Cross-Sectional Study of the Acquisition of Grammatical Morphemes in Child Speech. *J Psycholinguistic Research* 2:267-78.
Dickerson, Wayne B. 1975. The Wh Question of Pronunciation: An Answer from Spelling and Generative Phonology. *TESOLQ* 9:299-309.
----------. 1977. Generative Theory in TESL Practice. *MLJ* 61:179-87.
Dickinson, Leslie. 1971. The Language Lab and Advanced Teaching. *ELT* 25:32-42.
Diebold, A. Richard, Jr. 1965. A Survey of Psycholinguistic Research, 1954-1964. In Charles E. Osgood and Thomas A. Sebeok, eds., *Psycholinguistics: A Survey of Theory and Research Problems* (Bloomington, Ind.: Indiana University Press).
Diller, Karl C. 1971. *Generative Grammar, Structural Linguistics, and*

Language Teaching (Rowley, Mass.: Newbury House).

Di Pietro, Robert J. 1971, 1978-a. *Language Structures in Contrast* (Rowley, Mass.: Newbury House). (Revised edition, 1978.)

----------. 1975. The Twentieth Running of the Grand Prix. In Readers' Reactions and Comments, *MLJ* 59:195-7.

----------. 1978-b. Verbal Strategies, Script Theory and Conversational Performance in ESL. In C. Blatchford and J. Schachter, eds. 1978:149-56.

Disick, Renée S. 1975. *Individualizing Language Instruction: Strategies and Methods* (New York: Harcourt Brace Jovanovich).

---------- and Laura Barbanel. 1974. Affective Education and Foreign Language Learning. In G. Jarvis, ed. 1974-b:185-222.

Dodge, James W. 1968. Machine-Aided Language Learning. In E. Birkmaier, ed. 1968:311-41.

Dodson, Carl J. 1967. *Language Teaching and the Bilingual Method* (London: Pitman).

Dommergues, Jean-Yves and Harlan Lane. 1976. On Two Independent Sources of Errors in Learning the Syntax of a Second Language. *LL* 26:111-23.

Dooling, D. James and Roy Lachman. 1971. Effects of Comprehension on Retention of Prose. *J Experimental Psychology* 88:216-22.

Doron, Sandra. 1973. Reflectivity-Impulsivity and Their Influence on Reading for Inference for Adult Students of ESL. Unpublished manuscript, University of Michigan. Referred to by H.D. Brown 1980:94.

Drach, K. 1969. The Language of the Parent: A Pilot Study. In *The Structure of Linguistic Input to Children,* Working Paper No. 14, Language Behavior Research Laboratory, University of California, Berkeley.

Dreher, Barbara and James Larkins. 1972. Non-Semantic Auditory Discrimination: Foundation for Second Language Learning. *MLJ* 56:227-30.

Dressel, Paul, John Schmid and Gerald Kincaid. 1952. The Effect of Writing Frequency upon Essay-Type Writing Proficiency at the College Level. *J Educational Research* 46:285-93.

Dufort, Mary. 1962. *Foreign Language Attitude Scale* (Stanford, California: Stanford Center for Research and Development in Teaching).

Dulay, Heidi C. and Marina K. Burt. 1974-a. Errors and Strategies in Child Second Language Acquisition. *TESOLQ* 8:129-36.

---------- and Marina K. Burt. 1974-b. Natural Sequences in Child Second Language Acquisition. *LL* 24:37-53.

---------- and Marina K. Burt. 1974-c. A New Perspective on the Creative Construction Process in Child Second Language Acquisition. *WPB* 4:71-98.

---------- and Marina K. Burt. 1974-d. You Can't Learn Without Goofing: An Analysis of Children's Second Language "Errors." In J. Richards, ed. 1974: 95-123.

Dumas, G., Merrill Swain, and Larry Selinker. 1974. L'apprentissage du français langue seconde en classe d'immersion dans un milieu torontois. In S.T. Carey, ed., *Bilingualism, Biculturalism and Education: Proceedings from the Conference at Collège Universitaire Saint-Jean* (Edmonton, Alberta: University of Alberta), 83-90.

Dunn, Rita, Kenneth Dunn, and Gary E. Price. 1975. *Learning Style Inventory* (Box 3271, Lawrence, Kansas: Price Systems).

Dušková, Libuše. 1969. On Sources of Errors in Foreign Language Learning. *IRAL* 7:11-36.

Ecklund, Constance L. and Peter Weise. 1981. French Accent Through Video Analysis. *FLA* 14:17-23.

Eddy, Frederick D., ed. 1959. *The Language Learner*. RWCNECTFL (New York: Modern Language Association).

Edfeldt, Åke W. 1960. *Silent Speech and Silent Reading* (Chicago: University of Chicago Press).

Elkins, Robert J., Theodore B. Kalivoda, and Genelle Morain. 1972. Teaching Culture Through the Audio-Motor Unit. *FLA* 6:61-72.

Ervin-Tripp, Susan M. 1974. Is Second Language Learning Like the First? *TESOLQ* 8:111-27.

Estarellas, Juan. 1970. The Self-Instructional Foreign Language Program at Florida Atlantic University. *H* 53:371-85.

---------- and Timothy F. Regan, Jr. 1966. Effects of Teaching Sounds as Letters Simultaneously at the Very Beginning of a Basic Foreign Language Course. *LL* 16:173-82.

Fabian, Peter. 1973. The ARELS Oral Examination in English as a Second Language. Paper presented at the First International Conference of ATESOL, Dublin, Ireland, June 1973. Referred to by Jorstad 1974:238-9.

Fahmy, Nermine. 1979. An Investigation of the Effectiveness of Extensive Listening and Reading Practice on Students' Ability to Read English. Unpublished M.A. thesis, American University in Cairo. Referred to by Gary and Gary (1980).

Fanselow, John F. 1977. The Treatment of Error in Oral Work. *FLA* 10:583-93.

---------- and Ruth H. Crymes, eds. 1976. *On TESOL '76* (Washington, D.C.: Teachers of English to Speakers of Other Languages).

Farhady, Hossein. 1978. The Differential Performance of Foreign Students on Discrete-Point and Integrative Tests. Unpublished M.A. thesis, UCLA. Referred to by Farhady (1979-a).

----------. 1979-a. The Disjunctive Fallacy Between Discrete-Point and Integrative Tests. *TESOLQ* 13:347-57.

----------. 1979-b. New Directions for ESL Proficiency Testing. Draft manuscript (Los Angeles: TESL Program, University of Southern California). Referred to by Wesche 1981:563-5.

----------. 1979-c. Test Bias in Language Placement Examinations. In C. Yorio *et al.*, eds. 1979:162-70.

Fasten, Lynn A. and Charles A. Findley. 1976. The "Fantasy Journey" --A Valuable Tool in the ESL Classroom. In J. Fanselow and R. Crymes, eds. 1976: 75-88.

Fathman, Ann. 1975. The Relationship Between Age and Second Language Productive Ability. *LL* 25:245-53.

Fearing, Percy. 1969. Using the 8mm Film to Bridge the Gap from Drill to Creative Language Use. Unpublished demonstration, Northeast Conference. Referred to by J. Dodge 1968:326-7.

Feeny, Thomas P. 1976. Measuring Auditory Discrimination of Suprasegmental Features in Spanish. *IRAL* 11:195-209.

Ferguson, Nicholas. 1974. Some Aspects of the Reading Process. *ELT* 28:29-34.

Fiedler, Fred E., Terence Mitchell, and Harry C. Triandis. 1971. The Culture Assimilator: An Approach to Cross-Cultural Training. *J Applied Psychology* 55:95-102.

Fillmore, Charles J. 1968. The Case for Case. In E. Bach and R.T. Harms, eds., *Universals of Linguistic Theory* (New York: Holt, Rinehart and Winston), 1-88.

Fillmore, Lily W. 1976. The Second Time Around: Cognitive and Social Strategies in Second Language Acquisition. Unpublished doctoral dissertation, Stanford University.

Finlayson, Douglas S. 1951. The Reliability of Marking Essays. *British J Educational Psychology* 21:126-34.

Fisiak, Jacek, ed. 1981. *Contrastive Linguistics and the Language Teacher* (Oxford, England: Pergamon Press).

Fitts, Paul M. and Michael I. Posner. 1967. *Human Performance* (Belmont, Calif.: Brooks/Cole).

Flahive, Douglas E. 1977. Separating the g Factor from Reading Comprehension. In J. Oller and K. Perkins, eds. 1980:15-27.

Fleming, Gerald. 1964-a. Comic Cassettes for Language Classes. *Film User*, January 1964. Also available as ERIC microfiche ED 026 891.

----------. 1964-b. Language Teaching with Cartoons. *Film User*, June 1964. Also available as ERIC microfiche ED 013 015.

Flynn, Mary and Nora Trott. 1972. 300 Tongue Depressors. *FR* 45:654-6.

Foster, Dorothy P. and Clarence M. Williams. 1960. Aural-Oral-Written versus Aural-Oral in Teaching Spanish to Fourth Graders. *MLJ* 44:153-7.

Le Français élémentaire. 1956. (Paris: Publications du Centre de Documentation Pédagogique.)

Frank, Ted E. 1972. An Intensive Course in German. *U* 5:121-3.

----------. 1973. A Practical Approach to Intensive German. *U* 6:5-8.

Franke, Felix. 1884. *Die praktische Spracherlernung auf Grund der Psychologie und der Physiologie der Sprache dargestellt von Felix Franke* (Heilbronn, Germany). Referred to by several modern authors.

Frechette, Ernest A. 1976. Directions of Research in the 1970s. In G. Jarvis, ed. 1976:351-95.

Freed, Barbara F. 1976. Communicating Techniques and Teaching Reading. *FLA* 9:552-7.

Freeman, G. Ronald. n.d. *101+ Ways to Stimulate Conversation in a Foreign*

Language (New York: ACTFL Materials Center).
Freeman, G. Ronald, Thomas H. Geno, and Renate A. Schulz. n.d. *Getting Students Involved* (New York: ACTFL Materials Center).
Fries, Charles C. 1945. *Teaching and Learning English as a Foreign Language* (Ann Arbor, Mich.: University of Michigan Press).
----------. 1949. An Investigation of Second Language Teaching. *LL* 2:89-99.
----------. 1955. American Linguistics and the Teaching of English. *LL* 6:1-22.
Gaarder, A. Bruce. 1976. Elitism, Teacher Training, and Other Forbidden Topics. *MLJ* 60:150-5.
Gagné, Robert M. 1977. *The Conditions of Learning,* third edition (New York: Holt, Rinehart and Winston).
Gaies, Stephen J., Harry L. Gradman, and Bernard Spolsky. 1977. Toward the Measurement of Functional Proficiency: Contextualization of the Noise Test. *TESOLQ* 11:51-7.
Galisson, Robert. 1979. *Lexicologie et enseignement des langues* (Paris: Hachette).
Gallagher, William K. 1976. Investigation of the Relationship Between Memorization and Rule Acquisition --The Two Stage Language Acquisition Hypothesis. In J. Fanselow and R. Crymes, eds. 1976:89-99.
Galloway, Vicki B. 1980. Perceptions of the Communicative Efforts of American Students of Spanish. *MLJ* 64:428-40.
Garcia, Ernest F. 1966. Interference by Textual Stimuli in Selected Elements of Spanish Pronunciation. Unpublished doctoral dissertation, UCLA.
Garcia-Zamor, Marie and Mary J. Krowitz. 1974. Contextual Testing and Communicative Competence. Paper presented at the Annual Meeting of the Linguistic Society of America, New York City, December 1974. Referred to by R. Jones 1977:258.
Gardner, Robert C. and Wallace E. Lambert. 1959. Motivational Variables in Second-Language Acquisition. *Canadian J Psychology* 13:266-72.
---------- and Wallace E. Lambert. 1965. Language Aptitude, Intelligence, and Second-Language Achievement. *JEP* 56:191-9.
---------- and Wallace E. Lambert. 1972. *Attitudes and Motivation in Second Language Learning* (Rowley, Mass.: Newbury House)
----------, P.C. Smythe, and R. Clement. 1979. Intensive Second-Language Study in a Bi-Cultural Milieu: An Investigation of Attitudes, Motivation and Language Proficiency. *LL* 29:305-20.
Garfinkel, Alan. 1972-a. Teaching Languages Via Radio: A Review of Resources. *MLJ* 56:158-62.
----------. 1972-b. The Enrichment-Oriented Radio Program: A Medium for Building Listening Comprehension Skills. *H* 55:310-2.
----------. 1972-c. FL Packrats Always Collect for Teaching. *AACTFL* 3,ii:12-3.
Gary, Judith O. and Norman Gary. 1978. Why Speak If You Don't Need to? The Case for a Listening Approach to Beginning Foreign Language Learning. In William C. Ritchie, ed., *Second Language Acquisition Research: Issues and Implications* (New York: Academic Press).
---------- and Norman Gary. 1980. Comprehension-Oriented Foreign Language Instruction --An Overview. *LR* 23,3:4-5.
Gattegno, Caleb. 1972. *Teaching Foreign Languages in Schools: The Silent Way,* second edition (New York: Educational Solutions).
Gauthier, Robert. 1963. Tan-Gau --A Natural Method for Learning a Second Language. *Education* 4:33-6.
Genesee, Fred. 1976. The Role of Intelligence in Second Language Learning. *LL* 26:267-80.
----------. 1978. Is There an Optimal Age for Starting Second Language Instruction? *McGill J Education* 13:145-54.
---------- and Else Hamayan. 1979. Individual Differences in Young Second Language Learners. Unpublished research report, McGill University. Referred to by Stern and Cummins 1981:216.
George, H.V. 1972. *Common Errors in Language Learning* (Rowley, Mass.: Newbury House).
----------. 1973. Two Practical Experiments with Teachers-in-Training and Some Conclusions. In J. Oller and J. Richards, eds. 1973:145-56.
Gezi, Kalil I. 1965. Factors Associated with Student Adjustment in Cross-Cultural Contact. *California J Educational Research* 16:129-36.
Ghadessy, Mohsen. 1980. Implications of Error Analysis for Second/Foreign

Language Acquisition. *IRAL* 18:93-104.
Gibson, Robert E. 1975. The Strip Story: A Catalyst for Communication. *TESOLQ* 9:149-54.
Gingras, Rosario C., ed. 1978. *Second Language Acquisition and Foreign Language Teaching* (Arlington, Va.: Center for Applied Linguistics).
Goddu, Roland. 1976. Pursuing Continuing Education as a Foreign Language Teacher: An Overview. In G. Jarvis, ed. 1976:327-50.
Gold, Richard M., Anne Reilly, Robert Silberman, and Robert Lehr. 1971. Achievement Declines Under Pass-Fail Grading. *J Experimental Education* 39,iii: 17-21.
Gomes de Matos, Francisco. 1980. A Case for Selective Listening. *LR* 23,1:14.
Good, Carter V. 1945. *Dictionary of Education* (New York: McGraw-Hill).
Gorden, Raymond L. 1974. *Living in Latin America: A Case Study in Cross-Cultural Communication* (Skokie, Ill.: National Textbook Company).
Gordon, W. Terrence. 1976. Object-Oriented Expression Practice and Vocabulary Acquisition. *CMLR* 32:422-3.
----------. 1977. Communicative Exchange Through Oral Paraphrase. *CMLR* 34:71-5.
Gorsuch, Richard L. and Charles D. Spielberger. 1966. Anxiety, Threat, and Awareness in Verbal Conditioning. *J Personality* 34:336-47.
Gougenheim, Georges, P. Rivenc, R. Michéa, and A. Sauvageot. 1964. *L'élaboration du français fondamental (1er degré): étude sur l'établissement d'un vocabulaire et d'une grammaire de base* (Paris: Didier).
Gougher, Ronald L., ed. 1972. *Individualization of Instruction in Foreign Languages: A Practical Guide* (Philadelphia: Center for Curriculum Development).
Gouin, François. 1880. *L'art d'enseigner et d'étudier les langues.* (Paris: Fischbacher). (In English: London, Phillip, 1912.)
Gradman, Harry L. and Bernard Spolsky. 1975. Reduced Redundancy Testing: A Progress Report. In R. Jones and B. Spolsky, eds. 1975: 59-66.
Grauberg, W. 1971. An Error-Analysis in German of First-Year University Students. In G. Perren and J. Trim, eds., *Applications of Linguistics: Selected Papers of the Second International Congress of Applied Linguistics, Cambridge, 1969* (Cambridge, England: Cambridge University Press), 257-63.
Green, Jerald R. 1972. Purposes and Goals in Foreign Language Education: A Look to the Future. In D. Lange and C. James, eds. 1972:1-33.
----------, ed. 1973. *Foreign Language Education Research: A Book of Readings* (Chicago: Rand McNally).
Greenewald, M. Jane. 1980. Developing Communicative Competence in Oral Reading. *FR* 54:121-4.
Grittner, Frank M., ed. 1974. *Careers, Communication and Culture in Foreign Language Teaching* (Skokie, Ill.: National Textbook Company).
----------. 1977. *Teaching Foreign Languages,* second edition (New York: Harper and Row).
Guiora, Alexander Z., Benjamin Beit-Hallahmi, Robert C.L. Brannon, Cecelia Y. Dull, and Thomas Scovel. 1972-a. The Effects of Experimentally Induced Changes in Ego States on Pronunciation Ability in a Second Language: An Exploratory Study. *Comprehensive Psychiatry* 13:421-8.
----------, Robert C.L. Brannon, and Cecelia Y. Dull. 1972-b. Empathy and Second Language Learning. *LL* 22:111-30.
Guntermann, Gail. 1978. A Study of the Frequency and Communicative Effects of Errors in Spanish. *MLJ* 62:249-53.
----------. 1980. Factors in Targeting Proficiency Levels and an Approach to "Real" and "Realistic" Practice. *SSLA* 3:34-41.
Hadlich, Roger L. 1965. Lexical Contrastive Analysis. *MLJ* 49:426-9.
Hakuta, Kenji. 1974. Prefabricated Patterns and the Emergence of Structure in Second Language Acquisition. *LL* 24:287-97.
----------. 1976. A Case Study of a Japanese Child Learning English as a Second Language. *LL* 26:321-51.
Hall, Edward T. 1959. *The Silent Language* (New York: Fawcett).
----------. 1966. *The Hidden Dimension* (New York: Doubleday).
Hall, Robert A., Jr. 1966. *New Ways to Learn a Foreign Language* (New York: Bantam Books).
Halliday, Michael A.K. 1964. Syntax and the Consumer. In C.I.J.M. Stuart, ed., *Report of the 15th Annual Round Table Meeting on Linguistics and Language Study,* Monograph 17 (Washington, D.C.: Georgetown University), 11-24.
----------. 1975. *Learning How to Mean: Explorations in the Development*

of Language (London: Edward Arnold).
Hamayan, Else, Fred Genesee, and G. Richard Tucker. 1977. Affective Factors and Language Exposure in Second Language Learning. *LL* 27:225-41.
Hammelmann, William M.R. and Melvin L. Nielsen. 1974. The Native Paraprofessional: Identifying His Role in the Foreign Language Program. *FLA* 7:346-52.
Hammerly, Hector. 1964. A Study of the Spanish Spoken by a Bilingual Child. Unpublished manuscript, University of Texas at Austin.
----------. 1965. Results of One Year of Experimentation at Ohio State University. Unpublished report.
----------. 1970-a. And Then They Disbelieved Their Ears. *H* 53:72-5.
----------. 1970-b. Linguistics and the Teaching of Foreign Language Pronunciation. Unpublished doctoral dissertation, University of Texas at Austin.
----------. 1971-a. Recent Methods and Trends in Second Language Teaching. *MLJ* 55:499-505.
----------. 1971-b. Student Preference Between a Traditional and an Oral Approach to the Teaching of Spanish. *H* 54:100-2.
----------. 1973-a. The Correction of Pronunciation Errors. *MLJ* 57:106-10.
----------. 1973-b. Teaching Pronunciation and Generative Phonology. *FLA* 6: 487-9.
----------. 1974-a. *The Articulatory Pictorial Transcriptions --New Aids to Second Language Pronunciation* (Blaine, Wash.: Second Language Publications).
----------. 1974-b. The Myth of Language Laboratory Monitoring. *MLJ* 58:336-9.
----------. 1974-c. Primary and Secondary Associations with Visual Aids as Semantic Conveyors. *IRAL* 12:119-25.
----------. 1974-d. The Teaching of Oral Grammar. In H. Hammerly, ed. 1974-e: 172-93.
----------, ed. 1974-e. *Second Language Teaching '74,* Part II of the Proceedings of the 25th Annual Meeting of the PNCFL (Burnaby, B.C., Canada: Simon Fraser University).
----------. 1975-a. The Deduction/Induction Controversy. *MLJ* 59:15-8.
----------. 1975-b. The Relative Frequency of Spanish Pronunciation Errors. ERIC microfiche ED 119 504.
----------. 1975-c. The Teaching of Second Language Vocabulary. In H. Hammerly and I. Sawyer, eds. 1975:131-8.
----------. 1976. From Language Laboratory to Language Learning Room. *NALLDJ* 10,ii:40-4.
----------. 1977. The Teaching of "Ser"/"Estar" By a Cognitive Audiolingual Approach. *H* 60:305-8.
----------. 1978-a. On "Applied" Generative Phonology. In Notes and News, *MLJ* 62:38-9.
----------. 1978-b. The Unreliability of Visual Aids as Conveyors of Contextualized Sentence Meaning. Unpublished manuscript.
----------. 1979. Conveying Lexical Meanings in Second Language Teaching. *CMLR* 35:567-80.
---------- and Isabel Sawyer, eds. 1975. *Second Language Teaching '75,* Part II of the Proceedings of the 26th Annual Meeting of the PNCFL (Burnaby, B.C., Canada: Simon Fraser University).
Hancock, Charles R. 1972. Student Aptitude, Attitude, and Motivation. In D. Lange and C. James, eds. 1972:127-55.
Hanzeli, Victor E. 1968. Linguistics and the Language Teacher. *FLA* 2:42-50.
Harley, Birgit and Merrill Swain. 1977. An Analysis of the Spoken French of Five French Immersion Pupils. *WPB* 14:31-46.
---------- and Merrill Swain. 1978. An Analysis of the Verb System Used by Young Learners of French. *Interlanguage Studies Bulletin* 3:35-79.
Harris, Brian. 1978. The Difference Between Natural and Professional Translation. *CMLR* 34:417-27.
---------- and Bianca Sherwood. 1978. Translating as an Innate Skill. In David Gerver and H. Wallace Sinaiko, eds., *Proceedings of the NATO Symposium on Language, Interpretation and Communication* (New York: Plenum Press), 155-70.
Harris, Katherine S. 1958. Cues for the Discrimination of American English Fricatives in Spoken Syllables. *Language and Speech* 1:1-7.
Hartley, Peggy J. 1972. A Comparison Between Achievement in an Individualized Self-Paced Program and a Conventional Lockstep Program in Basic College Spanish. Unpublished doctoral dissertation, University of South Carolina.
---------- and Frances J. Dannerbeck. 1974. An Experiment in Self-Pacing in

Basic College Spanish and Subsequent Program Implementation. *H* 57:913-6.
Hatch, Evelyn. 1974. Research on Reading a Second Language. *J Reading Behavior* 6:53-61.
----------. 1978-a. Acquisition of Syntax in a Second Language. In J. Richards, ed. 1978:34-70.
----------. 1978-b. *Second Language Acquisition: A Book of Readings* (Rowley, Mass.: Newbury House).
Hatfield, William N. 1966. The Effect of Supplemental Training on the Achievement in Ninth Grade French of Students Weak in Sound Discrimination and Sound-Symbol Association Skills. Unpublished doctoral dissertation, Ohio State University.
Haugen, Einar. 1953. *The Norwegian Language in America* (Philadelphia: University of Pennsylvania Press).
Hawkins, Lee E. 1971. Immediate versus Delayed Presentation of Foreign Language Script. *MLJ* 55:280-90.
Hayes, Alfred S. 1965. New Directions in Foreign Language Teaching. *MLJ* 49: 281-93.
----------. 1968. *Language Laboratory Facilities: Technical Guide for Their Selection, Purchase, Use, and Maintenance* (London: Oxford University Press).
Hebb, Donald O., Wallace E. Lambert and G. Richard Tucker. 1971. Language, Thought, and Experience. *MLJ* 55:212-22.
----------, Wallace E. Lambert and G. Richard Tucker. 1973. A DMZ in the Language War. *Psychology Today* 6 (April):54-62.
Heilenman, Laura K. 1977. Foreign Language Vocabulary Learning and Native Language Processes. In R. Schulz, ed. 1977:43-52.
Hendon, Ursula S. 1980. Introducing Culture in the High School Foreign Language Class. *FLA* 13:191-9.
Henning, William A. 1976. Adapting Reading Materials for Individualized Instruction. *FLA* 9:542-7.
Heyde, Adelaide. 1979. The Relationship Between Self-Esteem and the Oral Production of a Second Language. Unpublished doctoral dissertation, University of Michigan.
Higa, Masanori. 1965. The Psycholinguistic Concept of "Difficulty" and the Teaching of Foreign-Language Vocabulary. *LL* 15:167-79.
Hill, Archibald A. 1958. *Introduction to Linguistic Structures; From Sound to Sentence in English* (New York: Harcourt, Brace).
Hill, Clifford A. and John S. Rittershofer. 1976. An Integrated Approach to Pronunciation and Spelling in ESL Curricula. In J. Fanselow and R. Crymes, eds. 1976:117-28.
Hill, Jane H. 1970. Foreign Accents, Language Acquisition and Cerebral Dominance. *LL* 20:237-48.
Hill, Joseph E. n.d. *Cognitive Style Interest Inventory.* Available from Oakland Community College, Bloomington Hills, Mich.
Hinofotis, Frances B. 1976. An Investigation of the Concurrent Validity of Cloze Testing as a Measure of Overall Proficiency in English as a Second Language. Unpublished doctoral dissertation, Southern Illinois University at Carbondale.
Hirschmann, Rudolf. 1975. An Intensive Approach to Culture and Civilization: The German Semester at USC. *U* 8:78-81.
Hocking, B.D.W. 1973. Types of Interference. In J. Oller and J. Richards, eds. 1973:88-95.
Hocking, Elton. 1967. *Language Laboratory and Language Learning,* second edition (Washington, D.C.: National Education Association).
Hok, Ruth. 1972. Cognitive and S-R Learning Theories Reconciled. *IRAL* 10:263-9.
Holley, Freda M. 1973. A Study of Vocabulary Learning in Context: The Effect of New-Word Density in German Reading Materials. *FLA* 6:339-47.
---------- and Janet K. King. 1971. Imitation and Correction in Foreign Language Learning. *MLJ* 55:494-8.
Hollingsworth, Rita. 1977. A Classroom Trip Through France. *FR* 51:175-9.
Horne, Kibbey M. 1970. Optimum Class Size for Intensive Language Instruction. *MLJ* 54:189-95.
Hosenfeld, Carol. 1975. The New Student Role: Individual Differences and Implications for Instruction. In G. Jarvis, ed. 1975:129-67.
----------. 1976. Learning About Learning: Discovering Our Students' Strategies. *FLA* 9:117-29.

Howatt, Anthony. 1974. The Background to Course Design. In J.P.B. Allen and S.P. Corder, eds. 1974:1-23.

Huang, J. 1972. A Chinese Child's Acquisition of English Syntax. Unpublished M.A. thesis, UCLA.

Huberman, Gisela and Vadim Medish. 1975. Spanish Multi-Channel Instruction: A Progress Report. *FLA* 8:49-52.

Humphreys, Lloyd G. 1939. Acquisition and Extinction of Verbal Expectations in a Situation Analogous to Conditioning. *J Experimental Psychology* 25:294-301.

Hunt, David E. n.d. *Paragraph Completion Test.* (Available from The Ontario Institute for Studies in Education, 252 Bloor St. W., Toronto, Ontario.)

Hunting, Robert. 1967. Recent Studies of Writing Frequency. *Research in the Teaching of English* 1:29-40.

Huser, Victor J. 1979. The Multiple-Choice Cloze Test: A New Way of Measuring EFL Proficiency in College Entrance Examinations. *Creativity: New Ideas in Language Teaching* (Instituto de Idiomas Yázigi, São Paulo, Brazil), No. 34 (July 1979):7-10.

Hymes, Dell. 1972. Models for the Interaction of Language and Social Life. In J. Gumperz and D. Hymes, eds., *Directions in Sociolinguistics* (New York: Holt, Rinehart and Winston), 35-71.

Ingram, Elisabeth. 1974. Language Testing. In J.P.B. Allen and S.P. Corder, eds. 1974:313-43.

Jakobovits, Leon A. 1970-a. Foreign Language Attitude Questionnaire. In J.A. Tursi, ed. 1970:9-30.

----------. 1970-b. *Foreign Language Learning: A Psycholinguistic Analysis of the Issues* (Rowley, Mass.: Newbury House).

----------. 1971. Psychological Perspectives on Individualizing Foreign Language Instruction. In H. Altman and R. Politzer, eds. 1971:88-102.

James, Carl. 1969. Deeper Contrastive Study. *IRAL* 7:83-95.

----------. 1970. A Rationale for Developing Foreign Language Reading Skills. *NALLDJ* 4,4:15-26.

----------. 1980. *Contrastive Analysis* (London: Longman).

Jarvis, Gilbert A., ed. 1974-a. *Responding to New Realities*, ACTFL Review of Foreign Language Education, vol. 5 (Skokie, Ill.: National Textbook Company).

----------, ed. 1974-b. *The Challenge of Communication*, ACTFL Review of Foreign Language Education, vol. 6 (Skokie, Ill.: National Textbook Company).

----------, ed. 1975. *Perspective: A New Freedom*, ACTFL Review of Foreign Language Education, vol. 7 (Skokie, Ill.: National Textbook Company).

----------, ed. 1976. *An Integrative Approach to Foreign Language Teaching: Choosing Among the Options*, ACTFL Review of Foreign Language Education, vol. 8 (Skokie, Ill.: National Textbook Company).

---------- and William N. Hatfield. 1971. The Practice Variable: An Experiment. *FLA* 4:401-10.

Jenkins, Evan. 1974. Grading Systems Return to the Basics --Grades. *New York Times*, April 14, 1974:7E.

Jenkins, Jacinto C. 1970. The Effects of Explanation with Spanish Pattern Drills. Unpublished doctoral dissertation, Stanford University.

Jenkins, Joseph R., Daniel C. Neale, and Stanley L. Deno. 1967. Differential Memory for Picture and Word Stimuli. *JEP* 58:303-7.

Jenks, Frederick L. 1974-a. 15-Year-Old Students Can Do Cross-Cultural Research. In F. Grittner, ed. 1974:65-71.

----------. 1974-b. Conducting Socio-Cultural Research in the Foreign Language Class. In H. Altman and V. Hanzeli, eds. 1974:95-123.

Jespersen, Otto. 1904. *How to Teach a Foreign Language* (London: Allen and Unwin).

Johansson, Faith Ann. 1973. *Immigrant Swedish Phonology: A Study in Multiple Contact Analysis* (Lund, Sweden: CWK Gleerup).

Johansson, Stig. 1973-a. An Evaluation of the Noise Test as a Method for Testing Overall Second Language Proficiency by Perception Under Masking Noise. *IRAL* 11:107-33.

----------. 1973-b. Partial Dictation as a Test of Foreign Language Proficiency. *Swedish-English Contrastive Studies Report No. 3* (Lund, Sweden: Dept. of English, Lund University).

Johnson, Keith. 1977. The Adoption of Functional Syllabuses for General Language Teaching Courses. *CMLR* 33:667-80.

Johnson, Raymond L. and Hebert L. Friedman. 1971. Some Temporal Factors in the Listening Behavior of Second Language Students. In P. Pimsleur and T. Quinn, eds. 1971:165-9.

Johnson, Ronald E. 1973. Meaningfulness and the Recall of Textual Prose. *American Educational Research J* 10:49-58.

Joiner, Elizabeth G. 1974-a. Communicative versus Non-Communicative Language Practice in the Teaching of Beginning College French: A Comparison of Two Treatments. Unpublished doctoral dissertation, Ohio State University.

----------. 1974-b. Keep Them Guessing. *AFLT* 4,ii:16-8.

----------. 1974-c. Tailoring Language Instruction to Student Needs. In G. Jarvis, ed. 1974-b:151-84.

----------. 1977. The Self-Directed Dialogue: A Technique for Conversational Practice. *FLA* 7:414-6.

Jonas, Sister Ruth A. 1969. The Twinned Classroom Approach to FLES. *MLJ* 53: 342-6.

Jones, George F., ed. 1964. *Foreign Language Teaching: Ideals and Practices.* RWCNECTFL (New York: Modern Language Association).

Jones, Randall L. 1977. Testing: A Vital Connection. In J. Phillips, ed. 1977:237-65.

---------- and Bernard Spolsky, eds. 1975. *Testing Language Proficiency* (Arlington, Va.: Center for Applied Linguistics).

Jonz, Jon. 1976. Improving on the Basic Egg: The M-C Cloze. *LL* 26:255-65.

Jorstad, Helen. 1973. Training Prospective Foreign Language Teachers at the University of Minnesota. *FLA* 6:521-3.

----------. 1974. Testing as Communication. In G. Jarvis, ed. 1974-b:223-73.

Kalivoda, Theodore B. 1972. An Individual Study Course for Facilitating Advanced Oral Skills. *MLJ* 56:492-5.

----------. 1975. Organization of Intensive Instruction: Dispelling Misconceptions and Facing Realities. *H* 58:114-21.

----------, Genelle Morain, and Robert J. Elkins. 1971. The Audio-Motor Unit: A Listening Comprehension Strategy That Works. *FLA* 4:392-400.

Keating, Raymond F. 1963. *A Study of the Effectiveness of Language Laboratories* (New York: The Institute of Administrative Research, Teachers College, Columbia University).

Kellerman, Eric. 1979. Transfer and Non-Transfer: Where We Are Now. *SSLA* 2:37-57.

Kellermann, Marcelle. 1981. *The Forgotten Third Skill --Reading a Foreign Language* (Oxford: Pergamon Press).

Kelly, Louis G. 1969. *25 Centuries of Language Teaching* (Rowley, Mass.: Newbury House).

Kelly, Thomas E. 1974. Interdisciplinary Studies. In G. Jarvis, ed. 1974-a: 129-59.

Kennedy, Graeme D. 1978. Conceptual Aspects of Language Learning. In J. Richards, ed. 1978:117-32.

Kessler, Carolyn. 1971. *The Acquisition of Syntax in Bilingual Children* (Washington, D.C.: Georgetown University Press).

King, Janet K., Freda M. Holley, and Betty N. Weber. 1975. A New Reading. In G. Jarvis, ed. 1975:169-217.

Kirch, Max S. 1956. At What Age Elementary School Language Teaching? *MLJ* 40:399-400.

Kirschenbaum, Howard, Sidney B. Simon, and Rodney W. Napier. 1971. *Wad-ja-get? The Grading Game in American Education* (New York: Hart).

Kirstein, Boni H.-J. 1972. Reducing Negative Transfer: Two Suggestions for the Use of Translation. *MLJ* 56:73-8.

Knorre, Martha L. 1975. The Role of Cognitive Processing in Second-Language Learning: A Study of the Effects of Depth Processing and Task Type on Measures of Student Learning in Elementary College Spanish. Unpublished doctoral dissertation, Ohio State University.

Kolers, Paul A. 1963. Interlingual Word-Associations. *JVLVB* 2:291-300.

----------. 1966-a. Reading and Talking Bilingually. *American J Psychology* 79:357-76.

----------. 1966-b. Interlingual Facilitation of Short Term Memory. *JVLVB* 5: 314-9.

----------. 1968. Bilingualism and Information Processing. *Scientific American* 218, 3:78-86.

Korchin, Sheldon J. and Seymour Levine. 1957. Anxiety and Verbal Learning.

J Abnormal and Social Psychology 54:234-40.

Krashen, Stephen D. 1973. Lateralization, Language Learning and the Critical Period: Some New Evidence. *LL* 23:63-74.

----------. 1978. The Monitor Model for Second Language Acquisition. In R. Gingras, ed. 1978:1-26.

----------. 1981. *Second Language Acquisition and Second Language Learning* (Oxford: Pergamon Press).

Kreidler, Charles W. 1972. Teaching English Spelling and Pronunciation. *TESOLQ* 6:3-12.

Kroeber, Alfred L. and Clyde Kluckhohn, eds. 1954. *Culture: A Critical Review of Concepts and Definitions* (New York: Random House).

Krohn, Robert. 1970. The Role of Linguistics in TEFL Methodology. *LL* 20:103-8.

Lado, Robert. 1957. *Linguistics Across Cultures: Applied Linguistics for Language Teachers* (Ann Arbor, Mich.: University of Michigan Press).

----------. 1961. *Language Testing: The Construction and Use of Foreign Language Tests* (London: Longmans).

----------. 1964. *Language Teaching --A Scientific Approach* (New York: McGraw-Hill).

----------. 1970. Language, Thought, and Memory in Language Teaching: A Thought View. *MLJ* 54·580-5.

----------, Theodore V. Higgs, and Joseph Edgerton. 1971. *The Relationship of Thought and Memory in Linguistic Performance: "Thought" Exercises in Foreign Language Teaching*. Final report for the Office of Education, Institute of International Studies, Contract No. OEC-0-70-1626 (Washington, D.C.: U.S. Office of Education).

Lafayette, Robert C., ed. 1975. *The Culture Revolution in Foreign Language Teaching* (Skokie, Ill.: National Textbook Company).

----------. 1978. *Teaching Culture: Strategies and Techniques*. Language in Education: Theory and Practice Series, No. 11 (Arlington, Va.: Center for Applied Linguistics).

---------- and Renate Schulz. 1975. Evaluating Cultural Learnings. In R. Lafayette, ed. 1975:104-18.

Lakoff, Robin. 1976. Language and Society. In R. Wardhaugh and H.D. Brown, eds. 1976:207-28.

Lambert, Richard D. 1973. *Language and Area Studies Review. Monograph 17* (Philadelphia: American Academy of Political and Social Science).

Lambert, Wallace E. 1963-a. Psychological Approaches to the Study of Language. Part I: On Learning, Thinking and Human Abilities. *MLJ* 47:51-62.

----------. 1963-b. Psychological Approaches to the Study of Language. Part II: On Second-Language Learning and Bilingualism. *MLJ* 47:114-21.

---------- and Robert C. Gardner. 1972. *Attitudes and Motivation in Second-Language Learning* (Rowley, Mass.: Newbury House).

---------- and John Macnamara. 1969. Some Cognitive Consequences of Following a First-Grade Curriculum in a Second Language. *JEP* 60:86-96.

---------- and G. Richard Tucker. 1972. *Bilingual Education of Children: The St. Lambert Experiment* (Rowley, Mass.: Newbury House).

Lamendella, John T. 1969. On the Irrelevance of Transformational Grammar to Second Language Pedagogy. *LL* 19:255-70.

----------. 1977. General Principles of Neurofunctional Organization and Their Manifestation in Primary and Nonprimary Language Acquisition. *LL* 27:155-96.

Lane, Harlan L. 1962. Some Differences Between First and Second Language Learning. *LL* 12:1-14.

----------. 1965. Models of Learning and Methods of Teaching. In E. Najam, ed. 1965:15-23.

---------- and Roger Buiten. 1966. A Self-Instructional Device for Conditioning Accurate Prosody. In A. Valdman, ed. 1966:159-74.

Lange, Dale L. 1968. Methods. In E. Birkmaier, ed. 1968:281-310.

----------, ed. 1970. *Britannica Review of Foreign Language Education*, vol. 2 (Chicago: Encyclopaedia Britannica).

----------, ed. 1971. *Britannica Review of Foreign Language Education*, vol. 3 (Chicago: Encyclopaedia Britannica).

---------- and Charles J. James, eds. 1972. *Foreign Language Education: A Reappraisal*, ACTFL Review of Foreign Language Education, vol. 4 (Skokie, Ill.: National Textbook Company).

Langer, Susanne K. 1951. *Philosophy in a New Key* (New York: Pelican Books).

Lawler, John and Larry Selinker. 1971. On Paradoxes, Rules, and Research in Second Language Learning. *LL* 21:27-43.

LeBel, C.J. 1950. Standards for Educational Recording Machines. *Quarterly J Speech* 36:520-3.

Lee, W.R. 1968. Thoughts on Contrastive Linguistics in the Context of Language Teaching. In J.E. Alatis, ed., *Report of the Nineteenth Annual Round Table Meeting on Linguistics and Language Study,* Georgetown University Monograph Series in Languages and Linguistics, No. 21 (Washington, D.C.: Georgetown University Press), 185-201.

Léon, Pierre, 1966. Teaching Pronunciation. In A. Valdman, ed. 1966:57-79.

Lepke, Helen S. 1978. Assessing Individual Learning Styles: An Analysis of Five Instruments. *FLA* 11:657-68.

Lester, Mark, ed. 1970. *Readings in Applied Transformational Grammar.* (New York: Holt, Rinehart and Winston).

Lim, Kiat B. 1968. Prompting vs. Confirmation, Pictures vs. Translations, and Other Variables in Children's Learning of Grammar in a Second Language. Unpublished doctoral dissertation, Harvard University.

----------. 1970. The Use of the First Language in Second Language Teaching and Learning. *RELC Journal* 1:66-76.

Lipton, Gladys C. 1969. To Read or Not to Read: An Experiment on the FLES Level. *FLA* 3:241-6.

Listerman, Randall W. 1973. Film Production in FL Study. *U* 6:24-5.

Littlewood, William T. 1980. Form and Meaning in Language Teaching Methodology. *MLJ* 64:441-5.

Locke, John L. 1970. The Value of Repetition in Articulation Learning. *IRAL* 8:147-54.

---------- and Fred S. Fehr. 1970. Subvocal Rehearsal as a Form of Speech. *JVLVB* 9:495-8.

LoCoco, Veronica 1975. An Analysis of Spanish and German Learners' Errors. *WPB* 7:96-124.

Logan, Gerald E. 1970. Curricula for Individualized Instruction. In D. Lange, ed. 1970:133-55.

----------. 1973. *Individualized Foreign Language Learning: An Organic Process --A Guide to Initiating, Maintaining and Expanding the Process* (Rowley, Mass.: Newbury House).

Lorge, Sarah W. 1964. Language Laboratory Research Studies in New York City High Schools: A Discussion of the Program and the Findings. *MLJ* 48:409-19.

Lozanov, Georgi. 1978. *Suggestology and Outlines of Suggestopedy* (New York: Gordon and Breach Science Publishers).

Lumsdaine, Arthur A. and Robert Glaser, eds. 1965. *Teaching Machines and Programmed Learning; A Source Book* (Washington, D.C.: Department of Audio-Visual Instruction, National Education Association).

Lusky, Mary H. 1981. Some Doubts About the Cultural Approach to Teaching Spanish. *H* 64:266-72.

MacCorquodale, Kenneth. 1969. B.F. Skinner's *Verbal Behavior:* A Retrospective Appreciation. *J Experimental Analysis of Behavior* 12:831-41.

----------. 1970. On Chomsky's Review of Skinner's *Verbal Behavior. J Experimental Analysis of Behavior* 13:83-99.

Mackey, William F. 1965. *Language Teaching Analysis* (London: Longmans).

----------. n.d. Unpublished manuscript referred to by McArdle 1968:268.

----------. 1973. Language Didactics and Applied Linguistics. In J. Oller and J. Richards, eds. 1973:4-15.

Macnamara, John. 1967. The Bilingual's Linguistic Performance --A Psychological Overview. *J Social Issues* 23:58-77.

----------. 1973. Nurseries, Streets and Classrooms: Some Comparisons and Deductions. *MLJ* 57:250-4.

----------. 1975. Comparison Between First and Second Language Learning. *WPB* 7:71-95.

----------, Joyce Svarc, and Sharon Horner. 1976. Attending a Primary School of the Other Language in Montreal. In António Simões, Jr., ed., *The Bilingual Child: Research and Analysis of Existing Educational Themes* (New York: Academic Press), 113-31.

Madsen, Harold S. and J. Donald Bowen. 1978. *Adaptation in Language Teaching* (Rowley, Mass.: Newbury House).

Maley, Alan and Alan Duff. 1978. *Drama Techniques in Language Learning* (Cambridge, England: Cambridge University Press).

---------- and Alan Duff. 1979. *Sounds Intriguing* (Cambridge, England: Cambridge University Press).

Mantini, Lawrence C. 1980. The Use of a Structured Sequence of Recorded Materials for Language Stress-Rhythm and Intonation Study. *FLA* 13:373-7.

Marks, Carolyn B., Marleen J. Doctorow, and M.C. Wittrock. 1974. Word Frequency and Reading Comprehension. *J Educational Research* 67:259-62.

Marshall, John C., Freda Newcombe, and Jane M. Holmes. 1975. Lexical Memory: A Linguistic Approach. In Alan Kennedy and Alan Wilkes, eds., *Studies in Long Term Memory* (London: John Wiley), 315-22.

Marty, Fernand. 1962. *Programming a Basic Foreign Language Course: Prospects for Self-Instruction* (Roanoke, Va.: Audio-Visual Publications).

----------. 1965. *Language Laboratory Learning* (Roanoke, Va.: Audio-Visual Publications).

Maslow, Abraham H. 1970. *Motivation and Personality*, second edition (New York: Harper and Row).

Mason, Charles. 1971. The Relevance of Intensive Training in English as a Foreign Language for University Students. *LL* 21:197-204.

Matluck, Joseph H. 1957. The Presentation of Spanish Pronunciation in American Textbooks. *MLJ* 41:219-28.

Matthews-Břeský, R.J.H. 1972. Translation as a Testing Device. *ELT* 27:58-65.

Mazurkiewicz, Albert B. 1976. *Teaching About Phonics* (New York: St. Martin's Press).

McArdle, Richard J. 1968. Teacher Education, Qualifications, and Supervision. In E. Birkmaier, ed. 1968:259-80.

McEwan, Angela and Roger Minkle. 1979. Why Am I Studying Spanish? An Evaluation of Student Response. *H* 62:89-97.

McGuignan, F.J. 1973. The Function of Covert Oral Behavior ("Silent Speech") During Silent Reading. *Linguistics* 112:39-47.

McNeill, David. 1966. Developmental Psycholinguistics. In F. Smith and G.A. Miller, eds., *The Genesis of Language: A Psycholinguistic Approach* (Cambridge, Mass.: MIT Press), 15-84.

Mead, Robert G., ed. 1966. *Language Teaching: Broader Contexts*. RWCNECTFL (New York: Modern Language Association).

Meade, Betsy and Genelle Morain. 1973. The Culture Cluster. *FLA* 6:331-8.

Meloni, Christine F. and Shirley E. Thompson. 1980. Oral Reports in the Intermediate Classroom. *TESOLQ* 14:503-10.

Miller, George A. 1951. *Language and Communication* (New York: McGraw-Hill).

----------. 1956. The Magical Number Seven, Plus or Minus Two: Some Limits on Our Capacity for Processing Information. *Psychological Review* 63:81-97.

Miller, W.R. 1963. The Acquisition of Formal Features of Language. *American J Orthopsychiatry* 34:862-7.

Mills, Geoff. 1977. Contrastive Analysis and Translation in Second-Language Teaching. *CMLR* 33:733-45.

Minn, Jay P. 1976. Clue-Searching: An Aid to Comprehension. In Renate A. Schulz, ed., *Teaching for Communication in the Foreign Language Classroom* (Skokie, Ill.: National Textbook Company), 93-100.

Mishima, Toshiko. 1967. An Experiment Comparing Five Modalities of Conveying Meaning for the Teaching of Foreign Language Vocabulary. Unpublished doctoral dissertation, Georgetown University.

Molina, Hubert. 1968. Transformational Grammar in Teaching Spanish. *H* 51:284-6.

Mollica, Anthony. 1976. Cartoons in the Language Classroom. *CMLR* 32:424-44.

Morain, Genelle G. 1968. French Folklore: A Fresh Approach to the Teaching of Culture. *FR* 41:675-81.

----------. 1971. Teaching for Cross-Cultural Understanding: An Annotated Bibliography. *FLA* 5:82-3.

----------. 1976. The Cultural Component of the Methods Course. In Alan Garfinkel and Stanley Hamilton, eds., *Designs for Foreign Language Teacher Education* (Rowley, Mass.: Newbury House), 25-46.

Morehouse, Ward. 1973. Foreword. In P. Boyd-Bowman 1973:iii-vi.

Morrey, Robert A. 1971. The Attitudes of Students and Teachers to Individualized Instruction. In H. Altman and R. Politzer, eds. 1971:21-52.

Morrison, H.W. and E.N. Adams. 1968. Pilot Study of a CAI Laboratory in German. *MLJ* 52:279-87.

Morrow, Judith C. and Lorraine A. Strasheim. 1977. Supplementing the Textbook Attractively, Effectively, and Responsibly. In R. Schulz, ed. 1977:74-91.
Morton, F. Rand. 1961. *The Language Laboratory as a Teaching Machine* (Ann Arbor, Mich.: University of Michigan Press).
Morton, Jacqueline. 1979. *English Grammar for Students of French* (Ann Arbor, Mich.: The Olivia and Hill Press).
Moskowitz, Gertrude. 1975. Make that Shock Lesson Shocking. *H* 58:894-6.
----------. 1978. *Caring and Sharing in the Foreign Language Classroom* (Rowley, Mass.: Newbury House).
Moulton, William G. 1961. Linguistics and Language Teaching in the United States 1940-1960. In Christine Mohrmann, Alf Sommerfelt, and Joshua Whatmough, eds. 1961. *Trends in European and American Linguistics 1930-1960* (Utrecht, The Netherlands: Spectrum), 82-109.
----------. 1962. *The Sounds of English and German* (Chicago: University of Chicago Press).
----------. 1966. *A Linguistic Guide to Language Learning* (New York: Modern Language Association).
Mowrer, O. Hobart. 1960-a. *Learning Theory and Behavior* (New York: John Wiley and Sons).
----------. 1960-b. *Learning Theory and the Symbolic Processes* (New York: John Wiley and Sons).
Mueller, Gunther A. 1980. Visual Contextual Cues and Listening Comprehension: An Experiment. *MLJ* 64:335-40.
Mueller, Klaus A. 1972. Judging the Competency of Teachers on the Performance of Their Students. *MLJ* 56:10-2.
Mueller, Theodore H. n.d. Individualized Instruction in French at the University of Kentucky. Mimeo.
----------, ed. 1968-a. *Proceedings of the Seminar on Programmed Learning* (New York: Appleton-Century-Crofts).
----------. 1968-b. Programmed Language Instruction--Help for the Linguistically "Underprivileged." *MLJ* 52:79-84.
----------. 1968-c. Programmed Learning Instruction Six Years Later. In T. Mueller, ed. 1968-a:38-49.
----------. 1971-a. Could the New Key Be a Wrong Key. *FR* 44:1085-93.
----------. 1971-b. The Effectiveness of Two Learning Models: The Audio-Lingual Habit Theory and the Cognitive Code-Learning Theory. In P. Pimsleur and T. Quinn, eds. 1971:113-22.
---------- and Robert Harris. 1966. First Year College French Through an Audio-Lingual Program. *IRAL* 4:19-38.
---------- and Henri Niedzielski. 1968-a. *Basic French --A Programmed Course* (New York: New Century, Appleton-Century-Crofts).
---------- and Henri Niedzielski. 1968-b. The Influence of Discrimination Training on Pronunciation. *MLJ* 52:410-9.
Mullen, Karen A. 1979. An Alternative to the Cloze Test. In C. Yorio *et al.*, eds. 1979:187-92.
Muller, Daniel H. 1965. The Effect Upon Pronunciation and Intonation of Early Exposure to the Written Word. *MLJ* 49:411-3.
---------- and Trinidad Muller. 1968. The Problem of Interference in Beginning Portuguese. *MLJ* 52:201-5.
Munby, John. 1978. *Communicative Syllabus Design* (Cambridge, England: Cambridge University Press).
Murdock, George P. *et al.* 1964. *Outline of Cultural Materials,* revised edition (New Haven: Human Relations Area File). Referred to by Seelye 1974.
Myers, Pamela J. 1979. Student Factors as Indicators of Continuation in Secondary School Study of French/German/Spanish as a Second Language. Unpublished doctoral dissertation, University of Minnesota.
Nachtmann, F.W. 1973. Let the Student Have the Last Word. *FR* 47:62-5.
Naiman, Neil, Maria Frölich, H.H. Stern, and Angie Todesco. 1975. *The Good Language Learner* (Toronto: Modern Language Centre, The Ontario Institute for Studies in Education).
Najam, Edward W., ed. 1962. *Materials and Techniques for the Language Laboratory* (Bloomington, Indiana: Indiana University Research Center). Also The Hague: Mouton.
----------, ed. 1965. *Language Learning: The Individual and the Process* (Bloomington, Ind.: Indiana University Press).

Nation, I.S.P. 1977. The Combining Arrangement: Some Techniques. *MLJ* 61:89-94.
Nattinger, James R. 1980. A Lexical Phrase Grammar for ESL. *TESOLQ* 14:337-44.
Navarro Tomás, Tomás. 1932. *Manual de pronunciación española*, 5th edition, revised (New York: Hafner, 1957).
Nemser, William. 1971. Approximative Systems of Foreign Language Learners. *IRAL* 9:115-23.
Nesset, Bonna C. 1973. *Minneapolis Senior High Schools: Grades for Fall, 1972* (Minneapolis: Research and Evaluation Department, Educational Services Division). Mimeo. Referred to by H. Jorstad 1974:253.
Neufeld, Gerald G. 1980. On the Adult's Ability to Acquire Phonology. *TESOLQ* 14:285-98.
Newmark, Leonard and David A. Reibel. 1968. Necessity and Sufficiency in Language Learning. *IRAL* 6:145-64.
Ney, James J. 1968. The Oral Approach: A Re-Appraisal. *LL* 18:3-13.
----------. 1971. Transformational-Generative Theories of Language and the Role of Conditioning in Language Learning. *LL* 21:63-73.
Nickel, Gerhard, ed. 1971. *Papers in Contrastive Linguistics* (Cambridge, England: Cambridge University Press).
----------. 1975. Problems of Syllabus, Curriculum and Testing in Connection with Modern Language Programmes for Adults in Europe. In R. Jones and B. Spolsky, eds. 1975:131-7.
Nida, Eugene. 1957. *Learning a Foreign Language* (New York: Friendship Press).
Nilsen, Don L.F. 1971. The Use of Case Grammar in Teaching English as a Foreign Language. *TESOLQ* 5:293-300.
Northeast Conference on the Teaching of Foreign Languages. Reports of the Working Committees. 1954-81.
Nostrand, Howard L. 1966. Describing and Teaching the Sociocultural Context of a Foreign Language and Literature. In A. Valdman, ed. 1966:1-25.
----------. 1967. *Background Data for the Teaching of French* (Seattle: Dept. of Romance Languages and Literature, University of Washington).
----------. 1974. Empathy for a Second Culture: Motivations and Techniques. In G. Jarvis, ed. 1974-a:263-327.
----------, David W. Foster, and Clay B. Christensen, eds. 1965. *Research on Language Teaching: An Annotated International Bibliography 1945-64*, second edition (Seattle: University of Washington Press).
Obrecht, Dean H. 1956-57. A Visual Aid to Pronunciation. *LL* 7:51-8.
Oller, D.K. 1974. Toward a General Theory of Phonological Processes in First and Second Language Learning. Paper presented at the Western Conference on Linguistics, Seattle.
Oller, John W., Jr. 1971. Dictation as a Device for Testing Foreign Language Proficiency. *ELT* 25:254-9.
----------. 1972-a. Scoring Methods and Difficulty Levels for Cloze Tests of Proficiency in English as a Second Language. *MLJ* 56:151-8.
----------. 1972-b. Testing Language Skills. *Language in American Indian Education*, Spring 1972:61-8.
----------. 1973-a. Cloze Tests of Second Language Proficiency and What They Measure. *LL* 23:105-18.
----------. 1973-b. Discrete Point Tests versus Tests of Integrative Skills. In J. Oller and J. Richards, eds. 1973:184-99.
----------. 1973-c. Some Psycholinguistic Controversies. In J. Oller and J. Richards, eds. 1973:36-50.
----------. 1976-a. Evidence for a General Language Proficiency Factor: An Expectancy Grammar. *Die Neueren Sprachen* 75:165-74.
----------. 1976-b. Language Testing. In R. Wardhaugh and H.D. Brown, eds. 1976:275-300.
----------. 1979. *Language Tests at School --A Pragmatic Approach* (London: Longman).
---------- and Christine A. Conrad. 1971. The Cloze Technique and ESL Proficiency. *LL* 21:183-95.
---------- and Dean H. Obrecht. 1968. Pattern Drill and Communicative Activity: A Psycholinguistic Experiment. *IRAL* 6:165-74.
---------- and Dean H. Obrecht. 1969. The Psycholinguistic Principle of Informational Sequence. *IRAL* 7:117-23.
---------- and Kyle Perkins. 1980. *Research in Language Testing* (Rowley, Mass.: Newbury House).

Oller, John W., Jr. and Elcho Z. Redding. 1971. Article Usage and Other Language Skills. *LL* 21:85-95.
---------- and Jack C. Richards, eds. 1973. *Focus on the Learner: Pragmatic Perspectives for the Language Teacher* (Rowley, Mass.: Newbury House).
---------- and Virginia Streiff. 1975. Dictation: A Test of Grammar Based Expectancies. In R. Jones and B. Spolsky, eds. 1975:71-88.
---------- and Seid M. Ziahosseiny. 1970. The Contrastive Analysis Hypothesis and Spelling Errors. *LL* 20:183-9.
Olsen, Solveig. 1980. Foreign Language Departments and Computer-Assisted Instruction: A Survey. *MLJ* 64:341-9.
Olson, Linda and S. Jay Samuels. 1973. The Relationship Between Age and Accuracy of Foreign Language Pronunciation. *J Educational Research* 66:263-8.
Olstad, Charles. 1964. Composition in Imitation. *H* 47:452-4.
Omaggio, Alice C. 1976. Real Communication: Speaking a Living Language. *FLA* 9:131-3.
Ornstein, Jacob, Ralph W. Ewton, Jr., and Theodore H. Mueller. 1971. *Programmed Instruction and Educational Technology in the Language Teaching Field* (Philadelphia: Center for Curriculum Development).
---------- and Robert Lado. 1967. Research in Foreign Language Teaching Methodology. *IRAL* 5:11-25.
Osgood, Charles E. and G.J. Suci. 1955. Factor Analysis of Meaning. *J Experimental Psychology* 50:325-38.
Ota, Akira. 1971. Comparison of English and Japanese, With Special Reference to Tense and Aspect. *The PCCLLU Papers, Working Papers in Linguistics* (University of Hawaii) 3,4:121-57.
Otto, Ernst 1921. *Methodik und Didaktik des neusprachlichen Unterrichts. Versuch einer wissenschaftlichen Unterrichtslehre* (Bielefeld: Velhagen und Klasing). Referred to by W. Butzkamm 1973.
Palmer, Harold E. 1917. *The Scientific Study and Teaching of Languages* (London: Harrap). Reprinted in 1968 (London: Oxford University Press). Pages given in text correspond to the 1968 printing.
----------. 1921. *The Oral Method of Teaching Languages* (Cambridge, England: Heffer and Sons).
----------. 1922. *The Principles of Language-Study* (London: Harrap). Reprinted in 1964 (London: Oxford University Press). Pages given in text correspond to the 1964 printing.
---------- and Dorothée Palmer. 1925. *English Through Actions* (Tokyo: Kaitakusha, 1955).
---------- and H. Vere Redman. 1932. *This Language-Learning Business* (London: Harrap). Reprinted in 1969 (London: Oxford University Press). Pages given in text correspond to the 1969 printing.
Papalia, Anthony. 1973. An Assessment of Attitudes and Behaviors of Foreign Language Teachers. *FLA* 7:231-6.
----------. 1976. *Learner-Centered Language Teaching: Methods and Materials* (Rowley, Mass.: Newbury House).
---------- and Joseph Zampogna. 1972. An Experiment in Individualized Instruction Through Small Group Interaction. *FLA* 5:302-6.
Parent, P. Paul and Simon Belasco. 1970. Parallel Column Bilingual Reading Materials as a Pedagogical Device: An Experimental Evaluation. *MLJ* 54:493-504.
Parker, William R. 1962. *The National Interest and Foreign Languages,* third edition (Washington, D.C.: U.S. Department of State, Government Printing Office).
Passy, Paul. 1899. *De la méthode directe dans l'enseignement des langues vivantes* (Cambridge, England: Association Phonétique Internationale).
Paulston, Christina B. 1974. Linguistic and Communicative Competence. *TESOLQ* 8:347-62.
---------- and Mary N. Bruder. 1974. *From Substitution to Substance: A Handbook of Structural Pattern Drills* (Rowley, Mass.: Newbury House).
---------- and Howard R. Selekman. 1976. Interaction Activities in the Foreign Classroom, or How to Grow a Tulip-Rose. *FLA* 9:248-54.
Pavlov, Ivan P. 1927. *Conditioned Reflexes* (London: Oxford University Press).
Pei, Mario. 1973. *How to Learn Languages and What Languages to Learn* (New York: Harper and Row).
Pelosi, Angelo G. 1973. What is "Grammar"? *MLJ* 57:329-35.
Perren, George E. 1967. Testing Ability in English as a Second Language:

3. Spoken Language. *ELT* 22:22-9.

Petry, Karla L. 1981. *La Chanson de Roland* in the Elementary School Classroom: A Case for Medieval Literature and Young Language Students. *MLJ* 65:137-40.

Phillips, June K. 1973. Syntax and Vocabulary of Mothers' Speech to Young Children: Age and Sex Comparisons. *Child Development* 44:182-5.

----------, ed. 1977. *The Language Connection: From the Classroom to the World,* ACTFL Foreign Language Education Series, vol. 9 (Skokie, Ill.: National Textbook Company).

----------, ed. 1979. *Building on Experience --Building for Success,* ACTFL Foreign Language Education Series, vol. 10 (Skokie, Ill.: National Textbook Company).

----------, ed. 1981. *Action for the '80s: A Political, Professional, and Public Program for Foreign Language Education,* ACTFL Foreign Language Education Series, vol. 12 (Skokie, Ill.: National Textbook Company).

Phillips, Robert. 1968. Using the Tape Recorder to Correct Student Composition. *H* 51:126-7.

Piaget, Jean. 1967. *Six Psychological Studies* (New York: Vintage Books).

Piazza, Linda G. 1978. Communicative Effects of Grammatical Errors Made by Americans Learning French. Unpublished doctoral dissertation, University of Rochester.

----------. 1980. French Tolerance for Grammatical Errors Made by Americans. *MLJ* 64:422-7.

Pimsleur, Paul. 1959. The Functions of the Language Laboratory. *MLJ* 43:11-5.

----------. 1963. Discrimination Training in the Teaching of French Pronunciation. *MLJ* 47:199-203.

----------. 1966-a. *Pimsleur Language Aptitude Battery* (New York: Harcourt Brace Jovanovich).

----------. 1966-b. Testing Foreign Language Learning. In A. Valdman, ed. 1966:175-214.

----------. 1971. Some Aspects of Listening Comprehension. In L. Chatagnier and G. Taggart, eds. 1971:106-14.

----------. 1980. *How to Learn a Foreign Language* (Boston: Heinle and Heinle).

---------- and Robert J. Bonkowski. 1961. The Transfer of Verbal Material Across Sense Modalities. *JEP* 52:104-7.

---------- and Terence Quinn, eds. 1971. *The Psychology of Second Language Learning. Papers from the Second International Congress of Applied Linguistics* (Cambridge, England: Cambridge University Press).

----------, Donald M. Sundland, and Ruth D. McIntyre. 1964. Under-Achievement in Foreign Language Learning. *IRAL* 2:113-50.

Plaister, Ted. 1973. Teaching Reading Comprehension to the Advanced ESL Student Using the Cloze Procedure. *RELC Journal* 4,ii:31-8.

----------. 1981. Teaching Vocabulary, Listening Comprehension, and Reasoning by Means of Analogies. *FLA* 14:25-9.

Politzer, Robert L. 1953. Student Motivation and Interest in Elementary Language Courses. *LL* 5:15-21.

----------. 1964. Pattern Practice for Reading. *LL* 14:127-35.

----------. 1965. *Teaching French --An Introduction to Applied Linguistics,* second edition (New York: Blaisdell).

----------. 1966. *Practice-Centered Teacher Training: French: A Syllabus for the Training of Teachers of French* (Stanford, Cal.: School of Education, Stanford University).

----------. 1968-a. An Experiment in the Presentation of Parallel and Contrasting Structures. *LL* 18:35-43.

----------. 1968-b. The Role and Place of Explanation in the Pattern Drill. *IRAL* 6:315-31.

----------. 1972. *Linguistics and Applied Linguistics: Aims and Methods* (Philadelphia: Center for Curriculum Development).

----------. 1978. Errors of English Speakers of German as Perceived and Evaluated by German Natives. *MLJ* 62:253-61.

----------. 1980. Foreign Language Teaching and Bilingual Education: Research Implications. *FLA* 13:291-7.

----------. n.d. *Practice-Centered Teacher Training --French* (Philadelphia: Center for Curriculum Development).

---------- and Charles N. Staubach. 1961. *Teaching Spanish: A Linguistic Orientation* (Boston: Ginn).

Politzer, Robert and Louis Weiss. 1966. *An Experiment in Improving Achievement in Foreign Languages Through Learning of Selected Skills Associated with Language Aptitude* (Washington, D.C.: Bureau of Research, U.S. Office of Education). Also available as ERIC microfiche ED 046 261.

---------- and Louis Weiss. 1969. Developmental Aspects of Auditory Discrimination, Echo Response and Recall. *MLJ* 53:75-85.

---------- and Louis Weiss. n.d. *The Successful Foreign Language Teacher* (Philadelphia: Center for Curriculum Development).

Pollio, Howard R. 1966. *The Structural Basis of Word Association Behavior* (The Hague: Mouton).

Pond, Karl S. 1963. A Language Teaching Tool: The Overhead Projector. *MLJ* 47: 30-3.

Porter, D. 1976. Modified Cloze Procedure: A More Valid Reading Comprehension Test. *ELT* 30:151-5.

Postman, Leo and Benton J. Underwood. 1973. Critical Issues in Interference Theory. *Memory and Cognition* 1:19-40.

Postovsky, Valerian A. 1971. Effects of Delay in Oral Practice at the Beginning of Second Language Learning. Unpublished doctoral dissertation, University of California at Berkeley.

Powell, John S.J. 1969. *Why Am I Afraid to Tell You Who I Am?* (Niles, Ill.: Argus Communications).

Powell, Patricia B. 1975. Moi Tarzan, vous Jane? A Study of Communicative Competence. *FLA* 8:38-42.

Powers, James R., ed. 1971. Professional Responsibilities. In J.W. Dodge, ed., *Leadership for Continuing Development*. RWCNECTFL (New York: MLA Materials Center), 15-50.

Preibusch, Wolfgang and Heidrun Zander. 1971. Wortschatzvermittlung: auf der Suche nach einem analytischen Modell. *IRAL* 9:131-45.

Preller, Arno G. 1974. Building Better Bridges in a Kaleidoscopic Society. In F. Grittner, ed. 1974:72-83.

Pressey, S.L. 1926. A Simple Apparatus Which Tests and Scores --and Teaches. *School and Society* 23:373-6.

Prince, Marilyn M. and John P. Casey. 1972. Programmed Instruction Helps Teach Spanish Grammar. *MLJ* 56:491-2.

Probst, Glen W. 1970. Two Basic Methods of Presenting Spanish at the University Level. Unpublished doctoral dissertation, Ohio State University.

Purcell, Edward T. and Richard W. Suter. 1980. Predictors of Pronunciation Accuracy: A Reexamination. *LL* 30:271-87.

Quinn, David J. 1971. Attitude and Verbal Participation in Second Language Learning. Unpublished doctoral dissertation, University of Oregon.

Quinn, Terence J. 1974. Theoretical Foundations in Linguistics and Related Fields. In G. Jarvis, ed. 1974-a:329-53.

Racle, Gabriel, ed. 1975. *A Teaching Experience with the Suggestopaedic Method/ Une experience d'enseignement avec la méthode suggestopédique* (Ottawa: Information Canada).

Ramsey, Robert M. 1981. A Technique for Interlingual Lexico-Semantic Comparison: The Lexigram. *TESOLQ* 15:15-24.

Raugh, Michael R. and Richard C. Atkinson. 1975. A Mnemonic Method for Learning a Second-Language Vocabulary. *JEP* 67:1-16.

Reeds, James A., Harris Winitz and Paul A. García. 1977. A Test of Reading Following Comprehension Training. *IRAL* 15:307-19.

Reilly, Richard R. 1971. A Note on "Clozentropy": A Procedure for Testing the English Language Proficiency of Foreign Students. *Speech Monographs* 38:350-3.

Reinert, Harry. 1972. Beginners Are Individuals, Too! In H. Altman, ed. 1972:89-101.

----------. 1974-a. Extending the Teacher: From Text to Context. In G. Jarvis, ed. 1974-b:275-98.

----------. 1974-b. Use of Student Opinion as a Basis for Curriculum Planning. In H. Hammerly, ed. 1974:5-10.

----------. 1977. ELSIE Is No Bull! or On Utilizing Information Concerning Student Learning Styles. In R. Schulz, ed. 1977:21-8.

Reynolds, Sue. 1975. Study-Travel Abroad. In R. Lafayette, ed. 1975:140-55.

Rice, Frank A. 1959. The Foreign Service Institute Tests Language Proficiency. *LR* 1,2:4.

Richards, Jack C. 1971. Error Analysis and Second Language Strategies. *LL* 17:12-22.
----------. 1973. A Noncontrastive Approach to Error Analysis. In J. Oller and J. Richards, eds. 1973:96-113.
----------, ed. 1974. *Error Analysis: Perspectives on Second Language Learning* (London: Longman).
----------. 1976. The Role of Vocabulary Teaching. *TESOLQ* 10:77-90.
----------, ed. 1978. *Understanding Second and Foreign Language Learning --Issues and Approaches* (Rowley, Mass.: Newbury House).
Richards, S. Earle and Joan E. Appel. 1956. The Effects of Written Words in Beginning Spanish. *MLJ* 40:129-33.
Richmond, Edmun B. 1973. Processing and Displaying Speech Patterns for Use in the FL Class. *U* 6:112-4.
----------. 1980. German Via the Airwaves, Phase Two: On the Beam with CB Radio. *FLA* 13:371-2.
Riestra, Miguel A. and Charles E. Johnson. 1964. Changes in Attitudes of Elementary-School Pupils Toward Foreign-Speaking Peoples Resulting from the Study of a Foreign Language. *J Experimental Education* 33:65-72.
Rivers, Wilga M. 1964. *The Psychologist and the Foreign-Language Teacher* (Chicago: University of Chicago Press).
----------. 1968. (Second edition, 1981) *Teaching Foreign-Language Skills* (Chicago: University of Chicago Press).
----------. 1971. Linguistic and Psychological Factors in Speech Perception and Their Implications for Teaching Materials. In P. Pimsleur and T. Quinn, eds. 1971:123-34.
----------. 1973. The Non-Major: Tailoring the Course to Fit the Person --Not the Image. In Kurt R. Jankowsky, ed., *Language and International Studies*, Monograph Series No. 26 (Washington, D.C.: Georgetown University Press), 85-97.
----------. 1975. *A Practical Guide to the Teaching of French* (New York: Oxford University Press).
----------. 1976. *Speaking in Many Tongues: Essays in Foreign-Language Teaching*, expanded second edition (Rowley, Mass.: Newbury House).
Robinson, Boyd E. 1969. Use of the Initial Teaching Alphabet in English as a Second Language. Classes for Spanish Speaking Adults. Unpublished doctoral dissertation, UCLA.
Rochet, Bernard. 1978. L'enseignement de la phonologie d'une deuxième langue aux adultes. *CMLR* 34:327-34.
Rodgers, Theodore S. 1969. On Measuring Vocabulary Difficulty --An Analysis of Item-Variables in Learning Russian: English Vocabulary Pairs. *IRAL* 7:327-43.
----------. 1978. Strategies for Individualized Language Learning and Teaching. In J. Richards, ed. 1978:251-72.
Rojas, Colette. 1971. L'analyse des fautes. *FdM* 81:58-63.
Roland, Lyn. 1966. An Experiment in a Pronunciation Problem. *IRAL* 4:255-9.
Ronjat, Jules. 1913. *Le développement du langage observé chez un enfant bilingue* (Paris: Champion).
Rosansky, Ellen. 1976. Methods and Morphemes in Second Language Acquisition Research. *LL* 26:409-25.
Rosenbaum, Peter S. 1969. The Computer as a Learning Environment for Foreign Language Instruction. *FLA* 2:457-65.
Rosenthal, Robert and Lenore Jacobson. 1968. *Pygmalion in the Classroom: Teacher Expectation and Pupils' Intellectual Development* (New York: Holt, Rinehart and Winston).
Roulet, Eddy. 1978. *Théories linguistiques et enseignement des langues* (Paris: Nathan).
Rubin, Joan. 1975. What the "Good Language Learner" Can Teach Us. *TESOLQ* 9: 41-51.
Ruiz, M.B. 1963. Weighting and Sequencing English Tense-Aspect Modifications for Hiligaynon Speakers. Unpublished doctoral dissertation, UCLA.
Sacks, Norman. 1967. "Modern Spanish" in an Intensive Program for Graduate Students: An Experiment and Some Reflections. *H* 50:310-9.
Saegert, Joel, Sue Scott, John Perkins, and G. Richard Tucker. 1974. A Note on the Relationship Between English Proficiency, Years of Study, and Medium of Instruction. *LL* 24:99-104.
Sampson, Gloria P. 1978. A Model for Second Language Learning. *CMLR* 34:442-54.

Sandstrom, Eleanor L. and Paul Pimsleur, eds. 1970. Foreign Languages for All Students? In J. Tursi, ed. 1970:105-33.

Saporta, Sol. 1966. Applied Linguistics and Generative Grammar. In A. Valdman, ed. 1966:81-92.

Sastri, H.N.L. 1970. The Bilingual Method of Teaching English --An Experiment. *RELC Journal* 1,ii:24-8.

Savignon, Sandra J. 1972. *Communicative Competence: An Experiment in Foreign-Language Teaching* (Philadelphia: Center for Curriculum Development).

Sawyer, Isabel. 1977. Talking to Students and *Voici les prévisions de la météo*: An Experiment in Using the Radio as an Auxiliary in the Language Lab --Two Presentations. In David P. Benseler, ed., *Second Language Teaching 77,* Proceedings of the 28th Annual Meeting of the PNCFL, Part 2 (Corvallis, Oregon: Oregon State University), 93-6.

Scanlan, Richard T. 1971. Computer-Assisted Instruction: PLATO in Latin. *FLA* 5:84-9.

Schachter, Jacquelyn D. 1974. An Error in Error Analysis. *LL* 24:205-14.

----------. 1981. The Hand Signal System. *TESOLQ* 15:125-38.

Schaeffer, Reiner H. 1981. Meaningful Practice on the Computer: Is it Possible? *FLA* 14:133-7.

Schane, Sanford. 1970. Linguistics, Spelling, and Pronunciation. *TESOLQ* 4: 137-41.

Scherer, George A.C. and Michael A. Wertheimer. 1964. *A Psycholinguistic Experiment in Foreign-Language Teaching* (New York: McGraw-Hill).

Schmidt, Richard W. and Jack C. Richards. 1980. Speech Acts and Second Language Learning. *AL* 1:129-57.

Schools Council Committee for Wales. 1978. *Bilingual Education in Wales, 5-11* (London: Evans/Methuen).

Schulz, Renate A., ed. 1977. *Personalizing Foreign Language Instruction: Learning Styles and Teaching Options*. Report of the Central States Conference on the Teaching of Foreign Languages (Skokie, Ill.: National Textbook Company).

Schumann, Francine M. 1975. Collective Storywriting: Teaching Creative Writing to ESL Children. In M. Burt and H. Dulay, eds. 1975:300-4.

Schumann, John H. 1976. Second Language Acquisition: The Pidginization Hypothesis. *LL* 26:391-408.

----------. 1978. The Acculturation Model for Second-Language Acquisition. In R. Gingras, ed. 1978:27-50.

---------- and Nancy Stenson, eds. 1974. *New Frontiers in Second Language Learning* (Rowley, Mass.: Newbury House).

Schwartz, Ralph J. 1967. Pattern Practice: Some Considerations. In Betty W. Robinett, *On Teaching English to Speakers of Other Languages --Series III* (Washington, D.C.: Georgetown University), 169-72.

Scott, Charles T. 1966. The Linguistic Basis for the Development of Reading Skill. *MLJ* 50:535-44.

Scovel, Thomas. 1979. Review of G. Lozanov's *Suggestology and Outlines of Suggestopedy*. *TESOLQ* 13:255-66.

Scriven, Michael. 1967. The Methodology of Evaluation. In Ralph W. Tyler, Robert M. Gagne, and Michael Scriven, eds., *Perspectives of Curriculum Evaluation* (Chicago: Rand McNally), 39-83.

Scully, Malcolm G. 1980. Taking Foreign Languages Out of the Classroom. *The Chronicle of Higher Education,* September 22, 1980, p. 9.

Seah, Hong Ghee. 1980. Contrastive Analysis, Error Analysis and Interlanguage in Relation to Adult Chinese Speakers Learning English as a Second Language. Unpublished doctoral dissertation, Simon Fraser University.

Seelye, H. Ned. 1968. Analysis and Teaching of the Cross-Cultural Context. In E. Birkmaier, ed. 1968:37-81.

----------. 1974. *Teaching Culture: Strategies for Foreign Language Educators* (Skokie, Ill.: National Textbook Company).

Seliger, Herbert W. 1979. On the Nature and Function of Language Rules in Language Teaching. *TESOLQ* 13:359-69.

Selinker, Larry. 1972-a. The Application of Linguistics to Foreign Language Teaching: The State of the Art. In J.C. Seigneuret and D.P. Benseler, eds., *Reports and Papers from the State Conference in Spokane, March 17-18, 1972* (Pullman, Wash.: Washington Association of Foreign Language Teachers). Also available as ERIC microfiche ED 065 015.

----------. 1972-b. Interlanguage. *IRAL* 10:209-31.

Selinker, Larry and John T. Lamendella. 1978. Fossilization in Interlanguage Learning. In C. Blatchford and J. Schachter, eds. 1978:240-9.

----------, Merrill Swain, and Guy Dumas. 1975. The Interlanguage Hypothesis Extended to Children. *LL* 25:139-52.

Semke, Harriet D. 1975. Peer-Teaching Helps! *FLA* 8:123-7.

Sewell, Penelope M. 1974/1975. Test Items --Objective and Otherwise. *Audio-Visual Language J* 12:147-56.

Sheen, Ronald. 1980. The Importance of Negative Transfer in the Speech of Near-Bilinguals. *IRAL* 18:105-19.

Shuell, Thomas J. and Claudia Z. Lee. 1976. *Learning and Instruction* (Monterey, Cal.: Brooks/Cole).

Shuldberg, Howard K. 1981. An Examination of the Importance of Focus on Form for Monitor Function. Research note in *TESOLQ* 15:81, based on a Utah State University M.A. thesis.

Shuman, R. Baird. 1971. Let's Get Foreign Language Teachers Out of our Public High Schools! *MLJ* 55:21-6.

Simon, Sidney B., Leland W. Howe and Howard Kirshchenbaum. 1972. *Values Clarification: A Handbook of Practical Strategies for Teachers and Students* (New York: Hart).

Sisk, Karin R. 1975. The Use of Instant Replay Television as a Tool for Teaching Oral Language --A Research Study. *FLA* 8:187-8.

Skinner, B.F. 1938. *The Behavior of Organisms* (New York: Appleton-Century-Crofts).

----------. 1953. *Science and Human Behavior* (New York: Macmillan).

----------. 1957. *Verbal Behavior* (New York: Appleton-Century-Crofts).

----------. 1958. Teaching Machines. *Science* 128:969-77.

----------. 1968. *The Technology of Teaching* (New York: Appleton-Century-Crofts).

Skirble, Rosanne. 1975. The Television Commercial in the ESL-EFL Classroom. In M. Burt and H. Dulay, eds. 1975:253-6.

Slobin, Dan I. 1973. Cognitive Prerequisites for the Development of Grammar. In Charles A. Ferguson and Dan I. Slobin, eds., *Studies of Child Language Development* (New York: Holt, Rinehart and Winston), 175-208.

----------. 1975. On the Nature of Talk to Children. In Eric H. Lenneberg and Elizabeth Lenneberg, eds., *Foundations of Language Development*, vol. 1 (New York: Academic Press), 283-97.

Smith, Melvin I. 1968. *Teaching to Specific Objectives* (Modesto, Cal.: Stanislaus County Schools Office).

Smith, Paul C. 1980. New Potential for the Old Dictation. *FLA* 13:403-4.

Smith, Philip D., Jr. 1967. Teaching a Modern Foreign Language Via Telephone. Unpublished doctoral dissertation, Ohio State University.

----------. 1970. *A Comparison of the Cognitive and Audiolingual Approaches to Foreign Language Instruction: The Pennsylvania Foreign Language Project* (Philadelphia: Center for Curriculum Development).

----------. 1980. A Study of the Effect of "Slowed Speech" on Listening Comprehension of French. *NALLDJ* 14,iii/iv:9-13.

Smith, W. Flint. 1969. The Language Laboratory and the Electronic Classroom: A Comparison of Their Relative Contribution to Achievement in Three Languages in the Comprehensive High School. Unpublished doctoral dissertation, Purdue University.

---------- and Frank J. Woerdehoff. 1970. The Attitudes of Modern Language Teachers Toward Instructional Media. *NALLDJ* 4,iv:27-37.

Snow, Catherine E. and Charles A. Ferguson. 1977. *Talking to Children* (Cambridge, England: Cambridge University Press).

---------- and Marian Hoefnagel-Höhle. 1978. The Critical Period for Language Acquisition: Evidence from Second Language Learning. *Child Development* 49: 1114-28.

Solé, Carlos. 1973. *Summary of Results of Student Evaluation Survey* (Austin: Tex.: Dept. of Spanish and Portuguese, University of Texas).

Spilka, Irène V. 1976. Assessment of Second-Language Performance in Immersion Programs. *CMLR* 32:543-61.

Spinelli, Emily. 1979. *English Grammar for Students of Spanish* (Ann Arbor, Mich.: The Olivia and Hill Press).

Spolsky, Bernard. 1969-a. Attitudinal Aspects of Second Language Learning. *LL* 19:271-85.

Spolsky, Bernard. 1969-b. Reduced Redundancy as a Language Testing Tool. Paper read at the Second International Congress of Applied Linguistics, Cambridge, England, September 1969. Available as ERIC microfiche ED 031 702.

----------. 1970. Linguistics and Language Pedagogy --Applications or Implications? In J.E. Alatis, ed., *Report of the Twentieth Annual Round Table Meeting on Linguistics and Language Study*. Georgetown University Monograph Series on Languages and Linguistics, No. 22. (Washington, D.C.: Georgetown University Press), 143-55.

----------. 1973. What Does It Mean to Know a Language; or How Do You Get Someone to Perform His Competence? In J. Oller and J. Richards, eds. 1973:164-76.

----------. 1978-a. *Approaches to Language Testing* (Arlington, Va.: Center for Applied Linguistics).

----------. 1978-b. *Educational Linguistics* (Rowley, Mass.: Newbury House).

----------, Bengt Sigurd, Masahito Sato, Edward Walker, and Catherine Arteburn. 1968. Preliminary Studies in the Development of Techniques for Testing Overall Second Language Proficiency. In J.A. Upshur and J. Fata, eds., *Problems in Foreign Language Testing, LL*, Special Issue No. 3, 79-101.

Stack, Edward M. 1971. *The Language Laboratory and Modern Language Teaching*, third edition (New York: Oxford University Press).

Stanislawczyk, Irene E. and Symond Yavener. 1976. *Creativity in the Language Classroom* (Rowley, Mass.: Newbury House).

Stansfield, Charles. 1977. Dictation as a Measure of Spanish Language Proficiency. Paper presented at the TESOL Annual Convention, Miami, April 1977. Referred to by R. Jones 1977:247.

Steiner, Florence. 1975. *Performing with Objectives* (Rowley, Mass.: Newbury House).

Stenson, Nancy. 1974. Induced Errors. In J. Schumann and N. Stenson, eds. 1974:54-70.

Stern, H.H. 1963. *Foreign Languages in Primary Education: The Teaching of Foreign or Second Languages to Younger Children*. Report on an international meeting of experts, April 1962 (Hamburg: UNESCO Institute for Education).

----------. 1974. Retreat from Dogmatism: Toward a Better Theory of Language Teaching. *CMLR* 30:244-54.

----------. 1976. The Ottawa-Carleton French Project: Issues, Conclusions, and Policy Implications. *CMLR* 33:216-32.

----------. 1981. Language Teaching and the Universities in the 1980s. *CMLR* 37:212-25.

---------- and Jim Cummins. 1981. Language Teaching/Learning Research: A Canadian Perspective on Status and Directions. In J. Phillips, ed. 1981: 195-248.

Stevick, Earl W. 1971. *Adapting and Writing Language Lessons* (Washington, D.C.: Foreign Service Institute, U.S. Department of State, Government Printing Office).

----------. 1973. Review of Curran, *Counseling-Learning: A Whole-Person Model for Education*. *LL* 23:259-71.

----------. 1976-a. *Memory, Meaning, and Method --Some Psychological Perspectives on Language Learning* (Rowley, Mass.: Newbury House).

----------. 1976-b. Teaching English as an Alien Language. In J. Fanselow and R. Crymes, eds. 1976:225-38.

----------. 1980. *Teaching Languages: A Way and Ways* (Rowley, Mass.: Newbury House).

Stockwell, Robert P. and J. Donald Bowen. 1965. *The Sounds of English and Spanish* (Chicago: University of Chicago Press).

----------, J. Donald Bowen, and John W. Martin. 1965. *The Grammatical Structures of English and Spanish* (Chicago: University of Chicago Press).

Strasheim, Lorraine A. 1981. Establishing a Professional Agenda for Integrating Culture into K-12 Foreign Languages: An Editorial. *MLJ* 65:67-9.

Stratton, Florence. 1977. Putting the Communicative Syllabus in Its Place. *TESOLQ* 11:131-41.

Strevens, Peter. 1978. The Nature of Language Teaching. In J. Richards, ed. 1978:179-202.

Stubbs, Joseph B. and G. Richard Tucker. 1974. The Cloze Test as a Measure of English Proficiency. *MLJ* 58:239-41.

Sugano, Marian Z. 1981. The Idiom in Spanish Language Teaching. *MLJ* 65:59-66.

Sutton, Donna. 1972. Problems of Individualized Instruction --How Successful Programs Deal with Them. In R. Gougher, ed. 1972:86-118.
Swain, Merrill. 1976. Changes in Errors: Random or Systematic? In G. Nickel, ed., *Proceedings of the Fourth International Congress of Applied Linguistics* (Stuttgart: Hochschulverlag), 345-58.
----------. 1978-a. French Immersion: Early, Late or Partial? *CMLR* 34:577-85.
----------. 1978-b. Home-School Language Switching. In J. Richards, ed. 1978: 238-50.
---------- and Barbara Burnaby. 1976. Personality Characteristics and Second Language Learning in Young Children: A Pilot Study. *WPB* 11:115-28.
----------, G. Dumas, and N. Naiman. 1974. Alternatives to Spontaneous Speech: Elicited Imitation and Translation as Indicators of Second Language Competence. *WPB* 3:68-79.
Sweet, Henry. 1899. *The Practical Study of Languages* (London: J.M. Dent and Sons). Reprinted in 1964 (London: Oxford University Press). Pages given in text correspond to the 1964 printing.
Tardif, Cécile and Alison d'Anglejan. 1981. Les erreurs en français langue seconde et leurs effets sur la communication orale. *CMLR* 37:706-23.
Tarone, Elaine E. 1978. The Phonology of Interlanguage. In J. Richards, ed. 1978:15-32.
----------. Some Influences on the Syllable Structure of Interlanguage Phonology. *IRAL* 18:139-52.
----------, Uli Frauenfelder and Larry Selinker. 1976. Systematicity/Variability and Stability/Instability in Interlanguage Systems. *LL*, Special Issue No. 4:93-134.
Taylor, Barry P. 1975. The Use of Overgeneralization and Transfer Learning Strategies by Elementary and Intermediate Students of ESL. *LL* 25:73-108.
Taylor, Harvey M. 1981. Learning to Listen in English. *TESOLQ* 15:41-50.
Taylor, H. Darrel and John L. Sorensen. 1961. Culture Capsules. *MLJ* 45:350-4.
Taylor, Linda L., John C. Catford, Alexander Z. Guiora, and Harlan L. Lane. 1971. Psychological Variables and Ability to Pronounce a Second Language. *Language and Speech* 14:146-57.
----------, Alexander Z. Guiora, John C. Catford, and Harlan L. Lane. 1969. The Role of Personality Variables in Second Language Behavior. *Comprehensive Psychiatry* 10:463-74.
Taylor, Stanford E. 1964. *Listening: What Research Says to the Teacher. No. 29.* (Washington, D.C.: American Educational Research Association).
Taylor, Wilson L. 1953. Cloze Procedure: A New Tool for Measuring Readability. *Journalism Quarterly* 30:415-33.
Teetor, Will R. 1972. Grading and Awarding Credit on a "Humane" and Sensible Basis: The Ithaca Experience. In R. Gougher, ed. 1972:149-65.
Teichert, Herman U. 1972. An Experimental Study Using Learning Packages in Beginning College German. *MLJ* 56:488-90.
Terman, Lewis M. *et al.* 1947. *The Gifted Child Grows Up*, 4 vols. (Stanford, Cal.: Stanford University Press).
Terrell, Tracy C. 1977. A Natural Approach to Second Language Acquisition and Learning. *MLJ* 61:325-37.
Thogmartin, Clyde. 1971. A Survey of Attitudes Toward Foreign Language Education Among 247 First-Year Language Students at Iowa State University. *ADFLB* 3,ii:39-45.
Thorndike, Edward L. 1927. The Law of Effect. *American J Psychology* 39:212-22.
----------, Elsie O. Bregman, J. Warren Tilton, and Ella Woodyard. 1928. *Adult Learning* (New York: Macmillan).
Titone, Renzo. 1968. *Teaching Foreign Languages: An Historical Sketch* (Washington, D.C.: Georgetown University Press).
Tran-Thi-Chau. 1972. The Concept of Difficulty in Second Language Learning and Teaching. Unpublished doctoral dissertation, University of Toronto.
----------. 1975. Error Analysis, Contrastive Analysis, and Students' Perception: A Study of Difficulty in Second Language Learning. *IRAL* 13:119-43.
Trescases, Pierre. 1981. Propositions pour une compétence culturelle de l'enseignant *et* de l'apprenant. Unpublished manuscript, Simon Fraser University.
Tucker, C. Allen. 1978. Evaluating Beginning Textbooks. Appendix 3 in H. Madsen and J. D. Bowen 1978:219-37.
Tucker, G. Richard and Alison d'Anglejan. 1972. An Approach to Bilingual

Education: The St. Lambert Experiment. In Merrill Swain, ed., *Bilingual Schooling: Some Experiences in Canada and the United States* (Toronto: The Ontario Institute for Studies in Education), 15-21.

---------- and Wallace E. Lambert. 1973. Sociocultural Aspects of Language Study. In J. Oller, Jr. and J. Richards, eds. 1973:246-50.

Tuckman, Bruce W. 1978. *Conducting Educational Research,* second edition (New York: Harcourt Brace Jovanovich).

Tulving, Endel. 1974. Cue-Dependent Forgetting. *American Scientist* 62:74-82.

Turner, Ronald C. 1970. CARLOS: Computer-Assisted Instruction in Spanish. *H* 53:249-52.

Tursi, Joseph A., ed. 1970. *Foreign Languages and the "New" Student.* RWCNECTFL (New York: Modern Language Association).

Twarog, Leon I. and E. Garrison Walters. 1981. Mastery-Based, Self-Paced Instruction in Foreign Languages at Ohio State University: A Report to the Profession on a Four Year Experiment in Individualized Instruction in Six Foreign Languages. *MLJ* 65:1-23.

Upshur, John A. 1968. Four Experiments on the Relation Between Foreign Language Teaching and Learning. *LL* 18:111-24.

Valdman, Albert, ed. 1966. *Trends in Language Teaching* (New York: McGraw-Hill).

----------. 1968-a. Problems in the Definition of Learning Steps in Programmed Foreign Language Materials. In T. Mueller, ed. 1968-a:50-62.

----------. 1968-b. Programmed Instruction versus Guided Learning in Foreign Language Acquisition. *U* 1,ii:1-14.

----------. 1978. Implications of Current Research on Second-Language Acquisition for Teaching Foreign Languages in the United States. In R. Gingras, ed. 1978:78-87.

---------- and Helen P. Warriner-Burke. 1980. Major Surgery Due: Redesigning the Syllabus and Texts. *FLA* 13:261-70.

Valette, Rebecca M. 1964. The Use of the Dictée in the French Language Classroom. *MLJ* 48:431-4.

----------. 1969. The Pennsylvania Project, Its Conclusions and Its Implications. *MLJ* 53:396-404.

----------. 1977. *Modern Language Testing,* second edition (New York: Harcourt Brace Jovanovich).

---------- and Renée S. Disick. 1972. *Modern Language Performance Objectives and Individualization: A Handbook* (New York: Harcourt Brace Jovanovich).

---------- and Cathy Linder. 1979. Measuring the Variables and Testing the Outcome. In J. Phillips, ed. 1979:199-232.

Van Teslaar, A.P. 1963. Les domaines de la linguistique appliquée. *IRAL* 1: 50-77 and 223-78.

Veidt, Frederick P. 1973. The Dialogue: An Aid to Oral Production in Beginning Language Study. *MLJ* 57:3-8.

Viëtor, Wilhelm ("Quousque Tandem"). 1882. *Der Sprachunterricht muss umkehren! Ein Beitrag zur Überbürdungsfrage.* (Third edition, Leipzig: Reisland, 1905).

Vigil, Neddy A. and John W. Oller, Jr. 1976. Rule Fossilization: A Tentative Model. *LL* 26:281-95.

von Restorff, H. 1933. Über die Wirkung von Bereichsbildungen im Spurenfeld. *Psychologie Forschung* 18:299-342.

Walker, John L. 1976. The Student View: Attitudes Toward Foreign Language Learning. In G. Jarvis, ed. 1976:129-50.

Walz, Joel. 1980. An Empirical Study of Pronunciation Errors in French. *FR* 53:424-32.

Wardhaugh, Ronald. 1970-a. An Evaluative Comparison of Present Methods for Teaching English Phonology. *TESOLQ* 4:63-72.

----------. 1970-b. The Contrastive Analysis Hypothesis. *TESOLQ* 4:123-30.

----------. 1974. *Topics in Applied Linguistics* (Rowley, Mass.: Newbury House).

---------- and H. Douglas Brown, eds. 1976. *A Survey of Applied Linguistics* (Ann Arbor, Mich.: University of Michigan Press).

Warriner, Helen P. 1980. Foreign Language Teaching in the Schools --1979: Focus on Methodology. *MLJ* 64:81-7.

Watson, John B. 1914. *Behavior: An Introduction to Comparative Psychology* (New York: Henry Holt).

----------. 1919. *Psychology from the Standpoint of a Behaviorist* (Philadelphia: Lippincott).

Wattenmaker, Beverly and Virginia Wilson. n.d. *Real Communication in Foreign*

Languages (New York; ACTFL Materials Center).

Weinreich, Uriel. 1953. *Languages in Contact: Findings and Problems* (New York: Linguistic Circle of New York).

Weir, Ruth. 1962. *Language in the Crib* (The Hague: Mouton).

Wesche, Marjorie B. 1981. Communicative Testing in a Second Language. *CMLR* 37:551-70.

Westphal, Patricia B. 1977. In Search of a Systematic Way with Words. *FR* 51:59-64.

----------. 1979. Teaching and Learning: A Key to Success. In J. Phillips, ed. 1979:119-56.

---------- and Elizabeth G. Joiner, eds. 1978. *Developing Communication Skills* (Rowley, Mass.: Newbury House).

Whitaker, S.F. 1976. What is the Status of Dictation? *Audio-Visual Language J* 14:87-93.

Whitman, Randal L. and Kenneth L. Jackson. 1972. The Unpredictability of Contrastive Analysis. *LL* 22:29-41.

Whorf, Benjamin. 1956. *Language, Thought, and Reality: Selected Writings*, J.B. Carroll, ed. (New York: John Wiley and Sons).

Widdowson, Henry. 1978. Notional-Functional Syllabuses: 1978, part four. In C. Blatchford and J. Schachter, eds. 1978:33-5.

----------. 1980. Models and Fictions. *AL* 1:165-9.

Wierenga, Leanne. 1979. A Practical Model for Listening Comprehension Activities. *FR* 52:866-72.

Wilds, Claudia P. 1962. Time Requirements for Foreign Language Achievement (mimeo) (Washington, D.C.: Foreign Service Institute).

----------. 1975. The Oral Interview Test. In R. Jones and B. Spolsky, eds. 1975:29-38.

Wilkins, David A. 1972. *Linguistics in Language Teaching* (London: Arnold).

----------. 1974. *Second Language Learning and Teaching* (London: Arnold).

----------. 1976. *Notional Syllabuses* (London: Oxford University Press).

Wilkins, George W. and E. Lee Hoffman. 1964. The Use of Cognates in Teaching Pronunciation. *LL* 14:39-43.

Winitz, Harris, ed. 1981. *The Comprehension Approach to Foreign Language Instruction* (Rowley, Mass.: Newbury House).

---------- and James A. Reeds. 1973. Rapid Acquisition of a Foreign Language (German) by the Avoidance of Speaking. *IRAL* 11:295-317.

---------- and James A. Reeds. 1975. *Comprehension and Problem Solving as Strategies for Language Training* (The Hague: Mouton).

Wolfe, David E. and Leland W. Howe. 1973. Personalizing Foreign Language Instruction. *FLA* 7:81-90.

Wolfe, David L. 1967. Some Theoretical Aspects of Language Learning and Language Teaching. *LL* 17:173-88.

Wright, Andrew. 1974. Audio-Visual Materials in Language Teaching. In J.P.B. Allen and S.P. Corder, eds. 1974:255-78.

Yeni-Komshian, Grace. 1965. Training Procedures for Developing Auditory Perception Skills in the Sound System of a Foreign Language. Unpublished doctoral dissertation, McGill University.

Yorio, Carlos A., Kyle Perkins, and Jacquelyn Schachter, eds. 1979. *On TESOL '79: The Learner in Focus* (Washington, D.C.: Teachers of English to Speakers of Other Languages).

Zampogna, Joseph, Ronald J. Gentile, Anthony Papalia, and Gordon R. Silber. 1976. Relationships Between Learning Styles and Learning Environments in Selected Secondary Modern Language Classes. *MLJ* 60:443-7.

Zelson, Sidney N.J. 1974. Skill-Using Activities in the Foreign Language Classroom. *AFLT* 4,iii:33-5.

Zenner, Walter P. 1970. Ethnic Stereotyping in Arabic Proverbs. *J American Folklore* 83:417-29.

INDEX

[illegible] E DAY [illegible]